D1261024

Philosophical Faith and the Future of Humanity

Helmut Wautischer · Alan M. Olson ·
Gregory J. Walters

Editors

Philosophical Faith and the Future of Humanity

 Springer

Editors
Helmut Wautischer
Sonoma State University
Philosophy
East Cotati Ave. 1801
94928 Cotati California
USA
helmut.wautischer@sonoma.edu

Alan M. Olson
Boston University
Religious Studies
Bay State Road 145
02215 Boston Massachusetts
USA
amo@bu.edu

Gregory J. Walters
Saint Paul University
Philosophy
Main Street 223
K1S 1C4 Ottawa Ontario
Canada
gjw@existenz.us

ISBN 978-94-007-2222-4   e-ISBN 978-94-007-2223-1
DOI 10.1007/978-94-007-2223-1
Springer Dordrecht Heidelberg London New York

Library of Congress Control Number: 2011940958

Printed on acid-free paper

Springer is part of Springer Science+Business Media (www.springer.com)

To the Memory of Leonard H. Ehrlich

Celebrating the 30th Anniversary of the Karl Jaspers Society of North America and Founding Members, Leonard H. Ehrlich, Edith Ehrlich, and George B. Pepper

Editors' Preface

Philosophical Faith and the Future of Humanity celebrates the 30th Anniversary of the Karl Jaspers Society of North America (KJSNA) founded on December 28, 1980. The prospect of forming a learned society devoted to the philosophy of Karl Jaspers emerged as Leonard H. Ehrlich, Edith Ehrlich, and George B. Pepper worked toward a systematic presentation of the philosophy of Karl Jaspers in the form of an English reader, *Karl Jaspers' Basic Philosophical Writings-Selections* (1986, 1994). During this process, the co-editors concluded that the organization of a learned society dedicated to the thought of Karl Jaspers and his contributions to twentieth century philosophy would greatly serve the interests of scholars concerned with contemporary and Continental philosophy.

Since its founding in 1980, KJSNA has held meetings in conjunction with the annual meetings of American Philosophical Association (APA) and occasionally with the Society for Phenomenology and Existential Philosophy (SPEP). KJSNA has also cooperated with the Jaspers Society of Japan, the Karl Jaspers Stiftung of Basel, and the Austrian Karl Jaspers Society in the planning and execution of six international conferences on the life and work of Karl Jaspers. The first international conference was held during summer of 1983 in conjunction with the XVII World Congress of Philosophy in Montreal, Canada, commemorating the centenary of Jaspers' birth. Since then, international Jaspers conferences have been held every five years at the World Congresses in Brighton, Moscow, Boston, Istanbul, and Seoul. The proceedings of these events have also been published in separate volumes.

Following the Fifth International Jaspers Conference at the World Congress in Istanbul (2003), the officers of KJSNA commenced the development of an online international journal in philosophy under the Jaspersian masthead, *Existenz: An International Journal in Philosophy, Religion, Politics, and the Arts*. The mission of *Existenz* is to provide the means whereby select essays presented at the annual meetings of KJSNA, as well as direct submissions of research and writing in philosophy and related fields, might be published in an accessible and sophisticated electronic format. Since the founding of *Existenz* in 2005, bi-annual volumes are produced under the co-editorship of Alan M. Olson and Helmut Wautischer. Volume 5/2 (2010) is devoted to the life and memory of Leonard H. Ehrlich by way of a lengthy philosophical autobiography and also to Edith Ehrlich's work in Nietzsche studies.

The anniversary volume at hand explores two basic issues in the philosophy of Karl Jaspers: the notion of philosophical faith, and Jaspers' abiding concern for the future of humanity. Thirty-four international scholars have contributed to an elucidation of these themes and issues, which are "fundamental," as the late Leonard H. Ehrlich put it, not only to the work of Jaspers, but to philosophy as such. Indeed, it can be argued that the notion of fundamentality is of even greater importance today, as philosophy finds itself drawn away from perennial concerns and into the position of becoming the handmaiden of the natural and social sciences.

We are very pleased, therefore, to provide, by way of the introductory section, a translation of Jaspers' *Grundsätze des Philosophierens: Einführung in philosophisches Leben, 1942/43*. These five principles, from the Jaspers *Nachlass* and so graciously provided by Hans Saner, Literary Executor of the Jaspers Archive, are strong and important reminders as to what Jaspers considered fundamental in the pursuit of philosophy by all who wish to philosophize. It is entirely appropriate that Springer Verlag has seen fit to publish these materials, given the longstanding relationship of this publisher with Karl Jaspers, dating back to 1913 with the publication of Jaspers' earliest major work, *Allgemeine Psychopathologie*, which has gone through eight editions; the 1919 publication of Jaspers' entry into the philosophy faculty at Heidelberg, *Psychologie der Weltanschauugen*; then in 1923 *Die Idee der Universität*; and the three volume edition of *Philosophie (3 Bände)*, first published in 1932. The Springer Verlag also published the first major work of Jaspers' famous student, Hannah Arendt, who completed her doctoral dissertation under his supervision, *Der Liebesbegriff bei Augustin* (1929).

For the continuing interest of the Springer Verlag, past and present, in the life and work of Karl Jaspers, and for the steadfast support of all who assisted us throughout the production of *Philosophical Faith and the Future of Humanity*, we would like to thank the editorial directors at Springer, Harmen van Paradijs, Ties Nijssen, Willemijn Arts and her assistant, Anita Fei van der Linden. We are also deeply indebted to Dr. Carl S. Ehrlich, the son of Leonard H. Ehrlich, upon whom we greatly relied when his father, due to failing health, was no longer able to supply us with pertinent information regarding his mentor Karl Jaspers, KJSNA, and the International Association of Jaspers Societies. We would also like to express gratitude to Dr. Kurt Salamun, Editor, *Jahrbuch der Österreichischen Karl Jaspers Gesellschaft*, for the tremendous work he has done over the years in providing a forum for the philosophy of Karl Jaspers and, of course, also to Hans Saner, Literary Executor of the works of Karl Jaspers. Last, but certainly not least, we would like to thank Brian Jenkins, doctoral candidate in philosophy, religion and science at Boston University, for his fastidious work as a fact-checker for most of the essays in this collection.

Boston, Massachusetts   Alan M. Olson
Ottawa, Canada   Gregory J. Walters
San Francisco, California   Helmut Wautischer
July 10, 2011

1. Gott ist.
2. Es gibt die unbedingte Forderung im Dasein.
3. Der Mensch ist endlich und unvollendbar.
4. Der Mensch kann in Führung durch Gott leben.
5. Die Realität in der Welt hat ein verschwindendes Dasein zwischen Gott und Existenz.

Karl Jaspers, 1942/43
Grundsätze des Philosophierens: Einführung in philosophisches Leben

Contents

Part I   Introduction, *Nachlassfragment*, Autobiographical, Science, and Linguistic

Introduction 3
Helmut Wautischer

Foreword to Karl Jaspers' *Principles for Philosophizing* 9
Hans Saner

Principles for Philosophizing: Introduction to Philosophical Life, 1942/43 11
Karl Jaspers

Philosophical Faith and the Future of Mankind 35
Leonard H. Ehrlich

An Interview with George B. Pepper 45
Gregory J. Walters

Karl Jaspers: Philosophical Faith of a Scientist 53
S. Nassir Ghaemi

Honoring the Messenger 65
Suzanne Kirkbright

Part II   *Philosophical Faith*: Critical and Historical Analyses

Philosophical Faith and Its Ambiguities 77
Alan M. Olson

Jaspers' Concept of Philosophical Faith: A New Synthesis? 99
Andreas Cesana

Faith and Affirmation 115
Gerhard Knauss

Certainty and Trust: Reflections on Karl Jaspers' Cosmo-Anthropology 123
Reiner Wiehl

Three Interpretations of the Content of Jaspers' Philosophical Faith . .   135
Raymond Langley

**Philosophy of Revelation: Remarks on Schelling,
Jaspers, and Rosenzweig**   147
Wolfdietrich Schmied-Kowarzik

**Thinking from the Origin: Critical and Personal Remarks
on Jaspers' Philosophy of Philosophizing**   159
Armin Wildermuth

Faith, Science, and Philosophy   165
Reinhard Schulz

The Philosophy of History in Hegel, Heidegger, and Jaspers   179
Stephen A. Erickson

Jaspers' *Achsenzeit* Hypothesis: A Critical Reappraisal   189
Michael Zank

Jaspers Meets Confucius   203
Charles Courtney

***Verstehen* in Historical-Philosophical Interpretation**   211
Andrew L. Gluck

Philosophical Faith, Periechontology, and Philosophical Ethics   227
Shinji Hayashida

**Can Corporate Capitalism Be Redeemed? Business Ethics
and the Search for a Renewed Faith in Work**   235
W. Michael Hoffman and Robert E. McNulty

**Reflections on Philosophical Faith and Faith
in the Twenty-First Century**   253
Filiz Peach

**Part III   *The Future of Humanity*: Global Communication
             and the Project of World Philosophy**

Philosophical Faith and the Foundering of Truth in Time   269
Gregory J. Walters

**Towards World Philosophy and a World History
of Philosophy—Karl Jaspers: His Work, Calling, and Legacy**   287
Richard Wisser

**Humanism and Wars: Karl Jaspers Between Politics, Culture,
and Law**   299
Chris Thornhill

On Recovering Philosophy: Philosophical Dialogue and Political Philosophy After 9/11 319
Tom Rockmore

World Philosophy: On Philosophers Making Peace 335
Anton Hügli

Philosophical Faith as the Will to Communicate: Two Case Studies in Intercultural Understanding 347
Tomoko Iwasawa

Faith as Humanity's Essential Communication Bridge 365
Hermann-Josef Seideneck

Freedom in the Space of Nothingness 375
Malek K. Khazaee

Philosophical Faith: The Savior of Humanity 387
Indu Sarin

The Second Axial Age: Fulfilling the Human Destiny 399
Czesława Piecuch

Karl Jaspers' Philosophical Faith for the Global Age: The Idea of Civilizational Continuity 409
Joanne Miyang Cho

The Factor of Listening in Karl Jaspers' Philosophy of Communication 419
Krystyna Górniak-Kocikowska

Appendix 435

Notes on Contributors 439

Name Index 449

Subject Index 451

Contributors

Andreas Cesana Department for Interdisciplinary Studies, Johannes Gutenberg-University, Mainz, Germany, cesana@uni-mainz.de

Joanne Miyang Cho William Paterson University, Wayne, NJ, USA, choj@wpunj.edu

Charles Courtney Drew University, Madison, NJ, USA, ccourtne@drew.edu

Leonard H. Ehrlich (1924–2011) University of Massachusetts, Amherst, MA, USA, ehrlich@philos.umass.edu

Stephen A. Erickson Pomona College, Claremont, CA, USA, stephen.erickson@pomona.edu

S. Nassir Ghaemi Tufts University, Medford, MA, USA, nassir.ghaemi@tufts.edu

Andrew L. Gluck Hofstra University, Hempstead, NY, USA; St. Johns University, New York, NY, USA, andy_gluck@msn.com

Krystyna Górniak-Kocikowska Southern Connecticut State University, New Haven, CT, USA, gorniakk1@southernct.edu

Shinji Hayashida University of Electro-Communications, Tokyo, Japan, hayasida-s@nifty.com

W. Michael Hoffman Center for Business Ethics, Bentley University, Waltham, MA, USA, MHoffman@bentley.edu

Anton Hügli Basel University, Basel CH-4058, Switzerland, anton.huegli@unibas.ch

Tomoko Iwasawa Reitaku University, Chiba, Japan, iwasawa3@livedoor.com

Malek K. Khazaee California State University, Long Beach, CA, USA, mkhazaee@csulb.edu

Suzanne Kirkbright University of Surrey, Guildford, UK, suzanne.kirkbright@gmail.com

Gerhard Knauss University of Saarbrücken, Saarbrücken, Germany

Raymond Langley Manhattanville College, Purchase, NY, USA, langleyr@mville.edu

Robert E. McNulty Center for Business Ethics, Bentley University, Waltham, MA, USA, RMcNulty@bentley.edu

Alan M. Olson Boston University, Boston, MA, USA, amo@bu.edu

Filiz Peach Mary Ward Centre, London, UK, fpeach@hotmail.com

Czesława Piecuch Pedagogical University of Krakow, Krakow, Poland, cechnap@op.pl

Tom Rockmore Duquesne University, Pittsburgh, PA, USA, rockmore@duq.edu

Hans Saner Curator of Karl Jaspers' Literary Estate, Karl Jaspers Stiftung, Basel, HansSaner@gmx.ch

Indu Sarin Punjab University, Chandigarh, India, indusarin@yahoo.com

Wolfdietrich Schmied-Kowarzik University of Kassel, Kassel, Germany, schmied-kowarzik@aon.at

Reinhard Schulz Carl von Ossietzky University, Oldenburg, Germany, reinhard.schulz@uni-oldenburg.de

Hermann-Josef Seideneck Ferna, Germany, hermann-josef-seideneck@hotmail.de

Chris Thornhill University of Glasgow, Glasgow G12 8RT, UK, Christopher.Thornhill@glasgow.ac.uk

Gregory J. Walters Saint Paul University, Ottawa, ON, Canada K1S 1C4, gjw@existenz.us

Helmut Wautischer California State University, Sonoma State University, CA 94928, USA, helmut.wautischer@sonoma.edu

Reiner Wiehl (1929–2010) Department of Philosophy, University of Heidelberg, Heidelberg, Germany

Armin Wildermuth University of St. Gallen, St. Gallen, Switzerland, wildermutha@bluewin.ch

Richard Wisser University of Mainz, D-67547 Mainz, Germany

Michael Zank Department of Religion, Boston University, Boston, MA, USA, mzank@bu.edu

Part I
Introduction, *Nachlassfragment*, Autobiographical, Science, and Linguistic

Introduction

Helmut Wautischer

As a trained psychiatrist, Karl Jaspers undoubtedly had keen insight into the nature of humans. Recognizing the importance of scientific methodology, he understood that "medicine draws little distinction somatically between man and animal."[1] Nonetheless there are distinct differences: "Man is not merely pattern, he patterns himself" (*GP* 8). Of course, the chosen methodology will dictate the range of results, and as such, the uniqueness of the human condition eventually leads to an antinomy. Humans are subjected to the methods of science with regard to physical, mental, and emotional qualities. Likewise, this ability to pattern oneself transcends human existence into a domain of Being where self-realization takes place in the context of communication with others. Such an Other can be any entity ranging from the mineral-, plant-, or animal kingdoms to humans, transcendence, and god.

Fully aware of the limits of any methodology, Jaspers maintained their importance for the acquisition of knowledge. In fact, from the very beginning of his academic writing, he developed a sense of openness and a willingness to engage in dialogue based on different methodologies, each of which may shed light to explore the complexity of Existenz. Already in his *General Psychopathology*, Jaspers attempted "to develop and order knowledge guided by the methods through which it is gained."[2] At the same time Jaspers was a fierce and compassionate critic when interpretations of facts occur on the basis of methodologies that are not suitable for the phenomenon under investigation. This is demonstrated, for example, in his elaborate critique of Ernst Kretschmer's constitution theory that assumes a correlation between body types and psychological dispositions (*GP* 641–668). For Jaspers, the concept of science included a much broader spectrum than merely research in the so-called natural sciences. With regards to the science of humans, a

---

[1] Karl Jaspers, *General Psychopathology*, trans. J. Hoenig and Marian H. Hamilton (Chicago, IL: The University of Chicago Press, 1964), p. 7. [Henceforth cited as *GP*]

[2] Karl Jaspers, "Philosophical Autobiography," in *The Philosophy of Karl Jaspers*, ed. Paul Arthur Schilpp (La Salle, IL: Open Court Publishing, 1981), pp. 1–94, here p. 20.

H. Wautischer (✉)
California State University, Sonoma State University, CA 94928, USA
e-mail: helmut.wautischer@sonoma.edu

H. Wautischer et al. (eds.), *Philosophical Faith and the Future of Humanity*,
DOI 10.1007/978-94-007-2223-1_1, © Springer Science+Business Media B.V. 2012

variety of methods is called for, without any one method overriding the relevancy of the others. For example, the criterion of testability in psychopathology reflects the dynamic between limits of empirical methods in contrast to philosophical assertions about human freedom. Likewise, in developing an axiomatic ground for scientific research, the boundaries of knowledge-belief-faith are not clearly demarcated, as an analysis of the difference between philosophical faith and religious faith demonstrates. Such analyses based on different points of observation are described in this volume. Jaspers reminds us that the human condition ultimately escapes objective accessibility. He endorses a plurality in the methods of understanding, and universality for the methods of justification: "What is known scientifically can be demonstrated and proven in such a way that any reasonable person at all capable of understanding the matter cannot evade the compelling truth of it" (*GP* 768). The Encompassing (*das Umgreifende*) as such transcends beyond justification; it is grasped by the individual in the immediacy of communication. In this context, "thinking is itself an act of the essence of the thinking person, an essence which produces itself by touching an Other, viz., Transcendence."[3]

At a first glance, an in-depth analysis of philosophical faith might appear irrelevant for understanding life in modern societies, given their seldom challenged acceptance of scientific dogma to govern and interfere with all aspects of personal existence throughout all stages of life. From therapeutic practice, Jaspers knew that any objectification of humans has limits. "There always remains the all-embracing precondition which we call the vitality of life, idea, creativity, the initiative of Existence itself" (*GP* 398). Such initiative is non-objective and occurs in one's philosophizing about the inevitability of foundering, in which Transcendence shows itself. Jaspers does not call for some remote or exclusive attentiveness to purely intellectual or spiritual practice. He knows of the defining layers of human existence and would not want to submit their corresponding drives into any hierarchical order. In his classification of drives he differentiates between the obvious somatic and sensory drives, the vital drives, and the drives of the human spirit (*GP* 319). He knows that, "man cannot, as it were, participate in nothing but purely intellectual or spiritual drives" (*GP* 320). If one does, most likely some form of pathology will develop.

By bringing attention to such references in the context of exploring philosophical faith, it should become clear that Jaspers is not some lofty philosopher disconnected from reality. It is quite to the contrary. Philosophical faith is the human endeavor on the path of temporal truth. How such path, in a Jaspersian context, can guide a person to live a truthful life is described, from various perspectives, throughout this book. Reason alone will not suffice, as can be demonstrated with examples of conflicting expert testimonies, denial of facts by authoritative experts, or with dogmatic applications of truth that serve ulterior motives where the dignity of others is being objectified for practical ends. Jaspers knew that an individual's awareness of truth is

---

[3] Karl Jaspers, "Reply to My Critics," in *The Philosophy of Karl Jaspers*, ed. Paul Arthur Schilpp (La Salle, IL: Open Court Publishing, 1981), pp. 747–896, here p. 849. [Henceforth cited as *RC*]

not just a given. It belongs to the drives of the human spirit, "drives to comprehend and give oneself to a state of being which manifests itself as an experience of absolute values, whether religious, aesthetic, ethical or pertaining to truth" (*GP* 319). For each participant in any historical age, this motivation needs to be nurtured anew without any reliance on dogma, be it religious, philosophical, or scientific. Such process of renewal is not just a destruction of the old, but requires an awareness of truth "whose fountainhead is at such level of depth where reason is approached by that which comes to light through reason."[4] Human progress requires more than simply destroying ancient wisdom by misclassifying it as dogma. It requires development of motivation and maturity for travelling on a path of knowledge. "Truth springs from the intertwinement of thought and life, while obscured awareness of truth springs from decay" (*VW* 2).

In this context it becomes clear that Jaspers offers valuable insight for maintaining and recreating a sense of humanity that is so drastically challenged in this current age of seemingly insurmountable struggles; such as the ever increasing world population, the global challenges that arise with an externally induced metamorphosis of cultures due to centralized political and economic regulation, and the increased efficacy in shaping human life to accept a shared global narrative that is presented through centralized global channels of communication with their claim of supporting freedom of expression. Manipulative democracy knows best how to highlight and mass-distribute selective voices on any subject matter for the purpose of guiding public opinion. The short-lived gains acquired through deceptive interaction eventually lose their value when measured against one's finite existence in eternity. While it is true that the key to life is in the hands of the individual, its functionality for opening one's comprehension of the Encompassing is acquired by authentic communication that transcends subject-object divisions. "Only thus can we gain the way to ourselves by becoming communicable, by communication and renewed recognition" (*RC* 791–792). In other words, communication is at the very core of human existence. But not just any communication will do. In the end, communication must include other humans and demand the same dignity be given to others than is expected for oneself. All other instances of communication can only provide for functionality. Jaspers' description of the doctor-patient communication describes such limits in regards to psychotherapy, where "the doctor limits what he tells and speaks authoritatively; the patient duly accepts and does not think about it but has blind confidence in its certainty ... doctor and patient instinctively adhere to authority as something reassuring" (*GP* 797). Such communication objectifies its participants and Jaspers does not leave it at that. He elaborates on a doctor-patient relationship that takes place as existential communication, reaching far beyond any therapy and "beyond anything that can be planned or methodically staged" (*GP* 798). Just like in this professional interaction between doctor and patient, most human interaction takes place within their unique parameter of diverse motives

---

[4] Karl Jaspers, *Von der Wahrheit* (Munich: Piper & Co. Verlag, 1958), p. 2, translated by the author. [Henceforth cited as *VW*]

and reasons for engaging in dialogue. Differences constitute a limitation but can be addressed by sharing "destiny as fellow-travellers within the frame of what is called Transcendent Being. Mere existence does not bind persons together, nor does Existence itself as such" (*GP* 799).

When communication is addressed in the context of a global communication related to the project of world philosophy, Jaspers' writings offer profound insight that is explored in Part 3 of this book. The focal point of discussion is directed to comprehending the difference between philosophical faith and religious faith, and the efforts by an individual to ascertain knowledge of the encompassing. Placing this effort on a global stage of world philosophy requires one to discuss the legitimacy and limits of authority. Public freedom of expression does bring empowerment to the individual, provided that there is an attentive listener. Most likely no reasonable person will object to the fact that screaming "Fire!" in a crowded place should be illegal unless there is indeed a fire. Most will agree that public search engines should not direct users to manuals for building explosive devices. But when authority uses deceptive rhetoric to justify its demand for obedience, the public is easily fooled due to lack of better knowledge. For example, the current state-of-the-art inoculation schedule for 0–3 year olds in pediatric medicine becomes increasingly demanding for the immature nervous system of this age group. Some even argue that post-vaccination effects are related to auto-immune and neurological disorder in children. Despite this controversy, a pediatrician who challenges this practice in favor of a more individualized inoculation schedule to support healthy development in the child will face authority challenges by the Medical Board. Jaspers identifies several reasons for and against the legitimacy of authority and he knows of the human condition that yields to, desires, and revolts against authority (*VW* 804–816). For any future of humanity, the moral challenge of global capitalism will have to be taken into account. While it is important to stress the responsibility of individuals, it is too simplistic to place the burden of moral compliance on individuals alone. In this context, one's willingness to engage in cunning communication becomes a tool of authority. Jaspers paraphrases Hannah Arendt when he addresses the moral obligation of a State: "No state today is only responsible to itself, but must ask itself what consequences its actions have for the possible free federative unity of mankind—and with this it is already on the road to renouncing its absolute sovereignty" (*RC* 754). In today's world such obligation best serves as a directive for multinational corporations with regards to their presumed perception of entitlement for the ownership and distribution of the world's resources. When communication is not direct but mediated through opaque technological gateways, democratic discourse can easily become a form of one-sided communication that is projected into a neutral domain of internet accessibility with no real knowledge who might engage with the material posted, if anyone at all. In his very perceptive way, Jaspers already anticipated such form of communication. "Everyone says anything. There is a chaos of irresponsibility. Within this context there are suggestions, deceptions, and sophistry for material gain and seeking power. This is used as a pastime of general speaking without continuity of education. All truths and falsities occur in random chaos as a form of speech act, where even truth becomes hollow and loses its relevance" (*VW* 809).

Not anything goes. Just as there are criteria for scientific communication, there are equal criteria for philosophizing, practicing religion, or truthful communication in transcendence. Such criteria are needed for the acquisition of knowledge, but Jaspers makes it clear that no individual can hide behind criteria to pretend truthful communication. Ultimately such communication requires the full participation of an authentic individual who recognizes himself by interacting with others in full awareness of one's foundering in Existenz.

The thirty-four contributions in this volume speak to this journey on the path of knowledge, starting with Karl Jaspers himself in a lucid and insightful outline of five principles for philosophizing.

San Francisco   Helmut Wautischer
July 10, 2011   Executive Editor

Foreword to Karl Jaspers' *Principles for Philosophizing*

Hans Saner

Abstract A summary statement about the five principles that define Jaspers' position of 1942/43, and a brief description of the circumstances for this hitherto unpublished writing of Jaspers.

The probate fragment of Karl Jaspers' *Principles of Philosophy: Introduction to Philosophical Life*, which is said to have secretly circulated in 1943 among the students of Heidelberg, consists of ten parts, of which five are transcribed and include about 350 printed pages. The parts VI–X, partly transcribed and partly in notes, consist of about 700 sheets. The project is like the hub of mature themes of Jaspers' philosophy which are then developed in the post-war period. They originate in philosophical faith that Jaspers characterizes in five principles:

1. God is
2. There is Unconditional Demand in Being
3. Man is Finite and Unfinishable
4. Man Can Live By Guidance Through God
5. Reality in the World has Diminishing Being between God and Existenz

Of these five principles he developed three in his later writings, namely, God; unconditional demand; and reality in the world has diminishing being between God and Existenz. The special feature of this writing of 1942/43 is its strong commitment which is otherwise quite atypical of Jaspers. It seems to reflect the crisis situation of the time, and something that he not only softened later, but also subjected to criticism. While the principles pertain to no particular religion, neither are they merely metaphysical, but indicate religious positivity, which may surprise many.

H. Saner (✉)
Curator of Karl Jaspers' Literary Estate
Karl Jaspers Stiftung, Basel
e-mail: HansSaner@gmx.ch

H. Wautischer et al. (eds.), *Philosophical Faith and the Future of Humanity*,
DOI 10.1007/978-94-007-2223-1_2, © Springer Science+Business Media B.V. 2012

Principles for Philosophizing: Introduction to Philosophical Life, 1942/43

Karl Jaspers

Abstract This original probate fragment of Jaspers' literary estate summarizes five principles that define Jaspers' philosophical position of 1942/43.

Preface

[...]
This writing may be an encouragement for philosophical living, a sort of modern *Protreptikos*. Its final aim is practical. It commands the seriousness of a self-engaged reader. It wishes to aid the awakening of the essential core within a human being. It encourages by affirming the encompassing, by truth, by looking at origins, by means of examples from human thought and abilities.
[...]

Introduction

[...]

The Overall Humaneness of Philosophizing and the Individual

Philosophy is the matter of an individual. It must originate from its age and bear fruits from its soil; but the uniqueness of philosophy fully comes to life in the context of including narratives from all of thoughtful humankind. General humaneness is claimed in the philosophical works of East Asia, India, the Occident as its kind of factual philosophizing by humans. Reverberating upon these works, one's

---

This unpublished manuscript was released by Hans Saner, curator of Jaspers' literary estate, for first publication and is translated from German by Helmut Wautischer. The ellipsis indicate redundant and duplicate text omitted by the curator for the sake of a more cohesive presentation of Jaspers' thesis.

H. Wautischer et al. (eds.), *Philosophical Faith and the Future of Humanity*,
DOI 10.1007/978-94-007-2223-1_3, © Springer Science+Business Media B.V. 2012

own self is found through philosophizing. Each work is an objective construct of thought—even though it is historically identifiable as belonging to a certain people and time and situation, and is cloaked by its own history—from the very beginning it addresses in principle a universal comprehensibility that is present in every human being. In dialogue throughout the millennia, one human shares with the other knowledge about oneself, the world, and God. Early attempts to protect philosophical insight as some secret to be shared with others only when they are ready to fully comprehend it at the level of their personal maturity soon proved to be futile. It is the task of philosophy to transmit itself to the public, and by avoiding the label of secrecy to remain an open secret that is available to each individual: in the freely accessible work, thoughts will be comprehended only by the one who engages them with self-awareness. [...]

Affirmation Truth and Philosophical Truth

Philosophy is not religion. A philosophical creed—in the sense of belonging or not belonging to a historical community of fellow believers—is a misnomer. Philosophy can bridge any abyss to coalesce each and every one, not necessarily by shared community and beliefs, but by means of listening and understanding and by engaging in a dialogue of questions and answers. As such we cannot put forward a catechism of philosophical creed, but we can develop principles for philosophizing.

Confession is faith in the content of dogmatically defined sentences, and confession is conforming: from my origin with others I affirm the deeds of my community. As such, affirmation truth is the objective disposition of a community in truth for all its members. This truth is the subject of religion and its authenticated institutions.

Philosophy lacks such firm ground in speech, deed, or form, but finds it in the context of objectively gained reminiscence which awakens and motivates. Philosophical propositions are not affirmations; they are outlines of possibilities, steps in thought processes, attempts in ascending to an authentic sense of self. The manifested universalities of such propositions suggest a direction to the reader for actualizing a concrete philosophical thought process. This ever-unique content is not a confessional content. The truth of philosophy, that is analogous to affirmation, is solely found in practice: in the conditioning of its historically well-founded ethos, in the unyielding nature of being-a-self. Such truth is not knowledge, but in its propositions has its ground of remembrance and appearance.

[...]

Philosophy proper is lost when it forms sects, foundations, or "schools"; it is also forfeited by founding restrictive traditions analogous to religions, orders, or states. Philosophy is public and common property—essentially bound only by writings, the possibility for free speech, and a certain inspiration for contemplation—it is free of purpose in the world, and constitutes a revealing quiet space of illumination in truth for each and every one who desires it.

Whenever principles for philosophizing can be formed, they constitute an indication for remembrance of primal experiences and the means of their elucidation. While such propositions can bring refreshment in truthful awareness of being, when taken alone they cannot constitute a complete teaching of truth.

Whenever a person communicates philosophy—and philosophizing is shared in this form alone—such philosophy cannot take on a form that is valid for all, or complete, or final. Our principles here are serious, but not a confession; they are carried by the faith in their implicit truth, but not a claim for unconditional acceptance; they try to seek approval of such truth by the other, but constitute simultaneously also an encouragement for the stranger to engage in questioning us, and all this as an expressed intent for clarification.

[...]

[...] Regardless of their own historical origin, there are ancient beliefs of universal applicability that form the foundations of philosophy and religion, in contrast to mindless thoughts of unphilosophy (*Unphilosophie*). In spite of their universality, these beliefs are not detachable binding truths for all, but they do have a historical coloring. As they are communicated, they remain in limbo for rationality. Their absolute demarcation would be untrue. [...]

[...]

Part 1. Philosophical Beliefs

The contents of faith are invisible. They cannot be shown in the world. They cannot be proven, since they do not depend on anything else.

When speaking of beliefs, this it is not done for the purpose of proving their truth through reason and by making them available to the senses, but it is done to circumnavigate them and guide to them by means of signs that are found indirectly in the facts of existing in the world. Contents of faith are to be awakened wherever a receptive individual can listen, but they cannot be handed over.

[...]

Philosophical beliefs differ from religious faith. Philosophical contents lack a specific religious ground in cults, rites, dogma, or religious institutions. They only know transmissions of thoughts derived from personal meditations. Rather than acknowledging a certain currently active authority, philosophical belief acknowledges only the authority of its origin in view of its history in human thought.

From the tradition I attempted to acquire in my own life, I postulate five beliefs.

God Is

Historical Examples of the Belief in God

When Jeremiah noticed the demise of all for which he had devoted his entire life, when his country and people were lost, when in Egypt even the last remnants had became unfaithful to Yahweh as they offered sacrifices to Isis, and when his disciple Baruch lamented: "I am tired of lamenting and I find no peace!", Jeremiah answers: "Thus spoke Yahweh: Behold, what I have built I shall tear down, and what I have planted I shall pull out, and you demand great things for yourself? Demand them not!"

In such a situation these words mean: That God is, already suffices. Whether or not "immortality" is possible, is not the question; whether or not God is "forgiving," such question is no longer relevant. The individual no longer matters, having a mind of one's own and concerning oneself with beatitude and eternity has diminished. Even more, it is understood as impossibility that the world as such should have purpose susceptible of fulfillment and that it will endure in some form; since all is created by God out of nothing and is in his hands. Attaching oneself to anything in the world means that the experience of joy also brings the experience of sorrow: the weakness, malice, taking pleasure in the pain of others, demise and death. When all is lost, one thing remains: God is. When even with presumed guidance by God one human in this world failed in spite of best efforts, one unshakeable reality remains: God is. As a person fully renounces himself, his goals, and any final reward, then this reality will show itself as the only reality. But it does not show itself in advance, or abstractly, and only when one descends into one's own existence will it show itself right at the boundary.

Jeremiah's words are rough words. No longer are they linked to a historical will to action in the world that used to affirm life and made possible such ultimate goal. These words are simple and free of any allusions about ultimate things; they contain unfathomable truth, precisely because of the renunciation of any claim and any fixation in the world.

Jeremiah positions absolute transcendence into the thought of an otherworldly creator. From this origin which at times is veiled, this belief permeates the Occident until today. A different form of transcendence is found in India since the time of the Upanishads. Whether as Atman-Brahman or as Nirvana, it is the essential being within and in relation to all worldly existence which, including gods, humans, animals, or plants constitutes Maya, disappearing appearances.

Even rougher is Shakespeare's knowledge of transcendence in Hamlet, simple in its lack of knowledge and by renouncing infinity. Upon completing in this world what was relevant to him, Hamlet speaks his last words prior to his death: the rest is silence.

Absolute transcendence is shared in India and the Occident, by finding some ground beyond worldly existence and its corresponding freedom for humans in their ability to bind themselves to some otherworldliness. All else though is radically different: In the occidental tradition, creative spirit is experienced in the totality of world creation by means of extraordinary efforts and by historical participation in world events including the demise of such world totality. In India, transcendence is not experienced by means of human activity in regards to shaping the world, it is also not experience in a historical awareness about the unfolding of human matters; instead, it is found through indifference toward this infinite and the alien hustle and bustle of the world, and by the individual's effort to cultivate awareness and one's "state of being." The divine creator becomes personalized, while transcendence in India remains impersonal.

Both forms of internalizing absolute transcendence have the capacity to experience their boundaries to avoid their respective manifestation of an abyss: The claims for exclusivity in the belief in God as found in Judaism and Christianity is manifested in human action and by its relation to secular goals; in such digression it is identified by the speculative, infinite, and deep concept of transcendence in India as Maya. The lack of historicity and world in Indian transcendence regresses from impersonal emptiness to passive inactivity; it is the might of a faith in a personal God that commands participation in world events, where it is through foundering and not because of avoidance that an otherwise abstract transcendence can be truly experienced.

The Reality of the Axiom: God Is

The axiom refers to God as reality per se. This reality is not already contained by just thinking of this proposition. Merely thinking about it leaves the proposition empty. Its meaning is to be experienced, if at all, by historical presence in transcending through reality beyond itself as the actual reality.

This reality is the Being of trust, despite the demise of a life, despite the moment when one's actions cease, despite individual foundering: in the end, all is well. Within the horizon of inner-worldly purpose and in one's judgment about the totality of perceived history, such awareness constitutes an anticipatory deception. Since in the world [. . .], the fate of an individual and the totality of foundering in the end remain indeterminate. [. . .] Being in the world as such is always reason for despair or for stubborn steadfast in view of absurdity. Appearances as such and without godly attributes manifest themselves as determinate as a perceived proximity to God, even without any indication of an actual God or a clearly descriptive language.

The axiom itself, more or less, relates nothing. Although the name God carries an infinite historical depth, it has to manifest itself first within an individual life. God is to be sought out, and not to be owned; but the actual search starts with the initial certainty that He is.

God is reality itself and not, as in mere thoughts, the boundary of the world, nor the external point without content, nor a mere nothingness of transcendence in contrast to the visible colorfulness of the world.

Therefore, the axiom "God is" takes on many shapes. Speculative: "It is Being" (the origin of Parmenides' thought). In historical presence: "God is;" "God is the living God." Revelation lets him speak directly: "I am who I am."

Believing that God is does not mean knowing what God is. Propositions used to justify that God is present themselves as proofs of God, while propositions that speak of God describe knowledge of God.

Proofs of God; That God Is

The axiom that "God is" has been denied. Recent attempts in philosophizing seem to circumvent it, i.e. neither confirming nor denying it. But whoever philosophizes has to stand one's ground. When there is doubt that God is, a philosophical answer is in order.

Yet, the existence of God escapes proof, regardless of numerous attempts throughout history in a rich variety of reflection. Most proofs start with the assumption of something in the world that can be found, experienced, or followed and then conclude: if this is the case, then God must be; by imagining the basic riddles of the existence of the world, they now serve as proof for God. Or, one engages in speculative reflection where awareness of one' own existence first is understood as awareness of being which then deepens into an awareness of God. Or, one views the reality of love; experiencing eternity within the context of love is like a language of God. At all times the constant flux of the world and the planning of human inventions and manifestations in the world lead to a boundary; when facing the abyss one will experience the void or God.

It is obvious that none of these proofs satisfy understanding, but they are pointers for reason. Proof for understanding relates to finite events in the world. Pointers actualize understanding. A proof is an inappropriate form for the affirmation of God. The affirmation of insights, of reflectivity, of transcendent thinking does not come about through proof, but through elevation (*Aufschwung*). A proven God is no God.

Cognizing God: What God Is

In our finite thinking God is constantly "not" this or that *definiendum* that we can think of or perceive. He is the "not" all finite, amounting in finite thinking to seemingly nothing. He is nothing when the sum of finitude is something, and each finite has an absolute manifestation. That God is perceived as nothing and opposite to all being in the world therefore suggests: he is not less but more than all reality, he is reality in itself, being as such. Restrained by empirical reality and being in the world, as long as I consider this for absolute, God is not.

Regardless, since time immemorial God is thought of and perceived. As he is seen in thoughts and similes, each thought or image is veiled. God seems to be nothing when we cannot allow ourselves any perception; he is hidden, as we attempt yet another inappropriate perception. Whatever God might be, is only seen through finite form. Such finite form becomes symbol (meaning, language, cipher). It is immediately out of place as soon as it should become God himself.

[. . .]

Foremost and most convincingly God is portrayed as a personality. [. . .] Also this view, albeit the most perceptive one, remains inappropriate, and this is not because God is less, but he must be more than personality. [. . .]

[. . .]

Faith and Testimony of Faith

Faith in God is the only ground that remains. The manifestation of such faith in perceptions, thoughts, or actions may be poor or rich; where faith truly is, it is necessarily deep and infinite.

But the testimonies of faith are preempted either in abstractions, in deisms of understanding, or finally in conventional colloquial expressions that ultimately can be linked to some factual nihilism. Or, the testimony digresses into perceptions that, combined with infinite fixations, lead to superstition. All testimonies of faith are but a play in an incessant movement of revocation. A single testimony can have a force of symbolic accuracy for memory to awaken or confirm in a given situation; it can become the *signum* for a firm position of consciousness. But all perceptions and thoughts can never replace by objective means the subjectivity of faith that humans are gifted with by God for realization.
[...]

The Immediacy of Faith in God Denies any Mediation

[...]
Of philosophical relevance is the fact that faith in God becomes real and without any fixations that would be unavoidable for anyone. Within historicity, an immediate, unmediated, and independent relationship takes place for the individual with God.

Historicity is not general for all. It does not constitute an absolute truth in its communicability or representation, but by means of it the absolute is grasped. The historical path of an individual is *his* way, not *the* way. Whence he arrives, it is the One, shared by all. What is perceived as an affirmation on the path, and it appears as a proof for its truth—even though it is not factual proof, since this would mean some superstition—is not a condition for all, but a historical form of infinite modifications.

Whatever God is, he must be real and absolute and not just in one of the historical appearances of his language in the language of humans. When he is, he must be immediate and perceivable without detour or mediator for humans as individuals.

There Is Unconditional Demand in Being

To my question, "What shall I do?" I receive answers in the world that state finite purposes and means. [...]

[...] Whence I set out to comprehend the commanding authority, I find myself with an authoritative demand of an alien "I ought to do so" or, "as it is written."

[...] All such orders apply whenever purpose or obedience is in place. They are conditional demands. Are there unconditional demands?

Conditional demands bring forth dependency on another, on purpose in being, or on authority. Unconditional demands originate within me. Conditional demands face me in opposition as a certainty that I may choose to obey. Unconditional demands originate from me in as much as they carry me.

The unconditional demand approaches me as a request from my actual self to my being. When the foundation of my will is unconditional, I resonate with it as a manifestation of myself because I ought to; and vice versa it is a manifestation of what I ought to be, since I am this resonance. Such becoming-in-contemplation is dim at the beginning yet bright at the end of my reflective clarity. Once becoming-in-contemplation is completed, all questioning finally ends in the certainty of one's sense of being—in the course of time such certainty cannot be owned, questions surface again, and in ever changing situations such certainty must be regained anew.

The unconditioned (*das Unbedingte*) is not to be understood as purpose since it precedes the purpose that it forms. Consequently, the unconditioned is not what is desired, but it is that from which desire stems. When captured as the purpose of will, the unconditioned is lost, because such reversal brings finitude and with it conditionality.

That the unconditioned becomes the foundation of action is not a matter of knowledge, but it is the content of faith. Inasmuch I recognize the reasons and goals of my actions, I remain within the finite and the conditioned. Once I cease to live in objective justification, I start to live from the unconditioned.

Historical Examples of Accepting Death

Unconditioned actions occur in the development of life, in love, in struggle. In any such occurrence, the hallmark of the unconditioned is one's readiness to chance life. All conditioned action builds upon life as necessity, while the unconditioned builds on a view where life itself is subject to conditionality rather than the final concern. By realizing the unconditioned, a restriction of existence takes place, since existence is subordinated to the unconditioned: an idea, a vocation, loyalty, communication, love. Only at the boundary to special or exceptional situations one can notice that acting from the unconditioned may lead to a loss of existence and to one's conscious choice of accepting the inevitability of death, regardless of the fact that the conditioned is ready, foremost and at all times, for paying any price to remain in existence, to live.

[...]

The most vivid example of this is Socrates. In the lucidity of his reason and by living in the encompassing of unknowing, he traveled his path steadfastly with no disturbance by passions of indignation, hatred, or righteousness; he made no concessions, did not cease his chance to flee and died in joyful spirit, risking all due to his faith.

There have been martyrs of purest moral energy in loyalty to their church, such as Sir Thomas More. Rather questionable are quite some other martyrs. To die for something and to confess it can easily create purposefulness and with it impurity of dying. As martyrs were driven by their desire to die in imitation of Christ, impurity increased with an urge to die that veils the soul with hysteric appearances.

Rarely do we find philosophers, even those without any essential affiliation to a community of faith in the world and left to themselves when facing God, who came to realize the Platonic dictum: Philosophizing means learning to die. While awaiting his death sentence for years, Seneca overcame his cunning efforts for rescue, so that he did not have to renounce himself in unworthy actions nor did he lose his resolve. Boethius died innocently due to a death sentence imposed by a barbaric ruler: all the while philosophizing in bright awareness attending to the actuality of Being. Giordano Bruno overcame his doubts and partial concession by yielding to his noble decision of steadfast and fearless resistance until sentenced to the stake.

The Purpose of the Unconditioned

The unconditioned does not become the unreflective given of human life. As unre- flecting beings, humans become the subject of psychology. Whatever I can know philosophically of myself or others is always submitted to the scrutiny of endless causes, reasons, and motives, and I never find an unconditioned. It is futile and deceptive to search for it in forms of spatial intuition. The unconditioned cannot be grasped when I perceive the essence of a person as his daimon. While such is under- stood as acting unconditionally from transcendence, nonetheless he is bound for any opinion to his dark and incomprehensible ground of mere suchness; hence despite his overpowering force of immediate action, he might suddenly grow weary and become different, showing himself forgetful and unreliable. The unconditioned also is not found in one's innate character that can transform itself due to decisions in freedoms of choice, metamorphosis, and rebirth. Innate character can also change for reasons that are accessible to empirical research. When asserting resolve like vitality, passion, or the demonic, all these manifestations of suchness are not uncon- ditioned, despite their perceived forcefulness. Even the case of a sacrificial death does not prove unconditionality (as animals also can sacrifice their life, without grasping their demise).

The unconditioned becomes manifest in a resolve of existence that results from reflection and is now simultaneously present as being and ought. The uncondi- tioned is from freedom rather than givenness. The unconditioned determines the final ground of a person, whether it has relevance or not. The unconditioned remains hidden, it can be felt only in boundary situations but even then without proof, despite the fact that it always carries life as it springs from existence.

Just as trees have deep roots when they grow tall, so also a full person's depth grounds itself in the unconditioned: all else is like brush, easily torn out, repotted, leveled down, and resilient *en masse*. But this analogy is not quite suitable, since the foundation of the unconditioned is best grasped as a leap into a different dimension rather than into the superlative.

Faith in the Unconditioned

When touched by the unconditioned, it becomes the most relevant reality, the unconditioned cannot be proven as knowable and cannot be shown as a being-in-the-world (all historical examples are mere references), thus the unconditioned is subject to faith. What we can see and know is always just an instance of the conditioned. What enriches one by an experience of the unconditioned is simply not present when measured in view of provability. In fact, a known and proven unconditioned is not really such; instead it is a strong force, fanaticism, savagery, spleen, or insanity. In response to the question whether the unconditioned actually exists, a skeptical response yields a better if not the only chance for persuasiveness.

For example: It is questionable whether or not there is love in the sense of the unconditioned rooted in its own ground rather than mere human affection, infatuation, habit, or contractual loyalty. A skeptic might argue that nothing can be manifest outside of itself, and thereby deny that existential communication can even be possible. All communication would be nothing more than the mirroring perception of monads that can perceive only their own states. Whatever can be shown psychologically in communication only captures presuppositions or derivations, perceptions or consequences, but not the communication by itself. Hence, psychological realities are subject to a variety of interpretations. It is quite possible to deny the reality of communication. Whatever can be shown is no longer unconditioned. Also, communication is real only at the time of its occurrence and by itself. Thus faith in the possibility of loving communication is a prerequisite for philosophizing about communication, and it is also a prerequisite to enable the possibility of practice to entertain the chance of fulfillment for a given historical life.

Such is the unconditioned. It truly is faith alone and for faith.

[...]

The Unconditioned in Time

The unconditioned in humans is not given like human existence. It grows in the person. Once we notice the effort in a person and we feel the path traveled where the unconditioned decision is manifested unmistakably, only then do we believe him. The trustworthy person remains concealed from the very beginning by the abstract imperturbability of finality and motionlessness of his soul.

The unconditioned has its source not in Being. It reveals itself in the experience of boundary situations and in the threat of becoming unfaithful to oneself. Inasmuch as it claims itself, it is available to a person through transcendence by means of deciding from inner action.

The unconditioned as such does not become temporal. Wherever it is, it is likewise transversely to time. It bursts into this world from transcendence from the path of our freedom. Wherever it is claimed, it remains genuine at each moment. Hence: Whenever temporal continuity appears to have resulted in its possession, at the very same moment all can be lost and betrayed. Contrariwise, when one's past seems to burden oneself to the point of demise, one can start anew at each moment by coming to realize the unconditioned.

[...]

Self-Empowerment and Transcendence

Reflecting upon the unconditioned almost inescapably leads to another reversal: Once I know what I want and what I do, such alignment can result in self-contentment. In it resides presumptuousness, as I now fail to see my own shortcomings and questionability; when I lose the foundational awareness of gifting myself within authentic being in favor of an exuberance, as if the creating of myself solely stems from myself and what I am.

An example: The authenticity of self-reliance reveals itself in one's ability to die. In existential plight, the reliance on one's own strength always offers as a last resort choosing to end one's life. Whoever knows how to die at the right time may claim that he did not allow bringing himself down. Such ability to accept death, such position to subsume life under certain conditions that would not be waived, contains a self-empowerment that is available to humans as humans. As such self-empowerment is relevant, where God uses human freewill as his tool and directly though through many interpretations touches one's soul; by freely choosing one's own death in bright awareness is a form of obedience against God, fulfilling the demand of its victim.

When self-empowerment misunderstands itself as originating in itself, when a person choses death—not in facing God but, as in the *Edda*, because of fame and in rebellious self-sufficiency while at the same time depending upon other people's opinions, then it is to be stated: such self-empowerment can be absolute only by saying "Nay!". It cannot rest upon itself, neither in Being nor in actual existence. Whenever it becomes affirmative, it is no longer through itself. By claiming Being it depends upon the world and nature, it could not gain duration and is bound to fail. By claiming itself it depends upon transcendence. It is not self-sufficient because it must be gifted by transcendence, through which it comes into being: hence the freedom of being oneself rests in God and not in oneself.

It is a downfall to think of oneself as absolute, such as in a disposition of stoical awareness: nothing ill happens to me, no one can harm me, I stand above things. At best this is an error in relatively favorable situations; at times there might be a superhuman and inhuman practice of enduring suffering. Nonetheless it is luck and not a result of achievement in avoiding exposure to extreme and horrific situations where a person would have no choice but to fail.

Humans stand between birth and death. One must endure to enter this world and to be situated without prior consent; one must endure the certainty of departure from this world. What one can manifest between birth and death, to what level of self-consciousness one can rise in love that is determined by the degree of clarity by which the person realizes the unconditioned when arriving at his boundaries.

Self-isolation through self-empowerment leads to emptiness, while the experience of boundaries leads to transcendence.

[. . .]

Man Is Finite and Unfinishable

There is an unconditioned for man and one can come to be certain of one's own unconditioned. But with regards to one's Being, man is finite, always conditioned, and fully aware of it. The unconditioned cannot be demonstrated by empirical observation or in scientific psychology; within objective science, there is no unconditioned. In contrast, the finitude of humans can be demonstrated in the fundamental features of one's existence. One feels the meaning and depth of personal finitude when one comes to know the unconditioned as a demand whose fulfillment points to an origin of one's existence that is different from the one noticed in one's finite existence. The unconditioned is the light that ties one in one's finitude to God. Finitude is not only determination of existence, but also becomes the fundamental of being created. While man shares this characteristic with all existence, with animals, our human finitude has an additional trait of incompleteness. Man cannot even reach the completeness attained by each animal. His incompleteness increases in finitude as his recognition of finitude comes to light. There is a sense of loss in him which seeds duties and possibilities. From here the proposition, "Man is finite and unfinishable" contains a faith whose certitude stems not only from provable knowledge of the finite, but also from the basic knowledge of one's being. This faith encompasses its unfinishedness and its possibility, its boundedness and its freedom.

Historical Examples of Human Self-Perception

The hallmark of human self-consciousness and the knowledge of responsibilities is found in the images man has created about his own existence. From the fields of history where such images are planted, I select a few characteristic examples in order to reflect upon how feebleness and forlornness were seen as a foundation for exceptional human possibilities.

The Greeks knew that no human should be praised as fortunate prior to one's death; one is exposed an uncertain fate; when losing sight of human judgment this hubris can lead to an even deeper fall. At the same time the Greeks also knew that while there are many mighty things, but nothing mightier than human.

The Old Testament addresses the insignificance of humans:

As for man, his days are as grass
as a flower of the field, so he flourishes.
For the wind passes over it and he is gone,
and the place thereof shall know him no more. (Psalm 103:15-16)
What is man, that you are mindful of him? (Psalm 8:4)

Christians were so radically aware of man's ultimate situation that they perceived it even in God became Man: Jesus experienced in deepest pain what he vocalized on the cross with the Psalm: "My God, my God, why hast Thou forsaken me." Man cannot rest upon himself.

The holiest of Christians can fail. When threatened by the hangmen and pressured by the intrusive maid's question, Peter denounced Jesus three times: "I do not know this man."

Paulus and Augustine understood the impossibility of a good person being truly good. When one acts properly, one must know about the proper action; but this knowledge is the beginning of self-adulation and arrogance. Without self-reflection there is no human goodness, and with self-reflection there is no innocent pure goodness.

Pico della Mirandola drew humans from the Idea that deity sketched of man who was born to the world on the last day of creation: God created man as his all-inclusive mirror image and spoke: No special place, no special endowment did we grant to you. All other beings in creation were given defining boundaries. You alone are nowhere restricted and you can take whatever and choose to be whatever you decide with your will. By your will and to your glory you shall be your own craftsman and sculptor and form yourself from the matter that pleases you. So you are free to fall to the lowest level of animal kingdom. But you can elevate yourself to the highest spheres of divinity. Animals possess from birth all of what there ever will be in their possession. In humans alone had the father sowed the seeds for all actions and the sprouts for all forms of life.

Blaise Pascal simultaneously saw the brilliance and wretchedness of humans. Man is all and nothing, he stands without ground in the middle between infinities. Irreconcilably formed in opposition, he lives with insatiable disquiet, neither as an appeased middle nor as a reclining in between. "What a fabrication is man! What distorted image, what confusion, what thing of contradiction. Judge of everything, foolish earth worm, glory and scum of the universe. . . . Man exceeds man infinitely. . . . So pathetic we are that we have a glimpse of joy. Within ourselves we carry an image of truth but we possess only confusion. We are incapable to know truly nothing nor to know with certainty something.

The Finitude of Man

First of all the finitude of all things is vital. Man depends on the environment, food, and sensory contents; man is subjected to the mercilessly silent and blind events of nature; and man must die.

Secondly, the finitude of man has to do with one's dependency on other humans and the corresponding worlds of shared realities. There is no reliance for man on anything in this world. Treasures come and go. In the orderliness of humans reigns not just a permeating justice, but also an appropriate might, which claims arbitrarily to be the executioner of justice and as such is simultaneously always based on untruths. States and populace can destroy people who have worked for all their lives in support of reality as a service to their idea. Only the loyalty of man in existential communication is truly reliable when it is void of shrewd motives. Reliability here is not derived from an objective provable being in the world. For the next human may very well fall ill, turn insane, or die.

Thirdly, the finitude of man has to do with the fact that even by tending to oneself he cannot take credit for it. One is not authentic to oneself through oneself. Just as one's existence in the world does not originate by one's will, to be oneself is the gift of transcendence. One must be gifted to oneself each time anew, if one does not want to miss out on oneself. As one affirms inner strength in life, and as one remains steadfast even at the time of death, one cannot get through this alone. What is helpful here is of a radically different nature than any other help in the world. Transcendence reveals itself by being true to oneself. That one can stand one's ground is possible by freely experiencing one's guiding hand from transcendence.

Each animal has its own well-being, in its limitations as well as in its perfection. It is only at the mercy of the cycles of nature that dissolve and birth anew; and it overcomes this fate without knowing of it. Only man knows death to be certain, and knows that one lives under constant threat. But simply knowing one's vital finitude is not really the decisive factor. Except that this knowledge of death differentiates man from all other life inasmuch as through freedom one knows of one's incompleteness and incompletability. Through this realization, one is in the most desperate situation of knowing the strongest demand of ascending through one's own freedom. And so, descriptions of man always point at stunning contradictions when man is described as the most wretched and the most sublime creature.

[. . .]

The Journey of Man Starts from Faith in One's Possibilities

The feeling of discontent arises because man knows the high demands upon oneself; the abyss of desolateness manifests itself because man can see the bright possibilities. But these polarities that nurture man's self-confidence, of discontent and demand, of desolateness and possibility, of feeble attachment and the unconditional demand of compliant ability, and of forlornness and freedom are not empirical realities: actually they occur just in one's faith. Through faith, one is certain of something invisible or undetectable. From this faith one's journey unfolds, if there is a journey at all and not just an unfolding of events in nature. Only faith becomes aware of its forlornness and of its potential.

Hence in the finitude and incompleteness of man there is not just despair, but also the path of one's way of life. This path is of truthfulness and purity of soul as conditions to manifest its contents. Both are an ability of being, an incomplete being-on-the-way.

The danger of man is a false self-confidence, by assuming that one already is what one strives to be. Faith that is merely motivation and hope turns into an erroneous possessing and being. It either turns into the arrogance of moral self-contentment (as if one is certain of one's actions inasmuch as they bring testimony to oneself due to their external reality), or faith turns into pride of one's own good heritage (as if it is innately present what is gifted transcendently in freedom but could have remained elusive).

Man Can Live by Guidance Through God

When man travels on the path of his self-becoming, fully aware of his finitude and incompletability, and when on this path he asserts the reality of God and experiences the unconditioned, then he lives in a reality that combines all of this: in the unconditioned, finite man believes to feel guidance through God.

When God guides one, the question arises: How does one hear what God commands? Is there an encounter of man with God? How does it come about?

Historical Examples

The search for God's guidance through prayer has taken place from time immemorial. Even a statesman like Oliver Cromwell prayed through the nights for gaining clarity to the point when he deemed his political decisions had matured to god-willed necessities.

Without the certainty of facts, humans knew how deep they were in the grace of God, whether God is near or far, protects them or forsakes them, if He reveals himself and then withdraws, and even if He disappears and is no longer.

Prophets announced they heard God's words and related them to the people.

Humans massively believed that God revealed himself through prophets and events of history, so that they can live obediently according to these directives.

Autobiographical works (for example of the mineralogist Franz Ernest Neumann) often describe the process of gaining sudden certainty that comes after a long period of doubt when pondering over difficult decisions in life. After being captivated by helpless wavering, this certainty constitutes the freedom of embracing action. In the clarity of certainty, the more a person of resolve knows his freedom, even more luminous is the transcendence through which he exists.

There are a sudden illuminations through speculative thought, until a jolt occurs in the transformation of self-awareness. No teachings can deliver what this is all about, they can only prepare one. Each and every individual must obtain it all through him or herself. But this action through and by oneself is experienced as if enacted by God, and since he cannot be made, there is no awareness of how it possibly could have happened. Philosophers have claimed that their most important thoughts were given by God (Anselm, Nicolas Cusanus, Descartes) or at least were inspired by God (Nietzsche).

Kierkegaard enacted his self-reflection with regard to God's guidance in such a way that he knew himself permanently to be in God's hands: Kierkegaard's actions and the events that occurred to him in the world led him to believe that he heard God and yet perceived all in its inconclusiveness. No guidance with certain accessibility or immediate and clear directives guided him, but leadership through freedom is lucidly bound by its transcendent ground.

Without fully comprehending it at first, Socrates listened to a daimon who forbad certain actions. Of his task Socrates relates in the Apology: "I receive from the gods, through oracles, dreams, and all sorts of signs by which God's will can be related to man."

Revelation (to the Individual as Generally Accepted Authority due to Tradition)

Communication by God is called revelation; in a more narrow sense revelation refers to a historically defined objective account of God's deeds and God's words; it claims to be a direct and universally valid exclusive truth as such. In a wider sense, revelation is that form of objectivity that is perceived by an individual as an indirect knowing of God's will.

Revelation in its narrower sense is in and by itself questionable, since a revelation that addresses everyone as an absolute truth can occur in the world only as a claim of people who insist that such revelation was made accessible to them. One can chose to believe such people and follow unconditionally the directives of revealed communications. One can also chose to establish criteria for testing the content of revelations, and only then it is determined if and to what extent such content could possibly come from God.

Revelation in the broader sense is only questionable inasmuch as the existence of God might be questionable. For the person who lives with God, there is also some form of revelation. Without revealing himself, God would remain simply a subject of sentiment. No objective and conclusive philosophical affirmation has been established for revelation, which allows for a variety of directions to perceive the possible language of God or his guidance.

aa. Revelation to Individuals: After weighing all possibilities, posing questions, and incessant pondering about the certainty of one's decision, man arrives unmediated and within the totality of one's personal fate at resolve that remains unpredictable and incomprehensible in all of its essential aspects. This certainty is borne by the seriousness of unconditional commitment. It is this disposition that can be interpreted as God's will, although it is never physically audible.

[. . .]

bb. Revelation as universally valid authority in the world: There are people—the prophets—who relate their experience of God to others by claiming their authority and stake their influence for others as God's instrument. There are institutions—the churches—that mediate by virtue of their authority related claims by prophets, and claim for themselves a character of holiness (for example the Catholic Church as corpus Christi).

cc. Revelation by means of tradition: God's guidance occurs overall through objectivities from tradition. It becomes the purpose for knowing in the absence of knowledge and the resolve in the multiplicity of possibilities. God speaks in the community of humans, in which I live in solidarity through communication and in a community of humans that refer to God throughout millennia.

The possible language of God is not just audible in selected passages of tradition, but in the totality of mental events that liberated humans by enabling the realization of one's finitude and incompletability and the possibilities of redemption. These events occurred in the Axial Age of history, the times between 800 and 200 BC in China, India, and the Occident. For us Westerners who live with biblical religion, God should be heard far beyond the Occident by his revelation through humans who came to realize transcendence even at the last earnestness. We do not need to get caught in a particular origin of religious tradition that might have had a complete character at one point but no longer possesses it today. Our endowment in the transmission of biblical religion is not compromised if it is experienced as the unique historical foundation for one's own life within the broad spectrum of truth.

[...] Given the necessity of interpretation, there are two possibilities for the acquisition of tradition.

Either there is an objectively transcendent becoming-in-itself, upon which I have faith based on certain manifestations and supported by certain humanly represented authority figures. I believe in this as an assured warranty within this world.

Or, there is an indefinite objectivity of images, thoughts, and claims that are represented by human actuality. It is a medium in which my awareness manifests itself, awakens, and remembers.

[...]

Ambiguity and Certainty

Revelation is perhaps at the core of an event or a narrative. When taken by itself it still remains veiled. What an individual can perceive from it and through it as one journeys through the world, when understanding it as God's guidance, it does not manifest itself objectively as revelation. Even when humans are trusted to have received revelation, or institutions are trusted to be the conveyor of revelation, still revelation as such is nowhere clearly present. All events in the world are ambiguous with regards to their transcendent meaning, and equally ambiguous are the humans who appear with claims regarding revelation. We know being only in its manifestation and revelation only in interpretation.

Within this ambiguity, the individual must nonetheless make an instantaneous decision "at a glance" within one's actual existence. The absence of knowledge is the space and the source within which decisions are made and never sufficiently comprehended by reason. Ambiguity remains the constant background of every temporal determination of certainty.

[...]

Universal Validity and Historicity

Experiencing God's guidance does not happen solely by insight into universally known facts but also through the language of historicity related to one's life. One

would not need a historical ground and guidance through God if all action, perception, thinking, and feeling could be derived from the universality of knowledge and
moral laws. The universally valid that is rationally comprehensible is as such not
God's voice. God's voice is historically directed toward the individual. Guidance
through God rests in history as its affirmation and incomprehensibility, yet as an
infinite dawning.

One must seek his path in the tension between universality (rational ethical) and
historicity. [. . .] One must accept guilt either by breaking through the universal in
favor of one's historicity, or by breaking with one's historicity through universality.
[. . .]

The historicity of community is guided by the revelation of God that is directed
to all. This communication must take place in a universally accessible form.
Universality commands obedience to something that cannot be comprehended and is
simultaneously somewhat absurd (for example, the belief in Yahweh's arrangement
with the people of Sinai and his prophecies about the Commandments and Christ
as God who is sacrificed in human form and is resurrected). Whatever could be historically true in first instance, is no longer the same in subsequent narrations. Since
God's revelation can only be absolute, unique, and also simultaneously unconditioned and without universality of communicability, it is for a philosophizing human
the fixation of God's voice to a specific revelation of a particular people, community, sect, or church already mistaken in its roots. Since the veracity of revelation
at the moment of rational discourse no longer remains what it was, philosophers
would not take revelation as a given objective in the world; for example, not as an
objective salvation for all, not as a universally valid canon, law, dogma, or sacra-
ment. Revelation tends to dissipate if one refers to it as a means to negate others in
the world; one can only show readiness to perceive it in unrepeatable historicity and
to build upon this for oneself.
[. . .]

Self-Empowerment and Obedience

Priests and theologians incessantly repeat the complaint about individual self-
empowerment that one should not philosophize about God. They demand obedience
toward God. One might reply to them as follows:

1. God acts through the free decisions of individuals. One believes to obey God
   when deciding from one's depth in perpetual risk of no objective guarantee to
   know what God's will is.
2. They confuse obedience toward God with obedience toward those institutions in
   the world where direct revelation is assumed to occur, such as in churches, with
   priests or books or laws.
3. A truthful coincidence between obedience toward objective authorities in the
   world and one's original experience of God's will is in principle possible.
   However, if the originally experienced will of God is played against objective

authorities, then one faces the temptation to avoid the risk of being obedient toward God and against objective authorities, as one perceives God's will in reality through the god-given medium of autonomy. This is due to the fact that because one can refrain from the duty of autonomy in favor of obeying authorities that objectively exist in the world, even though such authorities justify their status with reference to revelation and demand to be perceived as uniquely holy and directly authenticated by God.

As one reaches for guidance in trustworthy laws and commands by an authority, a downhill helplessness manifests itself. In contrast, one can give rise to energy through responsibility, by listening to the whole, derived from reality and depth.

Theologians notice the self-empowerment of individuals also in the self-contentment of a moral person. From the stoic claim that one should live in such a way to please oneself (instead of seeking influence in the world), all the way to the form of self-contentment that Kant already granted to a moral person, theologians object to a permeating high-handed self-contentment which is constituted already by Paul and Augustine, and even Kant himself with his theory of radical evil, asserts that the reason for human existence is corrupt in its roots.

In fact, man can never be fully and completely content with oneself; since any judgment about oneself cannot rest upon oneself. One asks for an assessment of one's action. This judgment becomes valuable to the degree of esteem of the judging person. As one becomes true to oneself, an increasing sensitivity occurs about the status of a person whose judgment and echo is now experienced in sympathy and antipathy. The judgment of average people or the masses, of vagrants or the blind, or of abandoned institutions no longer appears relevant. In the end, the ultimately relevant judgment does not rest with noble people either, even though their judgment is the only accessible one in this world; what ultimately matters is the judgment of God.

[. . .]

God's Voice in the Freedom of Self-Assertiveness

Through self-knowledge man comes to accept general moral commands. Considering such directives as God's commands has transported the presence of God into the ethical domain since the Decalogue. One can accept and comply with such commands without believing in God, in mere acceptance of permissible human action; in such cases the possibility of God's existence remains open, it is neither affirmed nor denied. However, to accept the seriousness of obeying the ethical law which is understood in one's freedom, often is combined with hearing God's voice precisely within such freedom.

Since concrete action cannot be sufficiently derived from the universality upon which it measures itself, God's guidance becomes more noticeable within the origin of historically concrete demands rather than in universality. In all certainty, taking such notice remains questionable; it does not become objectively certain within a freedom that affirms to itself the necessity of such an ought. Moderation is essential to obeying God's guidance due to the chance of failure. Moderation excludes the safety of certainty, prohibits the universalization of one's own action as a template for all, and avoids fanaticism. Even the purest clarity of a path, as it is seen under God's guidance, must not lead to self-assertiveness, as if such path would be the only true path destined for all.

[...]

The voice of God as the judgment of man has no other expression in time as in the judgment of a human upon oneself. In free and sincere ways of judging self-realization, in self-contentment, and in self-reproach man finds the indirect, and never final, yet always ambiguous judgment of God.

[...]

Reality in the World Has Diminishing Being Between God and Existenz

Human reality seems to teach the opposite: for man, the world and occurrences in the world are absolute. And one can say of man who has adopted so much as the final content of his essence: what you observe and what you do, that is in fact your God (Luther). Man cannot help taking things as absolute, whether one wants to or not, whether it is done accidentally and constantly changing or assertively and with continuation. For man, as it were, the absolute has a place. This place is unavoidable. He must fulfill it.

This fulfillment occurs in the chosen forms of one's being-in-the-world that constitute a symbol (simile, incarnation) of being, or it occurs by transcendence above all being-in-the-world, or it unites both.

Historical Examples of Transcending the World

Indian ascetics—as well as certain monks in China and in the Occident—left this world in the worldless meditation of internalizing the absolute. The world seemingly disappeared, while being was everything when perceived as nothing from the perspective of the world.

Chinese mystics liberated themselves from binding desires in order to achieve pure contemplation, where all being turns into the transparent language of dissipating appearances of the eternal and the infinite presence of its law. For them, time has erased in eternity in order to become the actuality of language in the world.

Occidental scientists, philosophers, poets, rarely also perpetrators went through the world as if—in spite of all dependency—they arrive permanently from an outside, as if they were originating from a distant homeland and find in this world themselves and objects; and from profound proximity to these objects traverse their temporal appearance in favor of remembering the eternal.

Harmony of Being and Disunity

World-optimism that perceives the world as a harmony of being is an error brought about by the relative delight of the charm of worldly fulfillment. Against such untruth, despair shows scornful anger as it faces the totality of reality: and this defiance can turn to godless nihilism.

Truthfulness must see through the double error of the harmony of being and nihilistic disunity. Both contain a generic judgment due to insufficient knowledge. Against the fixation of contrary generic judgments there is the readiness for incessant listening to the events, fate, and choice of action within the timeless course of life. This readiness includes:

(1) The experience of God's absolute transcendence to the world; *deus absconditus* moves into ever greater distance the more I attempt to grasp it in general terms with the desire to comprehend everything once and for all. This is unpredictable and due to the absolutely historical nature of language in ever-unique situations.
(2) The experience of God's language in the world: being-in-the-world is not by itself but takes place in the permanent ambiguity of God's language that becomes accessible only in historical terms without the permission to universalize, and has clarity as such only at the moment of existence.

When the absolute, being, and creation are described in totality and with certainty and accessibly, such as the hitherto most impressive scholars Thomas and Dante succeeded in doing, it still leaves the feeling of a prison door closing shut.

Being in Time

In our freedom for being the last concern is not the world as such and by itself. In this world encounters take place that are eternal as they appear temporal. All tasks in the world, solidarity among humans, and all else is between God and Existenz.

But as eternal being we can attain when being in the world, we experience for our self-knowledge nothing else but what transmits itself as real temporal appearance; since whatever exists for us must occur in the temporality of being-in-the-world, there is no direct knowledge of God and existence. There is only faith.

General Principles of Faith and Their Historical Fulfillment

General principles of knowledge apply for things in the world in whose reality or evidence they find confirmation. However, the truth of generally transmitted philosophical principles of belief in the world are experienced historically. The truth of principles of faith in their universality can only be felt to the extent that their fulfillment resonates in the world as the language of God. If God were to circumvent the world for the purpose of approaching existence, this would turn out to be incommunicable. The truth of general principles is communicated in a given form of transmission and their special acquisition in life: individual awareness has awakened in these persons to such truths; one's parents have said so; there is an infinite historical depth to the origin of formulae: "for the sake of his holy name"; "Immortality"...

The more general the principles of faith are, the less historical they become. They claim their high demand purely in abstraction. But no human can live with such abstractions alone, since they remain minimal in their failure to generate concrete fulfillment that can provide a golden thread to memory and hope. But at the same time such principles have a cleansing power: they liberate us from bodily fetters and superstitious narrowness and allow for proper acquisition of the great traditions to bring alive their relevance.

[...]

Retrospect

About the Five Principles

[...]

There is diffidence in speaking these principles straightforwardly. All too fast they are treated as knowledge and consequently lose their meaning. All too quickly they are treated as affirmations and put in the place of reality. In communicating these principles there is the temptation of an incorrect claim on the part of those who speak them. Yet they beg to be communicated, so that humans can get along with them, and assert their place in dialogue, so that they awaken those who willingly allow for it. But because of their clarity and precision these assertions mislead by becoming propaganda, as if by virtue of their dissemination truth would be more accurate and confirmed, as if it would be unavoidable to humans to believe anyway. But philosophy ends where propaganda begins.

Propositions require debate. Wherever we engage in thought, there is an immediate rift: we can either find truth or miss it, hence with all positive propositions there is also the repulsion of error, alongside the truthful path is also the wrong track, besides the orderly build-up of thoughts there is also reversal. Because of permanent intimidation in missing a point, the treatment of positive thinking is permanently spiked with negative judgments, demarcation and repulsion, apologetic and polemic. As long as one philosophizes, this struggle is not a battle for power, but an encounter on the path of lucidity by being questioned, whereby all the weaponry of intellect is available to the opponent as well, just as it is available for expressing one's own belief.

I am now forced to make this assertion in philosophizing about these questions: Is there God? Is there an unconditioned demand in being? Is man capable of completeness? Is there guidance through God? Is being-in-the-world vague and disappearing?—For their answer I am even more assertively forced to express the following antinomies when faced with propositions regarding faithlessness:

There is no God, because there is only reality and the rules of its occurrences; reality is God.

There is no unconditioned, because the demands I follow have developed through and infinitely conditioned by habit, practice, tradition, obedience.

The perfect human can exist, since a human can be a well-developed being; and like an animal, it is possible to cultivate perfect humans. *There is in principle no incompleteness*, no "original sin," in whatever form it might be understood, no frailty of humans at their core. Humans are not an in-between but complete and whole. Like everything else in the world man is transitory, but is self-made, self-sufficient, and self-fulfilled in his world.

There is no guidance through God; since this is an illusion and a comfortable self-deception. Man has the strength to guide himself and can only rely upon his own strength.

The world is everything; its reality is the one and only actuality. Since there is no transcendence, all that exists is transient, but the world is absolute, eternal and does not disappear, there is no fluctuating transitory state.

When faced with such propositions of faithlessness, it is philosophically relevant to first understand where they come from. They are possibilities of reflection due to a period of enlightenment, after dislodging themselves from understanding and turning to pure reason. They become reality by the lack of force of an encompassing faith, in whose presence any such empty propositions would be denied both from within me and within my environment.

Furthermore, since I advanced with an affirmative reply to these questions, these answers will in the end turn into an *analogon* of the confession (although it includes some sort of support, for the most part negatively and yet also in a directing and developing manner). The philosopher must not use lack of knowledge to withdraw from an answer altogether. Philosophically I will keep in reserve that I do not know, and that I also do not know if I believe: but I may say that faith, when expressed in principles, appears to be meaningful to me, and I dare to venture to believe this and to find the strength for living accordingly. When philosophizing there is always some tension between the seemingly indecisiveness of pending propositions and the reality of one's chosen conduct. Perhaps this is the contrast of a philosophical demeanor in contrast to one that is found amongst all dogmatists, to wit, the concealment of an already decided affirmation, knowledge, or opinion unresolved in practical behavior and inner emotional life.

The mistake in proposing principles of faith occurs when they are taken as proclamation for a material content. The meaning of each of these principles is not found in their material extension, may they be known or believed, but as ciphers for solidifying infinity. Wherever infinity is present in faith, the infinite becomes an ambiguous manifestation of this origin.

Our endeavor proclaimed five general principles of faith. The five propositions show a relationship to one another. Their closer analysis would demonstrate how they affirm each other and reciprocally originate from each other. But each one has its own convincing strength applying only to itself, has its own origin in a fundamental experience of existence, and consequently has its own sense of truth.

Philosophical Faith and the Future of Mankind

Leonard H. Ehrlich[†]

Abstract Leonard Ehrlich's final reflections on Jaspers' concept of "philosophical faith" prior to his death on 8 June 2011 and the concept for which Ehrlich was also famous. An account of the two phases of the philosophy of Karl Jaspers during which he developed and refined his notion of philosophical faith, the first being tied to his *Philosophie* in 3 volumes (1932) following World War I, and the second being tied to his *Von der Wahrheit* (1947), written immediately following World War II, and his political writings having to do with the partition of Germany, the Cold War, and hope for the future of mankind.

The point of departure for Jaspers' deep concern over the future at the midpoint of the twentieth century was the insight that for humankind the world had become *one* world. For us Jaspers' insight has become an obtrusive fact, with consequences Jaspers barely foresaw. In our situation, no less than 60 years ago, the question of faith is of central importance in both its negative and positive ramifications. Concern regarding the future is not only a matter for the philosophy of history; it is also political thinking, meaning thought with respect to people toward each other, even as politics in the larger sense is a matter of action that affects groups of people, whether within small political units or between nations.

The question of faith nowadays is firmly placed within the world-political concern regarding the future. For the Western mind, the juxtaposition of faith and politics may seem strange. Jaspers would agree with this insofar as the separation of faith and politics is a significant and irreplaceable achievement of the spiritual maturity of humankind. It is a separation, lapidarily chiseled in the constitutions of the free democracies of the West. However, what is meant by "faith" in this separation is the faith of a religion. Hence, it signifies that religious faith institutions are separated from access to the means of exercising political power. The separation does not mean the elimination of religion or religious faith. To the contrary, Jaspers sees in that separation the possibility of a genuine actuality of faith that, according to him, arises from free and original conviction, and not from coercion.

There are two phases in the unfolding of Jaspers' thought regarding these matters. The first is tied to his *Philosophie* in 3 volumes (1932), the second to his *Von der*

L.H. Ehrlich (✉)

H. Wautischer et al. (eds.), *Philosophical Faith and the Future of Humanity*,
DOI 10.1007/978-94-007-2223-1_4, © Springer Science+Business Media B.V. 2012

Wahrheit (1947). During the first phase of his great thought-work, Jaspers already took up the phenomenon of faith. Here he is concerned with the phenomenon of faith as such, where religious faith is merely one among other forms of faith. In order to understand Jaspers' meaning of the connection of faith and politics, it is important to recall his fundamental phenomenology of faith.

Jaspers encountered the actuality of faith in his young years, the earnestness of faith as well as its problematic side and aberrations with critical respect. In his teens he wanted to leave his church community for reasons of honesty. His father admonished him that many value the church and, since one is a member of society, one has to respect this fact. In old age, when that consideration no longer counts, one can leave. And in his later years Jaspers' father *did* indeed leave the Church.

In his twenties, Jaspers fell in love with Gertrud Mayer, a Jewish woman from a notable family that had lived in Prenzlau, Pomerania, since the end of the seventeenth century, thanks to a patent of privilege from the Elector of Prussia. The prospect of a Jewish daughter-in-law presented no problem for Jaspers' parents since they were what was then called liberal-conservative. However, a non-Jewish son-in-law was a problem for the Mayer family. Gertrud's father was President of the Jewish Community; and Father Mayer wanted to resign as president of the community, but the Rabbi of Prenzlau forbad it. Three decades later, the Rabbi was murdered by the Nazis.

When Jaspers was invited to Prenzlau he wore a hat, since the Mayer family was traditional and the men wore their hats, at the table. Father Mayer said, "You do not have to do that, my son." Fifty-five years later, my wife, Edith, and I were as moved by this as was Frau Gertrud Jaspers when she reported this brief event to us as if it had happened only yesterday. In his memoirs Jaspers wrote how he loved his father-in-law, almost like his own father. And yet, throughout his life he was pained by Father Mayer's initial reservations against his daughter's marriage to a non-Jew.

In the 1920s Jaspers worked out the aspects and the connections of the phenomenon of faith in terms of the fundamental phenomena of thought, i.e., without fundamental reference to institutional religion. However, the relation of faith to religion was unavoidable, even though Jaspers treats it as a philosophical phenomenon. He also juxtaposes philosophizing and religion, as well as philosophical faith and revelational faith or faith in revelation, and subjects the latter to a critique from a philosophical perspective. This means that according to Jaspers the customary contraposition of reason and faith is invalid.

Jaspers' phenomenology of faith points to the fact that in our thinking we cannot help taking something as absolute. This makes sense when we consider that in formal thought, for example, in mathematics and especially in formal logic, we base our thinking on axioms or on the law of non-contradiction even though we do not refer to axioms and formal presuppositions as fundamentals of faith. However, the principle is the same since in any thoughtful discourse certain presuppositions count as absolute. This does not mean that they are ultimately absolute, or as the scholastics call it, *simpliciter simplex* ("utterly simple"). A different discourse might rest on a contrary axiom. We know this from the example of the history of the parallel axiom in Euclidean geometry.

When Jaspers proposes that our knowledge, and even science, rests on a kind of faith, this may sound provocative to many. We must keep in mind, however, that in German "knowledge" is translated as *Wissen*, and "science" as *Wissenschaft*; and *Wissenschaft* comprises any disciplined inquiry, and is not restricted to the natural sciences, as in English.

What Jaspers means is that scientific knowledge neither is simply experience nor the generalization of experiences. Rather, science is the theoretical conjunction of experienced, possibly measurable, data, and the modes of conjunction rest on presuppositions that make the respective explanatory system possible and are valid insofar as they produce verifiable results. The presuppositions determine the meaning of the truth of evident knowledge; that is to say presuppositions themselves are believed, they are not known.

Faith in its fundamental sense is neither axiom, nor presupposition, nor principle, nor postulate. For the "absolute" of faith is simply absolute. Jaspers refers to faith as a mode of absolute consciousness, a term he adopts from Kierkegaard. As such, faith is not knowledge, because knowledge is derived, e.g., from experience or by deduction. Knowledge is relative to what is presupposed either concretely or by thought. Faith, on the other hand, is original and, hence, absolute in the originary sense. This does not mean that faith comes to us in a mystical way, because what we believe as faith comes to us through the education and culture (*Bildung*) that we experience from our earliest childhood long before we face the meaning of faith from a critical distance. Rather, what is meant by the originality, i.e. the absolute consciousness of faith, is the following: Faith is an act of freedom on the part of an individual person. What I believe, in the sense of faith, means that I stand by it; I not only adopt faith, but I testify to it by offering my temporality for it, to the extent that I have the courage to live out of it at my risk and at my responsibility. Faith is not a project of life but that out of which one lives.

Faith is not truth that is known. Despite what one knows, or what is generally known, faith is the motivation to live and to continue no matter what happens. The truth of knowledge does not need to be adopted in the manner of faith, much less to offer one's life for it. Jaspers illustrates this by reminding us of the difference between the situations of Galileo Galilei and Giordano Bruno. Both men had to appear before the court of the Inquisition at the time during which the controversial Copernican theory of the solar system motivated the beginnings of modern science. The heliocentric theory was taken up by the metaphysical thinkers of the Renaissance who, in turn, provoked the opposition of the Church and its theologians. Both Bruno and Galileo were accused of harboring and publicizing views connected with the Copernican theory that were contrary to faith. Both were in danger of suffering death on the pyre unless they recanted their teachings. In accordance with his scientific research, Galileo taught that the earth revolves around the sun, and not the other way around. This seemed not only to contradict the Bible but also to question the conception that the earth is the center of creation and the locus of divine revelation, especially of the salvific death of Jesus as the divine Christos. Bruno, on the other hand, passionately represented his vision of the infinite number of worlds that come to be and pass away, and of other solar systems with planets.

Upon interrogation, he could not deny that in his vision the earth and its history, including the life and suffering of Christ, are not unique and, consequently, that the earth cannot be viewed as the unique center of a universe that is God's creation.

The truth of Galileo's problematic theory rests on a scientific procedure that anyone, able to follow the steps of research and thought, can retrace. The validity of this kind of truth in no way rests on the empirical reality of vouching for it with one's life. We all know the apocryphal story according to which Galileo, after he abjured his controversial theory, is said to have murmured into his beard, "...and yet it turns" (*eppur si muove*). This legend informs us that the Copernican theory does not require the death of a person for its verification. The situation of Bruno is different. The truth of his theory could not be proven by scientific means but was the product of his cosmological vision. One does not need to share Bruno's vision, nor does one need to understand it or take it seriously, in order to see that for him it was a matter of faith. If he had abjured it, he would have been an exemplary image of the wretched self-traitor, disloyal to his truth and to himself. Hence, he had to die in the flames of the pyre, and is now counted as one of the martyrs among philosophers, along with Socrates and Seneca.

Jaspers goes so far as to maintain that faith rests on a unique kind of skepticism and what Nicholas of Cusa called learned ignorance (*docta ignoratia*). On the other hand, Jaspers considers it a perversion of faith to confirm or disprove faith by means of scientific, formal, or empirical methods. Disproofs are an ancient and perennial problem, as in the case of Job's friends. In our days the literature of disproof is rampant, mainly produced by Anglo-American analytical formalists. There also is a new field of inquiry that Jaspers would never have anticipated, namely experimental theology.

According to Jaspers, faith, as the foundation of life, is something personal. In order to further characterize the phenomenon of faith, we turn to two related questions: What is the content of faith? And wherein consists the actuality of faith? When we speak about the content of faith, we usually mean articles of faith, confessions, dogmas, or doctrines of magisterial authorities, or symbolic representation. All these are articulations through which personal inner faith attains a form of objectification transmitted from person to person, and from generation to generation. Jaspers refers to the old distinction that probably stems from scholasticism. He distinguishes *fides quae creditur* and *fides qua creditur*. Literally these mean "faith that is believed" and "faith as it is believed." In Jaspers' use we would say "faith in something" and "faith as that by which one exists." The former refers to the objective content of faith. The latter refers to the effect of what is believed within the actuality of life. The truth of a person's faith is not actual insofar as the objective content of faith, i.e. "faith in something" does not coincide with the subjective realization of faith, i.e., with "faith as that by which one exists."

The actuality of faith consists in its effectiveness. The truth of faith does not rest in its confession because in order for faith to be true, it requires that faith be rendered true in the proof of deeds, in the way a person lives her or his life, and in the offering of one's temporality. According to Jaspers, a confession of faith, without risking for it the conduct of one's life, is nothing more than reducing faith to its formal content. Faith must have effect or it is a void. In some Christian Churches, the mere confession of faith has been the path to salvation, especially in earlier centuries. We can see how Jaspers' phenomenology of faith developed independently of actual religious faiths.

The following is essential for our topic: One's own actuality of faith testifies to what is absolute truth for oneself. It does not testify to its being fundamental truth for anyone else, much less for everyone, or that the authority to whom one defers in one's faith is exclusively absolute. According to Jaspers, the one ultimate truth is absolute, and as such transcendent. It transcends every realization of truth on the part of human beings, of humankind, and of human history. The truth of faith that is actual and effective among peoples, no matter how comprehensive or catholic by virtue of conviction or by the sword, merely partakes of the one truth in its transcendent, encompassing absoluteness. Even the faith of every faith community is more than its actualization, no matter how wide and how detailed it is articulated, and no matter how tolerant it may be of other modes of faith. Jaspers maintains that every faith is itself encompassing in the sense that it includes both actuality and transcendence.

The situation in which a believer meets another believer can be characterized by faith against faith. The same thing can be said of the encounter between faith communities. This concerns especially those religious communities that rest on belief in special revelations. History shows how such a meeting can lead to a life-or-death battle.

What then is the significance of Jaspers' thoughts about the possible efficacy of the idea of a philosophical faith? On the basis of Jaspers' criticism of Christianity as a revelational faith, many have concluded that Jaspers means to contrapose revelational faith with philosophical faith. This notion has to be corrected.

First, Jaspers elaborates philosophical faith by expressing it in the form of a few statements that sound like articles of religious faith. Jaspers' five statements and brief elaborations in *Grundsätze des Philosophierens: Einführung in philosophisches Leben,* are particularly important in this regard.[1] His statements in this fragment are very abstract and are not meant to express a confession. Instead they are meant to evoke a consciousness of an encompassing ground of faith in which believers of various actual modes of faith can encounter each other in solidarity and not as opponents.

Second, Jaspers refers to the idea of philosophical faith in order to subject revelational religion, especially Christianity, to criticism. The title of his final major philosophical work, *Der philosophische Glaube angesichts der Offenbarung* (1962) literally means "Philosophical Faith vis-à-vis Revelation" and not as rendered in the title of the English translation, *Philosophical Faith and Revelation* (1967). Both formulations of this distinction could be the reason for misunderstanding. Even before

---

[1] See the English translation of this fragment of Jaspers' *Nachlass,* viz., "Principles for Philosophizing: Introduction to Philosophical Life, 1942/43" by Karl Jaspers, this volume.

the publication of this book, Karl Barth deprecated Jaspers' treatment of transcendence, and Fitz Buri, who was on friendly terms with Jaspers, considered that for Christian theology Jaspers' idea of the encompassing was the gift of a Trojan horse. Jaspers thought this to be a most apt judgment.

It would be wrong to think that Jaspers would advocate the abolition or the abandonment of revelational faith, or that this could take place with Jaspers' support. One can certainly find some sharp judgments in Jaspers regarding institutions founded on special revelation; for example that the Churches failed with respect to the evil of the Nazi-regime. This means that in their magisterial authority they failed and missed strengthening the moral motivation that is rooted in the faith of the believer to recognize evil and, personally undeterred, to resist and to counteract that evil. One can also read in Jaspers the extent to which, and how in spite of its many errors, he affirmed Christianity and the Church as being the buttress and teacher of the Western ethos, affirming the dignity of each individual human being before God, and thus before their fellow humans; as the teacher of the individual's freedom, in particular through Luther's teaching of the freedom of conviction; and finally, as transmitter of the contents of the Hebrew Bible, not only that of the unconditional moral and ethical demands placed on human beings, but also the challenge of the prophets to steadfastness in the fulfillment of God's will. Even though Jaspers, after his youth, did not enter a church to attend a service, he valued the magisterial mission of the Church, the extent of which can be seen that throughout his life he contributed his church tax while Frau Gertrud Jaspers submitted her religious tax to the Jewish community. One could comment at this point that in his 1947 Basel lectures on *Der philosophische Glaube* (in English, *The Perennial Scope of Philosophy*) Jaspers opined that if Christianity could abandon the doctrine of Jesus as divine Christ, Judaism could accept Jesus as one of the prophets. However, these were provocations. Jaspers well knew that the continuance of institutional Christianity, which he promoted, could not be imagined without faith in Christ's redemptive martyr's death. The problematic situation from which we look to the future cannot count on the end of faith in special revelations. Jaspers was no utopian, he was a realist. The problem of the future of humanity was rather the question as to how could there be peace on the basis of the actually existing revelational faiths.

According to Jaspers the problem is not revelational faiths as such, but their respective claims to exclusiveness. This claim means that the content of faith vouchsafed through believed revelation is Truth that excludes the validity of claims to truth on the part of every other faith construct.

For the Churches the abandonment of the claim of exclusiveness is a difficult problem, for not only would the Roman-Catholic Church and the Protestant Churches have to recognize each other in their respective differences as to the truth of faith, they would also have to recognize Judaism in its truth. Of course, there are ecumenical tendencies within Christianity. There is also the will no longer to deny the validity of the "Old" Testament on the basis of the "New." This is a will that arose spontaneously as well as programmatically in consideration of the almost completed success of exterminating European Jews and the concomitant destruction of European Judaism. However, while this addresses what for Jaspers is the problematic claim of exclusivity, it does not reach the root of the problem.

What Jaspers means may be expressed as follows: It is vital that a person not only affirm the other by way of noncommittal verbal assurances but also positively out of the origin and actuality of one's faith finding the reason and the strength to acknowledge not only the truth of the other's faith, but the other's humanity in the otherness of his or her truth.

If that were possible, it would be the work of philosophical faith. For what Jaspers understands by philosophical faith is not faith other than or separate from actual modes of revelational faith. Instead, Jaspers challenges believers of revealed faith to serve their faith in the manner of philosophical faith. Believing philosophically means believing with reason, i.e., believing with the insight that human beings, as creatures bounded in their temporality and in their time, are not masters of the full-ness of the absolute on which they might base themselves. It means, with respect to the absolute One, that humans have to content themselves with being bound in time. Human boundedness in time refers both to personal temporality as well as to the history of humankind, including the forms of humanity and the modes of faith that arose in and are transmitted in historical time. Speaking in theological terms, and also philosophically, we can say that believing with reason means to believe with the insight that God in his unfathomable trans-temporal eternity revealed himself out of his fullness in various forms, to various human beings, at various times—and he did and does so, not to sponsor strife about the absolute truth in the encounter between modes of faith, but so that human beings might prove themselves with regard to the truth of which they historically partake.

One can see here two of Jaspers' motifs at play: First, "I am not all." This refers to the individual in his or her pretense of being master over ultimate truth and, thereby, to claim control over the conviction of fellow human beings. And it also refers to the modes of faith on the part of world religions, including the revelational faiths, without regard to the extent to which they are spread and effective among the world's peoples, and how comprehensively they teach the scope of their validity to be. In his large work about the modes of truth for the time-bound human and for time-bound humanity, Jaspers treats the millennia old struggle between two realizations of the one and only truth. On the one hand there is "reason" aware of the transcendence of ultimate truth, and with respect to it reason strives to realize it within the meager scope of humankind's temporality. On the other hand there is what Jaspers calls "catholicity," referring not only to revelational religions with religious wars and forced conversions, but also to manifestations in history of a political nature, such as the *pax Romana* and the horrible totalitarian constructs of the twentieth century.

A second motif is his caution that one ought to content oneself with gratuitously given temporality and historicity. To content oneself, not out of humility, nor out of pride, but out of the earnestness of fulfilling the task as informed by one's respec-tive faith. Tasks derive from ever changing situations. In the situation following World War II, when Jaspers was so concerned about the future, the two dangers to humankind's progress toward freedom were the dangers of a world-empire and of an absolute annihilation of humankind through the use of atomic weapons.

Decades before that time, during the 1920s, Jaspers saw the danger resulting from the alienation of humanity from confidence in one's fatherland, in the solidity of one's faith community, in cultural values, and in the ethical behavior of one's fellow human beings. Such alienated people are likely to unite in like-minded masses, which, thanks to the growth of technological means, are easily absorbed into ideological movements that tend to appeal to the lowest common denominator and extend beyond the limits of cultures and nations in a globalization of leveling. In this way the indigenous spiritual substance is extinguished, and with it the foundation of the sense of life. Lost is trust in the conduct of life in solidarity with one's fellow human beings, and lost is the validity of authorities that relate human beings in mutual understanding. Masses of alienated people are ready, as are the technological means, to be re-formed into the political power of any ideology through manipulation, control, domination, and the abandonment of any sense of common humanity.

The connection between faith and politics, even before the ascendancy of Nazi rule, was treated in Jaspers' thinking and his writings quite literally in terms of an intertwining. This can be seen in his later magnum opus *Von der Wahrheit* (1947), as well as in his political tracts written immediately after World War II, such as *The Question of German Guilt* (1946), *The Origin and Aim of History* (1948), and even in *The Perennial Scope of Philosophy* (1947).

The connection between faith and politics, though natural for Jaspers, may seem perverse. I remember an incident at the Jaspers Conference in Istanbul (2003). It was known that for some 40 years I had been dealing with the phenomenon of faith in Jaspers, and in Istanbul I also took up this topic in a plenary session of the World Congress, including the in-Turkey-as-an-Islamic-state sensitive question of the relation of faith and politics. At that same Jaspers Conference, a young colleague gave a paper on Jaspers' political thinking with reference to the Federal Republic of Germany. After finishing his presentation, he turned to me and said, "What we need is more political thinking and less philosophical faith." Astonished, I wondered, had he not read the post-war German Constitution and the postulate regarding the dignity of each individual human being? Is that anything other than an item of philosophical faith, achieved with difficulty over time, yet nourished by the biblical doctrine of the value of the human creature before God?

In *The Question of German Guilt* Jaspers shows that while guilt and liability for evil deeds can be determined with respect to current law, or by norms of morality, or by standards of honorable political action, the citizens who are not guilty by these norms are not devoid of guilt. They carry the guilt of surviving, the guilt of looking away when the scoundrels did their evil deeds. In this way, Jaspers emphasizes that no citizen is so insignificant that he or she does not count as a political factor, nor that one not need prove oneself in one's freedom with respect to the supra-political that animates one's spiritual substance and determines one's worth as a human being. Jaspers calls guilt rooted in faith "metaphysical guilt," in other words, a matter of philosophical faith. The supra-political, the aspect of faith on which political behavior is based, is discussed at length in Jaspers' main political work, *The Atombomb and the Future of Mankind* (1956). Here Jaspers shows in various ways how much political consciousness and faith are intertwined. Among other ways he points to the failure of the authority of the churches as teachers of the biblical ethos of probity and uprightness, as well as to how the spiritual leveling and the alienation of humanity are the bases on which the perversions of faith arise that are so destructive of positive political convictions and that become effective as fatal political power, namely demonology, including especially the deification of humanity and nihilism. Such tendencies, nourished by the loss of spiritual substance, appeal to faith, but a faith devoid of content, and devoid of niveau or standard.

I provide two examples regarding nihilism from November 1938. First, the perplexed mother of a former student visited Jaspers, who had been forced into retirement, and reported how her son had participated in the rioting of *Kristallnacht* and had justified himself to his mother by claiming that one could see what vigor there now was in the nation. The mother said, "You cannot believe this!" whereupon, the son replied, "I do not believe it, but one must believe it." A second example is that while Italian Fascism does not compare with German Nazism as regards nihilism, we recall its motto: *Credere, obbedire, combattere* (believe, obey, fight).

Do we need to demonstrate the deification of an individual man that was staged with respect to the Führer? An example: About mid-1940 the plan became known according to which the Nazi regime would abolish Christianity and replace it with a religion of the German-Aryan folk based on Hitler's *Mein Kampf*. The front cover of the new "holy" book would show a sword in place of the crucifix of a standard Christian bible. This transformation would take place slowly but surely, since the ideologists knew that among the people loyalty to the Church could not be dismantled from one day to the next. Yet we must know that in the government file labeled "Opponents," both in the SD (namely, the SS security service) as well as the Gestapo (the SS police force), there was a folder labeled "Church" next to the folders for the Freemasons and the Jews. How seriously the matter of founding the new faith was can be seen in the fact that every couple received from the registry office, as a wedding present, a copy of *Mein Kampf*, together with an official dedication.

In 1949 Jaspers took up the question of the possible renewal of religion in its function as teacher of the biblical ethos. He continued to do so in the following years, the highpoint of his writing political tracts and books, from *The Question of Demythologizing* (1954) to his last work *Philosophical Faith and Revelation* (1962). From his philosophical perspective, he maintained a critical stance. He knew that such a renewal would take several generations. He thought that aside from the institutional religions, a renewal of what he called "biblical religion" might be motivated. What he had in mind was the Bible with its calls for high ethical and moral values, in particular for honesty, as well as humanity being addressed by the divine directly, without a mediator, yet through symbolism and what Jaspers calls the "cipher script of transcendence."

Jaspers was certain that humanity's freedom rests on faith, and that surmounting nihilistic tendencies could be assured only through the renewal of the spiritual substance that, in the West, speaks from the Bible as well as from the great philosophers. Only in this way would human beings have the capacity to make free and responsible decisions and to take the risk of being politically effective through their actions.

Jaspers regards the renewal of faith to be indispensable for an orderly life in politics, especially among the nations. Faith is the basis for discipline and the source of strength to combat human, all-too-human, irrational motives. On the basis of faith, laws are forged, to which violent tendencies must bow, and which promote the trust of citizens. Renewal of faith would also further tolerance among peoples and nations which encounter each other in the world that is now one world. Without tolerance there is intolerance and destruction. Hence, a renewal of faith would lead to self-restriction, especially with respect to the exercise of brutal power. Everyone would remain within the limits of his given historicity and his sphere of action and influence. In his *The Origin and Aim of History* (1948), Jaspers wrote this in the form of an appeal directed to rulers and persons of influence.

Yet, in the end, the call to a renewal of faith concerns individual citizens. In Jaspers' Germany, democracy was in the process of being established. But one must not overlook the caution expressed toward the end of Jaspers' penultimate political tract written in 1966, *Wohin treibt die Bundesrepublik?* (Whither is the Federal Republic driving?). He says that democracy does not consist in a form of governance, but in the active faith in democracy of every single citizen, and that this faith is not actual in one's conviction, but in the daily renewal of the democratic idea, by means of tolerance toward every fellow human being who thinks differently from oneself, and by accommodating those who have other interests than one's own. It is like Faust's last insight, but too late because he is about to die: "Only he deserves freedom and life itself, who must attain them every day." Faith in democracy is actual as *fides qua creditor* (faith as it is believed).

To conclude: Faith in the mode of philosophical faith—whether as the basis for living, as a religious confession, as a conviction of a political sort, or as something else—thrives on mutual tolerance. Yet, like everything human, tolerance hits against its limit, namely intolerance. In his readiness to engage in unlimited communication, Jaspers hit against this limit in his encounters with the unbending theologians of the churches. And, as he said, "One cannot talk with fighters for a faith." If the fighter for a faith is not content with the militant means of his authority but uses means of exercising political power, then it is indispensable to defend oneself with similar means.

A final word from Jaspers: "Do not use the name of God wickedly. In his seriousness, a man does not play with God's name. He does not invoke God when he claims anything in the world. It is wickedness to claim God for oneself in opposition against others" (*Kleine Schule*, p. 125).

And a last word from me: If by infidel is meant one whose faith is not my faith, well and good. But the use of infidel, in the sense that the one whose faith is not my faith denies God and shall be dealt with accordingly, should be extirpated. We should never forget the slaughter accompanied by the Crusaders' cry of *Deus vult!* (God wills it!), and always keep in mind the slaughter perpetrated in the name of God in our own times.

An Interview with George B. Pepper

Gregory J. Walters

Abstract In this Interview with George B. Pepper, co-founder of the Karl Jaspers Society of North America, Gregory J. Walters explores the role that Jaspers' philosophy played in George B. Pepper's teaching career at Iona College, New Rochelle, New York, his recollections surrounding the origin of the Karl Jaspers Society of North America, formative philosophical influences on his thinking (Socrates, Augustine, Galileo Galilei, Giordano Bruno, Dietrich von Hildebrand, Robert Pollock, and Hannah Arendt), distinction and relations between philosophy and religion, the Holocaust, Jewish-Christian-Muslim relations, and the Boston heresy case involving Rev. Leonard Edward Feeney. For Pepper, a key challenge related to faith and the future of humanity is communication across boundaries without deception and invasion.

Gregory J. Walters (GJW): George, you had a successful academic career teaching philosophy at Iona College (New Rochelle, New York). What role did Jaspers' philosophy play in your own teaching and philosophical thinking?

George B. Pepper (GBP): Jaspers' philosophy helped me bring together much of the Western philosophical tradition. I most frequently taught Plato and Socrates. Jaspers' philosophy became especially important to me when, as chair of the philosophy department, I began teaching an upper division seminar on "Contemporary Philosophy."

GJW: What philosophers did you teach in the seminar?

GBP: Along with Heidegger, Sartre, Marcel, and Camus, I used Jaspers' work on *The Great Philosophers*. I had tremendous success in helping students understand the importance of Jaspers' philosophy for our modern philosophical situation. Without an accurate understanding of the historical context of the world in which Martin Heidegger, Hannah Arendt, and Karl Jaspers lived, contemporary continental philosophy often becomes merely academic, Scholastic, in nature. Jaspers helped

Recorded in three sessions between December 7, 2010 and March 3, 2011

G.J. Walters (✉)
Saint Paul University, Ottawa, ON, Canada K1S 1C4
e-mail: gjw@existenz.us

H. Wautischer et al. (eds.), *Philosophical Faith and the Future of Humanity*,
DOI 10.1007/978-94-007-2223-1_5, © Springer Science+Business Media B.V. 2012

me, and helped many students, bring philosophical thinking into a perspective with which we could strive to live, both faithfully and authentically.

GJW: I first met you in 1982. This was just two years after the KJSNA was founded. What are some of your recollections surrounding the origin of the society?

GBP: I contacted various publishers that might be interested in a book on Jaspers' philosophy for American philosophers. I submitted inquiries to numerous philosophical colleagues within the American Philosophical Association's Eastern Division about the idea of a Jaspers Forum in the APA. This information got to the Ehrlichs. When they heard that I was interested in writing a book on Jaspers' philosophy for the upper division Philosophy Seminar, they invited me to join them at their home in Amherst, MA, to discuss Jaspers' philosophy. I deferred to the Ehrlichs continually. I consider myself a mere backup for them on the Jaspers Reader. I should have written my own book on Jaspers. I some respects, I got overwhelmed with the Ehrlichs' credentials and German knowledge of Jaspers' thinking, and the work took almost 10 years to complete.

GJW: Is that the first time you met the Ehrlichs? When did the conceptualization of the KJSNA come into play?

GBP: I thought Jaspers' deserved a bigger voice in contemporary philosophy than he was getting. I wrote letters about the desirability of pursuing studies on Jaspers and the Academy responded positively. The society would be well worth the effort, and the APA gave us a group program format. We began in 1980, and I am just delighted that it is still in existence.

GJW: How long did you and the Ehrlichs work on the Jaspers Reader?

GBP: It was an intense amount of work over many years. I did some of the backup minor editing work. The conception of the Reader was Leonard's idea, and I can take no credit for that. As to the importance of the Jaspers Society, I hold second place to Edith and Leonard H. Ehrlich as well.

GJW: From where do you take your classical philosophical inspiration? Plato, Socrates, Aristotle, the Pre-Socratics?

GBP: It was not so much Plato as Socrates, and his wisdom in the statement "know thyself." Man must dialogue with oneself. No matter what one learns, and no matter whoever says it, philosophy is commissioned to question critically and to be responsible in and for the world. Philosophy challenges us: How can I expose falsehood? How do I bring thinking and acting together? Europeans who did not stand up to Nazi Germany when they could have is a case in point. The human being is not able, nor willing, to stand up against and to confront the great evils of time, unless one is a person that dialogues with the self.... Jaspers' reading of Aristotle is, of course, another story. I think one may easily establish bridges between Aristotle's concern for reason, reasoned discourse, and natural law ethics, on the one hand, and Jaspers' philosophy, on the other hand.

GJW: Who were the most formidable philosophical teachers that influenced your thinking?

GBP: Dietrich von Hildebrand and Robert Pollock. Robert Pollock is a Canadian, who discovered Christianity. His lectures on the American pragmatists—James, Dewey and Pierce—were exhilarating and riveting. He had students flowing from the rafters. In my own case, I found that his seventeenth century lectures on Leibniz were also substantive. I said to myself: "Look, this is where I come from philosophically".... and then I discovered Jaspers. In fact, I discovered the very thinker that allowed me to live with all the different, conflicting, divergent influences in philosophy in our age.

GJW: Was that because of Jaspers' conceptualizations of periechontology? The Encompassing? His conceptualization of philosophical logic?

GBP: Yes, it was Jaspers' philosophical logic, ideas of horizons, and transcendence. He gave me the tools of conceptual analysis. I think that's what he meant to do. He left psychology, then as a medical doctor, he went over to philosophy. Jaspers must have thought: "How do I make sense of all this material?" The philosophical logic, *Von der Wahrheit*, was his answer. The logic works. And it allows you to see yourself clearly, to situate yourself within a historical context, and to situate the self interpersonally, as well. Jaspers' real challenge is this: How to communicate across boundaries without deception and invasion?

GJW: Many active members of the KJSNA today are women. It stands to reason that the society will programmatically explore Jaspers' philosophy and his inclusive sense of the spirit of philosophizing in relation to women philosophers and notable personages. Do you have any suggestions?

GBP: Yes. There is much work to be done on Jaspers and Arendt. I recently finished reading a biography of Hannah Arendt.[1] The biographer shows how we must understand the social and cultural setting that characterized the Germany of Jaspers, Heidegger, and Arendt. Clearly, Hannah Arendt took the philosophical frameworks of Heidegger and Jaspers into new directions—in original ways (for example in *The Origins of Totalitarianism*). She is a Jewish woman, a German. She witnessed the horror of the Holocaust in Europe. She was very critical of the Israeli government and most critical of the Jewish leaders in Germany they finagled with the Nazis as

---

[1] Daniel Maier-Katkin, *Stranger from Abroad: Hannah Arendt, Martin Heidegger, Friendship and Forgiveness* (New York, NY: W.W. Norton & Company, 2010).

to who would go to the death camps. She had an ongoing love affair with Heidegger for thirty years of her life and career. Jaspers perceives that Arendt fell in love with Heidegger. She was a woman who got turned on by an intellectual's mind, and as a woman she gives herself to Heidegger. Still she considers him a self-promoter. But she understands the greatness of Heidegger in reshaping the philosophical discussion.

GJW: At the 30th Anniversary of the KJSNA held in conjunction with the 107th Annual Meeting of the APA in Boston, December 2010, Leonard H. Ehrlich presented, via the reading assistance of his son, Dr. Carl Ehrlich, a final paper entitled "Philosophical Faith and the Future of Mankind."[2] Since you were unable to attend, what comments would you wish to offer in response to his text?

GBP: I felt a strong response to it. In fact, I had hoped to send Leonard a lecture pamphlet by Patrick Ryan on "Prophetic Faith and the Critique of Tradition"[3] that captures some key issues involved in the relationship between philosophical faith and the Abrahamic faith traditions. I wanted to send a copy to Leonard. Now that you have explained his health challenges I won't send it to him, but the truth of the matter has to come out.

GJW: What is the truth of the matter given your *prima facie* reading of the text?

GBP: Now look, the paper is a great *apologia* of the evils of his time. Leonard is offering an explanation of the Holocaust: how it came about and how it can be avoided. He relies on Jaspers' theory of truth to do this. In passing, he takes some swipes against the Church, especially, Galileo Galilee and Giordano Bruno, but he misses some things here. There is no mention of Augustine, for example, who is pivotal in Western philosophy to an important understanding of the politics-religion relationship. I refer to his work on the *City of God*. Many Neo-Kantians rightly see the importance of Augustine as revealing the clear limits of the state. The fact that Galileo is so prominently displayed as an example of church oppression completely ignores all the seventeenth century literature surrounding those who defended Galileo against the Church's condemnation.

GJW: Leonard Ehrlich writes that "Faith is not truth that is known." Isn't his contrast between the life, work, and faith of Galileo Galilee, on the one hand, and Giordano Bruno, on the other hand, used to illustrate faith and its relation to truth?

---

[2] See the "Philosophical Faith and the Future of Mankind" by Leonard H. Ehrlich, this volume.

[3] Patrick J. Ryan, S.J., "Prophetic Faith and the Critique of Tradition Jewish, Christian and Muslim Perspectives," presented as The Annual Laurence J. McGinley Lecture, November 15, 2010 Fordham University. http://www.fordham.edu/audience/mcginley_chair/images/documents/Fall%202010%20-%20Father%20Ryan%20text.pdf, last accessed July 4, 2011.

He notes two types of knowledge (*Wissen*) and the nature of science (*Wissenshaft*) that characterizes the relation and distinction between science and philosophy? Didn't Jaspers consider both Galileo and Bruno, along with Socrates and Boethius, as martyrs for philosophical faith?

GBP: Well, I think this is essentially correct, but I haven't got to my point clearly enough. He uses Giordano Bruno's burning at the stake to identify a gross injustice and religious intolerance on the part of the church. Tolerance is the primary virtue for Leonard. There is ample evidence of this. Within the history of the church, there is ample evidence to reveal why the church's treatment of Bruno is a terrible disgrace. So is the church's treatment of Galileo Galilee. The text lacks a sense of the development of dogma and theology that goes on in the church. Many Catholics were working alongside Galileo. For example, Athanasius Kircher (1602–1680) was a seventeenth century German Jesuit scholar who defended Galileo, along with many others at the time. The fact that the church condemned Galileo because he was out of step with Aristotle's cosmology is a blatant manifestation of church authority run amok. But the church consists of many dimensions. This sordid history ignores the fact that Pope John Paul II made his papacy, a papacy of "confession" and he publicly confessed the wrongness of the church in the Galileo affair. He personally apologized for the oppression and degradation of the Jewish people on the part of church leaders, past and present. I certainly understand why Leonard has written what he has: growing up in Vienna, oppression against the Jews, and the loss of his own family members in the Holocaust. He had to expose the evil that was there. He used Jaspers phenomenology of faith to expose that. But there is another story at work here. I have some data on catholic charities today. Do you know how much money goes to victims of oppression today? The works of charity and mercy that church workers do for oppressed women, children, and persons suffering from AIDS?

GJW: So what you are really saying, then, is that despite some textual lacunae, you agree with Leonard Ehrlich's observation that: "One's own actuality of faith testifies to what is absolute truth for oneself. It does not testify to its being fundamental truth for anyone else, much less for everyone, or that the authority to whom one defers in one's faith is exclusively absolute. [...] the one ultimate truth is absolute, and as such transcendent. It transcends every realization of truth on the part of human beings, of humankind, and of human history. The truth of faith that is actual and effective among peoples, no matter how comprehensive or catholic by virtue of conviction or by the sword, merely partakes of the one truth in its transcendent, encompassing absoluteness. Even the faith of every faith community is more than its actualization, no matter how wide and how detailed it is articulated, and no matter how tolerant it may be of other modes of faith. Jaspers maintains that every faith is itself encompassing in the sense that it includes both actuality and transcendence."

GBP: Yes, this is essential. Leonard and Jaspers are correct in my judgment.

GJW: In another context, Leonard Ehrlich reminds me of the problem of secularization of religious faith in the context of modernity, especially as the theme of secularization figures in Jaspers' book *Man in the Modern Age*.

GBP: Yes, but secularization is not the major problem. Some people see secularization as a corruption of religious truth. That is not the way that Talcott Parsons (1902–1979) and Robert Bellah saw and see the matter today. Their sociological writings and work on American civil religion, respectively, had an important influence on me. Dietrich von Hildebrand also had a great impact on me. His phenomenology of self-consciousness and faith, his fundamental morality on ethics, and his important book on metaphysics and epistemology (*What Is Philosophy?*) helped an entire generation of Catholic philosophers to understand secularization, in relation to the question of truth and faith. He fled Germany in 1934 and actively opposed National Socialism. His anti-Nazi newspaper, *The Christian Corporative State*, waged philosophical battle with the presuppositions of Nazi ideology. Von Hildebrand, like Jaspers, remained faithful to the autonomy of philosophy and the central importance of the question of truth in philosophy. This is why I found Jaspers work on philosophical logic (*Von der Wahrheit*) fruitful for my own life. It is crucial for an understanding of what is going on in the Western world today in relation to secularization, religious faith, and politics.

GJW: Well, clearly, Leonard Ehrlich admits that the key problem is not religious faith per se, nor the variety of revelational faiths as such. The real problem is their respective claims to exclusiveness. Is Leonard's critique, then, really a critique of religious fundamentalist claims to exclusivity? Is this not a critique of religious dogmatism, if not theological dogma, per se?

GBP: Right. Look, this problem was worked out years ago, in American Catholicism, when Father Leonard Edward Feeney went around the country telling everyone there was no salvation outside the Roman Catholic Church. From the early 1950s until 1958, Feeney and members of the Saint Benedict Center went to Boston Common every Sunday. They shouted and raged against the evils of the world and other faiths in order to win converts to their rigorously narrow catholic belief. In fact, Feeney and his followers were surrounded by the police. Students and faculty were bussed-in from Brandeis University, which made available a chapel to Roman Catholics on the Brandeis campus. The bishop condemned Feeney and excommunicated him. I made a close study of these events, and Feeney and his followers were clearly off the wall.[4] The church has repudiated Feeney's literal interpretation of *Extra Ecclesiam Nulla Salus* (no salvation outside the church).[5]

---

[4] George B. Pepper, *The Boston Heresy Case in View of the Secularization of Religion: A Case Study in the Sociology of Religion* (Lewiston, NY: Edwin Mellen Press, 1988).

[5] Pope Innocent III, ex cathedra (Fourth Lateran Council, 1215).

GJW: Leonard Ehrlich has given us his last words in this way: "If by 'infidel' is meant one whose faith is not my faith, well and good. But the use of 'infidel,' in the sense that the one whose faith is not my faith denies God, and shall be dealt with accordingly, should be extirpated. We should never forget the slaughter caused by the Crusaders' cry of *Deus vult*! (God wills it!), and always keep in mind the slaughter perpetrated in the name of God in our own time."

GBP: The problem of slaughter perpetrated in the name of God arises in the context after World War I—the "War to End All Wars"—and with the formation of the League of Nations. It was during the period after the World War I, and given political and military developments in Germany leading up to WWII, that the Western powers should have mounted their forces to stop Hitler. At the end of the day, however, Karl Jaspers was a stalwart and upright figure throughout the terror of National Socialism and beyond. These terrible events raise the philosophical problem of the Political order, as well as the role of the use of deadly force on the part of the state. Look at the role of the Gestapo. Who was to blame for the rise of Nazism? It wasn't so much the church's responsibility, as it was the failure of the League of Nations.

GJW: Ethical vigilance and wakefulness in response to violations of human rights, especially the human rights of women and children, seem a tall order of our current historic economic and political situation. Nietzsche rejected rights language on the grounds of herd morality and his critique of equality, and Kierkegaard rejects the aesthetic stage of life that characterized his age. Kierkegaard and Nietzsche, those oh so great disturbers of Modernity, are central to Jaspers' understanding of the sea-change shifts that took place in nineteenth century European philosophy. Who had the most significant influence on Jaspers?

GBP: It would take more time to discuss this question. We have Nietzsche, the supreme atheist, and, Kierkegaard, the supreme theologian and religious philosopher; they provide unique expressions of the importance of reflection for authentic selfhood. What it most significant is the depths of selfhood they painfully plumbed. What did they discover? The subject cannot penetrate the self, in spite of the most extreme rationality. Religious, secular, other organizations today are still attempting to define some precise understanding of human nature or the complete scope of self-hood. And yet, they all, and always, come up short. Nietzsche and Kierkegaard understood this. Jaspers saw in these two philosophers the voice of modern selfhood. Jaspers essay on Kierkegaard and Nietzsche is a pivotal expression of the depth of selfhood that they represent,[6] and as opening on to subsequent philosophical discussions of Modernity and Post-Modernity.

---

[6] Karl Jaspers, "Kierkegaard and Nietzsche: Their Historic Significance," in Edith Ehrlich, Leonard H. Ehrlich, and George B. Pepper, *Karl Jaspers: Basic Philosophical Writings* (Athens, OH: Ohio University Press, 1986), 37–53.

GJW: Looking forward in time to the reception of Karl Jaspers' philosophy, and to pose a Kantian question, in what may we hope? Can Jaspers' philosophy continue its legacy? Can he help us now, in a situation marked by seismic changes toward democratic urges in the Middle East, with the conflict of interpretations across cultures?

GBP: People will discover Jaspers and his philosophy when they read him. I may only say that I forged an intellectual bond with him that has lasted a lifetime. Jaspers' philosophical logic and phenomenological insights have deeply informed my own selfhood. Despite all of the world's current economic, political, social, and cultural problems, Jaspers throws us back on ourselves. He forces us inward and outward, but always into our own personal responsibility, whether to self, to others and to God, and he does so in creative and original ways.

GJW: Well, George, it seems we have come full circle! You emphasize the ethical dimension in Jaspers, the moral and the political dimension of his philosophy, and the importance for both of you of individual and state freedom, but always, our own existential responsibility.

GBP: Yes, indeed. Karl Jaspers reminds us, quite simply, of the wisdom and truth of Socrates' imperative: "Know Thyself!"

GJW: Thank you, George, for sharing your reflections with me and with all future readers of the Festschrift and for those interested in the philosophy of Karl Jaspers.

GBP: You are welcome.

Karl Jaspers: Philosophical Faith of a Scientist

S. Nassir Ghaemi

Abstract Karl Jaspers' concept of philosophical faith is a notion he developed in the latter part of his career, and it has been most carefully expressed in the work of Leonard H. Ehrlich. Jaspers struggled with the perennial dichotomy between reason and faith, and, in the face of modern perils, provided a rationale, and—more importantly—an example, of how one might live both. He does so with a sympathetic critique of science, and with an intuitive awareness of both the power of reason and the demands of emotion. Jaspers tried to combine Kant, Kierkegaard, and science as he developed his own belief system about existence.

Ever since Galileo murmured *Eppur si muove* ("nevertheless, it moves"), the Western mind has struggled with the conflicting claims of faith and reason, of religion and philosophy. We can take it further back to the debates between Ghazali and Ibn Rushd in the Islamic era; and further still to Epicurus and to Socrates himself, found guilty of blaspheming the gods. As long as mankind has thought, it has struggled with believing versus knowing.

In this past century, Karl Jaspers is a key thinker who took on this struggle most seriously. For those of us who came of age just after he passed away, we have come to know him through his books and through the testimony of his living students. Of these, for many of us in the United States, Professor Leonard Ehrlich is the prime figure, a man who has patiently taught us how to appreciate Jaspers.[1] For me, as someone who was born just about when Jaspers died, the presence of Professor Ehrlich has been a physical and spiritual source of connection. If Professor Ehrlich is a philosophical child of Jaspers, then those of us who have learned from him can claim to be grandchildren of the great thinker. We can take pride in this intellectual and even personal connection; in so doing, we must thank Professor Ehrlich for making it possible.

---

[1] See Leonard Ehrlich, *Karl Jaspers: Philosophy as Faith* (Amherst, MA: University of Massachusetts Press, 1975) [Henceforth cited as *PF*]; also Edith Ehrlich, Leonard H. Ehrlich, et al., eds. *Karl Jaspers: Basic Philosophical Writings* (Atlantic Highlands, NJ: Humanities Press, 1994). [Henceforth cited as *BPW*]

S.N. Ghaemi (✉)
Tufts University, Medford, MA, USA
e-mail: nassir.ghaemi@tufts.edu

H. Wautischer et al. (eds.), *Philosophical Faith and the Future of Humanity*,
DOI 10.1007/978-94-007-2223-1_6, © Springer Science+Business Media B.V. 2012

Leonard Ehrlich's role in the world of Jaspers scholarship has never been purely intellectual. All knew, from the moment they got to know him, that his commitment to Jaspers' ideas was inseparable from his commitment to Jaspers the man; the philosophical and the personal were intertwined, as they are for Ehrlich himself. All knew that Ehrlich and his family had experienced great suffering because of the Holocaust; all knew that Jaspers' ideas had great personal, and not merely intellectual, meaning for Ehrlich and his wife Edith, who also was a student of Jaspers. Their sensitivity to otherness was something I experienced from my first introduction to them. I said hello to both of them and to others gathered around at a conference in the United States, somewhere around the 2001 terrorist attacks. Someone asked where I was from originally; I said, without elaboration or explanation, "Iran." An uneasy silence ensued. Edith Ehrlich broke the tension: "Well, that's a conversation stopper." I appreciated her frankness; she spoke up for my sense of otherness. She touched on my deepest existence and stated a brutal truth.

This essay is my simple testimonial of thanks and respect to Leonard Ehrlich for his example and his teaching. I wish to take up the theme of philosophical faith, a topic which has been central to the work of Ehrlich, in his interpretation of Jaspers, and which has, I think, intense relevance to many of our most heated political and intellectual conflicts today. Though I mostly expound Jaspers' ideas, here and there I philosophize, as he would have wished.

Many scientists and philosophers have struggled with their relationship to faith or religion. They seem to take a few basic stances. Some scientists view science as refuting religion and faith; they view the two as simply antithetical, professing a clear and sometimes combative atheism. Examples in the past include Razi and Voltaire and Thomas Huxley and Marx and Freud and Sartre and Mencken,[2] and more recently the philosopher Daniel Dennett[3] and the geneticist Richard Dawkins.[4] Other scientists or philosophers share the materialist outlook of the first group, but this second group is noncommittal and noncombative; religion to it is matter of relative unimportance, neither to be defended nor fought. This group upholds a cheery agnosticism; in the past, it has included Ibn Rushd and Einstein and Darwin and the great physician William Osler;[5] more recently the philosopher Raymond Aron[6] and biologist Stephen Jay Gould.[7] A third group accepts science as much as the other groups, but it also accepts religion and faith. Science and religion are kept separate like oil and water. Six days a week, this kind of scientist practices and lives as if he was an atheist; on the seventh day, he goes to church. When asked, the scientist at best can only describe a personal belief, a faith that he can neither defend

---

[2] Henry L. Mencken, *Treatise on the Gods* (Baltimore, MD: Johns Hopkins Press, (1930) 1997).

[3] Daniel C. Dennett, *Breaking the Spell* (New York, NY: Penguin Press, 2006).

[4] Richard Dawkins, *The God Delusion* (New York, NY: Mariner Books, 2008).

[5] William Osler, *Aequanimitas* (Philadelphia, PA: The Blakiston Company, 1948).

[6] Raymond Aron, *Memoirs* (New York, NY: Holmes and Meier, 1990).

[7] Stephen Jay Gould, *Rocks of Ages: Science and Religion in the Fullness of Life* (New York, NY: Ballantine Books, 2002).

intellectually nor explain emotionally. Some great thinkers and scientists belong in this category: in the past, this group includes Ghazali[8] and the great neurosurgeon Wilder Penfield[9] and the neurologist John Eccles;[10] more recently the neurologist Michael Trimble[11] and the geneticist Francis Collins.[12] I believe the great mass of scientists belong to this third group (what Ghazali called, approvingly, the "faith of the old women"). A fourth category might be those who reject science and accept religion or faith: the great mass of human beings probably fall into this category, as do, among thinkers, Kierkegaard and Heidegger. And then there are those who reject science and religion—Nietzsche would surely lead this group (at least in some of his incarnations), along with his postmodernist followers: Foucault and likeminded French scholars. The average American teenager arguably belongs to this category as well.

Besides these categories, though, there is another group of thinkers that cannot easily fit into such schemata. These persons accept science completely, but they are neither atheist nor agnostic nor believers. They are unable to simply reject religion, as in atheism; they correctly apply the standards of science to unfaith, and realize that we cannot really know that God does not exist. They are unable to ignore religion, as in agnosticism; the ultimate questions of meaning and death matter too much to them to be ignored. They are unable to simply accept religion, as most believers do, and as most scientists do; tradition and authority are not enough. To atheists, these thinkers seem to be believers; to believers, they seem agnostic; to agnostics, they are a mystery. Here we have strenuous souls like the great William James, Wilhelm Dilthey, Hegel, Kant, and in recent years: Carl Gustaf Jung, Viktor Frankl, the psychologist Rollo May, and Karl Jaspers. This last group is not homogeneous, obviously, and I will focus on Jaspers and mention a few others along the way.

Years after he survived the Nazi concentration camps, the psychiatrist Viktor Frankl came to visit Jaspers. The sage of Basel commented: "Herr Frankl, I know all of your books, but the one about the concentration camp (pointing to it in his bookcase) belongs among the great books of humankind."[13] What Frankl had done was to write a memoir, in my opinion, about the ultimate test of Jaspers' existentialist philosophy. Indeed, the whole Nazi era was, among other things, a test of Western philosophy. When Frankl sat wearily in those concentration camps, after long days

---

[8] M. Ghazali, *The Incoherence of the Philosophers* (Salt Lake City, UT: Brigham Young University, 2002).

[9] Wilder Penfield, *The Mystery of the Mind: A Critical Study of Consciousness and the Human Brain* (Princeton, NJ: Princeton University Press, 1975).

[10] John Eccles, "Natural Theological Speculations on Death and the Meaning of Life," in *Mind and Brain: The Many-Faceted Problems* (New York, NY: Paragon House, 1987).

[11] Michael Trimble, *The Soul in the Brain: The Cerebral Basis of Language, Art, and Belief* (Baltimore, MD: Johns Hopkins Press, 2007).

[12] Francis Collins, *The Language of God: A Scientist Presents Evidence for Belief* (New York, NY: Free Press, 2007).

[13] Viktor E. Frankl, *Recollections* (New York, NY: Basic Books, 2000), p. 114.

of harsh labor, never knowing if and when he would ever leave there, seeing scores killed daily in the gas chambers—he had to repeatedly answer the question of a fellow prisoner ready to give it all up: Why should I live? What is there of meaning in life so that I should choose to go on existing? Or put more generally, what is the meaning of life?

Often it is said that the fact of death raises the question of the meaning of life, and this is partly true. When one becomes a conscious human being, one wonders what the point of this life is if it is to end; why should we care to live if we are bound to die? What is death anyway? Five year old children typically ask these questions. Middle aged parents, having avoided such questions since they were five themselves, evade an answer. And elderly adults ask them once more.

But the meaning of life arises not only because of awareness of death; it also grows out of boredom. In young adulthood often, when a long vista of life lies ahead and death is an abstract futurity, many people wonder what the point of living is about; nothing much seems to be happening, people rush to and fro, going to work, shopping, doing errands. Why bother? Jaspers struggled with these questions out of his personal illness, initially, and through the dark experience of Nazism, later. No wonder he thought personal and political considerations are inseparable from philosophy.

Jaspers was a scientist, a psychiatrist, a physician. He was trained formally in the sciences, not philosophy, and experienced, predictably, some of the opposition of academic philosophers to one who was not one of their own. Jaspers, in turn, drew the opposite conclusion: One could not be a philosopher, a real philosopher, unless he was not a philosopher. Meaning: unless he was not formally trained in philosophy alone, but rather in the sciences. Why science? There is more than an educational rationale here. Jaspers' view about why philosophers should be more than philosophers is based on his philosophy. The key distinction in the world of wisdom, according to Jaspers, is between knowledge and faith, between science and philosophy.[14] The parallel terms are more than synonyms. Knowledge is the same thing as science; faith is the same as philosophy. Philosophical faith is, in a sense, a tautology; like saying scientific knowledge. What is unscientific knowledge? Jaspers would say nothing. What is nonphilosophical faith? What is faithless philosophy? Jaspers would say nothing.

So here we have it: science leads to philosophy; and philosophy is the same as faith. Let's see what this means. Science leads to philosophy because we begin our search for understanding ourselves, the world around us, and the mystery of existence by trying to gain knowledge. How do we gain knowledge? Through science: we watch, observe, smell, taste, touch; we extend and purify the senses through our scientific experiments; with stethoscopes, microscopes, telescopes; with hypotheses and tests and statistics and measuring probabilities. Science is knowledge; it is the best knowledge; in fact, it is knowledge per se.

---

[14] Karl Jaspers, *Way to Wisdom* (New Haven, NY: Yale University Press, 1954). [Henceforth cited as *WW*]

But science is not positivism. It is not positive, absolute knowledge of facts producing complete certainty. In short, science is not what most of Jaspers' pre-war contemporaries thought; it is not the Victorian vision of Comte and his apostles, a vision which persists even today among many simple-minded scientists and the masses who know little of science. Jaspers was ahead of his time in recognizing this limitation; he came to it not just from Kant's critical vision, but from his own observations on the practices of the medical profession. A few contemporaries or immediate predecessors shared Jaspers' insights into the limits and strengths of science, such as William James, Wilhelm Dilthey, Charles Sanders Peirce, or Nietzsche.

Science has its limits; this is trivial now, but only Jaspers understood how this apparent weakness (if one thinks in absolutes) is the secret of its strength: "The essence of science is its incompletability; in it, however, the extraordinary fragment counts for more than any—merely apparent—completion" (*BPW* 492). Science is limited because we can only see so far, we can only taste so well, we can only touch so much; but when we know our limits, we see and taste and touch clearly and fully. Science is limited because it is probabilistic, not absolute; because it requires statistics to measure, rather than ignore, error; because it always is a mix of truth and error. Indeed, as Peirce said, it views truth as corrected error.

Having limits is not a problem; it is the solution. All greatness, Goethe once wrote, comes from an awareness of one's limits. Jaspers fully understood this wisdom in his great study of psychiatry, *General Psychopathology*,[15] where he discovered that different methods produce different results, and that each method has its own strengths and scope—and limits. This is not a limitation of psychiatry; it is the very nature of science, properly understood. Otherwise, science becomes religion, an absolute belief-system. It takes some philosophical awareness, in fact, to practice science: "philosophizing brings about an inner attitude that is beneficial to science through the setting of boundaries. . . .The psychopathologist must concern himself with philosophy not because it might teach him something positive as regards his field but because it clears the inner space for the possibilities of knowledge" (*BPW* 19–20).

None of this means that science is mere opinion, no better knowledge than literature or religion. Jaspers was not Heidegger. He was not anti-science. There is a reason why Michel Foucault and the bevy of Parisian postmodernists admired Heidegger fervently, yet avoided Jaspers. Jaspers is no postmodernist. He is too wise for that. Postmodernism here refers to an intellectual and cultural ideology—growing out of frustration after the world wars—which rejects the Enlightenment tradition. Not only is there a rejection of faith in Reason, capitalism, and progress; there is a rejection of science per se as a kind of knowledge any more valid than other opinions. All knowledge is seen as the mere expression of power. There is no real truth. All of life is seen as a struggle for dominance, and nothing else.

---

[15] Karl Jaspers, *General Psychopathology*, 2 vols. (Baltimore, MD: Johns Hopkins University Press, (1913) 1997).

Jaspers sees through this "intellectual opportunism" that "is versed in all methods but adheres strictly to none" (*WW* 114). Seeing his onetime friend Heidegger go down this path (and carry much of the Western world with him for the last half century), Jaspers could hardly be more vociferous in his denunciation of this facile anti-science attitude:

> We have heard the outcry: Science destroys faith. . . .These critics doubt the eternal truth which shines forth in modern science. They deny the dignity of man which is today no longer possible without a scientific attitude. They attack philosophical enlightenment. . . . They turn against liberalism. . . .They attack tolerance as heartless indifference. . . .In short they. . .advocate philosophical suicide. (*WW* 91)

Jaspers accepts science as true, as far as it goes, which is very far. Probabilistic knowledge is not relativistic; we can know things with 99.99% certainty, and this does not mean that one opinion is as good as another, nor that knowledge is merely a reflection of power, nor that money is the base of everything. Some scientific ideas are not that certain, and others are quite dubious. But with time, science tends to become more and more certain about some truths, and less and less certain about some falsehoods. Over time, science approximates the truth, as Peirce said. Nonetheless, there is some room for uncertainty at any point in time, and over time, there are some things that tend to remain uncertain.

Despite all these limits, we have to accept the power of science where it gives us real knowledge. This is quite liberating. If life is full of mysteries and tragedies, it is not unimportant that the number of mysteries and tragedies are today, thankfully, much fewer than they were even in Jaspers' age. The physician Lewis Thomas eloquently describes the progress of medicine from the pre-antibiotic era in the 1930s to the post-antibiotic era in the 1950s, in his own medical career.[16] Where a young boy with a cut finger could die of cellulitis (infection of the skin) in 1935, the boy was easily cured with penicillin in 1955. Where children and future presidents were felled with polio routinely in the 1920s, all were prevented by the 1950s. I would venture to say that most who read these words in this book about Ehrlich and Jaspers would have been dead before he or she could have read these words, had it not been for the progress of modern medicine. Without modern treatments, like steroids for asthma, it is also probable that the writer of this essay would not have been alive to write it. Those postmodernists who disparage science should stop taking their antibiotics, and avoid their vaccines in childhood, if they want to be logically consistent. But they are biologically, rather than logically, consistent: they need science to live, but then they live as if science did not matter.

So Jaspers accepts science as far as science will take us, which is very far. Nonetheless, despite its great successes, science has had its failures, and it still has, even in the best circumstances, its limits. It is here that we are left with the mysteries of existence, and where philosophy steps in, which is the same thing, in Jaspers' view, as having faith. This is what he means when he comments on Plato's famous

---

[16] Lewis Thomas, *The Youngest Science* (New York, NY: Bantam Books, 1984).

saying that to philosophize is to learn how to die; if this is so, says Jaspers, then "to learn to live and to learn how to die are one and the same thing" (*WW* 126).

What are science's failures? Two great failures, caused by and leading to postmodernism, are undeniable. One is Nazism. The Nazi ideology was, as the psychiatrist Robert Jay Lifton has shown, a biological politics.[17] The Nazis made a claim to being scientifically up-to-date, and simply applying the truths of science to society. They were not the only ones to do so; similar programs had begun in the United States. But in Nazi Germany, this ideology did progress to a euthanasia program against the mentally ill. This social Darwinist research program was, of course, a travesty of science, more Herbert Spencer and Ernst Haeckel than Charles Darwin; but it had all the trappings of scientific vernacular; it spoke the language of science, so it was treated the same. This is the hallmark of pseudoscience, as physicist Richard Feynman describes,[18] and it persists today when pseudoscience manipulates us into taking medication, or not taking them, or believing in certain psychotherapies, or not; at least it does not systematically commit genocide. The Nazis took this pseudoscience to that logical conclusion. Lifton argues that their killings were not random: they grew, partly, out of an ideology that claimed to represent science as absolute truth. Jaspers knew that science did not work this way; but many of his medical colleagues, being only partially educated about science, apparently did not. It is interesting to note that physicians as a profession were the most likely to join the Nazi party; about one-half did; they also supervised and acquiesced, as a whole, in the Nazi euthanasia of the mentally ill and in the Jewish genocide.

The second great failure of science was, in reaction to Nazism, the development of the nuclear bomb.[19] Here is another example of scientists run amok; and now humanity literally is able to annihilate itself. Science proves it has no morals, it can be used ill or well. Even if nuclear weapons finally forced Japan to end the Second World War, they also became a political tool for both sides during the Cold War. After the Soviet Union restructured, the impression arose that nuclear war was no longer likely; but recent events in the Middle East have returned nuclear risk to the stage of international conflict. Some, like the US and Israel, have weapons, unlike others such as Iran and Arab states, who aspire to acquire them. The former fear that the latter will obtain such weapons; the latter fear that the former will use them for intimidation. Each side debases the other, with political and sometimes military threats. Nuclear weapons continue to put human existence at risk.

There is no doubt, scientifically or conceptually or politically, that science has its limits. The only question is what these limits mean. Jaspers did not adopt postmodernist views, he knew that the benefits of science have far outweighed its harms; and the future benefits still outweigh future risks, as long as science is properly used.

---

[17] Robert Jay Lifton, *The Nazi Doctors* (New York, NY: Basic Books, 2000).

[18] Richard Feynman, *Surely You're Joking, Mr. Feynman!* (New York, NY: Bantam Books, 1989).

[19] Karl Jaspers, *The Atom Bomb and the Future of Man* (Chicago, IL: University of Chicago Press, 1961).

Science is not an absolute system of knowledge, but its achievements are powerful and tempting. Clearly science does not produce good by itself; it is easily used for ill purposes as well. Despite all the strengths and benefits of science, by itself science does not solve the problems of humankind. In fact science alone can worsen those problems. The question is what we are to make of ourselves and our world once we reach the limits of science.

One response is to refuse to face the problem. Those who value science may argue that science itself will solve problems that currently seem unsolvable; what appears to be the limits of science today will not seem limiting in the future. While this may be, up to a point, it seems likely that limits to science will continue to exist, even though such limits change and recede with time. In contrast, those who devalue science may argue that science is too invasive, and proclaim a return to traditional beliefs. Jaspers avoids both extremes. He accepts science, and he also accepts its limits. He faces the problem of the limits of science, and his solution is philosophy and faith, or as he calls it, philosophical faith (*PF*).

Jaspers famously equates philosophy with philosophizing. Philosophy is a verb, not a noun; a process, not an outcome; a source of insight, not a system; a tool, not a dwelling. When philosophizing, Jaspers is trying to understand what science cannot know. Science can push back the three scourges of mankind—as John Kennedy put it, poverty, disease, and war—but it cannot put them off indefinitely. Suffering and death still happen. And the living, thinking, aware human being—as possible *Existenz*—faces those tragic realities. Here Jaspers sees a mystery, as suffering and death, after all the work of science, still cannot be explained. At this point, philosophy and faith begin: Philosophy means knowing that one does not know.[20] It is an ignorant knowledge, a knowing ignorance. Philosophical man, the aware soul (*Existenz*) rather than the mundane mind (*Dasein*), stands facing this mystery—solemn, silent, serious. He or she has to take a stand. Not taking a stand is not an option for one who philosophizes. He thinks, therefore he suffers. The stand Jaspers takes, like Nietzsche and like Kierkegaard, is to accept such tragic realities, to know that they are and they cannot be wished away. At the same time, such acceptance is not passive nor is it unique.

All humans philosophize; we all try to make sense of mystery. We have what Jaspers calls "ciphers," or symbols. For some the cipher is belief in immortality—Heaven or Hell; for others, reincarnation; for others, unity with Nature. Specific ideologies follow in one or another symbolic belief-system. Jaspers neither acknowledges nor denies the truth of any single ideology; but, like William James, he passionately defends one's right to believe in any one. All he asks for is a commitment to one's beliefs, as we deeply engage with those who believe in their beliefs. For him, communication is a dry word, and he suggests a "loving struggle" between ideas to be more expressive. Ehrlich interprets Jaspers to say that truth

---

[20] See Gerhard Knauss, "Karl Jaspers on Philosophy and Science," in *Karl Jaspers's Philosophy: Expositions and Interpretations*, Kurt Salamun and Gregory J. Walters, eds. (Amherst, NY: Humanity Books, 2008), pp. 69–82.

has a "combative character" that can only be civilized by love (*PF* 97). Dare I use a misunderstood complex Arabic word for the same concept: did Jaspers mean that a loving struggle of different faiths is like a *Jihad*, a struggle or striving, between them? Does *Jihad* have to be physical or military, as it is commonly conceived, with winner and loser; can it not be intellectual, without victory or defeat? Perhaps the extension of the idea of a loving struggle to the idea of an intellectual struggle may be pushing the idea of loving struggle too far. In fact, there can be no victory or defeat in the realm of philosophizing and faiths, for Jaspers. There are only insights. Jaspers argues for tolerance, but he does not do so out of relativism (*PF*). He does not claim that all philosophies or faiths are equal. He clearly values some philosophies more than others. In the world of philosophy and faith, we cannot prove or know their truths. If we can prove or know the truth, then we are, by definition, engaging in science. After a certain amount of experience and experiment, if there is still notable doubt, then we do not yet have scientific knowledge. Doubt is the substrate of faith, as Ehrlich suggests that faith implies doubt, and philosophizing is uncertain, by definition (*PF*).

Still, one cannot believe in a faith while at the same time disbelieving in it. Having faith is total, not partial; otherwise it is not faith. Jaspers thinks that such faith, though passionate and definitive in the personal life of a person, is not definitive for another person. Each of us can have absolute belief in a faith, he thinks, but only for ourselves; we cannot prescribe such absolute faiths for others. This is because faith is not knowledge; religion is not science. Faith involves not knowing, being ignorant, and yet having a "fundamental certainty of being" (*PF* 58). This certainty is an individual feeling of an existing person; it is not something that can be enforced upon another. To paraphrase Ehrlich, there may be many intellectual truths for all of us; but there is only one existential truth for each of us (*PF* 69). Or as Jaspers puts it, "Although scientific truth is universally valid, it remains relative to methods and assumptions; philosophical truth is absolute for him who conquers it in historical actuality, but its statements are not universally valid" (*WW* 162).

Tolerance stems from such individualism of faith. At the same time, we have to be curious about the absolute faiths of others. Though we believe in our faith, Jaspers reasons, we do not know that our faith is true. So we must wish to understand the faith of another, in case we are wrong and he is right; we must seek to appreciate the faith of another, though we may not in the end accept it. Similarly, the other philosophizer, believing in his absolute faith, will wish to understand ours. This is the loving struggle—not a superficial and optional exercise in tolerance, but a profound and necessary effort to know the truth. Indeed, Jaspers holds that one cannot know the truth just by oneself, or only within one's own faith or tradition. One needs to engage in the loving struggle with another before one can get to truth: "The truth begins with two" (*WW* 124). Is this what Gandhi meant by *Satyagraha*, the nonviolent struggle for truth? Or what Martin Luther King meant with his nonviolent resistance where some truth is recognized on both sides of the struggle? Jaspers seems to have a similar insight:

> Peace is not the absence of struggle. But man can convert the struggle from a violent one into a spiritual and loving struggle. The violent struggle dies in communication. Instead of superiority in victory, the result is communal truth. By means of such struggle each individual comes to him or herself. The loving struggle places all means of power, also the means of intellectual forcefulness, which as a stronger rationality corresponds to physical strength, at the disposal of the partner in the same manner in which one makes use of them himself, and thereby cancels its fatal effects.[21]

The postmodern relativist may seem superficially tolerant; but deep down, he does not understand the faith of another; deep down, he devalues it. And the other person, sensing this, will burrow deeper in his fundamentalism. Jaspers is known for his assertion that it takes faith to understand faith. Each of us has a specific personal and historical existence, and we will have our own faiths. There is no single central axis around which all faiths can coalesce.

The consequence of this multiplicity of philosophies and faiths is that we will need to tolerate each other personally, intellectually and politically. At the same time, we must resist any attempt to enforce one faith upon all the rest; fundamentalism will be rejected. And, just as importantly, we must reject the rejection of all faiths. The bland postmodernism of contemporary society will not work for us; the notion that nothing is true and that nothing matters will not do. In the end, that apathy either becomes a new ideology, rejecting truth along with untruth, and leading to cultural and political decline; or it creates a vacuum inviting a new totalitarianism to rise.

Jaspers promotes a notion that is complex and does not easily fit into common molds. He is spiritual, but not in a personal or New Age sense. His God does not personally know him, there is no room for miracles, and prayer has no object. He positions God into the realm of what is not known to science; if science expands, that realm diminishes accordingly. Giving us the sense that divinity represents what is above and beyond and all around us, Jaspers uses concepts such as the Encompassing or Transcendence. The analogy to Nature, viewed as a much larger power than humankind, is hard to avoid. Such pantheistic interpretation, similar to the spiritual leanings of the Transcendentalists like Emerson, is not entirely inconsistent with Jaspers. But using the concept of philosophical faith, Jaspers activates reason and emotion to pull in the same direction. This is not simply liberal Protestantism—a unitarianism solely based on rational notions, a modern version of Jefferson cutting up the Bible to keep its rational bits and discard the illogical parts—it is rather a philosophical and rational approach to religion that builds upon instead of ignoring its emotional core. His view is based on the existential realities

---

[21] "Friede ist nicht Kampflosigkeit. Aber der Mensch kann den Kampf verwandeln aus gewaltsamen Kampf in den geistigen und in den liebenden Kampf. Der gewaltsame Kampf erlischt in der Kommunikation. Statt Überlegenheit im Sieg ist das Ergebnis die gemeinschaftliche Wahrheit. Durch solchen Kampf stellt alle Mittel der Gewalt, auch die Mittel der intellektuellen Gewaltsamkeit, die als stärkere Rationalität der stärkeren Muskelkraft entspricht, dem Partner in gleicher Weise wie sich selbst zur Verfügung und hebt damit ihre tödliche Wirkung auf" (trans. by the author). Karl Jaspers, "Wahrheit, Freiheit und Friede," in *Hoffnung und Sorge* (Munich: R. Piper, 1965), p. 174.

of despair and equality—that we all suffer, and that we do so equally. Despair is the emotional source of spirituality, the need to succor our suffering. Equality is the rational source of tolerance. Our specific responses to suffering are true for us, but cannot provide truths to others. We allow for the fact that each of us needs a salve for despair; while we dare not taking away our neighbor's remedy, we might not want to use it for ourselves either.

Jaspers does not rest on religion, traditional or non-traditional. An old Sufi saying proclaims that anyone who says he is a Sufi is not a Sufi. Similarly, Jaspers once wrote: "If one is sincere, one does not know *whether* one believes" (*PF* 62). There is no question of saying one has faith or not, that one is a believer or not. If one philosophizes seriously, Jaspers teaches, then one is both believing and non-believing; there is both faith and doubt at the same time, and neither can be avoided. We can find spirituality in his approach, but not in the personal sense, and not without specific philosophical content, including the acceptance of all that science has to teach us. This is not faith without philosophy; one cannot have faith unless one philosophizes and thinks deeply about what is known or not, and why. Knowledge and faith cannot be separated. But Jaspers' faith is not intellectual, it is existential. It is reached by use of Reason—which Jaspers valued so much—and emotions, as Wilhelm Dilthey, the teacher of Jaspers' teachers, so clearly states by referring to the will, the entire soul.[22] To paraphrase Ehrlich, Jaspers = Kant + Kierkegaard (*PF* 117). It is all of one, one's entire existence, that philosophizes and can have faith. For beliefs and disbeliefs—when I use only my intellect, or only my emotions, or only my will—are mistaken. Jaspers calls for more effort. Can we meet his standard?

Faced throughout his life with personal illness, and in the middle of his life faced with the challenge of Nazism, Jaspers lived philosophical faith impressively. Not giving into the political demands of Nazism, he maintained a belief in proper science when science was being misused, he believed in the rights of individuals, in human liberty; he accepted punishment by loss of his job, endured threats to his life, all without capitulating. He was one of the few intellectual German leaders who could stay in Germany throughout the Nazi era and stand straight and solid for his faith and his philosophy. After the war, he could speak to Germany about its guilt, and he could speak to the world about its responsibilities. He objected to postmodern nihilism, despite the upsurge in Heidegger's influence. He remained authentic when speaking to a world still at risk of self-immolation by nuclear weapons, and he was resourceful when addressing the mysteries of life and death, as he continued his unfettered zeal for philosophizing. His philosophical faith kept him going and kept him strong, in the face of tornados that wiped away many others with traditional faith or without any coherent philosophy at all. One could give the credit to his personality. Or one could give it to his life-long effort to think, and think well; one could give it to his belief in the deep importance of philosophizing. He himself

---

[22] Rudolf A. Makkreel, *Dilthey: Philosopher of the Human Studies* (Princeton, NJ: Princeton University Press, 1992).

credited the latter. But then again, his wise personality and his wise philosophizing might be one and the same thing.

Such a teacher produces a student like Leonard Ehrlich, a teacher for new generations, one who teaches philosophizing as an essential activity for anyone who wants to be free and to know and to exist fully, accepting the mysteries of existence, while in perpetual pursuit of knowledge—scientific and philosophical. In faithful vigor, he carries the torch for generations to come, and does justice to his great teacher.

Honoring the Messenger

Suzanne Kirkbright

Abstract What is the true language of Jaspers' works in English? Why are Jaspers' texts in English frequently regarded as unintelligible? How can a balance be struck between literary and literal translation? This chapter critically examines these questions in the light of selected examples of successful English translations. Furthermore, it shows how conveying the "otherness" of Jaspers' thought is intrinsically linked to the editorial and interpretative decisions which reveal the profound implications of Jaspers' central metaphors. Here, the question concerning appropriate language refers back to the age-old dichotomy of interpreting the message, yet without jeopardizing the originality of the linguistic idiom.

> "... like such a bird was Hermes carried over the multitudinous waves."[1]
>
> "To be or not to be:" that was the question. Let us remark in passing that there were very great men who were existentialists, or rather, let us say with Kierkegaard, existent men without knowing it. ... We see in the philosophy of the German philosopher Jaspers more intellectualized and generalized echoes of the same tendencies which were in Kierkegaard. It is no longer a question of relation to God and to Jesus Christ, but to an obscure background of which we have the feeling, but which we can never catch, except in partial and fugitive moments, so that finally we succumb and are in a certain manner the victims of a kind of shipwreck.[2]

In his illustrations of the French existentialists as distinct from Germany's philosophers of *Existenz* (Heidegger and Jaspers), Jean Wahl highlighted how the interweaving of different cultural and linguistic horizons accentuates a subtle change of perspective and even promotes the acceptance of new ideas. Jaspers' ideas were in homage to Kierkegaard and Nietzsche and his conception of "real existence"

---

[1] Homer, *The Odyssey*, Book V, "Hermes and Calypso–Odysseus Released and Wrecked," trans. Walter Shewring (Oxford, NY: Oxford University Press, 1980), p. 56.

[2] Jean Wahl, "Existentialism: A Preface," in *The New Republic*, October 1, 1945, pp. 442–444 (p. 442). [Henceforth cited as *EP*]

S. Kirkbright (✉)
University of Surrey, Guildford, UK
e-mail: suzanne.kirkbright@gmail.com

H. Wautischer et al. (eds.), *Philosophical Faith and the Future of Humanity*,
DOI 10.1007/978-94-007-2223-1_7, © Springer Science+Business Media B.V. 2012

(*EP* 442) showed that, if clearly illuminated, the reality of life experience may be reflected in a new light: Man is always something more than what he knows of himself. This classic inscription from Jaspers' philosophy conveys one of his essential arguments: namely, it is possible to experience a real breakthrough and realize the potential freedom of *Existenz*; in this sense, freedom is not beyond *Existenz,* but especially raises awareness of what Jaspers called the boundary situations of guilt, suffering, contest or struggle, and the ultimate barrier of death.

When we read of how the darker moments of despair, anguish or ultimate failure may be responded to in the light of Transcendence, Jaspers' thought "intensifies life and strengthens and moulds character."[3] His conception of man's *Dasein* as the reality of "being alive oneself" points a way forward to the potential for continual self-improvement.[4] The quest for answers to the ultimate questions about life leads to certain moral challenges–especially with regard to individual guilt or personal responsibility for actions–and Jaspers invites us constantly to reconsider any given position.[5] Jean Wahl elaborated this in his suggestive terms: "Hamlet [w]as an existent. . . . even Socrates, says Kierkegaard, was an existent man. And we may add the great foe of Socrates, Nietzsche" (*EP* 442).

On the one hand, the idea of the existent man (for instance, as exposed in the torturous questioning of Hamlet's soliloquy) is not so different from the actuality of being alive–at least it neither brings to mind a Nietzschean superhuman capacity, nor a cathartic release from a solitary state. On the other hand, an existent individual can grasp the prospect of dialogue with others as a way to plot a course of action. Leonard Ehrlich's *Erinnerungen eines Jaspersschülers* vividly captured these aspects to give a memorable tribute to Jaspers as an active thinker, who was alert enough even in his final years to engage in conversation with his young interlocutor:

> In conversation, he never stated things were this way or that; and whatever he explained was always valid within limits—nothing was based on certainty. Rather, going far beyond the provocation of the questioner's inquiry, the disconcerting aspect about Jaspers was that—even thinking with and through things—was valid only on the proviso of thinking for oneself. [6]

---

[3] Werner Brock, "Karl Jaspers and Existentialism," in *German Life and Letters*, Vol. 17/4 (July 1964), pp. 289–303 (p. 303). [Henceforth cited as *KJE*]

[4] Richard F. Grabau, "Preface," in *Karl Jaspers, Philosophy of Existence*, trans. Richard F. Grabau (Philadelphia, PA: University of Pennsylvania Press, 1995), p. xviii.

[5] Further in reference to moral attitudes or imperatives "The Act of Choosing Oneself," see Kurt Salamun, "Karl Jaspers on Human Self-Realization", in *Karl Jaspers's Philosophy Expositions and Interpretations*, eds. Kurt Salamun and Gregory J. Walters (New York, NY: Humanity Books, 2008), pp. 243–262 (p. 246).

[6] Leonard H. Ehrlich, "Erinnerungen eines Jaspersschülers. Begegnungen mit Karl Jaspers," in *Jaspers Jahr 2008, Wahrheit ist, was uns verbindet*ed, Reinhard Schulz, Oldenburg 2008, translated by S. Kirkbright. ["Er sagte dabei nie, dies sei so und jenes so; was er auch darlegte, galt innerhalb von Grenzen und nichts ruhte in Gewissheit. Vielmehr—weit über die Provokation der Fragestellung hinaus—war das Beunruhigende bei Jaspers, dass—selbst beim Mit- und Nachdenken—nur das Selbst-Denken Geltung hatte."]

Here, more than a fleeting glimpse is given of the living dimension of Jaspers' approach to thinking and his unique way of challenging his listeners or individual readers.

And yet the idea that we grace life as existent beings again calls to mind the circumstances of Jaspers' biography and their highly unique connection to his intellectual life. In suggesting *Navigations in Truth* as a subtitle for Jaspers' biography, the purpose was to highlight how this unusual coincidence of the life and works gives one essential illustration of how Jaspers' life experience shaped his position in respect of the German intellectual tradition. If the happy coincidence (from a biographical perspective) of the life and the intellectual work accentuated one thing, then this was that a possibility of achieving truth within a given lifetime is necessarily a persistent and ongoing challenge. When reading Jaspers' comprehensive investigation of truth, we learn to appreciate an intricately constructed concept of being as a unity, which is grasped by means of the rational concept of the Encompassing–so to speak, a band of truth that we are as the modes of existence (*Dasein*), consciousness as such (*Bewusstsein überhaupt*), spirit (*Geist*), *Existenz*, world, and Transcendence.[7] In the background, however, there is always the figure of a navigator, who was alluded to often enough, for example, in Jaspers' autobiographical descriptions of contemplating the open horizon near his native Oldenburg from a fixed position on the shoreline.[8]

Although Jaspers remained in many respects a solitary personality, he willingly set things in motion by his most courageous life decisions that were always taken looking ahead and seeking something beyond the present. In outlining some persistent linguistic difficulties of rising to the challenge of engaging with his works, the intention here is to outline how as scholars and "common readers"[9] we may inevitably be bound by certain idiosyncrasies of language that may necessarily condition our perceptions. Jaspers' readers worldwide benefit from an animated discourse in which a worldwide community of scholars is represented. It almost goes without saying that this discourse thrives as an ongoing venture because it was initiated several decades ago with the early conferences and resulting publications of the *Karl Jaspers Society of North America*.[10] Here, however, our attention briefly turns to certain issues that were under discussion before this unique forum of scholarship

---

[7] George B. Pepper, "The Encompassing, Foundering, and the Tragic Individual in the Philosophy of Karl Jaspers," in *Karl Jaspers's Philosophy: Exposition and Interpretations*, op. cit., pp. 263–287, here p. 265.

[8] Cf. Edith Ehrlich's translation of Jaspers' autobiographical self-portrait (freely spoken text for German radio, directed by Hannes Reinhardt, 1966/1967) as "Karl Jaspers—Ein Selbstporträt. A Self-Portrait," in: *Karl Jaspers Today. Philosophy at the Threshold of the Future*, eds. Richard Wisser and Leonard H. Ehrlich (Washington, DC, 1988), pp. 1–25.

[9] The common reader "Reads for His Own Pleasure Rather Than to Impart Knowledge or Correct the Opinion of Others." See Virginia Woolf, *The Common Reader* (First Series), ed. Andrew McNeillie (San Diego, CA: Harvest, 1984), p. 1.

[10] For a description of these activities and commendation of the translations of Edith and Leonard Ehrlich, see also Kurt Salamun, *Karl Jaspers* (2nd ed., Würzburg, 2006), pp. 131–134, here especially, p. 134.

was finally established by Leonard Ehrlich and Richard Wisser. One frustration had been aired about certain difficulties of translation—especially in English—when Charles Wallraff argued that Jaspers was in danger of remaining "incommunicado": "It is as though the more Jaspers is translated, the less he is read."[11]

In his analysis of *The Task of the Translator*, Walter Benjamin considered in greater detail how the translator is in a unique position to identify a "true language" or a linguistic register presenting "the tensionless and even silent depository of the ultimate truth which all thought strives for."[12] The translation process, as Benjamin described it, leads to a keen appreciation of the linguistic nuances of any given text by placing the original or primary text within the reader's grasp. Multiple translations of Jaspers' works are available across the globe and there are many anthologies drawing our attention to a wide variety of different strategies for translation. Perhaps, however, the very familiarity of English in some respects presents a barrier that in vain we seek to work with and around. Ideally, an effective-historical understanding of a given text should transform a translator into an "interpreter of the divine will who can interpret the oracle's language."[13] Benjamin traced this time-honoured dimension of Schleiermacher's description of the translation process to highlight the creative potential of coining novel language. Thus, the translator truly becomes a messenger, if his or her language actually conjures up a new means of expression and allows freedom to air specific differences between the thinker's original thoughts and their reanimation in different language. This process depends, too, upon whether or not the romantics' dichotomy of translation versus interpretation is bridged by establishing something approaching poetical language.

In other words, the success of any given translation may not be measured purely in terms of the literal equivalence of word for word, but also depends on whether the text in hand grows to be appreciated and perhaps even rises in esteem to be considered as a part of a new literary canon. A case in point is E.B. Ashton's enduringly elegant translation of Jaspers' magnum opus, *Philosophy*. But in the Preface to this work, Ashton included a detailed translator's note and highlighted what he seems to regard as considerable imperfections as a result of the dilemmas of translating this most lucid of Jaspers' philosophical works. Jaspers lived to read some of Ashton's early English versions of his *Philosophy* and, indeed, favorably received them. However, in the end, Ashton turned away from a completely faithful presentation of Jaspers' text. Furthermore, even in the aforementioned translator's preface, Ashton remarked how English readers of Jaspers' *Philosophy* must wrestle with

---

[11] Charles Wallraff, "Jaspers in English: A Failure of Communication," *Philosophy and Phenomenological Research* Vol. XXXVII, No. 4 (1977), pp. 537–548 (p. 537). [Henceforth cited as *JE*]

[12] Walter Benjamin, "The Task of the Translator," in *Illuminations*, ed. Hannah Arendt, trans. Harry Zohn (London: Fontana Press, 1973), pp. 70–82, here p. 77.

[13] Hans-Georg Gadamer, *Truth and Method*, trans. Joel Weinsheimer, Donald G. Marshall (London, 2004), p. 307. Adolph Lichtigfeld implicitly considers the question of translation from a Gadamerian viewpoint; see his "Jaspers in English: A Failure not of Communication But Rather of Interpretation," *Philosophy and Phenomenological Research* Vol. XLI (1980), pp. 126–222.

a perplexing kind of relativism that he saw as a consistent facet of Jaspers' basic philosophical vocabulary.[14] Wallraff highlights that in discussion of the pitfalls of an assumed Jaspersian style of relativism, Ashton went as far as to suggest relativity as a "key to words peculiarly identified with Jaspers" (*JE* 546). He therefore created a certain amount of confusion in assuming relativity as a working principle. Nevertheless, he undoubtedly devised an impressive interpretative scheme that was built into the composition of the English manuscript.

The results of Ashton's undertaking are available in print (albeit mostly now in university libraries) for readers to decide about the merits of all three translated volumes. Undoubtedly, this accomplishment stands as a remarkable literary achievement. But could there be a more accurate rendition of Karl Jaspers' texts? Given Ashton's eminent position as a translator, his suggestion that in the case of Jaspers it was more important to compose a literary as opposed to a literal or philosophical translation was perhaps the more obvious route to find favor with Jaspers' readers. And if Ashton's major contribution was that his work established a literary benchmark, his translation undoubtedly made Jaspers' magnum opus sound more familiar to English readers. Certainly, however, he had not necessarily put to rest the idea of Jaspers being incommunicado.

An Unfinished Chapter

Ashton's work is an impressive legacy or an implicit endorsement of the need for translators and editors of Jaspers' works to continue with this outstanding example and apply the same dedication in continual revision or refinement of linguistic solutions and novel schemes. Because of the considerable poetic licence that Ashton employed, it is useful to bear in mind the great variety of alternative English texts and anthologies. We then see clearly how the readability of Jaspers' basic texts in English is also dependent upon the manifold and often contradictory English renditions of Jaspers' basic terminology.

One English anthology that offers us an ideal opportunity to gain such insights is *Karl Jaspers: Basic Philosophical Writings*.[15] Edited and translated over two decades ago, this anthology offers a special benchmark, because it presents readers with the necessary tools to verify existing texts in English translation. In the editors' Preface we read as follows:

> In the translations and emendations the editors have aimed at achieving the greatest fidelity possible both to the thought and to the language of Karl Jaspers in order that he emerge as the human being paradigmatic of his philosophy.... Therefore, faithfulness to Jaspers's expression has controlled the translation effort even when more felicitous constructions would seem desirable. (*KJ* xii)

---

[14] Cf. also the introduction to *Karl Jaspers. Existentialism and Humanism: Three Essays*, ed. Hanns E. Fischer, trans. E.B. Ashton (New York, NY: Russel F. Moore, 1952), p. 11.

[15] Leonard H. and Edith Ehrlich with George B. Pepper, eds., *Karl Jaspers: Basic Philosophical Writings: Selections* (Athens, OH: Ohio University Press, 1986). [Henceforth cited as *KJ*]

Thus, identifying how certain poetical ideals may persistently interfere with the foremost requirement of a translation, i.e. that it remain faithful to the original source, our immense enjoyment in browsing this particular anthology is that upon reading Jaspers' texts we are honuring the work of the original thinker.

Here, the editors' choice was not necessarily to follow a path of least resistance, for their literal translations are not so much an easier option in comparison with the impressive literary style of E.B. Ashton's existing translation of *Philosophy*. To highlight one example among the many, if we turn to the second part of the anthology, we become aware of the vast scope of linguistic alternatives already available in English. This section entitled "What is Man?" presents the reader with an open invitation to compare the editors' choices with a relevant section of the first of Jaspers' books translated into English in 1951 by Eden and Cedar Paul—*Man in the Modern Age* (this title is emended in Ehrlich and Pepper's anthology as *The Spiritual Situation of Our Time*):

> Man is always something more than what he knows of himself. He is not what he is simply once and for all, but is a path; he is not merely a determinable fixed existence, but is, within that existence, endowed with possibilities through freedom. Out of this freedom he decides, even as he acts, what he is. . . . As freedom he conjures up being as his hidden transcendence. The meaning and aim of this path is transcendence. In the end, that which is authentically itself experiences shipwreck as mere existence.[16]

Leaving the reader to decide upon the most plausible, preferable or accurate translation, the quest for what Benjamin called "true language" simultaneously raises the question as to whether Jaspers' language can be reflected without making reasonable allowances for linguistic variations. Thus, fidelity may hardly imply that there is a single solution to the question of translation. Indeed, a brief comparison of these alternative translations of Jaspers' 1931 text suggests the ideal working principle would be—*vive la différence!* So not the relativity of the original terminology, but the versatility of the vocabulary (in the target language) seems to be an overriding concern.

Consequently, only by suggesting comparisons with previous translations might the nuances of Jaspers' works—the difficulties and all—be brought to the reader's attention. The beauty of this comprehensive anthology is that, among other things, the editors have already implicitly undertaken significant comparative research. The outcome of their choices in relation to each specific text reverberates throughout the anthology. Ultimately, one of the great incentives of translation must therefore be that this task is essentially unfinished.

---

[16] *KJ* 55f. Compare with the earlier translation: Karl Jaspers, *Man in the Modern Age*, trans. Eden and Cedar Paul (New York, NY: Anchor Books, 1957), pp. 159, 161: "Man is always something more than what he knows of himself. He is not what he is simply once for all, but is a process; he is not merely an extant life, but is, within that life, endowed with possibilities through the freedom he possesses to make of himself what he will by the activities on which he decides. . . . As freedom he conjures up being as his hidden Transcendence. The significance of this path is Transcendence. Mere life miscarries."

Scheitern, for example, may be interpreted as "shipwreck" or "foundering" (Leonard and Edith Ehrlich and George Pepper), "foundering" (E.B. Ashton), or "failure" (Ralph Manheim).[17] The words are hardly set in stone. For instance, take the title of *Man in the Modern Age*, Jaspers' book first translated by Eden and Cedar Paul, a work that was a bestseller in its time just before the rise of the Nazi party to power in 1931. The basic ideas of this text were attuned to the central metaphors respectively of the second and third volumes of his *Philosophy—Grenzsituation, liebender Kampf, Kommunikation von Existenz zu Existenz* or *Scheitern, Gesetz des Tages* and *Leidenschaft zur Nacht*. Thus, *The Spiritual Situation of our Time* and metaphor of shipwreck might be followed closely. Nevertheless, there is also the added complication of whether it is possible to refer to an accepted canon of translated texts and, if so, where the reader's preferences should lie?

A literary canon, which most accurately reproduces the originality of Jaspers' words, suggests on the one hand that a more poetical interpretation will lead to a more readable text. On the other hand, if readability is valued above all else, fidelity to the original could simply be lost in translation. Also, there may be additional valid reasons to sacrifice accuracy for novelty in translation, as Harald Reiche previously considered in his essay on "Sources of Jaspers' Style"[18]:

> Language is at its strongest, truest, and least deceptive only where it is the almost unconscious by-product of thinking.
> Thus far Jaspers. It is easy to see that he has here uncovered the roots of his own style: his avoidance of terminology, formulas, jargon, his language of metaphor to convey the universality and failure of metaphor. (*SJS* 110f.)

The idea of a literary canon of preferred translation texts may well burden the translator with the problem of divining the message of the oracle. Jaspers' metaphors, for instance, may accentuate a broad range of intellectual sources from Hegel to his particular fascination for Shakespeare's Hamlet as a dramatic figure. We may therefore also acknowledge that Hamlet constantly appears as a mirror and focal point for Jaspers' treatment of tragedy. In "boundary situations" in which the fragile spirit of humanity wins out against hardship, shipwreck (or foundering), there is a potent force of reality that intervenes to change the tide of events: "In tragedy we transcend misery and terror and so move toward essential reality" (*SJS* 80).

In the final act of Shakespeare's play, Hamlet seizes the opportunity of becoming at one with his destiny and his fate seems inescapable: Hamlet's quest in death is to

---

[17] Translations are found respectively in *Karl Jaspers. Basic Philosophical Writings*, op. cit.; Karl Jaspers, "Philosophy," Vol. II, *Existential Elucidation*, trans. E.B. Ashton (Chicago, IL: Chicago University Press, 1969–1971); Karl Jaspers, *Way to Wisdom (An Introduction to Philosophy)*, trans. Ralph Manheim (New Haven, CT and London: Yale University Press, 1951), (translation of: *Einführung in die Philosophie*, 12 radio broadcasts, Basel, 1950). [Henceforth cited as *WW*]

[18] See Harald T. Reiche, "Postscript: Sources of Jaspers' Style," in Karl Jaspers, *Tragedy is Not Enough*, trans. Harald T. Reiche, Harry T. Moore, and Karl W. Deutsch (New York, NY: Archon, 1969). The essay was appended to this translation of the abridged 140-page English excerpt of the final part of Jaspers' *Von der Wahrheit*. [Henceforth cited as *SJS*]

shape and mould his existence. His memorable soliloquy echoes throughout of his ultimate end:

> To be or not to be; that is the question:
> Whether 'tis nobler in the mind to suffer
> The slings and arrows of outrageous fortune.
> Or to take arms against a sea of troubles,
> And, by opposing, end them.[19]

If a willingness to embrace a personal end to all things amidst the historical circumstances of the play places Shakespeare's character in touch almost with a sixth sense or at least an innate desire to be at one with "the innermost being of each man" there is no received wisdom to prescribe the most desirable translation.[20] What Jaspers calls failure or foundering or shipwreck is also a powerful force that takes Hamlet to the edge of the known limits of existence. But a cathartic motif is not channelled into the illumination of a boundary situation where man's historic situation and innermost being are apparently juxtaposed. Such an appointment with one's destiny is again different from the reality of a true or existent self. And the tragic individual is only exposed through a realization of life's inadequacy in the face of which Jaspers finds recourse to the Shakespearean sentence: "The rest is silence" (*H* 688).

Living in a New World

Ultimately, how can the translator be sure of being on the right track? Jaspers identified a new philosophical language. He introduced a step change from the traditional focus in philosophy on the World, the Soul and God and fashioned, in turn, coining a new description as *Existenz* and *Transzendenz*. He identified three subdivisions of philosophical world orientation, the elucidation of *Existenz* and metaphysics (*KJE* 291). His approach to philosophy was even redefined, as the editors of the aforementioned anthology suggested, in a mode of *Erhellung* of the Illumination of Existenz. Perhaps, the verification of Jaspers' language is bound to acknowledge what Werner Brock described as Jaspers' philosophical faith or his "courage to follow straightforwardly and undauntedly his own inner light from publication to publication" (*KJE* 290).

By tracing the underlying progression of Jaspers' works and incorporating the different suggestions used to translate Jaspers' *Grenzsituation*, it is clear that this pivotal concept can again be translated variously as "boundary situation" (E.B. Ashton), "limit situation" (Leonard and Edith Ehrlich) or "ultimate situation" (Ralph Manheim). If an English equivalent from amongst these selections is found

---

[19] William Shakespeare, *Hamlet*, Act 3, Scene 1, in *Shakespeare. The Complete Works*, eds. Stanley Wells and Gary Taylor (Oxford, NY: Oxford University Press, 1998), p. 669. [Henceforth cited as *H*]

[20] *SJS* 36: "This Much Is Certain: It Is an Experience That Touches the Innermost Being of Each Man."

as the closest approximation to Jaspers' concept, then a central tenet of the anthology in question is to draw attention to the unique nature of Jaspers' contribution, for instance, as outlined in the selection of the following:

> Situations such as: that I am always in situations, that I cannot live either without struggle and without suffering, that I ineluctably take guilt upon myself, that I must die—these I call limit situations. They do not change, except in their appearance; as applied to our existence they possess finality. We cannot gain an overview of them; confined within our existence we see nothing else behind them. They are like a wall against which we butt, against which we founder. They cannot be changed by us but merely clarified, yet they cannot be explained or derived from an Other. They go together with existence itself. (*KJ* 96f.)

Ralph Manheim's translation note on Jaspers' *Grenzsituation* supplies another interesting clarification: "The ultimate situations are the inescapable realities in relation to which alone human life can be made genuinely meaningful. Ultimate situations cannot be changed or surmounted; they can only be acknowledged"(*WW* 20). But the choice of the most relevant word is still unclear, for if we read on in the present anthology, we discover: "The word *limit* expresses that there is an Other, but tells us at the same time that this Other is not for consciousness within existence.... Limit situation belongs to existence as the situations belong to the consciousness that remains immanent" (*KJ* 97).

The register of English that provides the most poetical or idiomatic patterns to render the translation task effortless may be, as Reiche suggested, found in Shakespeare, the King James version of the Bible, or language taken "from the English speech of our own day" (*SJS* 112). But any plea for contemporary language returns us to our starting point in the sense that Jaspers' style should retain the genuine difficulty of the original. In interpreting Jaspers' appropriation of his intellectual influences in the works of the German Idealists—Hegel, Kant, Schelling—many interpretations abound. In Camus's pronunciation of the absurd, one such interpretation was in the esoteric language of his main protagonist, Mersault, who voices the final flourish of *L'Etranger*: "As if the blind rage had washed me clean, rid me of hope; for the first time, in that night alive with signs and stars, I opened myself to the gentle indifférence of the world."[21]

We may conclude that the most apt words to represent Jaspers' works depend (in English) less upon the accuracy of translation than upon a challenge to interpret a unique attribute of Jaspers' philosophical language: namely, its otherness, which invariably makes reading Jaspers in English sound like an unintelligible exercise. But the role of translation remains as much about the impossibility of making the English vocabulary function in the same categorical way as the original. And this has been shown to honour the role of the interpreter who brings to light the nuances of original ideas and expresses these in the most convincing terms.

Given that Jaspers was neither a dogmatic thinker nor in acceptance of an ideological standpoint, his legacy is nowhere more aptly represented than when

---

[21] Albert Camus, *L'Étranger* Gallimard 1957, p. 179, translated by S. Kirkbright. ["Comme ci cette grande colère m'avait purgé du mal, vidé d'espoir, devant cette nuit chargée de signes et d'étoiles, je m'ouvrais pour la première fois à la tendre indifférence du monde."]

successive translators succeed in reanimating the humanist ideas upon which his philosophy is grounded. Anthologies of Jaspers' texts in other languages must therefore continue to accommodate those existing projects that give the clearest possible insights into Jaspers' understanding of the German intellectual tradition after Kierkegaard and Nietzsche. Here, the messenger's role seems unassailable in the light of Jaspers' appreciation of the ultimate Kierkegaardian antinomian situation: it is possible that any venture is likely to founder, communication may not meet its target or even language itself may not arrive at the most appropriate poetical style. However, if fidelity to the original text is called for, it is possible to conclude— "Man does not possess perfect truth but, as temporal existence, remains on the way" (*KJ* 257).

Part II
Philosophical Faith: Critical and Historical Analyses

Philosophical Faith and Its Ambiguities

Alan M. Olson

Abstract An analysis of the strengths and ambiguities in Jaspers' concept of philosophical faith in three related contexts: language, religion, and value. The linguistic and semantic context discusses subtle differences of meaning in the Latin, English, and German expressions of faith. The religious context focuses on reason and revelation in the monotheistic traditions of the Middle East. Questions regarding the nature and future of humanity are discussed with respect to truth claims and an axiology of value.

One of the striking features of Karl Jaspers' philosophy is his abiding faith in the human prospect. This optimism is particularly remarkable when Jaspers' thought is contextualized historically and contrasted with the pessimistic and even nihilistic outlook of many of his contemporaries. A literary production of over sixty books spans six decades of the early twentieth century, precisely the period during which over 100 million people were slaughtered by various means, whether Mustard Gas during WWI, or Zyklon B, incendiary and nuclear bombs during WWII, for various horrendous ideological reasons, especially ethnic and political cleansing.[1] Throughout this catastrophic epoch, Karl Jaspers never waned in his determination to write analytically and constructively about the human condition, whether his inquiries had to do with medical issues, spiritual and religious matters, the status of the university, the future of Europe and the *Bundesrepublik Deutschland*, or the prospects for cross-cultural communication and world philosophy in the latter half of the twentieth century. Like Kant, and especially Hegel, Jaspers believed that philosophy must be engaged with the vital issues of ordinary living, must be *Realphilosophie*, and that taking academic refuge in formalistic specialization is tantamount to the "end" of philosophy.

One of Jaspers' most memorable statements, in fact, can be found in his *Atom Bomb* book, a statement that rather encapsulates what he means by *philosophical*

---

[1] Incendiary bombs alone killed upwards of 2.5 million German and Japanese civilians during WWII. The Mark 77 bomb (MK-77), used in Iraq and Afghanistan, is the direct successor to the napalm cluster bombs that were outlawed following the Vietnam War in 1981. Encouraged to attend the 65th anniversary memorial of Hiroshima in 2010, President Obama declined on the excuse that such an activity on his part might be deemed "controversial."

A.M. Olson (✉)
Boston University, Boston, MA, USA
e-mail: amo@bu.edu

H. Wautischer et al. (eds.), *Philosophical Faith and the Future of Humanity*,
DOI 10.1007/978-94-007-2223-1_8, © Springer Science+Business Media B.V. 2012

faith: "Philosophy alone," he asserts, "yields clarity against the perversions of reason," and further, "Philosophical faith is not a content we believe in, but an activity we believe by."[2] The "perversions of reason" to which he refers in 1958 were the double threats of totalitarianism and thermonuclear holocaust during the Cold War, threats made possible, and even probable, by a certain kind of "instrumentalist rationality" (*Zweckrationalität*) as this concept comes to be known through Habermas. But Jaspers' occasional assertion in 1958 also sheds light on the deeper meaning of the somewhat enigmatic concept of *philosophical faith*; and since *philosophical faith* is closely, if not primarily, identified with the philosophy of Karl Jaspers,[3] it needs clarification relative both to the time in which it found initial expression and also in terms of what it might mean for us today.[4]

---

[2] Karl Jaspers, *The Atom Bomb and the Future of Mankind,* trans. E.B. Aston (Chicago, IL, 1961), pp. 209, 262; *Die Atombombe und die Zukunft des Menschen* (Munich: Piper Verlag, 1958), "Nur in der Philosophie gibt es die Klarheit gegen die Unphilosophie, d.h. gegen die Verkehrung der Vernunft" and "Philosophischer Glaube is nicht ein Inhalt, an den geglaubt wird, sonder ein Tun, mit dem geglaubt wird" (pp. 289, 366).

[3] Jaspers introduced this concept in 1947 by way of a series of six lectures at the University of Basel, published as *Der philosophische Glaube* (Munich: Piper Verlag, 1948), and translated into English by Ralph Manheim under the title, *The Perennial Scope of Philosophy* (New York, NY: Philosophical Library, 1949). Jaspers further developed this notion in the early 1960s, with specific attention to religion and theology, under the more expansive title, *Der Philosophische Glaube angesichts der Offenbarung,* translated into English by E.B. Ashton under the title, *Philosophical Faith and Revelation*, and published as Vol. 17 in the prestigious Harper & Row "Religious Perspectives" series edited by Ruth Nanda Anshen. It is important to note that *Der Philosophische Glaube angesichts der Offenbarung,* in its first German edition (Munich: Piper Verlag, 1962), was preceded by an essay entitled *Der Philosophische Glaube angesichts der christlichen Offenbarung*, Jaspers contributed to a 1958 *Festschrift* for his Basel colleague, Heinrich Barth, who is the only theologian quoted favorably in the book length manuscript bearing nearly the same title; I say nearly the same title, because while the Christian understanding of revelation remains central to Jaspers' discussion, the modifier *christlichen* is dropped in the book and the adverb *angesichts is* introduced as if to suggest a *vis-à-vis* stance regarding the tensions between philosophical faith and religions of revelation generally, although this tension is increasingly ameliorated by Jaspers' attention to world religions late in his career. It should also be noted that the principal American expositor of the notion of philosophical faith, and Karl Jaspers' philosophy generally, is Leonard Ehrlich, to whom this collection of essays is dedicated. See Leonard Ehrlich, *Karl Jaspers: Philosophy as Faith* (Amherst, MA: University of Massachusetts Press, 1975).

[4] As Chris Thornhill argues, correctly, in my view, "The central idea in Jaspers' philosophy of religion is the concept of *philosophical faith...* This notoriously difficult concept contains a number of quite distinct meanings. *First,* it means that true philosophy must be guided by a faith in the originary transcendence of human existence, and that philosophy which negatively excludes or ignores its transcendent origin falls short of the highest tasks of philosophy. *Second,* it also means that true philosophy cannot simply abandon philosophical rationality for positively disclosed truth-contents or dogma, and that the critical function of rationality has a constitutive role in the formation of absolute knowledge. In this respect, Jaspers revisited some of the controversies concerning the relation between religion and philosophy which shaped the philosophy of the Young Hegelians in the 1830s. Like the Young Hegelians, he insisted that faith needs philosophy, and faith devalues its contents wherever these are dogmatically or positively proclaimed. *Third,* this concept also indicates that the evidences of faith are always paradoxical and uncertain and that those who pursue knowledge of these contents must accept an attitude of philosophical relativism and discursive

In what follows, I explore the meaning of philosophical faith in three separate but related contexts. I begin with some of the linguistic and semantic ambiguities of *philosophical faith* in German and English. My general thesis in this section is that these ambiguities arise, at least in part, because of certain incompatibilities in the English and German usage of faith and its cognates which make it difficult to settle on what philosophical faith means with any precision cross-culturally, so to speak, betwixt the Germanic and the Anglo-American linguistic and philosophical worlds.

Following this, I turn to the context of what Jaspers refers to as "biblical religion," for when the concept of philosophical faith is scrutinized against the truth claims of specific religions, especially the monotheistic traditions of the Middle East, its ambiguities become readily apparent and, in many ways, insurmountable. I am not, of course, so presumptuous as to suggest that I know what philosophical faith means for *biblical religions* as a whole or Christianity for that matter. This would be quite impossible. My reference point will be the form of Christianity with which Jaspers was most familiar and within which he went through the rite of confirmation, namely, the Evangelical Lutheran Church of Germany during the early twentieth century, and more specifically, the relatively liberal tradition of northwest Protestantism in Niedersachsen, influenced and conditioned, both in temperament and geography, by Dutch Reformed Protestantism, but also pressured, as was the German church generally (both Catholic and Protestant), by Prussian nationalism prior to WWI and by the Nazi dictatorship in the years leading up to and including WWII. As Carl Friedrich von Weizsäcker puts it perceptively, "Karl Jaspers was a liberal who believed in political freedom, following in the tradition of the church of Saint Paul, and not that of the Empire into which he was born."[5]

Finally, there is the looming issue of "the future of humanity" and this I explore briefly within the context of values. When we speak about the future of humanity, many questions arise: Are we speaking about the role of human beings in the future of the planet and what now have come to be known as problems of sustainability? Does the future of humanity have to do with empirical questions regarding the future of human beings on the planet Earth and environmental pollution caused by unrestrained population growth and consumption? Or are we dealing only with the idea of humanity? While the latter is certainly the case for Jaspers, as well as Kant, what bearing does this idea have on the actual life of human beings today? Does the idea of humanity offer helpful guidance regarding decision-making as it relates

---

exchange: if faith results in dogmatism, it immediately undermines its claims to offer transcendent knowledge." See Christopher Thornhill's fine entry on Jaspers in the *Stanford Encyclopedia of Philosophy*. http://plato.stanford.edu/entries/jaspers.

[5] See Carl Friedrich von Weizsäcker, "In Memory of Karl Jaspers" in *Karl Jaspers Today*, eds., Leonard H. Ehrlich and Richard Wisser (Washington, DC: Center for Advanced Research in Phenomenology & University Press of America, 1988), p. 27. I am reminded of the highly nationalistic monument in front of the Saint Lamberti-Kirche in Oldenburg, where Jaspers was confirmed, which proclaims: *Ein Gott, Ein Volk, Eine Wahrheit*, a graphical indication of the political conservatism of the Lutheran Church during the late nineteenth and early twentieth centuries in Germany. It is interesting to note that Rudolf Bultmann, with whom Jaspers had a prolonged and inconclusive debate in *Die Frage der Entmythologisierung* (1954), also came from the Duchy of Oldenburg.

to our future, or is the notion wholly illusory? My argument in this final section is that "philosophy alone yields clarity against the perversions of reason" if and only if philosophy encompasses a "firmament of values"[6] which are truly humane; values which, as Jaspers argues, can provide a "way to wisdom"[7] and elucidate the future of humanity in concrete and specific ways without claiming to be absolute, final, and fixed visions of truth and value.

The Semantic Context

Jaspers' heroic proclamations regarding philosophical faith in the late-1940s, against the background of the almost total devastation of Europe following WWII, garnered for him the identity of one of the world's leading existentialists. Together with Gabriel Marcel, Paul Tillich, and Martin Buber, Jaspers was famously identified by Jean-Paul Sartre as a religious or theistic existentialist as contrast to atheists like himself and also, so Sartre thought at the time, Martin Heidegger.[8]

Jaspers' upbeat notion of philosophical faith did not quite catch on (or caught on only briefly) in the quasi-positivistic circles dominating Anglo-American philosophy after WWII. Another reason for this failure, however, is that the concept of philosophical faith is semantically ambiguous and remains so today. This semantic ambiguity has to do with subtle differences of meaning betwixt "faith" and its cognates and related terms in English and German, e,g., faith (*Glaube*) and knowledge (*Wissen*), belief (*Glauben*) and trust (*Vertrauen*), and believing (*Glauben*) and thinking (*Denken*). In other words, *philosophischer Glaube* and *philosophical faith* do not mean precisely the same thing in English and German. And the major difference, it seems to me, is that the Germanic use of *Glaube* in its various forms entails a certain amount of *thinking*, a thinking combined with feeling as a kind of intuitive but not a rigorous or pure kind of thinking. The use of "faith" does not imply thinking in English; in fact, it can usually means the opposite, namely, blind acceptance, trust, and even the negation of reason and rationality by way of emotivistically driven conceptions of faith.[9]

No doubt much of this semantic ambiguity has to do with the extent to which the English and German languages have been textured over the centuries by the

---

[6] J.N. Findlay's lecture on "The Systematic Unity of Value" (Lawrence, KS: University of Kansas, 1968) can be found in *Ascent to the Absolute* (London: Allen & Unwin, Ltd., 1970). Findlay's most complete statement on this subject can be found in his *Values and Intentions: A Study in Value Theory and the Philosophy of Mind* (London: Allen & Unwin, 1961), a study influenced a great deal by the realist ontology of his teacher at Graz, Alexius Meinong, and also by Franz Brentano.

[7] See Jaspers, *Way to Wisdom: Introduction to Philosophy,* Ralph Manheim (translator) provides the title for the English translations of these lectures (English editions, Yale, 1951 and 1954).

[8] See Sartre's famous essay on "Existentialism and Humanism" (1946), Walter Kaufmann, *From Shakespeare to Existentialism* (1950); and Will Herberg, *Four Existentialist Theologians* (1958).

[9] See A.J. Ayer, *Language, Truth, and Logic* (1936), required reading for students of philosophy in the 1940s and 1950s; also Richard Hare, *The Language of Morals* (1952).

Anglo-American and Continental philosophical traditions, and the manner in which these traditions want to preserve and honor the past; the *Past,* in this instance, having largely to do with the history of the continental European philosophical and religious tradition. For the British, and also for Americans, the past, in the long historical sense, tends to be far less important than it is for Continental philosophers who routinely differentiate themselves from their analytic Anglo-American counterparts and who, conversely, detect in Continental philosophers the aroma of too much piety and religion.

This split has much to do with the rise of the *Novum Organum* in the sixteenth century and the spectacular rise of the scientific method and empiricism. But the Baconian revolution has deeper roots extending back three centuries from Sir Francis Bacon to the thirteenth century British Franciscan Friar, Roger Bacon, who, in his own way, played a major role, as did his contemporary, William of Ockham, in the rise of inductive logic, scientific method, and the nominalistic challenge to medieval realism that would find its theological and political champions in Luther and Calvin. While medieval nominalism was far from being the anti-ontological nominalism that would eventually come to be the case in Post-Enlightenment empiricism, it nevertheless challenged, quite successfully, the authority of tradition, which meant Roman Catholic Tradition, for the European tradition and Catholic tradition are one and the same for well over a millennium.

I am suggesting, then, that these historical developments play a major role in the psycholinguistic coloring of the meanings of faith and *Glaube*, thinking and *Denken*, knowledge and *Wissen*, and even feeling and *Gefühl*, sensation and *Empfindung*, especially in matters religious and philosophical. It is fair to assert that the distinction between faith and thinking, *Glaube* und *Denken*, is particularly acute in German and English, since "thinking," as mentioned above, plays a role in *Glauben*; whereas "feeling" and the emotions, and not thinking in the deliberative sense, are usually what inform the meaning of faith in English. For example, if one is asked, "What do you think about such and such. . ." one is faced with a much more rigorous and demanding question than if one is asked simply "How do you feel about such and such?" What is the difference? Feeling encompasses the emotions but thinking does not or, at least, there tends to be a difference not only in degree but also in kind with respect to the use of feeling and thinking as heuristic devices.[10] Thus, if one says, "I feel that such and such is the case; and since I have no compelling evidence to indicate that it is not the case, I therefore believe that it is the case." Feeling in English therefore functions very much like *Glaube* in German when one says, "*Ich glaube, dass so und so der Fall ist.*"

Moreover, knowledge (*Wissen*) is more sharply identified with thinking than with believing in its German forms. Why is this the case? It may be that the democratic

---

[10] See Herman Stark's very helpful analysis of Heidegger's *Was Heist Denken?* in the contributed papers of the 20th World Congress of Philosophy. http://www.bu.edu/wcp/Papers/Cont/ContStar. htm.

traditions of Anglo-Americans, and the Lockean emphasis on the autonomous individual and his or her beliefs, whether rational or irrational, is a causal factor; in other words, the popular notion that the values and convictions generated by the emotions of the autonomous individual has reduced the distinction between thinking and believing in English usage. As Charles Taylor has observed, we live in the age of soft relativism and the "expressivist self" where everyone's beliefs and convictions, or the lack of the same, are to be recognized and respected no matter what they happen to be, so long as they do not intrude on the beliefs and convictions of other autonomous individuals.[11]

When an English speaker says, "I believe such and such. . ." it usually means that the speaker believes such and such is the case based upon generally held assumptions combined with personal feelings and intuitions. For example, when one flies on the airplane of a reputable company with a long-standing tradition of excellence, like Lufthansa, one is confident that it will get to the intended destination even though one knows absolutely nothing about the pilot flying the plane. One might not feel the same way about a more obscure airline company, one with a bad accident record, or an airline known for cost cutting even if one knows something about the impeccable reputation of the pilot. Why then do I believe that I will be safer on Lufthansa than Airline X? It may be that I have recently heard about an accident on Airline X, or it may be because the Germans have a greater reputation for technology and quality control, that the Germans are better at reason and analysis, and that this translates into the reputation of the high-end technology products of BMW and Mercedes-Benz. To know that this is the case, then, requires much more rigorous thinking than simply believing that such and such is the case.

While Hegel knew little or nothing about these ambiguities between German and English, he famously reacted to the reduction of reason (*Vernunft*) to understanding (*Verstehen*) and asserted that the philosophy of reflection would lead to the end of philosophy. He made his case early in his career with the publication of what has come to be known as the *Differenzschrift* (1801) and *Glauben und Wissen* (1802), both published in the *Kritisches Journal der Philosophie* he edited with Schelling during his Jena period. The latter piece, *Glauben und Wissen oder die Reflexionsphilosophie der Subjektivität in der Vollständigkeit ihrer Formen als Kantische, Jacobische und Fichtesche Philosophie*, is squarely aimed at what Hegel believed to be deficiencies in metaphysics, epistemology, and the abandonment of reason (*Vernunft*) in matters moral, religious, and spiritual.[12] Not only did he co-edit this journal with his then more famous friend, Schelling (who had already succeeded Fichte at Jena following Fichte's move to Berlin following the *Atheismusstreit*), but he also used this opportunity to define what he thought was lacking and inadequate in his contemporaries in order to define the parameters of his own philosophy.

---

[11] See Charles Taylor, *The Ethics of Authenticity* (Cambridge, MA: Harvard University Press, 1992), *passim;* also his recent major work, *A Secular Age* (Cambridge, MA: Harvard University Press, 2007).

[12] G.W.F. Hegel, *Kritisches Journal der Philosophie*, Bd. II, Stück I (Juli 1802).

When Hegel published what some consider his *magnum opus*, *Phänomenologie des Geistes* (1807), it became clear that he also thought Schelling to be among the inadequate voices of early nineteenth century German idealism and that it became his life project to define the critical terms *Glauben* and *Wissen, Vernunft* and *Verstehen*, and to assign their proper roles in philosophy, metaphysics, and religion.

Since Hegel is best characterized, perhaps, as a philosophical theologian and a lodestar, together with Kant, of the co-called continental tradition, it is helpful to consider briefly what he says about *Glauben* and *Wissen, Vernunft, Verstand,* and *Verstehen,* in philosophy and religion, in order to determine what role, if any, Hegel plays in the formulation of Jaspers' concept of *philosophischer Glaube.* In the preface to Hegel's famous essay on "Faith and Knowledge," for example, and in a gloss on Kant's remarks in his preface to the *Critique of Pure Reason* (A viii–x) where he famously speaks of metaphysics as once "queen of the sciences," Hegel makes his case against his contemporary philosophers of religion as follows:

> Reason (*Vernunft*) had already gone to seed in and for itself when it envisaged religion merely as something positive and not ideally. And after its battle with religion, the best that Reason could manage was to take a look at itself and come to self-awareness. Reason, having in this way become mere intellect (*Verstand*), acknowledges its own nothingness by placing that which is better than it in a *faith outside and beyond* itself. This is what has happened in the *philosophies of Kant, Jacobi, and Fichte.* Philosophy has made itself the handmaid of faith once more.[13]

Hegel makes it clear in this passage that he has little regard for faith (*Glaube*) and mere understanding (*Verstehen*) as substitutes for reason (*Vernunft*) and knowledge (*Wissen*); and that when religion is reduced to its external manifestations (*Positivität*), that is, when completely reduced to what Hegel calls the *cultus* or to what today would be concerns of the history and sociology of religion, it is trivialized altogether; similarly, if the primary function of religion is considered to be the attainment of happiness (*eudaimonia*), then religion is reduced to psychotherapy, as Nietzsche was later to observe. There are not two types of reason for Hegel, one for philosophy and the other for religion; there is only reason (*Vernunft*) and the Idea (*Idee*). Thus Hegel does not think, as Jaspers suggests, that there are two types of faith, namely, philosophical and religious. Reason and reason alone provides the intelligible route to the Absolute Idea, from which, in fact, it originates and draws its strength, and within which there is no separation between philosophical and religious knowledge and truth. But if the reason and proper to religion is mere understanding (*bloßer Verstand*), then the separation between philosophy and religion, as in Lessing's "broad and ugly ditch," cannot be surmounted. While it is true, for Hegel, that popular religion conveys its message through picture thinking (*Vorstellungsdenken*), it is the task of philosophy to elevate these stories and metaphors into the realm of reason and logic rather than leave them at the level of mythology. Thus the truth of a given religion, for Hegel, has to do with determining

---

[13] *Hegel Werke 2, Jenaer Schriften*, 1801–1807 (Suhrkamp Verlag, 1970), p. 288. [Henceforth cited as JS]

how true a given religion is to its concept or idea.[14] This is why he insists that religion must always be considered in terms of its ideality and not merely by its popular manifestations as a cultural reality. Those who fail to do so remain mere "clerks in the storehouse" of religions. Thus the subject-object problem, as defined by Kant and his successors, and which persists in Jaspers, remains the critical problem for Hegel since it is formulated upon an inadequate concept of reason and, of course, on a wholly inadequate conception of *Geist* since it is precisely the work of *Geist* to transcend the subject-object problematic.

The following passage, aimed at Kant, Jacobi, and Fichte, might also include Schleiermacher, Schelling and, indeed, Jaspers; with Kant, Fichte, and Jacobi understood as the devotees of objectivity, and with Scheiermacher, Schelling, and, indeed, Kierkegaard and Jaspers, understood as the apostles of subjectivity when it comes to determining the nature of religious faith and truth. Hegel continues:

> According to *Kant*, the supersensuous is incapable of being known by Reason; the highest Idea does not at the same time have reality. According to *Jacobi*, "Reason is ashamed to beg and has no hands and feet for digging." Only the feeling and consciousness of his ignorance of the True is given to man, only an inkling, a divination of the True in Reason, Reason being something subjective, an instinct, though universal. According to *Fichte,* God is something incomprehensible and unthinkable. Knowledge knows nothing save that it knows nothing; hence, it must take refuge in faith. All of them agree, as the old distinction put it, that the Absolute is no more against Reason than it is for it, because it [the Absolute] is beyond Reason. [*JS* 288–289]

In order to be happy, i.e., in order to be religious, it is assumed that one must have faith; hence the necessary split between philosophy and religion and the need, as Jaspers concluded regarding the two types of faith. Obviously Hegel does not concur and, in this instance, is far more Kantian than Kant, namely, by insisting that the issue is not whether the greatest good is happiness, or even if one deserves to be happy; it rather has to do with the status of reason and the idea within the overall structure of consciousness.

> This is the basic character of eudaemonism and the Enlightenment. The beautiful subjectivity of Protestantism is transformed into empirical subjectivity; the poetry of Protestant grief that scorns all reconciliation with empirical existence is transformed into the prose of satisfaction with the finite and of good conscience about it. What is the relation of this basic character to the philosophies of Kant, Jacobi and Fichte? So little do these philosophies step out of this basic character that, on the contrary, they have merely perfected it to the highest degree. Their conscious direction is flatly opposed to the principle of eudaemonism. However, because they are nothing but this direction, their positive character is just this principle itself; so that the way these philosophies modify eudaemonism merely gives it a perfection of formation, which has no importance in principle, no significance for Reason and philosophy. The absoluteness of the finite and of empirical reality is still maintained in these philosophies. The infinite and the finite remain absolutely opposed. Ideality (*das Idealische*) *is* conceived only as the concept. And in particular, when this concept is posited affirmatively, the only identity of the finite and infinite that remains possible is a relative

---

[14] See Hegel's *Lectures on the Philosophy of Religion*, trans. Peter Hodgson (Berkeley, CA: University of California, 1985).

identity, the domination of the concept over what appears as the real and the finite, everything beautiful and ethical being here included. And on the other hand, when the concept is posited negatively, the subjectivity of the individual is present in empirical form, and the domination is not that of the intellect but is a matter of the natural strength and weakness of the subjectivities opposed to one another. Above this absolute finitude and absolute infinity there remains the Absolute as an emptiness of Reason, a fixed realm of the incomprehensible, of a faith which is in itself non-rational (*vernunftlos*), *but* which is called rational because the Reason that is restricted to its absolute opposite recognizes something higher above itself from which it is self-excluded. [*JS* 288–289]

Jaspers recognizes the truth of which Hegel speaks in his philosophy of "limit situations" (*Grenzsituationen*); but he also believes that this truth can only be apprehended in ciphers and not through an absolute logic. In this respect Jaspers' notion of ciphers is much closer to the fleeting existential apprehensions Tillich refers to as "fragmentary but unambiguous visions of the unity of Being"; fragmentary because such experiences, as ecstatic, nevertheless remain temporal and cannot be objectified, even though unambiguous as windows into the Ground of Being, as in Schelling. When Jaspers speaks about the foundering of reason in the face of Being-Itself, he raises the need for a modified ontology by way of another enigmatic concept, namely, *perichontology* or the ontology that circles round (or within) the Being of *das Umgreifende*, but cannot offer a definitive statement regarding the essence of Being-Itself.[15]

Because Hegel's pneumatological "ascent to the absolute," to borrow the Plotinian phrase of J.N. Findlay, is considered impossibly Promethean by many,

---

[15] For a more complete discussion of perichontology, see *Karl Jaspers: Philosopher Among Philosophers,* eds., Richard Wisser and Leonard H. Ehrlich (Würzburg: Könighausen & Neumann, 1993), esp. pp. 135ff, where Leonard Ehrlich differentiates Heidegger's fundamental ontology from Jaspers' perichontology with respect to Heidegger's notion of *aletheia*, upshot of his argument being that Jaspers clearly has more regard for the truths of biblical revelation and Heidegger does not. See also Gerhard Knauss, "The Concept of the Encompassing in Jaspers' Philosophy" in *The Philosophy of Karl Jaspers*, Schilpp Edition, Vol. IX (Open Court, 1957), pp. 141–176. Knauss argues, correctly in my view, that the basic difference between ontology and perichonotology is that the former proposes to offer a definitive word (*logos*) about being (*ontos*), that is to say, the essence of Being. But Jaspers, as a Kantian, thinks this impossible since the thing-in-itself cannot be known and that reason (*Vernunft*) founders like a ship on the rocks in the face of such an attempt. Hence the task of perichontology, as Knauss argues, is to know what the Being of the Encompassing means "for us" by way of *Verstehensphilosophie* or hermeneutics. This *pro me, extra nos* conception of perichontology seems to me very close to theological conceptions of the Trinity and Jaspers' notion of perichontology may, in fact, have its origins in Patristic theology and the notion of *perichoresis* where the Fathers attempt to explain both the unity and the diversity of the three persons of the Trinity, i.e., that the three hypostases or instances of the Being of the Absolute as Father, Son, and Holy Spirit are separate but distinct revelations having their source or ground within the absolute unity of the Godhead or "the god above god," as in Pseudo-Dionysus the Areopagite. As such, Jaspers' notion also seems somewhat related to the *communication idiomatum* and the manner in which the divine properties or attributes of Christ are communicated in the various idioms of Christology, while the divinity of Christ, as such, remains absolute and "beyond Being," so to speak, the whole being greater than its parts. The notion of panentheism, as Tillich has it, seems to me also very close to what informs Jaspers' notion of the Encompassing.

the question becomes as to whether it might be possible to ameliorate the extravagant ontological claims of absolute idealism and still preserve the moral and metaphysical insights of totality or *Absolute Einheit*. John N. Findlay, who admired Jaspers greatly, believed there was such a way, namely, an ascent to the Absolute by way of an absolute theory combined with an axiology of value empowered by what he calls rational eschatology. The rational eschatology Findlay prefers is Hegel's, although there is no reason, he says, that some other eschatology, including various religious eschatologies, "might do as well."[16] The point, quite simply, is that for values to make sense they have to refer to something; and reference to something implies some kind of movement or teleology towards the goal of fulfillment. Such a goal does not merely have to do with empiricism or consequentialism, but rather with the eidetic reference point of an absolute unity of value like "God," and God-Talk (viz., *philosophical faith*) necessitates some kind of rational eschatology, in Findlay's view and, of course, also in Hegel's. The task, then, is to determine what kinds of absolutes are worthwhile or, to use Jaspers' terms, what kind of Absolute encompasses all others in terms of Unity (*Einheit*). Thus the task of an axiology of values within Jaspers' notion of *das Umgreifende* or any other concept of the totality of Being, is to determine the difference between the values and disvalues, both being necessarily included within any notion of totality.

The Religious Context

What, then, is philosophical faith within the context of religion? And how is it different from theological faith? What is the meaning of "faith" when modified by the adjectives "philosophical" and/or "philosophic"? And what does this mean within the framework of what Jaspers refers to as the "biblical religions"?[17] Does it mean "faith in God" or "faith in philosophy"? If so, how is this different from "faith in reason" since it is commonly understood that philosophy has to do with cultivating the life of reason? Are not "philosophy" and "faith" antonyms? Can faith be philosophical and if so under what conditions? If philosophy has to do with the work of reason, science, and rationality, can religious faith be reasonable, scientific, and rational? If so, on what terms and conditions? What is gained and what is lost if one accepts what Jaspers has to say regarding philosophical faith?[18]

---

[16] See J.N. Findlay, *Ascent to the Absolute* (Allen & Unwin, 1970), and other works, including: *Values and Intentions* (Allen & Unwin, 1961), and, of course, his Gifford Lectures, *The Discipline of the Cave* and *The Transcendence of the Cave* (Allen & Unwin, 1966, 1957). Findlay, like Ricoeur and also Jaspers, I think, thought it best to philosophize between Kant and Hegel.

[17] By "biblical religions" he means Judaism and Christianity. Since 9/11 it has become painfully obvious to many that this notion must also includes Islam, about which Jaspers and, before him, Hegel, says little or nothing.

[18] Fritz Buri, Jaspers' colleague in Basel and who was strongly influenced by him, wrote a book entitled *Theologie der Existenz*, in 1954, translated into English and published by Fortress Press in 1968 under the title of *Thinking Faith*.

Jaspers makes it quite clear, as mentioned above, that there are two quite different kinds of faith: philosophical and religious. They can be mutually exclusive, he says, and frequently are, but there can also be communication between them on the grounds of *mögliche Existenz* because both kinds of faith are historic, that is, both philosophical and theological faith are held by individuals conditioned by the particularities of the specific historical process within which they find themselves, a process which, when recognized and understood, negates all claims to absolute and final truth. As Jaspers puts it:

> Originally different ways of life, and of the faith that goes with them, [religious and philosophical faith] are indeed mutually exclusive: they cannot be realized in the same human being. But they do not exclude each other if they meet in different human beings. Each *Existenz* is historic; each can be earnest about loving the other; each can know that between him and the other runs an encompassing bond.[19]

According to Andreas Cesana, however, the conflict for Jaspers is not really between religious and philosophical faith, but between the project of *Weltphilosophie* and philosophical faith as originally conceived by Jaspers. Cesana argues, quite convincingly in my view, that the basic principles and categories in Jaspers' philosophy can be found in his earliest philosophical works, namely, *Psychologie der Weltanschaungen* (1919) and in his three-volume *Philosophie* (1930), and that these principles and categories remain constant throughout Jaspers' career. After 1945, however, the notions of *philosophical faith* and *world philosophy* are progressively released from the constraints of Western theological discussions and debates. This does not, however, represent an *Umkehr* for Jaspers, as in the famous case of his estranged colleague, Martin Heidegger, after 1933. Rather these terms represent, as Cesana suggests, the basis of Jaspers' "moral response" to the catastrophe of World War II. Cesana's argument is based on the observation that after the 1950s Jaspers increasingly began to identify religion almost entirely with *philosophia perennis*, that is, with the religiosity and spirituality antecedent to the rise of biblical religions, especially the Asian religious and philosophical traditions dating from the third millennium BC.[20]

Armin Wildermuth, on the other hand, asserts that the notion of philosophical faith is intelligible only if one first understands what Jaspers means by philosophy, especially vis-à-vis the implicit ontological claims in his notion of the All-Encompassing (*das Umgreifende*).[21] While I am in agreement with both Cesana and Wildermuth on these points, I also argue that it is also important to understand what Jaspers means by "faith" and, indeed, how faith fits into his philosophical and religious system.

---

[19] *Philosophical Faith and Revelation*, p. 363.

[20] See Andreas Cesana, "World Philosophy and Philosophical Faith," in *Existenz*, Vol. 2, Nos. 1–2 (Fall 2007), pp. 25–31. http://www.existenz.us/volumes/Vol.4-1Cesana.pdf.

[21] See Armin Wildermuth, "Jaspers and the Concept of Philosophical Faith," in *Existenz*, Vol. 2, Nos. 1–2, pp. 8–18. http://www.existenz.us/volumes/Vol.2Wildermuth.pdf. [Henceforth quoted as *JCPF*]

When considered strictly within the context of what Jaspers called "the biblical religions"[22] it is difficult, if not impossible (as Tertullian noted long ago[23]), to square the work of philosophy and theology, and hence the relative meanings and proper functions of reason and faith. No doubt this accounts for the tension between the philosophy of Karl Jaspers and the Middle-Eastern monotheistic religions of revelation, and why many practitioners and theologians within these traditions identify philosophical faith with relativism. There are good reasons for this since, as Paul Tillich once observed, "Jaspers is a humanist who wants to know what it means to be a person" (i.e., that Jaspers is basically a Kantian), whereas his contemporary and rival, Martin Heidegger, is an "ontologist" who wants to know "the meaning of Being."[24] As I have pointed out elsewhere, Heidegger, in spite of his controversial political views, has fared much better than Jaspers in theological discussions over the years, the reason being that fundamental ontology is much more in keeping with the longstanding debate betwixt Protestants and Catholics on nature and grace, whereas the Kantianism that increasingly influences liberal Protestantism has long been viewed with suspicion by conservative Protestants and Catholics.[25]

One of the sayings dear to evangelical and conservative Christians with respect to the nature of faith, for example, a saying attributed to Saint Paul in the Epistle to the Hebrews 11:1 (KJV), is as follows: "Now faith is the substance of things hoped for, the evidence of things unseen" ('Έστι δὲ πίστις ἐλπιζομένων ὑπόστασις, πραγμάτων ἔλεγχος οὐ βλεπομένων); that is, faith (πίστις) has to do with a belief or conviction in the existence of things, realities, happenings, or states of affairs, that are beyond any kind of empirical verification and are to be accepted by faith.[26] Indeed, it is only through faith that such truths can be known, as Jesus reminded the doubting Thomas following the resurrection (John 20:25–29).

---

[22] This would include Islam although Jaspers, like Hegel, says little or nothing about Islam. Indeed, Islam, for Hegel, is a "deviant denomination," so to speak, and a throwback to the medieval ages.

[23] Tertullian (160–220 AD), Carthagenian Montanist and the first great Christian fundamentalist, is famous for what has been called the *credo quia absurdum* and the question: *Quid ergo Athenis et Hierosolymis?* His answer, of course, being that the reference points of Athens and Jerusalem, reason and faith, are wholly incommensurable.

[24] See Alan M. Olson, ed., *Heidegger and Jaspers* (Philadelphia, PA: Temple University Press, 1994), pp. 14–28.

[25] I developed this theme at some length in my article, "Cultural Factors in the North American Reception of Karl Jaspers" during *Jaspersjahr* at Oldenburg (2008). See *Existenz,* Vol. 4, No. 1 (2009), pp. 40–51. http://www.existenz.us/volumes/Vol.4-1Olson.pdf; see also *Jahrbuch der Österreichischen Karl Jaspers Gesellschaft*, Vol. 22, pp. 71–96.

[26] Biblical scholars have pointed out that the famous and oft-quoted passage from Hebrews mentioned above probably did not come directly from the hand of Saint Paul but rather Barnabas, Paul's right-hand man in Rome. Others, like Adolf von Harnack, suggest it came from the hand of Pricilla, and still others suggest that it might have originated from Alexandrine authorities such as Clement and Origin. Whatever the case, it is an assertion informed by the notion that one should believe Jesus is the Christ because of the testimony of authorities, whether eye witnesses, the witnesses of witnesses or, in the case of Saint Paul, by way of an ecstatic conversion experience akin to his famous theophany on the road to Damascus.

The warrant or imperative of *sola fides* is essentially what comes to be known in philosophy as *fideism*. And this is not surprising since it is precisely the meaning of the Greek word for faith (πίστις) that carries over into the Latin *fides*, and the English *faith*, as in the *fides quaerens intelligam* or "faith seeking intelligibility" through reason (νόος or *intellectus*) in Augustine and Anselm, and which provides the basis for the long and powerful dialectical tradition of speculative and philosophical theology in Christianity, namely, *credo ut intelligam, intelligo ut credam* as the *foci* constituting the hermeneutical circle.[27]

Within Reformed Christianity one also recalls Luther's famous discovery on the privy upon reading that *Der Gerechte wird seines Glaubens leben* (The just shall live by faith, Romans 1:17), the exegetical insight leading to the rejection of scholasticism and the Roman Catholic hierarchy, and eventually to the Enlightenment and the so-called Post-Christian age. On the rather more banal side, some scholars have reminded us that because Luther suffered a great deal from constipation, this discovery may have had more to do with physical than spiritual relief, so to speak. But on the sublime side, Pauline injunctions regarding the nature of *faith* reinforced Luther's notion regarding the "priesthood of all believers" and that pious believers wanting to be justified or right-wised could do so by way of a direct, non-mediated, relationship with the Divine "by grace, through faith."[28]

But what does it mean to be "justified by faith"? Suicide bombers carry out their desperate actions on the conviction that their faith is faith in the "God of Justice." It is not surprising that skeptics and atheists should consider such actions the product of totally blind and fanatical faith.[29] In its less extreme and more traditional Christian form, this kind of faith had to do with belief in the resurrection of Jesus from the dead and, in the *eschaton*, the resurrection of the dead whereupon the just (or righteous) will reap the reward of everlasting bliss and the unlucky remainder will be "cast into eternal darkness." Needless to say, the consequentalist convictions of the terrorist regarding suicide and mass murder are qualitatively different from the personal belief that Jesus was the Messiah since, in the latter instance, there is a certain amount of historical data and testimony upon which to base one's judgment. Nevertheless, common *doxological* usage, so to speak, regarding "faith" in religious claims (for which there is little or no empirical and/or material evidence) usually means, "Well, it's all a matter of faith" and "If you do not have it, you need

---

[27] I argued as much in my book on Jaspers, namely, that this dialectic passes from Jaspers to Ricoeur and, indeed, also Lonergan and Gadamer, although Gadamer is usually understood has being more influenced by Heidegger's understanding of hermeneutics. See: *Transcendence and Hermeneutics* (Springer, 1979).

[28] "And Abraham believed and it was reckoned to him as righteousness" (KJV, Galatians 3:6); "*Gleichwie Abraham hat Gott geglaubt und es ist ihm gerechnet zur Gerechtigkeit*" (Luther Bible). Recent English translations prefer the term "righteous" to the German "*gerecht*" as being closer, perhaps, to the original Hebrew in the Abramic instance.

[29] See some of the current noisy voices in the current atheism discussion: Sam Harris, *The End of Faith* (Norton, 2004); Christopher Hitchens, *God is Not Great* (New York, NY: Hatchette, 2007); Richard Dawkins, *The God Delusion* (New York, NY: Mariner, 2008); and, more reasonably, Dan Dennett, *Breaking the Spell: Religion as a Natural Phenomenon* (Penguin, 2006).

to get it!" "Having faith" in this sense can mean, on the one hand, that if one has been bought up within a specific faith tradition, i.e., baptized, confirmed, and habituated within it, and remaining certain regarding its dogmatic truth claims throughout one's life, then one has faith and can be counted amongst the faithful. It is precisely this sense that informs the notion of faith as trust as found in the Hebrew Bible: "Trust in the Lord with all thine heart and lean not unto thine own understanding" (Proverbs 3:5, KJV).[30] But, on the other hand, if one is not amongst the "once born" or "the chosen" with this secure confidence and trust, then one needs to be "born again," that is, one needs to be counted amongst the regenerated who have, later in life, gone through a conversion experience and "accepted Jesus" as one's "personal savior."[31] William James famously called this the difference between the "healthy minded" and the "sick soul," the "volitional" and the "self-surrender" forms of conversion, and that the latter type needed to be taken seriously, at least for pragmatic reasons, and not dismissed as being altogether pathological.[32]

Jaspers clearly rejects this kind of *fidism*, considering it no different form other manifestations of psychopathology that lead to political disaster, as in the blind acceptance of a *Führer Prinzip*.[33] In speculating about the philosophy of the future immediately following WWII, Jaspers discusses the "willful belief of the unbelievable" wherein people believe as though "belief is a duty." In this instance, Jaspers writes:

> What matters is not what you believe but that you believe. This is a wonderful perversion; faith becomes faith in faith. . .nihilistic and positive at the same time. . .having donned the iron mask. . .of an absolute without content.[34]

While the "duty of belief" is clearly being a perversion of deontology, there also is a deeper dimension to this apparent fideism and philosophical faith, for that matter. For it seems to me that Jaspers' assertions regarding the nature of *philosophical faith* at times seem to echo the words of Luther who, in his explanation to the Third Article of the Apostle's Creed, the article on the Holy Spirit and the work of *Heiligung,* asserts: *Ich glaube, das ich nicht aus eigener Vernunft noch Kraft. . .glauben kann.* In this rather amazing passage, Luther confesses enigmatically that he "believes that he cannot believe," in other words, he believes (or thinks)

---

[30] "Verlaß dich auf den Herrn von ganzem Herzen und verlaß dich nicht auf deinen Verstand" (Luther Bible, 1545); *Verlaß*, as in the noun *Vertrauen*, meaning "trust" or "reliance," and *Vertrauen* is a cognate of *Glauben* in German. Fidelity and Trust (as in a financial trust) are analogues of faith in English.

[31] It is precisely this definition that informs those who, like Billy Graham's son, Franklin, doubt that Barack Hussein Obama II is a Christian.

[32] See William James, *Varieties of Religious Experience* (1906), *passim.*

[33] Indeed, Jaspers believes that all worldviews, especially religious worldviews, are contaminated by a certain amount of psychopathology. See *Psychologie der Weltanschauungen* (Springer, 1954).

[34] Jaspers, *The Perennial Scope of Philosophy*, trans. Ralph Manheim (New York, NY: Philosophical Library, 1949), p. 162. Faith as a "duty" is analogous to the notion in popular sports culture that "You gotta believe!" that the home team will be all-victorious, and that the consequence of "not believing." In my case, will be "excommunication" from "Red Sox Nation."

that he cannot comprehend the unity (*Einheit*) of the Trinity (or what Kierkegaard called the "absolute paradox" of the Incarnation) by "reason alone" and that such comprehension is possible only by way of *Geist*.[35]

Luther's nominalistic suspicions of Thomistic realism are well known, and much has been made of his pejorative references to Aristotle and the "whore reason." But as Rudolf Otto argues, the early Luther also stood in awe before the mysteries of the *deus absconditus* and believed that a primordial apprehension of *das Numinose* was at the core of his faith in God.[36] One's comprehension of this reality, however, was not immediate but mediate (as was also the case for Hegel), and this mediated comprehension was possible only by way of heeding the "call" (*berufen*) of the *Heilige Geist,* a call or summons that, for Luther, becomes determinate by way of the Gospel, the Sacraments, and fellowship in the *Geistliche Gemeinschaft* that is the Church. In other words, "reason alone" is prone towards a rationalization and justification of all sorts of perversions and disvalues and cannot, therefore, be the sole basis for a comprehension of the meaning of Being. There must be something more for this to happen, and this something more has to do with the nature of philosophy properly understood as the work of Spirit, that is, accomplished in the spirit of philosophical faith.[37]

Jaspers at times seems to share this view and it certainly is a view that makes sense vis-à-vis his assertion that "philosophy alone yields clarity against the perversions of reason," i.e., that reason alone and unmediated by value is capable of providing justification for almost anything, and that the dogmatic and value-free pretensions of rationality need to be held in check, especially in science and technology. Philosophy alone is capable, indeed, has the deontological duty to intercept and negate the "perversions" of facile, wrong-headed, and perverse forms of rationality.

---

[35] See Luther's *Small Catechism,* explanation to the Third Article of the Apostle's Creed which reads as follows in German: *Ich glaube, daß ich nicht aus eigener Vernunft noch Kraft an Jesus Christus, meinen Herrn, glauben oder zu ihm kommen kann; sondern der Heilige Geist hat mich durch das Evangelium berufen, mit seinen Gaben erleuchtet, im rechten Glauben geheiligt und erhalten; gleichwie er die ganze Christenheit auf Erden beruft, sammelt, erleuchtet, heiligt und bei Jesus Christus erhält im rechten, einigen Glauben; in welcher Christenheit er mir und allen Gläubigen täglich alle Sünden reichlich vergibt und am Jüngsten Tage mich und alle Toten auferwecken wird und mir samt allen Gläubigen in Christus ein ewiges Leben geben wird. Das ist gewißlich wahr.* This, of course, was the form that Jaspers had to memorize as a teenager for catechization and conformation in the Evangelical Lutheran Church.

[36] See Rudolf Otto's classic *The Idea of the Holy* (*Das Heilige, 1917*), trans. John W. Harvey (Oxford, 1923). Otto argues that Luther, especially the early Luther, was deeply influenced by Rhineland mysticism, especially that of Johannes Tauler, and that Jacob Böhmer may be viewed as a continuation of Luther's spirituality. It is not surprising that once embroiled in politics, as he was after 1520, Luther became less and less mystical. Jaspers' admiration of the Rhineland mystics, of course, is well documented in his works, especially *The Great Philosophers*, 4 vols. (New York, NY: Harcourt, Brace, & World, 1995).

[37] I believe that Luther's enigmatic assertion in his *Kleine Katachismus* (see n. 17) has a strong bearing on the formulation of Hegel's doctrine of *Geist*, and I argued as much in my book, *Hegel and the Spirit: Philosophy as Pneumatology* (Princeton, NJ, 1992). Given his interest in mystics such as Eckhart and Cusanus, the same can be said, I think, of Jaspers.

The reason that philosophy has this duty, for Kant as well as Jaspers, is that philosophy must not only be critical, that is transcendentally critical, but must also have an informed understanding of the *Good* (ἀγαθός).[38] This does not mean *the good* subdivided into natural and moral goods, as tends to be the case in contemporary value theory, but rather the good-in-and-for-itself, as in Kant and Hegel. This is the non-objectifiable Good; the Good that discloses itself in "ciphers of Transcendence", to use Jaspers' language, or instantiates itself from time to time in paradigmatic instances of Transcendence. In other words, we are not speaking about abstract, empty notions of worth and value, but the human capacity to recognize and understand the good through maxims and imperatives that expose and preclude disvalues and validate true values. I believe, for Jaspers, faith is preeminent in his constellation of values, precisely as philosophical faith, and that apart from it the human prospect on this or any other planet is exceedingly bleak.

The Values Context

There can be little doubt that Jaspers' discourse on Transcendence (*Transzendenz*), the Encompassing (*das Umgreifende*), Unity (*die Einheit*), origin and goal (*Ursprung und Ziel),* the unconditioned (*das Unbedingte*), etc., presupposes some kind of ontology. Because of a lack of clarity on these notions, as Wildermuth (*JCPF*) and others have argued, Jaspers is sometimes viewed as being both a primordialist and a transcendentalist, that he avows a psychologically modified Kantianism that remains vague and sometimes contradictory, and that he, like Schelling, ultimately enters an indifference point and a "night in which all cows are black,"[39] which is the perennial problem with pantheism and many forms of monism.

One might say that the issue ultimately comes down to the question as to whether Spinoza or Leibniz was more important to Jaspers, whether he thought that we are already "in God" as his notion of the Encompassing implies, or whether we have

---

[38] Biblical literature usually refers to God as "good" because he does "good things," like providing us with food as in the popular table prayer. In this instance I refer to "the good" the way Jesus does: "Why callest thou me good? There is none good but one, that is, God" (Mark 10:18, KJV); "Aber Jesus sprach zu ihm: Was heißest du mich gut? Niemand ist gut denn der einige Gott" (Luther Bibel), since this synoptic assertion provides the textual basis for the fusion of "the good" and "the One" in Judeo-Christian tradition as modified and transformed by Platonism. This transformation is taken for granted, not only by Jaspers, but also by Kant and Hegel, and certainly undergirds Jaspers' *First Principle of the Philosophical Life*, namely, "Gott Ist", *supra*.

[39] "Die Nacht, worin alle Kühe schwarz sind", Vorwort, *Phänomenologie des Geistes* (1807). Few scholars referring to this expression really understand what it means since it presupposes a time "before the power lines," in the phrase of Erazim Kohak, and the experience of looking for the cows at night in order to bring them in for milking. When it is dark, one looks for the "white" on Holstein cattle, which makes them easier to find than the Black Angus, for example, which was a breed developed for meat and not milk in Scotland during the early 1800s. Needless to say all farm animals and poultry in Hegel's day were "free range" creatures and not imprisoned in the "iron cages" of factory farms, such as is the case today.

God "in us" as his notion of Transcendence suggests, and whether, finally, it is necessary to chose between these alternatives in order to remain consistent philosophically. I personally do not think that it is necessary to choose because these options are the analogs, so to speak, of the hermeneutical circle, *credo ut intelligam, intelligo ut credam.*[40]

What Jaspers clearly values the most is communication and the "loving struggle" of human beings to understand one another, themselves, and the world more deeply in order to realize more completely their *Geschichtlichkeit* and *mögliche Existenz.* Philosophical faith is intended to facilitate this process in a responsible and constructive manner. Therein lies the status of philosophical faith as the highest value for Karl Jaspers who, at once, is a psychiatrist, philosopher and, in the best sense of the word, a *moralist*, or better, as Hegel put it, a *Volkerzieher,* with the capacity to educate his fellow human beings in the values and virtues required to develop true or authentic humanity. "Philosophical faith," he says, "is not about a specific content to be believed in" but rather something to "believe by," viz., the values underlying our "actions."[41] Having these values and being qualified to educate, is precisely what is required in order to aspire to authentic *paideia,* as defined by Socrates, and *Bildung* as understood by Schiller.

In a previous essay I argued that a deficiency in Jaspers' philosophy is the lack of any systematic development of value theory and hence further clarification of the content of that which he believes.[42] The values he avows are the values of a humanist, as Tillich rightly observed,[43] indeed, I would say a Christian humanist given the draft of his sources in the history of Western philosophy and theology; and therein lies the real content of his position. Human beings, if nothing else, are creatures of value, and not just creatures of value, but also creators of value and mediated by values. It is precisely this attribute that sets humans apart from other sentient beings as Lonergan has noted so well.[44] It may be that Jaspers failed to specify more clearly the specific content of his value theory and, accordingly, his ethics, as Christopher Thornhill and others have argued, because of his longstanding quarrel with Heinrich Rickert and with Neo-Kantian *Wertephilosophie.* One needs to recall that Jaspers, like Heidegger, wanted to wrest German philosophy from what they regarded as the threadbare, formal scholasticism of late-nineteenth and early-twentieth century Neo-Kantian epistemology. Jaspers accomplished this by revitalizing Kant by way of the revolution in Kierkegaard and Nietzsche studies

---

[40] The doxological prayer, "Preserve us in thy Truth, O Lord, all things begun and ended in Thee" (BCP) has a ring of the *All Encompassing*, needless to say.

[41] Op. cit.

[42] See my essay in *Existenz*, "Faith and Reason: Ishmael and Isaac Revisited," Vol. 1, Nos. 1–2 (Fall 2006), pp. 55–63. http://www.existenz.us/volumes/Vol.1Olson.pdf.

[43] Tillich, op. cit.

[44] See Bernard J.F. Lonergan, *Insight: A Study in Human Understanding* (New York, NY: Philosophical Library, 1957), *passim.*

during the 1920s, just as Heidegger revitalized existential phenomenology by way of a Neo-Aristotelian revival and his hermetic voyage into the Pre-Socratics.[45]

But when Jaspers asserts, "Philosophical faith is not about a content to be believed; it is the activity we believe by," his intention clearly seems to have a double motivation. On the one hand, and as Kurt Salamun has argued, it is precisely Jaspers' "anti-dogmatic" orientation to philosophy that defines his unique form of "liberality" and which might be summed up as "openness to communication."[46] On the other hand, and following Kant, Jaspers is primarily interested in practical philosophy. He is completely devoted to what he identifies as his second principle of philosophizing, namely, that we have an "unconditional duty"[47] to act morally as agents of truth in the world. He also recognizes the performative role of tradition in shaping the values we hold dear and that, as in the old saying goes, "Actions speak louder than words." But not just any actions, for the maxims we avow as the basis of action need to pass the deontic test of universalizability in the Kantian sense so that our actions can be undertaken without contradiction. The task of universalization, of course, has precisely to do with the axiology required for making specific values determinate, and about which Findlay speaks as something necessary in order to establish a "systematic unity of values." Only by the systematic axiological process of separating values from disvalues can one determine whether one's basis of action in *good faith* is also right, just, and therefore true.

Jaspers' philosophizing does, in fact, have the implicit teleology about which Findlay speaks; and while this may not be expressly developed in terms of rational eschatology, it is posited precisely as "transcending thinking," that is, the kind of reason that transcends through thinking, in other words, through *Vernunft,* towards its ultimate goal:

> This new, but ancient, thinking transcends the finite thought that cleaves to objects. As speculative thought it goes beyond the intellect to the source of thinking itself. Such speculative thought has a powerful effect on the thinker, and on the listening re-thinker. In concepts and conceptual movements, in images and metaphors, and in the strength of symbols, it has created a language over the centuries. It has many meanings, as if it was done in a room full of mirrors. When it stays pure and honest, it keeps all its words in a balance in which its seriousness can become sure of itself. But its existential weight is not recognizable by its content, by the way in which it is done.

---

[45] See Christopher Thornhill, *Karl Jaspers: Politics and Metaphysics* (London: Routledge, 2002), especially his section on Jaspers and Kant, pp. 31–54. Thornhill points out, rightly, I think, that Rickert was not only opposed to Jaspers' appointment to the Heidelberg Philosophy Faculty (since he was "a psychologist and not a trained philosopher"), but also a conflict as to who was the better friend of Max Weber, Rickert or Jaspers!

[46] Kurt Salamun, "The Concept of Liberality in Jaspers' Philosophy and the Idea of the University," in *The Tasks of Truth,* ed. Gregory J. Walters (Frankfurt am Main: Peter Lang, 1996), pp. 39–54. See also Kurt Salamun, "Der Fundamentalismus aus der Sicht von Jaspers' Philosophie," *Jahrbuch der Österreichischen Karl Jaspers Gesellschaft,* Vol. 23 (2010), pp. 71–86.

[47] Op. cit.

> If this transcendent thinking is due to the inadequacy of the world, it rises nevertheless from an encompassing, All Encompassing presence. It is not driven by the thing it transcends. *It is drawn where it is going.*[48]

To be actively drawn toward its goal is very similar to Hegel's concept of "true infinity," that is, consciousness drawn by the infinity that I am in my freedom to act, and not an alien conception of infinity as something wholly extrinsic to possible *Existenz*. Only within such a conception of transcending-thinking, that is, a thinking that transcends through thinking, does thinking have the eschatological feature of driving toward its ultimate goal; and transcending-thinking has this power because reason (*Vernunft*) is grounded within and arises from the Absolute of Transcendence-Itself. This is why we have notions of the Absolute in the first place, as Findlay argues in his "Absolute Theory."[49] For example, while Saint Anselm pondered "the Greatest beyond which nothing Greater exists" and may have presupposed the authority of revelation, his intention to do so was in its first instance a supersensible intuition of the Absolute. Indeed, the first of Jaspers' *Fünf Grundsätze* for philosophizing is his postulation that "God Is," which was not only a supersensible intuition for Jaspers, but also an evidental principle and/or proposition grounded in the history of religions, both East and West.[50] Therein lies the basis of his unfinished (and inherently "unfinishable") project of *Weltphilosophie*.[51]

There can be little doubt that Jaspers made tremendous strides in advancing his philosophical project and the project of *Weltphilosophie* in this regard, and he has not received the credit he deserves in the development of philosophical hermeneutics in the mid-twentieth century. Jaspers' understanding of the "historicity of Existenz," for example, has many similarities with Gadamer's notion of "effective history" (*Wirkungsgeschichtliches Bewußtsein*) or the "consciousness within which history is ever effective."[52] This means that while it may be impossible to bring about a formal reconciliation between religious and philosophical faith (as in Kant and especially

---

[48] *Atom Bomb*, p. 217. *Emphasis mine.* See my *Transcendence and Hermeneutics,* op. cit., which was, in fact, inspired by Jaspers' concept of *transcending-thinking* which I prefer to Ashton's translation., i.e., *transzendierenden Denkens* or thinking that transcends precisely because it is grounded in the Encompassing. The German text of the last lines is as follows: "Wenn of this Transzendieren aus Anlaß des Ungenügens in der Welt geschieht, Doch es entspringt aus der Gegenwart des Umgreifenden alles Umgreifenden. Es wird nicht getrieben von dem, worüber es hinausgeht. Es wird gezogen von dorther, wohin es geht."

[49] See Findlay's three lectures on "Absolute Theory" in *Ascent to the Absolute*, op. cit.

[50] See, in this volume, the *Nachlassfragment* of Karl Jaspers, *Principles of Philosophising: Introduction to Philosophical Life*, written in 1942/43.

[51] This, in fact, is the third of his five principles of philosophizing, viz., "man is finite and incomplete," and this incompleteness is the reason for transcending-thinking. *Supra.*

[52] Gadamer did not give Jaspers the credit he deserved for hermeneutical insights in his *magnum opus, Wahrheit und Methode* (1960) and, later in life, acknowledged this in *Philosophical Apprenticeships* (MIT, 1985), first published as *Philosophische Lehrjahre* (Klostermann, 1977). As he puts it regarding the impact of Jaspers' *Existenzphilosophie*, "What distinguishes Jaspers is that he was at once a great teacher and a great moralist. His all-encompassing spirit had at its disposal his broadly streaming and finely nuanced language, but it also experienced the fate of finiteness,

Hegel), there can be a productive and *humane* communication regarding religious and philosophical faith if interlocutors recognize both the value of their traditions and the historical contingencies of their positions. Humane communication, that is, communication or dialogue which results in understanding and respect of the *other,* depends upon the antecedent acceptance of Kant's metaphysical idea of humanity or something like it, metaphysical precisely because this judgment has to do with the supersensible and therefore a priori idea of humanity.[53] If this notion is rejected, that is, if interlocutors do not believe in universals and ultimate unity, but only in endless disparities and differences, there can be no ultimately effective or productive communication.[54]

Finally, and with respect to the title of this collection, what is the future of humanity? Needless to say, Jaspers was a devotee of the Kantian "idea" of humanity and that this idea has an a priori status in human consciousness even though it is so easily distorted and even negated by all sorts of *a posteriori* considerations, especially the machinations of instrumentalist rationality. Was Jaspers a humanist and, if so, what kind of a humanist? Does humanism have any special meaning and significance as we attempt to look into the future? Was he a Christian or a secular humanist"? Can the philosophy of Karl Jaspers serve as a special guide as we consider these questions and issues?

These questions have been debated throughout the history of Western philosophy, especially following the hegemonic rise of Christianity in the fourth Century. Small wonder that scholars interested in determining the proper relation between philosophy and religion should return, again and again, to the teachings of Augustine who was not the first, but certainly the most notable in the attempt to reconcile the disparate worlds of Athens and Jerusalem, philosophy and faith.

The world of Athens, for Augustine, was the quasi-dualistic world of Neo-Platonism, not the world of Aristotle. Reality, for Augustine, consisted of two spheres or realms, the sphere of the sacred and that of the secular, famously posited as the *City of God* and the *City of Man.* Jerusalem, on the other hand, was the site of revelation and reflections on the meaning of revelation, whether in the Bible or in the writings of the Apostolic Fathers. What this meant during the next 1,300 years, until the advent of the European Enlightenment, was that reason alone, in all instances, was subservient to divine revelation and the Catholic development of dogma and the authoritative meaning and the truth of revelation. Even the Promethean attempt of Thomas Aquinas and his followers to demonstrate that revelation could be completely harmonized with reason through the rehabilitation of Aristotelian categories, bowed in reverence to the absolute authority of revelation. The imprint of the God of

---

which he never forgot precisely in the unrealizability of his universal will to knowledge. . . There is no conclusion to the impact of Karl Jaspers," p. 167.

[53] COJ.

[54] Jaspers' notion of "metaphysical guilt" in *Die Schuldfrage* (1948) rests on this assumption, as I agued in an essay by the same title. See *Existenz*, Vol. 3, No. 1, pp. 9–19. http://www.existenz/volumes/Vol.3-1Olson.pdf.

Abraham and Isaac, Jesus and Mohammed, on Western consciousness was deemed absolute in all matters of truth.

Karl Jaspers defines Augustine, together with Plato and Kant, as one of the three "seminal founders of philosophical thought" in the West. Indeed, the nexus of philosophy and religion takes place in Augustine, not only for Jaspers but the history of philosophy generally. Jaspers' three ciphers of Transcendence, namely, God as Impersonal, God as Personal, and God as Incarnate, may be perceived as resting quite comfortably with Plato, Augustine, and Kant.[55] Even the latter instance, namely, the cipher of the Incarnate God, does not present an insuperable barrier to cross-cultural communication in the comparative philosophy of religion. As John Findlay reminds us, there are three possible directions of Spirit: "Away from the world," as in Socrates, in the ascent to the intelligible realm; "towards the world," as in Jesus, in order to save it; and towards a Nirvana "beyond both world and nonworld," as in the Buddha: "Of the three supremely paradigmatic men that our race has produced, Socrates, Buddha, and Jesus," Findlay reminds us, "one was a polytheist, one an atheist, and one a monotheist, a fit reminder that those best qualified to perceive and enjoy the Absolute also perceived it quite differently." [56]

To these three instances, Jaspers adds a fourth, Confucius, and it was prophetic addition in 1957, as it were, given China's present role in the process of globalization and communication. "Confucius", Jaspers reminds us,

> had no fundamental religious experience, no revelation; he achieved no inner rebirth, he was not a mystic. But neither was he a rationalist; in his thinking rather he was guided by the idea of an encompassing community through which man becomes man. His passion was for beauty, order, truthfulness, and happiness in the world. And all of these are grounded in something that is not made meaningless by failure and death. [57]

Whether there are three or four such paradigmatic individuals, or even five, including Muhammad, is a topic deserving additional inquiry.

---

[55] See *Chiffren der Transzendenz* (Munich: Piper Verlag, 1970).

[56] See J.N. Findlay, "The Absolute and Rational Eschatology," in *Ascent to the Absolute* (Allen & Unwin, Ltd., 1970). As he puts it eloquently, "Of the three supremely paradigmatic men that our race has produced, Socrates, Buddha, and Jesus, one was a polytheist, one an atheist, and one a monotheist, a fit reminder that those best qualified to perceive and enjoy the Absolute also perceived it quite differently" (p. 74). Jaspers, of course, identifies "four paradigmatic" individuals in Volume One of *The Great Philosophers*, and does so in 1956, namely Socrates, Buddha, Jesus *and* Confucius. That academic philosophy fails to recognize and, in fact, intentionally "neglects" these "suprahistorical figures who are our eternal contemporaries" is a sign of philosophy's "irresponsibility" and decline over the past 50 years, as Jaspers observes in 1957 (pp. vi–vii, Preface to the Original Edition).

[57] Karl Jaspers, *The Great Philosophers*, Vol. 1, (1962) p. 67.

Jaspers' Concept of Philosophical Faith: A New Synthesis?

Andreas Cesana

Abstract Philosophy begins where science ends. Philosophy has ceased to be a science. It is a source of its own. The limits of science make obvious that faith belongs to being human. Faith is either religious or philosophical. Faith is a main phenomenon of being human. It consists in the simple fact that persons have ultimate convictions. Philosophical faith is existential faith. Its certainty is tied to the individual. Philosophical faith cannot be achieved without personal effort, without acts of actual freedom, and without realizations of Existenz. Jaspers' concept of philosophical faith turns out to be a new synthesis of historical conditions and philosophical requirements.

> *I regard my thinking as the natural and necessary conclusion of Western thought until now, the unprejudiced synthesis by means of a principle that in its wideness is able to integrate all that is true in any sense whatever.*[1]

Man is the historic being. He produces and forms history, he determines himself within history, and remains bound to its changing requirements and situations. This double phenomenon of power over and dependence on history establishes the particular options and limits we have—even those of philosophical thinking. Man and his philosophy have their past with them. They are not capable of escaping from the historical situation to which they belong. "We are what we are only in relation to our whole past," Karl Jaspers declares categorically. History is therefore "the only great authority, the originator of all what we are."[2]

With the growth of historical consciousness in the nineteenth century it became irrefutable that philosophical thinking is historically limited, dependent, and contingent. This insight is an elementary precondition of Jaspers' philosophy of existence. The two German notions of *Historizität* and *Geschichtlichkeit* signify the historical

---

[1] *Von der Wahrheit. Philosophische Logik*, Erster Band (München: Piper, 1947), p. 192. Cf. Leonard H. Ehrlich, *Karl Jaspers. Philosophy as Faith* (Amherst, MA: University of Massachusetts Press, 1975), p. 219.

[2] *Weltgeschichte der Philosophie. Einleitung*, from the probate, ed. Hans Saner (München and Zurich: Piper, 1982), p. 33.

A. Cesana (✉)
Department for Interdisciplinary Studies, Johannes Gutenberg-University, Mainz, Germany
e-mail: cesana@uni-mainz.de

H. Wautischer et al. (eds.), *Philosophical Faith and the Future of Humanity*,
DOI 10.1007/978-94-007-2223-1_9, © Springer Science+Business Media B.V. 2012

conditioning of the present situation of thinking. In this context, Jaspers introduces a terminological differentiation which is significant for the comprehension of the peculiarity of his philosophy. He denominates our knowledge of the specific historical conditions of a present situation as "historical consciousness" (*historisches Bewusstsein*) and that in contrast to the "historic consciousness" (*geschichtliches Bewusstsein*). This second term signifies one's own specific way to be a historic being. The changeover from the historical consciousness to the historic consciousness occurs at the time when my "knowledge of history becomes a function of possible Existenz," when "beyond all historical research" the contents and images of history "point to me, if they appeal to me, challenge me, or repel me".[3] The historic consciousness means therefore a specific attitude towards and orientation on the past: History becomes a medium for self-being.

In Jaspers' terminology the concept of *Geschichtlichkeit* designates something beyond objectivity and scientific conceivability. It circumscribes the possibility of existential appropriation of the historic situation. Existential historic consciousness arises out of the course of an individual's live in which he gains identity with himself.[4]

In his work *Die geistige Situation der Zeit* of 1931, published in English in 1933 as *Man in the Modern Age*, Jaspers asserts that the deeper insight in the historicity of the existential dimension would have enabled philosophy to improve its understanding of the human situation. But philosophy did not seize the chance. From the second half of the nineteenth century on, the traditional philosophy became "an enterprise carried on by university schools which more and more seldom were communities of philosophic persons."[5] Philosophy tried to conform to the standards of pure science or to subsist as historical knowledge of its own history. Outwardly learned, inwardly rationalistic and "devoid of any relationship with the life of the individual," the philosophical schools "watered down the radical problem of philosophy until it could no longer be dangerous" (*GSZ* 131, *MMA* 141).

"The unsheltered individual gives our epoch its physiognomy," Jaspers asserts (*GSZ* 134, *MMA* 144). Philosophy is therefore the only refuge for those who, in full awareness, "are not sheltered by religion." The immense duty and responsibility of philosophy consists in the fact, that man, being no longer able to guide his life in accordance with the dictates of a revealed religion, can become aware of his own

---

[3] Karl Jaspers, *Philosophie, 2. Band: Existenzerhellung* (Berlin: Springer, 1932), p. 120. [Henceforth cited as *PH2*]; *Philosophy,* Volume 2: *Existential Elucidation*, trans. E.B. Ashton (Chicago, IL and London: University of Chicago Press, 1970), p. 105. [Henceforth cited as *P2*]

[4] Karl Jaspers, *Der Philosophische Glaube angesichts der Offenbarung* (Munich: Piper, 1962), p. 170. [Henceforth cited as *PGO*]; *Philosophical Faith and Revelation,* trans. E.B. Ashton (New York, NY: Harper & Row, 1967), p. 105. [Henceforth cited as *PFR*]

[5] Karl Jaspers, *Die geistige Situation der Zeit* (Berlin: de Gruyter, 1931), p. 131. [Henceforth cited as GSZ]; *Man in the Modern Age,* trans. Eden and Cedar Paul (London: Routledge & Kegan Paul, 1933), p. 140. [Henceforth cited as *MMA*]

true will only with the help of philosophical thinking (*GSZ* 132, *MMA* 141). Today, the significance of philosophizing consists in "our attempt to confirm ourselves in a faith that arises independently of revelation" (*GSZ* 132, *MMA* 142).

The experience of history is always an experience of loss and failed possibilities. In the history of philosophy it is the experience of ways of thinking which became impassable. Karl Jaspers developed his philosophy of Existenz and his concept of philosophical faith by means of a philosophical analysis of the situation of his time. He proceeded more or less systematically. The present contribution argues historically. Its aim is on the one hand to show that Jaspers' concept of philosophical faith gives an answer to the philosophical situation of his time (1–4), on the other to demonstrate that his philosophical re-assessment of faith is determined by the basic principles of his existential philosophy (5–8). The concept of philosophical faith turns out to be a new synthesis of historical conditions and philosophical requirements.

Kant's Critique of Philosophical Reason

Jaspers is Kantian. In the foreword to his *Philosophy* he describes Kant as "the philosopher *catexochen*" and characterizes him as "unmatched in the noble, deliberate humanity of a pure, keen, infinitely mobile thinking that never lets us touch ground."[6] At the same time he specifies his own philosophy as the venture to enter the "inaccessible ground of human self-awareness". This philosophy comprehends itself as the thinking "that transforms my consciousness of being". It is a thinking that "brings me to myself." No objective knowledge is able to do this (*PH1* vii, *P1* 1).

According to Jaspers' interpretation, Kant's critique of reason pursues a double objective: On the one hand, it is criticism of traditional metaphysics, based on the finding that pure reason is getting caught up in contradictions as soon as it transcends the limits of empirical knowledge. Thus Kant's critique of reason shows as well the limitations of positive scientific knowledge. On the other hand, this critique establishes the place of the genuine philosophical way of thinking. It is a third and middle way in between the empirical sciences and the speculative and dogmatic metaphysics.

For Jaspers it is certain that the critical claim to renounce metaphysics is illusionary. This renouncement is existentially impossible. In view of the great questions of metaphysics, it is of no avail to attempt to be existentially uninterested, as Kant has

---

[6] Karl Jaspers, *Philosophie, 1. Band: Philosophische Weltorientierung* (Berlin: Springer, 1932), p. viii. [Henceforth cited as *PH1*]; *Philosophy*, Volume 1: *Philosophical World Orientation*, 1969, trans. E.B. Ashton (Chicago, IL and London: University of Chicago Press, 1969), p. 2. [Henceforth cited as *P1*]

declared himself: "For it is in reality vain to profess *indifference* in regard to such inquiries, the object of which cannot be indifferent to humanity."[7]

In his important essay of 1786, "What is Orientation in Thinking?," Kant introduced the term *Vernunftglaube* to refer to a new type of rationality.[8] *Vernunftglaube* could be translated as "faith of reason" or "rational faith" or "rational belief." This surprising concept gives Kant an opportunity to specify the characteristics of philosophical knowledge based on pure reason (*WSD* 141): (1) Rational belief is based on no other data than those which are inherent in pure reason. It is a belief which is legitimized by rational arguments but not by empirical, i.e., objective reasons. (2) Like any other faith, faith of reason is a conviction of truth which is subjectively adequate but objectively inadequate. (3) Faith of reason is the opposite of knowledge. (4) Since the grounds for considering something to be true are not objectively valid, faith of reason can never become knowledge by any exercise of reason. (5) Kant calls the faith of reason a "*postulate* of reason." This does not mean that it is a matter of insights that are capable of satisfying all criteria of certainty. Rather it means that considering something to be true is in no way inferior in degree to any knowledge, "although it is totally different from it in kind" (*WSD* 141).

With his conception of the faith of reason Kant distinguishes his standpoint from two traditional positions: First, the faith of reason turns against all manifestations of uncritical use of reason, in particular against metaphysical rationalism and dogmatic faith, that is, against zealotry (*Schwärmerei*) and superstition (*Aberglaube*). Second, the faith of reason turns against the empirical limitation of reason and the conviction that reason accepts only what can be justified on objective grounds. This renunciation of faith of reason is rational faithlessness or rational unbelief (*Vernunftunglaube*): "an undesirable state of mind" which gives rise to the attitude of libertinism (*Freigeisterei*) (*WSD* 146).

This brief look at Kant's conception of philosophy shows Jaspers' explicit dependence on Kant's philosophy: Jaspers resumes Kant's distinction between *Verstand* and *Vernunft*. He, too, characterizes philosophical thinking as *Vernunftglauben* and as *philosophischen Glauben*, in contrast to *philosophischen Unglauben*. Both authors describe the thinking of reason as dialectical, but without developing it into a fixed procedure in the manner of Hegel's dialectic. And both conceive the rationality of philosophical thinking as a third and middle way between metaphysical or religious dogmatism on the one hand and scientific rationality on the other.

Compared to the binding and obligatory character of scientific knowledge, philosophical insight is less stringent, and compared to the absoluteness of religious doctrines, philosophy is less authoritative. Philosophical knowledge in terms of Jaspers' philosophy of existence can't require timeless validity. However, this

---

[7] Immanuel Kant, "Kritik der reinen Vernunft," in *Gesammelte Schriften,* Akademie-Ausgabe, Volume 4, Preußische Akademie der Wissenschaften (Berlin: Georg Reimer, 1903), p. 8 (KrV, A X).

[8] Immanuel Kant, "Was heißt: Sich im Denken orientiren?" in *Gesammelte Schriften,* Akademie-Ausgabe, Volume 8, Preußische Akademie der Wissenschaften (Berlin: Georg Reimer, 1912), p. 141. Cf. KrV, A 829, B 857. [Henceforth cited as *WSD*]

doesn't mean that philosophical insights are arbitrary. They have their own epistemological status. Philosophy has ceased to be a science. It is a source of its own. Philosophy is situated between science and faith in revelation.

The Turning Point in the Philosophy of the Nineteenth Century

Karl Jaspers begins his three-volume book *Philosophy* of 1932 with the basic questions: "What is being?," "Why is anything at all? Why not nothing?" or "Who am I" or "What do I really want?" And he explicates that when asking such questions he does not begin at the beginning. These questions arise from a specific situation in which, coming from a past, he finds himself (*PH1* 1, *P1* 43). It belongs to the situation of Jaspers' thinking that he cannot go back before Kant and his critical philosophy. Metaphysics in a pre-critical way is no longer possible. The efforts of Fichte, Schelling, and Hegel to reshape the critical philosophy of Kant into a speculative idealism have, according to Jaspers, failed.

Not only in Kant's critique of metaphysics but also in Kierkegaard's und Nietzsche's critique of reason identifies Jaspers decisive points which are not reversible. In 1935, Jaspers declares at the beginning of his Groningen lectures: "The present philosophical situation is determined by the fact that two philosophers, Kierkegaard und Nietzsche, who did not count during their own lifetime and remained for a long time without influence in philosophy, are constantly growing in importance."[9] Jaspers characterize them as the two "philosophers of our age who can no longer be ignored" (*VE* 11).

For Jaspers, Nietzsche's "*complete break* with the traditional historical substance" is unsurpassable. Nietzsche has thought the consequences of the new situation through and has analyzed the effects on the future of philosophy.[10] Whatever Nietzsche said in detail is for Jaspers not as important as his "immense earnestness of his life by breaking with everything" (*N* 441). Jaspers considers Nietzsche's ruthless analysis of the situation of his time as basically correct. Nietzsche's diagnosis, condensed in the formula "God is dead," has posed a continual challenge to philosophy, and Jaspers understands his own philosophy as an answer to this challenge. As long as we live from certainties without further reflection, philosophy is a "harmless activity among others" (*N* 422). Due to Nietzsche, philosophy became again "the matter of the whole human being". Nietzsche gave back to philosophy its "original and genuine problems."[11]

---

[9] Karl Jaspers, *Vernunft und Existenz. Fünf Vorlesungen* (Groningen: J.B. Wolters, 1935; Bremen: Johs. Storm, 1947; München: Piper, 1960), p. 11. [Henceforth cited as *VE*]

[10] See Karl Jaspers, *Nietzsche. Einführung in das Verständnis seines Philosophierens* (Berlin: de Gruyter, 1936), p. 440 f. [Henceforth cited as *N*]

[11] See Karl Jaspers, *Aneignung und Polemik. Gesammelte Reden und Aufsätze zur Geschichte der Philosophie,* ed. Hans Saner (Munich: Piper, 1968), p. 389.

One can correctly state that Jaspers has tried to think out the philosophy of Kierkegaard and Nietzsche. In his book on Nietzsche of 1935 he declares, Nietzsche's destruction of morals was brilliant (*großartig*) and "cleared the way again for philosophy of existence" (*N* 442). In this citation the word "again" needs an explanation. In his essay of 1941, *Über meine Philosophie*, Jaspers accentuates the "enormous break" in the thinking of the nineteenth century. Hegel is "an end of two and a half millennia." Though philosophizing with Kant is still possible, we can do it only if we realize what has happened in the wake of Kierkegaard and Nietzsche: "The feeling of being sheltered in the continuous philosophical thinking from Parmenides to Hegel is lost." Philosophy has to return to the ground of a "primordial thinking out of which the occidental philosophy of the somehow terminated millennia came into existence."[12] Philosophy of existence returns to the origins of occidental thinking; it is the timeless figure of philosophy.

Philosophic Reason and Scientific Rationality

A century after Hegel, Karl Jaspers develops a philosophy of Existenz. It is his response to the changed situation of philosophical thinking. An essential premise of the new philosophy is the assertion that philosophy and science have lost their previous unity. Philosophy has ceased to be a science. It is a resource of its own. Both philosophy and science have their own and specific forms and competencies of knowledge. The modern scientific approach has transformed the traditional ways of thinking. But as a result of its separation from science philosophy gained new relevance. Philosophy is "the carrier of our humanity," and without it, "we would lose ourselves" (*PGO* 96, *PFR* 51).

Due to its autonomy philosophy differs from the sciences and also from faith in revelation. The traditional distinction between rational cognition and cognition by faith is no longer appropriate: "We can become more aware than ever of the independent source of philosophy" (*PGO* 38, *PFR* 11). On account of this, the traditional separation between reason and faith is replaced by the modern tripartition of science, philosophy, and theology (*PGO* 95ff, *PFR* 50ff). More precisely, the new situation of thinking is to be described as follows: Today philosophy—similar to theology and yet quite different from it—takes up the position of insight by faith. There is no other position to take up ever since philosophy broke with her self-image as science. Philosophical faith is based on reflection, is existential faith, and gains certainty only for the individual person.

Scientific rationality and philosophical reason are dealing with different dimensions. The separation from science establishes philosophy as an independent and

---

[12] See Karl Jaspers, *Rechenschaft und Ausblick. Reden und Aufsätze* (Munich: Piper, 1951), p. 400 f. [Henceforth cited *RA*]

autonomous source between science and the faith in revelation. "The truth of this," says Jaspers, "is decisive for the treatment of all of our questions" (*PGO* 96, *PFR* 51).

Philosophy begins where science ends and knowledge reaches its limits. The scientific knowledge fails in all questions of existential relevance. It is unable to deal with vital issues and to satisfy the existential need for orientation. Some of Jaspers' formulations are reminiscent of the well-known words of Wittgenstein in the final passage of his *Tractatus*: "We feel that even when all possible scientific questions have been answered, the problems of life remain completely untouched." The continuation of the quotation however reveals the difference of the two positions: "Of course there are then no questions left, and this itself is the answer."[13] Jaspers, in contrast, demands an extension of the concept of rationality: The philosophical reason begins when the scientific rationality cannot get ahead anymore.

Jaspers who came to philosophy from medicine and psychiatry has experienced the narrowness of scientific knowledge and the failure of the scientific reason in the discussions of the great questions. The limits of science make obvious that science cannot replace philosophy. "The confusion of convictions out of which I live and knowledge which I prove deranges the whole human condition," Jaspers declares categorically (RA 410). Definitely he rejects the idea of a scientific philosophy. It is a main task of philosophy to separate that what can be known stringently from that what is based on unjustifiable knowledge. Just because scientific knowledge is particulate and aimed at objects, not at the being itself, science tends to say more than should be said. Scientific conclusions intermingle easily with worldviews, normative principles, and religious premises.

It is the insight in the boundaries of what we can know for certain, and it is the awareness of the phenomenality (*Erscheinungshaftigkeit*) of the world which "lift the self-sustained objectively extant world out of its hinges" (*PH1* 44, *P1* 83). This makes the feeling of being naively sheltered in the world impossible. It is evident that our knowledge of the world is existentially insufficient. We cannot live out of it. Due to the fact that the knowledge of the world has no absolute character, man has the chance to be aware of his autonomy, his possibilities, and his existential freedom. The insight in the limits of knowledge brings, as Jaspers says, "me to myself. I am myself when I am present, no longer withdrawing behind an objective standpoint which I merely represent, and when another Existenz can no more become an object for me than I can" (*PH1* 147, *P1* 172).

From today's standpoint, the importance of Karl Jaspers' philosophy is based on his concern to separate philosophy from science and to identify philosophy's particular form of rationality. In a time when the modern sciences transform the traditional thinking profoundly, a new and existentially relevant thinking gains significance. In 1954 Jaspers declares, if the various new approaches of philosophizing which we can summarize under the label "Philosophy of existence" (*Existenzphilosophie*)

---

[13] Ludwig Wittgenstein, *Tractatus logico-philosophicus. Logisch-philosophische Abhandlung* (Frankfurt am Main: Suhrkamp, 1963), § 6.52.

have anything in common," it is, negatively, the rejection of so-called scientific philosophy, and, positively, the affirmation of a moral earnestness foreign to mere knowing".[14]

Philosophy is no longer a part of science. Philosophy is not science. This view is shared by many. But if Jaspers declares that philosophy is "a source of its own, between science and the faith in revelation" (*PGO* 96, *PFR* 51), he takes up a position that is unexpected and surprising for most people.

Philosophy and Religion

Jaspers declares categorically: Faith belongs to being human. "Every human being needs a grounding in faith for everything that he is serious about."[15] This faith is either a philosophical or a religious faith. Either it is based on reflection and carried through to personal certainty, or it is grounded in religious tradition, that is, either in conscious, explicit adherence or as a thoughtless habit.

These general statements imply that not only religion but also philosophy is a universal phenomenon of mankind. Hence there is "no standpoint outside the opposition of philosophy and religion." Every person, Jaspers emphasizes, stands within this polarity on one side, and speaks about the other without personal experience.[16] Jaspers explains this polarity using the example of the difference between philosophy and the Christian faith in revelation. Revelation is not a reality but faith in revelation. Jaspers did not have access to this faith: "I do not believe in revelation; to my knowledge I have never believed in the possibility" (*PGO* 35, *PFR* 8). Thus there remains one last boundary of the ability to understand the faith in revelation—as Jaspers admits himself.

Philosophical and religious faith is, in the end, irreconcilable. While philosophical faith remains open and is not determinable because it is bound to the individual person, religious faith has fixed tenets. The experience of philosophizing, says Jaspers, makes it impossible to live in unquestionable authority.[17] Faith in revelation encounters such a position with a lack of comprehension—and with a lack of interest in communication. Possession of the truth of revelation makes one incapable

---

[14] Karl Jaspers and Rudolf Bultmann, *Die Frage der Entmythologisierung* (Munich: Piper, 1954), p. 36. Karl Jaspers and Rudolf Bultmann, *Myth and Christianity. An Inquiry into the Possibility of Religion without Myth*, trans. Norbert Gutermann (New York, NY: Noonday Press, 1958), p. 26.

[15] Karl Jaspers, *Provokationen. Gespräche und Interviews*, ed. Hans Saner (Munich: Piper, 1969), p. 72. [Henceforth cited as *PRO*]

[16] Karl Jaspers, *Der philosophische Glaube* (Zurich: Artemis, 1948; München: Piper, 1948), p. 60. Karl Jaspers, *The Perennial Scope of Philosophy*, trans. Ralph Manheim (New York, NY: Philosophical Library, 1949; London: Routledge and Kegan Paul, 1949), p. 76.

[17] Karl Jaspers, *Existenzphilosophie. Drei Vorlesungen, gehalten am Freien Deutschen Hochstift in Frankfurt a.M., September 1937* (Berlin and Leipzig: de Gruyter, 1938), p. 46. [Henceforth cited as *E*]

of engaging in dialogue because the other position has no relevance. Faith of revelation, rigidified in dogma and possessing tenets of faith as if they were knowledge,
lacks any understanding for the open and incompleteable character of philosophical
faith. The philosophical faithful cannot preach. He has to attain certainty in his own
faith.

Though Jaspers delimits philosophical faith sharply from faith in revelation, it
does not mean that he devalues the religious sphere on which we remain existentially dependent. Even on a personal level Jaspers always stressed his allegiance to
the Christian tradition of faith: "We Westernes, formed in this space, animated, motivated, and determined by this background, filled with images and concepts derived
from the Bible, are all Christians" (*PGO* 52, *PFR* 20). While for philosophical faith
religious doctrines have merely the status of ciphers, they are a reality for the religious faithful. Philosophical faith is with regard to its contents not definable. Even
a credo as "There is no God" can become a certainty of philosophical faith.

The open character of philosophical faith contrasts in particular with religious
fundamentalism. The return to the lost fundaments, to the old, simple, ultimate
truths, provides indeed orientation and the binding force of traditional religious
values gives shelter in a world of unquestionable certainties. But thereby religious
fundamentalism breaks out of the modern way of life which Jaspers considers as an
achievement. However, the fundamentalist escape from a presence which has lost
its orientation and which is an era of existential uncertainty is comprehensible. It
shows that the request of Jaspers' existential philosophy, to live out of uncertainty,
overburdens many.

Life-Sustaining (*Lebentragende*) Philosophy

In an interview of 1962, Karl Jaspers remembers the years of his studies. He tells that
he began the study of jurisprudence but did not attend many juristic lectures because
he preferred to go to the lectures on philosophy and art history. And then he states
laconically: "The philosophical lectures disappointed me. I didn't find what I was
searching for" (*PRO* 33). That the later physician and psychiatrist found his way
to philosophy at long last is in Jaspers' self-assessment quite consequent: "From
my experience of the limits of science the way directed me to the life-sustaining
philosophy" (*PRO* 35).

This programmatic expression, "life-sustaining philosophy" (*Lebentragende
Philosophie*), shows the concern of Jaspers' philosophical thinking. Philosophy is
life-sustaining only when it deals with the fundamental questions of life and when it
is ascertainment of what is lived out. In the epilogue of 1955 to the third edition of
his *Philosophie* Jaspers writes that his philosophizing originated in three premises:
firstly the "enthusiasm for scientific certainty," secondly "the experience of the limits of science," and thirdly "a yearning for such philosophy that will sustain us in
life" (*PH1* xxv, *P1* 13).

Life-sustaining philosophy is transcending philosophy. Transcending is philosophical transcending, that is, a process of rational thinking. And reciprocally, philosophizing without transcending became contradictory in itself. "Thinking that does not transcend is not philosophical. It is either scientific, involving the immanent and particular cognition of objects, or it is an intellectual pastime" (*PH1* 39, *P1* 78).

The justification for philosophical transcending consists in the fact that the boundaries of knowledge are crossed in the actuality of life even without methodically conscious transcending. It is an anthropological fact that man is dependent on images of the whole. Religion, myth, art, and ideology have the function of transmitting images of the whole. Jaspers' *Psychology of Worldviews* already made it clear that man is dependent on orientation, on images of the whole, and on ultimate principles. The term worldviews (*Weltanschauungen*) expresses something that is more than knowledge. It is the way in which a person evaluates things, in which he determines what has absolute validity, in which he lets himself be guided by ultimate principles. It is his inner stance in relation to that which is no longer knowable (*PH1* 241, *P1* 251).

Jaspers called his *Psychology of Worldviews* the "book of my youth."[18] The short preface begins with a quite ambiguous statement: "It has been a philosophical task to develop a worldview that is both: scientific knowledge and practical theory of life (*Lebenslehre*). The rational insight should ensure orientation." What does this mean? Is this philosophical task an earlier stage which today is no longer possible? Or, do Jaspers' cryptic words give a hint that his book in psychology actually deals with a different topic? Indeed, in the following sentence he points out that the book attempts to understand, "which are the ultimate positions of the soul and which are the moving forces." The factual worldview however is a matter of life. In the preface to the fourth edition of 1954 Jaspers states his position more precisely: "I formulated [in the first edition], psychology observes and understands all possibilities of worldviews. But philosophy, on the contrary, gives one worldview, namely the true one. Genuine philosophy is prophetic philosophy" (*PW* x). This comparison is indefensible, Jaspers states, but they clarified two things for him: first, the task and obligation of a philosophy which is not prophetic and proclamatory; and secondly, the task to distinguish and separate philosophy from empirical psychology. Due to this autocorrecting, Jaspers' statement in the first preface gains not only precision but also significance. Now it means: "It was once a philosophical task to develop a worldview that is both: scientific knowledge and practical theory of life. The rational insight should ensure orientation." Today, this is no longer a task, neither for psychology nor for philosophy. This example demonstrates how Jaspers' philosophy responds to a situation which coerces him into developing a new approach because the old ways of thinking are not passable anymore and philosophy is no longer a science among sciences.

---

[18] Karl Jaspers, *Psychologie der Weltanschauungen* (Berlin: Springer, 1919), p. viii. [Henceforth cited as *PW*]

Psychology of Worldviews is according to Jaspers' own statement "the earliest publication of the later so-called modern philosophy of existence."[19] The book brings to mind possible beliefs, attitudes, and images of the world. Such a psychology no longer means to be merely an empirical determination of facts; rather, it means to serve, by way of clarification of the possibilities of being-human, as an orientation for contemplation about oneself.

The core of all worldviews is not knowledge but faith. The real essence of a worldview is not a possible object of scientific analysis. Each lived worldview is the factual limit of world orientation. In the worldview—conscious or unnoticed—knowledge of the world is transcended, for human consciousness cannot avoid setting something as absolute. And if I would give up what is absolute for me, then something else would automatically take its place (*PH1* 250, *P1* 258).

Philosophical Faith is Existential Faith

Philosophy, which no longer is science, regains its independence. Philosophy is more than science and something different from it. It does no longer aim for knowledge which is "generally valid for every intellect" but rather aims for "the illumination of philosophical faith" (*PGO* 99, *PFR* 53). In 1937 already, Jaspers declared that philosophic faith is "the indispensable origin of all genuine philosophizing" (*E* 80).

The essential concern of philosophy is therefore the self-assurance of philosophic certainty of faith. But today it fails in its function. It no longer illuminates what men live by. "Its thinking loses the vigour of subsequent inner action. The philosophizer no longer thinks out of total involvement. His thinking becomes noncommittal, existentially lax in spite of acute logic and literary brilliance. It ceases to be philosophy" (*PGO* 102, *PFR* 55). Such decided declarations are numerous in his work of 1962. Again and again, Jaspers emphasizes that today philosophy can only survive as autonomous discipline if it rests on ascertainment of thinking and if it takes the shape of philosophic faith. Philosophy as faith is simultaneously philosophy of existence.

Faith is a difficult concept. An exact definition is not possible because of its broad meaning. But the core of its meaning is to some extent definable: Faith is an inner certainty and reliability which is not validly deducible and which is incapable of proof. In this respect knowledge and faith are in opposition to each other. What grants us orientation is not part of our knowledge; it has to be accepted as a matter of faith. Faith is either religious or philosophical. In both cases faith is a personal act of *Fürwahrhalten*, of considering something as true. Faith is a main phenomenon of being human. It consists in the simple fact that persons have ultimate convictions.

It is the philosophical-existential consciousness of having to believe which is the main point of difference between philosophy and modern science. This explains why

---

[19] Karl Jaspers, *Philosophische Autobiographie*, revised ed. (München: Piper, 1977), p. 33.

the relation between both is unproblematic: Philosophy and science are concerned with different realities; they go different ways. Compared with this, the relation between philosophy and religion suffers from a fundamental antagonism. Though both share the consciousness of having to believe, philosophy knows neither revelation nor dogmata and precisely determinable contents. Religions teach as objective actualities what, from the standpoint of philosophy, possesses merely the function of existentially effective images and parables. Philosophic faith knows that transcendence cannot be expressed, and it speaks of it only in ciphers. The error of religion consists in confusing the language of ciphers with objective reality. This confusion as well as the obedience of faith demanded by the religions has the consequence that the realization of existential freedom and authentic self-being become impossible. This is the main reason why Jaspers declares: "For the philosophizing person as such, faith is possible but religion is not" (P1 295 fn1).

Philosophical faith is called "existential" because it is the faith of the individual person. This faith belongs to the self-being of the individual, to one's existence. Existence is what can never become an object. Existence is "the never objectified source of my thoughts and actions. It is that whereof I speak in trains of thought that involve no cognition" (*PH1* 15, *P1* 56). The existential dimension is what constitutes me as being myself though it will never be a possible object of knowledge: "In Existenz I know, without being able to see it, that what I call my 'self' is independent. The possibility of Existenz is what I live by; it is only in its realization that I am myself" (*PH2* 1f, *P2* 3).

Philosophical Faith is Reflected Faith

Philosophy has the task to scrutinize all what we are, what we do, and what we could be. Through the existential analysis of ourselves we achieve a distance to all what we think, do and are; we achieve distance to ourselves.[20] Self-distance is the precondition for the procedural process of self-assurance or self-ascertainment. It initiates a process of thinking which leads to personal certainty. This process refers to the individual person. Only the individual has the authority to answer existential questions with certainty.

When dealing with arguments, insights and positions, with images and symbols, the process leads to certainty. The procedural method of self-assurance implies the readiness for unrestricted open-mindedness (*PGO* 140, *PFR* 82). Such thinking does not result in a certainty of the kind produced by the reliability of the certainty of revelation but it can achieve more than all certainty of revelation because it guarantees a personal certainty whose value consists in its existential commitment and meaningfulness.

The process of self-ascertainment is endless, is never complete, never finally determinable: The inquiring reflection always begins anew. At the same time the

---

[20] See Karl Jaspers, *Chiffren der Transzendenz*, ed. Hans Saner (Munich: Piper, 1970), p. 99.

philosophical reflection dispels "the security of our natural sense of being." Self-ascertainment "pulls the accustomed ground from under our feet" (*PGO* 142, *PFR* 84). Yet the aim of such thinking is not skepticism, the aim is ascertainment of philosophical faith.

Philosophical self-assurance does not only mean arriving at a personal decision and at one's own standpoint. It also requires that one remains open to different possibilities, that one does not take a position with finality but sees it in perspective. There is no mediation between these two opposing requirements: to commit oneself and yet to remain open. Attempts to overcome this intrinsically contradictory situation would contradict the existential actuality.

The process of self-ascertainment finds a provisional ending in an existential act of decision, determination, vote, choice and so on. By deciding, choosing, or voting I become myself. "By virtue of choosing I am; when I am not, I do not choose" (*PH2* 182, *P2* 160) The existential decision has the status of unshakable certainty and belongs as "my identity with myself" to what I am and what carries me (*PGO* 189, *PFR* 120). The existential decision is not deducible from facts, knowledge or insights because it is part of one's self. In Jaspers' words, "My decision and I are not of two sorts" (*PH2* 182, *P2* 160).

The process of self-ascertainment is aimed at certainty which is subjective certainty. It contains the momentum of decision on the one hand and the momentum of faith on the other. Existential certainty is partially based on irrational factors. Therefore some people say that they cannot justify their credo or conviction sufficiently and that there is something involved which is unexplainable, something which rests ineffable.

Certainty of philosophic faith is tied to the individual. This means that philosophic faith cannot be achieved without personal effort, without acts of actual freedom, and without realizations of Existenz.[21] Whenever the individual gains, in the process of philosophic-existential self-assurance, his personal conviction and certainty of faith, then—for that particular individual—these constitute in fact an absoluteness that, however, must not be tied to a claim to its exclusivity. It is evident that this individual—for himself—cannot and may not give up the absolute validity of his convictions and certainties of faith; if he were to do so, it would not be a matter of personal conviction and certainty of faith.

Being human means having to make decisions and choices. Numerous examples of world literature testify our ability to make a choice or a decision in terms of existential decision processes and to bear the responsibility for it. Socrates decides in favor of the maxim that it is better to suffer injustice than to commit it.[22] Camus lets Dr. Rieux say: "To my death I will refuse to love this creation in which children

---

[21] Karl Jaspers, *Nachlaß zur Philosophischen Logik,* eds. Hans Saner und Marc Hänggi (Munich and Zurich: Piper, 1991), p. 387.
[22] See Plato, *Gorgias* 469 c, 479 e; also *Crito,* 49 b–e.

are tortured."[23] Jaspers takes Giordano Bruno as an example, the "great martyr of modern philosophy—a greater hero than any Christian martyr, since he had to hold out solely on the strength of philosophical faith [...], standing alone before God" (*PGO* 90, *PFR* 46). And we should not forget Jaspers himself and his Jewish wife Gertrud and their decision, to prepare for joint suicide to evade deportation.[24]

Philosophical Faith in the Situation of the Time

"Philosophical faith is the substance of personal life" (*E* 79), Jaspers declared as early as 1937 and emphasized that while faith does belong to our condition of being human, religion does not necessarily do so. Faith is the main phenomenon, not religion. Man is therefore not *naturaliter religiosus*, as the traditional formula indicates, but man is, so to speak, *naturaliter credens*. Faith belongs to being human—inescapably and beyond religion, cultural background, or worldview. This is Jaspers' main point.

Faith belongs to being human. Jaspers failed in his attempt to give this fact a name. The notion "philosophical faith" could not gain acceptance. The intellectual provocation did not take place. There was no debate.

The term "faith" is religiously connoted. It is still misleading and far too narrow if this term is limited to religious faith. As long as an appropriate concept is missing the matter remains misunderstood. Faith, not religion, is a phenomenon of humankind. There is faith without god, and there is faith without religion. But the conception of nonreligious faith does not find acceptance. The history of the reception of Jaspers' pleading for philosophical faith demonstrates the futility of all efforts to introduce a new concept against the prevailing language use.

It is therefore doubtful if a philosophical faith which has nothing to proclaim can persist in the dialogue with religions whose doctrines provide authoritative orientation. Hans-Georg Gadamer remarked in the conversations which he held with Riccardo Dottori in the years 1999 and 2000 that Jaspers—in contrast to Heidegger—just had not been a religious person. In view of the threatening global crises Gadamer demanded to promote the dialogue between cultures and religions. Responding to the question if Jaspers' open concept of transcendence and his notion of philosophical faith could be helpful in this enterprise he answered tersely: "No, that is much too little." Given today's serious situation, existential elucidation is nothing but "moralistic bourgeoisie" and without grasp of the religious importance

---

[23] Albert Camus, "La Peste," in *Théâtre, récits, nouvelles* (Paris: Gallimard, 1963); (Bibl. de la Pléiade, 161), p. 1397: "Et je refuserai jusqu'à la mort d'aimer cette création où des enfants sont torturés."

[24] Karl Jaspers, *Schicksal und Wille. Autobiographische Schriften*, ed. Hans Saner (Munich: Piper, 1967), pp. 143–163.

and power of transcendence. Jaspers' "upper middle class reservation" (*großbürg-erliche Zurückhaltung*) cannot help us to escape from the threatening situation of our time.[25]

Gadamer, however, explained that, using Jaspers' conception of transcendence, one can describe the actual situation in the same way as he would do it. But this is due to the fact that Jaspers just as he himself is formed by the influence of the idea of enlightenment. And Gadamer makes aware of the fact, that the idea of enlightenment is "our issue and not that of the world (*LJ* 151).

Conclusion

"I regard my thinking as the natural and necessary conclusion of Western thought until now, the unprejudiced synthesis." Referring to Kant's critique of philosophical reason, influenced by the turning point in the philosophy of the nineteenth century, and in critical distance to the sciences as well as to the religions, Karl Jaspers' philosophy of existence comes to the conclusion that there are no universally valid answers to the questions of philosophy. As a consequence, the philosophy of existence ties philosophic truth to the individual person: I myself have to answer the irrefutable questions.

At the beginning of the twenty-first century and as a result of the advancing process of globalization religion returns as a decisive factor in politics and society. In the "post-secular society"[26] the public interest in religions grows. Religion remains the authority in questions of orientation. In today's world situation with its multiplicity of different religious traditions, which influence each other, arises, on the one hand, the paradoxical need for doubtless and absolutely certain orientation. On the other hand, the same process results in the fact that every claim to the absolute truth loses its power of persuasion and its credibility.

Faith constitutes—beyond all ways of religious faith—the possibility of self-determination and self-obligation. Philosophic faith is existential and reflected faith. Philosophic faith is the consequence of self-ascertainment. Existential certainty of faith is not negotiable. The existential certainty is a personal decision with absolute value. Certainty of faith is the existential *fundamentum inconcussum*.

---

[25] Hans-Georg Gadamer, *Die Lektion des Jahrhunderts. Ein Interview von Riccardo Dottori* (Münster: Lit, 2001), pp. 138 f. [Henceforth cited as *LJ*]

[26] Jürgen Habermas, *Glauben und Wissen* (Frankfurt am Main: Suhrkamp, 2001), pp. 12 ff.

Faith and Affirmation

Gerhard Knauss

Abstract During a discussion between Leonard Ehrlich and Richard Wisser at a philosophy congress, about the necessity of professing one's faith, it appeared at first that Jaspers' writings suggest a principal rejection of such obligation. Recent works about rationality and its limits in logic and game theory are put in the context of the discussion where external coercion is recognized as starting point for all forms of confession. Nonetheless, there are clear passages in Jaspers' Introduction to Philosophy that call for philosophical affirmation. The assertion of an essential truth that would be destroyed in case of denial or lack of affirmation seems to support the position of Ehrlich. But as the content of faith now is reduced to a free decision, it becomes empty. The idea of confession can be traced to the battle over religious creed. An externalized faith produces and attacks confession, and the actual political-theological situation demonstrates unavoidable consequences with such decision.

In the discussion following his presentation at a philosophy congress,[1] Leonard Ehrlich insisted that faith requires affirmation or avowal (*bekennen*), one must profess one's faith. A participant in this session, Richard Wisser, objected,[2] and this made me wonder what possibly could Ehrlich have had in mind when he refers to affirmation? He did not elaborate on this concept at the congress and to my knowledge he has done so nowhere else. What was on his mind when he said this? As a first reaction I remembered a passage in Jaspers that seems to negate such a claim, "philosophical faith...cannot become a confession. One's thought does not become dogma."[3] This seemed to have settled it, but Ehrlich insisted otherwise, so let us explore this matter.

Revelatory religions such as Christianity, Judaism, and Islam do refer to creeds. Those who attest to their faith are called believers. The content of faith can

---

[1] XXI World Congress of Philosophy, August 2003, Istanbul, Turkey. This essay is translated from German by Helmut Wautischer.

[2] See Richard Wisser's contribution to this Festschrift on pp. 287–298.

[3] Karl Jaspers, *Der philosophische Glaube* (Munich: Piper 1948), p. 15. [Henceforth cited as *PG*]

G. Knauss (✉)
University of Saarbrücken, Saarbrücken, Germany

H. Wautischer et al. (eds.), *Philosophical Faith and the Future of Humanity*,
DOI 10.1007/978-94-007-2223-1_10, © Springer Science+Business Media B.V. 2012

be communicated orally or in writing, and it can be criticized and revised. For example, whether to omit or include in the Nicean Creed a single word, "filioque," was debated in the Western church already at the time of Emperor Constantine Copronymus and continued to take place in the palace of Charlemagne during the ninth century. In fact, zealous Christians can still today become quite enthused about this debate. Such creeds are similar to a constitution of States, a minimally shared common denominator that allows for maximal consensus. Does Ehrlich think of such creed related to Jaspers' philosophical faith? After all, the event in Istanbul was a Jaspers symposium. Is someone who lives by philosophical faith a believer, while others are infidels? Jaspers uses very carefully the term believer in the context of philosophy. The one who philosophically believes is, in his terminology, not a believer but a philosopher.

There is a creed in the church, but is there also a creed in philosophy? Is there some sort of *Philosophicum*, just as there is a *Symbolum Nicaenum* and a *Confessio Augustana* and a *Professio fidei Tridentina*? It is worthwhile to inquire why all standard religions have some sort of confessions and creeds. From today's perspective we might see why this does not apply for philosophical faith where, first of all, it does not seem necessary that one must affirm or confess a particular creed. The problem of affirming and professing faith relates directly to the fate of the Abrahamic religions, Jewish, Christian, and Islamic, each derived from their inner source, later objectified and externalized, faced and fought one another to protect their existence and influence. Under such conditions a creed is demanded to differentiate friend and foe and to forge allegiance with others.

What then is actually believed within such worlds of faith has relevance only because of its external manifestations. Faith in a bellicose environment becomes confession, from the early Christians' struggle for survival to the writings of Augustine of Hippo whose confessions are affirmations of the truth of Christian faith as a right choice from the vast selection of worldviews in late Antiquity. Such affirmations are not seeking psychological relief from sin, as we might find it in the confessions of Jean-Jacques Rousseau. In the victorious times of the medieval Christian Occident no such affirmations were needed. Only later, at the arrival of Cathar heretics and with the great exodus of Protestants, did a real need for confessions emerge. The Lutheran *Confessio Augustana* triggered the *Catholic Professio fidei Tridentina.* And just as the Jews managed to escape the requirement of forced confessions in Spain, the philosopher Spinoza was asked for the same forced confession, but this time by Dutch rabbis. Spinoza's deep philosophical faith was of no interest to them; they demanded his affirmation to the synagogue. Spinoza's *deus sive natura* was similar to Giordano Bruno's *natura infinita,* and at this end the coerced confessions of the inquisition did not differ much from the powers of the synagogue.

As soon as faith becomes externalized, it demands affirmation. Where faith need not show itself, it needs no professing. One confesses for others, not for oneself. One need not confirm faith to oneself. Perhaps one might seek assurance, but this is an inward movement while others might attempt to enforce one's outward movement. There always have been, and still are, unaffirming believers without bishopric guidance or imamate directives. For example, there still exists in Japan a Christian creedless church of no church (Kin'en kyōkai kyōkai). Overall there is no requirement for affirmation in Buddhism. One seeks refuge but affirms no one and nothing. After all, what could one possibly confess in a faith with no self.

Reflecting on affirmation is accompanied with thoughts about constraint. A confession is demanded by force. The magnitude of religious icons is always measured, until today, by their resistance against force. For example, Luther enjoyed free speech in Worms; nonetheless he was confronted with political constraint. The broken promise for Jan Hus in Constance was not forgotten. Occidental might was aligned with coercion to confess. The externalization of faith consequently brings intolerance. In fact, in this "external" world there is room only for one monotheistic creed. By definition, a monotheist strives for achieving autocratic rule. A tolerance for two monotheistic creeds is, at best, a stopgap. By contrast, there is no restriction on the number of diverse thoughts in philosophical faith.

Affirmation comes from distress. The plight of distress forces one to confirm or to lie. Giordano Bruno used to be a Christian, without pressure, without affirmation; only later did he become an affirming philosopher. The more pressure the Roman Inquisition put upon him during his stay in prison, the more resisting and affirming did he become. Most fabrications come under stress. Predicaments force one to lie. The lie is perceived to be lighter, while the truth is heavier. In this case the lie consisted in denying what he believed and proclaiming to be true for what he did not believe.

What exactly is the confession of someone like Bruno? Unlike some Islamic Aristotelians, Bruno does not deny the soul but he calls it a monad. His all-encompassing *natura* is not too distant from Jaspers' encompassing. We do not know much about the last few hours of Bruno before he was condemned to the stake. Allegedly he screamed while his tongue was torn from his mouth. Apparently he did not commit to lie and professed his beliefs. Under the pressure of inquisition, his faith assumed the character of profession. This quality of professing faith could be seen as a criterion to differentiate between religious and philosophical faith. Philosophical faith is not a weakened religious faith; transcendence is not just another word for God. Philosophical faith is of a different kind. Religious faith is directed toward a person or a personal entity that can be revered and worshiped since it has qualities that are akin to one's own qualities. In a philosophically reflective way it would not make sense to claim that "I have transcendence," or "there is transcendence." Transcendence is not an object. Religious language takes place in a division of subject and object. The objects of religious faith are explicitly persons. For a philosopher it is rather awkward when transcendence is addressed in a quasi-objective manner. Persons, even when they are divine entities, are religiously affirmed or disowned. The encompassing in philosophy entails that something is and is not, one thinks and thinks not. To deny the personally known biblical Jesus was the utmost downfall for the Apostle Peter. Distress produces the lie. To dialogue without stress in philosophical faith can manifest as a feeling of joy or it might be a simple and trivial deception.

The foundational idea that is at the core of any understanding of philosophical faith is transcendence: human existence is immanent and its boundary defined by the human ability of rational conceptualization, and this boundary of existence is rationally absolute. The boundary between immanence and transcendence is rationally seen absolute and yet there is discontent with such confinement. Humans are not just rational beings, not just *animal rationale*. It is quite interesting to note that such a statement is not only daring, but can also be supported empirically by means of game theory and economy. For example, Herbert Simon and Nobel laureate Reinhard Selten used economic and game-theoretical analysis to demonstrate that a human is not just a *homo economicus*. The presupposition that humans would act primarily rationally contradicts observation and apparently also overtaxes the rational disposition of humans. Being irrational is a human need: stepping out of line, trying one's luck, seeking adventures. Schopenhauer's metaphysical need comes to mind, and also Pascal's wager. A restricted rational behavior is not yet proof for transcendence but a reminder that immanence does not always require being immanent, and being rational does not always assure rationality. From a rational vantage point, irrationality is permitted. Rationality, seen from an empirical perspective, does allow for crossing boundaries.

Economists and game theorists noticed a partial tendency for irrationality that apparently is fundamental from an anthropological viewpoint. Selten claims that we need a new theory of rationality, which he calls bounded rationality.[4] In a sense, Jaspers' idea of a foundational philosophical faith might constitute such new theory. The anthropological support for noticing a need to transcend rationality appears to me as fundamental as Arnold Gehlen's positioning of humans as scarcity beings, a position that can be traced back to Giovanni Pico de la Mirandola and his *De Hominis Dignitate*.

Jaspers has no aversion to use rational means for restricting rationality, as can be seen in his "formal transcending": To surpass logic by means of logical categories, to question all questioning by asking "why at all why," by searching for unity and using the category of unity to dismantle the entire system of categories. All this abolishes logic as such and leads to the idea of the encompassing which encompasses itself. When mathematicians use set theory to discuss the set of all sets, and either rejoice in or suffer from such paradox, they might not notice that Jaspers addresses this paradox with the encompassing, just like Jaspers himself did not notice that he has given a philosophical answer to this mathematical formulation.

Jaspers states that at the core and beginning of philosophy there are contradictions, tautologies, paradoxa. But what can one possibly make of such insight? Only a few contradictions are profound, most paradoxa are primarily ingenious, nearly all circularities are meaningless. Yet, some are deep and signalize transcendence. At my first visit with Jaspers in Heidelberg in June of 1946, he stopped my enthusiasm

---

[4] Reihard Selten, "Features of Experimentally Observed Bounded Rationality," *European Economic Review*, Vol. 42, No. 3, 1998, p. 443.

for Schopenhauer by pointing to the nonsense of his famous "the world is my representation," by continuing cynically, "and my representation is part of the world," He found it foolish (*töricht*) to believe in this simple circularity.

Arriving at the boundary of rational thought we might start to ask questions about immanence–transcendence boundary. It is both, boundary and no boundary. It is boundary, since we know that we cannot know anything transcendent. But nothing prohibits us from having faith in transcendence. Faith is a form of knowledge that knows of its lack of knowing. I conjecture that Socrates might have thought of his famous saying as a form of faith. Faith is much less defined than knowledge. Positivists can define knowledge with a few lines; by contrast, theologians cannot explain in vast tomes what faith is, and philosophers likewise cannot define it. "We do not know what faith is, since we have no organ for it, just as we have reason for knowledge," explains Descartes in his *Discourse*.

For Jaspers, all of this could relate to cipher. The logical boundary situation of formal transcending is a cipher. A cipher must be interpreted. The result is either trivial or profound and no one can really decide upon it. There is no deciphering code to be learned. I am the code. The interpretation of ciphers is a logical boundary situation. It is not a scientific determination between A and not-A, but rather an individual decision that allows me to believe, without really knowing that it is indeed a cipher, in other words, that it has transcendent meaning. The poet and intellectual Paul Valéry is known for considering Pascal's *Memorial* as nonsense and suggests that he should rather have build bridges. All beliefs are ciphers. If I have no faith in X, then X is not a cipher. The poet Valéry would not know it any better than the mathematician Pascal when he yelled, "Fire!" Both knew what fire looks like, regardless of knowing the formalities of a wager that were known to this probability theoretician. And yet, all we can say is that it appears to us that he had faith in his belief.

After all this discussion, supported by the passage on page 15 of Jaspers' *PG,* it is safe to assume that there is no *confessing* in philosophical faith. And yet, Ehrlich is correct: Jaspers did acknowledge the philosopher's duty to provide affirmation. In his *Einführung in die Philosophie* Jaspers notes that philosophers in his days would rather avoid the question regarding God, and goes on to say: "Whoever philosophizes must give affirmation." Moreover, "when there is doubt about God, a philosopher must give an answer."[5] So far, this does not suggest a creed. Here, Jaspers primarily addresses the unprincipled skeptics that he rallies against, which for him includes also Ludwig Wittgenstein with his infamous sentence, "whereof one cannot speak, thereof one must remain silent". Here, Jaspers mitigates. Confession yes, but when professing becomes martyrdom, it is advisable to reject it altogether. When paying for the strength of one's convictions with death, the intended goal becomes untruthful. Instead of speaking about affirmation, Jaspers refers to loyalty to faith.

---

[5] Karl Jaspers, *Einführung in die Philosophie* (Munich: R. Piper 1965), p. 40. [Henceforth cited as *EP*]

Jaspers did indeed address various forms of affirming philosophical faith in different passages of *PG* and *Von der Wahrheit*.[6] He developed this idea with the examples of Galileo and Bruno, and their behavior toward the inquisition under the perspective of a comparison between essential and nonessential truth: It is senseless to give one's life for a nonessential truth that does not affect my being; it is equally senseless to confess or deny under duress, since the truth-value of the contested assertion does not change due to my confession or denial. Galileo's behavior was reasonable and justifiable in view of protecting his own life.

Jaspers describes the essentiality of truth in many ways. It is relevant for essential truth, he says, that the denial of truth, namely the refusal of affirmation, itself jeopardizes truth. But what exactly is put in danger when the affirmation of truth is denied? It is the disaffirmation of God's transcendent existence that Jaspers rallies philosophers to resist, albeit transcendence here is not understood as something whose affirmation or disaffirmation would lead to a sacrifice of one's own existence. He does not call upon religious sacrifice. Transcendence is not divine revelation. This makes it difficult to comprehend in what and to whom a philosopher should give affirmation—since it is not a person, earthly or heavenly; neither writing, nor scripture, not created or revealed; no event of the past or still to come; no worldly treasure or sacred stone. Jaspers speaks of a secret (*PG* 11) and becomes almost religious when he speaks of a "betrayal of eternal being" (*EP* 52) that would render inauspicious (*unselig*) all remaining being.

Who actually demands an affirmation from a philosopher? First of all, it can come from external forces, such as the inquisition or some authorities. But ultimately it is an internal unconditional requirement derived from my authentic being as mere existence (*EP* 54). It is the demand of the "I" toward itself. At the origin of such demand is a decision that is identical with myself. The deciding party and its authority are identical. The deciding factor for an affirmation is the resoluteness to make such decision.

Essential truths that demand affirmation are truths that would vanish in the absence of professing them (*VW* 651). There are "performative sentences" whose being true is depending on their "being performed" and which will become false, of one denies the theme ("I speak"). But this is not what Jaspers is interested in. He is thinking of requirements, not sentences. And because these requirements do not have moral or theological content, they are becoming empty. The subject of the requirement does not have an object. It is identical with it.

The subjectification of philosophical truth makes it sound as if an affirmation simply confirms one's resoluteness to confess. The confessor affirms his readiness for confession. Any form of objectifying faith and affirmation would consequently lead to deceptive instrumentality. For Jaspers, the absolute demand to affirm philosophical faith allows for an exclusive form of existence that circumvents the subject-object division.

---

[6] Karl Jaspers, *Von der Wahrheit* (Munich: Piper 1947), pp. 651 ff. [Henceforth cited as *VW*]

Historical truth is quite different. Socrates died, even though he could have fled, and by this example he demonstrated to his pupils and the citizenry of Athens his loyalty to uphold the laws. Boethius affirmed his innocence to the king. Bruno was not ready to deny his eight theses, even when facing the inquisition.[7]

I end these reflections by deriving the following consequence from Jaspers' absolute demand for affirmation: If faith, even philosophical faith, needs affirmation, and if the form of affirming requires some external manifestation, such as a piece of clothing, a ritual, or something that is audible or visible, then the question remains still, whether any other person has to accept such external manifestation. If a Jaspers scholar would require from students some form of philosophical affirmation, this would be a violation of the German constitution which clearly states that in certain public spaces (such as schools) certain external signs of faith (such as head scarf) are prohibited. All affirmations are in principle external and could conflict with different faiths. Once philosophical faith is to be affirmed externally, given its political consequence, it would no longer differ from religious faith or faithful worldviews.

The reputable German scholar of constitutional law, Ernst Wolfgang Böckenförde, created furor with his provocative sentence that "the secular State lives with presuppositions that it cannot guarantee."[8] This means that even the secular State is based on judicial, moral, and metaphysical assumptions that are outside the reach of its purview. Once the secular State can no longer warrant its presuppositions, it is in a state of danger. Thus in "metaphysical silence" the roots of the secular State perish—so claims Böckenförde. But from a different perspective, one that Böckenförde does not consider, our earlier reflections make it clear that not only can the State not guarantee metaphysical ideas, but due to the potential for conflict, the State may also not permit external manifestations of such affirmations. Unrestricted permissions of confessions endanger the existence of the State. Hence the arbitrary permissions of liberalism would lead to havoc.

In the beginning of the age of enlightenment, freedom of worship was a step toward freedom from political monotheism. But it was just a step. An absolute and, for Jaspers unconditional, demand for affirmation could not prevent the danger of forceful implementation, even under the most tolerant circumstances. Hence one must ask if philosophers really would want to embrace affirmation in the manner of theologians.

Philosophical faith comprehends; Philosophical affirmation repels.

---

[7] In view of subjective self-opinioned exchanges, one is reminded of Michel de l'Hopital, the Chancellor of Henry IV of France, who declared on the eve of the Huguenot wars in 1562 that it is not relevant which one is the true religion; what matters is how people can get along living together. See Leopold von Ranke, *Französische Geschichte, Volume 1*, ed. Willy Andreas (Wiesbaden: E. Vollmer, 1957), vol. 1, p. 157.

[8] Ernst Wolfgang Böckenförde, *Der säkularisierte Staat* (Munich: Carl-Friedrich-von-Siemens-Stiftung, 2007), p. 71.

Certainty and Trust: Reflections on Karl Jaspers' Cosmo-Anthropology

Reiner Wiehl†

Abstract A discussion of the concepts of certainty and trust in Jaspers' cosmo-anthropology with special reference to Hegel's famous essay on "Faith and Knowledge", Kant's *Religion Within the Limits of Reason Alone*, and Heidegger's *Being and Time*. The chapter offers clarifications of Jaspers' understanding of certainty and trust by way of his psychology of worldviews and periechontology.

Hegel's renowned essay "Faith and Knowledge," published in the *Critical Journal of Philosophy* co-edited with Schelling, explores a complete range of forms for the reflective philosophy of subjectivity in Kant, Jacobi, and Fichte. The first sentence in this essay states:

> Civilization has raised this latest era so far above the ancient antithesis of Reason and faith, of philosophy and positive religion that this opposition of faith and knowledge has acquired quite a different sense and has now been transferred into the field of philosophy itself.[1]

With these words Hegel commences a critical assessment of reflective philosophy that used to be practiced in his time, pondering whether victorious reason has not suffered the same fate as faith by succumbing to it. Faith and knowledge, religion and reason are still hotly debated topics. Hegel's sentiment, written more than 200 years ago, reflects an analogous query for today, namely, what is the relationship between these two foundations that are pursued in reason and religion, in science, philosophy, and theology? In modern culture, which of these two foundations ought to yield to the other, which one must yield to the other? Even if one should be given primacy over the other, by what measure could this be accomplished at all?

---

[1] Georg Wilhelm Friedrich Hegel, *Faith & Knowledge*, trans. Walter Cerf and H.S. Harris (Albany, NY: State University of New York Press, 177, [315]), p. 55. An earlier version of this essay was presented at the International Symposium in Naples, Italy. Translated from German by Helmut Wautischer, except for quotations from references cited in English.

R. Wiehl (✉)

H. Wautischer et al. (eds.), *Philosophical Faith and the Future of Humanity*,
DOI 10.1007/978-94-007-2223-1_11, © Springer Science+Business Media B.V. 2012

Differentiating Philosophy from Science and Religion

The relationship between faith and knowledge and considering the possibility, perhaps even necessity of ranking one over the other is one of the primary questions in the philosophy of Karl Jaspers. One does not exaggerate when claiming that this topic permeates through all of Jaspers' work, beginning with his *Psychologie der Weltanschauungen* (1919) and *Philosophie* (1932), followed by *Von der Wahrheit* (1947) and in his later works as well. But when approaching the subject faith and knowledge, Jaspers did not call upon the same primary adversaries that one finds in Hegel. In contrast, Jaspers was inspired by Kant, whom he considered as measure and role model for philosophy, "the epitome of philosophers who is unmatched in his nobility of reflective humanity. . .whose humaneness is revealed as purity and acuity in infinite thought processes without ever becoming fossilized."[2] Here Jaspers also describes his intellectual-philosophical proximity to the author of *Critique of Pure Reason*: "Philosophy, the risky endeavor to advance into the uncharted depths of self-awareness, must fail when pursued as teaching of truths accessible to all."[3] For Jaspers, Kant is the harbinger of human subjectivity and existence in the philosophy of modernity, the one who placed human subjectivity into the center of his reflection. He is the one who opened the path for the real comprehension of human freedom, in the context of ethical, judicial, and political action. Therefore, Kant is for Jaspers also the focal point for addressing the problem of faith and knowledge in the questionable context of theoretical and practical reason. But Kant is the one who lost sight of his critique when he attempted to develop a foundation for metaphysics by means of pure reason. One of the first sentences in Jaspers' *Philosophie* states, "philosophy of existence is metaphysics."[4] With this distinction he demarcates the specific character of his philosophy of existence in relation to the existentialist movements of his time. At the same time he is aware of the fact that by striving for a renewal of a central concept in classical European philosophy, he

---

[2] Karl Jaspers, "Preface" in *Philosophie, Volume 1: Philosophische Weltorientierung* (Berlin, 1932), p. viii. [Henceforth cited as *P* with volume number.] Jaspers lists here also the great philosophers that he considers to be his companions: "Plotinus, Bruno, Spinoza, Schelling, the great metaphysicians and creators of dreams that become truths; Hegel with his riches of envisioning contents that he expresses with pure linguistic force in constructive thoughts; Kierkegaard who is trembled in his roots when philosophizing with integrity in view of nothingness but with passion for Being as the possibility for Other; W.v. Humboldt, the embodiment of German humanity throughout the entire world; Nietzsche, the psychologist and inexorable exposer of all deception who in the midst of his faithless world became the visionary of historic unfolding; Max Weber, who faced the destitution of our time and recognized it with profound knowledge, in a collapsing world that must rely upon itself."

[3] *P1* vii. For the relationship between Jaspers and the two philosophers Kant and Hegel see Richard Wisser and Leonard H. Ehrlich, eds., *Philosoph und Philosophien*, part 1 (Würzburg, 1993); especially the contributions by Andreas Cesana and Alan M. Olson.

[4] *P1* 27. The full text is, "Philosophy of Existence Is, in Essence, Metaphysics. It Believes in from Which It Originates." See also *P1* 33 ff.

aligns himself not with Hegel's speculative philosophy of the absolute, but instead with Kant's critique of reason.

In his attempt to renew metaphysics Jaspers was fully aware that the vital core of traditional metaphysics—which was the main objective in Hegel's philosophy of the absolute—was lost for good. Here I refer to the general ontology that was supposed to provide a philosophical account of God, the world and humans, along with a conceptual foundation for nature and culture. Jaspers' theory of ciphers demonstrates the loss of validity in any attempt to establish a general ontology. And with regard to worldview I use the term cosmology and speak of anthropology rather than the illumination of existence. I do this purposefully in order to view metaphysics and philosophy as the condition for the possibility of comprehending the world and consciousness. And I use the concepts of certainty and trust in close proximity to the concepts of reason and faith. All of these concepts refer most suitably to the aforementioned problematic of science and religion, as well as philosophy and theology. Certainty and trust are primal behavioral patterns in human life and denote primary needs of human existence, and our hunger and thirst for certainty and trust runs parallel to our hunger and thirst for justice.

Both of these concepts—certainty and trust—belong to the basic terminology of Jaspers' philosophy, as long as one is permitted to designate such basic vocabulary in the context of his philosophy given the historical loss of a universal ontology for a system of justification. Be that as it may, this basic terminology and basic concepts serve the spirit of Jaspers' philosophy as *signa* and ciphers. In addition to these foundational concepts there are two equally important key concepts—indecision (*Schwebe*) and foundering (*Scheitern*)—that are inseparably connected to the philosophy of human existence in the function of expressing the rational and critical component of existentialism.

Here we are confronted with a puzzle: On one hand we find the undisputed relevance of certainty and trust for human existence; while on the other hand we see the inseparable alignment of human existence with all kinds of uncertainties and a perpetual confrontation with the possibility of foundering. Does this indicate the originating philosophical ground that Hegel cleverly called a "fulfilling skepticism" (*vollbringender Skeptizismus*)?[5]

The antinomic structure of Jaspers' thought relates to his Kantianism. Already in his *Psychology of Worldviews*, we can find the truth function of the antinomy as starting point for identifying boundary situations. This is also addressed in the third volume of his *Philosophie* where Jaspers addresses the foundations of metaphysics:

It becomes apparent in boundary situations that all positive is inseparably aligned with its corresponding negative. There is no good action without potential and real harm; no truth without falsity, no life without death; joy is tied to woe, as actualization is tied to risk and loss. Human depth—which gives voice to transcendence—is positively linked to

---

[5] G.W.F. Hegel, "Einleitung," *Phänomenologie des Geistes*, Theorie Werkausgabe Volume 3 (Frankfurt am Main: Suhrkamp, 1970), p. 72.

destruction, disease, or extravagance, but this connection is not transparent due to its vast multifariousness. In all of being I recognize its antinomic structure.[6]

Jaspers was fully aware of the peculiarity of his existential metaphysics and coined a clear measure for engaging in its philosophical dialogue:

> Since philosophy does not exist as objective validity but comes to fulfillment in the singularity of its reflectice existence, the objective expression is for the listener of the language of the other; fully comprehending it would mean bringing the other to oneself. (*P1* 298)

This sentence expresses both, the exceptional truth claim of philosophy and also moderation and the apparent retraction of such encompassing claim. What this passage is all about is that "comprehending the language of the other" is more than just a hermeneutical effort or just a methodically successful interpretation of such language. For Jaspers, philosophy is something uniquely personal and at the same time something uniquely transpersonal—an indirect communication of one existing human to another: "No philosophy can be transmitted identically, and yet it must urge toward communicability; since philosophy is the means for communication between existences who constitute the authentic being of a philosopher" (*P1* 299). Engaging in this kind of philosophical communication could refer to someone I know personally, or to a stranger who now receives the philosophical content like a message in a bottle. The claim for truth and the simultaneous moderation of such a claim—such is the inherent contradiction in philosophical communication that finds its realization in the proximity of philosophy to religion, which takes on the philosophical task to differentiate between philosophical faith and faith in revealed religion. Mindful of this task, Jaspers writes,

> By differentiating itself, philosophy knows itself to be unfinished. Its truth claims are unconditional, yet it knows its limitation. It seems that the inspiration of some occasionally brings it to proximity with religion, but then it refuses to make this final leap, although it remains in a steady readiness. (*P1* 299)

In this context, Jaspers talks about the inspiring proximity between philosophy and religion in prayer, but he cautions us to meet this proximity with due distance: "Philosophy does not confuse worship, sentiment, or the uplifting presence of reading a cipher in prayer with an actual relationship to God" (*P1* 300). This self-imposed differentiation of philosophy from religion comes in different forms: It is the task of philosophy to fight religion when it succumbs to the heterodoxy of fanatical violence. Nonetheless, philosophy knows how to discern the truthful core of a religion and to respect it. In this self-imposed differentiation, philosophy demands above all the will to truthfulness with regard to objectivity in order to ascertain this differentiation with utmost clarity. Proximity and distance between philosophy and religion manifests within philosophy an awareness that the search for truth points to human existence, but that the truth of human existence always is and remains

---

[6] *P3* 221. See especially Martin Heidegger, *Sein und Zeit*, eight edition (Tübingen, 1957), p. 301, where he praises Jaspers' *Psychology of Worldviews* and the existential concept of boundary situations.

just a search. In a cryptic manner Jaspers writes: "If a theologian would object that, by placing truth into Existenz, one mistakenly identifies with God, since what was permissible to this one human, Jesus, is not permissible for others; these would be words that a philosopher simply could not understand."[7] The philosopher would not understand these words, since the truth of existence is and remains subject to a perpetual search and inquiry. Mindful of Nietzsche, Jaspers explicitly rejected the idea of prophetic philosophy, but for the purpose of philosophical communication he adopted a sense of veiled prophecy. Repeatedly he referred to appellation for expressing what he envisioned with such veiled prophecy. Jaspers was aware of the immediate danger with moving his philosophical communication too closely to the language of religion, and so one can find in his writings extensive efforts to steer in the opposite direction, since counter-measure occurs in the form of methodical inquiry. In its methodical search for truth philosophy feels obliged to the idea of science, even though it does not claim to be science; such self-differentiation from science—just as its self-differentiation from religion—belongs to the main tasks of philosophy.[8]

In whatever way the methodical character of Jaspers' philosophical reflections would be described, there will always be a reference to differentiation and self-differentiation becomes a most transparent instrument of philosophical inquiry about truth. This methodical trait of differentiation unmistakably moves his approach in proximity with the classical philosophical methods one finds in works from Plato to Hegel. Plato tests this method in his later dialogues, as for example in his *Sophist* in the form of a progressive division of presumed generic concepts that were consequently divided into dual patterns of species and sub-species. This progressive division into two components—where one side is discarded in favor of its opposing side—found its most complete manifestation in the speculative method of Hegel's dialectic. When we notice the proximity between this tradition of philosophical method and the methodical approach of Jaspers' philosophical thought, we must not forget that Jaspers' method of differentiation does not constitute the beginning of a general ontology. In fact, his method has intentionally left behind the tradition that culminated in Hegel's science of logic. The universality of conceptual being— which is a prerequisite for any universal ontology—has itself become the subject of a critique of reason, in the search for truth and at the same time trying to find a new philosophical logic of reason. Jaspers replaced a traditional universal ontology with what he calls a periechontology that is a logic of the encompassing. Instead of division and dialectic, here we find organization that is in alignment with the given facts. Such organization of unity is in itself perpetually questioned due to its interconnectedness with other organizations of unity. These forms of organization are not reduced to differentiations in concepts, but they reach beyond denotation

---

[7] For Jaspers' differentiation between philosophy and science, see Reiner Wiehl, "Die Philosophie in Karl Jaspers' Allgemeiner Psychopathology," in *Karl Jaspers. Philosophie und Psychopathologie*, eds. Knut Eming and Thomas Fuchs (Germany: Heidelberg, 2008), pp. 3 ff.

[8] For a general account of Jaspers' idea of the encompassing see Giuseppe Cantillo, *Introduczione a Jaspers* (Roma/Bari, 2001), p. 95.

and include basic reflection concerning argumentation for or against the point in question. The method that comes from periechontology manifests in earnestness, its impartiality is compelling but at times also compulsive and tiring. But this dull facticity is intentional. It forms the methodical counter-move to the appellative. This is the component that targeted by appellative philosophizing, namely an ethos of impartiality in deliberate contrast to the rhetoric and sophistry that were elevated to a methodical principle in the context of philosophical hermeneutics. The ethos of impartiality contains the imperatives of logic that proclaim: You ought to differentiate and ought to avoid hideous simplifications and incorrect generalizations; you ought to be wary of totalitarian ideologies.

Truth and Freedom

There are two basic themes that permeate Jaspers' philosophical thought; from its beginnings in his grand *General Psychopathology* (1913) to the already *mentioned Psychology of Worldviews* (1919), to his purely philosophical works, the three volume *Philosophie* (1932) and his grand work *Von der Warheit* (1947) and his philosophical late works. The two themes of inquiry have to do with the being of Being, and with truth. Central to both queries is yet another question that is inseparably linked to them. This is the inquiry about the human being, a question that any human could not cease to ask, in short: Who am I? In Jaspers' view, this question precedes the inquiry as to what I am. This question about human self-awareness cannot be separated from the two other queries, being and truth. The query into being is a question about true being, while the query into truth is a question about the being of truth; and more importantly, both questions decidedly link to the question about human existence. The question about true being and the question about the being of truth are the two fundamental questions in philosophy and of all humans. Accordingly, these include questions about human existence, human self-determination, and especially about one's true nature. These differentiations acquire a different meaning, namely the distinction between true being and the truthfulness of being human. This division rests on the difference between a true self-determination of a human as human being, which includes determination of consciousness, Being, and intellect; as well as determining the Existenz of a human. Periechontology—which is Jaspers' theory of truth—surpasses the classical Aristotelian exploration of the multiplicity of Being that accounted for the content of traditional ontology. It combines this exploration with the study of the manifold meanings of a sense of truth along with the being of human within the complex assessment of the encompassing.

Jaspers' periechontology is not a theory of pure truth, nor is it a theory of absolute being, and it also is no theory that would attempt to define the human as a finite being. Most importantly, though, the being of truth cannot be separated from the being of falsity, since both are inseparably connected to human beings. Wherever humankind manifests, in form of consciousness and Being, as intelligence and Existenz, there is also falsity and insincerity and untruthfulness toward oneself or the other; such traits of insincerity occur in social and political life, in the disparity of views about the power of reigning and subservient opinions. While Kant demands in his *Metaphysics of Morals* a duty of virtue for truthfulness, Jaspers sketches a realistic image about the actuality of truth and falsity in the context of exploring these three basic questions. Nonetheless, it was also his study of the Kantian "religion within the limits of pure reason," demonstrably exemplified in the events of his time, that motivated Jaspers to combine his query into evil with his query into truth.[9] Evil is a specific manifestation of untruthfulness. An exploration of truth in connection with an exploration of the human condition requires the exploration of the emergence of truth in its opposition to the tendency for untruthfulness and the powers of deceit in an attempt to open space for truth. A suitable philosophical exploration of such topics related to certainty and trust requires the inclusion of these variables into the logical space of methodological differentiation between the being of existence, the being of truth, and the being of being human. Certainty and trust can be located within these differentiations. They are the modes of being, types of being human, and last but not least the modes of truth. Precisely here, one can recognize the character of Jaspers' philosophy that became the subject of his philosophical critique related to the aforementioned Hegelian essay on faith and knowledge, namely, it is reflective philosophy where the philosophical method of differentiation aims at acquiring a knowledge of truth. But truth in itself must become subject of methodical differentiation. Given the manifold meanings of truth, the following differentiations are essential for the exploration of certainty and trust, namely, truth as an event, something that is sought by humans and has an origin and goal; truth as the occurrence of being human, where this form of existence manifests as awareness and being, as mind and existence; truth as an event that clarifies an occurrence of revelation that brings clarity, lucidity, and ultimately certainty.[10]

This occurrence of truth—an occurrence of revelation—is for Jaspers not a religion nor bound to a particular religion. The modality of truth as becoming is primarily an event of philosophy and philosophizing. Lucidity and clarity, certainty and trust are gained in the struggle of philosophical reflection and exacted from its corresponding negations. Certainty and trust is only present when lucidity arises, when truth reveals itself in a certain way. The methodical differentiations for the modes of truth include the differentiation between certainty and clarity, and especially also the differentiation between certainty in a broader and narrower sense. Jaspers calls certainty in a narrow sense a binding certainty. The most discussed concept in Jaspers'

---

[9] See for example Jaspers' lecture "The Radical Evil in Kant," presented at the Lesezirkel Hottingen, Zurich 1935, published in *Rechenschaft und Ausblick. Reden und Aufätze* (Munich, 1958), pp. 107 ff. See also his lecture, "The Unconditioned and the Evil," in *Das Wagnis der Freiheit, Gesammelte Aufsätze zur Philosophie*, ed. Hans Saner (Munich: Piper, 1996), pp. 86 ff.

[10] See the methodology developed by Karl Jaspers in *Nachlaß zur Philosophischen Logik*, eds. Hans Saner and Marc Hänggi (Munich: Piper, 1991), pp. 285–371.

reflective philosophy, his foundational concept of the philosophical cipher, is inseparably connected with differentiating the manifold meanings of truth, namely, the
concept of boundary. Boundaries (*Grenzen*) are to be found whenever philosophical
method guides philosophical thought. These are boundaries of differentiations that
demarcate one thought from another. And it is by virtue of philosophical thought
that a self-imposed boundary can be crossed or transcended. Jaspers never grew
tired of emphasizing that transcending is the task of philosophy. But transcending always presupposes demarcation and setting boundaries. Existential critique
of reason includes both, setting and crossing boundaries. It contains yet another
third quality, the critical reflection upon one's own crossing of boundaries. I have
already mentioned the conceptual importance of the relationship between setting
and crossing boundaries. Jaspers' corresponding term—boundary situation—is the
most renowned concept of his terminology and it found recognition in the scientific language of psychology and psychiatry, and even in popular German language
usage.

Inasmuch as certainty and trust become the subject of philosophical thought for
variations in truth, they are confined by the setting and crossing of boundaries. In
this context of discussing the terms boundary and boundary situation, I need to
address the philosophical exchange between Jaspers and Heidegger for its relevance
in philosophy and also for its precise relevance related to the current awareness of
the intellectual situation in our times. Jaspers' philosophical frame for the relationship between philosophy and religion, knowledge and faith is here very much to
the point. Equally pertinent are Jaspers' clear demarcations between focused and
factually gained methodical knowledge as opposed to mere rhetoric and oratory
techniques for affecting opinions, especially within the context of a society that
upholds one's right to form opinions as an unalienable basic right. Freely formed
personal opinions require a successful application of critical reasoning in opposition
to the techniques of oratorical manipulation and the attempts of influential forces in
public and socio-political circles to produce and direct opinions.

The philosophical dialogue between Heidegger and Jaspers starts with
Heidegger's brilliant review of Jaspers' *Psychology of Worldviews* that he personally sent to Jaspers. Jaspers appreciated and respected the ambitious work of his
younger colleague, but not without letting Heidegger know that Jaspers himself had
already noticed this aspect of Heidegger's critique.[11] Jaspers' book was very well
received and Heidegger wanted to see more in it than simply an ideal typology of
worldviews; instead he wanted to read it as an outline for a philosophy of existence
that had at its center the newly coined concept of boundary situation. The subject of
his critique was an ambiguity in presentation of this concept, on one hand emphasizing psychology and the then dominantly practiced philosophy, and on the other

---

[11] Letter to Martin Heidegger of August 8, 1921. In *Martin Heidegger/Karl Jaspers Briefwechsel
1920–1963*, eds. Walter Biemel and Hans Saner (Frankfurt am Main/Zurich: Piper, 1990), p. 23.

hand emphasizing a philosophy of existence. Jaspers' concept of boundary situation was most favorably addressed in *Being and Time*.[12] Jaspers had already noticed this unintentional ambiguity and dealt with it in self-critical consequence. In his *Philosophy*, Jaspers dissolves the ambiguity by differentiating between a psychological and sociological venue to understand human existence and the illumination of human existence in the context of philosophical thought. Jaspers demonstrates the conditions that bring forth this unavoidable ambiguity and in order to make them a transcendental necessity.

Jaspers did acknowledge the accuracy of Heidegger's critique in that review, he acknowledged that the ambiguity of the relationship between psychology and philosophy critically played out in his discussion of boundary situations, where he describes them as extreme situations of existential pressure that can be overcome by means of psychiatric help, but simultaneously views them as ultimate boundaries for human existence that each individual must freely address from within one's own efforts to find a suitable disposition for life. Nonetheless, it is certainly no exaggeration to claim that Jaspers' *Philosophie* is more than just an acknowledgement of Heidegger's critique and a subsequent revision of the noted philosophical shortcomings. Instead, his book is a critical reply to Heidegger's *Being and Time*: a methodical counterproposal to all central claims of Heidegger's sensational book. This counterproposal is under the motto of the quest for truth, and consequently addresses in a methodical manner from its very beginning the interrelation of questions regarding the being of existence, the being of truth, and the being of being human, all of which I described earlier as the methodical key for understanding Jaspers' philosophy. Jaspers' critique of the existential-hermeneutical analysis of being in *Being and Time* relates primarily to Heidegger's method, which is the blending of phenomenological description and construction. He critiques a premature determination of being-in-the-world that does not account for the uncertainty of presuming oneness in the world. This relates emphatically against a methodical starting point for the exploration of being in a presumed commonplaceness of human existence that permits the explication of a corresponding pre-ontological assertion of being. Against such methodical starting point Jaspers argues it is not recognized that—similar to Hegel's determination of a natural consciousness—humans, by virtue of their historic existence, are formed by their cultures; and that for modern humans such cultural influence is the impact from contemporary empirical science. The scientific specificity of the modern world is for Jaspers' philosophy the methodical starting point under the motto "world orientation" (*PI* 29).

The foremost objection that can be derived from Jaspers' *Philosophie* against Heidegger's *Being and Time* is the lack of critical reflection, namely, Heidegger's hermeneutical analysis of being omits the fact that such analysis takes place within a given philosophical self-awareness and takes place in corresponding philosophical concepts. When Jaspers aligns human world orientation primarily on knowledge

---

[12] Martin Heidegger, *Being and Time*, see Anmerkung p. 6.

gained from science, he certainly is influenced by Max Weber's assertion of occidental rationality. More importantly, however, is the fact that for Jaspers philosophical knowledge of humans derives its norms for certainty from the natural sciences. Here one must heed the fact that from a philosophical perspective, the assertion of a unified science is just as questionable as the assertion of a unified worldview. Even the traditional systematicity in the organization of the sciences as it was drafted in ancient Greece and was philosophically justified by Hegel in his *Encyclopedia of Science* has lost its binding nature. Jaspers explicitly refutes the fossilized dualism of natural sciences and humanities. For him, all contemporary empirical sciences are human sciences. Both are sciences of humans and by humans. Yet, from a philosophical viewpoint human sciences do differ inasmuch as they bring about a perspective concerned with the true being of humans. From such perspective, psychology and sociology play a major role in Jaspers' philosophy of science. It is precisely for their focus on the spiritual-mental and sociopolitical aspect of humans that they pose some sort of competition to philosophy. The empirical sciences in general and the sciences of psychology and sociology in particular have methodical relevance for philosophical insight. And all this is prior to the methodical relevance of everyday life as it is portrayed in Heidegger's *Being and Time*. Jaspers' view on methodical relevance is based in the specific modality of truth that becomes transmitted by means of scientific rigor. This is truth as a binding certainty. The binding quality of this certainty is a specific form of necessity, a binding certainty that grants a certain place to probability statements. The methodic relevance of scientific materialization for philosophy is in the relationship between philosophy and the contemporary empirical sciences.

This relationship of philosophy to the sciences is by analogy similar as its relationship to religion. It is the task of philosophy to differentiate itself from these sciences. Such self-differentiation claims that philosophy is not science, especially not empirical science. But it has a specific proximity to science. This difference is already stated due to self-differentiation. Concerning its proximity, this relates to the aforementioned method of facticity which allows for structured thought. Self-differentiation acts primarily in its critique of the sciences. It is the critique of a disproportionate importance of scientific knowledge. The compelling quality of scientific knowledge cannot constitute all truth. It is this indecision or suspension— a rather peculiar term to designate distance—that affirms philosophical insight in contrast to inappropriate truth claims, and is reminiscent of the critical disposition in philosophical phenomenology against material being and of the validity claim from awareness of being in the form of a methodical abstention from judgment. But Jaspers' philosophical method is not the method of phenomenology, neither the phenomenology of Husserl nor the phenomenological hermeneutics of Heidegger. Philosophical critique is not directed against the primary assertion of being a natural consciousness in everyday life, but against the primacy claim of scientific knowledge. For philosophy, compelling certainty is never the closing point in the search for knowledge and it is not the full picture of truth in the search for truth about human existence. Philosophy's critique of the sciences is directed not only against psychologism and sociologism, or against the claim to be a philosophical anthropology. In a more fundamental way this critique is directed against naturalism in the sciences, such as biologisms and brain mythologies, inasmuch as the claim is made that these forms of practice can decipher the true being of humans. The methodical critique of philosophy against the sciences is directed against claims of exclusivity for access to truth by virtue of objectifying methods that guide the path of knowledge in the sciences. The acquisition of knowledge by objectifying means is an indisputable prerequisite for philosophical world orientation. But the quest for knowledge transcends beyond all such objectifications. Its access to the world in an effort for world orientation brings a different modality of truth, for by transforming the compelling quality of scientific knowledge into a state of indecision, according to Jaspers it enables one to achieve a lucidity of perception that constitutes an exemplary mode of truth.

How different for philosophical knowledge are the methodical meanings of psychology and sociology can be derived from the fact that all relevant reflection about the true nature of humans takes place in the medium of differentiation between philosophy and the two subjects psychology and sociology (*P1* 200ff). This is true for the determination of boundary situations, and also for the basic concept in Jaspers' philosophy, human freedom.

First and foremost, freedom is freedom of the will. An appropriate approach to determine freedom requires that two variables are to be seen simultaneously, the freedom of will and the will to be free. Both have a psychological and sociological component. The sciences of psychology and sociology, and also psychopathology, provide important facts in helping us to understand the manifold limitations and hindrances in the unfolding of human will and freedom. Once again, philosophical insight becomes active in its self-differentiation. Against the scientific objectification of being and especially against the objectification of humans, it allows for a fundamentally different possibility of observation, namely the unique relationship of human consciousness to itself and to the other, where I am not the object, but encounter myself in the other. From the perspective of scientific knowledge, such encounter is incomprehensible and unexplainable. But there is such possibility of encounter with the other that elucidates me in distinctive and unmistaken ways. This is the possibility of the elucidation of Existenz and existential communication. This is the place where the truth of being and the truth of human meet. Thus Jaspers' Kantianism is a form of dualism, whether the dualism of empirical science and philosophy, or the dualism of truths. Occasionally Jaspers refers to this form of dualism or the duality of the Kantian critique of reason, namely, appearance and being-in-itself. This dualism, in effect, constitutes the starting point of his existential metaphysics. It is in the historicity of human existence where humans find the true being of possibility, the possibility of one's truth and the possibility of one's true freedom.

For Jaspers, truth and freedom are inseparably together. This togetherness is the exceptional possibility of true human existence. It is an idea and an ideal that forms within the practice of philosophy. In this context, Jaspers refers to the appellative character of philosophical thought. This appeal is directed to a person, every person.

It shows the exemplary possibility as a possibility for one's own existence. This is the possibility for philosophy in every person.

In my exploration of Jaspers' metaphysics I have not yet addressed the concept of trust, and trust can also be addressed in a dualistic way. But trust belongs to the most important aspect. It is preceded by loyalty as a basic value for the determination of one's history, in reflection upon oneself and in communication with others. Loyalty and trust belong together with the secret of true love. And what about foundering, the lack of ultimate knowledge, and the incomprehensible? There is no last word. Nor is foundering the last word. The real time is not the future, but the moment, the moment of fulfilling time. And even that is not the last word.

Three Interpretations of the Content of Jaspers' Philosophical Faith

Raymond Langley

Abstract Philosophical faith traverses the divide between the transcendental understanding of phenomena and the unknowable dimensions of transcendent reality. Human beings are transformed through their free act of either accepting or rejecting the descent of Being into time as a lived faith and non-cognitive form of knowledge expressed in the cipher language of culture. The content of Jaspers' philosophic faith is examined in three interpretations: Faith with belief, faith without belief, and faith beyond belief. The essay opts for philosophical faith as beyond belief. The basic argument is that such faith is neither knowable nor demonstrable. Revealed truth and dogmatic metaphysics excludes the relativity of existential historicity. In this manner, philosophic faith is grasped as "not a knowledge I have, but a certainty that guides me."

Introduction

Glauben und Wissen wax and wane. For a millennium religious faith spoke authoritatively about God, the world and man. Philosophy was the *ancilla* or handmaiden of theology. In recent centuries, logic and epistemology slowly evolved into scientific methodology and the truths of reason dominated belief. Historically, the pendulum continues to oscillate between opposing claims to know everything solely by reason or to know nothing with certitude apart from the revelations of faith.

In 1867, 13 years before Karl Jaspers' birth, Mathew Arnold wrote "Dover Beach."[1] Hearing the "eternal note of sadness" in the sound of waves pounding

---

[1] *The Norton Anthology of Poetry* (revised), eds. A. Allison, H. Barrows, C. Blake, A. Carr, A. Eastman, and H. English; (New York, NY: W.W. Norton & Company, 1975), pp. 850–851. Arnold, a chief inspector of public schools in England and Wales, also wrote *Culture and Anarchy* (1869). This influential work exhorted ancient Greek and Latin culture as the highest standard of human achievement. The "sweetness and light" of dead cultures was a way of making the best that had been thought and known available through general education, and it was the Victorian bastion against materialism and anarchy.

R. Langley (✉)
Manhattanville College, Purchase, NY, USA
e-mail: langleyr@mville.edu

H. Wautischer et al. (eds.), *Philosophical Faith and the Future of Humanity*,
DOI 10.1007/978-94-007-2223-1_12, © Springer Science+Business Media B.V. 2012

and withdrawing on the Dover coast as similar to those Sophocles heard in "the tur-
bid ebb and flow of misery" on the Aegean shore thousands of years ago, Arnold
found a communion with humanity as the only solace of his straightened faith:

> The Sea of Faith
> Was once, too, at the full, and round earth's shore . . .
> But now I only hear
> Its melancholy, long, withdrawing roar,
> Retreating, to the breath
> Of the night-wind, down the vast edges drear. . .
>
> Ah, love, let us be true
> To one another! For the world which seems
> To lie before us like a land of dreams,
> So various, so beautiful, so new,
> Hath really neither joy, nor love, nor light,
> Nor certitude, nor peace, nor help for pain;
> And we are here as on a darkling plain
> Swept with confused alarms of struggle and flight,
> Where ignorant armies clash by night.

There is more philosophic rigor but a similar seriousness in Jaspers' concept of
philosophical faith in his philosophy of existence. Existentialism can be read as a
neo-Kantian philosophy of subjectivity. This thesis is not too radical as Kant also
inspired romanticism, pragmatism, phenomenology, and positivism. One can argue
that for the last three centuries metaphysics has been trapped within Kant's dis-
junction between knowable phenomena and unknowable noumena. The opening
sentence of the first *Critique* announces a magisterial theme: "Human reason," says
Kant, "has this peculiar fate . . . it is burdened by questions which . . . it is not able to
ignore, but which, as transcending all its powers, it is also not able to answer."[2] The
un-ignorable bit is the transcendental dimension of reason and the un-answerable
part is the relation of transcendental reason to the transcendent, i.e., to the question
of Being-in-itself and its relation to existence.

Kant plunged into the enchanted forest of consciousness to map out exact path-
ways that objects must follow to arrive at verifiable truth. Along the way he stumbled
upon the "less traveled" path of pure reason, which tries to go beyond our valid
understanding of trees and think the whole wood. In the first *Critique*, Kant confined
understanding to phenomena and posted warnings against trespassing, i.e. reason's
attempts to know the forest in-itself. At the end, Kant conceded that practical reason
was more important to ordinary humans than resolving metaphysical dilemmas. He
enunciated the famous thesis that made him the inspiration for these philosophies
named above: "I have therefore found it necessary to deny *knowledge*, in order to
make room for *faith*" (p. 29). Kant concluded that all philosophy reduced itself
to one question: What is man? And the answer, like Caesar's Gaul, was divided into
three parts: what can I know, what can I do, and what can I hope.

---

[2] Immanuel Kant, *Critique of Pure Reason*, trans. Norman Kemp Smith (New York, NY:
St. Martin's Press, 1965), p. 7. Further references in the text of this essay are to this edition.

Jaspers says Kant's genius was to see the need for different methodologies to answer the questions of knowing, doing, and hoping as each part of human anthropology simultaneously defines and limits the others. In this Kant was using philosophical faith to transcend the limitations of pure reason. Jaspers' own philosophizing transcends objectivity to a domain of non-cognitive, subjective experience of transcendence in immanence. The human being undergoes an originary leap from mere existence to possible Existenz by Transcendence in immanence, the experience of eternal being within ones particular historicity. This act of philosophic faith transforms the existent as he has the freedom to accept or refuse the possibility of Transcendence in immanence and the descent of Being into time. To maintain openness to the possibilities of transcending and transcendent, Jaspers proposes a form of non-cognitive knowing and a cipher language to indirectly express and communicate the lived reality of a faith beyond the objectivity of the world, religious revelation or dogmatic ontology.

Jaspers' conception of philosophical faith combines two of the deepest impulses of mankind: the need to know and the need to believe. He considers the possibility of a synthetic unity between knowledge and faith. Each term has an opposite. Hence, philosophic faith must show a way to reconcile knowing and not knowing and faith and disbelief and the truth claims of all four. Against the possibility of synthesis stands the immense diversity of faiths, beliefs, religions, philosophies, and dogmas culminating historically in relativism acted out with incredible violence. Pope John Paul's encyclical *Fides et Ratio* (1968) is but one of the multiple attempts to reconcile faith and reason.

This essay attempts to distinguish Jaspers' philosophical faith from religious faith by examining their respective contents. The content of a religious faith is what I believe. For example, the Apostles Creed enumerates the content of Roman Catholic faith. And the wedding ceremony binds each participant to the other "from this day forward." Each partner is pledged to the other to "have and to hold" in "sickness and in health, for richer or for poorer, until the hour of your death." The meaning of "I believe" and "I do" is my belief that all these holdings are true.

The content of a philosophic faith is more problematic because the terms are disjunctive. If I know something then I can demonstrate its truth; hence, I do not need belief. And if I believe, then I do not know if my belief is true. When Jaspers was asked the content of his philosophical faith, he answered, "Faith in God as the realization of transcendence, Faith in man as the possibility of freedom, Faith in possibilities in the world as openness beyond the limits of knowledge."[3]

---

[3] Leonard Ehrlich, *Karl Jaspers: Philosophy as Faith* (Amherst, MA: The University of Massachusetts Press, 1975), p. 137 [Henceforth cited as *PF*]. The quotation is from Karl Jaspers, *The Origin and Goal of History* (New Haven, CT: Yale University Press, 1979 (1949)), pp. 219–220. Ehrlich also cites propositions from a radio address by Jaspers in 1949–1950: Karl Jaspers, *The Perennial Scope of Philosophy,* trans. Ralph Mannheim (New York, NY: Philosophical Library, 1949), p. 30: "God is. There is an absolute imperative. The world is an ephemeral stage between God and existence."

There are two obvious difficulties. First, there is little or any distinction between this description and the religious faith of a liberal Protestant. Second, when philosophers talk about God, man and world they usually mean Being and its modes or the transcendent or the absolute. Jaspers is no exception but since his concept of philosophical faith is complex, it is worth investigation. He came to philosophical faith by an existential, transcendental method of hermeneutic. A hermeneutic is an open interpretation, so it implies the possibility of other interpretations.

In this essay, I will adopt a line from a poem as a framework for interpretations of the content of Jaspers' philosophic faith. In 1946, when Jaspers was freed from 12 years of internal exile in Nazi Germany, he published his reflections on man, history, truth, and faith. In the same year, Wallace Stevens wrote about the death of a pilot whose plane exploded in air. "Flyers Fall" ends with:

> Profundum, physical thunder, dimension in which
> We believe, without belief, beyond belief.[4]

The content of Jaspers' philosophic faith will be interpreted as *belief, without belief, and beyond belief.*

Philosophical Faith with Belief

> *Unless you believe, you will not understand*
> *(Augustine, De Libero Arbitrio).*

The faiths of theology and philosophy draw us toward experiences that are not comprehensible satisfactorily through perception and cognition. Faiths point to extra-ordinary realms that open us to the possibilities of freely transcending our mundane existence to realize enlarged and vital selves in union with God/Transcendence/Being. Faiths agonistically split over truth. For theology, truth is revealed and God commands us to believe as a condition for salvation. For philosophy the content is "man's risk of faith out of a freedom that is grounded in an ineffable transcendence."[5] The "ineffable" part is the scandal that there is no reason for the original "upsurge" of freedom in Existenz or the possibility of transcendence in immanence. The risk, of course, is the freedom to refuse and deny the promptings of faith.

One can view Jaspers' thinking as interpreting the nature and history of philosophy as leading toward his concept of philosophical faith and its historical clashes with revelations from theological faiths. Certainly, the analysis and clarification

---

[4] "Flyer's Fall" in *Wallace Stevens, Collected Poetry and Prose*, eds. Frank Kermode and Joan Richardson (New York, NY: The Library of America, 1996), p. 250. Poem cited by Richard Kearney, *Anatheism, Returning to God After God* (New York, NY: Columbia University Press, 2010), p. 3.

[5] Karl Jaspers, *Basic Philosophical Writings*, edited, translated and with introductions by Edith Ehrlich, Leonard H. Ehrlich, and George B. Pepper (Atlantic Highlands, NJ: Humanities Paperback Library, 1994 (1986)), editors' introduction, p. 441.

of different ways of transcending served as a principle of organization in his works. The three volumes of his *Philosophy* are divided into encompassing realms of World Orientation (objectivity), the Illumination of Existenz (subjectivity) and Metaphysics as a synthesis of world and Existenz as glimpsed in the language of cipher or of Being in itself understood as the unknowable encompassing of all encompassings. And *Von der Wahrheit* was a systematic analysis of all forms of knowledge according to different methods of scientific and philosophical thought. And Jaspers two books on faith, *Perennial Philosophy* and *Philosophic Faith and Revelation* bring together the conflicts between religious and philosophical faith.

What does faith add to philosophy? First, the subject of philosophical faith, my self-being "for which I am responsible" addresses the "ineffable" upsurge of transcendence in immanence: "Unfathomable deity grants me the calm and the impulse to do what I can as long as there is choice."[6] Second, faith is the impetus for the non-cognitive knowledge beyond the limits of objectivity of world orientation. As Jaspers says, "I do not believe when I have reason to know." And so, philosophical faith provides an account of "not knowing what I know" that assists me in freely choosing what I believe.

Not knowing for Socrates is a necessary condition for the search for truth. Early dialogues end without answering the "What is X?" question as it is applied to justice, courage, temperance, friendship, etc. Scholars suggest that these early negative dialogues were closer to Socrates actual method of philosophizing. Aristotle, for example, claims that Socrates asked questions but he professed ignorance and did not provide answers. Here is a summary argument of the negative dialogues. Virtue cannot be knowledge since virtue cannot be taught. Yet every inquiry into a particular virtue shows that each depends on some form of knowing or measure that separates each excellence or virtue from its opposite, e.g. justice from injustice, temperance from intemperance, etc. This leads to the paradox that virtue is knowledge, but it is not the kind of knowledge that can be taught or bought or provided by man for men. The consequences of Socratic ethics are: if virtue is knowledge; then, vice is ignorance; and, in scary entailments, no man errs knowingly, and it is better to suffer injustice than to act unjustly. Socrates was put to death for "bad teaching" and he was the first philosopher to suffer injustice for his philosophical faith in truth.

Of course, the real reason that knowledge, truth and wisdom cannot be taught or provided by man for man is that you already know: hence, the injunction that "the unexamined life is not worth living" and the insistence that primary task is to know yourself. Socrates claimed that there was no greater excellence then to spend a life inquiring into your own soul and the souls of other men. Philosophizing is overcoming the resistance to not knowing what you know.

The world history of philosophy and culture provide ways of encountering the knowledge that is within you. For example, Socrates was asked what would happen if, as he claimed, he did not know the truth and someone presented the truth to him?

---

[6] Karl Jaspers, *Philosophy*, 3 volumes, trans. E.B. Ashton (Chicago, IL: The University of Chicago Press, 1969 (1932)), vol. 2, p. 245. [Henceforth cited as *P* with volume number]

How can you recognize the truth unless you already know it! Plato's answer is *anamnesis* or recollection, first described as a myth *(Meno)* and presented as an acceptable argument for immortality *(Phaedo)*. What we call knowing is really remembering. Truth is recollection of what we know already and this connects to philosophical faith with belief. Dialectic is the struggle to communicate transcendence in immanence as a transformation of the soul.

To Jaspers, faith adds to philosophy a way of describing the existential choosing of transcendence in immanence; it also adds a way of knowing this lived experience with fidelity. What, on the other hand, does philosophy add to faith? First, it incorporates a skeptical reason that excludes dogma, creed, confession, closed theological systems, the authority or catholicity of ecclesiastical institutions as well as superstition, magic, mystical intuitions and Gnosticism. The positive value of negative philosophical faith is that it offers a tradition of negative philosophy that parallels negative theology.

Thomas Aquinas devoted the first question of *Summa Theologica* to distinctions between the knowledge provided by reason and revelation. He argued that all rational proofs of God's existence (including his own five demonstrations beginning with empirical facts: an object is moved, it is an effect, and it is contingent, and possessed of degrees of perfection, and includes mindless objects that behave purposively) establish only the fact that such a being exists as prime mover, first efficient cause, necessary being, highest perfection and intelligence that directs material objects "as the arrow is directed by the archer." All other knowledge of God, aside the assertion that X exists, are indirect, non-proper and negative proofs. God's nature, mode of being, attributes, predicates and names are knowable only through revelation. Aquinas utilizes this negative line of reasoning: because human beings are finite, contingent, imperfect, temporal, and particular we know by negation that God is infinite, necessary, perfect, eternal and universal. But this seemingly positive knowledge of God's Being actually consists solely of negations. Therefore, we are dependent upon faith in Biblical revelation for access to the divine.

The scholastic tradition supplemented negative theology with a positive doctrine of the analogy of Being. All analogy presupposes some likeness or resemblance between the primary and secondary analogues, e.g. that the relation of a watch to a watchmaker has a similar likeness to the relation between the universe and its creator. This, plus the scholastic adage *agere sequitur esse*, action follows being, provided analogies such as the improbable religious notion that we are made in the image and likeness of God.

Jaspers rejected the doctrine of the analogy of Being on several grounds. The simplest is that all four legs of analogy cannot stand because, to cite Kierkegaard, the finite is incommensurate with the infinite. Jaspers rejected analogy to his cost since it would have complimented the non-cognitive but knowable experiences and in conjunction with a rigorous skepticism toward the objectification of transcendence in immanence. This mix of elements would have offered a fuller interpretation of the content of faith as a sustained belief in negative philosophizing.

Philosophical Faith Without Belief

> *"All things are possible to him who believes." Then Jesus expels demons from a boy possessed, and the father responds, "I do believe, help thou my unbelief"*
> *(Mark 9:24).*

According to Jaspers, human consciousness cannot help making something absolute. Wotan, god of stress and frenzy and chief of the quarrelsome pantheon of Teutonic divinities, lamented his dependency upon human belief. "We exist only as long as they believe in us." Soon after, his youthful admirer announced, "God is dead!" Both Wagner and Nietzsche were wrong. Gods do not die. It is faith that dies.

Our deepest longings for Being and Truth, knowledge and belief, intermingle in philosophic faith. As we have seen, belief is the difference that makes a difference in freely choosing to become one's true self in Existenz and Transcendence, and to developing a knowable fidelity of communicable trust. Belief provides the existential content for the abstract definitional content of possibilities of transcendence, freedom, and openness in the world beyond determinate thought and objectivity. Philosophy adds to faith a skeptical reason that doubts all claims to universal certitude and denies definitive answers to metaphysical questions about being or appearance, nature or world, mind or body or even of faith itself.

Philosophical faith is a lived experience that transcends objectivity and subjectivity, to become an existence infused by belief in ethical and spiritual activity. It is different from religious faith in that philosophical faith promises no reward and it has no definable content. This lack of definition results from the philosophical dimension of faith. A thinking faith is essentially negative as it is not a body of factual knowledge, not based upon propositions of science, and not revelation. Philosophical faith is cognitively negative; a *Nichtwissen* that finds expression in the tradition of not knowing what we know and it is stated in a meaningful language of ciphers that is not demonstrable. This non-cognitive language conveys the non-rational experiences of freedom and transcendence in immanence.

But philosophizing based on negations generates its own problems. Engels remarked that the most important borrowing Marx and he took from Hegel was the contention that the negation of the negation was positive. What if it turns out not to be true? In math, zero multiplied by any number remains zero. In logic, arguments follow weakness so negative premises yield negative conclusions. This was Wotan's problem; what if doubt turns upon itself and belief becomes unbelief? A negative philosophy is a powerful offensive weapon against other positions, but a belief implies that its opposite is just as likely to be true. A consistently negative philosophy inevitably leads to endless disputations, despair and nihilism. And, as Kierkegaard pointed out, the Christian faith specifically prohibits despair as the "the sickness unto death."

The second hermeneutic interpretation of the content of philosophical faith is Jaspers' remarkably consistent account of philosophical faith without belief. It begins with the argument that belief and unbelief are conjoined in form and content:

> There is no faith unless there is unbelief; and with faith predicated upon unbelief, unbelief in turn exists only in view of the faith it denies... Faith and unbelief are the poles of self-being; when the tension between them has an end, when they eliminate each other as antitheses, philosophizing also has an end—for it springs as much from unbelief as from faith" (*P1* 255–256).

Two aspects of this passage are of particular importance: First, the notion that faith is an agonistic tension between belief and unbelief as mediated philosophically by skeptical doubt; and second, that philosophy itself is constituted by tensional struggles over contradictions between world, existence and ontology.

The general systematic of Jaspers comprehensive philosophical view is demarcated by boundary situations, limits, leaps, and gaps. In the realm of world orientation known by objective cognition there exist enormous, scientifically inexplicable gaps between inorganic nature, organic life, soul and mind (*P3* 130). We do not know the processes by which inert matter becomes organic, becomes animated, and develops cognition. In the upsurge to transcendence in immanence there is a leap from mere existence to the possibility of Existenz and freedom.

At the limits of objective world orientation we discover the encompassing that we are. But illumination of Existenz is a realm of subjectivity opposite to objectivity. According to Jaspers the self is the infinitely researchable object of the sciences but simultaneously, the subjective modes of Dasein, consciousness-as-such, spirit, possible Existenz is the "ineffable" and unknowable individual who created science and technology, art, religion, philosophy and cultures and civilizations. In *Man in the Modern World* Jaspers points out that man has created for himself what no god has ever provided.

In metaphysics this tensional opposition continues as objectivity and subjectivity meet in the encompassing of all encompassings or Being. How appearances relate to Being-in-itself remains a mystery. In effect, the realms of the encompassing limit one another. This oppositional characteristic also applies to his periechontology. The prefix "periech" suggests ontological processes above, around, or beyond static domains of objectivity and subjectivity.

The freedom encountered in the leap from existence to the possibility of Existenz and Transcendence was the capacity to refuse transcendence. In his philosophic anthropology especially, Jaspers provides an analytic of finitude that makes Arnold's poem seem merely nostalgic and romantic. The heritage of existentialism portrays every human being as inexorably conditioned by guilt, suffering, death and conflict. Attempts to capture "the promise of Being" in philosophy, religion, culture and art end with shipwreck. Nothing can stand on its own in the world and we cannot cling to Transcendence as both could easily be nothingness or illusions. Every totalizing viewpoint cognitively produces what Jaspers calls "foundering," our inability to think beyond contradictions, antitheses, beliefs and disbeliefs. Jaspers' psychiatric training leads him to think humans lack peace as individuals and collectively in their historicity. Human unrest is exacerbated by distinguishable modes of consciousness, spirit and reason with their respective methods of communication and truths. All of this foundering and shipwreck is re-enforced by destructive, unconscious drives that Jaspers describes as "passions of the night" as well as our built in disposition toward defiance.

Faith and unbelief is reduced to the opposition in which one concept is defined by its opposite. All categories of the comprehension of reality, including reason and anti-reason, existence and being, transcendent and immanent, oscillate between receding horizons, boundaries and limit situations. Even the realms of encompassing and periechontology are caught in tensional negation. One can look at every major and minor concept in Jaspers' work as a struggle in which one is defined in tension with another. As he says, "The boundary situations reveal that all our positives are tied to corresponding negatives" (*P3* 194).

The interpretation of philosophic faith without belief reads like a philosophy resembling de Saussure's description of language. In a dictionary, every word is defined in terms of other words and language is defined oppositionally and no single word has any positive denotation, e.g. white means only non-black and vice-versa.

Philosophical Faith Beyond Belief

> *"For what man knoweth the things of a man, save the spirit of a man which is in him?"*
> *(Saint Paul, I Corinthians 2:11)*

Beyond is a strong word. It suggests surpassing, crossing boundaries, limits and conflicts. Beyond also carries the implication of a new beginning as in Nietzsche's usage in his book title, *Beyond Good and Evil*. In Jaspers thought, beyond culminates his metaphysics and periechontology. Within the arsenal of spatial metaphors that make up the spiritual geometry of Jaspers' philosophizing, beyond has deep reverberations. Philosophical faith is beyond philosophy, the encompassing is beyond objectivity and subjectivity, periechontology is beyond ontology, and philosophizing is beyond doctrines and disputations. What lies beyond is an authentic philosophic life committed to philosophizing and moral and political activity. Consider the engaged tittles of Jaspers' later works: *The Question of German Guilt, The Atom Bomb and the Future of Mankind, Perennial Philosophy, Von der Wahrheit, Philosophical Faith and Revelation.* Jaspers invents cipher language to communicate his conception of philosophical faith beyond the antinomies of belief and unbelief and the foundering and shipwreck of reason.

Beyond belief there is a resolute philosophic faith without fear or expectation of reward, a committed faith as *Existenzen* living beyond cognitive certainty and without authority of revelation, institutional religion or political ideologies. In sum, philosophic faith is beyond negation and affirmation and is elected freely for possibilities for man, for the world and for Transcendence.

Faith brings together the multiplicity of visions of Being and Truth that is lived beyond belief and unbelief:

> Faith is not a matter of the goals of volition, nor of the contents or reason that become purposes. For faith cannot be willed, it does not consist in propositions between which one has to choose ...We cannot make our own transformation the goal of our wills; it must, rather, be bestowed upon us, if we live in such a fashion that we experience the gift. . ."[7]

What is impressed through the originary upsurge of transcendence can be expressed indirectly. The transcendental method seeks the indeterminate metaphysical ground of being and of human freedom. Cipher language is Jaspers' original contribution to grasping the meaning of metaphysics of encompassing realms of periechontology as determinate realms of objects and subjects. All forms of human thought are determinate–intentionally about some object or subject–so thinking is inadequate. Ciphers are a language, a script, a communicable non-knowing that cannot be fully achieved or decoded. For Jaspers, ciphers are manifestations of imperfect truths. Ricoeur claims that ciphers are actually Jaspers' philosophy of religion. The content of philosophical faith is a mask for rational theology directed toward a hidden God. Ciphers are symbols and more than symbols. They function as non-cognitive lures that cannot be comprehended as determinate thoughts. But if ciphers are lived they are identical with philosophical faith itself.[8]

In contrast to Ricoeur's interpretation, Leonard Ehrlich pursues Jaspers' attempt to realize truth and freedom beyond the limits of world orientation and the foundering of subjectivity by interpreting the content of philosophical faith as an "ingenious synthesis" (*PF* Introduction, 5ff.). This interpretation of the content of philosophical faith argues as follows. Philosophy excludes transcendence in immanence as neither knowable nor demonstrable. And theology or revealed truth dogmatically closes philosophizing against the relativity and precariousness of the truths of existential historicity. Hence, only philosophical faith can go beyond philosophy and theology as its content is neither factual nor a supernatural revelation nor a description of the *fait accompli* of transcendence itself but rather, philosophical faith is a guide to transcendent communication as a synthesis of Existenz and Transcendence.

In Ehrlich's brilliant analysis and interpretation, "ingenuity" is a contributing factor of the "ingenious synthesis." As evident in the previous pages, the concepts and categories of Jaspers' philosophizing limit one another and their transcendence finds its boundary situation in foundering over oppositional thinking. Similarly Wotan's undoing was the unbelief born from a dying faith. But Wotan was resurrected by renewed belief as storm troopers marched beyond Germany into a Second World War. Both belief and unbelief are infected by philosophical skepticism, so

---

[7] Karl Jaspers, *The Origin and Goal of History* (Westport, CT: Greenwood Press, 1976 (1949)), p. 214.

[8] Paul Ricoeur, "The Relation of Jaspers' Philosophy to Religion" in *The Philosophy of Karl Jaspers, Augmented Edition*, edited by Paul Arthur Schilpp (La Salle, IL: Open Court Publishing Company, 1981 (1957)), pp. 611–642.

the ingenuity is to take reason beyond objective and subjective limits toward a loving struggle of persuasive communication rather than shipwrecked on the shoals of absolute disjunctions.

The second item of synthesis is periechontology, which discloses the modes of the encompassing in oppositional forms characterized by distinctions, irreducibility and inter-relation. The encompassing combined with the notion of a general fundamental knowledge is the essentially philosophizing out of historicity and openness above and beyond all closed ontologies or inert systems of abstract ideas. The third item of synthesis is "general fundamental knowledge" which confronts the multiplicity of versions of truth of Being. Jaspers deals with this systematically in his philosophic logic, *Von der Wahrheit*, and historically in the *The Great Philosophers*. These never completed tasks invoke something like a Jaspersian version of general and special relativity. In general terms, it is impossible to extract one truth of Being from multiple intellectual versions but it is equally impossible to deny that the truth might reside in a particular system. The special theory of cognitive relativity is Jaspers' synthetic notion that all systems in their historicity share partial truths and that no philosophical system owns truth exclusively.

The final element of the ingenious synthesis is philosophical faith itself as "the risk of thought concerning matters about which man is essentially ignorant . . . the basis of the multiplicity of human visions of ultimate truth... Moreover, the confirmation of freedom through the plurality of faiths and the founding of human communication and community on this plurality of faiths are, for Jaspers, the main promises of a philosophical reflection on the nature of faith" (*PF* 8).

This interpretation of the content of philosophical faith as beyond belief is more satisfactory than the previous two. It takes the content of faith as beyond the negation of the negation that culminates in reason's foundering. The ending of philosophical faith becomes the beginning of a living faith which creates its own content and is for Jaspers not a knowledge one has, but a certainty that guides one beyond all boundaries and limits and ciphers.

Philosophy of Revelation: Remarks on Schelling, Jaspers, and Rosenzweig

Wolfdietrich Schmied-Kowarzik

Abstract Franz Rosenzweig and Karl Jaspers both made references to Schelling's *Philosophie der Offenbarung*. Despite his overall favorable reception, Jaspers disagreed with Schelling's ontological certainty of faith; in contrast, Rosenzweig develops in his *Stern der Erlösung* how Schelling succeeded with overcoming idealism in favor of a "new thinking." From these two contrasting interpretations it becomes clear that careful study of Schelling's philosophy allows for a contemporary perspective to the problem of philosophical faith—a position that was demonstrated by Leonard H. Ehrlich.

Unfortunately Rosenzweig could no longer experience that Jaspers would prove to be a principle member of that "small circle" [of the "new thinking"]. For independently of Rosenzweig, yet under the influence of Kierkegaard, some motives are presented in that first major work by Jaspers [*Philosophie*, 1931] in the framework of a renewal of fundamental philosophy that are also to be found by Rosenzweig under the designation of "new thinking," among them above all sacrifice and the risk of one's own individual temporality as verification of one's own individual basic truth; the historicity of truth on which humans base themselves; and especially as the necessary basis of tolerance, the dialogical in the encounter of humans with varying basic truths (Jaspers calls it communication).[1]

Prefatory Remarks

The similarities in the philosophical approaches of Franz Rosenzweig and Karl Jaspers are not surprising, for they both belong to those thinkers who, in the first decades of the twentieth century and coming from entirely different directions, tried to overcome scholasticism by moving toward a new existential thinking. Their thinking exhibits striking differences that are not only biographically determined, but rather have to do with their different appropriations of philosophical tradition, which results in profound consequences for their thinking.

---

[1] Leonard H. Ehrlich, "Neues Denken und Erneuerung der Fundamentalphilosophie," in *Franz Rosenzweigs "neues Denken*," ed. Wolfdietrich Schmied-Kowarzik, 2 Vol. (Freiburg/München: K. Alber, 2006), pp. 76 f. Translation of this essay and all quotations from German to English by Josiah Simon.

W. Schmied-Kowarzik (✉)
University of Kassel, Kassel, Germany
e-mail: schmied-kowarzik@aon.at

H. Wautischer et al. (eds.), *Philosophical Faith and the Future of Humanity*,
DOI 10.1007/978-94-007-2223-1_13, © Springer Science+Business Media B.V. 2012

One of these points of difference comes from their similar-minded yet contrary continuation of a philosophical battle of giants over ultimate foundations for self-determination of humans in the world, which resurfaced through Schelling's critique of Hegel and Idealism. The opposition between the advocates of being and those of ideas, which Plato had already believed to have overcome dialectically,[2] became newly enflamed in unexpected complexity and radicality between the once adolescent friends Hegel and Schelling. For a time Hegel seemed to have won the battle for the advocates of ideas with his philosophical system of absolute Idealism. Yet lo and behold, his adolescent friend Schelling, who had once founded the thoughts of the absolute system together with him, arose and positioned himself as a critic of Idealism.

Hegel had summed up the unity of thinking and being—dialectically closing the fundamental ideas of Parmenides—as the overarching unity of thinking over itself and other. With this absolute Idealism Hegel believed to have completed a truly presuppositionless philosophy, for in the re-enactment of all forms of comprehended being it is at once self-awareness of the absolute Spirit that penetrates everything.[3]

Hegel's philosophy lives on a presupposition that evades closure, for it is based on a denial. Declaring itself to be presuppositionless, Hegel presupposes that there is only thinking and that being is only a predicate—even if the most immediate—of thinking (WL5 126ff). Being is thought of as its other—not as the other of thinking— that which thought is to comprehend and has comprehended. This absolute Idealism is indeed ingenious with its overarching dialectic, but it denies—right from the first thought—the independent existence of being. This denial had always occupied Schelling, although he managed to clearly address it in only his late philosophy as a critique of Hegel's absolute Idealism.[4]

Of course the comprehension of reality in all its forms remains an important task of philosophy as system, which Schelling calls purely rational or negative philosophy (SW11 255ff). But such a comprehension inevitably makes reality into an object, into its object, i.e., thinking is here from the outset the exclusive subject of comprehension, which, as encompassing spirit, secures for itself all beings as its object—as this, by all means, aptly paraphrases Hegel. But this can only be a representation of the paraphrasing of cognition, and does not reach our existential-practical orientation in the historical world, which is addressed in Schelling's positive philosophy. For as thinking individuals we find ourselves thrown immemorially (unvordenklich) into historical existence, which can certainly not be captured by thinking in general.

For becoming aware of this immemorial existence, thought must enter into ecstasis—as Schelling says—of its overriding will to know in order to allow the other of existence to come forth as the actual absolute subject and to understand

---

[2] Plato, Sophistes 246 a ff.

[3] Georg Friedrich Wilhelm Hegel, Wissenschaft der Logik II, Werke 6 (Frankfurt am Main: Suhrkamp, 1969), pp. 548 ff. [Henceforth cited as WL with volume number]

[4] Friedrich Wilhelm Schelling, Zur Geschichte der neueren Philosophie, in Sämtliche Werke X (Stuttgart/Augsburg: Cotta, 1856), pp. 126 ff. [Henceforth cited as SW with volume number]

itself from its perspective (*SW9* 229f). Only after this, can thinking lift itself up again and ask how it can comprehensively grasp its existential being from the primacy of existence, the occurring history. Schelling's positive philosophy does not deal with the comprehension of the world in universals, but rather with our very own orientation in the occurring history within which we already existentially find ourselves.[5]

Both Rosenzweig, as well as Jaspers, are fascinated with Schelling's awakening to an existential philosophy and definitely understand themselves as Schelling's successors. Yet they both hold Schelling's realization of his positive philosophy, which peaks in the *Philosophy of Revelation* (*SW13, 14*), as failed, but draw entirely different consequences from this failure. For Rosenzweig (following here his cousin Hans Ehrenberg),[6] Schelling's critique of Hegel and Idealism, and with this his reversal from a negative to a positive philosophy, plays the fundamental role in his thinking. Hence he understands his *Star of Redemption*[7] as completing what Schelling's *Philosophy of Revelation* could not accomplish. In contrast, Jaspers values Schelling's concern for a positive philosophy, yet he considers it Gnostic enthusiasm in its realization, and he contrasts it with a philosophy of illumination of existence (*Existenzerhellung*) that attempts to overcome revelatory faith with "philosophical faith."[8]

Schelling's *Philosophy of Revelation*

Positive philosophy fulfills itself for Schelling in his *Philosophy of Mythology* and the *Philosophy of Revelation,* which Schelling gave as lectures beginning in 1832 in Munich and after 1841 in Berlin.[9] Both lectures present Schelling's great and grandiose philosophy of the history of consciousness of humanity, admittedly applied in a focused manner only on the "necessary God-placing consciousness" (*notwendig Gott-setzendes Bewusstsein*). Here Schelling deals with the historical coming-to-ones-self of human consciousness, human freedom, in its relation to the absolute: in the face of God.[10] Historical philosophy does not mean here telling

---

[5] See Wolfdietrich Schmied-Kowarzik, „Sinn und Existenz in der Spätphilosophie Schellings" (Wiener diss., 1963).

[6] Hans Ehrenberg, *Die Parteiung der Philosophie. Studien wider Hegel und den Kantianismus* (1911) (Essen: Die Blaue Eule, 1998).

[7] Franz Rosenzweig, *Der Stern der Erlösung* (1921) (Frankfurt am Main: Suhrkamp, 1988), in *Der Mensch und sein Werk. Gesammelte Schriften* II, The Hague 1976. See also Franz Rosenzweig, "Das neue Denken," in *Zweistromland. Kleinere Schriften* in *Der Mensch und sein Werk. Gesammelte Schriften*, Vol. III (The Hague: Nijhoff, 1979).

[8] Karl Jaspers, *Der philosophische Glaube* (München: R. Piper, 1948).

[9] F.W.J. Schelling, *Urfassung der Philosophie der Offenbarung*, 2 vols., ed. Walter E. Ehrhardt (Hamburg: F. Meiner, 1992). [Henceforth cited as *UPO* with volume number]

[10] See Paul Tillich, *Die religionsgeschichtliche Konstruktion in Schellings positiver Philosophie* (Breslau: H. Fleischmann, 1910).

stories of the past, but rather finding the standpoint for one's individual present decisiveness with its directional "horizon" on the future, which is still to be determined and is placed within shared human responsibility.

Seen from the perspective of our present freedom, the *Philosophy of Mythology* is set, as it were, as pre-past. In it we realize the unconscious natural history of human awakening, the pre-conscious history to the freedom of consciousness. The mythological worlds of the Gods and the theogonous process, which happens through the history of myths, are no arbitrary inventions of humans, but instead very real and powerful. In its naturalness, the necessary process of consciousness is expressed here, in which the potentials of consciousness that have not yet come about, still independently rule over human consciousness as Gods and battles of Gods. Only in this way is it possible to explain how the mythological process is a collective happening that so totally occupies human consciousness that it can be driven to all possible forms of human sacrifice, bewitching magic, and religious ecstasy. Only in its later form of mythology of art and its treatment in tragedy does human consciousness push through to become self-conscious, of course comprehended still entirely in tragic opposition to the dominance of fate. Schelling illustrates this by using the figure of Prometheus (*SW12* 482).

With Schelling's *Philosophy of Revelation* we enter into the present of our human freedom. The figure through which we become conscious of this freedom—according to Schelling—is Jesus of Nazareth.[11] In Jesus of Nazareth human consciousness has entered into the complete independence of its freedom and yet it does not place itself as absolute here, but rather avows itself to its origin as Son of the Father. It is precisely through Schelling's avowal of Jesus of Nazareth as an act of freedom, where Jesus asserts, "I am not God," but rather, "I am sent from the Father"—precisely herein, according to Schelling, Jesus becomes Christ.

> The son could exist independently of the father in his own glory, he could be external to and without God the father, namely Lord of being, he could actually, indeed not according to his essence, be God. But the glory which he could have had independently from the Father was rejected by the son, and herein he is Christ. That is the basic idea of Christianity. (*SW14* 37)

Through this remaining difference between Father and son, God and man, a third horizon is opened, namely, the still outstanding horizon of the unification of Father and son, God and man in the spirit of love that is assigned to us.

With this we enter into our present consciousness of freedom. But it will still be a while before it is really our own freedom. This is the history of the emulation of Christ, i.e., the conscious appropriation of our freedom; this is the history of Christianity, which for Schelling is not yet closed. There is first the example of the Catholic church of Peter, in which human freedom is still represented through the authority of the church and in its moments of forgetting Christ

---

[11] Cf. Wolfdietrich Schmied-Kowarzik, „Vom Totalexperiment des Glaubens. Kritisches zur positiven Philosophie Schellings und Rosenzweigs", in: Wolfdietrich Schmied-Kowarzik, ed., *Franz Rosenzweig. Existentielles Denken und gelebte Bewährung* (Freiburg/München: K. Alber, 1991).

(*Christusvergessenheit*) places itself as a human institution as absolute and proceeds with brutal terror against all who are not obedient to it. And there is second the church of Paul adopting the figure of Protestantism, in which every individual is called independently into the freedom of emulation, which in its own moments of forgetting Christ degrades into the absolute self-glorification of humans with all their principles of realization of their interests. We stand in this epoch of disunity, but with a hope and an aspiration for a future church of John, which will be a philosophical community of solidarity, freedom, and love (*UPO2* 700ff).[12]

Jaspers' Critique of Revelation

Karl Jaspers' critique of Schelling's Philosophy of Revelation is in no way an external critique, rather a critique that takes Schelling's concerns very seriously, and tries to disclose the reasons for its failure. Initially Jaspers emphasizes that Schelling by no means starts from a revelatory faith (*Offenbarungsglauben*) and by no means completed a return to Christian faith as a philosopher, but only elucidates Christianity exegetically. He expressly emphasizes that revelation for Schelling does not represent the source of his philosophizing, but rather its object.[13]

Jaspers understands revelation as an "immediate, temporally and spatially localized proclamation of God through word, demand, act, and occasion."[14] It is justified and passed on through prophets, apostles and priests and it is secured through institutions, which hold together the religious community of faith. Schelling does not invoke all of these factors but strives, as he himself says, toward a still outstanding "philosophical religion," which he hopes to reach through his philosophical-religious historical penetration of mythology and Christian revelatory faith (*SW13* 133; *UPO* 60, 105).

It is here that Jaspers' actual critique begins. While Schelling's *Philosophy of Mythology* and *Philosophy of Revelation* represent a pioneering achievement for understanding myth and Christianity, he does nonetheless see religious testimonies all too often as historical factualities instead of regarding them as historical ciphers (*Chiffren*) of transcendence. Even though Schelling himself understands his positive philosophy as an "existential philosophy"[15] that attempts, above and beyond the science of reason of negative philosophy, to reach a positive meaning of man in his historical existence, he hardly succeeds "in finding a cipher out of his own existential experience that grasps it" (Aber es gerät ihm kaum, aus eigener existentieller Erfahrung eine Chiffer zu finden, die ergriffe, *SGV* 107). His realizations

---

[12] F.W.J. Schelling, *Urfassung der Philosophie der Offenbarung*, 1992, Vol. II, pp. 700 ff.

[13] Karl Jaspers, *Schelling. Größe und Verhängnis* (1955) (München: R. Piper, 1986), pp. 59, 103. [Henceforth cited as *SGV*]

[14] Karl Jaspers, *Der philosophische Glaube angesichts der Offenbarung* (München: R. Piper, 1962), p. 49. [Henceforth cited as *PGO*]

[15] Karl Rosenkranz, *Hegels Leben* (1844) cited from *SGV* 98.

always degenerate into a Gnostic knowledge dealing with ultimate things. Schelling attempts thereby, as he had already had in mind as a youth in the "Oldest System-Program of German Idealism" (1796) discovered by Franz Rosenzweig,[16] to reach the "foundation of philosophical religion" that embraces all humans.

Jaspers goes up decisively against Schelling's Gnostic "foundation of philosophical religion" (*SGV* 109; *PGO* 236) precisely in order to save the concerns of Schelling's positive philosophy. An existential-practical orientation in lived history that goes beyond the "science of reason," or rather scientific insights, can in turn not be reached through knowledge and also does not lead to a philosophically founded religion. That which alone can bring about a positive philosophizing, towards which Schelling declaredly strives, is the "existential illumination" (*Existenzerhellung*) of our being-in-the-world, which verdantly understands itself in the "philosophical faith" of an absolute context (*Sinnzusammenhang*). But both do not constitute knowledge, but rather move in ciphers, which indeed deeply touch our existence in the world and our orientation on transcendence but which we accept, at the same time, as provisional interpretations.

> As existence we think towards transcendence in objects that we call ciphers.... Yet the inadequacy of all ciphers is shown in that I can only adhere to them like pictures or like guidelines in the existential moment, not as a reality that secures me as such. (PGO 153ff.)

In this context Japers believes he must take up the dialectic, which is indeed "most richly developed by Hegel" but which, for Hegel, aspires to an "absolute knowledge" that philosophy can never hope to reach. Jaspers, therefore, alludes to the existential dialectic that Søren Kierkegaard developed in criticizing Hegel. In contrast to the supposed certainty of revelation, this dialectical speech of philosophical faith remains in the balance of ciphers (*in der Schwebe der Chiffren*): "The dialectical way of thinking is a form for sharing the ciphers of transcendence that speak to humans in that ambiguous balance, but which do not submit them to it" (*PGO* 181).

Because philosophy cannot withdraw itself from the problem of transcendence—the context of existence in which we are placed without ever catching up with it—Jaspers speaks of "philosophical faith." In contrast to revelatory faith (*Offenbarungsglaube*), which "deems to know the acts of God in self-revelation for the salvation of mankind," philosophical faith knows not of God but only "hears the language of ciphers. God himself is a cipher for it" (*PGO* 196). For philosophers there can be no revelation as an historically occurring proclamation of God, neither the self-naming of God "I will be who I will be" (*Ich werde sein, der ich sein werde*) nor the becoming human of God can be understood by philosophy other than as revelation of the transcendental in humankind. In this sense Karl Jaspers says:

> The religion of Christ contains the truths that God speaks to humans through humans, but God speaks through many humans, in the Bible through the line of prophets, in which Jesus stands as the last one; no human can be God; God does not speak exclusively through one human, and still through each ambiguously. (SGV 80)

---

[16] F.W.J. Schelling, "Das ältestes Systemprogramm des deutschen Idealismus," in *Mythologie der Vernunft*, eds. Christoph Jamme und Helmut Schneider (Frankfurt am Main: Suhrkamp, 1984); see also *SGV* 56.

Rosenzweig's Revaluation of Revelation

Franz Rosenzweig ties into Schelling's late philosophy much differently and more decisively, yet he also emphasizes that Schelling fails in the realization of his ingenious project. Writing the first two parts of the *Star of Redemption,* Rosenzweig attempts to redeem what Schelling intended to accomplish by way of the reversal from negative to positive philosophy.[17]

In the first part, Rosenzweig establishes the self-limitation of philosophy in ways similar to Schelling, leading to a reversal in philosophical thinking that Schelling characterized as the turn from negative to positive philosophy. Negative or "purely rational philosophy" can only comprehend general or abstract structure apart from which nature, man, and God cannot be conceived; but the existentially occurring reality, that we ourselves are historically part of, remains for it a miracle that reason cannot grasp. In the "Transition" to the second part, thinking undergoes "a turn," a "reversal" from purely rational philosophy, that wants everything to proceed from it without suppositions, to a thinking that tries to ground and understand historical occurrence in its multiple dimensions of meaning.[18]

The introduction to the second part "On the Possibility of Experiencing Miracles—*In theologos!*" refers to a miracle, yet nothing is meant by this that contradicts the philosophical knowledge of the world in its structural generality. Here the antecedent existence of an historically occurring reality itself comes into view, in which we as thinking people find ourselves immemorially (*unvordenklich*). Herein lays revelation in the broadest sense of the word, that the historical existence in which we find ourselves can be revealed to us as a context of meaning, and in it we can find the way to ourselves existentially.

The miracle of the historical reality in which we find ourselves as existing and in which we try to unlock in its meaningfulness is threefold: (a) the creaturely being of creation, (b) the linguistically disclosed meaning of revelation, and (c) being ethically oriented toward a kingdom of redemption. In these factors our existence unlocks in a threefold temporal manner: as continual past, as renewing present, and as assigned future. Just as the miracle of creation will be experienced through its ever-enduring being "already there"—and thus the miracle of revelation occurs in the "always-renewed present" of language, in the being-able-to-speak-together of mankind; and the miracle of redemption is eternally awaited in the "coming of the kingdom" which we strive towards through acts of neighborly love, even though its fulfillment does not lie in our power alone (*SR* 121, 174, 242). Only together do these three dimensions form the foundation of the historicity of human existence outline the horizons of meaning of human actions and our hopes in history. The new

---

[17] Franz Rosenzweig, *Briefe und Tagebücher,* I, in *Der Mensch und sein Werk. Gesammelte Schriften* (The Hague: Martinus Nijhoff, 1979), p. 701. See also Franz Rosenzweig, *The Star of Redemption,* trans. William W. Hallo (Notre Dame and London: University of Notre Dame Press, 1985), pp. 19f. [Henceforth cited as *SR*]

[18] See Wolfdietrich Schmied-Kowarzik, *Rosenzweig im Gespräch mit Ehrenberg, Cohen und Buber* (Freiburg/München: Alber, 2006).

thinking, as Rosenzweig formulates it in connection to Schelling, confronts this temporal being-placed-in-the-course-of-history as experiential, as narrative, and as historical thinking. Language pulsates in the center of the human search for meaning in its historical existence as the living site of all revelation and of everything becoming revealed (*Offenbarwerden*).

> [L]anguage, for all it is all there, all created from the beginning, nevertheless awakes to real vitality only in revelation. And thus nothing in the miracle of revelation is novel, nothing is the intervention of sorcery in created creation, but rather it is wholly sign, wholly the process of making visible and audible the providence which had originally been concealed in the speechless night of creation, wholly—revelation. . . . The human word is a symbol; with every moment it is newly created in the mouth of the speaker, but only because it is from the beginning and because it already bears in its womb every speaker who will one day effect the miracle of renewing it. But the divine word is more than symbol: it is revelation only because it is at the same time the word of creation. "God said, Let there be light"—and what is the light of God? It is the soul of man. (*SR* 111)

With this discovery, Rosenzweig found what Jaspers sought in vain when he wrote: "If it were possible to allow revelation as such to become a cipher, then a transformation in revelatory faith would come about" (*PGO* 505). Such transformation is now fulfilled Rosenzweig's *The Star of Redemption*, who found a new philosophical-theological form of expression for "existential experience" which Jaspers justifiably found lacking in Schelling, and he also sheds a new light on Schelling's *Philosophy of Revelation* which we can now understand and appreciate more deeply than Jaspers was able to do.

Philosophy as Faith

In the second part of the *Star of Redemption*, Rosenzweig was successful in giving the concept of revelation a fundamental philosophical-theological interpretation with which he anticipates an answer to Jaspers. However, he does fall into the firing line of Jaspers' critique with respect to the third part of *SR*, for Rosenzweig places himself in the immanent certainty of the Jewish and Christian community of faith, i.e., he is speaking here from the self-conception of the revelatory faith of Jews and Christians without reflecting on the cipher-like nature (*Chiffrenhaftigkeit*) of his speech. Moreover, Rosenzweig only grants a revelatory faith to Jews and Christians and discounts all other communities of faith—including the community of faith of Islam—as heathen religions still to be won over for revelatory faith.

In the first chapter of the third volume "The Fire or the Eternal Life"—the interior of the Star of David—Rosenzweig goes into the life of the Jews, which is determined by their dialogue with God who revealed them as eternally His people. The cycle of Jewish festivals and prayers is also determined by and steeped in this promise (*SR* 298ff). They are lifted out of the course of world history as is expressed in the liturgy of the annual Jewish festivals which all point to occurrences of revelation to the people of Israel confirming and sealing the eternal union of God with His people. The life and liturgy of Christian people is determined entirely differently, as Rosenzweig addresses in the second chapter, "The Rays or the Eternal Way"—external rays of the Star of David that lead out into the darkness of a heathen world. "Christianity must proselytize. . . . Indeed proselytizing is the veritable form of its self-preservation for Christianity. It propagates by spreading" (*SR* 341). Different than Judaism, which is bound to the eternal life of a particular people, Christianity is a broad community of believers that includes all people who believe in Christ and emulate him. Christianity therefore turns to everyone as potential believers and it can only procreate itself through the faith of each individual and his testimonial dissemination. The liturgy of all annual Christian holidays relate to the historical existence of Jesus of Nazareth on earth and point to Christ as the mediator of the new union of believers with God.

For Rosenzweig, the decisive point comes after his characterization of the contrasts between Jews and Christians, namely, the offer of a Jewish-Christian partnership that goes beyond the irresolvable separation. The entire truth lies neither in Jewish faith, which is rooted in the promised eternal life of the Jewish people, nor in Christian faith, which promises redemption by the emulation of the eternal way, for this truth is only to be found in God alone (*SR* 380), and this is the result of the third chapter, "The Star or the Eternal Truth." Both Jews and Christians can experience their boundaries and limits through each other. According to Jewish doctrine, the kingdom of redemption can first come about only when all the people of the world have returned to God and, for Christian doctrine, the people of Israel remain the witness of their ancient union with God. Thus both Jews and Christians are separated in the fulfillment of their individual tasks, yet mutually inter-dependant in order to fulfill their respective tasks. Only together are they guarantors of the promise, only together are they the fire-radiating Star of Redemption, ignited by God (*SR* 415ff).

Certainly Rosenzweig here has a grandiose vision of Jewish-Christian relations and dialogue, and it was only possible during his time in a small circle of friends and began after the Shoah in Europe between certain Christian churches and the Jewish religious community. Rosenzweig addresses the contents of faith for Jews and Christians, and only these two communities of faith, as realities in his vision of reconciliation. According to Jaspers, such expectation is not possible for philosophers, since pictures or images of faith (*Glaubensbilder*) can always only be ciphers. Taken as ciphers and applied to all communities of faith, Rosenzweig's proposition that the fullness of truth is only in God and within which Jews and Christians play their individual roles, we encounter a profound insight that harmonizes with Jaspers' proposition regarding the "impossibility to know God and the inevitability to think him" (Die Unmöglichkeit, Gott zu erkennen, und die Unumgänglichkeit, ihn zu denken, *PGO* 386). When taken as a proposition that was revealed only to Jews and Christians, we encounter a provocation for all the communities of faith that are left out, but rather forced to accept it, as Jaspers would say, "an impossibility" for philosophy as faith. Jaspers expresses this unequivocally in relation to the Christological foundations of Christianity: Christ, the God who became man, is philosophically impossible, but Jesus can speak as a unique cipher. Jesus, as man, is a cipher of being human: The reality of the human Jesus is an incomparable, unique cipher of the possibility of man before God. He is not the revelation of God, but through him something of God can become revealed to us.

In relation to Judaism, one can just as well say that as a reality the covenant of God with the people of Israel is a philosophical impossibility; but that as a cipher the people of Israel as chosen reveals the uniqueness of God as historically revealed and that the people of Israel will hold true to this cipher of the uniqueness of God until the day when all humans and peoples have found their way to such divine reflection (*Gottesgedanken*).[19]

Concluding Remarks

The philosopher, as Jaspers rightly noted, can never submit to a particular religious faith. The philosopher can and should attempt to understand and penetrate the religious ciphers of one or another religious faith and feel himself closer to an understanding of one or another faith; but these ciphers can never represent realities that are valid in place of philosophical reflection.

On this point Jaspers feels related to Schelling, who tried to philosophically penetrate the mythological contents of Christian faith with his *Philosophy of Revelation*. Admittedly Schelling wants too much when he tries to condense philosophical insight into a philosophical religion that does have a bearing on the existing denominations and thereby represents a higher form of religion reaching and including all humans by way of combining philosophical and religious thought.

If Jaspers had been familiar with the third part of the *Star of Redemption* he would have protested against Rosenzweig in a way similar to his protest against Schelling. For after Rosenzweig brilliantly found his way through the second part of *SR* to a new philosophical-theological discourse on creation, revelation, and redemption (which even outdoes in terms of its complexity what Jaspers calls illumination of existence), Rosenzweig then falls back again upon the assured faith of a specific religious denomination, more accurately, of two denominations. It is here that Rosenzweig shows an indiscriminate transgression of the threshold between philosophy and theology.[20]

Philosophical faith, as Jaspers understands it, is refused an understanding of the contents of faith of a religion other than as ciphers for transcendence. The feeling of security in the certainty of a historically developed community of faith is denied to the philosopher who can neither understand himself from here nor verify himself in it; with and before God one remains alone. Of course the philosopher also knows that his thinking is related to praxis, yet its horizon lies in the ethical verification of

---

[19] Hermann Cohen, *Religion der Vernunft aus den Quellen des Judentums* (1919) (Darmstadt: J. Melzer, 1966), p. 39. See also Wolfdietrich Schmied-Kowarzik, *Rosenzweig im Gespräch mit Ehrenberg, Cohen und Buber* (Freiburg/München: Alber, 2006), p. 127.

[20] See Leonard H. Ehrlich, *Karl Jaspers: Philosophy as Faith* (Amherst, MA: University of Massachusetts Press, 1975), pp. 222 ff.

being human, which he has to verify before God with a view towards all humanity together with those of like mind. Taken aback in face of the limits of communities of faith the philosopher asks: Do we not all belong as humans to the chosen people and are we not all God's children to love our neighbor to the fullest?

As such the philosopher is given another important task. In the end every community of faith remains self-referential and isolates itself from all others. It was always philosophers who did the work of translation beyond the limits of faith and made the claim for the understanding and acceptance of communities of faith for each other. Karl Jaspers belongs without a doubt to those thinkers for whom the work of translation from one religious world of thought to another is successful in an impressive manner and who contributes to the understanding and agreement of religions amongst themselves.

Thinking from the Origin: Critical and Personal Remarks on Jaspers' Philosophy of Philosophizing

Armin Wildermuth

Abstract The intention of Jaspers' thought aims at a philosophy of philosophizing. This gives a central role to one's existential experience of philosophies. In this context Jaspers' *Philosophie* (1932) is an instance of existential philosophy. However, from a biographical perspective it can be understood as an instance of transformative psychopathology. During the 1930s Jaspers developed the concept of the encompassing, which resulted in a departure from his previous existenz-philosophical impetus. Ontological presuppositions and his motivation to develop a philosophical systematic disguise his original impulse for existential illumination (*Existenzerhellung*). Even with such critique, the author concedes that Jaspers was existentially charismatic as a person and also in his achievements.

The Primacy of Philosophizing

Philosophizing is more important for Jaspers than any philosophy. This should not be forgotten when one examines and describes his own philosophy. Its essence, as has been recognised, is to understand and personally acquire philosophy. This philosophy of philosophizing assumes its particular meaning through Jaspers' own existence. Its vantage point lies outside abstract theoretical philosophy. This immediately recalls Kierkegaard, who approaches system-oriented philosophy from the standpoint of Christian faith, and who caused it to founder on the rock of subjectivity through his dialectic. Kierkegaard and Jaspers demand us to take a leap in order to find our way out of abstract philosophy and thereafter back into it. Jaspers strives to introduce philosophy to philosophisers. Failing existential involvement, philosophies remain mere intellectual pastimes. The aim of philosophizing is the failure of abstractly formulated philosophies, together with the experience that philosophies, in particular those of historical rank, lead beyond themselves to existence. What philosophies are good for at best is the creation of an awareness of transcendence. Philosophies are thus transformed into existential appeals that concern the entire existence of the philosophiser. In contrast to Jaspers, Kierkegaard deliberately

---

Translation from German into English of this essay and of all quotations by Mark Kyburz.

A. Wildermuth (✉)
University of St. Gallen, St. Gallen, Switzerland
e-mail: wildermutha@bluewin.ch

seeks to lead theoretical philosophy astray into the absurd and the paradoxical, in order to provoke a change into the simple faith of being a Christian. Jaspers invokes existential earnestness, Kierkegaard the humility of faith.

Without falling into the trap of deducing a philosopher's philosophy from his personal fate, it is nevertheless worth remembering that Jaspers stepped into the circle of philosophers from without, namely, as a medical doctor and psychiatrist. In the preface to the new edition of *Psychologie der Weltanschauungen* (1954), he observes that he had already thought and worked philosophically in his psychiatric practice. His philosophizing was unnoticed, but it became concrete in his meetings with patients, that is, individuals with real existences endeavouring to understand themselves and the world. Even if these notions of the self and world were absurd, as well as fantastic and incomprehensible in rational terms, what was at stake, in strict phenomenological terms, was the acceptance of such views as real to the individuals concerned. Jaspers recognised, however, that the original reality of fantasies, dreams, obsessions, hallucinations, that is to say, worldviews, lay not so not much in themselves but rather in their pre-psychological, subjective origin. That is, they were situated in a reality that eludes the horizon of psychology. Now traditional philosophies are also worldviews, formulated and more or less shaped by reason. Jaspers' daring step was to carry this methodical insight into philosophy, to enter it in this manner, and to test his therapeutic standpoint therein. This twofold aspect of being inside and outside philosophy finds expression, albeit not without provocation, in the title of his first major work, which is plain and simply *Philosophie*. This work is aimed at the origin of philosophy, which emerges from an autonomous process of cognition, that is, philosophizing, and which passes unnoticed at precisely that moment when "philosophy is undertaken."

Jaspers' biography is well known: his illness, which imposed on him an extremely disciplined life; his loyalty toward his Jewish wife, which drove him into isolation during Nazi rule and placed him at risk of death; his appointment as Chair of Philosophy at Heidelberg, which was pushed through without a doctorate in philosophy and against the will of Heinrich Rickert; his dispensation from his teaching duties between 1937 and 1945; his clean slate compared to Heidegger's following the liberation of Heidelberg by the Americans; and his self-exile to the University of Basel in Switzerland in 1948. The twists and turns in Jaspers' life are continually marked by a sense of the extraordinary. Notwithstanding all of these strokes of fate, which came from without, there is the sense of an existence that elects itself and also decides for itself which guided Jaspers. In other words, his was an existence that shaped matters from within. In short, we are confronted with an existence that, as Jaspers phrased it, "lives from the origin" (*aus dem Ursprung lebt*).

Whence came the strength and courage to speak about the guilt of the Germans, to make journalistic interventions in the politics of Federal Germany, and to appeal to the whole of humanity to undertake a moral reversal in his book on the atom bomb? Jaspers saw in Nietzsche a "missionary earnestness"—and one is tempted to see this also in Jaspers.

Jaspers' Charisma: Some Personal Remarks

For many listeners, Jaspers' public appearances had a charismatic aura. I would not exclude myself from this perception either. I first met Jaspers in 1949 when I was a student at the University of Basel. Personal contact remained minimal. He was the famous philosopher who, together with Heidegger and Sartre, was at the forefront of so-called existentialist philosophy after 1945. Sitting behind a low lectern, he would deliver his brilliant lectures to a highly mixed audience in an always fully packed lecture hall, speaking freely and only occasionally swiftly turning some pages in what were known to be fully written-out manuscripts. In my first semesters, this made an overwhelming impression on me. All other professors paled in my eyes, and seemed to draw, as it were, on the brilliance emanating from their colleague's academic presence and fame. His seminar was open to anyone interested, including the many Germans returning from the war and at the zero point of their lives as they decided to embark on academic studies. Besides Jaspers, the professorial faculty at Basel at the time included Edgar Salin, Karl Barth, Adolf Portmann, Werner Kägi, Fritz Buri, Walter Muschg, Harald Fuchs, and Heinrich Barth. Jaspers enjoyed very good conditions in Basel; he lived close to the University in Austrasse, would arrive in a taxi at the Collegiate Building on St. Peter's Square, his tall figure striding toward the lift shortly before five o'clock in the afternoon, from where he would go to the staff room and then down the long corridor to the lecture hall, whose windows, for health reasons, always had to remain closed even during hot weather.

After a few semesters, I adopted a critical stance and a certain distance set in, not so much toward Jaspers as a person, but toward a method that provided orientation rather than analysis. This sounds very vague. It may also be that his lectures on world philosophy, which also included Chinese and Indian philosophies, seemed to lead to an arbitrariness little disposed to the concentrated study of philosophy. As a consequence, many philosophy students gained the impression that Jaspers was more intent on being publicly efficacious than guiding students in their philosophical studies.

I received my own philosophical training in Heinrich Barth's seminars and lectures. Barth was quite the opposite of Jaspers. He was inconspicuous and physically handicapped, lacked rhetorical brilliance (instead his manner of speech was ponderous), and enjoyed no esteem among the student body. He would hold his lectures from 7 to 8 a.m. in the summer semester, and his seminar would run from 8 to 10 a.m. on Saturdays. Proceedings adhered strictly to reading texts in their original language, and personal interpretations and statements were required. Not a single meeting lapsed without a participant being obliged to take the minutes. After meeting him in person and attending his lectures, Leonard H. Ehrlich also noted Barth's hidden significance next to Jaspers. I sat for my doctoral examination on Jaspers' 77th birthday, and he served as the co-supervisor of my dissertation along with Barth. Notwithstanding his criticism of my research, Jaspers acknowledged the tangible earnestness of my philosophical endeavour.

The Category of Earnestness (*Ernst*) and a Look Behind the Encompassing

What sounds so colloquial carries extraordinary meaning for Jaspers: the "category of earnestness" is an existential cipher that is related to the "idea of the origin." What is the subject of comparison here can hardly be determined unequivocally within Jaspers' system. There is neither a category of earnestness nor an idea of the origin therein. And yet these notions are present in his writings. Indeed, without them, his work remains irrelevant. Earnestness represents a foundation of the illumination of existence, while "origin" stands for the transcendent source of philosophizing and of philosophy. The origin becomes present in *Ernst* or earnestness.

If we adhere to the idea of the origin, and if we heed the appeal emanating from this notion, then it appears as the conveying forward to a reality that is linked directly to the illumination of *Existenz* in *Philosophie*, his major work dating from 1931/1932.[1] However, the thought of the encompassing, which should actually illustrate thinking about the origin, remains rather foreign in a stringent philosophy of existence. The concept of the sevenfold-divided encompassing virtually conceals that which the illumination of existence invoked and made insightful. Jaspers' philosophizing became speculative after the publication of *Philosophie*. Therein, he attempts to indirectly recover the existential reality that was actually at stake through politics, world-historical orientations, appeals to philosophical faith, and a critique of revelation. It is significant that ordering principles and a tendency toward large surveys increasingly come to replace real philosophizing in his writings. All his virtually large-scale projects, for instance his unfinished world philosophy, are of utmost fascination. They also have value for intercultural dialogue.

The thought of the encompassing introduces into Jaspers' existential thinking a lack of clarity. The concept was supposed to denote the dimension of the origin pervading all being and thought. As such, it approaches Spinoza's thinking about God. Be that as it may, the thought of the encompassing (*Umgreifendes*) seeks to bring closer and enhance the awareness of the universal, creative origin of reality than all previous philosophies. And yet it achieves precisely what Jaspers always maintained ought to be avoided, namely, the ontologising of existence. He classifies it in the encompassing super-immanence. While existence becomes only indirectly present, it is nevertheless oriented toward the "quest for being" (*Das Suchen des Seins*, *P* 4ff) and the "becoming of the sense of being" (*Seinsinnewerden*).[2] A lack of being is what drives existence and philosophy at the same time. Its meaning lies not in the weight philosophical terms and concepts carry in themselves, but alone in the philosophiser's performance of thought. The core substance of all articulated philosophies lies behind their backs, as it were. In all articulations, the un-articulated therein must be illuminated. However, we should not be deceived:

---

[1] Karl Jaspers, *Philosophie* (Berlin: Springer, 1948). [Henceforth cited as *P*]

[2] Karl Jaspers, *Der Philosophische Glaube* (Munich: Piper Verlag, 1948), p. 15. [Henceforth cited as *PG*]

the non-articulable, non-objective is also related to the articulable and the objective, and thus to being. It is so precisely through its negation, even when it appears as its negation, for example under the name of transcendence or a mystically understood nothingness. Jaspers never grows tired of polemicizing against the having of being (*das Haben von Sein*), against gnosis, and against inversion (*Verkehrung*). He insists on the ascesis of revelation and on the recognition of scientific, interminable openness. But it is precisely a radical openness to the philosophical cognition of reality that he refutes. Following an intense reading of Jaspers' texts, the impression remains that notwithstanding the vastness of the encompassing aspired to, an impenetrable wall, consisting of an absolute knowledge of philosophical knowledge itself, becomes evident. Hence, we may say that the powerful supreme being (*Übersein*) and the transcending, which is at the same also invoked as the true being, proves to be an ontological or periechontological super-immanence.

Philosophical Faith and the Appearance of the Origin

Philosophical faith is captured within this ontological constellation. It is neither immediate nor psychologically grounded. It is a belief in cognition. More specifically, it is the cognising insight into the encompassing. Various obstacles to understanding need to be surmounted here. Its aim is the "becoming of the sense of being from the origin through the conveying of history and thought" (*PG* 15). The two philosophical hurdles having to be overcome are the so-called subject-object split and the "phenomenality of our existence" (*Erscheinungshaftigkeit*), a theorem that had apparently entered Jaspers' awareness through Kant. Moreover, the becoming of the sense of being is either shaped or conveyed by the respective historical and epistemological constellation.

In the following striking passage, the periechontological point of entry into philosophical faith is designated thus:

> If faith is neither content nor only an act of the subject, but instead has its roots in that which bears phenomenal appearance, then it can be envisioned only by what is neither object nor subject, but both in one, which is that which appears in the division between subject and object.—We call the being, which is neither only subject nor only object, but is rather a subject-object split on both sides, the *encompassing*. Although this cannot adequately become an object, we speak from and toward it when philosophizing. (*PG* 14)

The last word in this quotation–philosophizing–is decisive. Its origin and aim is termed identical. What does this identity mean? For the time being, a being comes into view that is "neither only subject nor only object." Thus access to a dimension of one's existential essence becomes open. The subsequent comment, however, namely, that this is a kind of being that exists "on both sides," destroys the existential thought and leads back to the schema of an aggrandizing ontological super-immanence.

Why this relapse into an ontological schema? Why does Jaspers not pause with the insight into what "appears in the division between subject and object"? What kind of appearance is this? It is certainly not an appearance that may apply to the phenomenal appearance of all existence (*Dasein*). And if we disregard the fact that this could merely be a linguistic metaphor, we may say that origin shows itself here in its own very peculiar fashion. Nor is it that which encompasses, but rather that which suggests the un-anticipatable (*Un-Vor-Greifliche*). By no means does it do so only cipher-like, but instead immediately and inevitably. Did Jaspers perhaps understand this appearing (*Erscheinende*) as the "last cipher in response to all ciphers" (*P* 877), namely, as "uninterpretability"? We must bear in mind, however, that a phenomenon that is itself uninterpretable but accessible to interpretation precedes all communication through ciphers. If this is the case, then this original appearance must be valid as a possible condition for being a cipher in the first place.

If philosophizing attains primacy over philosophy, then the force of the origin (*Ursprungs-Antrieb*) enters thinking. The merely theoretical cognition of the origin is by all means excluded. But such cognition is separated from the origin by reflection. While it knows of its existence, it does not think from its impulse. It can be said to be a hermeneutics of the origin, which occurs in abstracting distance from the unconditional experience of the origin. But philosophizing conscious of the origin must dare to take a step behind fixed philosophies, and even behind the ciphers. There, philosophizing becomes a philosophy that actualises itself; it becomes a cognising that brings forth, and does not merely use, ciphers. Other categories come into force there. In particular the above-mentioned category of earnestness, which takes the lead. Existence embracing itself now replaces reflection. Traditional philosophies and ciphers are its ossified outcomes. Thus, for instance, Jaspers refers to the Biblical notion of God, and reinterprets it existentially with reference to the origin:

> The One becomes the foundation for the consciousness of being and the ethos, the origin of the active sinking into the world. No other gods besides God, this is the metaphysical reason for the earnestness of the One in the world. (*PG* 38)

Jaspers does not oppose metaphysics, but he seeks to disclose its impetus and to lead it back to life. "We are shackled by these visions of the world and transcendence, wherein we perceive their earnestness, which has become real in the personality of the one thinking them."[3] Phrased differently, existential earnestness creates worlds and transcendences for itself. Tragically, these are no more than visions rather than a fulfilled knowledge of the world and of transcendence. Nevertheless, there are sentences in Jaspers where caution also seems to have been dislodged. He speaks of instances of the utmost affirmation of "the eternal in time," indeed that "a complicity with creation as it were" occurs.[4] Moreover, "Philosophising [is] an overcoming of the world, an analogue of redemption" (*E* 24).

---

[3] Karl Jaspers, *Die grossen Philosophen, 1. Band* (Munich: Piper Verlag, 1959), p. 619.

[4] Karl Jaspers, *Einführung in die Philosophie. Zwölf Radiovorträge* (Zurich: Artemis Verlag, 1950), p. 117. [Henceforth cited as *E*]

Faith, Science, and Philosophy

Reinhard Schulz

Abstract The ambivalence of advances in the natural sciences and technology at times leads to unavoidable risks that result in a probe of public trust. By comparing the positions of Carl Friedrich von Weizsäcker, Niklas Luhmann, Jürgen Habermas, Norbert Elias and especially that of Karl Jaspers with its philosophical roots in Kant and Kierkegaard, it becomes clear that any recourse about trust cannot take place without faith in reason. Here, one of the most difficult obstacles is what Jaspers called "science superstition" (*Wissenschaftsaberglaube*).

Modern societies are closely correlated to science and social future is to a great extent dependent on progress and technology. But how is science accepted in society? Studies have shown that the more the public comes to know about results in the sciences, the more their mistrust grows. In the light of this seeming paradox, an increasing number of scientific organizations and scientists are asking what they could do to avoid losing the trust[1] of an increasingly sceptical public. The relevance of trust in scientific research always becomes particularly clear when the public is confronted with real or perceived risks. All scientists who inform politics, economy, media, and the public about risks, move on a fine line between under- and overestimating risks, as for example the globally discussed swine-flu or the climate debate have recently shown. The credibility of opinions about publicly discussed risks also depends largely on the reputation of the scientist or the institution the scientist works for. It will be interesting to know, seeing the complexity of scientific knowledge, whether the relationship between the sciences is actually founded on the basis of mutual knowledge, respect, and trust, or whether there are some other forces at work? The following considerations are to show that the answer to this question moves on a very fine line. It is clear that modern society would simply not be possible without a basic trust in scientific-technical supported supply systems (such as energy, health, or traffic). At the same time, exaggerated trust in scientific experts and an irrational faith in scientific-technical knowledge can lead to great risks and

---

[1] A difficulty in the English version of this text is that "faith" in the German translation can mean faith as well as trust. That is why we decided to use faith for *Glaube*, and trust for *Vertrauen*. All translations in this essay are by the author.

R. Schulz (✉)
Carl von Ossietzky University, Oldenburg, Germany
e-mail: reinhard.schulz@uni-oldenburg.de

dangers. To negotiate ambivalence orientation, assistance is needed concerning the relationship of science and philosophy. At the end of this essay it will become obvious that Immanuel Kant and Karl Jaspers still today are significant dialogue partners for such position.

Carl Friedrich Weizsäcker: Scientific Faith

In 1964 Carl Friedrich Weizsäcker approached the complexity of the connection of faith and science in his book *Die Tragweite der Wissenschaft*,[2] where he first shows parallels between science and religions.[3] He argues that from a sociological point of view, religion is marked by three elements: common faith, an organized church, and a system of behavior patterns. Weizsäcker asks himself whether these elements can be applied also to the sciences. At first glance the comparison seems paradoxical, since in contrast to faith, science is based on rationality. Weizsäcker works with a distinction between intellectual credibility and existential trust to be the guiding element of faith, but he continues, this is also found in the sciences. Intellectual belief means to adopt knowledge without inquiry; such knowledge then becomes relatively meaningless for a person, because nothing much depends on it. In contrast, existential trust is of concern for the whole person and not merely for conscious behavior—that was faith according to Weizsäcker. What we learn in scientific studies usually we would take intellectually for real. When driving at night on the motorway, existential trust is required in the functioning of science and technology and the automobile industry to confidently undertake such night-time jaunt. This existential trust also plays a vital role in political decisions (e.g. about the transport of nuclear waste, health risks, or climate research). In such decisions, politicians mostly trust in scientific experts, although this might not be completely justified, for progressing scientific knowledge is always limited to a scientific subterritory and as such just an excerpt of reality. Weizsäcker assumes that for science, the mental disposition of a member of modern civilization is very similar to that of believers in a manifested faith. To illustrate this point, he creates analogies between the atom and an ulterior world and between a mathematical formula and a holy text, which could both be read by experts, but would have to remain secret to lay persons. Miracles which are perceived as superhuman power are to be found in Christian religion (feeding the poor, healing the ill) but also in the sciences (for example, modern medicine and war technologies). Generally, we believe in science and in technical results, without ever being able to gain insight into the corresponding scientific system or to know about it. In every scientific investigation only extracts can

---

[2] Carl Friedrich von Weizsäcker, *Die Tragweite der Wissenschaft*, 6th edition (Stuttgart: Hirzel, 1990).

[3] This part is a translated version of section 4.1, "Exkurs: Naturwissenschaft und Glaube," in Reinhard Schulz, *Naturwissenschaftshermeneutik. Eine Philosophie der Endlichkeit in historischer, systematischer und angewandter Hinsicht* (Würzburg: Königshausen & Neumann, 2004), pp. 175–178.

be perceived, but never the whole. Symptomatic for the believe in miracles is the observation that we would never doubt the technical system as a whole in the case of a non-functioning technical appliance, but would search only for obvious reasons for its being "out of order." In a nutshell, we can find that religious behavior as well as behavior regarding the handling of science is characterized by a diffuse, non-reflected trust. This excludes a categorical questioning of science and technology and instead promotes having faith in its accomplishments and progress.

Upon closer inspection, science does not have a church like religion, but has a priesthood of science, according to Weizsäcker, which is connected by a common truth. This common truth allows for reaching shared results in research projects, even when the social and cultural conditions of scientists embedded in completely different political systems are diverse. By such common holding of a truth researchers are pushed into a priestly role. Human experience of success and failure in terms of faith in science has put us into an ambiguous position. It consists also of potentially creating new problems each time science solves a problem, which becomes quite threatening in the advancement of science. These two theses of Weizsäcker are closely related, namely the existence of trust in science and the ambiguity of the effects of science. Only through faith in science do the ambiguities of scientific results become a serious threat for human civilization. Another aspect of this faith in science lies in the wide-spread opinion that all achievable knowledge is to be assigned to science, particularly to the empiric sciences taken together. We act as if there were not any new findings possible outside a methodical empirical approach to science. Real understanding, however, is only possible in contexts regardless of the instigation of science. But because these contexts underlie a constant historical change, the comprehension of science thus changes correspondingly. For example, evolution theory today is by now a commonly accepted fact, but when it occurred in the nineteenth century it was an immense provocation for the religious world view of that time.

In contrast to Weizsäcker's exploration of faith and science, we have to emphasize that the ambiguity is not confined to the dangerous effects of scientific technical progress. The real danger that can emanate from specific results of natural sciences does not merely consist in the ambiguity of its results, but in the ambiguity of its constantly restrained structure on reality and the exclusive study of methodologically determined model systems. This structure is concealed by scientific faith and thus creates conditions in which errors of judgment may occur in the application of scientific methods, and therefore may imply an unjustified expectation regarding the results of science.

These introductory remarks on science and faith are intended to make clear that a debate is necessary to broaden the approach and attitude towards science and technology, not so much our knowledge about science and technology or the content of this knowledge. These prove to be usually more extraordinarily resilient against critical objections than their validity in the context of accumulated holding of knowledge. How does this defensive attitude come about and how to overcome it? Nearly 50 years ago, when Weizsäcker published *Die Tragweite der Wissenschaft*, the ambiguity progress (e.g. population explosion through better hygiene and medical progress) was slowly starting to become evident. This fateful ambiguity has been taken for granted by plenty of examples, yet has not crucially unsettled scientific faith. On the contrary, this faith nowadays has even been intensified by proceeding from natural science to popular science as transmogrified in the media. In other words, one need not have faith in the sciences as such, but rather in popular science. To return to Weizsäcker's image, the church (that is, the recipients of science) has lost its members and now subscribes to various sects instead. For example, sales figures on the popular science book market list an increase of general reader interest with a simultaneous decrease in the number of students pursuing science subjects. These sects use elements of scientific knowledge to convey their messages in a more digestible way. Not to mention various esoteric currents, which have always existed, when therapists and management consultants are happy to enhance the persuasive powers of their concepts with apparently meaningful fragments of scientific findings, such as research in areas of self-organization and chaos, brain and genetic research, or socio-biology.

Given a presumed higher dedication of scientific laws, one might be less likely coerced to withdraw from the so-called hard facts of science than from its so-called non-scientific counterparts. With respect to the true sciences and their way of promoting change in technical scientific civilization, popular science by now has taken on the character of a substitute religion. The arbitrariness in the selection of scientific examples and statements in popular sciences would furthermore abet the increasing misjudging of scientific methods and contents, and thereby increasingly obscuring the perception of lay people. Here critical awareness training is required and philosophy is faced with great challenges.

Already in 1948 Karl Jaspers saw this development coming and analysed it relentlessly in *Der philosophische Glaube*:

> Superstition in science needs to be analysed and overcome. In our age of relentless lack in faith one turns to science as the presumed solid foundation, one has faith in so-called scientific results, blindly surrenders to presumed experts, believes in science and planning for arranging life in the entire world, and expects from science answers for purposeful life, something that science will never deliver—and hopes for insight about the totality of Being, which for science is unattainable.[4]

Modern science management has not yet been prepared to recognize such missing directives of science that Jaspers analysed. Quite on the contrary, for example, increased efforts by leading German science organizations are underway to intensify the so-called dialogue with the public under the title "Science in the Public Space." Its purpose is "to enable for all citizens an impartial and unbiased understanding of the ethical, political, economic, and societal implications of scientific knowledge and activities."[5] Planned measures included motivating young people to

---

[4] Karl Jaspers, *Der philosophische Glaube*, 6th edition (Munich: Piper, 1974), p. 132 [Henceforth cited as *PG*].

[5] *Wissenschaft im öffentlichen Raum*, Perspektivenpapier der Deutschen Forschungsgemeinschaft (DFG) (Bonn: Bad Godesberg, 2009), p. 1.

adopt a scientific career, developing target-oriented concepts for introducing academic education to educationally underprivileged groups, increased utilization of the new media, assessing co-determination of social opinion-forming and decision-making processes, and emphasizing cognitive processes instead of research results for public consumption. These efforts signal a comprehensive tendency for the transformation of science communication for the purpose of affecting social coexistence. Public trust in science and research is sought mainly by potential political sponsors and the economy, but the ambiguity of scientific progress or the borders of scientific cognition are not mentioned at all in such ambitious statements. It remains the task of philosophy to address these strategically omitted, but nonetheless crucial questions for orientation of the public.

Niklas Luhmann: Trust in the System

One central topic is an analysis what trust toward sciences could look like, without falling into superstition in science that Jaspers criticized. Here it will be helpful to distinguish between "personal trust and the trust in functioning of social systems like science," as did sociologist Niklas Luhmann in 1973.[6] Personal trust signifies trust in certain persons, for example in friendships. It requires continuity of self-expression by the trustworthy person, in whom the difference between introspection and external perception can be stabilized. In contrast, trust in the system comes through abstract achievements. These subjects manifest in form of expertise, where symbolically generalized communication, media, or contracts function as equivalents for certainty about expected performances, such as the results of scientific technical progress. But every trust needs specific congruence warranties. So, while personal trust is related to actions of concrete persons, trust in systems is bound to the effectiveness of particular media. As much as the economic system needs relatively stable money value for its readiness to trust and it can be assumed that the political system will not abuse power, then the scientific system can depend on the reliability of its research results. These kinds of trust have in common that they increase the manageable insecurities of systems by a greater tolerance towards distrust, because their permanent security cannot be granted. If one considers the paradox, as initially mentioned and clarified here, that with growing knowledge about science simultaneously distrust in science increases, then we encounter a massive difficulty.

> The difficulty has its origin in the fact that trust and mistrust. . .are symbolically mediated generalized dispositions, that are directed by subjective dispositions pertaining to a simplified processing of experience, rather than relating to specific identifiable objective causes. In this simplification, in the reduction of complexity there is a volatile, unpredictable situation. Once the concern about trust or mistrust comes to the open, the situation becomes more

---

[6] Niklas Luhmann, *Vertrauen. Ein Mechanismus der Reduktion sozialer Komplexität*, 2nd edition (Stuttgart: Enke, 1973) [Henceforht cited as *V*].

problematic, more complex, increases possibilities; while at the same time activating sim-
plifying processes of reduction and focussing on a reduced number of crucial experiences.
(V 83)

This sociological diagnosis by Luhmann can without doubt be transferred onto the
experience of ambiguity in scientific progress. Each progress evokes new unforeseen
possibilities that by any means cannot be overlooked in all its technical, economical,
political, or cultural dimensions. Similarly, examples from the past (crucial experiences) are used for the interpretation of this progress, in which something significant
showed itself, or something was a close shave, or actually did go wrong. Yesterday's
key moments shoulder an important function in understanding the expectations for
scientific progress of tomorrow, for nobody can foresee the future. With regards
to this necessary orientation about a bonding agent for modern highly engineered
societies, it has become quite common to converse about virtues and values and
to give this debate an ethical fresh coat. Francis Fukuyama, who was regarded as
the prophet for this debate,[7] presented in 1995 another book on trust in human
and institutional contexts.[8] Economic exchange and thus capitalism was strongly
promoted by an existing trust within manageable groups. Fukuyama talks about
spontaneous sociability when he refers to the ability of forming groups or knitting
a net of relationships upon a primary basis that rests upon values and virtues rather
than contracts. He examines the extent to which the existence of such spontaneous
sociability as a social capital has influenced the development of Western and Asian
industrial nations even up to now. Emergence of spontaneous sociability is more
difficult where families are the pivot of all social organizations. The family focus
that results in only trusting one's own relatives, often hinders or makes it impossible to build larger social entities, and in poorly trusting societies it hardly occurs
that large companies develop. According to Fukuyama, and against the assumption
of a West-East contrast of different socio-cultural unity, a picture of a very diverse
strength of social trust in the development of economy emerges from country to
country. It is easy to conclude that analogous to this, trust in science and technology is also coined differently and the large distinctions in the acceptance of key
technologies within Europe (e.g. nuclear technology in France and Germany) are
impressive examples. Fukuyama's claim seems unconvincing that liberal democracy
with Western characterization can be strengthened with more values and virtues in
order to weaken prevailing individualism, because with moral appeals against the
deterioration of social confidence-building, and against the ambiguity of technical
progress, and also the seduction through constant consumption it will not be coun-
tervailed. If each single member of modern societies is called forth to find one's
personal truth in the infinity of possibilities available in capitalist markets, the limits
of the virtue debate are quickly visible and remain eventually in the dialectic of trust
and distrust that Lehmann pointed out.

---

[7] Francis Fukuyama, *The End of History and the Last Man* (New York, NY: Free Press, 1992).

[8] Francis Fukuyama, *Konfuzius und Marktwirtschaft* (Munich: Kindler, 1995).

Societal perceptions of value are always in close relationship to social, economical, political, and scientific frameworks. As long as one does not reflect on these coherencies, a discussion on trust and orientation remains without consequences. Also the ethical question under which circumstances to present trust and when to avoid it, would not be of much help. The problem of trust would then be transformed into a problem of knowledge, although the root of distrust is exactly to be found in inadequate knowledge (e.g. about the consequences of scientific progress). There is one solution, namely to gain a completely new dimension for the question of orientation and trust, if neither the appeal for new virtues and values nor the restricted trust in the system (e.g. current crises in the financial, climate, or energy sectors) manage to show a way out.

> It is a generally known fact of life that humans and social systems alike will have more readiness to extend trust when there is an inherent sense of security, a kind of inner assertiveness that enables them to cope with potential disappointments, instead of empowering such potential assertion as a foundation for their actions. (*V* 86)

Hence what is asked for is an inner trusting that is ready to expect the worst and yet can do without certainties on the basis of somewhat reliable factual information. It is about a feeling of trust that believes in being able to cope with problems no matter where and when and in which form they might occur. Since "each collapse of a trusting relationship restores the oppressive complexity of the world. Fear lurks behind each trust and motivates to reinforce the relationship as long as it proves its worth in some way" (*V* 90). Fear and the readiness for trust are two closely related states of minds making one aware that trust cannot be regarded a valuable behavioral maxim and thus a long-term trust in systems such as science and technology cannot be formed. Depending on the situation, at times trust or distrust can be advisable. In order to assess a situation a judging self has to be presumed. Dependency on situations and the ability to judge make one aware of the crucial role that self-esteem plays based on personal trust and trust in the system, and also shows a connecting line between system theory and existential philosophy as it relates to this topic.

Karl Jaspers: Rational Trust

Since its earliest beginnings with Søren Kierkegaard, existential philosophy has posited a dialectic of fear and freedom that is closely related to trust and confidence building. Referring to a fairy tale by the brothers Grimm (*Märchen von einem der auszog, das Fürchten zu lernen*), Kierkegaard notes:

> Aspire learning to become fearful so that one does not lose oneself because of never having known fear or being immersed in fear; whoever has learned to be fearful has indeed exelled in learning.... Whoever believes that it is their great achievement to have never been fearful of anything, let me take pleasure to share this insight with you, it is due to your lack of wit to hold such belief.[9]

---

[9] Søren Kierkegaard, *Der Begriff Angst* (Frankfurt am Main: Syndikat, 1984), pp. 141 ff.

Kierkegaard clear-sightedly clarifies that no worldly tormentor would be in the position to surpass the anxieties that rise from one's inner self. Hence it is no surprise that renowned twentieth-century philosophers such as Heidegger, Jaspers, or Sartre have placed fear in the centre of their philosophies. For fear as a constant given, relentlessly confronts humans with the certainty of death; the temporality and historicity of human nature in, what Jaspers calls "our age of restless disbelief," gains increasing significance. Such disposition, however, does not find consideration in the results and products of modern science and technology and labels them as an "allegedly safe haven," a solid foundation in the shape of "scientific superstition," as Karl Jaspers and Carl Friedrich von Weizsäcker outlined it. But can fear also be educative, in a way Kierkegaard imagined it? Jaspers relates to Kierkegaard as follows: "Fear is the vertigo and trepidation of freedom when about to act.... When fear dissipates, humans become superficial."[10] In system theory and existential philosophy apparently we have to deal with two diametrically opposite tendencies in the evaluation of consequences from people's fears. From the perspective of system theory, the readiness for trust or distrust serves as a coming to terms with one's increasing inner fears in face of the giant complexity of the outer world by adopting stabilizing systems like science and technology. According to existential philosophy, the coming to terms with this fear in, what Jaspers calls borderline situations, means intrinsically being really human. How does this all relate to trust and faith in science and technology?

> Without using reason and simply continuing on the path of science and technology according to Jaspers will not address the dangers of our age. Rescue cannot come just from science and technology alone, since guidance is needed from ethos and the will for unrestricted communication. Herein Jaspers sees the value of reversal. It is reason as philosophical faith that Jaspers is calling for.[11]

Also for Jaspers science and technology are essential parts of modern society—now and in future a certain trust in the system and in modern science will be necessary. Such trust requires an understanding and a deliberate decision for rationality and thus the need for philosophy. In relation to science, Jaspers talks in a twofold way about faith, one is the negative version of scientific superstition and the other is its positive alternative of philosophical faith. In order to measure what kind of resistance this philosophical rational faith has to expect, it is worthwhile looking at a text which perhaps emerged simultaneously with Weizsäcker's *Die Tragweite der Wissenschaft*, namely Jürgen Habermas' *Technik und Wissenschaft als Ideologie*. Following Horkheimer and Adorno,[12] Habermas developed his famous two-dimensional society concept of system and lifeworld, which then in the context

---

[10] Karl Jaspers, *Philosophie, Volume 2: Existenzerhellung*, 3rd edition (Berlin/Göttingen/Heidelberg: Springer, 1956), p. 265; [Henceforth cited as *P* followed by volume number] and *PG* 67.

[11] Alfons Grieder: "Karl Jaspers: Philosoph im wissenschaftlich-technischen Zeitalter," in *Wahrheit ist, was uns verbindet. Karl Jaspers' Kunst zu philosophieren*, eds. Reinhard Schulz, Giandomenico Bonnani, and Matthias Bormuth (Göttingen: Wallstein, 2009), pp. 453 f.

[12] Max Horkheimer und Theodor W. Adorno, *Dialektik der Aufklärung* (Frankfurt am Main: S. Fischer, 1969).

of an unfolded theory leads to his leading magnum opus *Theorie des kommunikativen Handelns*.[13] Habermas identified technology and science as new conflict areas "within the system of population management through media."[14] With a "scientification of technology" (*TWI* 79), a development goes along in which all research is increasingly focused on technically usable knowledge where scientific progress can by implication no longer be aligned with civilizing aims. Under these general conditions a policy of practical constraints becomes social technology, and rationally communicated value increasingly loses its legitimacy. In doing so, one side of the equation is ever escalating uncritical adaptation tendencies toward "manipulative duress by technocratic-operative management" (*TWI* 83), while the other more severe side would consist of people not being able to recognize the difference to instrumental-rationally technical action communicated by language, because "the ideological force of technocratic awareness succeeds by cloaking such difference" (*TWI* 84). Habermas uses this as an occasion to substitute the traditional connection provided by Marx of productive resources and relations of production with the more abstract relation of labor and interaction (*TWI* 92), thereby passing criticism on Max Weber and Herbert Marcuse.

For Habermas the term labor is instrumental-rational or instrumental action that has to follow technical rules and is based on empiric knowledge. Interaction or his concept of communicative action, in contrast, is understood as a symbolically conveyed interaction which complies with social norms and can be understood in mutually subjective appreciation. Thanks to Habermas' analysis of "technocratic consciousness" from 1968, which is even more current today, we can discern two significant connecting factors for scientific and philosophical faith. Due to the concealing tendency of this consciousness resistance becomes more apparent than it would occur in philosophical rational belief as presented by Jaspers, or in view of the rescuing force that Habermas assigns to symbolic interaction; all this suggests that Jaspers' concept of philosophical faith could act as a motivating force. Although Jaspers and Habermas stand in the tradition of Kant's transcendental philosophy, nonetheless their origins are quite different. Their most important distinction of faith and knowledge is the relationship of science and philosophy. While Habermas has in mind a transcendental concept of language to support a model of objectification in an understanding of science with a "methodical preference in contrast to subject philosophy."[15] Jaspers' reference to Kant is neither to be found in language nor method

---

[13] Jürgen Habermas, *Theorie des kommunikativen Handelns,* 2 volumes (Frankfurt am Main: Surhkamp, 1981).

[14] Jürgen Habermas, *Technik und Wissenschaft als "Ideologie",* 5th edition (Frankfurt am Main: Suhrkamp, 1971), p. 100. [Henceforth cited as *TWI*]

[15] One can arrive at intersubjective validation of observations by means of experimentation, that is by orderly transformation of data perception. A similar objectification appears to be possible when the analysis of concepts and ideas takes place in grammatic structures that aid such transformation. Grammatic concepts are open to the public and allow for the comprehension of structures without the appearance of subjective preference. The example of mathematics and logic added further support to defer philosophy in general to the public sphere of grammatic concepts. Frege

nor knowledge, but above all in "the immediacy of a freely assumed ought and its inherent courage of nescience."[16] Jaspers points out that all approximation attempts of philosophy toward science undermine the possibility of genuine philosophizing. In view of the hypothetical character of science, the philosopher regards himself called upon for faith, thereby experiencing his spiralling and angst-ridden nescience or lack of knowledge, and also the unconditional nature of his own decisions, which provides the only hold against the relativity of scientific knowledge.

> Faith is not knowledge; faith derived from a holistic perspective ceases to be applicable knowledge in the context of political reality. Kant's reply: From our human perspective we cannot come to comprehend the totality of history, neither through theoretical insight nor by practical planning. We can only bear it in mind as an idea. Cognition in support of faith does not constitute applicability, rather it provides consolidation. It does not have the utility of available knowledge, but it supports the overall effectiveness of my political reflection and action. (*GP* 580)

Never before has modern society moved so far away from this perception evoked by Jaspers. Today scientific and research activity together are mainly adapted to applicability and utility as a role-model of science. Students are pulled along consecutive study objectives that do not allow for time to philosophize and the dependency of universities on politics and economy increases daily. Considering this background, the philosophical faith that Jaspers originated in 1948 with his *Der philosophische Glaube* unfolded to its full critical potential in 1950 with his *Einführung in die Philosophie*, followed in 1961 with his *Chiffren der Transzendenz*, and in 1962 with his *Der philosophische Glaube angesichts der Offenbarung*. Unlike the scientific faith cited by Carl Friedrich von Weizsäcker, philosophical faith occurs without cult, without security, and without denomination but merely as a philosophical ascertainment. It is different from Christianity's revealed faith because it cannot be bound, and it perceives freedom and thinking as an infinitely open and seemingly paradoxical hovering certainty, all of which leads to essentially being human:

> Such rushed alternatives, like revealed faith or nihilism, or radical science or deception serve as fighting tools to instil fear in souls, taking away God-given self-responsibility and giving into obsequiousness. They tear into divisiveness human possibilities that constitute the essential qualities of being human. (*PG* 10)

Fear and inner turmoil are two sides of the same coin for an utterly individualized society as modern society likes to describe itself, which has also become an anxiety-provoking society suffused by competition, commerce, and consumerism, since fear from lack of success or other forms of shortcomings has become a constant companion. It is no surprise that under these conditions the fear of competition on global markets related to scientific knowledge plays an increasingly significant role as competition factors, strategic resources, and readily sellable goods along

---

and Peirce mark the turning point." Jürgen Habermas, *Nachmetaphysisches Denken* (Frankfurt am Main: Suhrkamp, 1988), pp. 53 f.

[16] Karl Jaspers, *Die großen Philosophen*, 6th edition (Munich: Piper, 1991), p. 581. [Henceforth cited as *GP*]

with the idiom of a knowledge society (*Wissensgesellschaft*) all of which allowed to unfold its propagandistic power into all segments of society. Increased demand for networking and the interdisciplinary character of modern knowledge connote closer relationships for members in modern society, along with the consciousness of a larger mutual dependency. Forced upon its members by the structures of capitalist social circumstances, this dependency is not freely chosen. Today it is more important than ever not loosing track of intellectual autonomy and self-education, given our emphasis on applied efficiency and the cultivation of expertise in worldwide data networks. Here is a chance for a long-standing recognition of others by opening a fearless discussion utilizing different ideas and concepts of thinking, cultural forms of religions and arts, allowing for critique and judgment, enhancing personal responsibility, developing social competence, reflecting upon self-perception and social perception, as well as intercultural understanding. All of these requirements can be easily united in Jaspers, for "philosophical faith is inseparable from unrestricted readiness for communication" (*PG* 129). Communication becomes a means without alternatives against all forms of anxiety, violence, mistrust, diremption, and hopelessness and creates the necessary trust to address by its binding force the seeming pointlessness of every day events. "Without such faith, a purely empirical perspective on pointlessness comes to a halt" (*GP* 576).

> Philosophical faith means faith with reason, i.e., coming to realize that humans are confined by personal temporality and time, unable to be master of the absolute plenum from which we originate. This means—by utilizing the inherent contemplation of reason upon unity and connectivity—to remain modest in human temporality.[17]

One can suspect that this kind of modesty is essentially lacking in an age of science and technology, since human rational faith and temporality are to be replaced by an unreasonable faith in alleged scientific truths. How else could one explain that human sciences are in ambitious search for a transition from neuro-technologies to technologies of consciousness, are working on a trans-human surpassing of mankind via biological technologies and genetic engineering; and fund research in artificial intelligence, neuro-implants, and human enhancement technologies (HET). What remains completely unaccounted for is what price we will have to pay one day for such change. Yet, even by removing all limits of peer pressure and reducing rational ability for differentiation between true and false knowledge, nonetheless true and false action does not remain untouched, let alone the difference between the ones who decide and those who are affected, the ones manipulating and the ones being manipulated. In fear of this difference In his *Die Zukunft der menschlichen Natur. Auf dem Weg zu einer liberalen Eugenik?*[18] Jürgen Habermas combined in a remarkable way existential philosophy (Kierkegaard), anthropology (Helmuth Plessner),

---

[17] Leonard H. Ehrlich, "Die Glaubensfrage und die Zukunft des Menschen," in *Wahrheit ist, was uns verbindet. Karl Jaspers' Kunst zu philosophieren*, eds. Reinhard Schulz, Giandomenico Bonnani, and Matthias Bormuth (Göttingen: Wallstein, 2009), p. 204.

[18] Jürgen Habermas, *Die Zukunft der menschlichen Natur. Auf dem Weg zu einer liberalen Eugenik?* (Frankfurt am Main, 2001). [Henceforth cited as *ZMN*]

and the ethics of responsibility (Hans Jonas), and pointed at the consequences when the limits between the developed and the created are distorted in the ethical self-conception of the individual person. If an adolescent, for example, were to be informed by his parents about his own genetic programming, he would be faced with his own nature as designed by a third party. "Progressive eugenics influences ethical freedom to the extent of labeling the individual as rejected and irreversibly altered by the will of others, thereby denying the right to perceive oneself as author for one's own life" (*ZMN* 109).

Furthermore such human breeding would bring about an unknown asymmetrical personal relationship since the manipulated ones are genetically locked and unable to create their own design. One cannot excluded that basic human experiences such as death, sorrow, struggle, coincidence, or guilt—by which, according to Jaspers, in border situations "by a radical shock of one's existence the subject awakens to Existenz (*P1* 56)—in the foreseeable future will become incomprehensible for humans, because such domestication and would allow us merely to differentiate between adapted and maladjusted dispositions of our body and our consciousness. Borderline situations would only happen in those areas "where an existential gap opens due to an error in physical and psychical programming."[19]

Given such a scenario it becomes apparent where to look for Jaspers' inspiration in Kant's faith in man and reason. It is not the empiricist who gets daily attention by the human sciences; nor is it the real man, who tries to be well equipped for daily social political challenges, nor is it about social elites who in spite of numerous crises continue to believe that they can control through networking the fate of humanity by means of science, economy, and politics. What matters instead is "the idea of man in man" in its limited historical options, for "to have faith in humanity is a prerequisite for having faith in the purpose of history which enables one to act in a morally and politically" (*GP* 76). As a medical scientist and psychiatrist, Jaspers had a precise conception of the difference between scientific and existential knowledge. He knew that ever so successful scientific mastery of nature would still leave unanswered questions about existential orientation for human beings. The more one can find out about man scientifically, the more faith in man is needed if one does not want to be consumed by the delusion of set human functions determined by science.

> Truth either does have a universal character and is then identical for all humans. Such is the understanding of scientific truth, yet it applies always only for specific subjects, spesific circumstances, is derived by means of specific methods that target in effect a relative truth. Or truth is unconditional, believed in and realized by man, but for the price that its claims, like rationally conveyed faithful claims, are not universally applicable. This means: unconditioned truth is historical, since as possible Existenz we are absolutely historical.[20]

Jaspers coined here an existential philosophical and historical term for the contrast between knowing and believing as conveyed by Kant who picked up again the theoretical thought pattern of subjective credibility in the chapter on "having an

---

[19] Gerald Hartung, *Philosophische Anthropologie* (Stuttgart: Reclam, 2008), p. 120.

[20] Karl Jaspers, *Philosophie und Welt: Reden und Aufsätze* (Munich: Piper, 1963), pp. 165 f.

opinion, knowing, and believing"[21] in the transcendental method of his *Critique of pure reason* and in his *What is orientation in thinking?* Rational belief here, gains its opposite determination of knowledge, which is also still valid for Jaspers:

> Every opinion, even a historical one, must be rational (since the final test is always reason); yet, rational faith does not refer to other facts, it is contained in pure reason alone. Each opinion is subjectively sufficient, but an objectively insufficient holding-to-be-true in consciousness; and as such is contrary to knowledge.[22]

What looks like a negative definition against objectifying knowledge in the sciences is in reality something completely different than the presumed universal validity as it is established by science—which in fact wants to strive ever more into areas that are measureable, but cannot as of now expunge the particular character of the rightness of scientific technological knowledge. Jaspers talked time and time again about a bond of reason to establish a connection between the particular correctness of science and technology and human existence. This is where the concept of communication, which is inseparable from reason, finds its place. Here, communicability compared to universal validity comes to the fore.

> Philosophical faith includes reason as an imperative moment.... Reason expands in sharpness of hearing, is flexible in readiness for communication, adaptable for new experiences, but all of this is anchored in a reason, steadfast in loyalty, lively in all present memory of everything that it noticed once for real.... Reason demands boundless *communication*, it is by itself the unrestricted will for communication.... The shape of revealed truth in time.... Philosophical faith that can also be called faith in communication. (*PG* 38–40)

Finally, I would like to remind you of Carl Friedrich von Weizsäcker's differentiation between intellectual credibility and existential trust which served for his diagnosis of scientific faith on the basis of existential trust. For Weizsäcker, intellectual credibility contains a limitation of knowledge that Kant and Jaspers would not subscribe to in this way, because they would keep a positive definition for rational faith versus the negative definition of scientific faith. We have seen from Kant and Jaspers that faith in rationality cannot be separated from faith in man. This is true particularly in times of enforcing global research in scientific knowledge along with its currently exceptionally ineffable expectations for healing, and also the endangerment of future man in the remembrance of rational faith that "cannot be grounded on any other data" particularly for those of significant actuality, who will also in future be concerned with creatureliness, historicality, and the freedom of man. Because the scientific technological mindset, always tied in certain boundary conditions, in combination with the global slogan of "knowledge-embracing society," must remain utterly strange for Kant and Jaspers, who developed a thought pattern of unconditional philosophical rational faith.

---

[21] Immanuel Kant, *Kritik der reinen Vernunft* (Hamburg: Meiner, 1976), B 848–B 859, pp. 739–748.

[22] Immanuel Kant, "Was heißt: sich im Denken orientieren?" *Berliner Monatsschrift*, Oktober 1786, pp. 304–330, and "Was ist Aufklärung?" *Berliner Monatsschrift* (Hamburg, 1999), pp. 43–61, here p. 54.

In search of adequate means for orientation to be able to face the numerous threats and conflicts of our civilization, the sociologist Norbert Elias pointed in 1983 at the overestimated prestige of sciences, whose models and methods von Weizsäcker estimated and cited in the beginning as attributes of science that eventually will be distributed to other disciplines such as sociologists, who want to claim their works to be scientific. This is exactly what can be observed today in large parts of Germany in a desired scientific political transformation of sociology from a former critical social theory into a future prestigious and money-oriented empirical experimental social technology. Elias points out that this trend fails to recognize that models of causal links and methods of quantifying measurements are cut to fit the sciences rather than for the study of social problems. He introduced the interdisciplinary term of human sciences (*Menschenwissenschaften*).[23] I propose to bringing back Kant's and Jaspers' idea of man, as a remedy against all previously described dangers of a programmed and fully engineered future of personhood through scientific technological progress, and that we start talking about a society of individuals rather than a knowledge society. Already a century ago, Jaspers was very aware that philosophy could only address the individual and that this will probably not be very different in future, one will not be able to count on the enlightenment of the great masses of people in modern society.

> The precondition for the technical transformation of our existence is modern science. Intellectually, this science—rather than technology—provides a deep incision into the history of humanity that is noticed by only a few, and is also effectuated by only a few, while the majority of humans continue to live in prescientific mental constructs and merely use the results of science without comprehension, just as primal people used European top hats, tail coats, and glass beads. (PG 131)

---

[23] Norbert Elias, *Engagement und Distanzierung* (Frankfurt am Main: Suhrkamp, 1983).

The Philosophy of History in Hegel, Heidegger, and Jaspers

Stephen A. Erickson

Abstract I am concerned to explore the ways in which some major European philosophers, particularly Hegel, Heidegger, and Jaspers have reflected both upon their time and upon the meaning of History itself. My purpose is to encourage a similar reflection among contemporary philosophers regarding our current early twenty-first century era and the spiritual future it may portend. An underlying assumption is that Hegel was right in claiming that philosophy is both the child of its time and should also be its time comprehended in thought. However future oriented, Heidegger believes the same and embodies the nostalgic urge for a return to origins and thereby an escape from the corrosive effects of modernity. By contrast Hegel represented a sense of his particular time as a celebratory consummation of essential trends from the spiritual past. Jaspers, in turn, displays far more caution and a wise uncertainty regarding these matters. Through this stance he provides more realistic promise than either of those of his major predecessors whom I consider in these reflections. (This essay was previously published in *Existenz*, Vol. 1, Nos. 1–2, Fall 2006, pp. 31–36. An earlier version was published in *International Readings of Theory, History and Philosophy of Culture*, 21: "Dynamics of Values in Contemporary Culture," pp. 191–200, UNESCO-EIDOS publication, St. Petersburg, Russia, 2006.).

A Tribute to Leonard and Edith Ehrlich

It is a great honor to offer this essay to the Ehrlich *Festschrift* and I do so with gratitude. As one who first met Leonard and Edith Ehrlich through the *Karl Jaspers Society of North America*, I have been deeply impressed by their dedication to Jaspers scholarship. Their masterful and precise translations of Jaspers' work and Leonard Ehrlich's insightful book, *Karl Jaspers: Philosophy as Faith*, have contributed greatly to a better understanding of Jaspers' philosophy of human existence and to an appreciation of European philosophers more generally, particularly such thinkers as Kant, Heidegger, Kierkegaard, Buber, and Barth. "For Jaspers," as Leonard Ehrlich writes, "faith is thought which seeks to master the disparateness of what can be known. . . . However, philosophical faith not only means mastery of

S.A. Erickson (✉)
Pomona College, Claremont, CA, USA
e-mail: stephen.erickson@pomona.edu

H. Wautischer et al. (eds.), *Philosophical Faith and the Future of Humanity*,
DOI 10.1007/978-94-007-2223-1_16, © Springer Science+Business Media B.V. 2012

the diversity of knowledge by means of trans-cognitive unities; it also means mastery of what is known."[1] Ehrlich comes to the conclusion that philosophical faith is not indifferent to the concreteness of knowledge and therefore is not otherworldly. This insightful analysis has been a helpful contribution to the understanding of much of the canon of theological-oriented European philosophy of the last few centuries.

Leonard and Edith's eloquent and elegant presence at the Jaspers' Society meetings were a joy to behold. I have learned much from Leonard's critical observations. As a Continental, mostly Heidegger, scholar I had not delved very much into Jaspers' philosophy until I began attending the Jaspers Society meetings some 15 years ago. And only through the Jaspers Society have I come to appreciate the work of the compassionate and spiritual man Jaspers was. In a world where the wide sweep of philosophical and historical overviews are becoming "endangered species," being replaced by more narrowly focused studies and the virtual reality of cyberspace, I have come increasingly to value the enduring image of "the European intellectual," an image that both Jaspers and Leonard and Edith Ehrlich exemplify. The Ehrlichs' contributions to the world of philosophy, both through writings and translations, as well as through the founding of the *Karl Jaspers Society of North America* are truly invaluable. They represent the best of what the professional life and scholarship have to offer. With this essay I wish to salute and honor both Leonard and Edith. May their work endure and continue to enlighten many a philosopher, young and old. May their work contribute to the spirit of philosophy itself.

I wish to make some comments on History[2] as a subject of philosophical reflection—an object of inquiry, first in Hegel, then in Heidegger, and finally in Jaspers. By comments I mean observations, not analyses, though I will also make a few recommendations along the way regarding the notion of History (and its future) as a fit topic for pursuit in what will turn out to be our particular time.

Two claims might be said to dominate Hegel's view of the relation of philosophy to History, and we have heard them stated often enough: first, that philosophy is the child of its time; second, that philosophy is its time comprehended in thought.

That philosophy is the child of its time tells us, of course, that philosophy arises out of and is bounded by historically definable time periods, what we might call eras. Philosophy lives within these eras. They define philosophy and through them philosophy receives its nourishment and lives its life. In different time periods, it would follow, philosophy will not only live differently, but might be something different with respect to its goals and methods. The notion of philosophy as a timeless, unchanging or perennial activity must, thus, lose all but edifying force.

---

[1] Leonard Ehrlich, *Karl Jaspers: Philosophy as Faith* (Amherst, MA: University of Massachusetts Press, 1975), p. 117.

[2] I capitalize "History" throughout this essay to adumbrate narrative possibilities transcending the organization of fact, yet not insisting on alleged necessities. This capitalization, thus, points to a dimension neither quite empirical nor metaphysical. At best such capitalization opens us to problems deserving further reflection.

Stepping back for a moment from Hegel himself—who surely would have been most uncomfortable with the implications I have so far drawn from one of his own remarks—let us consider. Times do change. One era is in fact succeeded by another, though confirmation of this occurrence, even an initial judgment that it has actually happened, usually comes only retrospectively. But there is a genuine and even today an abiding mystery surrounding this circumstance. The underlying movement of time relevant to the transition from one era to its successor can be measured only externally by the ticking of the clock or by the flipping of the calendar. Historical time periods do rise and fall, come into being and pass away for timely reasons, but their temporally measurable durations, the durations of the temporal punctuations between them, and the proverbial Newtonian time line on which these various durations are placed, are external to the timeliness of differing eras and external, also, to the timing and the nature of the time involved in the transition from one era to another.

In the *Phenomenology of Spirit* Hegel tells us, following such figures as the brothers Schlegel and Novalis, "that time ripens slowly in hidden places." In terms of our normal sense of time this statement is at best poetic and at worst silly. But if we think of "time ripening" as "time periods" (eras or epochs) gestating and then emerging, declining and then disappearing, we can make much sense of Hegel's remark. We are usually well into an age—another term for era or time period—before we recognize it for what it is. And though a new era does not hide from us, it is often hidden from us by activities we engage in which belong to an era that, usually we say in retrospect, was soon passing or had essentially already passed.

What defines Hegel's particular time for Hegel? The best answer is probably the French Revolution. For Hegel it had a specific meaning which he discusses in that section of *The Phenomenology of Spirit* entitled "Freedom and Terror." The main issue is the relation of social, political and cultural institutions to the needs and legitimate interests of human beings. Are those needs and interests being met? If not, might they come to be met through reform? If not, then revolutionary action is required. Why? Because humans are meant to be free, and freedom does *not* mean being left alone and uninterfered with, thus allowed to do what you want. This is a notion of freedom that through Isaiah Berlin is popularly known as the negative conception of liberty. As we know, this notion has woven its way through the works of such thinkers as Hobbes, Locke, Constant and Mill, and forms a significant portion of the fabric of any contractarian utopia. For Hegel, on the other hand, and by contrast, freedom means finding your interests and needs nurtured, reflected, recognized, acknowledged, responded to and met in the various institutions that form the milieu in which your life is led.

The meaning of the French Revolution—which for Hegel defines his specific time—is thus freedom itself, positively construed. Therefore, the meaning of Hegel's very time is itself this same freedom as just defined: a complementary congruence between institutional realities and human interests and needs, individual and social.

As we know, the Hegel of the *Phenomenology* is concerned, always, to bring the meaning of things, which Hegel often calls their certainty, to their truth, i.e.,

to bring the purposes of things to their conceptual completion and actual fulfillment. So if the meaning of the French Revolution is freedom, how is this freedom
then achieved? In one sense—and it must be carefully qualified—the answer is that
for Hegel positive freedom is brought about in part through terror, at least terror
is involved. How so? What we are told in the "Freedom and Terror" section of
the *Phenomenology* is that the destruction of an existing order may have one of
three outcomes: continuing chaos, a better order or a worse order. At that agonizing
and often extended moment of uncertainty regarding the outcome of an intended
and accomplished institutional convulsion, the honest and appropriate response to
the existing and transitional situation is terror, for the transition itself as genuine
transition is terrifying. Groundlessness exists. There is no place to stand.

But in Hegel's retrospective judgment, as we well know and which elicited
Marx's outrage, the transition worked out positively—perhaps not altogether in
France, but in Prussia, where the *purpose* of the French Revolution, its "truth"
could have its gains, the achievement of positive freedom, consolidated by non-
revolutionary means. Hegel, thus, saw his era as the era of freedom, positively
defined, and the purpose of philosophy as reconciliatory, i.e., as showing how it
was the case that various forms of institutional reality on the one hand, social, political, and cultural, and the needs and legitimate interests of individuals on the other
hand, coincided and could be rationally comprehended as harmonized.

Often noted, and rightly I believe, is that Hegel cheats in multiple ways. Since
many of these bear on senses of History that succeed Hegel's, a few of them deserve
mention. First, Hegel's time periods, the eras of central concern to Hegel, are essentially Western. The narrative that constitutes their sequence works its way through
Athens, Rome, Jerusalem, and Florence to Prussia, albeit with various useful detours
and pit stops along the way. Second, what first appeared to be somewhat separated
if not separate time periods, turn out through a rationally retrospective lens to give
sequential rise to one another, with each successor accumulating the essential components of its predecessor. Assumed is that there *are* essential components, that they
unfold in an historical sequence, and that they can be comprehensively preserved,
appreciated, and made institutionally accessible in the present. Thus, though Hegel
does say, and is often so quoted, that philosophy is the child of its time, he does not
actually quite mean it. Hegel only means it, if we accept the qualifying claim, not
so covert in Hegel, that Hegel's time is comprehensive and consummatory.

If these—and a few other—assumptions are granted, History, of course, has been
completed. Not only is it completed in the sense that all of the essential components of previous time periods have been accumulated into the present, but it is
completed in the sense of now being over. History for Hegel is now over in that:
(a) freedom in the positive sense has been recognized and, if not fully achieved,
at least mapped in extensive outline and catalogued with respect to its specifics
within an affirmative and reassuring categorical system; and (b) all essential human
possibilities have been made institutionally and individually available in a co-
respondent and mutually reinforcing way; and (c) all that could happen subsequently
comes to be construed either as a falling away from or a failure to achieve these
circumstances. "Falling away," presumably, would be a nearly uniquely Prussian

possibility, whereas "failing to achieve" might occur nearly anywhere else and certainly outside of Europe for some time to come.

Note once more that on this account philosophy, construed first as reconciliation of thought with the world but then soon as the articulate recognition that this reconciliation has already taken place, becomes less the child of its time, than the adult for all times. It becomes this adult because all times get construed as living not just in the past but, in their humanly essential components, in the present, in Hegel's time.

Note still once more, for it is critical to Hegel's account of History, that progress is assumed, but that complete accumulation is claimed as well. Perhaps the best single term for this sense of History is History as Preservation. Clearly Hegel saw this as one of his very major bequests to posterity, a bequest first made possible through his historical acquisition of those ideas which define the philosophical West. For Hegel this acquisition had been made fully and convincingly possible through the further and extraordinarily happy circumstance that the full sequence of relevant ideas had reached their completion only, but also definitively in Hegel's own time. Proof of their definitiveness could be found, Hegel was in turn convinced, through Hegel's and then our Hegelianly indebted capacity to comprehend these ideas within and as a system. If anyone were to doubt this strong strain in Hegel's philosophy of History, they need only read the last page of his *Phenomenology of Spirit*. Here he more or less states it, and through making the claim guides us toward seeing the whole of the *Phenomenology of Spirit* as the preface to his subsequent philosophical writing.

The essential historical period for Hegel, thus, *is* the present. But in another sense History itself has now collapsed. It has collapsed as something past, for what matters of the past is now fully found in the present. And History has collapsed as future as well, for the future is only possible as the further discovery, recapitulation, and/or recapture of this present. What might be "future" can only be further detail, latent in a present, Hegel's present and ours, already essentially and comprehensively— though not thereby exhaustively—articulated.

Hegel's celebration of History is simultaneously its extinction and wake. All the essential sounds of History are symphonized in the present, Hegel's present. Moving "forward" in calendar time, after Hegel, all that is possible are re-soundings— perhaps themselves resounding. Otherwise there can only be disharmony, atonality, muted sound, possibly just noise, or silence.

I will return to the notion of silence in a few moments, for, as I will soon suggest, it is within that silence which is offered through Hegel as an unattractive and therefore implausible alternative to Hegel's own philosophy of History that a deeply disharmonious and discordant, if nonetheless poignant and even somewhat appealing, Heidegger finally comes to live.

But first a footnote to what I have said regarding Hegel. Hegel not only said that philosophy was the child of its time. He also said that philosophy was its time comprehended in thought. Hegel could not only say this, but also believed that the project of comprehending his time fully in thought was possible, because he unwaveringly—dialectical machinations notwithstanding—distinguished the essential from the accidental. It was this distinction that not only drove his account of History, but gave him the confidence to believe that he had comprehended History, had comprehended History fully, and thus, when all was said and done, had buried it with a dramatic conceptual eulogy to console those for whom its death would be experienced as a loss.

A moment ago I connected Heidegger with silence. But there is much Heidegger, or should I say many Heideggers, before this silence is reached. Heidegger shares with Hegel—apparently an occupational hazard for German philosophy professors—the view that the history of philosophical ideas is the driving engine of History itself. Unlike Hegel, however, Heidegger understands the historical sequence of philosophical ideas to demonstrate not progress but decline, a conceptually accelerated, if also growingly sophisticated falling away from a set of encounters most extraordinary.

For purposes of brevity I am going to recount this in fact largely enduring dimension of Heidegger's philosophy of History as a story. Once upon a time there was an extraordinary sense of wonder and amazement over the fact that things were and how they were. There arose the emerging and enduring *physis,* out of which later came physics. Intimately and unavoidably intertwined with *physis* there simultaneously emerged a letting things be, *logos,* out of which all too soon came reason, logic, and eventually manipulation and technology.

Though it would not have been within the very limited confines of Heidegger's even more limited supply of generosity to admit such, were it in fact the case, Heidegger's account of the extraordinary advent of *physis-logos* is perfectly compatible with and might have been influenced by long conversations with Jaspers, in whom an account of something called the dawn of the Axial Age had been gestating. For Jaspers the axial age—explored by Heidegger most explicitly and without attribution in his *Introduction to Metaphysics,* circa 1935—involved the bifurcation of our human world into reality and appearance, liberation and bondage, enlightenment and confusion, light and darkness, and somewhat later, eternity and time. At the dawn of the axial age human life gradually unfolded, to those who sought to comprehend it, as a journey: through appearance to reality, from bondage to liberation, out of confusion to insight, and through darkness toward the light.

It is not hard to understand Heidegger—all reference to possible Jaspersian influence aside—as standing, or at least through heroically intuitive re-appropriations of pre-Socratic fragments, attempting to stand, at the dawn of this axial age. If little else is certain, something that is evident is that Heidegger not only thought philosophy had begun in wonder, but that the only hope for philosophy and, thus, for humanity as philosophy's child, was that philosophy return to that wonder which had spawned it and, possibly simultaneously, had also spawned us humans in our specific humanity.

Considerably indebted to a subtle, though not thereby particularly controversial reading of Nietzsche, Heidegger understood the rise of post-Socratic Athenian philosophy as introducing or at least highlighting and intensifying the time/eternity bifurcation in axial thinking. The journey of human life not only sought a way out of appearance, bondage, confusion, and darkness, it also sought escape from time. The goal of the journey was not just reality, liberation, enlightenment and light. It was also eternity. In Heidegger's account, the early axial experience of *physis* became transformed into the quest for what lay behind *physis*, the metaphysical, something soon identified with form or primary substance. For this metaphysical pursuit to offer hope of success, *logos*, which was first a focused and benignly concentrated "letting things be," got transmuted into "reason," "dialectic," "logic," "episteme," and, more generally, conceptual thought.

The result of this assault of Greek metaphysical philosophy upon human axial history was from Heidegger's point of departure catastrophic. Once the enduring and abiding became the eternal and unchanging, the goal of History—the quest of the "religions of the Book" Platonized—became the escape from History. It was acceptable for appearance to belong to time, and thus History, but for time, and thus History to belong to appearance progressively implied that time, and thus History, were just appearance. Beyond them and intimately intertwined, it came to be believed, were reality and eternity, a reality that was eternity, and an eternity that, equally, was the only true reality.

For Heidegger, thus, the task is not to bring History to completion. Neither is it to bring History to its end or help us find ways to escape or transcend it. Pardoxically, the task is to get us back into History. It is not that we have ever actually left it, but the deep spiritual therapy needed is to make unavoidable the understanding that time and, thus, History are the only place we can ever be. It is as if Heidegger were claiming that "the fall of man" were not a fall into *time*, but in fact a deeply deceptive quest or possibly even deluded belief that we existed in our essential being outside of time. If there were a fall, on this Heideggerian account, the fall was from within time toward a nonexistent domain outside of time. Humanity has thereby lost any authentic History. If much of religious thinking later in the axial age involved delivering us *from* time and History, Heidegger's thinking strove to return us to History, to push our thinking back into that inescapable History we had never left.

A moment ago I mentioned the notion of authentic History. If philosophical History has been for Heidegger the further fixating of a misguided because a-historical purpose, the transcendence of time and History, what then might an authentic History look like?

An anti-enlightenment thinker significantly indebted to romanticism and figures such as Fichte and Herder, Heidegger understands History to be the History of a people who are the bearers of something spiritually significant. To be such bearers becomes especially significant, even desperately important, in the wake of the death of God, Nietzsche's proclamation which on Heidegger's reading is Nietzsche's accurate but for Nietzsche himself not fully comprehended announcement that the axial age had ended—however many decades or even centuries might be required for this circumstance to be fully absorbed.

Without an eternal and liberating reality beyond appearances—in short, without religion as traditionally and Platonically conceived—something else must sustain human existence. And what might this be? For Heidegger it appears to be a people. It is a people not so much because they so choose as because they are chosen, but because it is their *Geschick*.

But who or what chooses them? The Heidegger who is enduringly influenced by Nietzsche, and at best benighted through arrogance and misunderstood political opportunity, comes, however briefly, to see the people themselves, his people, choosing themselves. After the death of God, not only does the transcendent go, with it departs chosen-ness as well, except as a collective act of will. We can safely see what has been called Heidegger's decisionism as very much alive in at least a significant portion of the thirties. The account of History it suggests has a remarkable and further parallel with something else in Nietzsche.

Nietzsche was prone to think of History as a series of long and insignificant detours in the service of a few great individuals. His list once included Goethe, Heine, Schopenhauer, Wagner, and himself. Gradually the list suffered attrition born of disillusion or anger, and we know that by his end, tragically documented in *Ecce Homo*, only Nietzsche remained on that list. I suggest that Heidegger at one point understood peoples in a similar manner, but there were and always remained for him just two such peoples: the Greeks and the Germans, speakers of those two "most spiritual of languages," Greek and German. A middle Heidegger, neither early nor late, partly under the influence of Nietzsche, saw actual history as ordinary in a manner beneath philosophical interest—not, by the way and as we know, an atypical stance taken by a number of philosophers of History—and Heidegger saw two peoples, one long ago and his own people in his own post-Weimar Republic time as worthy of an authentic History and having had or possibly soon having one.

And there is the later Heidegger, for whom not only the gods, but Being and History have fled, for whom all that remains for us regarding History is a waiting and expectant silence and even silence about this silence, for, as is finally stated, and deliberately as a posthumous remark, "only a god can save us."

When we turn to Jaspers we find subtleties found neither in Hegel nor in Heidegger. In one sense Jaspers might be termed a pre-Hegelian enlightenment thinker. Made more influential through the writings of Habermas, communicative reason plays a major role in Jaspers' thinking. Through what Jaspers sometimes simply calls communication—which involves the recognition of differing perspectives and the attempt at least to understand, if not always to overcome them—people and peoples are granted equal standing and mutual recognition in a process of reciprocal comprehension. The dignity of people as peoples receives acknowledgment and support.

Jaspers, however, is not an "enlightenment" thinker, if by this is meant someone oblivious to the importance of History or someone optimistically and confidently directed toward its progressive completion or its end. For Jaspers we are enmeshed in History, and, having knowledge neither of its origin nor of its goal, are in no position to know its purpose nor to glimpse beyond it toward its presumptive ground (or grounds). To recognize oneself as enmeshed in History has as a consequence a considerable measure of humility regarding any claimed narrative meaning to History.

For Jaspers as well, to experience oneself as historical and thereby grounded by History, is also to accept that History may not be one's only ground. If Hegel turns eternity into History and then reabsorbs History into a present that collapses History, then Jaspers, through *Existenz*, accepts History as unavoidable and as unavoidably suggestive of a ground that transcends it and upon which it may rest.

If Heidegger spurns eternity in the name of a specific post-Nietzschean History, and then flees this History, or at least its overt acknowledgment, in the name of a yet to be found future History, Jaspers finds glimpses of an elusive Transcendence while always acknowledging his and our historical circumstances, our pluralized hopes and in some painful ways our human guilt over opportunities lost and actions committed.

There is a strong tendency to demand a unified narrative History, unifying and simultaneously convincing. In its absence there is an equally strong tendency toward understanding History as incommensurable and as incompatible histories, histories very much conflicting and plural. Perhaps worse, there is the abandonment of hope with regard to narrative philosophical History and an abdication of historical reflection in deference to those painstaking and deservedly respected gatherers and their gatherings of information. Jaspers, however, shows us another way—or perhaps it is many ways: These many ways involve living in the largely irreconcilable tensions of varying Historical narratives that co-exist in our twenty-first century, histories either ignoring or speaking at, not *to* each other. In his notion of communication and the humility that the recognition of our entanglement in History requires of us, Jaspers may suggest our one hopeful, though never safe nor sure philosophical opportunity to reinstate and to explore the philosophy of History.

Jaspers' *Achsenzeit* Hypothesis: A Critical Reappraisal

Michael Zank

Abstract Jaspers idea of a grand shift in the spiritual paradigm of unrelated civilizations, located rather generously somewhere around the middle of the first millennium BC, inspired only few historians, but a closer reading reveals that Jaspers was always more concerned with what we can learn for the situation of our own time from what is generally true about our perception of antiquity. Jaspers made this argument twice, namely, in 1931 and again in 1949. The post-modern situation, globalization, and the question of how we understand human existence under these conditions are still of obvious relevance. This essay also brings Jaspers' idea of an axial age to bear on an ongoing study of the millennial history of Jerusalem.

Imagining Jerusalem

I imagine writing a book about Jerusalem. Proceeding in chronological order, this imaginary book tries to elucidate the relation between the histories and the meanings of a city shaped by the vicissitudes of monotheists and monotheism. I am in fact writing a book about Jerusalem, but it is not the one I imagine. When people ask me what kind of book I am writing (after all, Jerusalem is an ancient city, it has a long "history," many books have been written about it, and how close to the present was I planning to go), I tell them about my imaginary book as follows:

"I am trying to answer the question why we, that is, Jews, Muslims, and Christians, care about this city as we do," without specifying the differences and difficulties obscured by this "we." "The answer," I continue, "has something to do with scripture;" using "scripture" in a generic sense that might include the agglomeration of respective text and interpretive traditions sacred to Jews, Christians, and Muslims for whom revelation comes in the form of, or in interaction with, holy writ. "If it is the authority or experience of scripture that configures what we see in

M. Zank (✉)
Department of Religion, Boston University, Boston, MA, USA
e-mail: mzank@bu.edu

H. Wautischer et al. (eds.), *Philosophical Faith and the Future of Humanity*,
DOI 10.1007/978-94-007-2223-1_17, © Springer Science+Business Media B.V. 2012

Jerusalem, then the history of Jerusalem may be divided into three major historical periods, namely: before scripture, since scripture, and 'in' scripture."[1]

To be sure, the phrasing of the task is ironic. Aside from the *longue durée* of the history here envisaged, which forces the narrator to use chronistic tools, the irony of this project rests on the impossibility of delineating the entrance of scripture into history in the manner in which revelation enters scriptural narrative whose authority is, in turn, grounded in the revelation it historicizes. Our assumptions about there being something like history is always already grounded in an engagement with scriptural revelation, perhaps even with the plurality of such revelations. Hence a "before scripture" is not strictly speaking possible for us. *Qua* event, scripture is primordial, auratic (in Walter Benjamin's sense), *unvordenklich,* and hence cannot be neatly coordinated with a political history of the city of Jerusalem that is not already caught up in its scripturality. The very idea that there ought to be a correlation between the major destructions and reconstructions that serve as demarcations in the chronology of the city's history in time and space, and the history of the city as an emblem, sign, symbol, representation, or synecdoche of belief, is suggested by scripture itself (it may be its *raison d'etre* and the reason why it has a hold on us), namely by the fact that the city appears in scripture (which *is* the connection of, at once, a sign and a signified). It is a scriptural idea. To separate what is united in scripture appears artificial or rather as a self-consciously applied sleight of hand, which serves to remind us of the artificiality of every historical critique. Far from transcending the perspective of scripture or breaking its hold on us, historical critique merely serves to emphasize and enhance this always present effect of scripture which we are not able to transcend or circumvent by means of a historical critique. Replacing biblical narrative with quasi-objective historical narration we replace one story by another. But the triangulation of before scripture, in scripture, and after scripture goes a step further. Only thus do we realize the degree to which we live and read in the shadow of such story even when we try to take a position on its outside. It would require a more complete secularization or alienation from tradition than we can aspire to or wish for, a point at which the monotheistic traditions will have receded into the past to such a degree that they truly no longer matter for us to be able to know or understand the history of monotheism, its signs, or its manners of signifying. But then our lack of interest may prevent us from understanding what no longer concerns us.

My imaginary book is more of a thought experiment than an exercise in historiography, and it is quite possible that one cannot really carry out such a program in a concise, chronological, or chronistic fashion. It is history by allusion, a history organized by symbols or generalizations that are meant to point out certain characteristics about our attitudes toward and infatuations with something like the Holy City. The experiment is nevertheless warranted by our concern with "monotheism" and with the way in which Jerusalem is enmeshed in it (or vice versa).

---

[1] See "Jerusalem in the Religious Studies Classroom: The City and Scripture," in *Jerusalem Across the Disciplines*, eds. Miriam Elman and Madeleine Adelman (at the time of this writing, August 2010, this volume is under consideration with Syracuse University Press).

Treating the history of Jerusalem in relation to the Abrahamic monotheisms as religious worldviews grounded in a particular history of prophetic revelation and having this history rotate around the axis of scripture rather than around a particular moment in the history of the actual city allows me to coordinate the three major book-religions of Judaism, Christianity, and Islam without prioritizing one over the other. I believe this is not just a matter dictated by liberal guilt but recommended by methodical circumspection. That there were Jews before there were Christians, and that there were Jews and Christians before there were Muslims, may be mere truism or possibly a fallacy. We know Jews, Christians, and Muslims only as co-existent and always already laboring under mutual influence and in competition with one another. To attribute higher dignity in the life of the spirit or culture to the first or earliest form of a cultural formation is a mere prejudice that is furthermore contradicted by the very biblical critique of the prevailing of the human laws of primogeniture in the economy of divine election. At least, it may be said that our scriptures display references to both exclusiveness of election (and hence a scarcity of resources) and the promise or prospect of universal inclusion. Not just in politics (more precisely: in the question of just rule) but also in the realms of culture and religion the later formation may well be the most accomplished and hence, in a transcendental sense, the original one from which the earlier ones receive their ultimate meaning and belated legitimacy. I happen to like the early Muslim idea that casts Islam as a restoration of the original and uncontested religion of Abraham, attributes equal value to all prophetic scriptures, and elevates Jewish, Christian, and Zoroastrian communities to "people of the book"—a legal fiction that allows Islam to tolerate them as God-pleasing, though in error, and thus care for their continued existence within the House of Islam. It is an eminently wise and exemplary arrangement that allows for peaceful coexistence between alternative though clearly related cultural formations.

Applying this insight to the history of Jerusalem, the first advantage of this approach is that it allows me to applaud and recognize the great achievements of Islamic civilization as not just commensurate with the spirit of biblical prophecy and Christian love but as an indication that our scriptural religions are in fact capable of extending themselves toward the possibility of a harmonization of their particularities. The importance of this possibility is obvious.

The Axial Age Hypothesis: First Impressions

I became interested in Jaspers' notion of an axial age before I read his book on *The Origin and Goal of History*, where it makes its first appearance.[2] I read this book with the suspicion that the notion of an axial age was a mere *deus ex machina*, a suspicion, I found later, that occurred to Jaspers himself. To be sure, Jaspers' ideas about history may have been misrepresented by those who picked up the axial age

---

[2] Karl Jaspers, *Vom Ursprung und Ziel der Geschichte* (Munich: Piper, 1949). [Henceforth cited as *UZG*, all translations by the author]

hypothesis most vigorously, among them biblical scholar Benjamin Uffenheimer[3] as well the popular religion author Karen Armstrong.[4] Uffenheimer turned to Jaspers in support of Yehezkel Kaufmann's claim that the notion of ethical monotheism stood at the beginning rather than then the end of a long development that, according to Uffenheimer, may well have begun at the time of the biblical patriarchs. Karen Armstrong whose retellings of the history of the Abrahamic religions revolve around the notion of God's preferential option for the poor sees the axial age formation of biblical prophecy as on the one hand alive in Judaism, Christianity, and Islam and on the other hand perpetually threatened by political theologians exploiting the claim of divine favoritism.

I came across the axial age hypothesis in form of derivative adaptations. My impression was that it served apologetic purposes and shed no distinct light on the actual complexities of the history of culture and religion. I felt particularly disconcerted by the notion that the appearance of ethical monotheism or something akin to it should be considered a turning point in human history. To me this seemed both unsettling and somehow unhistorical. After one reads Jaspers himself, however, one will almost certainly conclude that his thesis has been employed by careless readers to whom it appealed for the wrong reasons. This is not to say that Jaspers' philosophy of history is entirely satisfactory, and I say this with chagrin since I cannot help noticing that my own approach to the (imaginary) history of Jerusalem as a symbol or a cipher has much in common with Jaspers' philosophy of history.

Jaspers' Theory of History: Review and Critique

Let me introduce the axial age hypothesis in its context, Jaspers' aforementioned book *Vom Ursprung und Ziel der Geschichte*. The book is divided into three parts, dealing respectively with World History, Present and Future, and the Meaning of History. Here, as in another related work first published in 1931,[5] the existentialist philosopher is most concerned with the present, but in contrast to the earlier work

---

[3] See Benjamin Uffenheimer, *The Origins and Diversity of Axial Age Civilizations,* ed. S.N. Eisenstadt (Albany, NY: State University of New York Press, 1986). Uffenheimer represents the Yehezkel Kaufmann school, which is still prominent in Hebrew University biblical scholarship (M. Weinberg et al.) and popular among many American biblical studies scholars. Kaufmann presented his theory in an elaborate multi-volume work on the "History of Israel's faith" (*Toldot Ha-Emunah Ha-Yisra'elit*) on the basis of Hermann Cohen's philosophy of religion and in polemic against the Wellhausen school. By Uffenheimer see further *Nevu'ah Ha-Kedumah Be-Yisra'el* [*Early Prophecy in Israel*] (Jerusalem: Magnes Press, 1999).

[4] See K. Armstrong, *The Great Transformation: The Beginning of Our Religious Traditions* (New York, NY: Knopf, 2006).

[5] Karl Jaspers, *Die geistige Situation der Zeit* (Berlin and Leipzig: Walter de Gruyter, 1931), appeared as volume 1000 in the popular *Sammlung Göschen* of "brief and generally accessible" introductions to the latest state of knowledge in all fields, a series akin to the ongoing "Very Short Introductions" published by Oxford University Press. Jaspers' book appeared in several further printings and is referred to as a companion piece in the 1949 *Vom Ursprung und Ziel der*

he now attempts to anchor our situation within the broad sweep of human history. Jaspers invokes a structure of history that can be compelling only because it is also grounded in indisputable empirical facts and observations. Thus, for example, there is an obvious divide between the vast stretches of prehistory, the hundreds of thousands, even millions of years during which the *genus homo* acquired the traits that set us apart from other animals and connect us beyond all cultural and genetic differences. Prehistory is not yet history but it structures human history. The natural evolution of our species is not at hand but it is in that Promethean age that our common human traits were shaped. This generates a fundamental uncertainty with regard to any assertion about the difference between natural and acquired traits, between cultural values and natural behavior. Any assertion about human nature is therefore profoundly doubtful. As something beyond our grasp but essential in having shaped the entire human species, prehistory is in fact the token or the historical expression of our awareness of a common origin.[6] In the symbolic terms employed by Jaspers, and—to anticipate—in an expression shaped in one of the axial age moments of lucidity, when we look at ourselves in historical terms, we see ourselves as descended from a single origin and hence, as it were, descended from Adam.

History, as distinct from prehistory, is limited to the past six millennia for which we have access to written records. In other words, history begins when we perceive humans to emerge from silence and to begin speaking to us. Our ability to listen to the voices of the literate members of ancient societies was only recently extended beyond the previously available Greek, Latin, and Hebrew sources from which the West nourished its great Humanistic revivals since the fifteenth century. In and through the modern spirit of exploration, generated in part by this retrieval of ancient rational and religious traditions from which the West had already been nourished, albeit in the attenuated forms of late antiquity, the moderns eventually extended the limits of knowledge in methodological, geographical, and historical terms to the point at which they were compelled to relativize and question their own place in the larger historical and geographical world that we now inhabit. The great question of Jaspers' historical meditation is, in fact, what we mean by this "we" that inhabits the globe, and whether and how this "we" can shape a common humanity.

This philosophy of history has its center of gravity in the question of history itself, or rather in the question of whether it is possible to speak of history in the singular, that is, in the emphatic philosophical sense in which we have become used to referring to this thing called history and that is really limited to a blip of six millennia, compared to which natural history, including the natural history of the

---

Geschichte. The theme raised in 1931 is technology and its implications for the human spirit. This remained a central concern for existentialist philosophy and was taken up by Heidegger as well.

[6] In his review of Peter E. Gordon's book on Rosenzweig and Heidegger, Charles Bambach offers a significant meditation on the problem of origin and the crisis of historicism in twentieth century German thought. Though Bambach does not touch on Jaspers, the latter clearly speaks to and out of this very crisis. See Charles Bambach, "Athens and Jerusalem: Rosenzweig, Heidegger, and the Search for an Origin," *History and Theory*, Vol. 44, No. 2 (May, 2005), pp. 271–288.

genus homo, is an unfathomable abyss of time and of unknown and unknowable facts and factors that determine what we are as a species in decisive but perhaps irretrievable ways. The notion of an axial age was Jaspers' attempt to move beyond the myth of a common origin of the West that is still implicit in the title of the 1931 work, which speaks of a "spiritual situation of the present" in the singular and without any consideration of a non-Western situation or present. The 1949 book is Jaspers' attempt at retaining the possibility of speaking of the origin and goal of history in the singular while recognizing a plurality of points of departure for human orientations toward this unified conception of history.

The idea of the axial age represents a point of orientation in a historical horizon that is on the verge of a world historic turn in a more acute sense, namely, a future determined by what today we would call globalization. Jaspers' book is really a statement on whether the past offers us any help in orienting ourselves toward this uncharted future. Significantly, Jaspers now recognizes, at least in principle, a plurality of such points of orientation. Here are some of the things Jaspers says about the axial age and its role as a structural moment in history.

- The axial age followed a period of decline of the ancient high urban civilizations that stretched from North-Africa and the eastern Mediterranean via Mesopotamia to Persia, India, and China in a narrow band of geographical regions nourished by rivers, reliable precipitation, arable land, and favorable climates. It also preceded the rise of new vast empires that tended to base themselves on elements of axial age insights that they used to legitimize their hold on power.
- Wedged between these imperial ages we find personalities that expressed profound insights into the human condition. Their forms of human self-expression still speak to us immediately, whereas we are less profoundly touched by earlier sources, some of which appear no less intricate but ultimately leave us cold and, in any case, have not been part of a continuous cultural memory. It is rather from the axial age expressions of humanity that later civilizations have repeatedly renewed themselves.
- Expressions of axial age insights into what Jaspers calls *Menschsein* (being human), include, among others, the Hebrew prophets, the great poets and philosophers among the Greeks, Zoroaster in Persia, the Buddha in India, and Confucius in China.
- A defining characteristic of the axial age moments is their occurring at roughly the same time, without any evidence of mutual influence. Lasting discoveries of this sort were made around 800–200 BCE, or the middle of the millennium before Christ, though separated from one another across vast geographic distances. This rules out mutual influence and suggests more of a coincidence that is, however, not entirely without structural parallels. In all cases, axial age movements followed a decline or collapse of preceding empires that had dominated vast but relatively self-enclosed regions.
- Jaspers does not claim to be the first to have observed this parallel phenomenon. In contrast to Hegel, who tried to bring India, China, and the West (including Persia) into a dialectic relation that culminated in the development of western

civilization, Jaspers emphasizes that the great axial age personalities emerged independently from one another.

- Jaspers emphasizes the spontaneity of the axial age discoveries. It is important to him that it is difficult and perhaps impossible to explain the rise of certain ideas, such as prophetic monotheism. It is a hallmark of their authenticity that they cannot be causally derived from what preceded. Instead the fact and phenomenon of the axial age in its undeniable factuality evokes amazement and hence points to a kind of immanent transcendence, a token of the human spirit and the heights to which it attained in several places almost at once. Jaspers describes the axial age appearance of the human being with whom we continue to be concerned as a kind of anthropophany. Echoing Kant who referred to freedom as "the miracle in the phenomenal world" (*das Wunder in der Erscheinungswelt*), Jaspers describes the idea of humanity as a miracle in the world of historical causality.

- Jaspers' description of the contrast between the ancient high urban civilizations and the axial age personalities that gave us the idea of freedom in the face of limit situations (*Grenzsituationen*) anticipates the central concern of his book, which is the struggle for freedom and liberty in an age characterized by the ubiquitous trappings of technology and the virtually complete attenuation of all traditions rooted in the axial age. In other words, Jaspers' real concern is with the question of whether the notions of humanity that had hitherto guided us, and that first appeared in the first pre-Christian millennium, can still guide us in a situation characterized by global war and mass murder.

- Jaspers does not stipulate that the ancient personalities and their ideas have eternal and unalterable meaning that merely needs to be retrieved in our new situation. In fact, as Jaspers says (p. 42), even the axial age was ultimately a failure. In a remark toward the end of the book, Jaspers rules out the possibility of repristination:

> Our sketch of world history attempted to derive the unity of history [*geschichtliche Einheit*] from an axial age that was common to humanity as a whole.
> What we meant by axis was not the hidden interior around which the foreground of the appearances always revolves, while itself remains timelessly stretched through all ages, wrapped in the dust-clouds of the merely present. Rather, what we called axis was an age around the middle of the last millennium before Christ, for which everything that preceded may seem like preparation and to which everything that followed relates in fact and often in bright consciousness. From here, the world-history of being human [*Weltgeschichte des Menschseins*] receives its structure. It is not an axis for which we may claim an absoluteness and uniqueness that lasts forever. Rather, it has been the axis of the brief world history until now, that which, in the consciousness of all people, could serve as the ground of their historical oneness, recognized in solidarity. Then this real axial age would be the incarnation of an ideal axis around which being-human [*Menschsein*] aggregates in its movement. (*UZG* 324)

- To simply rely on axial age statements therefore misses the point, which is, after all, to take history seriously. The ancient positions as such are no longer tenable or compelling in their literal sense, though their symbolism may continue to serve us as orientation. But the core of the humanity that first appeared in form of axial age personalities is the humanity itself that appears in those personalities rather than its doctrinal residue that became the basis of philosophical and theological schools.

• In contrast to the age of mythology and ritual that gave the appearance of permanence to the first urban civilizations, the axial age prophets and philosophers articulated the fragility of humanity, the infinite value of freedom, the uncertainties and ambiguities of human nature, and the limitations of reason. In regard to such insights we have not made any progress.

This is almost all Jaspers has to say about the axial age as a historical period. The real center of gravity of the 1949 book is not the axial age as such but the future of those Western values that are rooted in the texts and traditions that first appeared in the middle of the millennium before Christ and from which Western civilization renewed itself until the modern technological age destroyed the plausibility of every and all tradition. In 1931, Jaspers makes many similar points about the crisis of modernity as in 1949 but there he pays no attention to non-Western sources. In 1949, with greater emphasis on globalization as the new challenge, attention to non-Western sources is still more modest than one might expect. Jaspers sees the modern process of globalization as the result of a Western development and links it with the age that dawned around 1500, the age of discovery that was enhanced by the Western renewal and transformation of its own axial age sources. Nothing comparable happened in the east, which was in decline when the Western nations began to expand and conquer.

Taken as a claim about a historical phenomenon rather than a structural device in a historiosophical contemplation, the axial age hypothesis is open to a number of critical objections. I will list these in the order in which they occurred to me as I was reading *Vom Ursprung und Ziel der Geschichte*.

Jaspers considers the place of primitive people in the unity of world history. Where they are not absorbed into historical nations and empires he regards them as the mere rudimentary organs of prehistory. Either they were annihilated or they are gradually integrated. So far so good; but what about the rudimentary organs of the axial age? What about people or nations that brought forth axial age personalities but then failed to transform themselves any more into axial age civilizations than the post-axial age empires that oppressed them? Of course I am thinking in particular of the Jews. How does Jaspers explain the cultural conflict and religious wars between axial age civilizations? How are conflicts to be resolved and what is their place in Jaspers' schema of world history? Is the progression toward unity possible without reducing and homogenizing those nations and civilizations that fail to behave according to the general theory of cultural decline and religious attenuation?

According to Jaspers world history moves from the ancient geographic parataxis, where all history is local or regional, toward global unity via exploration, conquest, colonization, and the technological shrinking of the globe into a single interconnected unit. He does not consider the many ways in which this schema may be questioned. Pre-modern interactions between originally separate regions were not limited to equestrian hordes but included trade along the silk road, which Jaspers does not mention at all. In general, Jaspers is not informed about the role of

Islamic civilizations in the early medieval world. Another indication that the pre-modern world was more hypotactic than Jaspers thought are the nomadic nations that crossed borders and boundaries all the time, including the Jews and the Gypsies.

The core of the axial age hypothesis is the great personality who appears in a certain place and, without obvious connection to any predecessors, articulates a great and lasting insight into our humanity. One of the great individuals of the ancient world who might fit this classification, the Egyptian pharaoh Amenophis IV, also known as Akhenaten, is never mentioned since he falls outside the time frame of the axial age by almost a millennium.[7] Furthermore, Jaspers' views on the biblical prophets appears dated since biblical scholarship no longer considers either Ezekiel or Daniel as personalities at all but emphasizes the composite nature and late date of composition of the books that merely bear the names of these prophets. (Moses, by the way, is not considered at all by Jaspers, presumably because the historicity of that personage was already doubtful when he went to school.) Similar concerns have arisen with respect to the historical Zoroaster and the formation of the Zoroastrian corpus of scriptures on which we rely when speaking of this prophetic figure of the Persian religion.[8] By the same token, one must ask why Jesus and Muhammad, both undoubtedly historical founders of great movements, are never considered as axial age breakthrough personalities. It is because of such historical problems that the axial age hypothesis appears to me as a *deus ex machina* within a larger historical schema rather than a truly persuasive statement of fact. It seems to allow Jaspers to be rather vague about the common, though accidental, emergence of notions of humanity that are still with us.

There is a streak of elitism in Jaspers' understanding of humanity to the detriment of far more pervasive aspects of humanity that are likewise embedded in literary texts such as the Bible, such as the value of hospitality. If any value may advance us toward a global ethic, why not the ancient and inviolable virtue of hospitality?

Given the weakness of the axial age hypothesis as a thesis about actual historical phenomena it is not surprising that it had little impact on serious historians of the ancient world and that its popularity has been limited to semi-scholarly works on biblical religion, such as Karen Armstrong's book on the axial age, that took the authority of Jaspers' thesis for granted and used it to enhance a theologizing view of biblical prophecy and its ultimately inexplicable appearance in ancient Israel. Ultimately it is the god of monotheism, himself, who appears on the historical scene as somewhat of a *deus ex machina*, as an unexplained historical or inexplicable

---

[7] Jan Assmann's prolific *oeuvre* may be said to be devoted to the project of having Egypt considered as an "axial age" civilization. See, among others, J. Assmann, *Ma'at: Gerechtigkeit und Unsterblichkeit im Alten Ägypten* (Munich: Beck, 1995).

[8] On Persian religion see Carsten Colpe, *Iranier–Aramäer–Hebräer–Hellenen. Iranische Religionen und ihre Westbeziehungen. Einzelstudien und Versuch einer Zusammenschau* (Tübingen: Mohr, 2003). On Persian history see Josef Wiesehöfer, Ancient Persia: From 550 BC to 650 AD, trans. Azizeh Asodi (London and New York, NY: I. B. Tauris Publishers, 1996). The book includes excellent bibliographic essays.

meta-historical phenomenon. Jaspers was aware of this situation and considered the objection that his entire thesis might appear as a *deus ex machina* (*UZG* 39f).

In Defense of Jaspers

Here is how I read Jaspers. Those who take him too literal and think they can rely on the axial age hypothesis as a positive insight into an otherwise enigmatic set of phenomena are misreading Jaspers. Although Jaspers probably thought that he was describing the phenomena he discussed accurately, he would not have to object to my objections to defend the larger point he was trying to make. What is decisive to Jaspers is what Jan and Aleida Assmann call "cultural memory."[9] There is no doubt that Jaspers is right when he speaks of expressions of humanity that have been with us since antiquity and in whose light we have repeatedly sought guidance on the origin and goal of history. The very elements of history and existence in light of history, the notion of decision and of freedom in light of limit situations, etc. are indeed the legacy of what we might locate somewhere in the second half of the pre-Christian millennium when the major textual bodies we have since drawn on seem to have originated. Likewise, Jaspers' diagnosis of the problems of our time, whether in the formulation of 1931 or in that of 1949, is as sharp as any diagnosis of the crisis of modern civilization. Like others Jaspers accepted the critique of modern culture that had been decisively expressed by Kierkegaard and Nietzsche; like others he felt that philosophy was compelled to go beyond cultural pessimism; and like others he sought to retrieve what could be retrieved from the ancient sources, including the biblical sources, without compromising the modern standard of absolute truthfulness that he felt, as others did, derived from no other source than the prophetic ethos of the Bible itself. At that bizarre moment of loss of tradition, the tradition began to speak anew, and Jaspers' attempt of opening a space for a renewed engagement with the demands of history by means of a strong reading of our ancient sources appears as fresh and engaging today as it did in 1949. None of this depends on the historical accuracy of the axial age hypothesis as Jaspers presented it. What matters is not what actually happened or when, but what is present to us. "True is what connects between us" (*Denn wahr ist, was uns verbindet, UZG* 30). What interests Jaspers in his axial age personalities is that, in his perception, they were the ones who articulated human freedom in contrast to the "peculiar dullness [*Dumpfheit*] combined with extraordinary style in the achievements of art, esp. in architecture and sculpture" (*UZG* 33) that was typical of the great empires.

In Jaspers' mind, the fact that the axial age occurred (or that axial age formations exist and have enduring value) carries the promise or holds out the possibility of a new axial age that might arise in the future and carry us beyond the menace of a tyrannical world order or a sinking back into a prehistoric form of existence.

---

[9] See Jan Assmann, *Das kulturelle Gedächtnis: Schrift, Erinnerung und politische Identität in frühen Hochkulturen*, 6th edition (Munich: Beck, 2007).

The center of gravity of Jaspers' historical contemplation is really the future. In the face of the technological ability to destroy the globe and mindful of the nihilistic alternative, Jaspers reaches for global sources as models by which we might bestir ourselves in the pursuit of the "eternal tasks" of freedom and humanity. What necessitates the historical detour is the realization that these eternal tasks themselves first made their appearance in history and that their authority is fragile.[10] To articulate what is needed requires the use of symbols that continue to speak to us, and indeed are indispensable, even though their original meanings have long since been abandoned.

The Relevance of Jaspers

Here I break off this all-too-brief and fragmentary discussion of Jaspers' lucid prose, but hope I did not mangle it too badly. I conclude with a few comments on the echoes I found in Jaspers that reverberated with my imaginary project of writing the history of Jerusalem as a symbol.

Like Jaspers I am not a historian but a philosopher writing about history. My writing about Jerusalem is an exercise on the history and historiography of something like Jerusalem, or a contemplation on the past, present, and future of our monotheistic formations. Jaspers' 1931 predecessor to *Ursprung und Ziel der Geschichte* was less of a meditation on history but it was more openly Christian or based on Christian symbols than *Ursprung und Ziel,* but even in 1949 Jaspers does not hide the fact that he believes we have no better or more significant way of structuring history than the one we inherit from the Christian or Judeo-Christian tradition. As I have mentioned earlier, the three parts of *Ursprung und Ziel* address the past or common origin of humanity, the present situation of humanity, and its future. The question of origin and goal concerns the pursuit of a unity for which the globe is merely the external symbol and foundation in space or empirical reality. The real unity is an elusive goal, but that it is what we must strive toward is expressed in the form of an immanent eschatology. Origin and goal of history are transcendent, what is at hand are the present and the short moment of world history. What moves us are care and responsibility not just for ourselves but for others. The task is to move from individual and subjective insights into the character of history to a commonality based on a new and extended range of communication reaching for universality.

Similarly, my project also rotates around an axis—namely scripture—that is both historically empirical and symbolic. Like Jaspers' axial age, scripture is both anchored in historical processes and linked to its moments of origin and linked to later ages as their perpetual source of renewal. Scripture has its history of reception and interpretation. It has remained present; it determines how we see the past and what we look for in the past; and it impacts on what people are taught to expect of

---

[10] I cannot resist pointing out that, when speaking of *ewige Aufgaben*, Jaspers consciously or unconsciously echoes a phrase prominently used by Hermann Cohen.

the future. Scripture's influence is not just beneficial; much of it must be considered untenable and rubs against the critical spirit that it helped to spawn. All of this is also present in Jaspers but I would argue that by presenting a claim that is more limited and specific, I am closer to the historical specificity that Jaspers envisions, namely, a phenomenon pertaining to our scriptural religions, the religions of the people of the book.

Like Jaspers I look at the variety of scriptural religions as parallel phenomena, even though in the case of Judaism, Christianity, and Islam, to use the conventional and broad qualifiers, there is an evident element of influence and historical priority. But, in contrast to our biblical sources, the Judaism that is still with us is not the Jewish environment that spawned the Christian movement. In fact, just as Jaspers reminds us that the appearance of the great breakthrough personality in his axial age cannot be linearly derived from its antecedents, there is much to be gained from resisting the common and pseudo-historical platitudes about Christianity having grown from Judaism and Islam having grown from both of its antecedents, as if these movements were a kind of organism. Like Jaspers in 1949 I find it refreshing to think of our monotheistic formations as parallel phenomena rather than look at them in terms of filiation because that is how they have been present. Rabbinic Judaism, the Christian denominations and political formations, and the Islamic *umma* all emerged around the middle of the first millennium after Christ and thus it is just as reasonable, or more so, to treat them as a common axis as it was for Jaspers to speak of the widely distributed and disconnected formations of the middle of the first millennium before Christ as a common axis.

I agree with Jaspers where he speaks of the problem of romantic views of history. Romanticism was a movement that attempted to locate its view of communitarian perfection and the wholeness of faith in an actual past, namely, in the Middle Ages as conceived by the romantics. Jaspers' own impulse is somewhat similar in that he locates what makes us human in an actual historical moment, the axial age. He foregrounds the axial age because its expressions of humanity are more fragile, and formulated in an age between empires. Unlike the romantics, he approves of the freedom and individualism of renaissance and enlightenment but he wishes to bind these back to the ethos of the biblical prophets. Jaspers explicitly rejects Catholicity as the radical alternative to reason (*UZG* 349 fn). Jaspers dismisses the romantic attempt to use modern scientific means to locate their mythological ideal of the past in actual history:

> Where empirical research finds the remnants of this primordial age [*Vorzeit*] it finds no confirmation of such dreams. Those primordial ages were rough, the human being infinitely dependent and exposed. We can grasp what it means to be human only through what becomes spirit and can be communicated. (*UZG* 303)

Since 1967, Israeli archeologists have had greater access to what is generally believed to be the location of first and second temple Jerusalem. This has boosted the previously existing but marginal Jewish religious nationalistic movement which has usurped crucial archeological work in Jerusalem. Right now, attempts are underway to produce evidence of the City of David in the village of Silwan. The archeological park established in this area south of the Haram ash-Sharif or Noble Sanctuary is run by a settler organization supported by Irving Moskovitz, an American Jewish millionaire, and the scientists excavating are supported by the Shalem Center, a right-wing think tank, supported by the same source. I propose that,

> to say, there was no Jewish temple in Jerusalem is a historical lie (in the interest of de-legitimizing legitimate Jewish claims to their history in the city); to say Palestinians are not a people with distinct roots and attachments to the Holy Land is also a lie, used to de-legitimize the Palestinian sense of history and belonging.
>
> To say, we don't have evidence of a united Jewish kingdom at the beginning of Israelite history, i.e., to deny the veracity of the biblical stories about David and Solomon is not a betrayal of the Jewish nation of today but based on the belief that authentic nationhood cannot be based on unverified and unverifiable myths of origin at the expense of scientific veracity. To say that some biblical stories are contrived is not to declare the entire corpus of ancient Judahite historiography a literary contrivance. It matters, especially in connection with the repeated international calls among academics for a boycott of Israeli institutions of higher education, whether Israeli and Jewish scholarship elsewhere meet the highest standards of excellence. It is therefore of utmost importance that archeological explorations of sensitive places, such as those conducted in Silwan, the so-called "City of David," are conducted under the auspices of internationally recognized bodies such as UNESCO.[11]

What I formulate here is based on Jaspers' consideration of the conditions for a common future.

There are other ways in which I find myself stimulated by Jaspers. I find his characterization of the post-Christian empires interesting and helpful in exploring the difference between Catholic and Protestant perspectives of Christian history. From a Protestant perspective, early Christianity was what the Protestants made of it, what they wrested away from Church hierarchy, and what eventually emancipated itself even from its Protestant ecclesiastic forms, namely, the discovery of the existential challenge of faith, the freedom of the human being who stands before God directly and without the mediation of a cult or a priesthood. But this is historically problematic. The forms in which the Christian experience became institutionalized and historically efficient were ecclesiastical, cultic, and ultimately political. The strange though tense affinity between prophetic faith and political authority is an important theme in Jaspers and it is important for me in trying to understand the invention of Jerusalem as a Christian Holy City in the fourth century under the imperial guidance of Constantine and his successors.

Further important in both historical and philosophical or symbolic terms is the question of political freedom. Jaspers attends to the distinction between spiritual freedom and political freedom. Jaspers does not believe that the Western form of political liberty, democracy, and the rule of law are necessary conditions for the attainment or preservation of one's humanity, which does not mean that he would not stand up for human rights in China, for example. But he declines to commit to any one-size-fits-all-solution to our global political problems. In my own project I found that biblical prophecy is misrepresented if we only look at its most universalistic

---

[11] Source: URL http://unholycity.blogspot.com/2009/12/bad-science.html. Accessed August 9, 2010.

formulations, anticipating a reign of peace on earth. When it comes to Jerusalem-related prophecy before the Babylonian exile, the prophetic project is concerned with the freedom of a land-owning class from the tribute imposed by foreign powers, represented by their "foreign" gods. It seems to me that Jaspers does not distinguish within the religious traditions between political and spiritual impulses. This lack of perception derives from a conflation of Jewish and Christian traditions, as in general he does not see the enduring power of distinct religious formations.

In conclusion, Jaspers' anamnesis of the present situation in the historical past is not without problems but it is nevertheless profound. His diagnosis of the present situation is subtle, insightful, and moving. His prognosis is powerful in a neo-Kantian and normative way, indicating where we ought to go, but it is not so powerful as forecast or prophetic speech. He emphasizes, of course, that prognosis is not prophecy. Jaspers did not see the possibility that the religious formations of the past might endure and, in fact, return in force to determine, for better or worse, our bumpy path toward some end of history. Although Jaspers extended his horizon to consider China and India as independent and parallel sources of axial age insights, he might have perceived a global future through his own cultural lens. Otherwise he would have noticed that the phenomenon of an attenuation of religion he saw in his own culture was not at all a global phenomenon. To be sure, such perception that the European model applies to other places is not unique to Jaspers.

Jaspers Meets Confucius

Charles Courtney

Abstract I place Jaspers' discussion of Confucius in the context of his project of writing a universal history of philosophy. But I say that Jaspers *meets* Confucius because he acknowledges the critical scholarship about dating and the authenticity of the texts attributed to Confucius and then goes on to form a picture of his subject that he claims has all its original freshness. Philosopher meets philosopher. I consider to what extent Confucius is a representative of the Axial Age. Jaspers emphasizes how Confucius gives priority to existential enactment over mere form. I suggest that the role of custom and ritual for Confucius is played for Jaspers by philosophical communication. Finally, I compare them as public figures.

Before discussing *what* happens when Jaspers meets Confucius, we should note that it is remarkable *that* they meet. Many leading philosophers from the West and from Asia do their work without encountering thinkers from the other tradition. In two of his most important works, *The Origin and Goal of History* and *The Great Philosophers*, Jaspers pays attention to Asia.

The former book, which appeared in 1949 and was already translated into English by 1953, proposes a universal view of history. Jaspers opens the concluding part by saying,

> We wish to understand history as a whole, in order to understand ourselves. History for us is the memory which is not only known to us, but from which we live. It is the groundwork which is laid down and to which we remain bound, if we do not want to melt away into nothing, but desire to win a part in humanity.[1]

This quotation makes two important points: First, history is not just information, but has existential import; second, if humanity is to be more than an abstract idea, we must try to grasp history as a whole. There is a contrast here with Hegel, who also offers a universal view of history. While Hegel sees Asia as a phase superceded

---

[1] Karl Jaspers, *Vom Ursprung und Ziel der Geschichte* (Munich: R. Piper & Co., 1949), p. 222. English translation, *The Origin and Goal of History*, trans. M. Bullock (New Haven, CT: Yale University Press, 1953), p. 231. The translation loses the music of *die Erinnerung* (memory) and *zerrinnen* (to melt or vanish).

C. Courtney (✉)
Drew University, Madison, NJ, USA
e-mail: ccourtne@drew.edu

H. Wautischer et al. (eds.), *Philosophical Faith and the Future of Humanity*,
DOI 10.1007/978-94-007-2223-1_18, © Springer Science+Business Media B.V. 2012

by Greece, Rome, and Modern Europe, Jaspers lets it stand on its own and enjoy continuing relevance.

The most famous concept advanced in the 1949 book is that of the Axial Period, the six centuries between 800 and 200 BCE, with the axis itself around the year 500. Jaspers claims that during this period, in China, India, and the West, the mythical age was left behind and philosophers appeared for the first time. He lists the characteristics of the Axial Period as follows: (1) there is a consciousness of Being as a whole, of self, and of human limitations; (2) humans experience the terror of the world and their powerlessness; (3) they ask radical questions; (4) in face of the void, they strive for liberation and redemption; (5) while recognizing their limits, they set for themselves the highest goals; and (6) they experience absoluteness in the depths of selfhood and the lucidity of transcendence. All of this was accomplished by reflective thought which accomplished a step into universality which provided a common frame of historical self-comprehension for all peoples (*UZG* 14–15, *OGH* 1–2).

Jaspers' quest for a universal history led his student Hannah Arendt, in her essay in the Jaspers volume of the Library of Living Philosophers, to call him a citizen of the world.[2] Here, she makes it clear that it is a philosophical term, linked to Jaspers' idea of mankind. If being a citizen means being a member of a sovereign state, Jaspers could not be a citizen of the world, because no such entity exists. Moreover, Jaspers argues against such an all-powerful state. He wants to preserve the diversity of political and cultural traditions, but break their dogmatic authority. Arendt puts it nicely: once "the shell of traditional authority is forced open" (*CW* 542), all the great contents of all the traditions are available to all. The faith in the comprehensibility of all truths *and* the good will to reveal and to listen make possible the limitless communication, which is the philosophical foundation for the unity of mankind. Arendt says that Jaspers' philosophy of communication

> will not abolish, not even criticize, the great philosophical systems of the past in India, China and the Occident, but will strip them of their dogmatic metaphysical claims, dissolve them, as it were, into walks of thought which meet and cross each other, communicate with each other and eventually retain only what is universally communicative. (*CW* 546–47)

The ones who communicate are existing thoughtful individuals who, in our time, face new and urgent questions. Jaspers himself concludes the chapter on the Axial Period by saying that "it is a question of the manner in which the unity of mankind becomes a concrete reality for us" (*UZG* 32, *OGH* 21).

---

[2] Hannah Arendt, "Karl Jaspers: Citizen of the World," in *The Philosophy of Karl Jaspers*, P.A. Schilpp, ed., Second Augmented Edition (LaSalle, IL: Open Court, 1981 [1957]), pp. 539–549. [Henceforth cited as CW] I got myself into a little trouble with Arendt over this term. The closest I got to studying with Jaspers was to take Arendt's seminar on Plato at Northwestern in the Winter Quarter of 1961. The next year, when I asked her to write a letter supporting my application for a Fulbright Fellowship, the form asked for her nation of citizenship. Not knowing, and not knowing any better, I put "Citizen of the World." She agreed to write the letter, but cautioned against such whimsy on official documents.

I write these words as Afghanistan lies in waste and the hunt for Osama bin Laden is still on. So, before getting to Confucius, I quote Arendt's concluding thoughts:

> Nothing, according to the implications of Jaspers' philosophy, should happen today in politics which would be contrary to the actually existing solidarity of mankind. This in the long run may mean that war must be ruled out of the arsenal of political means, not only because the possibility of an atomic war may endanger the existence of all mankind, but because each war, no matter how limited in the use of means and in territory, immediately and directly affects all mankind. The abolition of war, like the abolishment of a plurality of sovereign states, would harbor its own peculiar dangers; the various armies with their old traditions and more or less respected codes of honor would be replaced by federated police forces, and our experiences with modern police states and totalitarian governments, where the old power of the army is eclipsed by the rising omnipotence of the police, are not apt to make us over-optimistic about this prospect. All this, however, still lies in a far distant future. (*CW* 549)

In *The Great Philosophers,* the first volume of which appeared in 1957, Jaspers puts his ideas of universal history and philosophical communication to work. The latter comes into play because for Jaspers practicing the history of philosophy is itself a way of philosophizing. As we have just noted, texts make possible philosophical communication across vast divides of time and culture. The universal history he calls for in *The Origin and Purpose of History* is made operative precisely because he deals with thinkers from China, India, and the West. *The Great Philosophers* is organized according to types of thinker, and he enters into communication with three from China. Confucius is one of the Paradigmatic Individuals or Exemplary Men with which he opens the book; Socrates, Buddha, and Jesus are the others. Lao-Tzu is one of the larger group of Original Metaphysicians; among the others are Anaximander, Plotinus, Nicholas of Cusa, Spinoza, and Nagarjuna. Finally, Chu Hsi is one of the Creative Orderers; the others are Aristotle, St. Thomas, Hegel, and Shankara. Those of you who know the history of philosophy and the thought of Jaspers perhaps didn't see some names that you expected to be among the great philosophers. Plato, St. Augustine, and Kant are there, to be sure, but they constitute a group by themselves, the Seminal Founders.

Even though they are not philosophers strictly speaking (only Confucius among them wrote at all), the Paradigmatic Individuals come first. This is because, as Professor Ehrlich puts it, "the human actuality in which the exemplary lives of Socrates, Buddha, Confucius, and Jesus can be and have been lived is the alpha and omega of philosophy."[3] It is also because "each one of them was the only crucial individual for large parts of mankind, and as a matter of fact has remained so even since the others became known."[4] This last point applies to Confucius more than to any of the others because in China even today for many the argument turns on the extent to which the nation, the culture, a policy, or an individual is Confucian.

---

[3] Leonard Ehrlich, *Karl Jaspers: Philosophy as Faith* (Amherst, MA: University of Massachusetts Press, 1975), p. 214.

[4] Karl Jaspers, *The Great Philosophers,* Vol. 1, ed., Hannah Arendt, trans., Ralph Manheim (New York, NY: Harcourt, Brace & World, 1962), p. 13. Original German, *Die grossen Philosophen: Erster Band* (Munich: R. Piper & Co., 1957). [Henceforth cited as *GP1e* and *GP1g*]

Jaspers approaches Confucius aware of the critical scholarly debate over dating, authenticity of text, etc.; he cites many of the most reputable studies available when he wrote and consistently takes a moderate position. He says:

> The findings of historical criticism cannot be ignored, but they cannot produce a picture of the historical reality. For when we sift out the historical certainties, the result is a very scant minimum. When we strip off the accumulated layers of tradition to arrive at the original reality of the great men, it evades us. . . . The historical reality of these great men can be discerned only in their extraordinary impact on those who knew them and in its later echoes. . . . Pictures of these men were conceived from the very beginning and . . . such images are themselves a historical reality. . . . The people of every epoch have seen these images of the paradigmatic individuals as a reality and this is what we must do today, but under new conditions. Critical analyses of the traditions have prepared us to see beyond the documents. In studying the sources, we let the image take form within us. Like the men of all other periods, we may look at the reality directly, independently of the defined, fixated, faith. Criticism, to be sure, imposes limits on this vision and demands a certain preparation. But, once gained, the vision has all its original freshness. It remains indemonstrable and cannot be arrived at by reasoning. . . . Critical doubt joined to a feeling for the tradition cannot but encourage us to risk forming a picture of the historic reality. (*GP1e* 97–98)

Some of these points apply more to the other three exemplary men than to Confucius, and each one of them could be contested if my subject were on hermeneutics. But they prepare us for Jaspers' encounter with Confucius. What does Jaspers find when he meets Confucius, and more basically, who is Confucius for Jaspers?

Jaspers says that, "In China, Confucius was the first great flaring up of reason in all its breadth and potentiality" (*GP1e* 68). But his actual discussion of Confucius seems to fit better with potentiality than with breadth. For example, although Confucius is Jaspers' exemplary figure for the Axial Period, he does not apply all the characteristics of that period to Confucius. Yes, Confucius is conscious of himself and his limitations, but several other characteristics, such as consciousness of Being as a whole, experiencing the terror of the world and human powerlessness, striving for liberation and redemption in face of the void, and experiencing absoluteness in the depths of selfhood and the lucidity of transcendence apply better to Lao-Tzu. And, indeed, it is in connection with Lao-Tzu that Jaspers develops those points. On the other hand, Jaspers finds in Confucius an individual who asks radical questions and sets for himself the highest goals.

Jaspers overstates it when he says in the original German that through Confucius' wisdom run basic thoughts that take on a conceptual character, and the translation adds to this by referring to "certain basic ideas that form a kind of conceptual system." (*GP1g* 167, *GP1e* 59). Concepts and system emerge in China in the development of Neo-Confucian philosophy, which came to its fullest expression many centuries later in the great orderer, Chu Hsi, who lived from 1130 to 1200 of the Common Era. Neo-Confucian thinkers debated the nature and principle of humanity and things, for example, material force (*ch'i*), yin and yang, and The Great Ultimate (*T'ai-chi*). Wing-Tsit Chan says:

> Confucius had nothing to do with these problems, and never discussed them. In fact the words *li, yin, yang,* and *t'ai-chi* are not found in the . . . *Analects*. The word *ch'i* appears

several times, but is not used in the sense of material force. And Confucius' pupils said that they could not hear the Master's views on human nature and the Way of Heaven.[5]

Do these limiting and critical remarks count against what Jaspers says about Confucius? I think not. Rather, they allow what Jaspers finds in the *Analects* to stand out even more boldly. In what follows, I will lift up a few features of Jaspers' picture of Confucius.

First, even though Confucius does not discuss the principles of *li* (ritual, customs) and *jen* (humaneness), his critical awareness of their relation catches Jaspers' interest. He says, "In Confucius there is nothing absolute about the *li*. 'A man is awakened by the Odes, strengthened by the *li*, perfected by music.' Mere form, like mere knowledge, has no value without the originality that fulfills it, without the humanity that is enacted in it" (*GP1e* 55). The key term here is "enacted." Human being is not a given, but must be achieved. It is achieved through acting according to the forms that have been developed by the human community.

Jaspers' interpretation is supported by Robert Neville, who writes:

> The ontological importance of the ritual-humanity norm for human affairs is that value is given to the creativity of the present moment.... The true norm for life is ... the realization of human harmony with personal investment in it.... Confucianism focuses attention on special obligations to create the human world with its unique values. Fidelity to human norms thus supplants authenticity regarding origins. Origins, of course, remain extraordinarily important; witness the emphasis on filial piety and the ancestor cult. In Confucianism, however, the emphasis shifts from conformation to utilization of the past; achieving true filial piety is the present making of a man.[6]

I think here of a saying from the *Analects* not quoted by Jaspers but connected with the theme of enactment: "It is man that can make the Way great, and not the Way that can make man great."[7] On this point, the English translation gets only half of Jaspers' meaning. The English says that Confucius' basic idea is "The Renewal of Antiquity," whereas the German original says that his basic thought is "The Deliverance of Humanity through the Renewal of Antiquity" (*GP1e* 53, *GP1g* 157). Jaspers holds that

> Confucius finds a living solution to the problem of *authority*, which for him is not merely a monopoly on the exercise of violence. Here, for the first time in history, a great philosopher shows how the new, merging with the tradition flowing from the source of eternal truth, becomes the substance of our existence. He points the way to a conservative form of life, made dynamic by a liberal open-mindedness. (*GP1e* 54)

Antiquity, through custom and ritual, does deliver humanity, but rather than being something done once and for all, this deliverance is best regarded as a journey that is never completed. For example, although Confucius made it his vocation to improve

---

[5] Wing-Tsit Chan, *A Source Book in Chinese Philosophy* (Princeton, NJ: Princeton University Press, 1963), p. 14.

[6] Robert Neville, *The Tao and the Daimon* (Albany, NY: SUNY Press, 1982), pp. 142–143.

[7] Confucius, *Analects* 15:28, quoted in Chan, *A Source Book in Chinese Philosophy*, 44. [Henceforth quoted as *A*]

and reform his society by advising rulers and even holding public office, his efforts met with only modest success. The quality of leadership was always changing, so constant vigilance was required. Individual lives are unfinished as well. Although contemporaries and successors saw Confucius as a superior man and although he devoted much attention to portraying the superior man, Confucius said, "The way of the superior man is threefold, but I have not been able to attain it. The man of wisdom has no perplexities; the man of humanity has no worry; the man of courage has no fear" (*A* 14:30, 42).

The incompleteness of human existence is echoed in Jaspers' own philosophy. In the section on "Universal and Existential Community" in the second volume of *Philosophy*, Jaspers says several times that achieving community is a task. All humans have things in common which can be stated objectively, but "none of these common unities is perfect in temporal existence."[8] Jaspers makes a related point in his presentation of Confucius as one who was not a rationalist but who "was guided by the idea of an encompassing community, through which man becomes man" (*GP1e* 67). Jaspers acknowledges the this-worldly character of Confucian human-ism by using the term "encompassing" to apply only to the horizon of the human community and not as a periechontological term for Being itself. As to the relation of Existenz to Existenz, he says, "Intrinsic truth remains unconditional, not a stand-point; ... historic, not timelessly valid; en route, not perfected" (*P2* 371). While Jaspers holds that the reality of existential community "is more vigorous the more comprehensively and boundlessly the intelligible realm is crossed and constantly held on to as a medium of expression" (*P2* 371), Confucius would say that the common medium conducive to the good society is custom and ritual.

Outcomes are not in our control. Jaspers sees Confucius as one whose "passion was for beauty, order, truthfulness, and happiness in the world. And all these are grounded in something that is not made meaningless by failure and death" (*GP1e* 67). The *Analects* confirm this point with this verse:

> When Tzu-lu was stopping at the Stone Gate for the night, the gate-keeper asked him, "Where are you from?" Tzu-lu said, "From Confucius." "Oh, is he the one who knows a thing cannot be done and still wants to do it?" (*A* 14:41, 43)

Confucius' passion and will to do is grounded in the Mandate of Heaven, a mandate which does not call him away from the world but impels him toward involvement with the world.

I will close with some reflections on Confucius and Jaspers as public figures. It is known that Confucius' desire to reform society was frustrated. For example, his experience led him to say: "Do not enter a tottering state nor stay in a chaotic one. When the way prevails in the empire, then show yourself; when it does not prevail, then hide" (*A* 8:13, 34). His adult life was an alternating series of periods of engage-ment and withdrawal, most of the years being withdrawal. But he used those periods

---

[8] Karl Jaspers, *Philosophy* Vol. 2, trans., E.B. Ashton (Chicago, IL: University of Chicago Press, 1969), p. 370. [Henceforth cited as *P2*]

for personal study and for teaching and scholarship. Chan says, "he was the first person in Chinese history to devote his whole life, almost exclusively, to teaching. He sought to inaugurate private education, to open the door of education to all, to offer education for training of character instead of for vocation, and to gather around him a group of gentlemen-scholars" (*A* 17). The irony is that the Confucian style of education, created in his time of withdrawal, produced the literati who have dominated Chinese history and society until recently. Jaspers registers both Confucius' goal to shape the world and the importance of his school, but observes that "his limitation, which explains the insuccess of his world idea, is that in the face of evil and failure he merely laments and suffers with dignity, but derives no impulsion from the abyss" (*GP1e* 103).

And how is it for Jaspers? Jaspers did not aspire to public leadership. Perhaps it is just as well. Can we name a single happy conjunction between philosophers and political power? Not among Plato, Aristotle, Descartes, Heidegger, or William Bennett. But Jaspers led a public life in so far as he was a licensed physician and a university professor. He had an influence through his teaching and writing. His radio broadcasts sought to bring philosophy to the wider public; *Way to Wisdom*[9] is based on twelve radio addresses. He used the radio to address an urgent public issue, namely, nuclear weapons; those talks are the basis for *The Future of Mankind*.[10] Three different times, once in response to Heidegger's notorious Rectoral Address at Freiburg, he wrote about the nature of the university. After World War II, he accepted leadership of the University of Heidelberg. Even more telling is the fact that, in the very darkest of times of the war, although in involuntary academic exile, he remained in place. Friends would have assured for him and his Jewish wife safe passage to France. But he declined their offer. Confucius-like, he placed integrity and honor over personal advantage and expediency. In his discussion of Confucius' personality, he finds "the essential" in a saying by the Master which I think applies to both men: "The one thing over which a man is master is his own heart. Good or ill fortune is no yardstick of a man's value (*GP1e* 67).

What can we conclude from this brief account of the meeting between Jaspers and Confucius? Jaspers' philosophy was not formed by Confucius, but upon meeting him Jaspers found a kindred mind and heart. Confucius, as presented to us by Jaspers, is made more accessible and challenging than otherwise would be the case. As witnesses to this meeting, we are better ready to listen to what Confucius said: "He who learns but does not think is lost; he who thinks but does not learn is in danger" (*A* 2:15, 24).

*A slightly different version of this essay was first given as a talk at a session of the Jaspers Society of North America in Atlanta, Georgia, December 2001. I was pleased and honored that Leonard and Edith Ehrlich and George Pepper were in the audience.

---

[9] Karl Jaspers, *Way to Wisdom,* trans. Ralph Manheim (New Haven, CT: Yale University Press, 1951 and 2003).

[10] Karl Jaspers, *The Future of Mankind,* trans. E.B. Ashton (Chicago, IL: University of Chicago Press, 1961).

Verstehen in Historical-Philosophical Interpretation

Andrew L. Gluck

Abstract This chapter takes its starting point in a paper of Leonard H. Ehrlich on hermeneutics, in which he discussed the validity of valuation in understanding. The chapter discusses schools of history of philosophy, attitudes towards valuation and the relationship between philosophy and other academic disciplines. Jaspers' early teachings are examined, in particular his work on worldviews, as a means of elucidating the history of philosophy. Jaspers' concept of existential will is offered as a means of unraveling the significance and legitimate potential of the study of the history of philosophy.

Introduction

It seems that the very term "philosophical faith" conveys a value-laden concept that many contemporary philosophers might object to. In Western minds it might also suggest some destiny of humankind. Conjoining faith with reason is objectionable to some philosophers.[1] This essay will specifically explore the conflict between evaluative and non-evaluative methods in the history of philosophy. Here I delve into territory that has already been explored by others, including Leonard Ehrlich, but I do not claim support from him or anyone else for the conclusions offered. It is for the spirit of inquiry that I imitate him and Karl Jaspers. As a starting point, I use Ehrlich's essay "Jaspers' Method of *Verstehen*: Its Basis for History, Psychology, Translation" in *Existenz*, Volume 3, No. 1, Spring, 2008, initially presented at the annual meeting of the Karl Jaspers Society of North America in December 2007 in Baltimore. Ehrlich describes it as an "offshoot" of his book, co-authored with Edith Ehrlich, *Choices under the Duress of the Holocaust: Vienna 1938–1945, Theresienstadt 1941–1945.*

---

[1] This is separate from the possibility that reliance upon reason might require an implicit faith commitment. If that underlying attitude of faith is all there is to Jaspers' philosophical faith it might encounter little opposition. However, as we will see, I consider his notion a much more radical and controversial one.

A.L. Gluck (✉)
Hofstra University, Hempstead, NY, USA

St. Johns University, New York, NY, USA
e-mail: andy_gluck@msn.com

H. Wautischer et al. (eds.), *Philosophical Faith and the Future of Humanity*,
DOI 10.1007/978-94-007-2223-1_19, © Springer Science+Business Media B.V. 2012

The Hermeneutical Issue

Current philosophers are all heirs to at least two distinct traditions in the history of philosophy. One stems from traditional philosophy, which feels no compunction regarding stating preferences and other normative viewpoints. Traditional philosophers are quite willing to subject their views to scrutiny, the test of reason, and human experience. They nearly always question and seek reasons, unlike many of those without philosophical temperament or training. Nonetheless, an additional normative element is not only allowable in the traditional school but even celebrated as proof of the true philosophical nature of such writings. And since, at the very least, not all preferences regarding ends can be supported by reasons, it is practically inevitable that a certain intuitive element should be present in many of the writings of traditional philosophers, both past and present, even when addressing the history of philosophy.

A later school of history of philosophy, exemplified by Eugenio Garin's work in the 1950s and 1960s[2] would follow a "historical" model rather than a traditional philosophical one, and scrupulously avoids ultimate judgments of value, except when the commentator regards how well a historical figure made his or her case. Needless to say that analytical and logical positivistic schools tend to be a-historical with less interest in traditional philosophical thought compared with historians of philosophy. But since this essay addresses the interpretation of past philosophers, the methodologies of positivists, linguistic analysts, and other analytical schools are less germane to our discussion.

Intellectual history has liberated itself from religion, theology, and philosophy to a great extent and I believe this to be an essentially healthy development. We can now look back at great thinkers in the past who misunderstood their predecessors for apologetic reasons, even if those motives were unconscious. It is similar to the liberation of science from religion and philosophy and I, like most contemporary scholars, breathe that atmosphere of non-evaluative historical research and attempt to largely adhere to it. Nevertheless, we should also be aware of the side effects of this contemporary trend. Unlike good scientists and good historians (who may do so if they wish) a good philosopher must question contemporary intellectual paradigms. And that attitude of questioning should include one's own methodology. This general distinguishing characteristic of philosophy sets it radically apart from purely historical research. The latter only reports on the facts and never evaluates them from a perspective beyond the temporal.[3] To the extent that historians indulge

---

[2] See Eugenio Garin, "Osservazione preliminari a una storia della filosofia," *Gionale Critico della Filosofia Italiana*, Vol. 38, 1959, pp. 1–55.

[3] For example, the historian and philosopher Quentin Skinner assert that History by uncovering more archaic modes of thought can guide us in thinking aright about political or perhaps religious issues. Drawing the disciplinary lines somewhat differently, I argue that a historian who draws normative conclusions from historical investigations is no longer doing history but philosophy. All such labels are somewhat arbitrary but descriptive of substantive areas in which philosophy

in evaluation from either a timeless or teleological point of view they are no longer doing purely historical research.

As philosopher, one has every right to question the triumph of history over some of the other disciplines. Though many will yield to Santayana's warning that those who neglect history are doomed to repeat it, we find historically knowledgeable people taking opposite sides on many of the most crucial issues of our day. It is quite possible that the so-called "liberation" of intellectual history might actually signal a new hegemony of history over both philosophy and religion. Whether we ought to go quite that far in characterizing it is debatable but we can (and perhaps ought to) raise questions. From my point of view, the three major defects of such liberation of intellectual history are intellectual relativism, the failure to see the inevitability of value judgments (or perceptions of value), and the extreme estrangement of such scholarship from a non-scholarly public.

Such defects might not apply in other academic fields aside from philosophy and closely related studies. Why then is philosophy exceptional? A philosopher, even when eschewing metaphysics, must attempt a different view of reality than would be required in other academic fields. This is the reason for asking the sometimes-annoying philosophical questions. The impulse to philosophize is basic for humankind and quite likely to become a subterranean current that is powerful for its invisibility. When philosophical questions cease to be asked we must suspect that some metaphysical or other type of orthodoxy has achieved the status of consensus, perhaps unconsciously. We should also remember that scholarly consensus is often short-lived.[4]

The history of natural science is fairly clear. It is now almost completely free from religious and philosophical influences. I say almost, because there may indeed be areas where this is not the case (such as teleological assumptions in biology). For the natural sciences, philosophy is often viewed as an old fashioned parent, perhaps loved or despised, but surely irrelevant to one's active research. The major areas of contention seem to be in the humanities and the social sciences where philosophy may still have a relevant role as a living foundational discipline. If that is the case, the liberation of history of philosophy (along with intellectual history) from traditional philosophy may be problematic from a philosophical standpoint, even if one continues to adhere to it as a methodological principle. Such a divorce of methodology from philosophy is surely justifiable in areas of practical interest where heuristics oftentimes rule the day. Whether such divorce is justifiable in theoretical disciplines is an open question.

---

has something to contribute, especially since history is so occupied already. See Quentin Skinner, *Regarding Method* (Cambridge, MA: Cambridge University Press, 2002), p. 21.

[4] For an excellent summary of the historical relationship between philosophy/religion and intellectual history see Gabriele Boccaccini, *Roots of Rabbinic Judaism* (Grand Rapids, MI: William B. Eerdmans, 2001), pp. 15–41. In his final summation he suggests that "the emancipation of intellectual history from philosophy stands today as a consolidated achievement of Western civilization."

Leonard Ehrlich on *Verstehen*

The following quote is a jumping-off point for beginning a conversation. I do not claim that here is Ehrlich's final position on a very difficult subject:

> One last characteristic of understanding is that valuation walks in lockstep with under-standing. In other words: to be understood also means to be appraised. The minimal value inherent in understanding is consistent with reference to true-false, correct-incorrect, but extends also to right-wrong, good-bad, good-evil, worthy-reprehensible, loyal-treacherous, etc. Valuation pertains to the understanding of the author, and *a fortiori* to that of the reader. In fact, the author cannot avoid the reader's valuation that accompanies his understanding of what he reads, and *volens* or *nolens* the author provokes the reader's valuation. Sarcasm, innuendo and obfuscation are often an author's surreptitious but deliberate means of evoking a certain valuation on the part of the reader, short of clearly stating it himself, be it for lack of evidence or certainty. The tendency of judging what one understands is an ever present and ever ready personal hermeneutic context. What other researchers into a topic of interest to us have produced by way of direct or implied value judgments would be of invaluable help to us in posing questions, searching for factualities, illuminating hermeneutic contexts, and establishing plausible understanding—and valuation.
>
> The inevitable resonance of valuation with understanding may interfere with methodical inquiry. In the natural sciences this can take many forms. Prior to the rise of modern science Aristotelian teleology prevailed because it supported the biblical view that God, in creating the universe, "saw that it was good." Yet while the reaction to it led to the rise of inquiry into (the truth of) what is actually the case and into the calculable causes for it, i.e., a methodical inquiry conducted for its own sake, it was in turn impelled by the possible valuable use to be made of the result of the inquiry. The intertwining of scientific inquiry and the (largely technological) application of whatever knowledge is gained persists to this day. That scientific research (pure or basic science) can proceed only by *suspending* value considerations has been a stumbling block to its acceptance, from Galileo's theory of heliocentrism to Darwin's evolution of species. The problematic nature of Max Weber's principle that natural scientific inquiry be free of value—though not devoid of value—is well known. And yet scientists proceed under that supposition as they aim at suspending valuation. Scientific inquiry and its useful results cannot be a matter of command performance. The pioneering nuclear scientists are neither praiseworthy for benign, not guilty of horrific applications of the results of their research, unless they participate in the realization of that application.
>
> Can there be an analogous demand of keeping methodical understanding free of value judgment, considering that, since it is inextricably linked to understanding, it can hardly be suspended? What is called for is the enactment of a distinction between judging and pre-judging; keeping an open mind in inquiry; maintaining a posture of justness and fairness; since opposites are equally plausible, seeking out the alternatives of contextual interpreta-tions and weighing their respective plausibility; and to be critically mindful not only of the limits of the understanding and judgment of what others have presented, but of one's own.[5]

What particularly concerns me here is what I perceive as some equivocation in Professor Ehrlich's thinking regarding the role of value judgments in academic disciplines and particularly in philosophy. I certainly share that ambivalence and perhaps it is of interest to others as well.

---

[5] Leonard H. Ehrlich, "Jaspers' Methodology of *Verstehen*: It's Basis for History, Psychology, Translation," *Existenz*, Vol. 3, No. 1, Spring 2008, pp. 188, here p. 6. http://www.existenz.us/volumes/Vol.3-1Ehrlich.pdf.

Scientific inquiry proceeds by suspending value judgments, even if it was initially motivated by them. But this is not only the case in theoretical science. Whenever we are attempting to assess a situation for practical purposes it might often appear best to first look at the facts without distracting and complicating judgments of value and their emotional consequences. Yet that may be impossible for, as Ehrlich says, "valuation walks in lockstep with understanding." Perhaps without such valuation we only see a pale, dry, and not well-understood version of reality. Yet for many people it is only non-evaluative science that tells them about reality. Is it possible that non-evaluative scientific disciplines are actually lacking in understanding? What about the "Aha!" moment in scientific discovery? Yet there is indeed the possibility that understanding is more limited in science than it is in philosophy. This conjecture does not in any way imply a critique of science or an anti-scientific attitude but simply an attempt to place vertical, if not horizontal, limits on something that is undoubtedly of great value. Of course, the fact that a discipline might lack a degree of understanding does not entail that its practitioners do. Understanding or *Verstehen* may simply be outside the scope of the discipline itself. I think this brings us back to the discussions of Karl Jaspers that have been so influential for us and to the basic distinction that he made between science and philosophy (as those categories are currently defined). We know that valuation has a rather free rein in the arts and a tighter one in the sciences and, partly as a result of that difference, there is often a severe communication problem between them. Witness the following excerpt from G.-Albert Aurier:

> It has been peculiar to the nineteenth century to try to introduce science everywhere, even where it is least concerned—and when I say science, one must not think of mathematics, the only real science, but of those obtuse bastards of science, the natural sciences. But these natural sciences, being inexact. . .lead therefore inevitably to skepticism and to the *fear to think*. They must, therefore, be accused of having made this society lose faith, become earthbound, incapable of thousands of those intellectual or emotional human utterances which can be characterized by the term devotion. They are therefore responsible—as Schiller has already said—for the poorness of our art, which they have assigned exclusively to the domain of imitation, the only quality that can be established by experimental methods. . .If we have understood this, is it not time to react, to chase away science, as Verlaine said, "the intruder of the house," the "murderer of oratory," and to enclose, if that is still possible, the invading scientists in their laboratories?. . . To love is the only way to penetrate into a thing. To understand God, one must love Him; to understand a woman, one must love her; understanding is in proportion to love.[6]

Such a visceral reaction to science often occurs when that which a person prizes most is perceived as being depreciated as an illusion. As Ehrlich points out in the earlier quote, "that scientific research (pure or basic science) can proceed only by suspending value considerations has been a stumbling block to its acceptance, from Galileo's theory of heliocentrism to Darwin's evolution of species." This same stumbling block exists for historical research, especially when it impinges upon religious,

---

[6] Cited in Herschel B. Chipp, "Essai sur une nouvelle méthode de critique," translated by H.R. Rookmaaker and Herschel B. Chipp, *Theories of Modern Art: A Source Book by Artists and Critics*, Berkeley, CA: University of California Press, 1968, p. 87.

ethical or nationalistic sensibilities. Some, however, appreciate such non-evaluative empirical studies but reserve the right to evaluate nonetheless. I would argue that this is legitimate.

In the fields of intellectual history and history of philosophy it is often considered bad form to make value judgments. Yet when we read the works of the real masters in those fields it is difficult not to detect some implicit judgments of value. I suspect that this results from the transcendence of mere technical mastery of details and the achievement of understanding or *Verstehen*. Yet we also sense that there are limits to this evaluative engagement with the facts and with thinkers if we are to retain academic credibility. In the earlier quote, Ehrlich has offered criteria that help us define what it means to be a philosopher. Such criteria might be very useful in the history of philosophy as well. Nonetheless, we all know quite competent scholars in various fields who lack that sense of humility and fairness and who push their particular points of view just as far as they can go without any apparent sense of limits except, of course, the prohibition against manufacturing evidence. To be fair to such scholars, one would want to say they lack philosophical temperament, and their work, as valuable as it may be, does not lead to dialogue but to argumentation.

Philosophy and the Non-evaluative Sciences

We seem to have arrived at the suggestion of a distinction between philosophy and many of the other academic disciplines. On the one hand, it could perhaps be argued that like science most academic disciplines require a non-evaluative stance in the sense of suspension of value judgments. Perhaps philosophy does not require that in all of its operations.[7] There was indeed a period, not so long ago, when normative ethics was practically *verboten* in philosophy proper and in some circles, such as the history of philosophy, it is still quite suspect. Nowadays, with the decline of the authority of religion among educated people, philosophy is often looked to as a training ground for ethicists and few of us would want to turn down lucrative career opportunities. I suspect that such financial pressures will continue to move philosophy in the direction of normativity even if a very substantial segment continues to disagree with that trend and attempts to deny the ethical exceptionality of philosophy. Ehrlich does not seem to be among them. He very much desires that philosophers should be "keeping an open mind in inquiry; maintaining a posture of justness and fairness." I suggest that many good scientists and historians do

---

[7] Some argue that history is also sometimes evaluative. For example, as Leo Strauss once pointed out, the description of a historical figure as cruel is evaluative yet sometimes inescapable. But the disallowance of value judgments in history seems to do less damage to its traditional character than such a proscription in philosophy would accomplish. There are other humanistic disciplines such as art criticism and literature that also seem to evade the academic proscription against value judgments but even in those fields it is debatable whether the allowance of evaluation is as global as in traditional philosophical discourse.

not exhibit such traits and yet we consider their work quite valuable. This seems to imply that the values of communication, dialogue, and fairness are somehow uniquely required by philosophy.

The History of the Problem

In the beginning, of course, most thinkers did not strictly distinguish between the "is" and the "ought." We can already see an intensification of those kinds of distinctions in Aristotle but it did not really come to fruition until the twentieth century. Nevertheless, there were strong attempts to ground philosophy on value-laden concepts from the Renaissance on, and such conscious attempts seem to indicate the perception of a problem. That problem essentially has to do with the nature of cognition and its purported grounding in sensory perception and logic as well as tradition. The latter grounding seems to conflict somewhat with philosophical values yet the two former ones seem insufficient. We now know that much theoretical knowledge is not completely dictated by logic and sense data. Tradition and/or current fashion determines much conventional wisdom in academic disciplines. And it is the philosophers who come around exposing those ephemeral fashions and enduring traditions. The exceptionality of philosophy, therefore, may not reside so much in its interest in ethics but in its concern with epistemology. Even philosophers who are relatively unconcerned about ethics ask penetrating and unconventional epistemological questions that scientists and historians often fail to ask, unless they have philosophical training or temperament. The exceptionality of philosophy may ultimately have to do with the pursuit of truth and a philosophical interest in ethics or valuation might be a part of that broader cognitive concern. The other academic disciplines of course are concerned with truth as accurate correspondence with reality but only philosophy questions the meaning and nature of truth. This leads to questions regarding whether philosophy has a valid methodology for answering such questions or are they asked in vain.

There are relatively few people who consider the search for truth an end in itself and many more are attracted to those who at least appear to have found the answers. There are those who find themselves somehow dissatisfied with the sciences and ask whether there might be more to life than the reality they describe and explain, but the humanities do not always offer them what they seek. They quite often seek religious type answers. If we follow Jaspers, we will admit that even philosophical faith does not offer redemption, as do religions, but only a kind of understanding. Yet that is still saying quite a lot! Is it conceivable that philosophy has a certain intuitive grounding that the other academic disciplines simply don't possess? The Hegelian attempt to ground history, philosophy and religion in some sort of historical necessity seems to be just such an enterprise. I am sure that it left deep traces in the thinking of people like Karl Jaspers and Leonard Ehrlich, yet it would perhaps be fair to say that the Hegelian method does not resonate very well in the contemporary world and has not been very popular for some time.

I think there is another somewhat more modest theme that we can trace from the Renaissance on in thinkers such as Ficino, Pico, Vico, Dilthey, Weber, and Jaspers. That theme is the transcendence of abstract reason by the unique and irreplaceable nature of the human individual. It seems to me to be peculiarly relevant to both the humanities and the social sciences. It is more modest than the Hegelian synthesis. It fails to make bold claims about history but only about the nature (or lack thereof) of humankind. Since it makes no claims about human intellectual evolution, it is somewhat more compatible with the more or less successful revolt in intellectual history that was previously described. Its failure to assert any inevitability in human development also lends itself to a vital connection with human pragmatic concerns. I am sure that it is a major trend in modern thought, but also one that has been suppressed from time to time by various attempted solutions. One can see how prominent it is in modern thought by comparing the latter with ancient and medieval thought, both of which practically ignored the question of the individual altogether.

Thinking in abstract categories is inevitable, but one can also sense an inner quality that is more robustly individual. This leads to inescapable quandaries as when students want to know whether the Aristotelian forms are universal or individual. I don't think this was nearly as big a problem for the ancients. Because they failed to see the unique power of the individual, they often failed to see a conflict between logic and ontology. A dawning of this awareness is in Aquinas' famous distinction between *ens, essentia* and *ente*. For him, unlike Plato, Aristotle, and Avicenna the essence of a being no longer fully explained its existence. There is always a conflict of sorts between logical and ontological categories, yet it is only with the former that one can think. Every now and then we can recognize the limitations of such cognitive methods, for example, by falling "madly" in love. It is quite understandable that some philosophers viewed love as a cognitive disease. But viewed in a different way, it is also conceivable that the logical categories, being divorced from the ontological sources of power, cannot really exhaust reality.

Ordinarily, things can be viewed as entities of a certain kind or as instantiations of more general categories. This led Plato to believe that over and above the phenomenal world lays a realm of Forms, from which the things of this world take their essential natures. Aristotle, following in the same general path, transferred those Forms to the physical objects themselves as their very inner form or essence. The Aristotelian view still arguably functions as a sort of default way of viewing the world, with one rather major exception: the human psyche. Where Aristotle viewed that psyche as intimately related to the general forms of the things that it perceives, our view of psychic reality is quite different, viewing the psyche as *sui generis*. I am quite cognizant of the fact that the various sciences have fought mightily against that prejudice, which some now attribute to the diseased thinking of Descartes. Nevertheless, we still tend to think in terms of essences as regards objects and about individuals as regards ourselves and other people.

While we cannot attempt an entire history of this way of viewing the human psyche, I would just like to mention two Renaissance thinkers: Marsilio Ficino and Giovanni Pico della Mirandola. Ordinarily they are classified in the same school and that is more or less correct but there is a crucial difference between them that bedeviled subsequent Renaissance thought. While both followed Aquinas in opposing Averroes' (commonly understood) interpretation of Aristotle[8] as endorsing a common material intellect for all of humankind, they opposed that view from two very different standpoints.

From the standpoint of Ficino, the human soul was a special creation of God. From the standpoint of Pico, humankind was not given a special form or essence by God at all but the freedom to become anything in this world or even to become an angel or purely spiritual being. While this freedom that Pico espoused was not quite the Kantian noumenal freedom that so many post-Kantian interpreters have stamped upon it, I see no need to deny the clear words of Pico's *Oration* either, especially since they were not exactly popular with the authorities of his day. At any rate, this view of a radical kind of human freedom (whether it was really Pico's view or not) and its ramifications for the understanding of the very being of humankind must not be ignored. It seems to me that Pico's rather extreme view was reflective of his youthful age and immaturity and, ironically (since Ficino was a priest and he was not) more dependent upon orthodox religion, than was Ficino's. This turn towards orthodox religiosity became more apparent and pronounced in his *De Ente et Uno*. But, unlike the modern age, the philosophical tradition was not overly skeptical and coexisted quite well with religiosity. Religious faith in the medieval and Renaissance periods was often an antidote for an *anti-philosophical* skepticism.

When discussing the human mind, it is easy to assume that it has a history of an almost geological nature and this has been reinforced by the influential work of Foucault. There is much to commend that paradigm. We can date human artifacts almost as reliably as we can date geological strata, but with human products, style rather than physical substance, is the normal method of identification. It must be admitted that from time to time human beings come into being with an extraordinary display of originality that only fits in to a general historical pattern after the fact and after they have obtained followers. This is as true in philosophy as it is in art. When we look at Plato, for instance, everything about his philosophy is colored by his subsequent effect upon human intellectual history. That sometimes prevents us from viewing him as he really was. Of course, we are much better at doing that than our medieval or Renaissance forebears were and can now proudly distinguish between Plato and his Neoplatonic or Christian interpreters. Nevertheless, the attempt to view Plato objectively is doomed to failure, whether we view his soul from a Ficinian or Pichian perspective: as a unique creation or as an equally unique individual appropriation of what came before him.

---

[8] Ficino's motives were similar to Aquinas' criticism of the purported views of Averroes as expressed in his *Long Commentary* to the *De Anima*. His *Middle Commentary*, expressing somewhat different views, was unknown to the Christian world until the fifteenth century. See Alfred Ivry, *Averroes Middle Commentary on Aristotle's De Anima* (Provo, UT: Brigham Young University Press, 2002), pp. xiii–xxiv.

The Current Situation

For some time now philosophers have been wrestling with the place of values in a universe of facts. The traditional method was to attempt to ground both facts and values in abstractions. We now tend to have a more nuanced view of reality, sometimes even admitting interpretation and *Verstehen* into our view of the physical universe. The unique nature of philosophical inquiry is not confined to questions of value, but extends to matters of fact and truth. While philosophers can delve into the possible implications of the new physics or theoretical problems in evolutionary theory, it suffices to say that philosophers of science nowadays are not nearly as certain about the basic structure of physical reality as they once were. Add to that the traditional perplexities regarding historical reality and it becomes more and more difficult to believe that one can escape from traditional philosophical problems of an ontological, metaphysical, or ethical nature by a retreat into either history or science. So what does a philosopher do with conflicting worldviews if he or she wants to remain faithful to the philosophical values of fairness and open-mindedness?

The easiest solution is to simply accept that there is no objective truth. Yet that would spell the end of dialogue and philosophical inquiry as we know it and substitute a methodology (doubt) for a desired end (wisdom). I think that part of the exceptionality of philosophy has to do with its intuition regarding the profound nature of the human condition and the profound difference between human being and other forms of being. Yet this is precisely what so many other academic disciplines deny! And perhaps that partly explains why intellectuals can often be so wrong while knowing so much. This is not simply a case of mistaking information for knowledge as is often the case with non-intellectuals who have a great deal of the former and simply assume that the future will resemble the recent past. Deluded intellectuals, on the other hand, often have real theoretical and historical knowledge that still blinds them to the actual facts. This is an even more problematic condition than that of most laymen and perhaps can be described as a disconnection of theoretical knowledge from the real ontological powers that move this world. This unfortunate tendency might be ameliorated considerably if people would be more willing to listen to one another. So the philosophical interest in dialogue on the part of Jaspers and Ehrlich is not necessarily some touchy-feely illusion, but could actually be an interest in that which is most real in the spatial-temporal realm: the reality of the human person. The recognition of this reality might even lead to a rather radical questioning of the applicability of theoretical science, even for one who believes very much in its universal validity.

I am sure that many readers of this *Festschrift* will already appreciate how Jaspers attempted to resolve these problems even though far too much time has passed for us to be content with merely copying what he had written. Instead, we should be attempting to add to his wisdom in a way that only a contemporary person can because only we can make the thought of the past relevant to the age in which we live. Yet the basic methodology of Jaspers is still sound and I believe this is also true of Ehrlich's methodology; it requires attention to all fields of human knowledge. No one can be expert in all those fields, so it makes sense to be respectful of them and interested in their findings. It also requires sympathy with spiritual strivings of all kinds and with the fundamental fact of human bewilderment that is present even in children. I would, therefore, like to go over some of the early thoughts of Karl Jaspers when he was still attempting to reconcile the field of psychiatry with philosophy and with the fundamental human condition.

Karl Jaspers on Worldviews

Jaspers' position on worldviews forms the bridge between his early work in psychology and psychopathology and his ultimate leap into philosophy.[9] In fact, this leap is even more pronounced than it might normally be construed to be since the kind of philosophy that Jaspers attempted to produce was not simply historical or analytical, but prophetic, even functioning for some as a replacement for religion. Unfortunately, Jaspers' *Psychologie der Weltanschauungen* has never been translated into English. I will utilize excerpts that have already been translated along with some of the other writings of Jaspers. My reason for including the work on worldviews has to do with the crucial transition from the factual and theoretical to the axiological, something that is seriously questioned nowadays.

Already in the *General Psychopathology* Jaspers had despaired of reducing the human condition to an object that can be studied in the manner of other things in the world. Psychopathology is concerned with the ill person as a whole, in so far as he suffers from a psychic illness or one that is psychically determined:

> If we knew the elements that constituted the human psyche and all the forces at work we could begin with a broad outline of the psyche and leave details to be filled in later. But we need no such blue-print, since we conceive the psyche as an unending effort at comprehension, an effort which can never be concluded wholly, though we are always advancing through the many methods of research. We have no basic concept in terms of which we could define man nor any theory that would wholly cover his actual, objective existence. We must, therefore, as scientists, keep an open mind for all the empirical possibilities and guard against the temptation to reduce human existence to one common denominator. We have no psychic master-plan, but we shall simply discuss a number of horizons within which our psychic realities present themselves.[10]

That view of the psyche as an "unending effort at comprehension" and the prescription of viewing it from "a number of horizons" may deserve some additional discussion. But before we do, we will look at what Jaspers had to say in his next book on worldviews. "When we speak of *Weltanschauungen*, we mean ideas,

---

[9] For his more purely philosophical treatment of worldviews see *Philosophy, Volume I* (Chicago, IL: University of Chicago Press, 1969), pp. 250–268. [Henceforth cited as *P*]

[10] *General Psychopathology*, Seventh edition (Chicago, IL: University of Chicago, 1963), p. 6.

what is ultimate and complete in man, both subjectively, as experience, power, and conviction, and objectively as the formed world of objects."[11]

Jaspers speaks there of a subset of human ideas (worldviews) as being both subjective and objective. This may become of greater significance later on. Chapter I of the book treats those ideas from the subjective viewpoint (attitudes) and Chapter II from the objective pole (worldviews). But Chapter III attempts a synthesis of the two perspectives and it has been argued by Edwin Latzel (*PW* 184) that for Jaspers those syntheses of the subjective and objective perspectives (spiritual types) "surpass the attitudes and worldviews which in themselves are abstractions." While Jaspers' concept of ultimate situations is crucial to an understanding of worldviews, I will here only dwell on the more general distinction that he makes between human ideas as subjective and objective, and the even more interesting synthesis of the two perspectives that would best reflect reality. Ultimate situations, in which one's values and beliefs are shaken, give rise to worldviews, both in the subjective sense of attitudes and in their objective correlates, but also in the living totality of a spiritual type, which is the synthesis of the two. It might be worth asking why Jaspers felt the need to incorporate what appears to be a Weberian concept of ideal types into a psychological investigation of worldviews. Perhaps he saw this as the key to the transition between psychology as an empirical and theoretical discipline and philosophy, but apparently at the time when he wrote the *Psychology of Worldviews* he still thought that he was doing psychology and only later realized that he had gone over the line. So it is possible that his initial motivations were to set up scientifically useful constructs but that he later realized that they reflected reality in a more fundamental way than a scientific construct needs to do. Jaspers seems to have used a concept from the philosophy of the social sciences (ideal types) to bridge the gap between empirical science and philosophy even if he did not realize it at the time. This leads to serious questions regarding the boundary between social science and philosophy and to a suspicion that they might be more fluid than even Weber and Jaspers thought.

There is another excerpt from the *Psychologie* that I find crucial to my discussion and it appears in his discussion of ultimate situations in the context of how an individual experiences them as historically unique and not as necessary or inevitable:

> No matter how true this may seem to the acting human being, he stands beyond all particular situations in certain decisive, essential situations, which are related to man's being as such, a being which is unavoidably given with finite existence; situations beyond which his vision does not carry, since his gaze is directed upon objective things within the subject-object dichotomy. These situations, which are felt, experienced, conceived, everywhere at the limits of our existence, we call "ultimate situations." [*PW* 184]

---

[11] Translated from *Psychologie der Weltanschauungen*, second edition (Berlin, 1922) by Edwin Latzel. See "The Concept of the Ultimate Situation," *The Philosophy of Karl Jaspers*, second augmented edition, edited by Paul Arthur Schilpp (La Salle, IL: Open Court, 1981), p. 183. [Henceforth cited as *PW*]

Beyond the subjective and objective poles of human existence and beyond the specific unique and ultimate situations that one finds oneself in are the "essential situations" that are related to "man's being as such, a being which is unavoidably given with finite existence." This perspective is the essentially philosophical one that both allows for and demands a kind of discussion of values that would not be normally allowable in science or even in history. Jaspers states this quite explicitly in his later philosophical writings and distinguishes that type of evaluation from one that is concerned only with truth vs. falsehood:

> The solid subject, ever available for professional teaching, was the history of philosophy. But what is handed down in this fashion becomes increasingly meaningless if we regard the great philosophies as doctrines that are right or wrong and that can be learned. The point is to consort with the philosophers, to sense the existential will expressed in their doctrines. The task, then, was to develop cogitative means for the understanding and adoption of great philosophy. First, of course, this would involve learning concepts and studying trains of thought, but no learning and studying helps if it does not become a matter of man's true concern. As a teacher I tried to appeal to the conscience of my students—not just to the intellectual conscience that would hold them responsible for correct thinking, but to their existential conscience that would condemn a noncommittal, merely intellectual occupation with so-called "philosophical problems." My *Philosophy* seeks to produce the inner posture that will let us deal meaningfully with the wealth of grand historic doctrines. A large part of philosophical literature will be discarded as moot, as mere endless, random, intellectual toil. But the other part, the part that bespeaks reality and truth, will glow so much more brightly. [*P* 8]

I think that in this passage Jaspers comes as close as he can to articulating a nuanced view of philosophy and the history of philosophy in a manner somewhat analogous to his earlier interest in psychiatry and psychology.[12] And perhaps while attempting to draw a clear line between the disciplines, he also sees them as running along parallel though separate tracks. They are all concerned with "man's true concern" and not simply the interests of intellectuals. They are all concerned with the "unending effort at comprehension" and viewing that psyche from "a number of horizons." Even the history of philosophy which might appear to be the study of the dead creations of once living psyches, demands the development of "cogitative means" for understanding them and in order to "sense the existential will expressed in their doctrines." This is much more important to him than whether they are "right or wrong." Those "grand historic doctrines" are therefore more than of purely historical interest. They may demand engagement in an evaluative manner. While Jaspers surely avoids judging the history of philosophy from some timeless standards of truth, at the same time he seeks that "existential will" which is both imbedded in the particularities of history yet also transcends them. While we cannot pursue this much further, it may perhaps add much to our understanding of the human condition.

---

[12] Jaspers shows himself to be an intentional realist, believing in inner conscious, intentional states and also an intentionalist, using them as explanatory accounts. For a good discussion see Karsten Stueber, "Intentionalism, Intentional Realism, and Empathy," *Journal of the Philosophy of History*, Vol. 3, No. 3, 2009, pp. 290–307.

The Limits of Historical Understanding

Perhaps we can now see a bit more clearly what the previous discussion of Renaissance philosophy has to do with Jaspers, Ehrlich and the understanding of previous philosophers. Like Jaspers, the Renaissance philosophers were intensely interested in psychology, philosophy and religion and entranced by the individual psyche. Like the more commonly accepted interpretation of Pico, Jaspers stresses human freedom and in-determinability, but like Ficino he also insists upon a universal, essential human condition from which previous thinkers can be judged. I think it is no accident that Jaspers uses the words "existential will" to describe what is most important in the "doctrines" of philosophers. It reminds me of what Ehrlich wrote about "right-wrong, good-bad, good-evil, worthy-reprehensible, loyal-treacherous, etc." All of those polarities go beyond mere description of the facts and at least two of them pertain to the human will. This is a rather radical departure from the norms of philosophical research of most of the major schools as they have developed up to the present day. Perhaps it explains what is so refreshing about Jaspers, the importance of his early work in psychiatry and also perhaps why for some others he is so difficult to fathom. Such beliefs regarding "existential will" certainly preclude a complete modeling of the history of philosophy after evolutionary natural history or even descriptive natural history. The attempt to extract from the writings of a dead thinker an objective and non-evaluative historical sighting as if we were looking at rare species of birds is doomed to failure because the thing most dear to that thinker, whether we view it as consciousness, will, freedom, etc. can't be sighted at all and can only be inferred in a rather flawed and simulated manner. The existential will is for Jaspers the essence of any philosophy. Yet from his perspective it is that unseen, unique mental stance towards a situation that reflects "man's being as such, a being which is unavoidably given with finite existence." In other words, the uniqueness of each individual is somehow inextricably linked to the basic human condition and it is that relationship to "man's being as such" that makes a philosopher great and relevant to us. This stands a certain contemporary viewpoint, which insists that the essential human condition is defined by historical conventions, on its head. Perhaps in order to truly understand a historical person we need to do a kind of simulation and in a sense pretend that he or she is alive and can answer our questions. In contrast, with a living philosopher we can have an actual conversation, ask probing questions, engage in loving or contentious dialogue, etc. While our view of a living philosopher cannot be finalized as his or her thinking is still evolving, that very lack of "objectivity" gives us the ability to have a more intimate view of the psyche in question and how it reflects the more universal situation of humankind. That perhaps is one other reason that dialogue has philosophical value, goes back to the very beginning of philosophy in the Platonic dialogues, and shows the superiority of living human communication over the written word. The values of dialogue and communication, rooted in an intuition regarding the essential nature of humankind, cannot be totally abandoned when we study the history of philosophy if we are to obtain the most from that study. As would be expected, however, each treatment will reflect the particular bias and intuition of its author.

Conclusion

From the philosophical perspective of both Jaspers and Ehrlich no understanding of the history of human thought is even remotely complete without some intuition into the essential human condition, which includes the will. And such an intuition regarding the human essence practically excludes the strictest prohibition against value judgments that is quite justifiable in the natural sciences and perhaps to a somewhat lesser degree in history, the social sciences, and certain specialized areas of philosophy itself. This may place philosophy in a powerful foundational role regarding those latter disciplines, somewhat akin to the age-old dependence of culture on religion. Value judgments not only inform the kinds of research and dialogue that lead to understanding, but also are always present in that understanding. Without evaluation we cannot speak of the future of humanity in any profound sense. This does not completely absolve us from dealing with the philosophical problem of values, however. Where we draw the line between facts and values in philosophy would now become a tactical decision, based to a great extent upon practical considerations (targeted audience, purpose of discussion, etc.) as well as the values of fairness and desire for loving dialogue, all of which are inherent to philosophy.

Philosophical Faith, Periechontology, and Philosophical Ethics

Shinji Hayashida

Abstract In Jaspers' philosophy as philosophical faith, knowledge has a noteworthy feature that inward action of subject is reflected in it. So, his philosophy supplies ethics, whose knowledge presupposes an inward action of the ethical subject, with justification as a unique field of learning. Furthermore, Jaspers' periechontology (ontology of encompassing) as the framework of infinitely manifold heterogeneous belief offers us the methodological foundation for the construction of a comprehensive ethics, which is a systematic unification of many heterogeneous ethics. Jaspers' philosophy accomplished by the correlation of philosophical faith and encompassing-thought has tremendous significance for the philosophical ethics.

Jaspers' concepts of "philosophical faith" and "the encompassing," initially developed separately in *Vernunft und Existenz* (1935), are so closely interrelated that they cannot be considered apart from each other in *Der philosophische Glaube* (1948) and *Der philosophische Glaube angesichts der Offenbarung* (1962). A correlation of both essential concepts made it possible for Jaspers to complete his united philosophy as it ought to be in the age of scientific-technology and heterogeneous beliefs.[1] The eminent significance of Jaspers' philosophy, accomplished by the correlation of philosophical faith and the encompassing, is also necessary for the foundation of philosophical ethics as a unique field in philosophy. Furthermore, Jaspers' periechontology, or philosophy of the encompassing, in correlation with philosophical faith has a special significance for the organization of a comprehensive philosophical ethics.

---

[1] I treated the "Correlation of Philosophical Faith and Encompassing in Jaspers' Later Philosophy" in detail in *Karl Jaspers: Historic Actuality in View of Fundamental Problems of Mankind*, eds. Andreas Cesana and Gregory J. Walters (Würzburg: Königshausen & Neumann, 2008), pp. 47f. [Henceforth cited as *A*]

S. Hayashida (✉)
University of Electro-Communications, Tokyo, Japan
e-mail: hayasida-s@nifty.com

H. Wautischer et al. (eds.), *Philosophical Faith and the Future of Humanity*,
DOI 10.1007/978-94-007-2223-1_20, © Springer Science+Business Media B.V. 2012

Faith and Philosophical Faith

Even before his clear formulation of the concept of philosophical faith, faith plays an important role in Jaspers' philosophy. In his first main work *Philosophie* (1932) faith is understood as the fulfilled absolute consciousness peculiar to *Existenz*. In *Von der Wahrheit* (1947), faith is the way of perceiving the truth characteristic of *Existenz*. But faith in these works is only one mode of the absolute consciousness or one mode of beliefs (*Überzeugungen*) that is also one mode of certainty (*Gewißheit*). While this is one of the important concepts of his philosophy as *Existenzphilosophie*, it is not a fundamental conception that would represent his philosophy as a whole.

In *Der philosophische Glaube* (1947), faith is defined by the encompassing, and its various modes are presented according to the "modes of the encompassing." Jaspers says, "in order to understand what faith is, we have to elucidate the Comprehensive (*das Umgreifende*)"[2] and "faith is life out of the Comprehensive, it is guidance and fulfillment through the Comprehensive" (*PSP* 17). As Jaspers says, "I have formulated clearly the philosophical faith in *Der philosophische Glaube*,"[3] the concept of philosophical faith has been definitely shown by its correlation with encompassing thought.

In *Der philosophische Glaube angesichts der Offenbarung* (1962), such an understanding of philosophical faith in correlation with the encompassing is so advanced that both fields are correlated in an inseparable unity (*A* 49f). As the result of such an inseparable correlation with the encompassing, which is the methodological core concept of his later philosophy, the idea of philosophical faith is completed as the fundamental conception which characterizes Jaspers' philosophy as a whole. In fact, this matter is shown clearly in this work. Philosophy, which is distinguished from science and theology, is expressed in other words as "philosophical faith," which is distinguished from faith in revelation and rational cognition.[4]

The distinctive feature of the concept of philosophical faith defined by the encompassing, which comprehends the subject-object dichotomy, is that faith is considered as the whole that synthesizes the subjective and the objective. This way of thinking about faith is suggested already in his earlier works. In *Philosophie* the concept of faith is elucidated in two ways. "Subjectively," Jaspers states, "faith is the way in which the soul, without sufficient concepts, is sure of being, of its roots, and of its goal. Objectively we express faith as a concept that will remain unintelligible in itself."[5] This way of thinking is advanced and deepened by the correlation of faith with the encompassing in later works. In *Der philosophische Glaube*, Jaspers says "the faith through which I am convinced, and the content of

---

[2] Karl Jaspers, *The Perennial Scope of Philosophy*, trans. R. Manheim (Hamden, CT: Archon Books, 1968), p. 11. [Henceforth cited as *PSP*]

[3] Karl Jaspers, *Philosophische Autobiographie* (Munich: Piper & Co., 1968), p. 119.

[4] Karl Jaspers, *Philosophical Faith and Revelation*, trans. E.B. Ashton (New York, NY: Collins, 1967), p. 61. [Henceforth cited as *PFR*]

[5] Karl Jaspers, *Philosophy Vol. 2*, trans. by E.B. Ashton (Chicago, IL: University of Chicago Press, 1970), p. 243. [Henceforth cited as *P* with Volume number]

faith, which I comprehend—the act of faith, and the faith that I acquire by this act—are inseparable. The subjective and the objective side of faith are a whole" (*PSP* 7).

Faith as philosophical faith is considered to be the matter in which the subjective inward action to believe and the objective contents of the belief are inseparably united. This understanding of faith means that the concept of the faith in Jaspers' philosophy expresses a special mode of the human knowledge in which subjective action and objective contents are united. It will be a noteworthy feature of knowledge as belief that the inward action of the subject is reflected into outward knowledge, in contrast to scientific knowledge in which the subjective is normally excluded.

Because philosophical faith in Jaspers' later philosophy is considered to be the conception which represents his philosophy as a whole, the feature of knowledge as belief indicates at the same time an important feature of Jaspers' philosophy itself, where knowledge is the knowledge into which something subjective is reflected. Fundamentally speaking, in his *Existenzphilosophie*, knowledge originally contained such subjective features. Jaspers addresses this in his Foreword to *Philosophie*: "In philosophizing I cannot look once again for the satisfaction I derive from knowing things in the world. What I seek in it and what it takes is more; it is *the thinking that transforms my consciousness of being* as it awakens me and brings me to myself" (*P1* 1). This original feature of Jaspers' philosophical knowledge is also confirmed by the understanding of philosophizing as practice. About his own philosophizing he says "philosophizing is *practice* (*Praxis*), but peculiar kind of practice," and the practice in this case is "inward action, in which I become myself."[6] In any case, knowledge in Jaspers' philosophy is the knowledge into which something of the thinking subject is reflected and which should be distinguished from scientific knowledge which is acquired when the subject is separated from the object.

Peculiarity of the Ethical and Ethics

Jaspers' conception of philosophical faith has great significance for the foundation of philosophical ethics when distinguished from the other fields of learning. In order to clarify this significance, we have to point out the peculiarity of the ethical and matters which have some ethical significance, and of knowing the ethical in view of the original situation of its appearance to human beings.

First, the ethical, as pertaining to matters of good and evil is a question for human beings and only for human beings. We should also bear in mind the fact that ethical matters do not come about as issues for all mankind in the same way or for mankind in general as living creatures. Nor do ethical issues pertain to infants. For ethical matters to come into question, a person must be able to comprehend some ethical

---

[6] Karl Jaspers, "Über meine Philosophie," in *Rechenschaft und Ausblick* (Munich: Piper & Co., 1951), pp. 401f. [Henceforth cited as *ÜMP*]

significance about himself or his world. In this case, the expression that "the ethical" comes into question for certain people does not mean the assertion that there exist some definite ethics and such matters come into question for a particular person. On the contrary, the ethical matters, at least originally, appear or come out for the human being by whom those matters are experienced or accepted as something ethically significant, namely as the matters pertaining to good and evil of his own personality. Some matters, first experienced as the matters of ethical significance, are comprehended as ethical, and then become relevant for a concerned person.

Now, in order to experience and comprehend ethical significance, one must be a free and spontaneous subject, to be concerned and participate actively in worldly matters. Moreover, because the ethical has principally to do with matters pertaining to good and evil, one must be able to experience and comprehend the ethical by way of spontaneous inward action that desires or aspires to realize a better (higher, greater, stronger, etc.) way of being. Such an individual, as the subject of the spontaneous inward action to whom the ethical originally appears and comes into existence, is called an ethical subject. As Jaspers says "conscious of his freedom, man desires to become what he can and should be" (*PSP* 67), and also expresses *Existenz* as "being which in the phenomenality of existence *is not*, but *can be, ought to be*" (*P2* 3), we can consider that such an action of the ethical subject belongs to human nature itself. That is, the individual, insofar as he or she is human, has an ability of the inward action of the ethical subject as original human nature. This understanding of the nature of humanity has many philosophical expressions, above all in the thought of Søren Kierkegaard.[7] Since a free inward action occurs for individuals desiring to be better human beings, the nature of the ethical is inevitably called into question. The sphere of ethical matters, which is called in question and is experienced through inward action based on human nature, is a unique and peculiar sphere to be distinguished from other spheres of human interest.

Furthermore, when starting from the consideration of the original appearance of the ethical, one can define ethics formally, confirm its substantial content, and decide systematically its main problems and its fundamental problem.[8] Then we shall be able to understand ethics as a unique learning about the ethical, which

---

[7] Kierkegaard says, for example, "But if the task of becoming subject is the highest that is proposed to a human being, everything is beautifully arranged... For even if the individuals were as numberless as the sand of the sea, the task of becoming subjective is given to each... First then the ethical, the task of becoming subjective, and afterwards the world-historical." *Concluding Unscientific Postscript*, trans. D.F. Swenson (Princeton, NJ: Princeton University Press, 1941), p. 142.

[8] Conclusive understandings about such problems, omitting the consideration in detail, are as follows: Ethics, defined as the comprehensive, is comprised by two inseparable moments, namely, man as ethical subject, and the ethical object-world as the object of inward action of the ethical subject. The substantial content of ethics is defined as the matter concerning good and evil of man as man. The fundamental problem of ethics is the problem of ethical man. The main problems of ethics are (a) problems of quality that the ethical subject intends to realize, namely, problems of value in a wide sense, good and evil, etc. (b) Problems of occasion where subjective action is concerned with the outer object-world, such as problems of duty and human relation, etc. (c) Problems of occasion where subjective action is concerned with the self, namely, problems of conscience

is inevitably called into question. Because ethics is considered to be a system of knowledge regarding the ethical, and in order to justify ethics as a specific field of learning and to confirm its foundation, we must first of all investigate the character of knowledge on the ethical and clarify its peculiarity.

The original appearance of ethical matters having some ethical significance is the fact that such matters are directly experienced by the ethical subject who desires a better way of being. Such directly experienced matters that a moral subject is forced to call into question are, in many cases, consciously examined and reflected upon by the subject of the action who then forms some knowledge or thought on its ethical value. The decisive peculiarity of such knowledge is that something of the ethical subject is reflected in the ethical knowledge. The peculiarity of this knowledge on the ethical will be shown also through the consideration of the special manner by which one thinks about the ethical. The ethical subject that experiences and reflects on matters of ethical significance is the person who is the subject of inward action intended to realize one's better being. Reflection or thinking, in this case, will take place in the subject accompanied by the inward intention to be better. Such thinking by the ethical subject is nothing but thinking as practice, which, according to Jaspers' understanding, is an inward action of self-being in which the subject becomes himself (*ÜMP*). Subjective qualities, such as one's personality or manner of thinking, are included and reflected in knowledge of the ethical, as they are acquired through such thinking as practice.

In any case, knowledge about the ethical is inseparable from the subject and it reflects something subjective. Accordingly, ethical knowledge must be clearly distinguished from the knowledge of general sciences that is acquired by contemplative thinking from which subjectivity is excluded. Ethics, as a system of special knowledge on the ethical, is to be distinguished from all other fields of human inquiry, since it can be demonstrated that its field is clearly different from the fields of any other scientific learning.

Of course, we are able to possess some objective knowledge about many matters generally regarded as ethical. In each society there exist, for example, norms such as custom, convention, or morality, which continue to exist independently of the individual and his or her inwardness. The people in a given society usually have some common cognition or general knowledge about social facts and realities regarded as ethical matters. When such knowledge is systematically arranged as the object of scientific research and the subject of research is clearly separated from the object, such objective and exact sciences may still be regarded as ethical sciences inasmuch as the research objects are regarded as ethical matters.

When this occurs, social facts or realities of the research objects cannot themselves be identified with the ethical, since it has special significance and must be distinguished from all other human matters. Objects regarded as ethical will possess special ethical significance only when they are considered as matters in which some

---

and moral sense, etc. And (d) Problems in the specific situation where subjective action is actually realized, namely problems about conduct.

moments of subjective reflection are included. Such matters are sufficiently ethical when each individual in a given society, obeying or resisting conventional norms, intends to realize his own better way of being. The social fact or reality itself cannot be regarded as the ethical insofar as it includes nothing of the subjective. Moreover, the way of thinking in this case is entirely different from ethical thinking as practice in which something subjective is reflected. It is true that systems of knowledge, such as the moral sociology or the science of customs, are universally approved exact sciences; but they are not the unique and peculiar ethics that needs to be distinguished from all other sciences.

In contrast to other sciences, ethics—as a system of knowledge in which subjective personality is reflected—has great influence on people who have some sympathy with the personality of the founders of such value systems, for example with Spinoza, where regardless of its significance, his theory could not be approved universally, since any ethics cannot avoid the weakness of subjective narrowness. How, then, can ethics including such weakness maintain justification of status as a unique field in philosophy?

Ethics is a system of knowledge on the ethical which appears originally in the ethical subject, and which is experienced and becomes conscious presupposing the inward action of the subject. In the knowledge of the ethical both the subjective action and the objective contents are inseparably included. This knowledge, which is the unity of the subjective and the objective, is precisely Jaspers' understanding of philosophical faith in correlation with the encompassing. In Jaspers' philosophy, knowledge is also regarded as a belief in the unification of the subjective and the objective. Ethics, as I have described here, has the very same character as knowledge in Jaspers' overall philosophy. Jaspers' thoughts on the relationship between philosophical faith and the encompassing show how ethics has its foundation as a unique field of philosophy with justification as a special field of learning, namely, as a philosophical ethics.

Periechontology and Comprehensive Ethics

Periechontology provides Jaspers with a basis for the development of a comprehensive philosophical ethics. The contents of philosophical faith, which are limited to biblical religion in *Der philosophische Glaube* (1948) are expanded in *Der philosophische Glaube angesichts der Offenbarung* (1962) by way of his notion of ciphers. In the latter work, just before the sections "On Ciphers (Part 4)" and "The Struggle in the Realm of Ciphers (Part 5)," Jaspers elucidates "The Philosophy of the Modes of Encompassing (Part 3)" (*PFR* 61f). This order (Parts 3–5) of the sections will mean that extremely manifold ciphers are unfolded on the premise of elucidation of the encompassing. In this work, philosophy of the encompassing is named also "philosophical basic knowledge as periechontology," in contrast to basic knowledge as traditional ontology. While traditional ontology has to do with the presentation of total knowledge regarding being as a whole, periechontology, or ontology of encompassing, does not make claims regarding the definite contents of material knowledge (*A* 50f). In spite of the weakness of substantiality, Jaspers' periechontology as the philosophy of encompassing, is understood to provide the basis or framework for the consideration of all original philosophies. Herein lies the significance of periechontology as the framework within which the infinitely manifold contents of philosophical faith find their proper position and their meaning to be unfolded (*A* 50f).

Philosophical ethics, for Jaspers, is the knowledge in which the subjective and the objective are united in the same way as knowledge understood as belief is constituted. Because periechontology is considered to be the framework of substantial philosophical thoughts and of knowledge as belief, periechontology provides the framework within which philosophical ethics finds its proper location. Furthermore, since periechontology is identical with his philosophy of encompassing, including the modes of encompassing, its elucidation is, according to Jaspers, an "awareness of how we find ourselves in the world" (*PFR* 61f). The elucidation of modes of the encompassing in periechontology is understood as the self-consciousness of our own original being in the world. Thus the ethical and matters of ethical significance appear to the ethical subject in the place where he participates in his world, desiring to realize a better way of his own being in his world. This very quality of humans as ethical subjects, as stated above, belongs to human nature itself. Accordingly, the modes of the original human being, which are presented by the elucidation of the modes of encompassing, are considered to be the original modes of the ethical subject to whom ethical matters make their appearance.

Jaspers enumerates four modes of encompassing in their subjective aspects: existence (*Dasein*), consciousness at large (*Bewusstsein überhaupt*), mind (*Geist*) and self-being (*Existenz*) (*A* 51; 58 n35, n36). Because these modes are four aspects of original human beings, and because the quality of man as an ethical subject belongs to the nature of human beings as such, each mode of the encompassing can be considered as an original mode of the ethical subject. When the ethical subject, in each mode of encompassing, desires to realize a better way of being and to participate in his objective world, matters of ethical significance appear and, in many cases, consciousness and knowledge of ethical matters will be clarified. When this knowledge is arranged and systematized, the philosophical ethics according to the each mode of encompassing comes into existence or actuality. The same four patterns—but now of philosophical ethics—emerge: existence, consciousness at large, mind, and *Existenz*. These patterns are considered in their interrelationship, according to the relation of the mutual regulation of the four modes of encompassing. While each mode of encompassing has its peculiar significance as an original being, each of them cannot avoid limitation, since the most fundamental mode is existence, and its most significant is *Existenz*. Thus the four modes of encompassing interrelate and provide foundation and significance for one another.

We can now conceive the systematic unification of four patterns of philosophical ethics, in which each pattern has its proper place, each preserving its unique significance and, at the same time, approving its limitation. Hence we are able to call such a systematic unification a comprehensive philosophical ethics, which can avert the deficiencies of philosophical ethics when considered separately.

The modes of encompassing are presented, according to Jaspers' description, with consideration to the experience of our ancestors.[9] Because these modes as a whole, at least formally, comprehend all the original meaning of being human as an ethical subject, we can understand that a systematic unification of the four patterns of philosophical ethics—at least in terms of methodology—can comprehend all the historic forms of philosophical ethics and be regarded as a comprehensive form of philosophical ethics. As mentioned above, because Jaspers' classification of the modes of encompassing is composed as provisional,[10] unification of the four patterns of philosophical ethics cannot be the final systematic unification of philosophical ethics. Nonetheless, we can assert that Jaspers' conception of periechontology presents us with the methodological foundation for the possible organization of a comprehensive philosophical ethics. Jaspers' conception of philosophical faith, accompanied by his views on periechontology, has tremendous promise for the foundation and justification of philosophical ethics as a unique sphere of human inquiry, and also for the organization of a comprehensive philosophical ethics.

---

[9] Japers' description as to the classification of the modes of encompassing: "Die von uns unterschiedenen Weisen des Umgreifenden sind in ihrem Gedachtsein geschichtlich, das *Resultat unseres abendländischen Bildungsprozesses*. In ihrem Räumen haben unsere Ahnen gelebt und gedacht." *Von der Wahrheit* (Munich: Piper & Co., 1947), p. 125.

[10] Jaspers' description: "We are drafting a pattern that must always be provisional... Insight into the modes of encompassing remains in suspension and brings us into a state of suspension" (*PFR* 89).

Can Corporate Capitalism Be Redeemed? Business Ethics and the Search for a Renewed Faith in Work

W. Michael Hoffman and Robert E. McNulty

Abstract This chapter investigates the relationship between faith, work, corporate capitalism and business ethics. The faith perspective with which it is concerned—though sharing some common elements with the faith associated with some religious traditions—is not tied to a particular religion or theology, but constitutes an existential commitment that guides people amidst the limitations inherent to human understanding. The authors assert that all work is guided by a faith that gives it purpose. However, over the last century the dominant system for organizing work has been corporate capitalism, which is guided by a faith according to which the ultimate purpose of work is profit maximization and personal enrichment. It is argued that this is a debasing faith and that work needs to be redeemed by a faith consistent with business ethics that affirms the dignity of work through service to the greater good.

To be sure, these are perilous times for the legitimacy of business. The perception of the moral bankruptcy of business constitutes a real social danger that compels us to examine the relationship between faith, work, corporate capitalism and business ethics. The faith perspective with which we will concern ourselves—though sharing some common elements with the faith associated with some religious traditions—is not tied to a particular religion or theology. Rather, we will briefly reflect on the phenomenology of faith as a form of existential commitment that, for better or worse, guides us amidst the limitations inherent to our human understanding. Faith, from this perspective, pervades human action and informs the way in which we face the world and approach our work. Work has long been understood to occupy a spectrum of forms from toil to transcendence. Underlying these varying interpretations there is a faith that motivates and informs us of the meaning of work. Over the last century the dominant system for organizing work has been corporate capitalism, which like all systems of work, is guided by faith. The faith conventionally associated with corporate capitalism, but which is not inherent to it, is one that understands the ultimate purpose of work as profit maximization and personal enrichment. This faith, we believe, debases work, humanity, and even corporate capitalism itself. We

W.M. Hoffman (✉) · R.E. McNulty (✉)
Center for Business Ethics, Bentley University, Waltham, MA, USA
e-mail: MHoffman@bentley.edu, RMcNulty@bentley.edu

H. Wautischer et al. (eds.), *Philosophical Faith and the Future of Humanity*,
DOI 10.1007/978-94-007-2223-1_21, © Springer Science+Business Media B.V. 2012

interpret the relentless lurching from business scandal to global economic catastrophe as a manifestation of a misguided faith writ large. If we hope for more than a patch on the fundamental brokenness of contemporary corporate capitalism, it must be redeemed by infusing it with a faith in an ethic that affirms personal dignity through service to the greater good. Karl Jaspers begins his book, *Philosophical Faith and Revelation*, with these words: "Religious perspectives represents a quest for the rediscovery of man."[1] In a similar spirit, in this paper, we wish to consider business ethics as partaking in a quest to redeem work by rediscovering it within the context of corporate capitalism.

On the Place of Existential Faith in the Human Experience

The scholar of religion, Alan M. Olson posed the following question: "Does *faith* have any place in postmodernity and what would a *postmodern faith* look like if such a faith were possible?"[2] This is an interesting question and one that asks us to reexamine the meaning of faith in an age where intellectuals are expected not to accept the tenets of any faith on faith alone. But even if we were to accept a certain duty to doubt, would this mean that postmoderns occupy a space stripped of faith? We would suggest that the answer to this question depends on what is meant by faith.

The concept of faith is not easily defined.[3] Typically, faith is associated with doctrinal beliefs that cannot be empirically verified, such as certain tenets of religion or other metaphysical notions, such as the purpose of life, the phenomenological experiences of other species, the nature of eternity or the afterlife. As such, faith may be associated with the Grand Narratives post-modernists seek to eschew. Faith, however, is not a simple concept and even if one were to eliminate one form of faith, such as adherence to a particular religious doctrine, that does not necessarily mean that one is living without faith. Moreover, even if some members of society give up faith in a particular narrative (for example, such as those embodied in certain mythic or shamanistic world-views), will there not be a faith that fills the gap? Whatever the narrative to which one holds ("grand" or not), to the extent that it involves an existential commitment that is not subject to empirical verification, is not the holding to it an expression of faith? Our position is that, indeed, it is.

Unlike ordinary beliefs, which can be easily changed, existential faith is more deeply held. I may believe that Los Angeles is the capital of California, but I do not have faith in this, and as soon as I am informed by a credible source that my belief

---

[1] Karl Jaspers, *Philosophical Faith and Revelation*, Religious Perspectives, V. 18, trans. E.B. Ashton (New York, NY: Harper & Row, 1967), p. xix.

[2] Alan M. Olson, "Postmodernity and Faith," *Journal of the American Academy of Religion*, Vol. 58, No. 1 (1990): p. 37.

[3] An article that provides a concise and helpful review of the term in the context of a Christian-Buddhist dialog is John B. Cobb, Jr., "Faith," *Buddhist-Christian Studies* Vol. 14 (1994), pp. 43–55.

is wrong, I can quite comfortably change my belief. As will be further discussed, changing one's faith is far more difficult, though not impossible. A guiding view that we will take in this essay is that it is impossible to live without faith, and that the faith to which we hold can substantively influence our encounter with the world. We get out of bed in the morning with the faith that there will be a floor on which to stand, and this faith leads us to assume the same holds everywhere. Although we have solid evidence to support this position, our faith is not based on science, or rational analysis, but reflects a worldview so broad that it includes suppositions that extend far beyond any data we have. Our ancestors would have argued with similar certitude that the sun revolves around the earth. Similarly, we spend decades caring for our children never doubting our faith that they are true, flesh and blood living human beings and not just memes implanted by engineers into a brain floating in a vat. The ways in which we start our day and approach our work are expressions of faith. We will refer to this general, basic faith as an "existential faith," as it reflects deeply held beliefs regarding the nature of existence as experienced and interpreted by the individual.[4]

The Faith of a Culture

Although a person may be incapable of articulating what his or her existential faith is, this in no way suggests a lack of faith. Existential faith need not be articulated, but it forms the background parameters of what is generally understood to be real and valuable. To the extent that this faith is shared by the wider society, it could be considered the "faith of a culture," by which we mean the tacit norms that constitute the framework with which the vast majority of people in a society generally understand to be the essential elements of reality and how one's experience ought to be evaluated. A person who partakes in the culture of Islam, for example, takes the existence of God as given whereas one who partakes in the culture of Hinduism or Buddhism takes it as given that one's lifespan is but a single episode in a series that stretches back through countless previous lifetimes. And yet, while the Muslim and the Buddhist may have different faiths regarding the nature of divinity, they may both partake in capitalist cultures in which it is taken as a given that a successful life is one that is associated with the accumulation of wealth. In the faiths of various cultures, we will find both distinct and overlapping elements. These various elements lead to changes in culture over time.

Like all forms of faith, the faith of a culture consists of ontological and normative elements. This form of faith embodies a collective understanding of basic metaphysical principles regarding what is real—such as whether or not there is purpose to the universe, spirit, or physical determinism—and what is of fundamental value, such as

---

[4] The term "existential faith" has appeared in a number of books and articles often with different interpretations. Therefore, while we will not claim originality, our coinage is not based on that of other authors.

wealth, honor, power, holiness, or physical attractiveness. Individuals are born into cultures, and from birth the faith of their culture is continually reinforced. It is not a matter of personal choice since it is embedded in cultural norms into which people are inducted from birth. Notions of family, personal purpose, religion, power relationships, and archetypes of goodness and evil are examples of some core cultural concepts. People are unable to simply opt in or out of these views at will. Like the regional accent that we inherit, so too, faith is woven into our mental formation. If one were to adopt incompatible faith elements, it would be seen as odd, unrealistic, or perhaps even nonsense to most other members of a society.

We are not suggesting that cultures are immutable or hermetically isolated. Individuals are capable of questioning and changing cultures, but even when they do so, it is against a background of the received view on what is real and valuable. It is a rare individual who is able to have a significant impact in changing the faith of a culture; Einstein, Gandhi and Martin Luther King are a few examples, and even with them, it took many years for the impact of the changes they helped to usher in to permeate the broader culture. In all but rare instances, our cultures are acted upon at the margins, while at the core they remain intact. We will argue that our view of work is part of the faith of our culture, and as such is embedded in the ways that we organize our societies and evaluate the meaning of work in our lives.

Broadening the Genealogy of Faith: Some Thoughts on Kant, Jaspers and Tillich

The kind of existential faith we are talking about may be linked with a doctrinal faith, but certainly need not be. It may have been with this orientation that Kant famously justified his metaphysical enterprise with the assertion, "Thus I had to deny knowledge in order to make room for faith."[5] What did Kant mean by faith? Perhaps, in part, his intent was to defend religious faith from the onslaughts of Enlightenment skepticism. However, his intent may have extended further. Kant sought to map out the terrains that together comprise the human mind, and therein his intent may have been to recognize that faith, though related to empirical knowledge, went beyond it.[6] Here we find a point of contact with Karl Jaspers'

---

[5] Immanuel Kant, *Critique of Pure Reason*, trans. Paul Guyer and Allen W. Wood (Cambridge, MA: Cambridge University Press, 1998), p. 117.

[6] Drawing on Kantian terminology, might it be that one of the characteristics of faith is that it provides a point at which the noumenal is indirectly accessible to phenomenal consciousness? Edward Ames proposes the following interpretation: "But for Kant, that destructive exposure of the claims of the understanding was only a preliminary step in clearing the way to what he regarded as a far more impressive substantiation of the fundamental things of religion. It was his purpose to show that religion belongs to a higher realm of faith. Above the bounds of reason and independent of it, rises the region of the spirit, secure from any intrusion of the earthbound senses and natural science." Edward Scribner Ames, "The Religion of Immanuel Kant," *The Journal of Religion* Vol. 5, No. 2 (1925): p. 173.

"philosophical faith." His philosophical faith offers a means for reconciling the apparent antinomies associated with knowledge and faith. Thus we read:

> Philosophical faith, the faith of the thinking man, has always this distinguishing feature: it is allied with knowledge. It wants to know what is knowable, and to be conscious of its own premises.... Philosophical faith must also *elucidate* itself. When I philosophize, I accept nothing as it comes to me, without seeking to penetrate it. Faith cannot, to be sure, become universally valid knowledge, but it should become clearly present to me by self conviction. It should become unceasingly clearer and more conscious, and by becoming conscious unfold more of its inner meaning.[7]

Jaspers' philosophical faith bridges faith and knowledge without slipping into a knowledge-denying nihilism or faith-sufficient solipsism. This faith is a faith in philosophy inasmuch as it represents the quest for understanding that is at the heart of the philosophical enterprise. As Leonard Ehrlich put it, "Jaspers... contraposes mysticism and positivism, and upholds philosophical faith as the third possibility."[8] Kant and Jaspers provide us with tools for better understanding faith as bridging the epistemic and transcendent. They offer a basis for understanding another perspective on faith provided by Paul Tillich.

Like Kant and Jaspers, Paul Tillich, offers a view of faith that straddles the realms of theology and philosophy. The strength of Tillich's view, as we see it, is that he articulates an understanding of the omnipresence of faith in human thinking generally: "Faith," Tillich states, "is the state of being ultimately concerned: the dynamics of faith are the dynamics of man's ultimate concern."[9] Faith in this sense universally pervades human consciousness. Even the most apathetic and listless of souls holds something as ultimate, be it one's own life, his country, or his contempt for others. In this regard, Tillich states, "If a national group makes the life and growth of nation its ultimate concern, it demands that all other concerns, economic well-being, health and life, family, aesthetic and cognitive truth, justice and humanity be sacrificed" (*DF* 2). As someone who was forced to flee his German homeland, Tillich could see very clearly that it was a faith in an extreme form of nationalism that provided the cognitive and emotional framework that permitted the growth of the Nazi abomination.

Tillich's view of faith is an insightful perspective into the phenomenology of faith independent of the objects of faith. That which claims "ultimacy," he notes, "demands the total surrender of him who accepts this claim, and it promises total fulfillment even if all other claims have to be subjected to it or rejected in its name" (*DF* 1). Faith in this Tillichian sense could be understood as falling within the broader understanding of the faith we are describing as "existential faith," and his perspective on faith as "ultimate concern" sheds light on its motivating capacity.

---

[7] Karl Jaspers, *The Perennial Scope of Philosophy* (Hamden, CT: Archon Books, 1968), p. 7.

[8] Leonard H. Ehrlich, *Karl Jaspers: Philosophy as Faith* (Amherst, MA: University of Massachusetts Press, 1975), p. 54.

[9] Paul Tillich, *Dynamics of Faith* (New York, NY: HarperCollins, 1957), p. 1. [Henceforth cited as *DF*]

Faith, as we see it, is a deeply powerful force that has served as the fuel that has enabled much of the development of human civilization in its manifold forms. What gives it this capacity is that it issues from our deeply held, often unconscious understanding of the nature of the world and what in it truly matters. In some respects, the characteristics of faith will vary from person to person, and from time to time within a person's lifetime. And yet, because faith is embedded in our sense of what ultimately is real and valuable, despite its seeming fluidity, we are unable to change our faith at will or with any rapidity.

Because faith—be it one's existential faith or the faith of a culture—is so deeply enmeshed in one's view of the world and one's place in it, one's personal identity is bound up with one's faith; indeed, our very moral core is founded on faith. And when faith is understood in the Tillichian sense of ultimate concern, such ultimacy serves as the benchmark against which we evaluate the relative goodness and badness of actions.

On Faith and Work in Corporate Capitalism

Work, like faith, has roots that reach deeply into the human psyche and there, through the intermediation of faith, work is infused with meaning and purpose in a way that places it in a category of human experience that is qualitatively different from simple action.

The meaning and purpose of work has assumed various forms depending on cultural and historical circumstances. Just as there is a "faith of a culture," so too corporate capitalism represents one cultural mode of work that is embedded in a particular form of faith. As with many forms of faith, on inspection we can discern elements that are both strong and weak. Although corporate capitalism responds to strong human desires, it is based on a faith that is prone to serious problems. However, the faith that is undergirding corporate capitalism is not fixed, and with appropriate reform, we will argue, corporate capitalism can be redeemed.

What Is Work?

Let us ask a basic question: what is work? Work has assumed many different forms depending on social and historical circumstances. This much is clear. What is less widely recognized is that the existential context in which the shape, purpose, and meaning of work is formed is largely a function of faith. The work of a monk praying in his cell bears little resemblance to that of the nineteenth century robber barons or the contemporary social entrepreneur seeking ecologically responsible solutions to the threat of global warming. What makes these examples so different? Distinct forms of faith, we would suggest, guide them.

Let us clarify what we mean by "work," first by offering a provisional definition and then by reflecting on the phenomenology of work. We understand work to be purposeful action aimed at some productive outcome, typically associated with economic gain.[10] Work, however, may be done to fulfill some personal or social purpose, such as when it done in response to a "calling," in which case it may be voluntarily pursued even when so doing results in no economic gain and may even violate one's ostensible self-interest.

But rather than settle for a definition, let's take a brief phenomenological look at a few of the more prominent contours of work.[11] Like culture—which influences every aspect of our experience—work is so central to human existence as to render it difficult to discern. To elucidate, consider two contrasting perspectives. First, work has long been associated with travail.[12] According to the Bible, it was sinfulness that resulted in the expulsion of Adam and Eve—understood in the traditional Judeo-Christian outlook to be our primal ancestors—from paradise and forced them into an existence of hardship and struggle. Thus, speaking to Adam, God condemned man, "In toil you shall eat of it [the earth] all the days of your life" (Genesis 3:17),[13] while woman was fated to the painful "labor" of childbirth. This theme of work as toil has persisted throughout history and, sadly, is vividly illustrated with all too many painful exemplars—from Europe's feudal serfs and America's slaves, to the impoverished workers of the Victorian era so powerfully depicted by Charles Dickens, as well as today's oppressed sweatshop workers laboring in places from Dhaka to Pretoria. Today, we disparagingly speak of "grunt work" as work that is laborious, tedious, and unfulfilling, be it manual labor or the drudgery associated with corporate bureaucracy. Despite the progress of centuries, the cursed toil of Adam's lot often holds as true today as it did in biblical times.

But this coin has at least two sides. Returning to the Bible, we read, "So God blessed the seventh day and hallowed it, because on it God rested from all the work that he had done *in creation*" (Genesis 2:3, *OAB* 13) [Emphasis added]. The world is depicted as the supreme manifestation of God's creative work and after creating the world in six days, "God saw everything that he had made and indeed, it was very good" (Genesis 1:31, *OAB* 12). It is worth noting that the first use of the term "good" in the Bible was to describe God's creative work.

From the prehistoric cave paintings to the contemporary artists, scientists, and social entrepreneurs, work may be a vehicle by which one gains access to the transcendent and through which one's creative capacities are expressed. Indeed, the

---

[10] The economic gain need not accrue to the worker. Through various exploitative circumstances, people may be forced to work in ways that benefits others but not themselves.

[11] Given the constraints of space, this "phenomenological look" is barely a glance. For a more in depth review of the nature of work, please see, Robin Patric Clair, *Why Work?: The Perceptions of a Real Job and the Rhetoric of Work through the Ages* (West Lafayette, IN: Purdue University Press, 2008).

[12] Indeed, "travail," in French means "work."

[13] Michael David Coogan et al., eds., *The New Oxford Annotated Bible with the Apocryphal/ Deuterocanonical Books*, Augmented, 3rd ed. (Oxford, NY: Oxford University Press, 2007), p. 15. [Henceforth cited as *OAB*]

treasures of human civilization all bear witness to the idea that through work humanity's inspired capacity for genius is realized.[14] To the extent that we consciously
aspire to leave a legacy, it is through our work that we aim to do so. In this sense,
work is vital to the possibility of human fulfillment. These two extremes—work as
toil and transcendence—may represent the poles between which lie a continuum of
alternative experiences of work.

Human Identity and the Purpose of Work

Based on our previous discussion, we would suggest that one of the reasons why
faith is so durable is because of its place in our personal and cultural identity. Who
we are and the nature of our culture are taken as articles of faith that are continuously
being subjected to empirical tests and modified as needed, and in the process of
identity creation, "work" occupies a central role. Not only is it through our work
that we are identified by others, it is how we conceive of our identity to ourselves.
If a person can take pride in him or herself, it is often in relation to his or her work.
Work is central to who we perceive ourselves to be.

For a somewhat different angle on the meaning of work, let's ask the question:
"Why work?" If you ask a person why he or she works, typically the response will
be, "To make money." As realistic as this may sound, it fails to capture the complex motivations that lead people to work. Aristotle observed, "Every art and every
investigation, and similarly every action and pursuit, is considered to aim at some
good. Hence the Good has been rightly defined as 'that at which all things aim.' "[15]
While Aristotle's universal teleology may be largely incompatible with the modern
Darwinian outlook, it is undeniable that at least human action is purpose-driven.
Unlike random activities or autonomic responses, all human work is done for a purpose. A person working is a conscious agent who participates in the purpose of the
work, and in this way, work is an expression of the identity of the person as agent.

We should also acknowledge the multiplicity of purposes associated with work.
To illustrate, let us consider Rosie, a worker in a weapons factory. The owners of
the company may be producing a product for the purpose of national defense. The
weapon, however, may be used for the external purpose of harming the innocent.
Rosie's internal purpose for engaging in this work as a factory worker may be to
earn money, but if questioned why she wanted the money, she would reply that she
needed it to support her family. Although this is true, if we asked her if she would

---

[14] According to some interpretations, it is through work that humanity discovers its role as
"co-creator" with God. For example, Raymond Baumhart, S.J., the former president of Loyola
University Chicago writes, "God presented you and me with an incomplete world and invited us
to help in its completion. . . . This cooperation is certainly a major source of our human dignity."
Raymond Baumhart, S.J., "It's Not Easy Being a Manager and a Christian," *Loyola Magazine*
(Fall 1990): p. 6.

[15] Aristotle, *Ethics: The Nicomachean Ethics*, trans. J.A.K. Thompson (London: Penguin Books,
1976), p. 63.

take a job murdering enemies of the mafia to support her family, she would say "no" because such work would be morally objectionable. In this way we can see that as a conscious purpose-driven person, Rosie cannot do the work without also considering how the product of her labor will be used, i.e., its external purpose. As the working agent, she is the bearer of the internal and external purposes of her work and both contribute to creating her sense of personal identity. This identity is neither fixed nor immutable, but it does characterize her as a person and as such is of great existential importance.

This connection between personal and professional identity has sometimes been captured in family names and transmitted down through the generations, as if part of one's genetic endowment. Thus, some popular English family names are Smith, Baker, Miller, Banks, Wright, Carpenter, Taylor, Cook, and Fisher.[16] It is this linkage between work and human identity that reveals the essential inadequacy of the idea that work is simply a vehicle to make money. It is through work that we lay claim to our personal identity, and yet this point is lost, given the faith that dominates the popular interpretation of work in our corporate capitalist culture, which is a significant defect.

On Work and Faith in the Culture of Corporate Capitalism

As long as there have been people, there have been people working. Corporate capitalism, however, is new... new due to the way in which the work is organized under the structure of large, technologically sophisticated, and administratively complex corporations. Consider these examples of different organizational forms of working: a student writing a poem; a son shepherding sheep on a family farm; a high energy physicist operating a particle accelerator; a hedge fund manager taking a company private. Among these, one that differs significantly is the hedge fund manager because this profession depends not simply on highly sophisticated computational capacities; it also requires a society in which there is an established system of corporate capitalism.

What is corporate capitalism? "Capitalism" is generally understood to refer to a free-market economy in goods and services in which the means of production and distribution are privately held by individuals or corporations. Corporate capitalism refers to a capitalist economy in which the dominant economic actors are large business organizations legally identified as limited liability corporations or "persons."

---

[16] This connection between employment and identity was illustrated in a recent New York Times article on the effects of joblessness that followed from the recession. Therein, the author states, "Nearly half of the adults surveyed admitted to feeling embarrassed or ashamed most of the time or sometimes as a result of being out of work. Perhaps unsurprisingly, given the traditional image of men as breadwinners, men were significantly more likely than women to report feeling ashamed most of the time." Cited in: Michael Luo and Megan Thee-Brenan, "Poll Reveals Trauma of Joblessness in US," *New York Times* (2009). http://www.nytimes.com/2009/12/15/us/15poll.html? emc=eta1. Accessed on December 18, 2009.

In the history of work, one of the great innovations of the nineteenth and twentieth centuries has been the ascendency of corporate capitalism, in which advances in technology and management have permitted the development of commercial organizations on a scale previously unattainable.[17] Illustrating this, Charles Perrow notes that "today (i.e., around the year 2000), well over 90% of the workforce works for someone else—as wage and salary employees—up from 20% in 1800; over half of the gainfully employed people in the country work for organizations with 500 or more employees, up from 0% in 1800."[18]

The US has been capitalist from its inception. It is only over the last century, however, in which corporate capitalism has come to dominate and spread around the world. In the United States and elsewhere, this development has ushered in unprecedented economic growth and improved living standards for countless millions of people. In the process, corporate capitalism has exercised enormous influence not simply by virtue of its economic contributions, but by embodying a culture, complete with its own norms, symbols, and folklore. If economic growth were equivalent to ethical good, the moral character of corporate capitalism would be secured. And indeed, this view is implied by its apologists. For example, early in the current "Great Recession," Steve Forbes wrote a piece entitled, "How Capitalism Will Save Us." Therein he points to the considerable economic growth experienced in the United States and globally during the period from the early 1980s to 2007. This he called, "an economic Golden Age."[19] He concludes his piece by affirming, "Free-market capitalism will save us—if we let it."[20] Our purpose is not to argue economics, but what we see as telling is the messianic language that Forbes uses in which he gives voice to the faith of corporate capitalism. Around the same time, *The Economist* magazine took a similar position: "Capitalism is at bay, but those who believe in it must fight for it."[21] Here again we see an implication that capitalism in itself constitutes a moral good worthy of our faith and, hence, is worth defending.

Corporate capitalism also has its critics, some of whom see it as irredeemably bad.[22] As evidence, they point to the deleterious environmental effects caused by

---

[17] We must emphasize that this is not to say that corporate capitalism was first invented in the twentieth century. One ancient institution, the Catholic Church may represent the primogenitor of the modern global corporation, and from the seventeenth to mid-nineteenth centuries, the East India Company was an early example of a commercial corporation operating virtually on a global scale.

[18] Charles Perrow, *Organizing America: Wealth, Power, and the Origins of Corporate Capitalism* (Princeton, NJ: Princeton University Press, 2002), p. 1.

[19] Steve Forbes, "How Capitalism Will Save Us," *Forbes* (November 10, 2008): p. 18.

[20] Ibid., p. 26.

[21] "Capitalism at Bay," *The Economist*, Vol. 182, No. 9 (October 18–24, 2008): p. 16. Although *The Economist*, speaks of capitalism generally, it can be understood that the form of capitalism which is being referred to is "corporate capitalism."

[22] In recent years, some of the harshest critics of corporate capitalism have been found among the opponents of globalization. An indication of the intensity of feeling and popularity of this view is the anti-globalization protests that have become a permanent feature of World Trade Organization

industrial polluters, the harm caused by businesses that sought to maximize profits at the expense of safety, the violation of the human rights of workers for the sake of producing cheap exports, and so on. How can we reconcile these contrasting views?

To understand the ethical significance of corporate capitalism we must distinguish between corporate capitalism as a theoretical construct on the optimal modes of business organization, and corporate capitalism as a culture that is central to the experience of business for most people in the developed world.

Taken simply as a form of organization, corporate capitalism is like an instrument that in itself is morally neutral. It is like a knife that can be used for good or bad but itself lacks moral content. The moral content of corporate capitalism emerges when it is adopted and forms a culture among its practitioners. If we take corporate capitalism as a lived culture, what is the faith, or "ultimate concern" of its devoted followers? The way in which that question is answered will give shape to the character of corporate capitalism by giving expression to the deeply held beliefs regarding its aspirations and the moral parameters by which it is guided.

Based on many years of close observation, we believe that the evidence clearly suggests that the faith of corporate capitalist culture is contained in two essential tenets: profit maximization for the corporation and personal enrichment for the individual. Support of this view is constantly and clearly demonstrated through the behavior of businesses and individuals around the world, and it is the paradigm that has been and continues to be taught in our most prestigious business schools.

The idea of profit-maximization as the ultimate concern for the corporation was famously given voice to by the Nobel Prize winning economist, Milton Friedman, who asserted, "there is one and only one social responsibility of business—to use its resources and engage in activities designed to increase its profits so long as it stays within the rules of the game, which is to say, engages in open and free competition without deception or fraud."[23] According to this view, as long as companies do not break the law, they could legitimately carry out all sorts of injustices in the name of profit maximization. Indeed, there are countless examples to support that view.

Writing in the prestigious *Harvard Business Review* a couple of years before the publication of Friedman's piece, Albert Carr, claimed quite brazenly that businesses were perfectly justified in lying, cheating, and bribing, all in the name of achieving business objectives. "If the law as written gives a man a wide-open chance to make a killing, he'd be a fool not to take advantage of it. If he doesn't someone else will. There is no obligation on him to stop and consider who is going to get hurt. If the law says he can do it, that's all the justification he needs. There's nothing unethical

---

ministerial meetings. For an example of a recent study on the anti-corporate globalization movements see Jeffrey S. Juris, *Networking Futures: The Movements Against Corporate Globalization*, Experimental Futures (Durham, NC: Duke University Press, 2008).

[23] Milton Friedman, "The Social Responsibility of a Corporation Is to Increase Its Profits," in *Business Ethics: Readings and Cases in Corporate Morality*, eds. W. Michael Hoffman, Robert E. Frederick, and Mark S. Schwartz (New York, NY: McGraw Hill, 2001), p. 160. This article originally appeared in the *New York Times Magazine* on September 13, 1970.

about that. It's just plain business sense."[24] In the same article, Carr goes on to assert the legitimacy of lying on one's résumé, engaging in industrial espionage, and adulterating the contents of consumer goods in order to maximize profits. Even when strictly adhering to Friedman's principle of acting within the law, if profit maximization is one's ultimate concern, then service to others, product quality, etc., will all be subordinated to that overriding goal.

The idea of personal enrichment as the other pillar of faith within the corporate capitalist culture is illustrated with many examples. Let us be clear, we are not suggesting that, in itself, personal enrichment is a bad thing. However, when personal enrichment is taken as an ultimate concern, then all other moral concerns will be subordinated and this inevitably leads to corruption and injustice. Examples from the recent past are telling. In the 1990s, there was a huge run-up in the stock market due to the dot-com boom. Millions of ordinary Americans came to believe that the stock market was a sure path to riches, and this misconception was reinforced when countless weak technology firms were misrepresented as strong, and contributed to an inevitable collapse in the late 1990s. Feeding off this market exuberance, the energy giant, Enron became the period's emblem of a corporation in which the company's leadership and its traders in particular thrived in a culture of personal enrichment in brazenly contemptuous disregard for the public good. Emblematic of its corporate culture, the company achieved astonishing growth through fraudulent means including manipulation of energy markets that led to rolling blackouts across California. Despite the catastrophic consequences, Enron executives claimed that their acts were not illegal, and hence, were acceptable. As another example, around 2005 the news emerged that many corporate executives were increasing their compensation through a process of stock option backdating. Because it was a form of unfair enrichment, it was always done in secret. And yet after the practice came to light, it was defended by many as "not illegal" and hence, permissible. Finally, in 2007, the global economy went into the worst recession since the Great Depression, caused in large part to a "housing bubble," brought about above all by awarding subprime mortgages on a colossal scale to unqualified borrowers, in a practice known as "predatory lending." According to Edward Gramlich, "From essentially zero in 1993, subprime mortgage originations grew to $625 billion by 2005, one-fifth of total mortgage originations in that year, a whopping 26% annual rate of increase over the whole period."[25] The loan originators, working in banks and other financial institutions across the United States and elsewhere, were able to enrich themselves by bundling the mortgages and selling them as securities, before the homeowners went into default. Because of the crisis, the national unemployment rate exceeded 10% and in response, the government was forced to intervene on an order of trillions of dollars, thereby ensuring the indebtedness of the country for generations to come. And yet, here again, in the inquiries that followed this catastrophe, leaders from the

---

[24] Albert Z. Carr, "Is Business Bluffing Ethical?," *Harvard Business Review*, Vol. 46, No. 1 (1968): p. 146. [Henceforth cited as *BBE*]

[25] Edward M. Gramlich, "Booms and Busts: The Case of Subprime Mortgages," *Economic Review* Vo. 92, No. 4 (2007): p. 106.

institutions that came close to bankrupting the country justified their actions as not being illegal.

Another glaring demonstration of the faith of corporate capitalism is executive compensation. The *Wall Street Journal* reports that in 1960 the average Fortune 500 CEO pay was twice the salary of the president of the United States. By 2006, these CEOs made 30 times that of the US president and 212 times as much as the average worker's salary. By comparison, in Japan, the average CEO's salary was 11 times greater than that of the average worker.[26] In 2007, the year in which the United States collapsed into recession, the CEO of Goldman Sachs was given a bonus of $53.4 million,[27] and his compensation was small compared to the income of a number of hedge fund managers. It could be argued that from a moral perspective, it is unfair to group "legitimate" CEO compensation with predatory lending. However, these examples all depict actions that were within the law and demonstrated a faith in the "virtues" of profit-maximization and self-enrichment. This faith was unflinchingly described in a notable article by Michael Lewis in which he examines the collapse of Wall Street following the subprime mortgage debacle. At one point, he recounts a meeting with John Gutfreund, the former CEO of the investment bank, Salomon Brothers:

> He [Gutfreund] thought the cause of the financial crisis was "simple. Greed on both sides—greed of investors and the greed of the bankers." I [Lewis] thought it was more complicated. Greed on Wall Street was a given—almost an obligation. The problem was the system of incentives that channeled the greed.[28]

Elsewhere in the article, Lewis says that the "truly profane event" was "the growing misalignment of interests between the people who trafficked in financial risk and the wider culture." He quotes a hedge fund manager who describes the situation in this way. "We fed the monster until it blew up."[29] By this he meant that they fully knew they were part of a process inexorably leading to a crisis, but they leveraged the system to maximize their profits until collapse made that impossible.

We see the designation, "Wall Street" as a metaphor for the corporate capitalist faith in its most distilled and concentrated form. Lewis is correct in acknowledging the givenness of greed on Wall Street, but we doubt that it is possible to constructively channel this greed. Why? Because greed is an excessive desire for self-enrichment, which by its nature, will never be satisfied no matter how much it is fed. The more that one "feeds the monster," the more rapacious it grows. Explosion is inevitable—and, hence, the cycle of boom and bust continues, resulting in much suffering for many.

---

[26] Lauren Etter, "Hot Topic: Are CEOs Worth Their Weight in Gold?," *Wall Street Journal* (January 21, 2006), p. A7.

[27] Michael J. de la Merced, "At Goldman, Lieutenants Also Reach Top Pay Levels," *International Herald Tribune* (February 23, 2007), p. 16.

[28] Michael Lewis, "The End," *Portfolio* (November 11, 2008). http://www.portfolio.com/news-markets/national-news/portfolio/2008/11/11/The-End-of-Wall-Streets-Boom/.

[29] Ibid.

And this points to a fundamental flaw in Milton Friedman's theory of business responsibility that follows from a faith in profit maximization and self-enrichment.[30] Profit maximization only makes moral sense if profits are understood to be instrumental and for some other good. Profit for the sake of profit (i.e., profits as ultimate concern) continues not only ad infinitum, but ad nauseum. It is pointless and ultimately destructively exhausting. If corporate capitalism is to legitimately flourish, it is in need of a deeper and truer faith. Doing so, however, would be exceedingly difficult because it would require a transformation of the culture under which corporate capitalism is preserved and defended.

The Culture of Corporate Capitalism: Individuals in Corporations

Earlier in this essay we noted that the "faith of a culture" consists in the "tacit norms that constitute the framework within which most individuals in a society generally understand the essential elements of reality and how to evaluate his or her experience." We also suggested that faith is not simply a matter of personal choice because it is embedded in the norms into which people are inducted from birth. This, however, does not mean that cultures are monolithic or immutable. To the contrary, cultures, both at the geographic and organizational level, are highly heterogeneous and dynamic. As Jones and Zeitlin note:

> One important implication of historical studies of firm culture is that culture is dynamic, and that firms are always drawing inspiration and ideas from the cultural materials at hand.... There may be numerous subcultures striving for power within an organization.... Far from being an impediment to change, moreover, a complex and contested firm culture can also serve as a source of competitive advantage.[31]

The power and flexibility of organizational culture is both a threat and opportunity to those who seek to conduct business ethically. As we suggested, culture is undergirded by a kind of faith. When a person joins a company he is admitted to an organizational culture and in so doing is inducted into its collective faith. The corporate norms are captured in the everyday practices that convey the message, "This is our faith and this is how things are done around here." Since one's paycheck is at stake, there is a strong incentive to adopt the norms and keep the faith. The risk in this is that by conforming to the organizational culture, normally ethical persons can be induced to engage in clear moral transgressions. Indeed, it was not long ago that people were encouraged to leave their personal morality behind when they engaged

---

[30] It could be objected that Friedman advocates profit maximization, not personal enrichment. However, while it is possible to seek profit maximization for reasons other than self-enrichment, it would lead to a different model of capitalism and that was never espoused by Friedman.

[31] Geoffrey Jones and Jonathan Zeitlin, *The Oxford Handbook of Business History*, Oxford Handbooks in Business and Management (Oxford and New York, NY: Oxford University Press, 2008), p. 611.

in business. Hence, Theodore Levitt infamously wrote in 1958 "business must fight as if it were at war. And, like a good war, it should be fought gallantly, daringly, and, above all, *not* morally."[32] Similarly, Albert Carr asserted, "the basis of private morality is a respect for the truth. . . ." However, he claims, "that business operates with a special code of ethics." What is this code? According to Carr, "As long as [businessmen] comply with the letter of the law, they are within their rights to operate their business as they see fit" (BBE 48, 52, 143). Such assertions are not unique; they are symptomatic of the business paradigm of the faith of corporate capitalism.

On the other hand, because organizational culture is changeable, the individual may have the opportunity to influence the culture's development. Indeed, according to Edgar Schein, "the only thing of real importance that leaders do is to create and manage culture."[33] The key question, we would submit, is this: What is the faith to which a business leader should cleave as he or she takes on the monumentally significant challenge of seeking to guide the development of an organization's culture?

On the Faith of Business Ethics

The discipline of business ethics arose out of the need to challenge the anomie of the misguided faith of profit maximization and self-enrichment that has taken corporate capitalism hostage. This unhealthy faith required people ordinarily of goodwill to bifurcate their moral life into two, one for business and the other for their personal life. Business ethics seeks to restore moral wholeness to persons participating in corporate life. To do this business ethics must be founded on a faith that can be consistently held by organizations large and small, and individuals inside and outside of business. What then distinguishes business ethics from the ethics of ordinary life? Simply this: business ethics is particularly sensitive to the ethical problems typically associated with business. Business ethics follows from the recognition that businesses are organizations comprised of people who do not lose their status as such when they engage in business.

In its simplest form, the faith of business ethics is this: work in all its forms should be consistent with moral goodness. But let us add a bit more detail. As we understand it, the faith of business ethics rests upon the following three pillars:

- Dignity
- Service (or stewardship)
- Accountability

---

[32] Theodore Levitt, "The Dangers of Social Responsibility," *Harvard Business Review* Vol. 36, No. 5 (1958): p. 50.

[33] Edgar H. Schein, *Organizational Culture and Leadership*, 3rd ed. (San Francisco, CA: Jossey-Bass, 2004), p. 11.

Let us briefly look at these three principles. The Dignity Principle can be summarized as follows: All human beings, irrespective of their ethnicity, gender, economic or social status, or any other factor, have intrinsic worth or dignity by virtue of their being a person and no individual or group has the right to deny them of their inherent dignity.[34]

Obviously, the Dignity Principle gives expression to an understanding that is central to Kantian ethics as well as the Golden Rule that is central to the ethical teachings of Christianity and many other religious traditions. Moreover, the Dignity Principle can be seen as underlying human rights. This is especially important because as more and more businesses are global in reach, they must act on principles that accord the same respect to people everywhere, especially to those who have a stake in the actions of the business, be they customers, employees, shareholders, regulators, or the public at large in all countries and cultures in which the business operates.[35]

The Service or Stewardship Principle follows on the idea that all work should be conducted in a spirit of service or stewardship. Rather than thinking of work as simply a vehicle for profit maximization or self-enrichment, the Service Principle recognizes that all our work has effects on oneself and others, and the criterion of success is whether one's work can be seen to serve the greater good or not. The profit motive is not incompatible with the Service Principle. To the contrary, no company can expect to survive if it is not profitable and, therefore, profitability is seen as a necessary element of the Service Principle. Nor is the Service Principle incompatible with the idea of personal enrichment. However, profit and enrichment, rather than being taken as ultimate concerns, are subordinated to a higher purpose of work as service that is respectful of the dignity of all affected parties.[36]

Finally, the Accountability Principle seeks to reconcile the tension between personal moral autonomy and organizational authority. Accordingly, an accountable organization is one in which the individual and institution are both accountable to each other and the broader society. If the individual and organization are both committed to the principles of Dignity and Service, then both sides are on an equal footing. It is the individual's responsibility to exercise the autonomy needed to act as an ethical agent, and the company is responsible to exercise its authority to create a framework of values to support its business objectives. The integrity and agency

---

[34] A variation this "axiom" appeared in an article we previously published. See Robert E. McNulty and W. Michael Hoffman, "Business Ethics Perspectives on International Negotiations," in *ABA Guide to International Negotiations*, eds. James R. Silkenat, Jacqueline Klosek, and Jeffery M. Aresty (Chicago, IL: American Bar Association, 2009), p. 39.

[35] This contrast is captured in the difference between shareholder v. stakeholder theory. For more on this, please see, R. Edward Freeman, *Strategic Management : A Stakeholder Approach* (Boston, MA: Pitman, 1984). The term "stakeholder" refers to those affected by the actions of a business and hence have a stake in the company.

[36] The Service Principle is related to the idea of "Servant Leadership," that was so well understood and articulated by Robert Greenleaf. See for example, his book Robert K. Greenleaf and Larry C. Spears, *The Power of Servant-Leadership: Essays* (San Francisco, CA: Berrett-Koehler Publishers, 1998).

of both the individual and the corporation are thereby respected. Moreover, the Accountability Principle follows from a recognition that all stakeholders are bound by common rights and duties, and while there will inevitably be conflicts and tensions, they should all be resolvable provided all are prepared to act according to the common moral norms, including the Dignity and Service Principles.

Like Jaspers' philosophical faith, business ethics follows from a faith that is rational and critical, as well as transcendent, in that it is informed by a view of ultimate goodness. If one is of a religious orientation, his or her notion of goodness may conform to religious insights or an experience of God. Those who may lack religious faith will be guided by a more secular notion of what is ultimately good. In either case, given the generally secular nature of business and modern polity, we believe that such variations, though not meaningless, need not be insurmountable.[37]

Seeking the Redemption of Business

Why is business ethics so often greeted with skepticism if not outright derision? We would submit it is because business ethics is profoundly countercultural. Business ethics rejects as flawed the faith of corporate capitalism. Because the faith of corporate capitalism, based on profit maximization and self-enrichment, is so entrenched, the idea that there could be an alternative is seen as preposterous. And yet, consider this: just over 90 years ago, women in the United States were denied the right to vote based on the view still held by many men (and some women) that women lacked the rational capacities to qualify them for this right. Today, less than a century later, for the first time in history, women make up over 50% of the US workforce and almost 60% of college graduates.[38] A century ago, these facts would have been deemed ridiculous. This type of cognitive dissonance pervades our views on business. We can see its brokenness, and yet we can't believe there is an alternative. But the truth is that the faith of profit maximization and self-enrichment is not just weak, it follows from a colossal misunderstanding of the nature of business. For if the conventional faith of corporate capitalism is correct, then profit maximization and self-enrichment are ends in themselves, and humanity is subordinated to business. Why would anyone embrace this? Because it reflects the long held view that in a world of work as toil people are condemned to a life of economic warfare. Accordingly, the best one can hope for is to build a financial bulwark sufficient to permit the isolation of oneself from the incessant conflict.

According to the faith of business ethics, while work may indeed involve pain and toil, if it is approached in a spirit of dignity, service, and accountability, the possibility of work as a calling is found. And in responding to such a calling, we find the possibility of work redeemed—not only in the lofty sense in which through our

---

[37] Secular societies around the world are populated by people of faith. In most instances we find that the two orientations are generally compatible.

[38] See "Female Power," *The Economist* (January 2–8, 2010): pp. 49–51.

work we tap into the creative potentialities inspired by a sense of the transcendent, but also redeemed in the sense that despite the pain, tedium, and toil of work, it still represents our heartfelt offering to the world.

In some instances, by all outward appearances, work done according to the faith of conventional corporate capitalism may be identical to that done according to a faith informed by business ethics. And yet, because the faiths are so different, the phenomenology of work as experienced will be sharply different. Rather than "feeding the monster" or being a "cog in a machine," work guided by the faith of business ethics aims at moral goodness and, in this way, is affirming of what is best in our humanity. Rather than being dehumanized by work, work is humanized by one's spirit of service. Rather than interminable toil from which we seek liberation, redeemed work is an essential vehicle for the realization of a purposeful life. And rather than seeking to maximize what we can take through self-enrichment, in redeemed work we seek to maximize the value of what we can contribute to our community and the world. Business ethics in the sense we are here describing provides us with the philosophical grounding for a faith in work that is rescued from the exhausting and exploitative faith associated with corporate capitalism. In its place, business ethics offers an opportunity to reinvent corporate capitalism in a way that opens the door to the creative potential of work informed by a spirit of dignity, service, and accountability. Too long have we accepted the tyranny of work malformed by a misguided faith. We know better. It is time to work better.

Reflections on Philosophical Faith and Faith in the Twenty-First Century

Filiz Peach

Abstract One of the fundamental concepts in Jaspers' existence philosophy is the notion of philosophical faith. In this chapter, I shall focus on the notion of faith and its manifestation in today's society. Faith and belief in God are quite different today from what it was like say 500–600 years ago. Clearly, Jaspers' concept of philosophical faith has a very special existential meaning, and it is not easy to compare it with faith as understood in our time. The questions that will be discussed are: How is faith perceived in the twenty-first century and to what extent does Jaspers' view of philosophical faith relate to today's understanding of faith? The connection between faith and globalization will also be explored.

Introduction

When discussing the notion of faith and its manifestation in today's society there are a number of elements which need to be taken into consideration such as political, economic and socio-cultural aspects of communities, the effect of cultural differences on the individual's beliefs within a particular society, technological progress and globalisation, and so forth. The first question to address, however, is: what do we mean by faith? Faith can be described as one's absolute commitment to a particular belief or a set of values. It is regarded as neither rational nor logical; but faith matters, because it affects not only how we feel and act towards others but also how we function in day-to-day existence. For some, it can also be a source of hope for the future. On the whole, the term *faith* has been associated with religious faith. A vast number of people identify themselves with and choose to follow the security and protection that various religions claim to offer to individuals. Faith remains personal. One could also describe faith as one's worldview or *Weltanschauung*, which represents what one holds to be true through reflection. Faith manifests itself mostly through inwardness, which may or may not relate to the outside world. It may not be intelligible or communicable but the power of the individual's inner feelings that faith creates is strong. The individual in solitude or in communication can

F. Peach (✉)
Mary Ward Centre, London, UK
e-mail: fpeach@hotmail.com

H. Wautischer et al. (eds.), *Philosophical Faith and the Future of Humanity*,
DOI 10.1007/978-94-007-2223-1_22, © Springer Science+Business Media B.V. 2012

experience these inner feelings. These profound experiences are said to constitute one's particular worldview. There are of course different types of faith such as religious faith, faith as a secular worldview, existential notions of faith including Jaspers' philosophical faith and so on, and they must be differentiated.

In what follows, I shall explore how Jaspers' view of philosophical faith relates to today's understanding of faith, and how faith relates to globalisation.

Jaspers' Notion of Philosophical Faith

Jaspers' notion of philosophical faith is one of the fundamental concepts in his philosophy of existence. It is fundamental because it is above all concerned with one's self-being and is a necessary condition for the realisation of selfhood. It must be made clear at the outset, however, that Jaspers' notion of philosophical faith has a very special existential meaning, and it is not always easy to compare it with faith in general terms and faith as understood in our time.

For Jaspers, faith can be described as one's attitude, belief and commitment to that which goes beyond what is objectively known. He states that philosophical faith is personal and closely tied to broader aspects of human experiences, particularly existential ones. In other words, the truth of faith is a matter of personal commitment. For Jaspers, faith is immediate in contrast to everything that is mediated by understanding. Although he acknowledges that philosophical faith is not verifiable in any scientific sense, he maintains that it can disclose or elucidate some fundamental aspects of human existence. Since philosophical faith cannot be universally valid, it does not relate to anything objective within the empirical realm. The truth of statements about human existence, particularly the transcendent aspect of the individual, are non-objectifiable and cannot be confirmed or refuted. Jaspers repeatedly says that matters of faith are subjective, cannot be verified or falsified, and transcend what can be evidentially known.

It should be noted that Jaspers' concept of faith does not mean blind faith in something beyond one's comprehension, nor does it mean the irrational. He believes that philosophical faith must elucidate itself for each individual in his reasoning to reveal its subjective truth. Reason, he reiterates, is a vital part of one's philosophical faith. One of the most notable characteristics of philosophical faith is its irreducibly subjective roots within each individual. In Jaspers' words: "Philosophical faith is real only in the individual himself, in his experience and insight, and in his reason, based upon his possible Existenz. It is in the roots of the whole human being, not by the mere intellect of consciousness at large, that philosophical ideas are heard and understood."[1]

---

[1] Karl Jaspers, *Philosophy*, Volume 1 (Chicago, IL: University of Chicago Press, 1969), p. 19. [Henceforth cited as *P* with volume number]

In his formulation of the concept of philosophical faith, Jaspers often links it with Existenz, Transcendence and self-being. He emphasises that existential reflections drive the analysis of human existence to its extreme boundaries where faith arises. The recognition of the limitation of empirical knowledge highlights the significance and the role of faith. For him, some subjective human experiences, for example the experience of the *Augenblick*, are matters of philosophical faith and unlike sciences they cannot offer any objective propositions or theories. In Jaspers' view, by preparing ourselves in philosophical thinking, we can face certain threatening situations more consciously, particularly in boundary situations. This kind of philosophical reflection, namely transcending-thinking, belongs to self-awareness and it can help the individual to realise his/her potentialities and self-being. In this respect, philosophical faith is also connected with what Jaspers calls "unconditional acts" (*P2* 255–261).

Jaspers discusses his concept of philosophical faith extensively in *The Perennial Scope of Philosophy* and *Philosophy*. Although Jaspers asserts that philosophy and religion are connected through faith, he makes a clear distinction between philosophical faith and religious faith. In his view, in religious faith what is given as truth by the mediators of religion is accepted as truth for everybody without further questioning; whereas for Jaspers philosophical faith is personal. He reminds us that religious faith is based on revelation, it is mediated by Scriptures, institutions, and the clergy, whereas the most important notion in philosophical faith is freedom which negates the certainty and protection that religions claim to offer to individuals. The very essence of Jaspers' philosophy is the free spirit of exploration (of human existence and Being) that rejects all authority. Jaspers dissociates himself from religious faith because of its tendency to objectify Transcendence and its symbols, namely ciphers. He also rejects the idea of one set of truths that are valid for everybody within a specific group. For Jaspers, philosophical faith, unlike religious faith, does not rely on revelation and institutionalisation but on the individual's subjective truth within the framework of his unconditional freedom. According to Jaspers, questioning and seeking truth through transcending-thinking, existential communication and the unconditional freedom of the individual are cardinal elements that separate philosophical faith from religious faith and dogma.

Kierkegaard's influence on Jaspers' thinking is clear. But there is a sharp distinction between Jaspers' notion of philosophical faith and Kierkegaard's concept of religious faith. These two concepts are incompatible and at times Jaspers is openly critical of Kierkegaard's view of faith on the grounds that it is mediated in the name of divine authority. For Jaspers, then, philosophical faith is an expression of one's attitude towards life, one's conduct toward the Encompassing of subject and object, but without a religious commitment. Jaspers maintains that the content of philosophical faith is historic in that it is closely connected with the individual's concrete historical situation. Jaspers maintains that whatever the individual does, one's freedom in choices and decisions shapes one's existence and historicity.[2] One's historicity indicates the specificity of the individual's self-being which is unique.[3]

Jaspers argues that philosophy and religion are connected through faith, and that there is tension between the two. Despite this tension, Jaspers, unlike Heidegger, does not break the relationship between the two. Heidegger avoids dealing with the concepts of faith and transcendence in his Being and Time and leaves them to the confines of religion. Jaspers on the other hand believes that this tension between philosophy and religion enables one to develop one's own philosophical worldview.

Jaspers further asserts that there is a tension and struggle between the poles of faith and unbelief and that it is an essential component of the process of attaining one's self-being. If the faith-unbelief polarity disappears, according to Jaspers, then "faithlessness" appears and this greatly undermines one's transcending-thinking. Jaspers expresses this kind of tension in philosophical faith as a constant dialectical movement whereby various conflicts in existence may turn into insoluble antinomies.

So this is just a brief outline of Jaspers' concept of philosophical faith. How does Jaspers' view of philosophical faith relate to today's understanding of faith? Does it relate to it at all? And how is faith perceived in modernity? Why is religious faith getting stronger in some societies? Now let us address these questions.

Faith in Modernity

The understanding of faith today seems quite different from what it was like say 500–600 years ago. Faith in modernity manifests itself in different forms, for example, it may simply be one's private secular worldview either in solitude or in communication. Although it may sound similar to Jaspers' view, there is no reference to Transcendence, Existenz or reading ciphers in this case. In other words, there is no transcendental or spiritual element in this form of faith and it certainly is not philosophical faith in the Jaspersian sense. Or faith can be related to an alternative mode of being in the world. Here I am referring to the so-called "new age"

---

[2] I should like to express here my gratitude to Professor Leonard Ehrlich. While working on my doctoral thesis on Jaspers' concept of death during 1998–2004 I had some valuable discussions with him at various philosophical conferences regarding philosophical faith as well as related notions of historicity, Being and ciphers. I found his remarks, explanations and interpretation of them, whether in correspondence or discussions, clear and helpful. I often referred to his knowledgeable comments and his books on these issues in my thesis. I am particularly grateful for our personal communication in 2003. I should also like to add that I found the translation of some of Jaspers' ideas such as Existenz and philosophical faith much clearer in *Basic Philosophical Writings* than Ashton's translation in *Philosophy*. See *Karl Jaspers–Basic Philosophical Writings–Selections*, eds. Edith Ehrlich, Leonard H. Ehrlich, and George Pepper (Athens, OH: Ohio University Press, 1986). [Henceforth cited as *BPW*]

[3] *P2* 106 and *BPW* 81. See also Alan M. Olson, *Transcendence and Hermeneutics: An Interpretation of the Philosophy of Karl Jaspers* (The Hague, Boston, MA and London: Martinus Nijhoff Publishers, 1979), p. 25.

ideology which primarily focuses on nature and which applies to a small group of people—this is seen as being engaged in spiritual life in a new form without any religious commitment. It is regarded as a new spiritual connection with the individual and social life. In the absence of interest in inherited religion, people seek direct spiritual experience today and have a choice of a vast number of spiritual alternatives. Because individualism is prevalent, particularly in western European countries, people tend to disconnect themselves from communal belief.

In most cases faith appears purely as religious faith emphasising the individual's personal connection with God with absolute commitment. This commitment may or may not be expressed in a traditional way. Since it seems to be the strongest type of faith at present, I will focus on the manifestation of religious faith in modernity for the moment.

There are some significant changes in the form and content of the perception of faith in modernity. Some thinkers claim that traditional religious faith cannot survive the changes in the twenty-first century and that the decline of religion is inevitable. One could argue that modernity does not necessarily entail the disappearance of religion although it certainly raises questions about the institutional position of religion. Religious faith has evolved and transformed itself over many centuries, and now it survives in various forms. The perception and the sense of faith one has varies from culture to culture and can change within the same culture over many years. It may have been weakened and to some extent faded from the public domain in some communities, particularly in Western Europe, but it continues to exist mostly in a private sphere concentrating itself in personal belief and practice.

Atheism and agnosticism have been on the rise since the seventeenth century and it is noticeable that today many churches remain almost empty. Religious faith in some European countries has been loosing its power steadily over the past couple of centuries and one can see the signs. It must be a seriously anxious time for the church leaders. In fact, in November 2009 something unusual and remarkable has happened which demonstrates this anxiety within religious circles and is worth mentioning here. The Roman Catholic Church (representing Pope Benedict) invited those traditionalist Anglicans who have been disillusioned with certain changes within the Anglican Church such as women's ordination and acceptance of gay clergy. Following this, the Archbishop of Canterbury Dr. Rowan Williams visited the Vatican to protest personally to the Pope expressing his concern with the Vatican's apparent lack of consultation. It was reported that this was the most strained encounter between the Church of England and the Catholic Church since the 1960s.[4] This event clearly indicates that there is uneasiness, disquiet, and anguish regarding the matters of Christian faith in both the Catholic Church and the Anglican Communion. It also suggests an indication of worry about the fading Christian faith.

---

[4] See http://www.guardian.co.uk/uk/2009/nov/22/williams-faces-pope-on-converts. Last accessed November 8, 2010.

This is indeed a significant historic event in the religious realm. It may be a reaction to the declining numbers of believers and churchgoers. The idea behind it may have been the belief that the unification of the two Churches may overcome this problem. It may also be an attempt to protect Christian values in the West against the threat of the Islamist ideology that is on the rise. On the one hand, this move may be a step taken to strengthen the declining religious faith in the Western world by uniting two branches of Christianity. On the other hand, it could negatively affect relations between the Catholic Church and the Anglican Communion. It may even lead to a deeper division of Christian faith between the two, although it was said that there was an important endorsement of continued talks on unity.[5]

As previously mentioned, manifestations of religious faith and belief in God are quite different today from what it was like in the Middle Ages. In the past religious faith used to be primarily the expression of the unconditional love and worship of the divine being, whereas now it is generally seen as a social structure that advocates a moral conduct in society or it is represented within the framework of a political ideology. Although in some countries, for example in the United States, religion is resistant to secularisation; modernity and secularisation have been closely linked. Modernity is also linked with the world of differentiation which entails deep-seated changes in communities. These changes stem from our perception of the self, society, economics, and nature all of which challenge religious views in politics, sciences, and arts.

While religious faith has been steadily declining in some western European countries, its strength has been growing in some other parts of the world. During the last 20–30 years it has become increasingly more politicised and radicalised in some cultures, for example, Islam in the Middle East. But it is not only in the Middle Eastern countries that Islam has been gaining strength. The increased presence of Muslims within Western societies is also becoming more vociferous. In one of his articles, a Pakistani journalist, Eqbal Ahmad, confirms the view that religious faith has a different perspective in today's communities. He points out the politicised nature of faith and writes about modern Islamists that they are "concerned with power, not with the soul; with the mobilization of people for political purposes rather than with sharing and alleviating their sufferings and aspirations".[6] I should point out that similar changes also occur in the Jewish and Christian worlds.

This kind of politicised and passionate religious faith sometimes gives way to dramatic and violent action against people in different parts of the world. It certainly creates fear, tension, and unrest in these communities. Obviously, religious conflicts are not new in our world history. A resurgence of religious uprising occurs usually as a reaction to a particular historical situation at a particular time. Throughout history quite often there have been unrest, fighting, and violence in the name of religion

---

[5] The crucial unanswered question is how exactly Catholics and Anglicans propose to move toward unity after years of progressive mutual alienation. It will be interesting to wait and see whether there will be a move toward conversion.

[6] Cited by Edward W. Said, "The Clash of Ignorance", *The Nation*, October 22, 2001. http://www.thenation.com/article/clash-ignorance. Last accessed November 8, 2010.

or God, for example, the Crusades in the eleventh to thirteenth centuries and the conflicts between Muslims, Jews, and Christians for the last 1,300 years.

People often ask questions: Why is religious faith so politicised and radicalised and why now? Is it a serious threat to society in the future? What can we do to leave behind a non-violent world, a peaceful global community for the next generations? There is, of course, no simple answer to these questions. Some scholars, including Anthony C. Grayling and Richard Dawkins, argue that religion is at the root of society's ills. In their view, religion has become more assertive, more vocal in the public domain. Dawkins, for example, thinks that eradicating faith in God is the best hope for the elimination of violence. But is it realistic to assume that religious faith can be eradicated? Religions and religious faith have survived in some form or other since the appearance of mankind on earth; it is unlikely that religious faith will disappear altogether. Nor is there a guarantee that eradicating religious faith will eliminate violence.

The fundamental source of conflict in the world today seems, in most cases, to be due to ideological, economic, and cultural differences. Conflicts often arise as a result of the lack of understanding of such differences. If we focus on the cultural perspective, we find that many cultural elements are in fact closely and inseparably connected with one's faith.

First, let me address what we mean by culture. Generally speaking, culture refers to a particular shared way of thinking about the world as well as a reflection on that world in art, literature and other social and cultural activities. Each community has its own distinct culture, as Jaspers himself stated which distinguishes it from other communities. Different cultures have different behavioral codes and different relationships of meaning systems. When we say we do not understand the actions of people from a culture other than our own, we are acknowledging our lack of familiarity with the meaning of their acts. It is important to recognize that there are no social values that hold true for all peoples at all times. Values are matters of opinion depending on specific cultures and in accordance with the code of behavior in one's society. In connection with cultural differences, Jaspers acknowledges that cultural experiences are expressed in terms of particular ciphers that may be shared in a particular community and he argues that ciphers are not universal. While Jaspers acknowledges differences between cultures, he also believes that there are at least some normative codes of conduct for humanity.

Cultural differences are real and important, and do not necessarily lead to conflict or violence. However, when there is a vast number of conflicting worldviews (religious and non-religious) in a pluralistic society, and when there is a breakdown in communication, then such differences between cultures create a fragile and unstable world. That is why Jaspers insisted that without existential communication there would be no unity of mankind or philosophical faith.

For Jaspers, communication is a matter of being with others while actualising one's potential self-being. Existential communication is an intrinsic part of philosophical faith, because it is the medium through which the transcendent aspect of the individual can be disclosed and this is essential for possible Existenz in the achievement of selfhood. It is this relationship between existential communication and the transcendent aspect of the human being that provides valuable insight in the area of self-understanding. This in turn helps the individual to understand others and form a better relationship with others.

How does culture contribute and relate to worldviews? All knowledge, including the most basic knowledge of everyday reality, what Jaspers would call *Grundwissen*, is derived from and maintained by social interactions. Culture reflects the ways in which individuals and groups participate in the creation of their perceived social reality. When people interact within a group, they do so with the understanding that their common interest and common knowledge of reality are acknowledged and shared. The understanding of the importance of culture is in a sense the process of constructing social reality. Over time, shared cultural elements, such as systems of meaning, become worldviews within a particular society. A worldview (*Weltanschauung*) represents a descriptive model of the world. It can be described as the framework of ideas and beliefs through which an individual interprets the world and interacts in it. It serves as a framework for generating various dimensions of human perception and experience such as language, knowledge, politics, history, moral values and most importantly religion all of which are appropriate to specific cultures. Worldviews are shared by people across generations. Some people see them as organic unity, operating at the same time at a community level and mostly in an unconscious way.

Globalisation

In order to understand the relationship between Jaspers' philosophical views on faith and manifestation of faith in modernity, one first has to look into the impact of culture and globalisation on societies in the world today. It also is necessary to bring cross-cultural communication into the discussion, as it is a major part of intertwined global and cultural issues. Cross-cultural communication, individual freedom and responsibility, human rights and conflicts, all are some of the defining features for the twenty-first century. Communication at different levels is a part of our everyday reality in our global community. But first, I will discuss globalisation and global community.

Globalisation is a dynamic process involved in political, economic and socio-cultural aspects of communities in the world. The process reshapes social relations through social and technical networks. Due to globalisation, there is a constant movement and cross-border interaction between individuals and nation states, and this can alter the familiar order of things and the social fabric of society.

The manifestation of faith in modern times cannot be separated from the global and cultural issues that have a huge impact on cross-cultural conflicts. Although globalisation brings peoples of the world together, paradoxically it can also lead to the fragmentation of societies. Some people see it as de-nationalisation of the nation state. The more communities are brought together, the more they seek their cultural, ethnic, or religious identity. In this regard, Samuel Huntington wrote an article in

1993 in which he claims that the clash of civilizations will dominate global politics. In his view, religion reinforces ethnic identities. He then suggests, "the processes of economic modernization and social change throughout the world are separating people from longstanding local identities. They also weaken the nation state as a source of identity. In much of the world religion has moved in to fill this gap. . . . The revival of religion. . .provides a basis for identity and commitment that transcends national boundaries."[7]

Nation states have certain characteristics such as historic specificity, the patterns of political and social organisation and their connection with modernity. All these elements make up one's national identity. People do not like radical changes. When there are societal changes due to globalisation perceived as threats to national identity people may turn to religion in order to re-establish their identity among like-minded people of faith, so to speak. In turn, the protection and security that religious identity provides may ironically lead to conflict and clash between different faiths.

Another source of conflict today is identified as the attitude of the West towards non-Western communities perceived as less advanced economically and politically; an attitude regarded by some as selfish and arrogant. Non-Westerners see the West as the power that uses international institutions, military power and economic resources to control the world according to their wish in order to maintain imperial interests and promote western political and economic values. It has been argued that the West, particularly the United States, tries to impose its values of democracy and liberalism upon others. Non-Western societies do not always welcome Western ideas of individualism, democracy, and a secular morality and they do not accept them as universal values. Such values provoke reaction both in their social and political realm, and this, in turn, deepens the hold on their traditional religious faith and identity. In some cases, the resentment of the West turns into anger, and the support for religious fundamentalism, particularly by the younger generation, becomes stronger. In these circumstances religious faith re-emerges as a unifying force, as a reaction to the common enemy as it were. So, the reason why we are experiencing a heightened presence of religious faith at present could be due to a reaction to the West's attitude.

How does philosophy relate to this? In globalisation the intellectual mode, as well as the political and economic conditions, is in flux. Philosophy is an intellectual activity that entails reflection and communication in order to make sense of the world when we interpret things around us and make judgements. We question assumptions, analyse them and form opinions and beliefs. Philosophising is closely connected with reasoning and the development of worldviews. Jaspers believes that tension between philosophical thinking and religious faith enables one to develop one's own philosophical worldview.

What is the impact of having different worldviews on globalisation then? Worldviews have various effects on different communities, some positive and some

---

[7] Samuel Huntington, "The Clash of Civilizations," *Foreign Affairs*, Vol. 72, No. 3, 1993, p. 26. [Henceforth cited as *CC*]

that provoke a hostile reaction. The significance of worldviews in connection with cross-cultural communication became increasingly clear during the twentieth century for a number of reasons, such as increasing contact between cultures, and the progress of sciences and technology in many areas of human existence. This kind of activity between various cultures led to a global movement. Worldviews are a significant part of cross-cultural communication, which is itself a necessary component of globalisation.

Worldviews are based on a number of basic beliefs which cannot, as Jaspers argued, be verified or falsified. Most of us acknowledge that values, behaviors, and worldviews differ from people to people, and we respect that. Some of us agree that different perspectives from different cultures contribute to various worldviews and this enriches human understanding. In fact, one can learn from and about different religious, political, and social organisations by examining their culture. It is possible to explore their internal dynamics and authenticity in a mature and rational way. This kind of attitude might enable us to understand others better and to have genuine communication with them in our pluralistic society. Creating dialogues between communities, however difficult it may be, is the first step towards a peaceful world.

What I am trying to point out here is that globalisation, communication, culture and worldviews are linked inseparably. Given that globalisation is here to stay, at least it seems so, then the question becomes how best to achieve effective cross-cultural communication to help us to have a peaceful world. Is it really possible to integrate different worldviews successfully? Are the cultural differences reconcilable? Such contemporary issues preoccupy politicians and philosophers.

I like to believe that Jaspers' cross-cultural appeal to humanity is still philosophically relevant today. If two different worldviews have sufficient common beliefs, it is possible to bring people together and have a constructive dialogue between them. If people are willing to communicate, conflicts can be resolved. It may be a wishful thinking but if we try harder, it is not impossible to achieve successful cross-cultural communication in today's global community, as Jaspers would wish.

Conclusion

After looking at various aspects of faith and discussing related issues in modernity such as communication, cultural perspective and globalisation, what conclusions can be drawn? Jaspers' notion of philosophical faith is quite different from traditional religious faith and from faith as understood today. For Jaspers, philosophical faith is inseparably connected with his concept of existential communication and self-being. For him, existential communication has its roots in the relationship with the other, that is, self-being is real in communication with another self-being. Jaspers thinks that one's relation to other human beings and the way in which one deals with others shape one's everyday existence. In his elucidation of human existence, Jaspers clarifies and highlights the importance of one's faith and truth in connection with cross-cultural communication. Philosophical truth, he says, is a function of communication with the other.

Jaspers' existential ideas are attractive because they are not dogmatic and they transcend cultural boundaries. The question, however, is to what extent are his views of philosophical faith and in connection with it existential communication relevant to today? In other words, can Jaspers' account of philosophical faith and existential communication relate to the understanding of faith in our time? It does not seem so. Let me explain.

When we reflect on Jaspers' philosophical views, it is clear that he is interested in shared human experiences grounded in history and he believes that this would provide a historical basis for the unity of mankind. He talks about harmony and communication between individuals. He also talks about the meeting of the minds. For Jaspers, communication is a matter of being with others and described as the loving struggle for mutual understanding. Jaspers indeed believes that understanding and communication between peoples would unite humanity, because we all share certain fundamental characteristics. For him, communication is essential in the understanding of philosophical faith as it is only in communication that we gain a profound awareness of Being. He also believes that philosophical faith transcends cultural and ideological differences between communities through existential communication.

All of this sounds positive and possible in an ideal world. However, today's so-called global community and cross-cultural communication do not always seem to be operating in harmony. The reality is that effective cross-cultural communication between some cultures is not happening and, perhaps, cannot happen. If we look around us, there does not seem to be much unity or peaceful communication between some communities and individuals. There is a lack of understanding and tolerance between different groups from varied cultural backgrounds. Unfortunately, Jaspers' view of harmony and the "meeting of the minds" between individuals do not seem to prevail in modernity. Instead it seems that most modern societies are fragmented, and unity and harmony seem to be missing in today's global community.

At an individual level, the skill of face-to-face communication with others seems to be deteriorating. Some argue that we have lost the skill of communicating with others in this age of technology and computerisation. Even if there is communication between individuals, it is not always constructive. At a societal level, it also seems problematic to have peaceful communication between some cultures. There is struggle but one cannot call it loving struggle in the Jaspersian sense. Tolerance between different cultures seems to be diminishing as some try to impose their own beliefs and values on other cultures. In some cases, violence is used in order to attain their goals. It seems to be getting more and more difficult to achieve harmony between some nation states. What we see indicates the fragmentation of societies rather than their being united in communication. It may seem a pessimistic view but it is clearly visible all around us, as in many parts of the world there is ongoing fighting and unrest. We witness on the news how cross-cultural conflicts destroy societies. Even within the same culture, tribal or ethnic violence and terror occurs.

Granted, Jaspers acknowledges the limits of communication. But he seems to disregard the destructive side of communication, when some worldviews can become obstacles in the paths of others, leading to massive destruction. I wonder whether

Jaspers' views of communication and philosophical faith were too optimistic, or even Utopian. Can different worldviews be successfully articulated and positively represented? Will existential communication remain as an elusive goal? These are some of the relevant questions when addressing Jaspers.

To do so, one has to acknowledge that cultural divisions exist and there can be irreconcilable differences and tensions between cultures, particularly in Western and non-Western communities. There are, of course, numerous reasons for this kind of tension and unrest. It seems that religious and cultural differences and a lack of understanding are the major causes for it. Is it possible at all to reconcile cultural differences? Jaspers himself asked a similar question, "What can unite all man?" His answer was, "truth is what unites."[8] For him, truth exists through communication. However, is this a realistic answer and is it still valid in modernity? Today, Jaspers' notions of truth and communication seem ignored and it seems that there is not much interest in philosophical faith in the Jaspersian sense. As far as religious faith is concerned, Jaspers does not give an analysis of the politicised and radicalised form of religious faith. It seems that in modernity philosophical faith fades into oblivion whereas the grip of religious faith on societies seems to be strengthening.

Although the present situation is problematic, it is not impossible to overcome difficulties. One way of looking at this is that since we are all part of the world history, perhaps we should try to see parallels between different cultures. Furthermore, perhaps our differences are not as great as we might think. It might be better to think not in terms of division of cultural sections but rather in terms of universal principles of justice, secular politics, critical understanding and informed analysis of the interdependence of societies. According to Daniel Dennett we have a huge range of intellectual tools, including psychology, neuroscience, genetics, and cultural history that ought to be used for better understanding the phenomenon of religious faith. He suggests that all sides should be prepared to examine and revise their own assumptions and should engage in dialogue with each other. It sounds very sensible, but in the light of the religious passions now raging in the world, perhaps not very probable.

One further point I should like to make here is that Jaspers' notion of philosophical faith is a contentious issue among some philosophers. First, one could argue that Jaspers' concept of philosophical faith is not much different from religious faith and mysticism given that there are some mystical elements in his existence philosophy. For example, Jaspers' existential concepts of Being, the Encompassing, and Transcendence are similar to what is in some religions called the concept of God. Jaspers' term Existenz is not identical but not dissimilar to the traditional concept of soul. Jaspers also takes the view, not unlike some religious doctrines, that one's finitude can be transcended, not as a person, but as Existenz, non-phenomenal aspect

---

[8] *P2* 57. Jaspers says that philosophical truth belongs to Existenz, and is closely connected with philosophical faith. Accordingly, philosophical truth, philosophical faith, and one's awareness of Transcendence are inseparably linked.

of the self. It can be argued that some of his metaphysical concepts in his philosophy point to religious faith. Some even consider him doing philosophy of religion.[9] Although Jaspers' metaphysical concepts are meant to be non-religious, it is a valid argument that certain elements in his philosophy can be interpreted as some aspects of religious faith. However, one must reiterate that Jaspers is concerned with the individual's philosophical faith and its manifestation and he often states that his existence philosophy has nothing to do with religious faith or mysticism.

While it is easy to be critical of Jaspers' use of terminology in his existence philosophy, one cannot deny the enormous difficulty of formulating such metaphysical concepts coherently. The misunderstanding is perhaps partly due to the limitation of language and partly to the absence of physical objects to refer to in the explanation of metaphysical issues. Jaspers often reminds us that such highly complex subjective experiences cannot be adequately expressed in ordinary language. Hence he uses the indirect language of the phenomena, namely ciphers, which provides a metaphysical link to the transcendent realm. Jaspers also points out that issues regarding ciphers, Transcendence, and Existenz are a matter of philosophical faith for the individual and that there is no certainty in such matters. What is real and present is relative to one's frame of reference. Scientific theories lead to predictions that can be used to settle some disputes. Metaphysical concepts, however, are intellectual constructs of the mind that try to help us to understand, interpret, and make sense of reality. Furthermore, they are supposed to give meaning to our temporal lives. It will suffice to say that such metaphysical concepts connect to one's subjective experiences, are grounded in one's philosophical faith, and thus such statements are not open to objective verification.

Secondly, his existential philosophy has been criticised as irrational due to his emphasis on philosophical faith and subjective truth.[10] Furthermore, Jaspers has been heavily criticised for connecting faith with reason. Reason, says Jaspers, is a vital part of one's philosophical faith. This is similar to the thought of the eleventh century theologian St Anselm of Canterbury whose *credo ut intelligam* appears in

---

[9] Paul Ricoeur, Julius Löwenstein, Soren Holm, and Adolph Lichtigfeld are among those who consider Jaspers' philosophy as religious. See their articles in *The Philosophy of Karl Jaspers* (La Salle, IL, 1974), pp. 611, 643, 667, 693 respectively. [Henceforth cited as *PKJ*] See also Marjorie Grene, *Introduction to Existentialism* (Chicago, IL and London: The University of Chicago Press, 1948), p. 136. Also Hartt thinks that God is "before us" in Jaspers' concept of Transcendence. See Julian Norris Hartt, "God, Transcendence and Freedom in the Philosophy of Jasper," in *The Review of Metaphysics*, Vol. 4/2, December 1950, p. 252.

[10] Thyssen in his analysis of foundering and Transcendence writes: "the hostility towards objective knowledge (if we may put it that way), a basic character of irrationality, is not only a feature of Jaspers, but is shared by existentialism and other current trends. See Johannes Thyssen, "The Concept of 'Foundering'" (*PKJ* 334). In his *Reply to My Critics* Jaspers states that existential concepts such as foundering and Transcendence "cannot be pulled down to the level of objective knowledge, even though talk about it must take place in the medium of objectivities" (*PKJ* 832). Indeed Jaspers is aware that his philosophy is labelled as irrational and absurd by some objectors as he calls them (*P1* 19). He is also aware that some existential concepts can be irrational but he prefers to use the term suprarational rather than irrational (*P2* 115).

many ways compatible with what Jaspers asserts. Can faith and reason really complement each other? Many contemporary philosophers argue that faith in any form is incompatible with reason and there is no room for it.

To conclude on a positive note, the heightened passion of religious faith appears at different times throughout history to depend on political, economic, and regional circumstances. Let us hope that the present unrest will fade into a historical moment in human existence. As Huntington observes, "For the relevant future, there will be no universal civilization, but instead a world of different civilizations, each of which will have to learn to exist with the others" (*CC* 49). Since we are all part of the world history, we have a duty to respect values and worldviews of other cultures. However much our feelings are challenged, we must try to understand cultural conditioning and learn tolerance towards the practices of others. In fact, careful examination may reveal that cultures do not differ nearly as much as it appears. Perhaps one day, existential communication as well as philosophical faith will re-emerge as a unifying force in our global community, as Jaspers envisioned.

Part III
The Future of Humanity: Global Communication and the Project of World Philosophy

Philosophical Faith and the Foundering of Truth in Time

Gregory J. Walters

Abstract If a revolutionary age is an age of action, then our age is marked by Internet advertisement and publicity, informational capitalism, and the rise of global police violence in response to post-9/11 security threats and pro-Democracy movements in the Arab world. Taking Kierkegaard as point of departure, the text festively explores the nature of philosophical faith, global catastrophic risks that threaten the future of humanity, and the inevitable foundering of existence, Existenz, and truth in time. What role will philosophical faith, foundering, and active sufferance play on our present historical stage? Periechontological orientation and existential "redirection" open on to absolute consciousness in faith and love that may bring about greater communicative solidarity among human beings and take *humanitas* further up the road to the future than technologies of "radical enhancement" projected by transhumanism. The poem *Verstehen*, dedicated to the founders of the Karl Jaspers Society of North America, is presented in the Epilogue.

> In our times, when so little is done, an extraordinary number
> of prophecies, apocalypses, glances at and studies of the future
> appear, and there is nothing to do but to join in and be one
> with the rest. Yet I have the advantage over the many who bear
> a heavy responsibility when they prophesy and give warnings,
> because I can be perfectly certain that no one would think
> of believing me. . . .[1]

Preliminary Expectoration

"If a revolutionary age is an age of action, then our age is one of advertisement and publicity" (*PA* 6). Like Kierkegaard, we too live in a revolutionary age, the information age. We have real-time Internet advertisements and publicity everywhere, instantly, what-you-see-is-what-you-get publicity, in old and new avatars. E-mail

---

[1] Søren Kierkegaard, *The Present Age: On the Death of Rebellion*, trans. Alexander Dru (New York, NY: Harper & Row Publishers, 1962), p. 61. [Henceforth cited as *PA*]

G.J. Walters (✉)
Saint Paul University, Ottawa, ON, Canada K1S 1C4
e-mail: gjw@existenz.us

H. Wautischer et al. (eds.), *Philosophical Faith and the Future of Humanity*,
DOI 10.1007/978-94-007-2223-1_23, © Springer Science+Business Media B.V. 2012

communications ad infinitum; smart handsets incessantly tugging with raucous ring-tones like small children whining and needing to go out. Tiresome text messages whose quantity and consequences exceed, if not the sands-of-shore, then at least the combined number of impaired cell phone users. Communications marked by end-less and free-flowing *pourriel* (spam). The generational gaps entailed by declining education for political and economic democracy loom larger with each younger generation whose identities are marked by the next round of wireless devices, paradoxically, used less and less for telephone communication.

Nothing ever happened, until recently. Then we watched live footage of unedited images, too close to one's own sensibilities to be ignored. The collapse of the twin towers in New York, or Iranian protestors being shot and beaten by police and secu-rity guards. Horror stories about political oppression are distributed through social networking outlets, changing political realities in Tunisia, Egypt, and Libya, with Yemen and Syria not far behind. The Cold War problem of military force recedes, while the protection of homelands and terrorist activities legitimates new struc-tures of domestic force, i.e., paramilitary policing, in the wake of 9/11. A revised understanding of security is underwritten with vast amounts of taxpayer money and invariably trumps privacy. Racial profiling proliferates. The revolutions of 2011 in the Arab world and the rise of global violence on the part of Para militarized police forces,[2] make questions concerning "political consciousness in our time" and "the future of humanity" as pressing today as during the height of the Cold War and Jaspers' 1958 atom bomb book.[3]

The atom bomb book is a testimony, one of the most substantive books on the nuclear age by any twentieth century philosopher. The book was a direct response to objections and questions elicited from his German radio audience (see below). It won the prestigious Peace Prize of the German book trade in 1958. Jaspers acceptance speech, *Wahrheit, Freiheit und Friede*, provided the opportunity to phi-losophize on a theme that encapsulates much of his moral and political philosophy. "First, no outer peace is sustainable without the inner peace of humanity. Second, peace exists only through freedom. Third, freedom exists only through truth."[4] The aim of politics is peace, but not peace at any price. Peace requires freedom, and democratic freedoms require truth in political communication. "We have," Jaspers tells us, "a breathing spell. If this interval is not utilized to prevent war as such, the doom of mankind seems inevitable.... Man will escape perdition only if he is changed in the Kantian concept of a 'revolution of the way of thinking.' Today

---

[2] Jack A. Goldstone, "Understanding the Revolutions of 2011," *Foreign Affairs*, Vol. 90, No. 3, May/June 2011, pp. 8–16.

[3] Karl Jaspers, *Die Atombombe und die Zukunft des Menschen. Politisches Bewußtsein in unserer Zeit* (Munich: Piper, 1958).

[4] Karl Jaspers, "Wahrheit, Freiheit und Friede (1958)," in Karl Jaspers, *Hoffnung und Sorge: Schriften zur deutschen Politik, 1945–1965* (Munich: R. Piper & Co., 1965), pp. 173–185, here p. 174 (author's translation).

he faces a great choice: the doom of mankind, or a transformation [*Wandlung*] of man."[5]

Above all, modern age is an age of marketing and the diffusion of a global "informational economy."[6] Information age economics ushered-in a global recession in 2008. US Federal Reserve chairman Alan Greenspan's instrumentally-rationalist-derivatives-calculation-framework, "the Model," didn't work. In wake of this failure, an economic tsunami is left, rooted in the most egregious and grotesque greed and sub-prime mortgage debt. Wages, jobs, homes, and, above-all, truthful communication, are on the global clearance table.

There is a role for philosophical faith, the foundering of truth in time, absolute consciousness, and active sufferance to shape the future of humanity. Transformations will have to be effectuated for moving forward into an unknown, yet open, future.

Despair and the Question Concerning the Future of Humanity

Reason understands that possible Existenz experiences truth via philosophical faith and despair. Existential concern over truth in its unity arises from a similar existential exigency. Despair inevitably arises because all existence contains the seeds of its own destruction. The question of the unity of truth in time arises out of our own most concern. Søren Kierkegaard warns that the "sickness unto death" is despair, and despair is sin. The state in which there is no despair is this: "In relating to itself and in willing to be itself, the self rests transparently in the power that established it. This formula. . . .is the definition of faith."[7] Possible Existenz *either* loses itself in despair in the face of nothingness, or is given to itself in "the certainty of eternity."[8] Thinking truthfully about the future of humanity may lead the self into despair, even fear. Well, then, let us despair and fear the future prospects for humanity, but for the right reasons!

Presumably the sun will eventually burn out. Some argue that the planet will become uninhabitable until swallowed-up by a black hole and possibly reborn into

---

[5] Karl Jaspers, "Kant's 'Perpetual Peace,'" in *Philosophy and the World: Selected Essays and Letters*, trans. E.B. Ashton (Chicago, IL: Regnery, 1963), p. 123.

[6] On informational economy and some of its ethical challenges, see chapter 3, "The Informational Economy, Work, and Productive Agency," in Gregory J. Walters, *Human Rights in an Information Age: A Philosophical Analysis* (London and Toronto: University of Toronto Press, 2001), pp. 80–116.

[7] Søren Kierkegaard, "The Sickness unto Death, a Christian Psychological Exposition for Upbuilding and Awakening (July 30, 1849) By Anti-Climacus. Edited by S. Kierkegaard," in *The Essential Kierkegaard*, eds. Howard V. Hong and Edna H. Hong (Princeton, NJ: Princeton University Press, 2000), pp. 350–372, here p. 372.

[8] Karl Jaspers, *Philosophy is for Everyman: A Short Course in Philosophical Thinking*, trans. R.F.C. Hull and Grete Wels (New York, NY: Harcourt, Brace & World, 1967), p. 112. [Henceforth cited as *PE*]

new forms of cosmic dust. Should we understand ourselves as mere specks of dust in the eternal hourglass of existence? Would the idea of eternal recurrence gain greater force as a prod to humankind's self-sublimation? Would the idea release the trouble-hook pulling humanity toward a possible shore of global human foundering?

A larger perspective on the question concerning the future of humanity is needed now more than ever. Over fourteen billion years of cosmic history is not a bad run in time and space, from the presumed Big Bang to the origins of organic life on earth, to the evolution of homo sapiens sapiens some 40,000 years ago. Humans are, as a part of the cosmos, beings through whom the universe is speaking; and yet, we remain human since our hominid origin, and at times, all too culturally human. The British philosopher, Bertrand Russell, emotively responded to news about the development of the hydrogen bomb and stated something to the effect: "Remember your humanity and forget all the rest!"

The historical track record for human existence is neither stellar nor sapiens. Consider the history of warfare from 10,000 BCE to the present. It has been said that every weapon of human destruction ever been created has been used. While this is an empirical question, at an intuitive level, the history of human warfare—rape, pillage, and plunder—gives the intellect troublesome pause. Could we really ever have a perpetual peace? History gives any reason to believe that a resounding "No" is the answer.

Without quibbling over a few stone, iron, steel, chemical, biological, nuclear, or nanotech weapons, the question concerning what role philosophical faith will play in the future of humanity is contemporary with our historical-technological situation. If "thinking is as thinking does,"[9] so too is, in the memorable words of *Forrest Gump*, "Momma says stupid is as stupid does."[10] With respect to Jaspersian moral and political *Umkehr* (turn-around) there is "a breathing spell," as this fragile planet uncontrollably coughs hydrocarbonic phlegm. Politicians have foundered in the implementation of an American universal health care system, a public policy dream that lay dying in the corridor of a diseased economy. The body-politic is politically divided and American politicians overall seem to have forgotten the importance of non-bipartisan politics in hard times. To be sure, a few "reasonable politicians" have prevailed in the post-Cold War period, but we remember that, and analogous to mutual fund investment, past political performance is no guarantee of future social democratic returns. The intellect's negations seem to give us little hope about the myriad possibilities of human self-destruction by means of political violence and warfare. We may or may not lovingly communicate, albeit we do so via "struggle." We work together to avoid stupid human actions that could wreak havoc on our planet and fragile social structures. There are actions we *can* change. We confront challenges and threats to the future of humanity that we *cannot* change. Do we have the *wisdom* to know the difference?

---

[9] Elisabeth Young-Bruehl, *Freedom and Karl Jaspers's Philosophy* (New Haven, CT and London: Yale University Press, 1981), p. 39.

[10] See http://en.wikiquote.org/wiki/Forrest_Gump, accessed July 8, 2011.

Problemata

We children of the bomb, children of early informational capitalism, children of late Modernity, swim perilously in shallow waters. The potential omni-destruction of our species, as well as other organic life forms on the planet, might well come to pass. No hype intended here, but we really do confront "global catastrophic risks." The phrase lacks sharp definition but, at a minimum, refers to risks that have the potential "to inflict serious damage to human well-being on a global scale."[11] Examples include volcanic eruptions, pandemic infections, nuclear power facility accidents, large-scale conventional war, nuclear terrorism, nuclear war, nuclear winter, worldwide political and economic tyranny, out-of-control nanotechnology experiments, catastrophic climatic change, and cosmic hazards such as asteroid and comet impacts.

Catastrophic global events would impact a fragile social order, with social disruption and collapse following in its wake. Nuclear terrorism and pandemic disease would have similar second-order effects on the social order. Asteroid impacts, volcanic super-eruptions, and nuclear war would all spew massive amounts of soot and aerosols into the atmosphere creating global climate change and chaos. We skate on thin ice because we are in a "climate of denial," where the media monger in fear and the merchants of pollution sell their goods to global tourists out to catch a glimpse of one last species before it too goes extinct. The animal we call "truth" is dying. All the while heat, mega-floods, melting ice, tsunamis, and earthquakes make the nightly newscast read like "a nature hike through the Book of Revelation."[12]

Our situation has its apocalyptic dimensions, false hopes, panaceas, pseudo-scientific solutions, and full-fledged future programs. Remember Y2K? While the event was hype and feeding-frenzy for PC companies, the machine world did not come crashing down at the stroke of midnight. The coming cyberwar will be neither hip nor hype. The "boys in the back room" (Dr. Suess) are planning for just such unexpected attacks. We may call such a war, with slight variation on a theme, a potential future human existential threat that will not be bloodless because conducted in the virtual realm. Sprinkle-in a few "nukes" or dirty-bombs and we really understand the meaning of *Wandlung* anew.

Consider also the widespread, but pseudo-scientific "doomsthought" that the world will end in 2012. Planet X, so-called Nibiru, will return to our solar system in 2012 and disrupt earth's polarity. Nibiru is at best a fantastic-freaking-fiction. Pseudo-science in extremis, made possible by software programs that morph reality along with real-time thinking and acting. Solar flares that may engulf the earth and knock-out the electromagnetic spectrum, and, thus, early-warning systems that sound ominous warnings of security threat, appear to be a concern of NASA. In fact,

---

[11] Nick Bostrom and Milan Ćirković, eds., *Global Catastrophic Risks* (Oxford and New York, NY: Oxford University Press, 2008), p. 1.

[12] See Al Gore, "Climate of Denial: Can Science and the Truth Withstand the Merchants of Poison?" *Rolling Stone*, Issue 1134–1135, July 7–21, 2011, http://www.rollingstone.com/politics/news/climate-of-denial-20110622, accessed July 8, 2011.

we are currently in a solar minimum; some might just be happy to have a warmer winter to alleviate pain. Predictions about the future of mankind, whether resulting from global catastrophic risks or human stupidity are a difficult subject matter for a non-risk assessment analyst, much less a poet, even a Legend like Bob Dylan.

In his "Song to Woody [Guthrie]," Dylan sings about a world that "looks like it's a dyin, and it's hardly been born."[13] We currently have a global population of seven billion in 2011. Global population is projected to reach nine billion by 2045.[14] What will the world look like then? Answers will depend on the decisions global capitalism and each of us make today. Understood in context, however, demographic data reveals declining birthrates. The problem that needs to be solved is poverty and consumption of limited resources. Preaching sexual abstinence and condemning condom use as a moral evil in countries where many are dying of AIDS would seem imprudent and potential immoral itself. Malthus thought, positively, that unchecked population growth would get us off our duffs and awaken new modes of thinking to cope with exponential growth of the human population. Perhaps most of us just see more hungry children dying of diarrhea and starvation.

Theories and ideas abound about the positive role that technologies of radical enhancement will bring to our lives and for the future of a transhumanity. The idea of radical enhancement involves "improving significant human attributes and abilities to levels that greatly exceed what is currently possible for human beings."[15] Some examples include improving human intelligence beyond the genius of Einstein, Picasso, and Mozart, boosting athletic abilities, and extending the human life span beyond the "122 years and 164 days achieved by the French super-centenarian Jeanne Calment" (*HE* 1).

Transhumanists suggest that radical enhancement will make us "posthuman."[16] Transhumanist philosopher Nick Bostrom defines the term as referring to "an intellectual and cultural movement that affirms the possibility and desirability of fundamentally improving the human condition through applied reason, especially by developing and making widely available technologies to eliminate aging and to greatly enhance human intellectual, physical, and psychological capacities."[17]

---

[13] Bob Dylan, "Song to Woody," *No Direction Home: The Soundtrack. A Martin Scorsese Picture. The Bootleg Series*, Vol. 7, http://www.youtube.com/watch?v=rt7MVy6cN_Q, accessed July 8, 2011.

[14] See Robert Kunzig, "Population 7 Billion," *National Geographic*, Vol. 219, No. 1, January 2011, pp. 32–63.

[15] Nicholas Agar, *Humanity's End: Why We Should Reject Radical Enhancement* (Cambridge and London: The MIT Press, 2010), p. 1. [Henceforth cited as *HE*]

[16] Nick Bostrom, "Why I Want to Be a Posthuman When I Grow Up," in *Medical Enhancement and Posthumanity*, eds. Bert Gordijn and Ruth F. Chadwick (Dordrecht: Springer, 2009), p. 108. [Henceforth cited as *WWP*]; cited in *HE* 4. See also the Transhumanist FAQ, "What is a Posthuman?" http://humanityplus.org/learn/transhumanist-faq/#answer_20, accessed July 8, 2011.

[17] Nick Bostrom, "A History of Transhumanist Thought," *Journal of Evolution and Technology*, Vol. 14, No. 1, 2005 at Bostrom's homepage http://www.nickbostrom.com, accessed July 7, 2011. See also, James Hughes, *Citizen Cyborg: Why Democratic Societies Must Respond to the Redesigned Human of the Future* (Cambridge, MA: Westview, 2004).

A posthuman is "a being that has at least one posthuman capacity," that is, "a general central capacity greatly exceeding the maximum attainable by any current human being without recourse to new technological means" (*WWP* 4–5). These general capacities include the individual's "health span" or ability "to remain fully healthy, active, and productive, both mentally and physically;" it includes intellectual capacities such as "memory, deductive and analogical reasoning, and attention, as well as special faculties such as the capacity to understand and appreciate music, humor, eroticism, narration, spirituality, mathematics;" with respect to our emotions, posthuman capacities include "the capacity to enjoy life and to respond with appropriate affect to life situations and other people" (*WWP* 4–5).

Transhumanists envision an outline for the future of humanity that invokes the role of computers, genetics, nanotechnology, and robotics. Ray Kurzweil,[18] artificial intelligence (AI) pioneer and inventor of speech recognition software that has enabled visually-impaired persons and others to use computers, advocates a "Law of Accelerating Returns." He means that computer technologies are improving at such an accelerating rate that, eventually, technological change will morph instantaneously into new form. Humans will upload brain data into machines, eventually migrating ourselves into machines. Exponential developments in genetics, nanotechnology, and robotics provide real technological hope. Genetic manipulation will make us smarter and healthier. Nanobots will cure high cholesterol and glitches in memory without having to insert or delete or transpose the neoclide base pairs (ACTG) of DNA in the human genome. Robotics will allow us to completely escape human biology. When the robotics revolution comes, we will arrive, c. 2045, at "the Singularity." This means "a future period during which the pace of technological change will be so rapid, its impact so deep, that human life will be irreversibly transformed....[to a mind] about one billion times more powerful than all human intelligence today."[19] The purchase of a new Smart Handset, with user-friendly Beam-me-up-Scottie technology, is probably as far as most of us will go before swapping gray-matter with cerebral nanobots and robotic replacements. Such technological developments will certainly represent a different level of consciousness, and presumably an unimaginably higher level of consciousness for posthumans.

Philosophical Faith and Absolute Consciousness

Jaspers provided a useful, albeit indirect, definition of philosophical faith in a *Reply* to his philosophical critics. Philosophical has an independent origin, one that communicates itself in the thinking of reason.

---

[18] See Ray Kurzweil, *The Age of Intelligent Machines* (Cambridge, MA: The MIT Press, 1990); *The Age of Spiritual Machines: When Computers Exceed Human Intelligence* (London: Penguin, 2000); and *The Singularity is Near: When Humans Transcend Biology* (London: Penguin, 2005).

[19] Ray Kurzweil, *The Singularity is Near*, p. 136; cited in *HE* 5.

The intent of my philosophizing, in the succession of philosophy which has lasted for thousands of years, is the affirmation of the independent origin of philosophical faith. . . .

My philosophizing does not, therefore, fit into the scheme which opposes faith and intellect, religion and science, Christianity and nihilism, in such fashion as to think that these alternatives are exhausting the problem. My thinking proceeds from a third, which does not occur in those alternatives and which is rejected by both sides as something impossible or as a compromise or as a blunting of the edges.

In the tradition of Plato, Bruno, Spinoza, Kant, Lessing, and Goethe, I would like once again to emphasize the eternal independent origin of all philosophizing, the philosophical faith which communicates itself in the thinking of reason. This faith is neither confessional theology nor science, neither a church-creed nor unbelief. It recognizes itself again in the great ancestors, even in those of India and China.[20]

Philosophical faith is colored by periechontological orientation. "Periechontology tells us what Being consists of, provides us with no determinacy of Being, constructs no edifice. It aims at a *systematic of what is*."[21] The systematic reveals itself in the distinction between the "encompassing which we are or can be" (Subject-being) and the "encompassing that is being itself," (Object-being). Philosophical faith also entails a common fundamental knowledge whose relevant idea is "that once we know the encompassing as our common meeting ground, we can leave each other free to live by our separate and vastly different sources."[22]

Perhaps the shapes, lines, and shades of philosophical faith are best expressed in the testimonial portraits of Socrates and Giordano Bruno? Are they quasi-saints of philosophic faith, martyrs for their singularly unique cipheric life-scripts? Socrates was criminally charged for the capital crime of "irreverence" because he failed to show due piety toward the gods of Athens. As a citizen he had the right to forgo his own criminal hearing, yet allowed the suit to proceed uncontested. He also had the right to voluntarily exile himself from Athens (*Crito* 52c).[23] He exercised neither right, but made his simple plea, but to no avail. Giordano Bruno was not as lucky as Socrates in drinking hemlock. He was burned at the stake as a heretic. His heresy case had nothing to do with his writings in support of Copernican cosmology. There was no official Catholic position on the Copernican system at the time, and belief in the system was not a heresy. Bruno's pantheism, on the other hand, led him into "seven years of incarceration and constant moral coercion." The Inquisitors of the

---

[20] Karl Jaspers, "Reply to My Critics," in *The Philosophy of Karl Jaspers*, ed. Paul Arthur Schilpp (La Salle, IL: Open Court, 1981), pp. 747–896, here p. 777.

[21] *Karl Jaspers: Basic Philosophical Writings–Selections*, eds. L.H. Ehrlich, E. Ehrlich, and George B. Pepper (Atlantic Highlands, NJ: Humanities Press International, 1994), p. 199 (italics in original). [Henceforth cited as *BPW*]

[22] Jaspers, *Philosophical Faith and Revelation*, trans. E.B. Ashton (New York, NY: Harper & Row, 1967), p. 88. [Henceforth cited as *PFR*]

[23] Debra Nails, "Socrates," *The Stanford Encyclopedia of Philosophy (Spring 2010 Edition)*, ed. Edward N. Zalta, http://plato.stanford.edu/archives/spr2010/entries/socrates/, accessed July 8, 2011.

Church "could not force him to recant his philosophy."[24] His heroic love is marked by "self-sacrifice, being consumed and not merely putting oneself at risk" (*GP3* 64). Rightly and reverently, Jaspers ruminates that the "history of heresy is largely one of truth, of men whose original Existenz made them suffer heroically for their truth."[25] "*Es lebt die Wahrheit der Ketzer in der Kirche*" (The faith of the heretic lives in the church).[26] It is even possible, he thought, that "the fate of the Western world will be decided by what will become of the churches" (*BPW* 444).

The ciphers of transcendence that summon us through philosophical faith are embedded in language, art, science, religion, and myth. How well we interpret faith and understand ciphers could break the back of the planet, contribute to human perpetuity in peace, or simply morph into new historical forms. The jury is still out. Humble acknowledgement of what we do and do not know regarding future risks and threats is a good start.

In volume two of *Philosophy*, Jaspers philosophizes about an experience of immediacy as a fundamental, yet fleeting, certainty of being in his concept of "absolute consciousness." In this consciousness the risk of faith is original. Love, faith, and creative imagination are forms of the fulfillment. Absolute consciousness, as the consciousness of Existenz with respect to the source of its being (*P2* 225), is an antipode of the "intellect" or consciousness-as-such. It is more like an *original motion*, a motion of not-knowing, a motion with respect to the losing, or gaining of one's self, a motion that respects and protects consciousness in forms of irony, play, shame, and composure. The intellect can find no referent to the expression "absolute consciousness." The gap between word and reality cannot be closed without some kind of violation. "Concrete reality calls for silence," Jaspers notes, "yet philosophy, combining a will to the utmost directness with a knowledge of its impossibility, will defy that pressure for silence and force itself into generally worded statements after all" (*P2* 241).

Love and faith are inextricably related to not-knowing, doubt, and ignorance, even as truth for man in time is not present in its unity, but rather stands *in between* origin and goal (*VW* 461ff). We do not know absolute consciousness as existence but in our forms of not-knowing. Searching the best science knowledge, and with a will to know, we know that we do not know. Not-knowing then becomes a kind of certainty with respect to the decisive inner and outer actions that we undertake. Love sustains our not-knowing and restores us to "assured being" from our cognitive "dizziness and trepidation" (*P2* 242). Faith and love are original. They can neither be willed nor proved. Faith is neither solely subject and neither solely object. The faith through which I am convinced and act—*fides qua creditur*—and the content of

---

[24] Karl Jaspers, *The Great Philosophers*, Vol. 3, eds. Michael Ermarth and Leonard H. Ehrlich, trans. Edith Ehrlich and Leonard H. Ehrlich (New York, NY, San Diego, CA, and London: Harcourt Brace & Company, 1993), p. 59. [Henceforth cited *GP* with volume number]

[25] Karl Jaspers, *Philosophy*, Vol. 2: *Existential Elucidation*, trans. E.B. Ashton (Chicago, IL and London: University of Chicago Press, 1970), p. 340. [Henceforth cited as *P2*]

[26] Karl Jaspers, *Von der Wahrheit, Philosophische Logik, Erster Band* (Munich: R. Piper & Co., 1947), p. 857 (author's translation). [Henceforth cited *VW*]

faith—*fides quae creditur*—are inseparable.[27] Faith is linked to action because the world is the arena for the realization of freedom. Human testimony of love and faith requires temporal actuality. Action is faith as it appears objectively in the world of purposive action, but especially in unconditional action in the world. Human actions gain objective appearance in the state, religion, education, literature, arts, culture and tradition. These objectivities shape and socialize the self into faith. They become the horizon within which the moral "ought" and faith, as the active form of love, make claims upon the self. However, we must not confuse the cogent, but relative, "ought" with the unconditional demands of faith. Faith may require breaking through the moral imperative in the same way that Kierkegaard's teleological suspension of the ethical gives way to the religious stage on life's way and a shift from humane rational religiosity to paradoxical Christianity or "Religiousness B."[28]

Faith may require breaking through the rule of conventional law, even as possible Existenz affirms the necessity of institutions and orders. And yet, as possible Existenz, one is far from the false claim of self-absolutizing individualism leveled against the subjectivism of Kierkegaard and Jaspers.[29] For Existenz does not accomplish or make its own freedom, nor exist by its own means. "I am myself, and free, as I freely *feel* the source of my freedom, and as I *think* the source together with my freedom" (*PFR* 6).

Faith struggles against faith. Philosophical faith struggles with revelational faith and vice versa. It is an inevitable relation of possible Existenz to other possible *Existenzen*. In faith we collide as the truth we are ourselves, and with the faith manifest in the other truth. "It takes faith to understand faith," Jaspers writes, "at the bounds of intelligibility the unintelligible is experienced as akin to myself but alien to me in the originality of the other faith" (*P2* 377).

Where faith is concerned with transcendence, meaning and absurdity take on an identity. Not even speculative reflection has access to this identity. The key to meaning is unlocked as the absurd founders and the disjointedness of being prods possible Existenz toward the ground of being, freedom, and the experience of presence (*Gegenwärtigkeit*) in the twin polarities of the encompassing. Presence is an experience, a source of its own that "I cannot will, but through which I will, am, and know" (*PSP* 20).

In the struggle of faith against faith, we inevitably press on toward a more fundamental unity in relation to the truth of difference. An existential concern for the unity of truth in time is necessary, lest human cognition becomes schizophrenic, but any proposed unity is always insufficient. All worldviews collapse under the

---

[27] Karl Jaspers, *The Perennial Scope of Philosophy*, trans. Ralph Manheim (New York, NY: Philosophical Library, 1949), p. 13. [Henceforth cited as *PSP*]

[28] Karl Jaspers, *The Great Philosophers*, Vol. IV, eds. Michael Ermarth and L.H. Ehrlich, trans. Edith Ehrlich and Leonard H. Ehrlich (New York, NY: Harcourt Brace & Company, 1995), p. 256.

[29] See Alasdair MacIntyre, *After Virtue: A Study in Moral Theory* (Notre Dame, IN: University of Notre Dame Press, 1984), pp. 39–45; Jürgen Habermas, *Observations on "The Spiritual Situation of the Age:" Contemporary German Perspectives*, trans. Andrew Buchwalter (Cambridge, MA and London: MIT Press, 1984), p. 3.

weight of internal contradictions and finite historicity. Gaps between Reason and Existenz, between Truth and Being, remain unbridgeable. Jaspers would not affirm, as Nietzsche, that "it is only as an *aesthetic phenomenon* that existence and the world are eternally *justified*."[30]

We are always, inevitably, thrown-back by philosophical faith, thrown-back to *my* thinking and living, to my acts of "synthetic openness" and "skeptical relativizing." Philosophy as faith is inevitably forced to think an "ingenuous synthesis"[31] of being, and to understand truth in time as encompassing. Philosophy as faith requires periechontologic orientation and unending "existential redirection" (*BPW* 229) via the horizons of being and within the encompassing. We steer our vessels toward the harbor of the "encompassing of all encompassing," but we inevitably founder in existence and Existenz.

Truth, Politics, and Lies

Can politics abide in truth, or will we merely repeat the "old politics," after the fall of the Berlin Wall, after the rise of complex terrorism, and given new technological means for killing? What about the dangers of totalitarianism today? Is the totalitarianism of the "old politics" really gone? "Totalitarianism," in an earlier definition, "is the universal, terrible threat of the future of mankind in a mass order. It is a phenomenon of our age, detached from all the politics governed by principles of a historic national existence of constitutional legality."[32] It thrives wherever rapid historical change and symbolic dislocation occur as a result of technological change. Total rule exploits the severance of ties to tradition and offers its own "program" as means of salvation. Persons become shallow, hollow, and refuse to remain loyal to themselves and to their transcendence. Everyone becomes functionalized. Obedience is the watchword. The challenging of political authority through peaceful demonstration, whether police or dictatorial authority, brings purges, persecution, and pain.

Technology does not *causally* bring about a totalitarian state of affairs. Global Internet communications are not as yet a mass ordering of humans, despite the push-technologies that drive-up telecommunications stocks. Information and communication technologies have been crucial in pro-Democracy protests. They help liberate persons and save lives. When governments shut down servers and control the flow of information on the part of citizens, we recognize totalistic impulses

---

[30] Friedrich Nietzsche, *The Birth of Tragedy*, trans. Walter Kaufmann (New York, NY: Random House, 1967), p. 52.

[31] Leonard H. Ehrlich, *Karl Jaspers: Philosophy as Faith* (Amherst, MA: University of Massachusetts Press, 1975), pp. 8, 29.

[32] Karl Jaspers, "The Fight Against Totalitarianism," in *Philosophy and the World: Selected Essays and Letters*, trans. E.B. Ashton (Chicago, IL: Regnery, 1963), p. 69.

and the ideologically control of communications in order to preserve the political status quo.

What perdures in totalistic thinking is the principle of the lie. Abhorrent lies and deeds springing from the will to power. Power structures that have a monopoly on truth can kill, maim, and rape with absolute impunity. Internet publicity reveals all too clearly the darkness of the will to power. And yet, all truth is mixed with untruth. The truth-untruth dialectic is certainly not a matter of abstract thinking to those who know the thin veneer of conventionality that may be stripped from society at any moment, who know that appearances and reality must be kept separate and distinct, while yet retaining the "objectivities" entailed by their conflation. Consider Plato's idea of the noble lie. Lies must be created by those most suited to create myths. In this case, myths about the gold, silver and bronze-iron classes that legitimate the socio-economic status quo in ancient Greece.[33] Such myths propose to give us meaning and purpose; they ensure a stable society.

When protesters around the world are illegally seized, raped, tortured, and shot, even in real time, we are forced to ask, again, *Quis custodiet ipsos custodes?* (Who guards the guards themselves?) The phrase comes from the *Satires* of Juvenal in the first/second century. The origin is hotly debated by classicists, translators, and philologists, but the following translation holds consensus: "I know the plan that my friends always advise me to adopt: 'Bolt her in, constrain her!' But who can watch the watchmen? They keep quiet about the girl's secrets and get her as their payment; everyone hushes it up."[34] Who is guarding the guards themselves? For all persons whose bodies have been unjustly branded or maimed by the guardians, it becomes imperative to recall that once you are labeled, turned into a pale criminal, your being is negated. Perhaps the ancient myths have become deadly?

Periechontology, Power, and Publicity

Periechontogical orientation holds fast to the belief that reason is the bond within us, the superglue that holds the encompassing of our modes of being together. The "Singularity" is confronted with a philosophically singular idea, i.e., there can be no finished theory of Being. The aim of periechontology is "to open the dimensions of Being in which human realizations of truth take place and encounter each other. . . .it can thus provide a basis for human beings of fundamentally different perceptions of Being to meet, if not in like-minded communication, at least in communicative solidarity, each vying with the other for the clarity of his truth in a space encompassing

---

[33] Plato, *Republic*, trans. Benjamin Jowett (1817–1893). "The Republic," Project Gutenberg. http://www.gutenberg.org/files/1497/1497-h/1497-h.htm, accessed July 7, 2011.

[34] Wikipedia, "Quis custodiet ipsos custodes?" http://en.wikipedia.org/wiki/Quis_custodiet_ipsos_custodes%3F, accessed July 7, 2011.

both" (*BPW* 200). Why not a blog, tweet, chat room, Skype video/audio space, website? The question begs another: What is truth?

> Truth—the word has an incomparable magic. It seems to promise what really matters to us. The violation of truth poisons everything gained by the violation.
>
> Truth can cause pain, and can drive one to despair. But it is capable—merely in virtue of being true, regardless of content—of giving deep satisfaction: There is truth after all.
>
> Truth gives courage: if I have grasped it at any point, the urge grows to pursue it relentlessly.
>
> Truth gives support: here *is* something indestructible, something linked to Being.
>
> But what this truth might be that so powerfully attracts us—is not particular determinate truths but truth itself—that is the question.[35]

Truth and power are often in conflict with each other because power wants and needs secrecy to function, whereas truth wants and needs publicity. In 1964, Radio Bavaria invited Jaspers to give thirteen televised lectures, a half an hour each, on philosophy and published under the telling German title, *Kleine Schule des philosophischen Denkens* (*PE*). In the Foreword, Jaspers writes that his lectures "shall again and again come to questions at the limit of the empirical and the logical. First we get answers, but no answer will be the final one; each leads to new questions, until the final question meets with silence, but not because it is an empty question. Rather it is the silence of fulfillment in which man's own essence can speak directly to him through his inmost self, through his own demands, through reason, through love" (*PE* xviii).

The lecture on "Publicity" begins with the story of the editors of the German periodical, *Der Spiegel*, who were falsely accused of treason for publishing the truth about the government department in charge of protecting the Constitution that had ordered unconstitutional wiretaps on telephone conversations. The *Spiegel* editors were accused of treason, and there followed "a wave of arrests all too reminiscent of the days of police terrorism" (*PE* 77). The *Spiegel* incident poignantly poses questions about the real meaning of freedom of the press and the inviolability of the German Constitution, but also about existential truth. A German public servant in charge of protecting the Constitution blew the whistle on unconstitutional wiretapping. Is this ground for "treason?" One begins "to think seriously about the violation of the public interest by the unconditional pledge of officials to secrecy" (*PE* 77). The public interest requires truth, not secrecy, and therefore oaths of loyalty to public service or government can and do run into existential walls.

The *Spiegel* whistle-blowing case illustrates the conflict "between power, which wants secrecy, and truth, which wants publicity" (*PE* 77). The case also demonstrates the personal conflict between mendacity and secrecy of the self in relation to one's own truth. As human beings we are neither completely angels, nor are we completely beasts. We exist betwixt the two. The existential problem arises because the adversary of truth in ourselves is the will to power. If we could abolish the will

---

[35] Karl Jaspers, *Philosophy of Existence*, trans. and Introduction by Richard F. Grabau. Editor's note by John R. Silver (Philadelphia, PA: University of Pennsylvania Press, Oxford: Blackwell, 1971). The citation is from *BPW* 240.

to power, then "secrecy would melt away" (*PE* 78). There exists a tensive relation between truth, the will to power, mendacity, and the human urge toward communicative openness and truth, on the one hand, and the urge toward mendacity, secrecy and power, on the other hand. The conflict is existential and political.

> As we are human, not only is this conflict inherent in us, but also the demand that we become authentic human beings by struggling with the adversary within us who works against ourselves.
>
> The will to power likes to pose as truth, paying lip service to truth and using it as a means of domination. It turns lies into truth. Mendacity is its native element, where it reigns supreme.
>
> The will to power assumes this form all the more readily when the will to violence lurks in the background. Violence by intellectual superiority, by defiance, by threats, by deception. The will to power as such, however, can be honest, and truth itself is a power (*PE* 78).

Journalists have great public intellectual power today. Fast forward to Julian Assange and WikiLeaks, the not-for-profit media organization, whose goal is to bring important news and information to the public. Because power wants secrecy it should come as no surprise that WikiLeaks has been the target of legal, political, and especially cyberwar attacks, even coming from "five major US financial institutions."[36] The attacks are apparently designed to silence the organisation, its journalists and anonymous sources. WikiLeaks seeks to defend freedom of speech and media publishing. Its basic principles are derived from the Universal Declaration of Human Rights, especially Article 19, which affirms the human right "to freedom of opinion and expression, freedom to hold opinions without interference and to seek, receive and impart information and ideas through any media and regardless of frontiers."[37] Governments and major financial institutions, alike, have attacked WikiLeaks. From the *Spiegel* case to WikiLeaks, it seems that the more things change, the more they remain the same. Will we move in consciousness toward a sense of the global public interest? Will WikiLeaks and Julian Assange withstand the power and mendacity that seek to silence freedom of speech? Censorship is less and less an option in an information age.

Foundering, Active Sufferance, and the Will to Communication

Foundering in existence and Existenz is the ultimate cipher, one that may lead to the *amor fati*, the daring and courage to appropriate one's own foundering . I may fail in this task, but I do what is in my power in the face of pain and suffering. "It is precisely in the acts of my most lucid and forthright self-being that I must experience its foundering" (*P2* 194). No assurances here initially, only default and loss. The leap of philosophical faith in the limit situations of suffering and death, so

---

[36] See   http://www.wikileaks.org/IMG/pdf/WikiLeaks_Response_v6.pdf,   and   http://www.wikileaks.org/Banking-Blockade.html, accessed July 10, 2011.

[37] See http://www.udhr.org/UDHR/udhr.HTM, accessed July 7, 2011.

very similar to Kierkegaard's "knight of faith" but in opposition to Hegel's theory of mediation, expresses the ultimate freedom of possible Existenz at the heart of the paradox of existence. To live life with one's hands closed tight, to live without *transcending* in thinking and action, to sink into the absolutization of one mode of being—whether body, intellect, spirit, or world—is possible. Philosophical faith requires a "leap" in the ultimate situation of foundering in order to hold together eternity and temporality, infinity and finitude, Transcendence and the world.

Philosophical faith marches forward in time, especially in light of the foundering of truth in time, by means of active sufferance. In philosophical faith, the leap from anguish to calm, from fear to serenity, is effectuated beyond the realm of rationality.

> That he succeeds in it [the leap] must be due to a reason beyond the Existenz of his self-being. Undefinably, his faith ties him to transcendent being....active sufferance [*Dulden*] allows me to experience the foundering of all existence and yet to engage in realizations as long as an ounce of strength remains. In this tension I gain composure. Sufferance sustains the world of one who is receptive to reality and has become sensitive to transcendent being. In sufferance lies the not-knowing of the kind of faith that makes men active in the world without any need to believe in the possibility of a good and definitive world order...sufferance means that he will cling to being *in spite of* his foundering, where the cipher of foundering fails him.... That there is being suffices. Whatever we think we know about the deity is superstition; truth lies where a foundering Existenz can translate the ambiguous language of transcendence into the simplest certainty of being. (*P2* 209)

The essential aim and meaning of philosophical faith is the will to communication. Only in a loving-struggle for communication may we gain a deep awareness of being, love's illumination, and "long-sufferance" that leads to peace in the face of the foundering of truth in time. If we have the strength to endure foundering, we do so via philosophical faith, in authentic communication, and in freedom as possible Existenz in relation to transcendence. Posssible Existenz stands in relation to transcendence, or it does not stand at all, and opens the individual to embrace the absurd *in spite of* foundering, *in spite of* the failure of the cipher of foundering itself, and *in spite of* the pain and suffering.

Conclusion

"What man is and what is [exists] for him are in some sense bound up with communication."[38] Global Internet communications mark our common situation. Do we have more time to communicate, really communicate? Will networked communications, paradoxically, lead to greater ruptures in human communication? Perhaps we should start taking existential freedom more seriously. There can be no world peace, no "new politics," no safe-steering through the twin shoals of foundering, without existential freedom. And yet, there can be no existential and political freedom without truth, including the truth of the foundering of truth in time as existence

---

[38] Karl Jaspers, *Reason and Existenz*, trans. William Earle (New York, NY: Noonday Press, 1955), p. 79.

and Existenz. There is truth in science and there is real truth in existence. The road to Philadelphia and the road to Jerusalem are not the same. There is no completion of truth in time this side of the grave.

We are consigned to our fragile communication, communication between science and religion, between Mars and Venus, between human-being and all other sentient-being, even communication between humanists, post-humanists, and transhumanists! To philosophize is to seek boundless communication. There are false prophets proclaiming "the Day of the Lord," but there are no true prophets capable of predicting the future, as if this capacity even has anything to do with Biblical prophets of old. Humanity may founder in existence by means of natural causes, techno-scientific "innovations" gone askew, stupid human actions based on reductionism within object or subject-being that fail to balance the modes of being that we are, or, quite possibly, unforeseen and unimaginable catastrophic cosmic events that impact the earth. Existence and possible Existenz are sailing toward Shipwreck Island some way or another.

The question concerning philosophical faith and the future of humanity becomes a challenge of existential-political freedom and truth, a challenge of faith and love operating in purposive and unconditional action in the world. Will we think and act out of absolute consciousness? Will we lose ourselves in despair and nothingness in light of the foundering of truth in time as existence and Existenz? "Real life in the world," Jaspers writes, "is permeated by this awareness of eternity or it is futile. It is not lost when our empirical existence is shipwrecked. We are moral as mere empirical beings, immortal when we appear in time as that which is eternal. We are mortal when we are loveless, immortal as lovers. We are mortal in indecision, immortal in resolution. We are mortal as natural processes, immortal when given to ourselves in freedom" (*PE* 112).

Freedom and truth are decisive in both the private and public sphere. Private mendacity leads to public mendacity. If we are to avoid catastrophic warfare, to outlaw warfare, then we need freedom. The individual, in freedom, stands in relation to his or her truth. "Man always lives with some outline of Being. Within its framework he becomes aware of Being as he thinks and expresses it. The actuality of such an outline within one who knows it has a wider significance than specific items of knowledge. It is the pervasive form and the condition of his knowledge, the mode of his relation to the divinity or to nothingness" (*BPW* 201).

Philosophical faith, an understanding of the foundering of truth in time, and active sufferance in love all have a positive role to play in the future of humanity? Humanity may effectuate a positive "existential redirection" into an unknown, yet open, future. Apart from global catastrophic risks beyond human choices and control, the existential risks we face all depend on the singularly unique individual, you and me, and how we will act.

The decisive (point) is this: There is no law of nature and no law of history which determines the way of things as a whole. The future depends upon the responsibility of the decisions and deeds of men and, in the last analysis, of each individual among the billions of men.

It depends upon each individual. By his way of life, by his daily small deeds, by his great decisions, the individual testifies to himself as to what is possible. By this, his present actuality, he contributes unknowingly toward the future. In doing this, he dare not think of himself as unimportant, just as he dare not do so in elections where his is just one among millions of votes. . . .philosophy is not without politics nor without political consequences. . . .what a philosophy is, it shows in its political appearance.[39]

Faith and love, that is, a kind of faith and love that help bring about communicative solidarity, can actually take humanity and *humanitas* much further along the road to the future than all the new technologies of hope.

Epilogue

So I do not ask that any one should make a cross in their calendar or otherwise bother to see whether my words are fulfilled. If they are fulfilled, then people will have something else to think about than my accidental being and if they are not fulfilled, well, then I shall simply be a prophet in the modern sense of the word—for a prophet nowadays means to prognosticate and nothing more. In a certain sense a prophet cannot do anything else. It was providence that fulfilled the words of the older prophets, so perhaps modern prophets, lacking the addition coming from providence, might say with Thales: what we predict will either happen or not; for to us too has God granted the gift of prophecy. (*PA* 61–62)

Verstehen[40]
A little boy, an adult child, fell.
Three founders, in solicitude, looked on.

The first said:
"The observable facts are not enough for understanding
what there was to understand. No final understanding. . .."
He spoke of Vienna and War.

The second said,
"My God, the banality of evil!
I pray for you, everyday.
May you understand
The stages on life's way."
He spoke of Socrates and the Church.

The third said,
"To love woman is *not* to hate life."[41]

---

[39] Karl Jaspers, "Philosophical Autobiography," in *The Philosophy of Karl Jaspers*, ed. Paul Arthur Schilpp (La Salle, IL: Open Court, 1981), pp. 1–94, here pp. 69–70.

[40] See Leonard H. Ehrlich, "Jaspers' Methodology of *Verstehen*: It's Basis for History, Psychology, Translation," *Existenz: An International Journal in Philosophy, Religion, Politics, and the Arts*, Vol. 3, No. 1, Spring 2008, p. 2, http://www.existenz.us/volume3No1.html, accessed July 8, 2011.

[41] The expression—"To love woman is to hate life"—is a gloss on Friedrich Nietzsche. The context is Nietzsche's philosophical counsel to Dr. Josef Breuer (1842–1925), Austrian physician, physiologist and key forerunner with his student Sigmund Freud of psychoanalysis, in Irvin D. Yalom, *When Nietzsche Wept: A Novel of Obsession* (New York, NY: Perennial Classics, 2005), p. 243.

Her eyes spoke with Care:
"Embrace *l'absurde.*
Leap now, to calm and serenity!"

Then the little boy, an adult child, took flight,
with broken wings,
still slowly beating.
He came to *Understand:*
Gift of the Founders,
Gifts of Self to others.

Our Watchword Still—"Unlimited publicity for truth!" (*PE* 79)
Umkehr, Faith and Love—*sine qua non* for the Future of Humanity and *Humanitas.*

Towards World Philosophy and a World History of Philosophy—Karl Jaspers: His Work, Calling, and Legacy

Richard Wisser

Abstract Professor Wisser's address to students during the Summer Semester of 1995 at the University of Mainz (Germany) regarding the contributions of Karl Jaspers on world philosophy, a history of world philosophy, and the value of his thought for philosophizing in general. Discussion of the semantics of seeing, hearing, and learning and what Jaspers has to offer as regards the continuous project of *Bildung* as contrast to other major figures in the history of Western philosophy and theology.

When preparing a treatise, the author focuses on a given subject and elucidates its details for the intended reader; in contrast, in a lecture, the presenter is mutually aware with and mindful of the audience.[1] He will have to direct his attention not only to the subject itself, but also to ensure that his audience will perceive the subject not just by its words but also feel its relevance. As important the focus on the subject might be, with the spoken word—where one's tone of voice triggers emotional responses as well—it becomes paramount to acknowledge and notice the audience's mood. Besides paying attention to the subject, the speaker must also pay attention to the audience. It is not enough just to portray a subject, but to consider simultaneously the various circumstances of an audience along with their immediate historiographical circumstances and educational preparedness; while at the same time directing the audience's attention toward and encourage reflection about the subject. This is the spirit of the opening phrase, "dear fellow comrades," which expresses the shared focus and togetherness for such task. Furthermore, each lecture provides opportunities to engage in dialogue, even in disagreements, with the audience; while upon the completion of a treatise, it remains uncertain if and when a critical discourse with the readers ever takes place. In memory of the lectures by professor Leonard Ehrlich, guest professor at my university in Mainz where I was a listener in the audience, I dedicate in fond memory to him and to his wife, Dr. Edith Ehrlich, intentionally not a treatise but the first two meetings of my lecture on the philosophy of Karl Jaspers.

---

[1] This text contains the first two meetings of my Summer 1995 lecture. Translated from German by Helmut Wautischer.

R. Wisser (✉)
University of Mainz, D-67547 Mainz, Germany

H. Wautischer et al. (eds.), *Philosophical Faith and the Future of Humanity*,
DOI 10.1007/978-94-007-2223-1_24, © Springer Science+Business Media B.V. 2012

Dear Fellow Comrades,

It is quite a picturesque offering of themes listed in the catalogue that will allow each of you to find a course, either because of immediate interest in the subject, or because it fulfills a requirement toward the major in philosophy. But to some of you, this abundance of offerings might just bring the opposite reaction that is contrary to a major tenet in philosophy, namely "to hear and see."

We have learned from behavioral science in anthropological research that there are so-called sign stimuli, also called releasers, which prompt our behavior into specific directions. Essentially, and quite usual for nature as such, these stimuli are imprinted in nature rather than spirit and serve procreation and survival of species rather than personal growth. For personal development, different features than sign stimuli or releasers are needed; it is mental dispositions that allow one to reach for contents in the domain of spirit and to account for one's choices.

A vital role in the fields of philosophy and the humanities is given to perceptions and horizons of imagination, to intellectual attitudes, or borrowing a modern expression, to mental dispositions. These will prove relevant in other activities as well, for example when tennis star Boris Becker introduced besides his infamous Becker Hecht of struck Volley (*Hechtsprung*) also a revisiting of the concept "mental," and shaped the tennis world in his very unique way. In other words, what matters is perspective and the sharp determinations derived from perspectives that govern and determine our quest for knowledge and insight. Our epistemological interests— to use another slogan albeit already introduced by Immanuel Kant and skillfully adopted by the Frankfurt School—are framed by such chosen perspectives that illuminate and attract our interest, in suspense creating a horizon of expectation that usually motivates us to engage with it once we have decided that the topic is neither boring nor tiresome and we are ready to spare neither trouble nor expense.

Today, a university education is nearly free, at least in comparison with my own experience when we did have to pay for it, so it is no longer a matter of expense but primarily of effort, and that is the same today as it was before. It is with good reason that the word "study" refers to the peculiar efforts of striving due to one's interests, that is, *inter esse* or an essential being-in-a-subject with affection in studious, diligent, and carefully passionate "effort" to find worthwhile answers for our knowledge interests. Take for example the meaning of "school"—may it be a school of thought, a high school or elementary school, a preschool or grade school, a trade school or university—its etymological Greek origin *scholá* (χολή), here you notice my emphasis on the second vowel, suggesting a forward movement; in contrast, the Latin use of schola (that is incorporated in the German word *Schule*) places the emphasis onto the first vowel: One can literally hear the difference in emphasis and mentality that recognizes time for muse and musings, as well as a literal sense for time of effort—a effort needed to avoid the dangers of procrastination.

As I have previously mentioned, today's university education is nearly without charge, at least for the time being, which might result in the absence of a motivating stimulus, namely to embrace the effort because of the cost factor, literally to spare neither trouble nor expense. Nowadays, when someone shies no efforts in the original meaning of *scholá* (Gk. χολή; Lat. *schola*; Ger. *Schule*), referring to advanced studies, or "high" schooling, such person does not play high and mighty but mingles with interest and on behalf of the study subject. Whoever acts in this way also has a particular motivation, and this is where I would like to direct your attention, to focus away from myself and pay attention to your own motivation. I invite you to reflect upon your own motivation for choosing to attend this particular lecture today. In other words, I would like to assist you in self reflection, since it is only through a thorough analysis of one's self-interest that one might potentially be ready to ponder about the perspective derived from self-interest. We always move within a given horizon defined by perspectives of different diameter and circumference that mark one's own measures, one's own views and perspectives, one's narrow and broad visions. We can opt for a frog perspective or a church tower perspective.

It is equally important to render account for one's own horizon. I use the word "horizon" intentionally, since it provides a suitable and descriptive image that had been used to highlight the philosophy of Karl Jaspers. A *Festschrift* that explored Jaspers' philosophy had the symbolic title *Open Horizon* (*Offener Horizont*). This is rather peculiar, since the word horizon—with its Greek origin *horizein* (ὁρίζω) referring to boundary, enclosure, bringing closure—designates something that cannot be surpassed or overcome, in other words, horizon actually limits or encircles or encloses everything within its range.

The characteristics of Jasper's philosophy are aptly described with "open horizon," inasmuch we transcend such typical horizon that one cannot reach beyond—the expression "this goes beyond my horizon" actually means, "I do not understand"—so that we are no longer faced with a more or less closed horizon but with an open one. This play with words should demonstrate that in Jaspers' philosophy there is no definitive or closed description of horizon or horizons, instead the concept designates an opening for a variety of mental dispositions, for example belonging to the Occident or the Orient, with an invitation to utilize this open horizon for overcoming such boundaries that would otherwise lead an individual to shake one's head in disbelief and resigning into "this goes beyond my horizon."

A remarkable feature in Jaspers' philosophy is the attempt to explore and utilize a method that does not obstruct such an open horizon. And here is something that you might want to note right from the beginning, such procedure will not see the other as an other, perhaps even with an opinionated attitude against any dialogue with such a person—in contrast, one core concept of Jaspers' philosophy is communication, to open one's eyes to see the other, and open one's ears to hear the other. What this exactly means in detail, I will demonstrate in due course. Already for now it should be clear that Jaspers' philosophy is not just another nuance to existing philosophies, and it is also not just excluding other philosophies. In view of Jaspers' comprehensive oeuvre this means, in a nutshell, for example, that one must not rush to Karl Jaspers' so-called existential philosophy without paying attention to his rational philosophy, which in turn requires one to pay attention to his illumination of existence while at the same time staying away from his metaphysics in order to make room for incorporating his ciphers of transcendence as well as his political philosophy; all of which cannot be just sorted out on the basis of one's own interpretation but in view of such "open horizons" that allow one an inclusive engagement with the encompassing while paying attention to the silver lining that unites these horizons. When this happens, we have arrived at Karl Jaspers.

But let us shift focus back to my earlier invitation that you might want to ponder your own reasons as to why you decided to attend this lecture. As you reflect upon conditions such as perspective, disposition, sign stimuli and releasers, it is quite important to assess why each one of you decided to attend a lecture about Karl Jaspers, or at least give it a try, in spite of the wide offerings available to you this semester.

Certainly each one of you has a number of reasons, and while such analysis would be very helpful, it cannot take place at the moment. Perhaps one of the reasons—here I allow myself some vanity and venture into the possibility of some rumors—is that the lecture about Karl Jaspers is given by someone who, while being a student just as you are, today, wrote a letter to Karl Jaspers exactly 45 years ago. That I did so, is actually nothing special. What is remarkable, however, is the fact that professor Jaspers did reply by return mail, and this developed into a life-long correspondence and a mutual relationship that prompted me to engage with the philosophy of Karl Jaspers, and to never leave it behind or to pass it by, but to journey with it. As you see, my personal initiative had significant consequences, and it is most appropriate to share such personal facts in the context of a lecture about Karl Jaspers, given that, in contrast to many other philosophers, Jaspers has always stressed the importance of including personal details into philosophical reflection. By philosophizing, a person is not in subjective or objective opposition to the content of reflection but engages with it, similar to the position in French existentialism. For this reason it is quite appropriate to address also the matters that at a first glance might appear insignificant.

Perhaps rumor might also have it that this student, who now gives a lecture about Karl Jaspers, has a reputation that he did not spare the proverbial trouble or expense to team up with Professor Leonard Ehrlich—a colleague from the United States at the University of Massachusetts at Amherst who has lectured about Karl Jaspers as a guest professor at our University of Mainz—for the purpose of organizing and chairing already three international congresses on the philosophy of Karl Jaspers in conjunction with the World Congress of Philosophy (in Montreal, Brighton, and Moscow) and published its Proceedings in three extensive volumes, and is currently undergoing preparations for the upcoming Jaspers conference in Boston.

Perhaps the reason for your interest in this lecture is of more mundane nature, simply to learn something about the philosophy of Karl Jaspers, without realizing that this is not some random offshoot of philosophizing or some approach that recently became popular, but that it was Jaspers' intention from the very beginning to save philosophy as a discipline when he wrote his three volume tome *Philosophie*. One must understand that during the nineteenth century and at the beginning of the twentieth century, quite into the time of Jaspers' academic life, science started to proclaim the legitimacy of disregarding philosophy. This is quite apparent as we look at our own university, where research subjects that were traditionally aligned with philosophy are now weaned off the breasts of its mother and proceed legitimately on their own. Take for example pedagogy and psychology. My own teacher was professor of philosophy, psychology, and pedagogy, and I studied with him in order to continue offering philosophy for psychologists. Other examples would be sociology or, and this is not known to many, even geography. Remember Immanuel Kant who as philosophy professor also was required to teach lectures about geography; in fact he left behind a very impressive and comprehensive study on geography.

A similar development also took place when theology denied philosophy its own legitimate place, leading to the known dictum that philosophy serves as the hand-maid to theology (*ancilla theologiae*). Jaspers recognizes and counters the even bigger danger, not only that philosophy might become an *ancilla scientie*, but also that science might replace it altogether and take away its legitimate right to exist. Jaspers' contribution differs from the kind of specialized philosophies as theoretical foundation research or philosophy of history. For Jaspers, the primary focus was philosophy as such, a *philosophia perennis*, a living and permanent philosophy that surpasses time and change.

Perhaps yet another reason for you to attend this lecture could have been its title, "Philosophy Toward 'World History of Philosophy' and 'World Philosophy' " and the emphasis on "world." This raises another idea, namely that it is generally not sufficient to reflect solely on the reasons that might have brought to you to attend this lecture, but also to ask about the meaning of world. What then, is "world"? Does it designate the common meaning typical of a tourist who is about to travel around the world, or is it a classification used by historians, for example, the "ancient world" or "the Greek world," with its exorbitant claim to illuminate a world of separation from barbaric and uneducated foreigners and brutes that are not perceived as full human beings? Does world designate the Roman Empire, the empire of the Caesars that defines any law and order with its Roman law? Does world refer to the homeland of Germanic people? Does world refer to its geographic designation of "old world" and especially the "new world" as discovered by Columbus?

Could we assume that none of these reflections went through your mind? In other words, what matters is to arrive at clarity regarding what is triggered by the sign stimulus or releaser "world." Is it an understanding known from the ancient world that at its end, the world is boarded up,[2] even to the point that there are reports from travelers testifying that the world is indeed boarded up at its ends. Johannes Olorinus Variscus (in German aka Johann Sommer) already reports such lies (as he calls them) in his *Ethnographia mundi* (Magdeburg 1608). For someone who believes that the philosophy of Leibniz is not only most relevant for German philosophies but for philosophy in general, "world" refers to God's creation and to "the best of all possible worlds." Perhaps you had come across Voltaire's 1759 satire, *Candide, ou l'optimisme*, now in the context of his 300th anniversary, where he parodies of such perceptions about the world. Perhaps one of you thought about Goethe and

---

[2] The German expression is, *mit Brettern vernagelt*. See Gunther Haupt and Winfried Hofmann, *Geflügelte Worte. Der Zitatschatz des deutschen Volkes, gesammelt und erläutert von Georg Büchmann* (Berlin: Haude & Spener, 1972), p. 147. [Henceforth cited as *GF*]

what possibly could have been on his mind as he responded to his lost love, Frau von Stein, in his famous poem *An den Mond* in 1777: "Blessed is who secludes from the world, without hatred"? And perhaps one or the other might have thought about Martin Luther and his often cited and misunderstood reference to "world" in his defying song, "and if the world would be full of devils"—misunderstood because Luther does not count on human gesticulation or efficacy or strength, instead he writes in verse, "with our powers nothing gets done" (*GF* 139). Now I ask myself if perhaps someone did associate with "world" the often cited and most of the time also misunderstood passage in Hoffmann von Fallerslebens' *Lied der Deutschen* (1841): "Deutschland, Deutschland über alles,/ über alles in der Welt," which does not refer to a conquest of the world, but instead brings a declaration of love, just as one is able to and desires to love one person more than any other in the world.

There are still many more associations to "world" that come to mind and that we could entertain. For now I have only brought your attention to some of the historical perceptions and commentaries about "world." My primary intention, however, was to inspire you to reflect for yourself what you associate with this word, so I can cease to suggest further historical references. After all, nowadays one might associate with "world" some sort of institution such as a world shop, a business that explicitly avoids trading in exploited third world products, in the sympathetic but perhaps naïve attempt to support those who make them. One might also think about the world organization of the United Nations, UNO, even when the reality of this institution often consists in demonstrating the disunity of nations, thereby highlighting the problematic complexity of a so-called one world and a lack of effectiveness contrary to one's hopes. Regardless of what one might associate with "world" or what you might associate or feel or resonate with it, this is always an indicator or pointer worthwhile of reflection. I invite each one of you to engage in such reflection and to attest your meaning of the concept "world"—not Wisser or Jaspers, or perhaps Jaspers as read by Wisser, but your motivation in attending this lecture, and hopefully to stay with it and to anticipate with curiosity what Jaspers has to offer to philosophy and by means of his philosophizing. It will be necessary to dissect the concept of philosophy, and this must be more than just adding up beliefs and names that are associated with philosophy to weave and sweep a dubious carpet. We will need to address how Jaspers coped in philosophical terms with the fact that the world is round and that it turns on its axis.

In other words, it will be necessary to clearly determine that philosophy is not just a general term suitable for all kinds of uses, such as the profit-philosophy of a business enterprise, the designs of a fashion house, or the ideas of a soccer trainer, but to analyze the concept "philosophy" to make it suitable for today's world, which as I mentioned, is round and turns on its axis. That the world is not a disk, and consequently the so-called ancient pillars of Heracles according to the perception of Hercules close the passage of Gibraltar, so that no one falls off the disk is not an accurate understanding we understand since Copernicus and Galileo, and we know it as a fact since we have seen photographs from the orbiting earth. We now understand that we could indefinitely circle the globe, but in principle we are in a finite situation that eventually will bring us back to the original starting point. What brings a sobering realization to our desire for travelling is the fact that after visiting all countries on this planet—and not just for the reason of cheaper lifestyles than in Germany or Austria or Switzerland—is the increasing market of possible space travel to finance an adventure trip to the moon; all this should be reason to reflect further, without losing equanimity.

In all seriousness, there is a new understanding that round is not just obese or curvy, or chubby-cheeked, but also means closed circumference, orbit, circling, interconnectedness of all and everything, and that axial turns are not just confusing but also bring change that results from its underlying organization. Jaspers has noticed very early that the so-called times for local and regional histories, State and Nation histories, or to gaze at one's own belly button and to refuse to look beyond one's church tower is perhaps still alive but no longer sufficient and can serve at best as one perspective among many. The role of philosophy is universal applicability in a matrix of diverse communication. It is certainly insightful to note what bureaucrats at the UNESCO section-philosophy have already established this in actuality and not just in thought. Last year I became aware of this institution in the context of a philosophy congress in Ankara, Turkey with the title "Philosophy on the Threshold to the 21st Century." Here, an attempt was made to organize and schematize all "philosophies" of the "entire world," at least to the extent that they make themselves known. It is precisely such attempt that makes me say: Do not repeat the paradigm of Heracles and his sign, "here and no further," but instead form a paradigm of one world, which means that our world is one world. I will discuss Jaspers' approach to this topic and his solutions in the upcoming lectures. (April 25, 1995).

Dear Fellow Comrades,

At the beginning of last lecture I made a reference to hearing and seeing—and I hasten to add that such brief review is valuable, since it does not just repeat what had been said already, but it brings back to attention matters in view—and I expressed full understanding for someone who might be overwhelmed by the sheer amount of lectures and the panoply of topics and perspectives to a point of not knowing whether on is coming or going; it is precisely the openness to hearing and seeing that counts as a prerequisite without which philosophy could not exist.

My comment about hearing and seeing is not just a literary device. Rather, I brought your attention to the two most vital senses by which we can acquire meaning, which allow us to understand something or someone, or to place ourselves in someone else's position: First of all by means of one's ear that allows us to notice someone's voice and to become aware of a word; such voice (*Stimme*) will trigger an ambiance (*Stimmung*) and also an emotional disposition when we assess if this voice that we hear also communicates accurately (*stimmt*) with words that are aligned with their content (*über-ein-stimmt*). Secondly by means of one's eye that allows us to perceive (*sehen*) such alignment by comprehending (*sehen*) and understanding (*sehend*) its written and literary content as we go beyond mere reading or reading-up, and instead gain insights (*ein-sehen*) and understanding. This reference to eye and ear is more than just a remark about one's eyes and ears—it describes a human experience that is already addressed in *Isaiah* (42:20): "You see many things, but you do not observe; your ears are open, but you hear nothing"—apparently it does not suffice to open one's eyes and ears absent-mindedly, but to keep them open in order to learn accurate hearing and seeing.

Accurate hearing is one of the prerequisites for preliminary engagement especially in our context of academic activity, this was already stressed by Pythagoras, the creator of the Pythagorean theorem that in comparison to his contribution about hearing is rather insignificant or harmless at least from a humanitarian perspective. It was Pythagoras' contribution that, still today, you are considered an audience (*Hörer*) as you come to hear (*hören*) my lecture in the so-called auditorium or lecture hall (*Hörsaal*); because Pythagoras identified hearing as the first step of a comprehensive education leading to permanent knowledge (*Bildung*) in a life-long process of becoming human, as opposed to mere training (*Ausbildung*) in a particular field of knowledge or to give into vanity (*Einbildung*). For Pythagoras it was not a question that attentive listening (*Hören*) is something that one needed to learn; to prick up one's ears rather than just opening them for the purpose of practicing the various forms of listening (*Anhören*, *Hinhören*, *Zuhören*, *Erhören*) are prerequisites for comprehending or engaging in depth with a person or a subject. By providing systematic and organizational means, Pythagoras had an impact on academic learning when he insisted that prior to learning the actual subject matter, the audience first must be instructed how to open their ears; in other words academic learning does not start with the facts of a subject matter, but with the preparation of the learner for self-assessment and readiness for attentive dialogue. In systematic and organizational ways Pythagoras insisted that presuming open ears of students is not enough, but that they needed to be opened. He did not know the miraculous "be-opened"-word from the New Testament, Ephphata (εφφαθα, Armaic ethpathach). He also did not know of the person how put his saliva on the ears of the deaf in order to make them hear. Instead, Pythagoras developed a targeted and effective method for listening in the sense of learning (*Hörschulung*) rather than opening deaf ears (*Gehörschulung*), by teaching attentive listening to those with auditory capacity and readiness to engage in a long standing process of practicing conscious comprehension in full realization that this is not a gift from the Gods ("He who has ears to hear, let him hear" *Matthew* 11:15) but a result of one's efforts.

So much for the ear and listening. But what should one make of the other sense, the eye? Here we focus on Plato, who did not emphasize the ear, but the eye. Plato effectively demonstrated in detail that it is not through sensory means that vision occurs but it is through innate ideas that our eyes are opened to perceive beauty and all other things that we notice. The Greek *idein* (ἰδεῖν) literally refers to the process of unmediated conscious knowing. Also the Indo-Germanic and Indo-European roots *id-*, *vid-*, and *wis-* as well as the Latin *videre* suggest that knowing relates to seeing. Actual seeing takes place by virtue of such knowing. This, for example, prevents that we would not see the forest for its trees, or in the words of Wieland, "Folks of this ilk are blinded by too much light;/ they lack to see the forest for its trees" (*GF* 171). Such comprehensive seeing prohibits that "while seeing we do not see" (*Matthew* 13:13), or that we become aware of "what no reason of rational creatures can see" (I quote here Schiller, but also 1 Corinthians 1:19) as we realize the unique quality of an inner eye. In today's world, one obstruction to Plato's *idein* is found in television which, in reality, is only a closed vision of distant events, a form of vision that removes distance in such a way that events from most distant locations in the world are delivered into our dwellings, or whatever name you want to give to your home. Now we are facing a screen [the colloquial German word is *Glotze*, suggesting a dumb staring at something] and absent-mindedly we stare at it. This is far from Plato's remembrance of archetypes that form the basis of perception, and it is also far from philosophical insight gained from such perception.

This is precisely the crux of the matter, one might lose any desire "to hear and see" because of an abundance of confusing offerings in the schedule of classes, unless one simply overlooks systematically any courses that are not caught by his eye, or simply ignores courses for which he has no ear. But such naïve exclusion of topics does not help with the confusion that comes from the abundance of detail related to the history of philosophy or the systematic treatment of themes in different disciplines; here an eclectic cherry-picking does not resolve the confusion that comes from different intellectual positions that oftentimes mutually exclude each other, and benevolent attempts to understand philosophy by way of a particular school of thought might be in vain. With that we arrive at a fundamental question that cannot be avoided, unless one would opt to run recklessly away from the problem, and this is the question, "what is philosophy?" Unless we want to avoid this question by selecting any one school of thought and pretend that this is what philosophy is all about, we will find no escape from it. In fact, this is a question where is not enough simply to ask it, but we must also face it.

One attempt for an answer, published in 1976 as *What is Philosophy?* (and this is a first suggestion for your reading list) was compiled by Hans Saner, assistant to Karl Jaspers for many years and also the curator of Jaspers' works, who selected a number of chapters from the collected works and also some of Jaspers' essays to form, what he calls in the subtitle, a reader (*Lesebuch*). Trained as a linguist-aesthetic philosopher, *Lesebuch* for Saner does not mean that a reader would turn pages randomly or flip to chapters on a whim, instead he had in mind a vintage (*Auslese*), an exquisite (*Erlesen*), a selective (*Auserlesen*) treatment addressing the complexity of this question. Saner organizes in broad themes that in due course we will also have to consider and explore. For example, Jaspers did not just address foundational questions of philosophy, but he also resonates about the role of philosophy for today and its historic relevance. Likewise, Jaspers does not just demarcate philosophy from science, religion or ideology (*Unphilosophie*), but he also ponders upon the media for philosophizing, such as the role of language or something that normally we would not associate with media for philosophizing, namely how the tragic touches upon and accompanies philosophy with its final assessment of being in the world derived from strict analysis of deep and permeating worldviews and life experiences. Whoever is marked by such tragic worldviews and derives insights into the world and human existence from such experience, will recognize one's place in such a medium that shapes, determines, and regulates philosophy.

Because of its complexity I mention this book of Jaspers' writings. And since Saner is an excellent connoisseur of Jaspers' collected works, given the scope of the publication he has not overlooked any relevant subjects and thereby provided an instructive overview. It was for this reason that the *Lesebuch*, as Saner calls it, was published in 1978 only two years after its initial appearance in 1976 and already in its second edition, followed by a paperback edition in 1980 in the DTV-Series, and already in 1982 with the second edition of the paperback version. For the next lecture I will provide a handout with an extensive bibliography, so that I need not spend too much time with bibliographical references.

In the previous lecture I brought your attention to a second problem that is related to this matter. Right now I want to remind you again that my lecture today does not simply repeat what I have already addressed, but is an attempt to deepen the subject matter and further explore its meaning. In other words, I attempted to increase your curiosity about what Karl Jaspers has to offer, and also about what I might have to say about Jaspers, and to confront you with Jaspers and my Jaspers interpretation. I have also attempted to make you understand that it is of equal importance, perhaps even greater importance, that you confront yourself with yourself. This means that I encourage you to reflect upon so-called foreign objects and also to ponder your own motivation as to why you decided to attend this particular lecture on this particular topic. In the course of this objective, I invited you to acquire clarity about your own motives and dispositions that are not detached transparencies or slates that are imprinted by me so you can carry them home, but that you form your own reality by engaging with topics and persons and also with yourself. This process, just like your conversations about what you have heard and seen, belongs to the prerequisites for a comprehensive engagement with philosophy and is a permanent condition for true philosophizing including one's own situation in the form of a lived engagement rather than looking at a topic as something distant or foreign.

To recapitulate, just as my first point, emphasizing hearing and seeing will not suffice for a comprehension of my second point, namely that you would simply attend as spectator or listener. This will not suffice if you participate in the somewhat naïve expectation of simply waiting for things to happen. None of you is a *tabula rasa* and we all bring to this event our personal histories as well as our projections and expectations regarding the future. You might pay attention to one thing and ignore another: just as one's actions are shaped by sign stimuli and releasers at the level of species survival, so also at the level of personal development one is shaped and impacted by thought processes, perceptions, and mental dispositions, as in the alert and insightful Mephistopheles in Goethe's *Faust I* wanted to bring this insight into this one well-known formula: "Thinking to push, thyself art push'd along" (*Walpurgisnacht*). Philosophers are not served by engaging in objectifying reflection about subjects that are perceived separated from oneself, but it requires a perpetual reflection about one's subjective states that contributes in significant ways to one's comprehension or misunderstanding of oneself, others, or a topic. For those of you who are familiar with my philosophical anthropology and the so-called critical-crisis basic disposition, you will know that a structural assessment of these topics that I have touched upon here in this lecture is presented in several of my publications.[3] What has hopefully transpired by now is the importance of meeting oneself in the context of philosophizing. So I tried to bring to your attention that it is not enough to bring a sharp pencil but to reflect upon yourself, to examine one's own horizon that always filters and decides about acceptance or rejection of what is heard and seen. You might also interrupt the flow of information, perhaps not by interfering with the lecture but by allowing your mind to interrupt silently but equally disruptive for your own comprehension of the topic.

Apropos *tabula rasa*! Already Aristotle argued in his *Perì Psūchês* (*Περὶ Ψυχῆς*, Lat. *De Anima*, III, 4) that one's soul can be compared to "a writing tablet on which as yet nothing actually stands written" (ωσπερ εν γραμματειω ω μηθεν υπαρχει εντελεχεια γεγραμμενον). Here is an essential difference in the rebellious student of Plato, who, as his teacher, claimed that ideas are immanently present in the soul, constitute the essential quality of soul, and, in effect, suggest that the soul is the totality of all that had been perceived. Moreover, the soul is the prerequisite for our ability to focus visual perceptions by identifying actual things instead of gibberish, making sure that we attentively hear and see, and that we notice the forest in spite of all the trees, since it is not just an empty page. In contrast, Aristotle believed that the soul is an empty page up to the point when perceptions are imprinted upon it. Aristotle's followers simply copied their master, mostly in a variation of the theme that is know to you as *tabula rasa*. To clarify, it was Albertus Magnus who used this phrase in his treatise *De Anima* (*About the Soul*, III, 2, 12) and was later copied by his pupil Thomas Aquinas who was well trained in Aristotle's philosophy and repeated in his *Summa Theologiae* (I, *Quaestio* 97a 2) that "human intellect is a flat tablet without any inscription" (*intellectus humanus . . . in principio es sicut tabula rasa, in qua nihil scriptum est*).

Being a Platonist, the rationalist René Descartes (1596–1650) also recognizes innate ideas (*ideae innatae*) but identifies additional ideas in the soul of which he is not sure that they actually belong there, such as ideas that we produce ourselves (*ideae a me ipso factae*) and also ideas that come to us or reach us (*ideae adventitiae*), all of which hinders or at least negatively affects our attempts for arriving at a solid foundation for philosophy. Descartes wanted to avoid that such types of ideas block or affect our reception of actual ideas which would interfere with finding a solid foundation (*fundamentum inconcussum*) for philosophy. He urges us to remove everything from philosophy—by making a *tabula rasa* of everything—that does not contribute to our understanding of truth (*veritas*) and of whatever lacks the character of clear and distinct perception (*clara et distincta perceptio*). Descartes went even so far to expunge in a *tabula rasa* all that what has historically accumulated in philosophy, in other words, to clean up philosophy from past errors.

A very short period later, the renowned anti-Cartesian Italian philosopher Giambattista Vico (1668–1744) claimed that with such drastic action all collective

---

[3] See for example Richard Wisser, *Kein Mensch ist einerlei. Spektrum und Aspekte "kritisch-krisischer Anthropologie"* (Würzburg: Verlag Königshausen & Neumann, 1997).

experience of intellect and soul that has shaped humanity by means of education and culture would fall prey to a problematic clear cutting. Vico was the first to pay attention not only to particular events in history, but to history as such, and took very serious its specific unfolding and the role of philosophy in formulating and observing such development thereby literally advancing as one of René Descartes' most serious critics.[4]

Friedrich Nietzsche, who was rightfully described by Sigmund Freud as the great-psychologist-judge-of-character, made it clear that philosophy is not served by Descartes' notion of intellect and its corresponding soul, since it does not constitute a specific instance of reality; instead, intellect and soul are impacted shaped by perspectives that affect and unconsciously determine its courses of action. In fact, Nietzsche refers to perspectivism as "the fundamental condition of all life."[5] It was also Nietzsche who calls upon philosophers to unearth prejudices that cloud our evaluations and estimations, especially the so-called "prejudices of philosophers" that he sees in the contrast of good versus evil and its implicit assumption of a presumed opposition of values. Such presumptions would lead to a glorification of metaphysical ideas at the expense of earthly matters and stand in the way of a value free reception of current events. Nietzsche introduced the idea of scrutinizing, or getting to the bottom of philosophical analysis (*hinterfragen*) that nowadays is incorrectly used in the meaning of "making sense" instead of "having sense" when we refer to the quality of preliminary perspectives, "... perhaps they are not even viewed head-on; perhaps they are even viewed from below, like a frog-perspective, to borrow an expression that painters recognize" (*BGE* 6).

---

[4] See Richard Wisser, "Von der Entdeckung des 'wahren' Vico: Geschichtsmächtigkeit des Menschen und Verstehbarkeit von Geschichte," in *Philosophische Wegweisung. Versionen und Perspektiven*, ed. Richard Wisser (Würzburg: Verlag Könighausen & Neumann, 1998), pp. 63–92.

[5] Friedrich Wilhelm Nietzsche, *Beyond Good and Evil: Prelude to a Philosophy of the Future*, eds. Rolf-Peter Horstmann and Judith Norman, trans. Judith Norman (Cambridge and New York, NY: Cambridge University Press, 2002), p. 4. [Henceforth cited as *BGE*]

Humanism and Wars: Karl Jaspers Between Politics, Culture, and Law

Chris Thornhill

Abstract This chapter examines the changes in Jaspers' thought brought about by the experience of National Socialism and World War II. It argues that, whereas his Weimar-era works were focused on a reconstruction of the metaphysical tradition and a critique of the anti-metaphysical impulses in neo-Kantianism, his post-1945 publications were marked by a cautious privileging of practical reason and a more sympathetic reading of neo-Kantian principles. The war stimulated a move away from the earlier metaphysical dimensions of his thought, and after 1945 he committed himself to a brand of humanism founded in principles of practical reason. In its conclusion, the article re-evaluates Jaspers' later political thought, generally considered damaging to his theoretical reputation, and it examines elements of his late work that still warrant positive reconstruction for political theory.

Humanism and Wars: Law, Politics, or Culture?

The development of humanism in the philosophical tradition to which Jaspers belonged is closely bound up with wars and resultant experiences of the fragmentation of political authority, and most major philosophical positions in German intellectual history have been immediately shaped by reflection on military conflict and its consequences. As a result, the conceptions in this tradition of what it might truly mean to be a human being are often directly linked to conceptions of what it might truly mean to live under acceptable and legitimate conditions of peaceful political governance. Most particularly, humanism in Germany is very often correlated with *legal* arguments and with *legal* analysis of human determinacy, so that theories of acceptable legality and legitimate laws of state commonly reflect underlying ideas about the authentically realized human being.

Many famous cases of this relation between humanism and legal thinking were directly provoked by experience of wars. Examples of this are found especially in thinkers who assumed a role of direct political intervention or commentary—for example Melanchthon in the later 1520s and 1530s; Kant and Fichte after the wars of the French Revolution; Schelling and Hegel during and after the Napoleonic wars.

C. Thornhill (✉)
University of Glasgow, Glasgow G12 8RT, UK
e-mail: Christopher.Thornhill@glasgow.ac.uk

H. Wautischer et al. (eds.), *Philosophical Faith and the Future of Humanity*,
DOI 10.1007/978-94-007-2223-1_25, © Springer Science+Business Media B.V. 2012

All of these thinkers argued that the political system is most truly legitimate if it can develop a legal order which gives expression to the human person in its ideal form, and if it can guarantee conditions of order which acknowledge and represent the ideal nature of human being. All also implied that, if a system of this kind is established, the likelihood of war and revolution will be restricted—or, in Hegel's case, that peace can at least be assumed to be the most common relation between states. Most crucial in these debates, however, is Kant's perspective. Kant can be seen as marking the apotheosis of legal humanism in Germany, and, of all these philosophers, Kant was perhaps also the most concerned with the threat of war. Kant viewed the deduction and prescription of law as the process in which human beings give practical expression to their true rational natures and so found legitimate public order in universalizable principles of reason. The resultant circumscription of state power leads states from wars, and it leaves the political system centered on a generalized conception of rational human being, to the laws originating from which all rational human beings might accede. At the heart of Kant's philosophy, therefore, is the notion of the human being as the legal subject, constituting the invariable substructure for a legally universalized system of public order, which will minimize the probability of the violent or arbitrary exercise of power.

In the history of political humanism, it is not surprising that law should be of such central importance. This is because law has a special relation to metaphysics, and because in many respects metaphysical law, as an account of the order of the world before the incursion of the human, remains the abiding dialectical problem of humanism. As divine law or divine-natural law, for instance, law might articulate ways in which human life is related to an originary condition of pure created-ness, over which human reason has no control.[1] Yet as rational law or consensual law, law might also describe and define the state of human being in distinction from all original order. In classical metaphysics, therefore, law is the medium in which human being interprets its relation to immutable sources or principles of order. Then, in enlightened metaphysics or post-metaphysical reflection, "law" is the term under which reason defines itself as other than metaphysics, conceived as pure heteronomy, and in which human being explains itself to itself as fundamentally accountable for and implicated in the production of the forms which organize its life. In post-metaphysical thinking, in consequence, reason places itself at the causal heart of the universe, and it cements this autonomy through the ongoing deduction and prescription of laws. On one level, these are laws which supersede metaphysics. However, these laws also retain an attachment to metaphysics, for they always describe that original act of self-authorization through which human reason proclaims itself to be unconditionally self-causing, and through which it

---

[1] In particular, I mean the scholastic or neo-scholastic argument that observes the world as shaped by an absolutely pre-determined law. See for example Thomas Aquinas, *Summa Theologiae*, ed. and trans. D. Burke and A. Littledale, 61 vols. (London/New York, NY: Blackfriars, in conjunction with Eyre and Spottiswoode, 1969), vol. V: p. 21; Gottfried Wilhem Leibniz, *Essais de Theodiceé sur la bonté de Dieu, la liberté de l'homme et l'origine du mal* (Amsterdam: Isaac Treyel, 1712), p. 363.

claims as its own the possibilities which were originally only contained in metaphysics. In the history of political humanism, therefore, law delineates the end of metaphysics and the beginning of the human—but it always marks the beginning of the human as a dialectical trace or as an echo of metaphysics. This is most perfectly expressed by Kant's doctrine of rational autonomy and legitimacy in the legal state.[2] Yet both Fichte and, to a lesser extent, Hegel, can also be seen as offering an account of political legitimacy in which law anthropologically articulates a human or post-metaphysical relation to pure metaphysics: they too were thinkers who viewed political legitimacy as the discernibly human form of metaphysics. On these grounds, in any case, it can be concluded that law provides a terrain for a quite particular type of humanism, which reacts critically against the pure-metaphysical legacy and which has its center in an account of human-being as a capacity for accountability and for legal recognition and authority. This type of humanism usually comes to the fore in climates of acute political instability, where the essentialist ideas of legal humanism promise at least some enduring hold for social order.

It is important to note, though, that in Jaspers' own political and philosophical background the translation of metaphysics into humanism has not always been at ease with law as the medium for transposing originally metaphysical contents into accounts of human-being. The very early Schelling, for instance, showed similarities with Kant in imagining law, and political order, framed in rationally sanctioned laws, as the form in which human being can manifest its essence and ultimately approach perfectibility.[3] The early Schelling was thus close to a metaphysical-humanist account of law, which claimed that legitimate laws in political life reflect the primary identity of human consciousness. However, the later Schelling eventually moved to a much more cautious view on law, depicting law first merely as the place-holder for higher expressions of freedom,[4] and then ultimately as indifference against revealed freedom. The late Schelling was finally much happier with the idea of culture, or religiously informed culture, as the objective condition of human self-realization.

After Schelling, the later nineteenth century witnessed the emergence of distinct lines of cultural and political philosophy, which depreciated the status of law as the most integral mode of human self-creation. In mainstream political debate, this was manifest in the dominance of positivism as the theoretical orthodoxy of the

---

[2] I refer to Kant's claim that the human being is only truly a "person" where it is the "subject of moral-practical reason" (Immanuel Kant, "Metaphysik der Sitten," in *Werkausgabe*, ed. Wilhelm Weischedel, 12 vols. (Frankfurt am Main: Suhrkamp, 1976), vol. VIII: pp. 309–634; 569). That is to say, the human being only fully elaborates its humanity where it makes its will transparent to self-given *laws*, where it is "self-legislating", and where it spontaneously creates itself or autonomously causes itself to be through the deduction of moral laws (Kant, "Grundlegung zur Metaphysik der Sitten," in *Werkausgabe*, vol. VII: pp. 11–102, 65).

[3] Friedrich Wilhelm Joseph von Schelling, "Vom Ich als Prinzip der Philosophie oder über das Unbedingte im menschlichen Wissen," in *Werke*, ed. Manfred Schröter, 12 vols. (Munich: Beck and Oldenbourg, 1927–1954), vol. I: pp. 73–168; 122.

[4] Schelling, "Stuttgarter Privatvorlesungen," in *Werke*, vol. IV: pp. 309–376; 354.

political system of Imperial Germany. Positivism offered a model of legitimacy in which power and law are divested of all humanist or metaphysical attachments, and in which public power is reflected, neither as an expression of human essence nor of any determinate personality, but merely as a legally constructed fact. This tendency culminated in the deep denunciation of metaphysics and personalism in the works of Hans Kelsen who claimed simply, "All great metaphysicians have opposed democracy and favored autocracy." Metaphysics opposes democracy, he concluded, because it seeks to recreate the absolute personality of God in an authoritative and absolute political order, and, accordingly, metaphysical views struggle to accept the objective neutrality of law, on which legitimate law depends.[5] This prevalence of the positivist hostility to metaphysics in political-theoretical debate was flanked by the increasing influence of late-historicist and early sociological views, exemplified by Nietzsche, Dilthey, Weber, and Simmel, which also expressly positioned themselves against the types of legal humanism growing out of the Kantian Enlightenment. Nietzsche, Dilthey, and Simmel sought cultural paths beyond what they experienced as the formalization or impoverishment of human experience under the conditions of post-Enlightenment legal humanism or legal metaphysics. Analogously, Weber identified pure politics as an expression of human-being which evades the formal rationalization of existence under modern law, and so escapes the technical and purposive constraints of post-Enlightenment metaphysics.[6]

It is therefore clear that the intellectual background from which Jaspers emerged was already marked by a set of debates which expressed great skepticism about the overcoming or translocation of metaphysics through legal doctrine, and which adopted rival cultural and political terms for the reconstruction of metaphysics and the foundation of humanism. At the same time, however, it is also worth bearing in mind that Jaspers was also very well informed about the lines of Kantian practical philosophy and juridical humanism which reemerged in Marburg, Freiburg, and Heidelberg around 1900. These neo-Kantian thinkers were still more emphatic than Kant himself about the status of rational law as the limit of metaphysics and the inception of the accountably human. The theorists of the Marburg School, most especially, construed law, or acts of rational legislation, as the moments in which human beings account for the unity and consistency of their thoughts and actions, and so constitute themselves as truly human. As self-legislative agents, they explained, humans are able to deduce binding imperatives for the organization of thought and behavior, and so to free themselves from that "pathology" which is heteronomy, i.e. determination by natural, material or pure-metaphysical principles and forces.[7] Underlying all writings in the distinct schools of neo-Kantianism in

---

[5] Hans Kelsen, *Staatsform und Weltanschauung* (Tübingen: J.C.B. Mohr, 1933), p. 25.

[6] Hence Weber's claim that political responsibility manifests a "humanly genuine" ethic and even constitutes the ethical form of "the genuine person." See Max Weber, "Politik als Beruf," in Weber, *Gesammelte politische Schriften* (Tübingen: J.C.B. Mohr, 1988), pp. 505–560; 559.

[7] Hermann Cohen, *System der Philosophie, zweiter Theil: Ethik des reinen Willens* (Berlin: Bruno Cassirer, 1904), p. 309. [Henceforth cited as *ERW*]

the later nineteenth century was the belief that human reason validates itself most supremely by deducing the prior conditions of the unity of human consciousness and then by imputing these conditions as the inner-worldly foundation for all acts, practical and cognitive. Human consciousness, which can regulate its own unity, is fully autonomous, and it therefore expresses itself in law—either in the deduction of binding values (in Freiburg and Heidelberg) or, as in Marburg, of binding objective laws (*ERW* 70). For the Marburg theorists, notably, the supreme realization of the unity of consciousness (that is, the end of metaphysical heteronomy) occurs in the political form of the legal state, constructed by the universal stipulations of a self-enacting autonomous consciousness (*ERW* 74).

On the eve of World War I the dominant positions in the debates on humanism around the early Jaspers were divided into three broad camps. His immediate intellectual horizon was pervasively shaped by views which insisted on the central association of humanism and (self-)legislation (neo-Kantianism), perspectives which viewed politics—freed from the restrictions imposed by formal law—as the most perfect expression of human being (Weber), and other outlooks tending to endorse cultural humanism, such as late historicism and Nietzschean philosophy. It is extremely striking, however, that the balance between these rival versions of humanism altered quite radically in the aftermath of World War I. The political, cultural, and intellectual climate emerging after 1918 was almost universally characterized by vehement hostility towards legalism, and by opposition both to the thin legal superstructures of the states that had entered the war and to the legalizing brands of humanism and juridical accounts of human authenticity that had supported and justified these states—especially those characteristic of neo-Kantianism. In pure political debate, this is clear enough in the influential writings of Erich Kaufmann and Carl Schmitt, both of whom set themselves against normative models of human reason and formalizing models of political legitimacy. In philosophical debate, this tendency was also manifest in the works of Georg Lukács and Martin Heidegger, both of whom objected, for obviously very distinct political reasons, to the focusing of humanist argument on legal postulates and formal conceptions of autonomy. Indeed, it is no exaggeration to say that, across all political divides, the major philosophical and political-theoretical concerns in the Weimar Republic were linked to the fragmentation of neo-Kantian doctrine, and to the quest to propose non-juridical accounts of human essence, representation and self-realization.

Most crucially for Jaspers, this widespread hostility to legal humanism after 1918 focused directly on the relation between law and metaphysics. In fact, the political critique of neo-Kantianism in the 1920s commonly asserted that neo-Kantianism impoverishes human existence because it denies metaphysics and because it stabilizes the human being around narrowly rationalized ideas of formal self-legislation, thus excluding all possibilities of metaphysical experience. For example, Erich Kaufmann argued against neo-Kantian humanism because he felt that its rationalization of metaphysical principles as cognitive and practical laws leads to a "de-metaphysicization" of humanity, and so smothers all vital and cultural impulses in human existence.[8] Carl Schmitt was also prepared to countenance, at least rhetorically, a reintegration of metaphysical contents into the political order, and he claimed that political legitimacy depends on the political system's ability to represent non-material principles of order.[9] Even Paul Natorp who, in his early work, had been intent on emphasizing the necessary juridical autonomy of reason, began in the early 1920s to advocate a creative-metaphysical model of the legitimate polity and a metaphysical model of the true human being.[10] Central to this model was the claim that the conditions of particular and collective authenticity cannot be produced exclusively or autonomously by practical reason, but require ideas originating outside the inner structure of reason. At the same time, Heidegger and Lukács also proposed an alternative political critique of neo-Kantianism. Both argued, in overlapping yet politically polarized terms, that the experientially depleted and formalistic character of neo-Kantianism, and of the types of humanism arising from it, result from the fact that it has not yet shed its attachment to metaphysics, and it remains structured around universal-normative metaphysical schemes. Neo-Kantianism, both claimed, commits the cardinal theoretical crime of extrapolating truth-claims from the practical reality of social being itself, and so of falsely organizing human existence around spuriously hypostatized laws and values, distilled in malignant abstraction against being itself. Famously, for example, Heidegger argued that all humanism, and especially that in the Cartesian/Kantian tradition, "is either founded in metaphysics or it makes itself the foundation of metaphysics."[11] Reflecting a simultaneous agreement with and intense hostility towards Heidegger, Lukács argued that idealist and neo-Kantian constructions of human consciousness locate consciousness in a formalistic relation of "contemplative duality" toward the contexts and objects of its historical being. Through this metaphysical abstraction, human consciousness is reduced to a sequence of temporally evacuated and factually inhuman functions, both subject and object are divided into distinct and mutually indifferent monads,[12] and the subject loses its ability to obtain truthful knowledge of the objective conditions which surround it (*GK* 266). Both Heidegger and Lukács, therefore, advocated a historical mediation of consciousness as the path beyond the bad metaphysics of the Marburg and South-West schools of Kantian theory, and they indicated that the constitutively human processes of law-production and self-authorization could only be addressed as historically immanent and inner-worldly manifestations of common consciousness.

---

[8] Erich Kaufmann, *Kritik der neukantischen Rechtsphilosophie. Eine Betrachtung über die Beziehungen zwischen Philosophie und Rechtswissenschaft* (Tübingen: J.C.B. Mohr, 1921), p. 61.

[9] See the theory of representation in Carl Schmitt, *Verfassungslehre* (Berlin: Duncker und Humblot, 1928), p. 209.

[10] Paul Natorp, *Sozial-Idealismus. Neue Richtlinien sozialer Erziehung* (Berlin: Julius Springer, 1920), p. 73. [Henceforth cited as *SI*]

[11] Martin Heidegger, *Über den Humanismus* (Frankfurt am Main: Klostermann, 1949), p. 13.

[12] Georg Lukács, *Geschichte und Klassenbewußtsein* (Neuwied: Luchterhand, 1968), p. 273. [Henceforth cited as *GK*]

For all their differences, in sum, the key critiques of neo-Kantianism in the 1920s had a shared point of departure in their negation of the relation between law and metaphysics in Kantian thought, and in their rejection of formal law as the terrain of the human. Some of these perspectives criticized Kantian legal humanism for being too metaphysical, whilst others criticized it being not metaphysical enough. Yet the critical focus remained analogous in both lines.

The Ideas of Humanism

We might therefore argue that the wars of the French Revolution and the Napoleonic wars initially gave rise to diverse variants on legal humanism, which intimated that the originally metaphysical idea and possibility of human freedom might be most effectively secured in law—especially in the necessary order of rational state law. This tendency toward legal-political humanism also described and enacted a move away from purely epistemological philosophy towards an ascription of greater importance to practical reason relative to pure reason, and toward a privileging of ethical ideas relative to the regulative ideas of knowledge. Kant's own rationalist humanism was clear, although extremely cautious, in its intimation that practical reason and the production of ethical law might assume primacy over the deduction of the ideas which found pure cognition.[13] However, subsequent perspectives in idealist and post-idealist philosophy were much more insistent in claiming that rational consciousness obtains its highest unity as it reflects and enacts the practical idea of necessary freedom. This inclination towards a privileging of the practical in fact became increasingly influential through the latter part of the nineteenth century. Even later thinkers of the nineteenth century who explicitly broke with the idealist tradition did so, not lastly, because they suspected that idealist definitions of practical reason were not practical enough, and remained incarcerated in formalized and atomized conceptions of rationality and self-realization. In a more direct idealist lineage, the final triumph of practical reason over pure reason was accomplished simultaneously (for different reasons) in the rival schools of neo-Kantianism. In Marburg, the idea of necessary freedom, deduced as the legislative foundation of reason and concretized as universalizable ethical law, was proclaimed as the unifying idea of consciousness and the guiding idea of all human operations.[14] Further to the South, Rickert imported elements of practical reason into his account of rational judgment, and he argued for the invariable "primacy of practical reason" in the autonomous deduction and application of values.[15] On this basis, therefore, the post-Kantian trajectory of German philosophy, which sought to give a determinately

---

[13] Immanuel Kant, "Kritik der Urteilskraft," in *Werkausgabe*, vol. X: p. 412.

[14] Law, Cohen argues, is the "foundation of the self" (*ERW* 269).

[15] Heinrich Rickert, *Der Gegenstand der Erkenntnis. Einführung in die Transzendental-philosophie*, 6te Auflage (Tübingen: J.C.B. Mohr, 1928), p. 437.

anthropological description of human autonomy, found in practical reason—the science of law—the key instrument for combating pure metaphysics and for founding humanism at the limit of metaphysics.

It is notable, though, that the cult of practical reason in post-Kantian thinking was far less in evidence after World War I, and through the years of the Weimar Republic. During this period, together with Jaspers himself, a number of influential thinkers emerged who argued that human consciousness does not obtain unity through the deduction of its legislative foundation and that the ideas through which human defines its authenticity are not merely inner-worldly moral regulatives. Apart from Jaspers, examples of such thinking are found in the reconstructions of neo-Kantian theory set out in the 1920s, albeit very diversely, by Natorp and Heinz Heimsoeth, both of whom showed elements of commonality with Jaspers. Common to their views was the claim that the envisioning of human reason and acting as mere self-regulating realities of juridical validity and autonomy serves only to truncate intellectual experience against its proper contents, and so to deprive human consciousness of its fundamental possibilities for *freedom*. Such thinkers argued that true human consciousness cannot be taken as an invariably legislated reality of autonomy; that consciousness is not yet complete, and it cannot, most surely, be stabilized in practical-juridical form against the events of the world. On these grounds, with Jaspers at the fore, the 1920s also saw a cautious turning to doctrines of pure reason as a source for a self-critique of reason's mere autonomy and as an account of reason's desire for transcendent experience (*SI* 240, 243). Such perspectives suggested that the ideas of pure reason, against practical reason, could disclose vital and challenging experiences for human reflection, which might correct the reduction of human freedom to the practical processes of regulation and legislation.

In my view, it is against the background of these post-Kantian debates on humanism, on the relation of humanism and metaphysics, and on the legal founding of the human in Kantian thinking, that the greatest importance of Jaspers' early philosophy can be best understood. One key implication of Jaspers' early thought is, against standard neo-Kantian outlooks, that human consciousness which merely regulates its cognitive and practical operations on the ground of a unity generated a priori invalidates and excludes its most vital experiences, and limits the possibility of its authentic formation. Authentic human existence is in fact the self-interpreting unfolding of consciousness, and the most existentially valid experiences are those in which consciousness and existence know themselves drawn beyond the limits of their existing unity. This argument was clearly intended as an experiential reconstruction of Kantian thought, and especially of *Kritik der reinen Vernunft*. Indeed, Jaspers' early thought is based in a transposition of Kant's transcendental ideas into a metaphysical doctrine of realms of human experience, and it develops the Kantian antinomies of pure reason as antinomies of lived existence, through which consciousness obtains ever more unified understanding of its own transcendent(al) form. In escaping the common interpretations of Kant's humanism, however, Jaspers also draws on theoretical residues that directly question the Kantian legacy, and he clearly opposed both the claim for the primacy of practical reason and the anti-metaphysical line of argument selected by most interpreters of Kant. Schelling's later metaphysical theory of the open system, in which reason defines itself as a positive relation to transcendent contents which are not generated as its own rational products, is evidently an important (yet very critically reconstructed) force in the background to Jaspers' metaphysical re-reading of Kant.

The early Jaspers approached the question of humanism through a metaphysical account of human consciousness, distinct from all stable anthropology or legal-moral positivism. Authentic humanity, he suggested, is nothing but the continual yet decisive self-interpretation of human consciousness, freed from prior juridical or foundational structure, and so lacking any prior unity or categorical form—either in ethical or epistemological reflection. It is for this reason that communication has such importance in Jaspers' philosophy. Communication is the temporal disclosure and self-interpretation of consciousness, reflected by cultural, religious and philosophical ciphers towards its limits and unity, but not instituting these as pure principles or ideas, and surely not as practical conditions for self-legislation. This doctrine of communication might be illuminatingly compared with the more directly neo-Kantian communicative theories of the Marburg School. For the Marburg School, communication occurs as an act of reciprocal self-reflection between one consciousness and another, in which each consciousness constructs the conditions of its own autonomy as reciprocally dependent on that of another, so realizing itself as an autonomously pure will—which then becomes the ground of valid law (*ERW* 201). For Jaspers, in contrast, communication does not refer consciousness to the prior conditions of its autonomy, but it discloses to it the lived contents of its possible freedom, and so frees it from any primary legislative base. Communication, in other words, is always the freely metaphysical openness of consciousness to those contents which cannot be internally derived from its own autonomous acts. Jaspers' early approach to the question of humanism therefore directly subverted all common perspectives in the Kantian legacy. Most especially, however, he suggested that the customary interpretation of humanity as a post-metaphysical capacity for self-authorship and self-legislation negates the innermost ideas and possibilities of human-being.

After World War I, in short, Jaspers belonged to a line of thinking which took its lead from a rejection of legal humanism and political humanism, and which argued that existential self-realization occurs, largely, in independence of law and politics. This theoretical lineage reflected a suspicion that the struggle against metaphysical heteronomy under the practical-rational banner of Kantian legal autonomy had led to a fateful curtailment of authentic human freedoms and human experiences. In consequence, this philosophical line opted squarely for metaphysical epistemology, for culture, and especially for religiously and metaphysically informed culture, as the elusive ground of human freedom, and of humanism itself.

Notwithstanding this seeming anti-practical and anti-political reflex, however, Jaspers' early metaphysical thinking still hinges on an argument which, in my view, has crucial implications for legal and political thought. This, namely, is the claim that autonomy is not the same as freedom, and that freedom cannot be made static in the juridical operations of consciousness or in the institutions prescribed by these. Autonomy alone, Jaspers might be seen to intimate, provides only for vainly abstracted accounts of human self-realization, endlessly referring human reason back to what it already is. Freedom, however, is an expansive and deferred metaphysical condition, fleetingly present in ciphers and in the authentic communication at the limits of established autonomy. The demand of practical reason is, therefore, that human beings should be authenticated only as agents who postulate the prior conditions of practical autonomy, and who exclude from themselves all contents which deflect from this autonomy, ultimately only offers a most depleted account of human being. In fact, such humanity is inhuman, and the political forms which express such inhuman humanity cannot represent the most essential freedoms of human-being. For the early Jaspers, therefore, as in fact also for Adorno, humanity cannot be conceived entirely without metaphysics; humanity always contains a metaphysical component, which indicates humanity as difference from its own autonomy. Owing to his aversion to practical-rational models of authentic being, Jaspers' account of human freedom and authenticity is always articulated through a very depoliticized vision of social order. In fact, apart from his allusions to the necessity of ideal-political or cultural elites, the earlier metaphysical Jaspers barely touched on the actual configuration of the good polity. However, it is precisely because he was prepared to abdicate the common field (practical reason) of post-Kantian humanism, and to aim instead at a metaphysical-epistemological theory of truthful human existence, that he was able to develop this crucial, and surreptitiously practical-political, argument.

The *après-guerre* and the Cold War: A Change of Consciousness

After World War II, Jaspers' understanding of humanism underwent certain clear modifications. In his very first writings after 1945, especially *Die Schuldfrage*, he appeared keen to resuscitate a culturally orientated humanism. However, in his influential writings of the 1950s, marked by the experience of World War II and shadowed by the onset of the Cold War and by the threat of nuclear conflict, certain perspectives begin to emerge which indicated that his thought was being drawn to more standard post-Kantian humanist political arguments and to more familiar positions in post-metaphysical political philosophy. Above all, at this stage Jaspers attempted to give a much more determinate and responsible account of legal and political existence than in his earlier works, and to avoid the metaphysical exuberance arising from the previous experience of military defeat in Germany.

Even after 1945, certain central ideas of Jaspers' work still survived from 1920s to 1930s. As in *Die geistige Situation der Zeit*, the fundamental reflex in Jaspers' later political thought was still to define acceptable political order as a "minimal state," which guarantees and preserves space for cultural interaction and communication, but which does not intervene excessively in such processes. Indeed, excessive political regulation is always shown to characterize states which are beginning to demonstrate totalitarian features. As in his earlier works, therefore, Jaspers continued to argue that politics itself is not the highest intellectual resource or the highest expression of human spirit, and he was still only willing to offer an extremely cautious theory of democracy. He claimed still that too much democracy, as popular sovereignty, or excessively extensive politicization of properly non-political arenas of social exchange, are always likely to lead to the erosion of democratic substance.[16] The active component of democratic formation is, therefore, given only nominal treatment in his post-1945 analysis of the necessity of democracy, and he remained very skeptical about organs of political coordination, especially political parties. The greatest importance of a democratic polity is in fact merely its idea of itself: the central component of democracy is "the idea of democracy" (AZ 277), through which it gives scope and content to the "path of reason" (AZ 280) and to the practical ideas of freedom in human consciousness. Most questionably, Jaspers never abandoned his earlier approving attitude to government by quasi-charismatic statesmen, bolstered by processes of elite-training and political selection (AZ 239, 293). In fact, he expressly persisted in claiming after 1945 that the foundation of democracy is, not "the visible organization, the community in institutions," but the "community of the reasonable," i.e. government by benign and reasonable elites who give shape to moral ideas and exercise a pedagogic influence on the people (AZ 187, 294).

Despite his cautious view on democracy, however, the extent of Jaspers' political transformation in his late political writings was surely evident in his willingness, like other thinkers in the 1950s, to tone down his earlier metaphysical interpretation of Kant, to accept original Kantian positions on legality, citizenship and political form, and, above all, to follow Kant in viewing legitimate political order as a truly valid representation of authentically realized human beings. More specifically, his political positions of the 1950s show a much more positive evaluation of Kant's practical reason than his earlier thinking, and the theory of "existential reason" or "existential communication" which he earlier distilled from pure reason were transposed here into a doctrine of political communication or communicative citizenship, in which reason is—at least ostensibly—integrally implicated in the shaping of political order.

Owing to this change of mind about Kant, the fundamental thrust of Jaspers' late work is to oppose and counteract all types of totalitarian governance, and to outline humanist alternatives (either rational, cultural or legal-ethical) to the dogmatic certainties of ideology (Totalwissen) and to the corrosive influence of technical reason and technological politics, all of which, he argued, threaten to bring about universal destruction in the Cold War. On a direct continuum with Kant, therefore, his late work favors the rule of law as the essential guarantor of national and international socio-cultural order. At times, it gives privilege to the legal state, built on a catalogue of basic rights, over the cultural state (AZ 275). It also aims at the institution of the international rule of law, envisaging a confederation of free states with neutral centers of legal accountability and sanction (AZ 86). These ideas are at the core of

---

[16] Karl Jaspers, *Die Atombombe und die Zukunft des Menschen* (Munich: DTV, 1961), p. 279. [Henceforth cited as *AZ*]

Jaspers' conception of "new politics", based on a limitation of national sovereignty, overcoming dogmatic distinctions of friend and foe, and directed towards peaceful international communication (*AZ* 327). With these aims in mind, Jaspers' late political works envision the acceptable polity as one which is guided by universal ethical or "supra-political" principles (*AZ* 209), and which represents a "political ethos" or a set of principles which inform politics and to which politics gives content, but which are not themselves intrinsically the results of political interaction or debate (*AZ* 328).

In more specifically institutional terms, the later Jaspers viewed legitimate democratic government as hinging on a constitution containing programmatic rights, and reflecting overarching ethical decisions, to which all subsequent decisions and, indeed, all political interactions are referred. Constitutional representation is therefore a crucial hallmark of stable democratic societies. In this, to be sure, Jaspers differed from more usual accounts of representative government as representation of the general will or of the particular interests of the people. Instead, he claimed that the state is most truly legitimate, and most truly representative, when it gives authentic shape to the moral ideas of human practical consciousness, which then provide a guide to human reason and a manifestation of its ideal contents and potentials (*AZ* 272). Therefore, if Jaspers' late model of democracy plays down the aspect of foundation and participation characteristic of pure-republican types of democracy, and if it also limits the regulatory functions of democratic systems usually championed in social-democratic accounts of democracy, it gives especial priority to the ethical-representative nature of democratic governance, and to the state as moral-legal person: it might therefore be classified as a theory of "pedagogic democracy."

At this point, Jaspers came close to a limited doctrine of constitutional patriotism or existential republicanism, in which the constitutionally inscribed laws of state define a normative framework for civic identity-formation, based in responsibility, tolerance, non-dogmatic universality and repugnance towards prejudice (*AZ* 277). At this juncture, to a large extent, he abandoned the existential relativization of politics which colors his earlier thinking, and he became much more skeptical about the endorsement of extreme existential experiences at the expense of commonly shaped order (*AZ* 278). Here, human self-experience is closely linked to political ideas and legal-constitutional forms, so that valid existence is construed as the conferring of lived content on political ideas, namely, on the ideas of democracy and legally enshrined freedom. "The democratic idea," Jaspers explained, "is founded in the task of the person to realize himself in reason" (*AZ* 281). Indeed, it is only through the practically manifest idea of democracy that cultural "rebirth from the origin of the Western tradition" might be possible (*AZ* 293).

However, this tone of existential constitutionalism should not, in my view, be taken to mean that the late Jaspers was an eminently political philosopher. By emphasizing the ideal nature of democratic and constitutional forms, he still remained, in many respects, an advocate of de-politicization, and he still adhered to many typically nineteenth-century conceptions of the state as a transcendent concretion of common ethical life, framed in minimal yet binding moral laws. Indeed, it might be argued that Jaspers' transition from metaphysical philosophy to practical philosophy was not fully or convincingly accomplished in these late works, and his earlier metaphysical reconstruction of Kant's doctrine of pure reason still intrudes rather awkwardly in his later practical-philosophical reflections. Even in the late work the exercise of practical reason, in the communications of citizens, does not possess that defining characteristic which Kant imputes to practical rationality: namely, that it is constitutive of the *laws* which frame the legitimate polity and that it can hold the political apparatus to account where it deviates from these laws. As discussed, Jaspers explained reasonable democracy and its constitution, guaranteeing rational rights and freedoms, as an idea which might appear at the limits of existing political consciousness, and which might then guide political consciousness as a non-materialized regulative. But ideas of this kind are not materially produced by public reason as documents of its own autonomy, as prescriptions on which it can practically and with evidential justification insist, or even as manifest conditions of its freedom. In certain respects, therefore, Jaspers' later political conversion still produces an outlook that interprets the operations of practical reason on a conceptual scheme deduced from his early metaphysical interpretation of pure reason: that is, as an account of the practical-metaphysical self-realization and self-interpretation of consciousness. Most importantly, the later Jaspers still retreated from the key anthropological assertion of the practical-rational line of Kant-reception namely, that human beings authenticate themselves by producing laws and by instituting these laws as the sole legitimate source of political power. Instead of this, he upheld his earlier claim, although now with a practical intonation, that human beings become authentic through their own ideal self-disclosure. Even in his very last writings, when his thinking closely followed the radicalization of political discourse in the Federal Republic of the 1960s, his political critiques (i.e. his condemnation of the emergency laws of 1968 and his rejection of the demand for unification as a party-political prerogative) still draw more on transcendental-ethical considerations than on directly political or legal perspectives.

It is therefore not difficult to see major problems in Jaspers' late political thought. Clearly, there are moments in his later thought which are indelibly marked by a great skepticism towards mass-democracy, resulting presumably from his own experiences of the possible results of political massification between the late 1920s and 1945. More fundamentally, though, there are also instances where his early metaphysical reflections sit incongruously with his later ideas on law and politics—especially because his metaphysical views hinge on the claim that human freedom cannot be reduced to law or politics. More critically, in fact, it might also be argued that the theoretical strength of Jaspers' earlier philosophy resides precisely in the fact that it refuses to stabilize the freedom of human-being around statically juridical, scientific or anthropological ideas of the person, and it insists on the irreducibly antinomical or metaphysical alterity of human freedom to its instituted forms. This provides a dynamic and dialectical perspective from which he was able effectively to criticize false dogma and easily satisfied political visions in the works of his critics and opponents. In his late work, however, Jaspers clearly tries to give a more expansive and more concrete description of what being human or being free might practically and politically entail, and he endeavored to politicize his idea of the authentically existing person by locating it at the creative-communicative center of political order. However, after 1945 it seems that Jaspers, for quite obvious reasons, was reluctant to endorse an existential-democratic or even agonistic-antinomical account of political foundation, which might naturally have emerged from a thorough politicization of his earlier philosophy, and, in consequence, his initial metaphysical conception of authentic human freedom proved very difficult to integrate into a notion of the human being as an active citizen. The result of this, then, was that he merely transferred his earlier existential and metaphysical ideas into a thinly universalized or quasi-transcendent quality of "humanity" or "freedom," which, stripped of all antinomical or even existential character, he imputed as the basis of legitimately representative politics.

We might therefore tentatively speak of a failure of politicization in Jaspers' late works. These writings forfeit some of the most important elements of his earlier existential-metaphysical work, yet (in my view, at least) they do not profit from this sacrifice by plausibly installing the person, as citizen, at the center of political order. The path from metaphysics to politics remains rather inconclusive, and the late works are suspended rather unhappily between metaphysics and politics, without effecting a fusion of the two. In practical terms, authentic human being emerges in Jaspers' late thought only as a general condition of cultural interaction and non-technical communication, beneath a guaranteed legal order, protected from excessive political engagement by the political influence of benign elites. It is only in the laws and actions of these elites that the ideas of human freedom obtain fully palpable form, and that the idea of democracy can figure as an active regulative for human self-reflection. Even for the late Jaspers, therefore, political legitimacy and political freedom are still secured only by a limitation of politics against itself, and legitimate democracy is defined solely by its ethical, transcendental, or transcendent content. The greater political specificity of Jaspers' late thought is, in sum, not necessarily a theoretical advantage. Indeed, it might in some ways be seen as a deficiency; for even in those works which directly treat questions of politics and law, politics and law remain, ultimately, restricted in their scope and influence. Law, to be sure, provides "reliability" which "makes common life possible," but it can only be "external" next to the true "dependability" provided by "reasonable communication" (*AZ* 183). Likewise, political organization cannot give full expression to reason. Reason, as such, "is not organized" and it is not "localized as authority" (*AZ* 214). What, then, we might ask, can reason actually do?

More sympathetically, though, perhaps the most far-reaching political significance of Jaspers' late work is demonstrated in his attacks on technology and political technocracy. On technology, he obviously directed his polemics against the purely strategic deployment of scientific knowledge in politics, detached from all broader cultural and ethical considerations. He clearly construed this as one cause both of the political triumph of the National Socialists and of the Cold War. On the question of technocratic governance, he turned vehemently against restorative political thinkers the early years of the Federal Republic. Above all, he aimed his critique at the technocratic theorists of the 1950s, who disconnected political foundation from representative principles, and who thus saw legitimacy as a simple technical variable in the operative self-reproduction of the political system.

In the 1950s this category of theorist included Hans Freyer, Arnold Gehlen, Helmut Schelsky, and Ernst Forsthoff, although Niklas Luhmann eventually also emerged from this lineage. All of these thinkers were acutely contaminated, more or less, by their association with the National Socialist Party. All of these thinkers described the restoration of the political system in the Federal Republic in terms which, to Jaspers' perspective, deliberately omitted the necessity to stress a radical reformulation of political ethics. All also tended to view the operations of the political apparatus in semi-authoritarian terms, limiting the rational or active input of citizens to a functional minimum, and often openly advocating government by semi-accountable executive elites. All, in sum, interpreted political order as a mere process of problem-solving, administrative self-reproduction and technical self-stabilization, and they construed legitimacy, not as representation, but, at most, as a demonstration of managerial or technological competence. For Jaspers, all such thinkers were guilty of the unforgivable mistake of defining the mere "means" of politics—the technical apparatus itself—as the actual "end" of politics, and so of transforming the human being—the true "end" of politics—into a neutral factor in the mechanics of systemic self-perpetuation (*AZ* 149). For Jaspers, therefore, technocratic theorists of governance are always, expressly or implicitly, on the side of totalitarianism, and they all more or less directly collude with the forces of technical and military rationalization which threaten moral and political culture. Most fundamentally, all technological and technocratic thinking obstructs Jaspers' great hope for a decisive reorientation of humanity on the ground of its cultural and ethical-rational resources.

At times, Jaspers was on slightly shaky ground with this antagonism towards technocratic political principles. As discussed, he himself did not provide for a model of active political participation, and he only offered an ethical or transcendental account of political legitimacy. It was, consequently, not easy for him to denounce the technocratic theorists for their exclusion of mass participation from the polity, or for their limitation of political consensus to the level of a functional variable. His own model of elite-democracy in fact shows a degree of common ground between himself and certain more openly authoritarian technocratic theorists. Despite this, however, Jaspers' insistence that political democracy cannot merely withdraw from representative accountability, and that a political system is most legitimate when it discloses its origins in ideal human nature, does surely provide an adequate foundation for a rejection of technocracy. Likewise, his interpretation of politics as a set of processes centered on (and limited by) "the purposes of the existential well-being of the human being" offers an important check on technical-democratic political models, which relegate or instrumentalize human beings as mere bearers of functional sequences (*AZ* 151). Most importantly, his sense that political order is only valid if it rejects all total knowledge of political necessity and if it reflects itself as limited by higher forms of ethical life surely directly undermines any political system which claims objective legitimacy for itself, or which views its legitimacy, in a technocratic manner, as a given reflection of its own functions.

To conclude this section, therefore, it seems clear enough that after 1945 Jaspers, however problematically, renounced some of his most central earlier views. These include his relative indifference to politics and law as spheres of human self-realization, his privileging of pure reason over practical reason in his reception of Kant, and his subordination of ethical-political questions to metaphysical and epistemological debate. Perhaps it might be assumed that Jaspers came to regret his own metaphysical depreciation of political life after World War I, and that after World War II he linked the widespread metaphysical rhapsody of the 1920s to the sad lack of democratic substance which beleaguered the first German democracy. In any case, it seems quite clear that Jaspers' thinking was directly marked by his experience of war and of the threat of war during and after the National Socialist dictatorship, and that the wars he witnessed impacted immediately and distinctly on his approach to the questions of humanism, politics, law, religion, culture, and metaphysics.

As discussed, it is not difficult to pick holes in Jaspers' late political thought. Apart from the obvious merit of their contribution to the revitalization of democratic debate in post-war Germany, however, it is also possible to identify several ideas in these works which retained some value well beyond the extremely cautious climate of the 1950s and which actually set the foundation for important later innovations in political theory. These aspects include the following points: first, his attempt to separate and preserve a sphere of non-administered interaction from corporate, technical, and scientific regulation; second, his insistence on non-administered interaction and tolerant communication as basic resources of democracy; third, his attachment to the constitution as an ethical semantic in which the moral contents of citizenship can be defined, enacted and internalized; fourth, his resolute opposition to all political perspectives which claim a full or ideological monopoly of truth; fifth, his rejection of all political systems which distil legitimacy from their own functional exigencies or which proclaim legitimacy as an instituted component of their own operations. On these grounds, it is at least arguable that Jaspers' work informed all important theoretical positions in post-1945 German political theory which negate simply technical or prerogative accounts of legitimate order: his works most surely set the tone for all subsequent outlooks within a broadly humanist tradition of political reflection.

Jaspers' Later Politics Reconsidered

In many respects, Jaspers' political writings of the 1950s have proven to be very inimical to his general theoretical reputation. This results in part from the extreme hostility towards them displayed in the attitudes of the leading representatives of the post-1945 German Left, especially Lukács, Bloch, Adorno, Horkheimer, and—to a lesser degree and with a stronger sense of indebtedness—Habermas. However, his case for consideration as a front-line political theorist has also suffered because of his initial clear support for Adenauer and Erhard, and because of his enthusiasm for their policies regarding the Western Alliance and the social market economy. More broadly, though, his connection with the 1950s, a period of German intellectual history long perceived as bereft of serious theoretical commentary, has also been major obstacle for attempts to urge a re-evaluation of Jaspers as political thinker. In fact, however perverse it may appear, the decline of Jaspers' political reputation is in part due precisely to the fact that he was such a noteworthy opponent of the Nazis and that he then set out his stall for cautious policies of democratization after 1945. Theorists as badly compromised as Heidegger and Schmitt are now often the objects of fervent admiration, and the standing of Lukács as a topic for constant discussion, has not been damaged by his nefarious political associations. In many cases, thinkers tainted by extreme political affiliations carry a touch of intellectual danger and glamour which attracts modern readers, whereas thinkers who merely provided a theoretical underpinning for modern-style liberal democracies do not benefit from such dubious charm.

Naturally, though, the marginal appeal of Jaspers' political works is not only the result of contagion. The elite-democratic perspective, the extreme reserve towards the participatory aspect of democratic foundation, and the tone of pedagogic admonishment in these writings mark them clearly as belonging to a period of extremely precarious and uncertain re-foundation, and this stands in the way of their positive reception as a whole. Indeed, even those contemporary readers who are willing to speak enthusiastically for a new interpretation of Jaspers as a political thinker usually do adopt an attitude of theoretical filtration to these works, sieving out the apparent high-handedness and elitist personalism.

In my view, nonetheless, there are certain political implications contained in Jaspers' late work, which are not fully drawn out in his own express political pronouncements, but which might be reconstructed as challenging and quite radical supplements to established and orthodox perspectives in contemporary political reflection.

These implications are outlined as follows, although there are surely other implications which might equally be included here:

• Jaspers argued for a polity based around communication, in which the certainty of argument is always transcendentally obviated by the knowledge of each consciousness that it is limited by other consciousness, and that disclosure of its own truth hinges on its alteration and relativization by others. Here, Jaspers' work contains a direct similarity with that of the early Habermas, and he obviously anticipated Habermas in certain ways. However, Jaspers' account of democratic communication as communication on the ground of a deferred idea, the idea of human democratic freedom, actually provides for a more radical and vital climate of political discourse than Habermas's doctrine of legislative speech acts. The true polity, for Jaspers, cannot be derived from certain prior capacities for consensus-finding or practical legislation, and he imagined instead a political reality of constant re-figuration and discursive transformation, in which the truth of communication is always both present and withheld. It is, in my view, perhaps to be lamented that Jaspers hedged this transcendental-communicative model of politics into such a defensive conception of democracy, and that he chose not to explicate its possibilities for theories of committed political foundation. Equally, in my view, it is regrettable that the implicit notion of the relation between theory and praxis in this perspective, which explains theoretical ideas as emerging from and guiding practical communication, not as conferring categorical value upon it, was not placed more firmly at the center of a doctrine of political existence. If stripped of the defensive connotations which it carries in his own work, in short, Jaspers' idea of transcendent and transcendental communication might provide the basis for a most important intervention in contemporary political debate. Indeed, his suggestion that legitimacy and representation are not the origin of democratic power, but its task and objective, remains a tantalizingly unexplored view in political theory.

- Jaspers' political thought imagines the reality of political exchange as essentially antinomical; that is, he claimed that true political discourse, albeit within a minimal legal-constitutional fabric, always refers itself to new antinomies, new limits and new ideas on the way to the idea of freedom. Unlike his interlocutors on left and right, therefore, Jaspers accounts for the epistemological underpinning of political life not by projecting a static model of human consciousness endowed with certain capacities and certain needs, which might be satisfied by instituted political forms or principles. Authentic consciousness, he observed, can never settle into finally stable or enduring prescriptions, and it remains ceaselessly self-interpreting and self-communicating. In my view, it is truly a great shame that Jaspers did not make more of this argument, and that he did not base his analysis of political order on this concept of antinomical consciousness.

- As discussed, one most important implication in these points is that, in his metaphysical reading of Kant, Jaspers, once more like Adorno, suggested that "autonomy," as envisaged by practical reason, is not the same as "freedom."[17] Autonomy, construed as the reality of human cognitive and practical self-legislation, is in fact a timelessly empty and recurrent condition, in which the most essential and most liberating contents of authentic experience are ostracized from human consciousness by its demand for internally consistent self-causation. Freedom, in contrast, is a reality of change and transformation, in which the true contents of consciousness are always being communicated, never finally accounted for. This idea is at the heart of Jaspers' early work, and it also informs his later political thinking, with its reluctance to cement political foundation and legitimacy in categorically instituted terms. Unfortunately, though, once again this most vital political insight is not really pursued to its full conclusiveness, and the consequences of Jaspers' thinking for a politics of freedom, not of autonomy,

---

[17] I remain intrigued by the relation between Jaspers and Adorno, and I suggest that Jaspers' metaphysical and experiential reading of Kant might easily be seen as reflecting and sharing ground with the critique of pure immanence in Adorno's negative dialectics. See my attempt to make sense of this in Karl Jaspers and Theodor W. Adorno, "The Metaphysics of the Human," in *History of European Ideas*, 31/1 (2005), pp. 61–84.

can only be guessed at. However, we might perhaps surmise that, as Jaspers saw freedom as communication, he might also have seen political communication as a process which founds and re-founds political freedom as something quite radically other than an expression of prior rights, prior autonomy and prior self-ownership. A politics of spoken freedom thus seems to be hovering just below the lines of Jaspers' political thought; indeed, it is inchoately manifest in his idea of communication on the ground of the democratic idea. If tied to a more pressing insistence on the constitutive role of political communication, this argument, in my view, would form a key position in modern debates on political humanism. The intimation here that human being and human freedom are always temporally and communicatively contested and unfinished might even assist the elaboration of a humanism which would evade the common post-structural allegation that humanism always imposes reductive or simplificatory categories on our intensely plural sense of what it means to be human.

• Jaspers' political thought also deserves very serious reconsideration for the manner in which it combines a theory of decisionism with a theory of difference and tolerance. He argued that authentic consciousness is consciousness which follows intensely individualized directives; indeed, authentic consciousness is defined as such by its unconditionedness, by its confrontation with the limits of its given forms, and by its decision to overcome these by acting without any external regulation. Unlike other models of decisionism in twentieth-century Germany, however, Jaspers' idea of unconditioned action outlines a theory of decisionism which is always expressly for tolerance. Each unconditioned decision is defined and authenticated as such only by the extent to which it senses and communicates itself as limited by other possible decisions, and so as limited in itself. As the decision arises from the confrontation of consciousness with its limits, each decision always holds the possibility of other limits and other decisions. On this basis, the concept of self-overcoming consciousness in Jaspers's philosophy might be seen to provide a quite unique model, however paradoxically, for a politics of intense tolerance and decisively democratic plurality. Once again, the full impact of these ideas is offset by the extent to which in the 1950s Jaspers underplayed the formative impact of existential experience and interaction on political institutions. Perhaps, though, he might be excused this on historical grounds.

The major point which I wish to make here, or rather the point which encompasses all the above issues, relates to my earlier critical description of Jaspers' later political thought as "a failure of politicization." As discussed, perhaps the greatest problem with these late works is that they revolve around a squared circle, or at least an uneasy compromise, between his early experiential reconstruction of metaphysics and Kantian pure reason and his later commitment to political theory and practical reason. This is especially problematic because at the heart of Jaspers' early metaphysics is a rejection of all interpretations of human consciousness as juridical form and a consequent rejection of human freedom conceived in the medium of law. My point then is merely that, as yet, we lack a reconstruction of both periods of Jaspers' philosophy which might effectively weld the earlier metaphysical insights to a convincing model of shared political life. In my view, Jaspers himself did not quite accomplish this, and the relation between his earlier metaphysics and his later politics is always one of awkwardly unresolved tension.

Conclusion

To conclude, the trajectory of Jaspers' thinking, and especially of his thinking on humanism, was integrally bound up with his experience of wars. In this he was not alone; the same might be said of most major German philosophers and political theorists. In Jaspers' case, however, the impact of war resonates most clearly in his decision sometimes to privilege one aspect of Kantian philosophy and sometimes to privilege a different one as a foundation for a theory of humanism. This means, more specifically, that after World War I his thought condensed a deep hostility to legal universalism, to formalized accounts of humanism, and to legal-political form almost per se; it focused, therefore, on a cultural-metaphysical reconstruction of Kant's theory of pure reason. After World War II, by contrast, this outlook was replaced by a far more sympathetic reading of Kant's doctrine of practical reason. His earlier cultural-metaphysical humanism thus came to sit alongside a theory of politics and law which accentuates their status as integral (yet still limited) domains of human self-realization and self-interpretation.

In my view, however, the late Jaspers did not more fully integrate his ideas on culture, politics, and law into a more encompassing notion of humanism and human political liberty. As discussed, what emerges from his late writings is a challenging, but occasionally rather haphazard overlaying of metaphysical and practical-rational reflections on politics, law, and legitimacy. This is extremely regrettable since, if assimilated to a genuinely practical account of political formation, the earlier ideas of existential communication, of the antinomical unfinishedness of consciousness, and of unconditioned decisions, could lay the groundwork for a very significant re-conception of political humanism. Unfortunately, after his experiences with the Hitler regime and its conclusion in World War II, the possibility of a consistent politicization of Jaspers' earlier existential and metaphysical thought was obstructed by his extreme (and understandable) caution regarding popular democratic responsibility. For this reason, I take issue with his insistent interpretation of democratic forms as universal ideas of consciousness, not as the practically and existentially founded bedrock of the acceptable polity. Wars therefore clearly shaped the development of Jaspers' political humanism; he manifestly saw his humanism as contribution to reflection on how wars might be avoided, and wars determined the course of his thinking between different available models of humanism. However, wars might also be seen to have stood in the way of fully elaborating his humanism.

On Recovering Philosophy: Philosophical Dialogue and Political Philosophy After 9/11

Tom Rockmore

Abstract Once upon a time, it was thought that philosophy was indispensable for the good life. That meant it did not need to justify its continued existence. But this time belongs to the past. Hence it is important to ask, if philosophy is to survive or at least to continue in a meaningful way, whether it still has anything worthwhile to say in an age of globalization. This theme, which is constitutive of Western philosophy, is compounded by the events of 9/11, which, as I write are clearly still with us. This essay will urge two points. On the one hand, I think that we need to take steps to recover philosophy. This is a perennial problem, which does not depend on 9/11, since philosophy is always in the position of needing to justify its social utility. This is not provoked by any specific recent event, but is so to speak always on the agenda, always something philosophers need to wonder about. On the other hand, I think we need to take steps now to begin to recover political philosophy, which, in the wake of 9/11, and for specific reasons, is in danger of becoming simply irrelevant.

On Recovering Western Philosophy

I know too little about Eastern philosophy, which has a long and varied past, to make any specific claims about it. In talking about the need to recover philosophy, I have in mind Western philosophy. Philosophers react differently to this theme. Some are content to assume, with Kant, Husserl and many others, the intrinsic social relevance of philosophy to any and all social concerns; a claim that, if true, would mean that no one would need ever address concrete difficulties. Others are concerned to take up specific themes. Karl Jaspers is, in this respect a shining example of someone who, after the Second World War, was concerned to bring philosophy to bear on concrete

T. Rockmore (✉)
Duquesne University, Pittsburgh, PA, USA
e-mail: rockmore@duq.edu

H. Wautischer et al. (eds.), *Philosophical Faith and the Future of Humanity*,
DOI 10.1007/978-94-007-2223-1_26, © Springer Science+Business Media B.V. 2012

issues, such as the problem of guilt[1] as well as such more specific questions as Martin Heidegger's turn toward Nazism.[2]

At stake is the question of the recovery of philosophy focused on human concerns. This theme can be introduced through reference to John Dewey, the American pragmatist, who, more than eight decades ago, suggested the need for reconstruction in philosophy. In an important book, he argued two main points: first, philosophy grows out of the distinctive affairs of human beings, or, as he vividly said, the stresses and strains of existence; and, second, in wake of the First World War the situation had changed in a way calling for a recasting of philosophy as it was then known.[3]

I think Dewey was both correct and incorrect. He was correct that after the War philosophy needed to be reconstructed. The world had changed and philosophy needed to change as well to continue to remain in touch with it. But he was wrong to think that philosophy only needed to be reconstructed because of the War. Philosophy in general perennially needs to be reconstructed if it is to be relevant to human beings. This is also a time in which philosophy needs to be reconstructed since, after 9/11, there has probably never been another moment in our increasingly globalized world when dialogue and cultural exchange have been more important. At least potentially, philosophy has a significant role to play. And yet, at least from the Western perspective that I know best, the relation of philosophical dialogue to the good life as widely defined remains as elusive as ever.

I will focus on what I detect as the need for philosophical dialogue in relation to knowledge. There is a crucial difference between knowledge, which may or may not result from dialogue, and philosophical dialogue. To bring out my point, I will call attention to the relation between normative conceptions of knowledge and of philosophical dialogue. In philosophy as well as in other pursuits, certain views of knowledge threaten dialogue in tending to transform it into mere monologue. This difficulty, which is extremely general, is present in different ways across a broad spectrum in politics, theology, philosophy and many other domains, each of which in its own way sometimes, but not always aims at knowledge of a kind that impedes or even precludes dialogue.

Now this claim might not be easy to grasp, I will make a few references to the philosophical tradition. A good place to begin might be in considering the obvious question of the usefulness of philosophy other than as a mere end in itself. I have in mind a conception of philosophy that aims to surpass mere debate about philosophical questions, hence the specific interests of the philosophers themselves, in further

---

[1] See Karl Jaspers, *The Question of German Guilt*, trans. E.B. Ashton (New York, NY: The Dial Press, 1947).

[2] Jaspers' relation to Heidegger is complex. Suffice it to say that he was consulted after the war by the Denazification Committee, which denied Heidegger the right to teach, and that in his correspondence he tried unsuccessfully to persuade Heidegger to acknowledge his mistakes. See Martin Heidegger/Karl Jaspers, *Briefwechsel 1920–1963*, eds. Hans Saner and Walter Biemel (Frankfurt: Klostermann, 1990).

[3] See John Dewey, *Reconstruction in Philosophy* (Boston, MA: Beacon Press, 1960).

contributing to the wider community. Since the beginnings of Western philosophy in ancient Greece, it has often been claimed that philosophy is socially useful, even indispensable. There is certainly no reason why we should accept this suggestion on faith. This needs not only to be proclaimed, but also to be shown in some way. An instance is the German phenomenologist Husserl's turn in the early 1930s to philosophy, as it was originally understood in the West as a supposed bulwark against the rise of National Socialism. He recommended a staunch defense of the ancient Greek distinction between opinion (*doxa*) and knowledge (*episteme*) to respond to Nazism understood as the rise of unreason.[4] This is only a recent instance of the view that philosophy is socially useful.

An assertion of the usefulness of philosophy presupposes a view of what philosophy is or at least could be. In this respect, the two main claims seem to be that (1) philosophy is socially indispensable as the minimal condition for the good life however defined, or that (2) philosophy is intrinsically relevant in some undefined way to the good life. Both claims presuppose an unspecified link between the true and the good. According to this view, the good life depends on knowledge. Philosophy is either the sole source of knowledge in the full sense of the term, or, in a slightly different formulation, a source of socially relevant knowledge.

Now knowledge in the full sense of the term is not necessarily socially relevant, nor useful for the good life. The venerable view of the social relevance of philosophy is firmly linked to the supposed usefulness of philosophical dialogue. At the dawn of Western philosophy, Plato depicts Socrates in conversation in texts that have come down to us as dialogues. Socrates is typically depicted as engaged in trying to define specific virtues in debate, which ends without any resolution. It is arguable that without the Socratic concern with ethics, Plato would not have come on his specific theory of knowledge. Be that as it may, though Plato often depicts others in dialogue, after Plato the Socratic dialogical approach was except in rare instances later abandoned in favor of a basically "monological" approach, an approach that may or may not take other views into account in seeking a definitive solution of the problem or problems under consideration.

The later turn away from the early Greek interest in philosophical dialogue is not merely accidental. It is related to a specific philosophical view of knowledge invented after Socrates by Plato. Dialogue is philosophically useful if epistemological claims are not absolute but relative, or limited in some way. In that case, no one claims to know and each of the participants in the debate must search for the truth on the assumption that it will result from free and fair discussion. Different approaches are possible. But most commonly different thinkers suggest that claims to know are not independent of, but rather dependent on context, perspective, point of view, conceptual framework, philosophical tradition, the language in which they are formulated, or in some other identifiable way.

---

[4] See Edmund Husserl, *The Crisis of European Sciences and Transcendental Phenomenology: An Introduction to Phenomenological Philosophy*, trans. with introduction by David Carr (Evanston, IL: Northwestern University Press, 1970), p. 12.

In this respect, there seem to be two views of dialogue I will be calling pseudo-dialogue, and incessant dialogue. Pseudo-dialogue aims at truth that, if it could be attained, would preclude further discussion, hence would lead beyond dialogue to monologue. Pseudo-dialogue aims to bring debate to an end in real time. It assumes philosophy can reach unimpeachable knowledge beyond time and place, which is not susceptible to further revision. Hence, from this perspective philosophical closure, which effectively brings the debate to an end, is always a real possibility. Incessant dialogue aims, on the contrary, at no more than ongoing debate between representatives of different points of view. Since it cannot be brought to a close, for instance by reliably claiming to reach unimpeachable knowledge, it is in principle always ongoing, hence endless. Since no view can ever be shown to be wholly true, and no position can ever reliably claim to leave the need for further debate behind, discussion only begets more discussion. Now these two forms of debate are basically dissimilar. The first view is only apparently dialogical, but potentially monological. Its aim is not further dialogue but rather to bring dialogue to an end in monologue. The second view, which eschews monologue, is dialogical in regarding ongoing, incessant debate, debate that is not terminable but rather interminable, as constitutive of philosophy itself.

These two views of debate rely on different ways of understanding knowledge. The relevant difference lies in normative conceptions of knowledge as either absolute or relative. In the *Republic* Plato draws a distinction between appearance, or the changing world in which we live, and an unchanging world of reality. According to this view, there is a way that reality, or the unchanging world, really is; to know is to know reality as it really is, that is reality beyond mere appearance; and at least some of the time such knowledge of the world as it really is is in fact possible. Plato suggests that on grounds of nature and nurture some exceptional individuals—he calls them philosophers—can literally "see" the invisible real. Some two millennia later, Descartes and Kant aim at a similar result through inventing new methods. According to Kant, such an innovation is the condition of entering on the secure road of science.

Others reject the very model of absolute knowledge in opting for weaker, relativistic claims to know, which are indexed to time and place, for instance a particular cultural background, historical moment, language, culture, religion, or other point of view. A relative claim for knowledge is very different from an absolute claim. There are different cognitive domains in which knowledge is sought. Examples might be physics, mathematics, theology, perhaps poetry, and, depending on the point of view, even philosophy. Cognitive relativism only means that the claim for knowledge is not absolute, hence wholly independent, but is in some way relative. A conception of cognitive relativism is not unusual in many cognitive domains, including the social sciences, and even natural sciences, which revise even the most basic theories from time to time. This is a recurring dream, which is not confined to our particular historical period. It was common late in the nineteenth century, when it was thought by many observers that just about all that one needed to know was in fact already known. This was before the discoveries of relativity theory and quantum mechanics that obliged us to reconstruct modern physics.

But this dream is very difficult to exorcise, since it exerts a permanent fascination. Later observers often think they are brighter than their predecessors. All too often the thought arises that we already have or at least soon will have the last word. This view, which has never entirely disappeared, keeps reappearing at irregular intervals in the discussion. It is even now making the rounds. At least some contemporary scientists believe that we are now getting to the point where it might be possible to formulate a final theory, hence bring the pursuit of science to an end. It seems difficult to believe that even our most cherished views are immune to the possibility of change. Yet I wonder who thinks that 5,000 years from now we will hold the same scientific views? Even the most important advances in science, advances which at the time they are made appear likely to stand forever, are sometimes later refuted. Illustrations might be the change from Newtonian mechanics to relativity theory and quantum mechanics early in the twentieth century. This suggests our claims to know, however well worked out, however carefully formulated, and however strongly held, are later subject to refutation, hence relative. I have in mind, as early mentioned, the view that claims to know are finally relative to what we believe in a given historical moment, hence historically relative.

Relativism about knowledge has long been out of favor, since we like to be able to say that we know in some final sense. Yet in most spheres of knowledge, a view of relativism about knowledge later comes into the picture at some point and in some way. In most cases, there is an ongoing contest between the immodest conviction that certain views are literally untouchable, hence cannot be revised under any circumstances, and the competing conviction that either a particular view can be changed or, more generally, that no view, none whatsoever, is in principle beyond revision. Yet a relativist conception of knowledge is unusual in Western philosophy. Ever since early in the Greek tradition, a succession of important thinkers has defended variations on the view that philosophical claims to know are not relative in any way but absolute, in a word demonstrable once and for all, not to be modified under any circumstances. It is then hardly surprising that important thinkers like Descartes, as mentioned, and Kant, construct their theories on the assumption that they are immune from any later change under any circumstances.

There are numerous exceptions among the philosophers to the immodest claim to know in a final, unrevisable way. The German polymath, Leibniz, formulates an early form of relativism. He believes that each of us looks at the world from a different perspective, from a different point of view. In the middle of the nineteenth century, Humboldt and Herder argue in different ways that claims to know are indexed to language and culture. Peirce, the inventor of pragmatism, thinks that knowledge claims are always subject to revision. But Western philosophy has mainly favored stronger, non-relative, allegedly apodictic cognitive claims.

Many things could be said about the idea of an unrevisable conception of knowledge. Philosophy since Plato, if not earlier, has been committed to the view that knowledge must be absolute, not relative. It typically resists relativistic epistemological claims on the basis of a specific ontological commitment, or a claim about what is, which goes all the way back to early Greek philosophy and forward to many present-day thinkers. These and many other thinkers are committed to the idea that to know means to know the way the world is, or in more technical language, to know the mind-independent world as it is, or again the world beyond appearance as it is in itself. This view is widely present in the contemporary debate, especially in analytic philosophers such as Putnam and Davidson, but also in such continental thinkers as Husserl and Heidegger. In different ways each of them features a version of the ancient Greek conception of knowledge as knowing the world as it really is.

This view, which is often called metaphysical realism, is perhaps natural but not necessary, hence no more than normative. Claims for knowledge routinely aim at knowledge of the real. Yet there are different forms of realism, different ways to formulate the claim for reality as an object of cognition. Metaphysical realism, which is widely accepted as the standard of knowledge, is simply incompatible with any form of relativism, including philosophical dialogue.

The underlying principle of philosophical dialogue is that there is something to be learned by debating with others. Yet if one can reliably claim to know the way the mind-independent world is in a way beyond doubt of any kind, then one does not have to settle for merely relative knowledge. Put another way, an absolute cognitive commitment suppresses the interest of philosophical dialogue, which becomes pointless, a waste of time, not productive, without any redeeming philosophical value. If we can be certain that either we already know or will some day know or at least in principle can know in a way that will never need revision, it is useless to conduct a dialogue in order to learn from someone else, mere false humility to pretend to weigh the merits of views different from our own. To put the point bluntly: if one really knows that one knows, then dialogue of any kind is pointless. If we know that we know, we can enter into discussion with someone else to explain what we already know. But we cannot embark with that person on a search for truth if we already have it. At most we can consent to explain to someone else what we already know but we cannot enter into dialogue.

The belief in absolute knowledge is frequent but unjustified. There is, in this respect, little difference between absolutist claims for knowledge of the trained philosopher and the naïve conviction of the ordinary, untrained individual, the person without philosophical training or sophistication. Both the philosophically untrained individual and the trained philosopher believe there is something akin to absolute, unrevisable knowledge, and that in the right circumstances there is access to it. The difference between them mainly lies in the fact that the ordinary person merely asserts this claim dogmatically, that is without what could plausibly count as a philosophical justification. But the philosopher believes it on the assumption one can in fact prove that one knows in an absolute, unrestricted way, in a way, as the phrase goes, beyond time and place.

Theory of knowledge, a main concern in the Western philosophical tradition, is routinely understood as leading to an ongoing effort by numerous talented individuals over many centuries to identify the conditions of knowledge of the way the mind-independent world is. Many of the participants in this discussion agree that we either do or at least can potentially claim to know the world as it is. Epistemological debate mainly turns on finding a convincing argument to demonstrate this point. Yet, and despite intensive study by many talented individuals, there is still not and probably never will be any single generally accepted approach to theory of knowledge understood in this or indeed any other way. Despite our best efforts over some two and a half millennia, nothing resembling consensus has yet emerged from the discussion.

It might be useful to say a word about the various roads to knowledge. Three main strategies for knowledge include epistemological intuitionism, epistemological foundationalism, and the causal theory of perception. Epistemological intuitionism is widespread in ancient philosophy, for instance in Plato and Aristotle. But since intuition is private, it is not public; hence it is not shared. For this reason, a theory of knowledge based on intuition is infrequent in the modern debate, which turns away from private, hence in principle unverifiable knowledge claims. In modern philosophy, Spinoza, who still relies on intuition, is an exception. Roughly since the middle of the seventeenth century, epistemological intuitionism has been largely replaced by epistemological foundationalism. This is an ancient approach, which Descartes refocused in modern times in a particularly influential way as a strategy that, when correctly applied, supposedly leads to apodictic knowledge of the world as it, in fact, really is.

Cartesian foundationalism invokes an analogy between a building and a theory of knowledge. This strategy consists in placing the discussion of knowledge on a so-called foundation, or allegedly unshakeable structure underlying and supporting the theory constructed upon it. Foundationalism, which is popular, though not always under that name, is formulated in many different ways. In the Cartesian formulation, it is based on an initial principle, known to be true without reference to any further principles, and from which the remainder of the theory can be rigorously deduced. Suffice it to say that this strategy is still very popular. Yet despite his best efforts, Descartes was unable to show that, to use his terminology, ideas in the mind correctly grasp material things outside the mind. And centuries of effort to improve his argument have been failed to demonstrate that we in fact ever bring the mind in touch with the world.

Cartesian foundationalism is related to the widespread, influential causal theory of perception widespread in modern philosophy. Both the continental rationalists and the British empiricists are committed to the overall thesis that ideas in the mind, what Kant later calls appearances, are caused by the mind-independent world. From both perspectives, a solution to the problem of knowledge lies in the reverse inference from ideas to the world, or from the effect to the cause. In the final analysis, modern philosophy from Descartes to Kant is dominated by the assumption that the world, which supposedly causes our ideas about it, can be known through some form of this reverse influence. The Cartesian belief that clear and distinct ideas are true and the very different Lockean conviction that simple ideas necessarily match up one to one with the world overlap on this crucial epistemological point.

Kant provides a new focus for the epistemological problem. It is not often noted that he inconsistently defends two incompatible strategies for knowledge: a representationalist approach based on the analysis of representations to objects, and a constructivist approach centering on the claim we can only reliably claim to know what we in some way "construct." Kantian representationalism is arguably the most sophisticated form of the causal theory of perception, a form never later surpassed, which consists in the relation of representations to objects, which are said to appear to an observer. Representationalism relies on a correspondence theory of truth. In such a theory, we can say we know if and only if the representation, or idea in the mind, corresponds to objects outside the mind. Kant's constructivism, which illustrates a different strategy for knowledge, substitutes for the failure of his representational model, and indeed any form of a causal theory of perception, that is, any strategy to demonstrate that we know the mind-independent world as it is.

Kantian constructivism is another name for Kant's celebrated Copernican revolution in philosophy. Kant never uses this term to refer to his position, which observers in his own time applied to his theory. Kant's Copernican revolution consists in two main claims. First, we do not and cannot know that we know mind-independent objects. This claim undercuts any form of the causal theory of perception. Kant experiments with representationalism before coming to the conclusion that there is no way to show that ideas in the mind correctly grasp, represent, or otherwise reliably tell us about the way the world really is. It follows that for Kant the solution to the problem of knowledge cannot lie in saying that we uncover, discover, reveal, or find what we claim to know. Second, his main insight is that we can only know what we in some sense "construct." Kant's constructivist approach to knowledge lies in claiming that we produce, construct, or make what we know as a condition of knowing it.

Hegel's conception of philosophy as the thoughtful grasp of its own time[5] suggests it is situated within and belongs to the social context. This thesis is countered by the widely known claim that the philosopher is in time but not of time, or independent of time and place. This rival claim derives from the widespread commitment to knowledge from no perspective at all. As soon as this supposition is abandoned, two things immediately become clear. On the one hand, all philosophers consciously or more often unconsciously think out of their time and place. On the other hand, claims to know are formulated within and influenced by prevailing views, the so-called *Weltanschauung*, or *Zeitgeist*, or again the normative conception of philosophy holding sway within a particular historical moment.

This point is crucially important. It is a mistake to think we can reliably identify the only possible approach to knowledge. There seems to be no way to formulate a theory without presuppositions, which are in turn always contestable by other thinkers. A normative conception of philosophy as not independent of, but rather as dependent on, the wider cultural context which opens the way to consider the relevance of other approaches. If claims to know are irrelative, or absolute, there is no point in dialoguing with other cultures, which are perhaps interesting but philosophically irrelevant. But they become relevant as soon as we re-conceive philosophy in relation to its context.

---

[5] See G.W.F. Hegel, *Philosophy of Right*, trans. T.M. Knox (London: Oxford University Press, 1967), p. 13.

I would like now to illustrate this claim as concerns the view of art and art objects, and with respect to the philosophical conception of knowledge. Over time, someone interested in Western art can master the Western canon. Yet to master the Western canon is not to master aesthetics as such, since many forms of art fall outside anything known in the West. Thus one of the first things one discovers in visiting museums in China is that in the East calligraphy is every bit as important as painting. Then there is the collection of the terra cotta warriors (兵马俑, bīngmǎ yǒng) near Xian, the ancient capital. Artistic creation of a very high order is involved in the figures of these soldiers that, since they are unlike anything to be seen in the West, cannot simply be understood in terms of Western criteria, in terms of the Western canon.

The difference between what counts as an art object in Western and Eastern aesthetics corresponds to different views of aesthetics itself. Western aesthetics, which is concerned with the relation between beauty and truth, is in that regard unlike Chinese aesthetics.[6] A simple way to put the point is that Chinese aesthetics recognizes rules and methods (*fa*) to be matched by enlightenment (*wu*) for the purpose of "intuitive mastery." This emphasizes the unity of naturalness and regularity, and stresses living rules (*huo fa*) as against dead rules (*si fa*) in following the so-called rules of nature.[7] Yet at least since Plato, Western aesthetics has been concerned with both beauty as well as truth and knowledge, for instance in imitating nature by following rules, but also, as Kant claims in his view of genius, in going beyond rules in creating new ones. In a letter at the beginning of the twentieth century, the French painter Paul Cezanne says: "I owe you truth in painting and I will tell it to you."[8] The history of Western aesthetics reveals a struggle between partisans of Plato, who claims that art strives for, but fails to attain, truth, and those who, like Cezanne two and a half thousand years later, believe, on the contrary, that art is successful in this task.

The differences in Western and Chinese aesthetics call attention to an important tradition significantly older than the Western one. If Western aesthetics does not exhaust the available ways to consider art and art objects, it becomes interesting to study other, non-Western aesthetic approaches. There is little attention in Western philosophy to Eastern models of knowledge. Yet here as well I imagine there is much to be learned. An example lies in the Daoist idea, contained in the famous first line of the *Dao de jing*: "dao ke dao fei chang dao"—that reality lies beyond language, hence beyond thought, which arguably points toward cognitive relativism.

---

[6] See Li Zehou, *The Path of Beauty: A Study of Chinese Aesthetics*, trans. Gong Lizeng (Hong Kong: Oxford University Press, 1994).

[7] See Karl-Heinz Pohl, "An Intercultural Perspective on Chinese Aesthetics," in *Frontiers of Transculturality in Contemporary Aesthetics. Proceedings Volume of the Intercontinental Conference, University of Bologna, Italy, October 2000*, eds. Grazia Marchianò and Raffaele Milani (Torino: Trauben, 2001), pp. 139–140.

[8] "Je vous dois la vérité en peinture, et je vous la dirai." Lettre of Paul Cezanne to Emile Bernard, dated 25 October 1905, cited in Jacques Derrida, *La Vérité en peinture* (Paris: Flammarion, 1978), p. 6.

I have so far stressed the link between the traditional Western interest in an absolute view of knowledge, understood as a claim to know the way the world is, and the related Western disinterest in philosophical dialogue. Yet no convincing argument has ever been proposed to justify claiming to know the way the world is. Unlike Kant, perhaps we do not wish to embrace constructivism, a strategy that I personally find very appealing. Yet if, as I also believe, one cannot justify claims to absolute knowledge, then knowledge claims should be understood as at best relative, imperfect, fragile, relative to what we now happen to believe. Thus in the seventeenth century, following Newton, it made perfect sense to think that because of gravitation large heavenly bodies like planets follow elliptical orbits. But in the twentieth century it made more sense to believe, following Einstein, that planets move along geodesics within a spatio-temporal gravitational field.

If claims to know are relative to the historical moment, then the best we can do is to apply theories we happen for whatever reason to favor in a given time and place, while awaiting further developments in the discussion. This suggests two points. On the one hand, one should abandon any effort to surpass dialogue in monologue based on the alleged identification of the final view of knowledge whether in philosophy, science, mathematics or in another cognitive discipline. On the other hand, it becomes interesting to dialogue with others outside the Western tradition, whose views, once we give up the pretense of conceptual finality, become relevant to our own.

It is tempting to believe that our most cherished theories are immune to the ravages of time. Yet, as noted above, it may later turn out that most of what we now think will later be abandoned. Dialogue is a way of testing the limits of our theories against other theories. Philosophy is best regarded as hypothetical, hence uncertain, and, for that reason, as perpetually in need of dialogue, never in need of monologue. It has been well said that the history of Western philosophy is comparable to a giant Socratic dialogue in which different perspectives confront each other. To escape the dogmatic "absolutization" of our own current views, there is no alternative to dialogue. The enormous interest of philosophical dialogue in a time of globalization is that for the first time it is really possible to engage in dialogue on the level of the entire world.

Western philosophy is often depicted as the Platonic tradition, hence understood in relation to Plato. Yet under his influence, at least since Greek antiquity Western philosophers have often favored a view of philosophy that excludes the relevance of philosophical dialogue. Socrates, as depicted in Plato's dialogues, examines existential questions while claiming to know only that he knows nothing. Though we do not know Plato's own view and cannot now recover it, in the *Republic* he influentially depicts knowledge as requiring an intuitive grasp of mind-independent reality.

The difference between the two views of philosophy is huge. Socrates comprehends philosophy as dialogue between representatives of different points of view leading to claims that are never absolute and are always indexed to the ongoing discussion, which simply cannot be brought to an end. From this perspective, philosophy engages with, hence is relevant to, the lives of ordinary individuals, whose problems it discusses, and to which it is directly applicable. For a Socratic philosopher, since we never really know, there is no reasonable alternative to debate bringing different hypotheses and their consequences into play. After Socrates, who advances a dialogical view, philosophy changes radically beginning with the Platonic claim to grasp the world, or mind-independent reality, as it is, hence to go beyond the need for dialogue in theories whose relation to the good life is at best tenuous, and often unclear.

Plato features Socratic dialogue, which he implicitly rejects through his absolute conception of knowledge. The influential Platonic view of philosophy as a way to know the real as it is, is compatible with monologue, but incompatible with dialogue. Since there is no prospect of knowing that we know the way the world really is, we do better to focus on debate linked or perhaps better indexed to the ongoing discussion in limiting our claims to know merely to dialogue. I conclude that in returning behind the monological Platonic view of philosophy as grasping the real as it is to the dialogical Socratic conception of philosophy indexed to the ongoing discussion, we can hope to recover a form of philosophy that is socially useful.

9/11 and Political Philosophy in an Age of Globalization

I have been arguing that there is a perpetual need to recover philosophy as dialogue. This need is only strengthened after 9/11 with respect to political philosophy, whose relevance to the contemporary world is questionable. We are still too close to 9/11 to more than dimly grasp its nature and intrinsic significance. I suspect that its importance will later be seen as obvious, as a given, as something one does not need to defend, but only to understand. Yet perhaps a case still needs to be made, right at the beginning, that 9/11 in the wider sense, that is not merely the events on that day but those prior to and after it, and which are still continuing, signals not merely an inconvenience, nor a temporary disruption, nor even a momentary hindrance to business as usual, but rather a basic change.

If that is correct, then I think two points need to be emphasized. First, we must see that the differences, which are real, are not so-called ruptures in the fabric of history, not something wholly new, hence not unknowable. Rather, they are the result of the continuity and maturation of an ongoing historical process, which has not often received the attention it requires and whose results cannot be foreseen but which, as a historical process, can be understood. Second, whatever else it does, political philosophy, if it is to remain relevant to human beings in the historical context, needs to scrutinize and to ponder the historical problem or problems we can designate as 9/11.

The time is ripe for reconstruction in political philosophy for at least three reasons concerning the problem of the general relevance of philosophy to human life, the main thrust of political philosophy in its current form, and specific changes in the political and social world. To begin with, political philosophy, like philosophy itself, is increasingly irrelevant to the real-world concerns of human beings, and mainly relevant at present to the interests of the self-appointed philosophical priesthood.

The first reason concerns the link between philosophical rigor and breadth. The steady emphasis on rigor from, say, Descartes through Kant, and in more recent analytic thinkers, increasingly compensated by an unfortunate lack of breadth, which tends to make it not more but less relevant. It is perhaps too late to recover the very broad traditional conception of philosophy within which political philosophy would have its place. Yet the proliferation of different forms of study of the wider political domain suggests its students do not find room for their interests, which are arguably political, within political philosophy as currently constituted. Interests that fall outside the contemporary paradigm of political philosophy include, in no particular order, black studies, women's studies, Holocaust studies, post-colonial studies, genocide studies, and so on. These concerns are real, not fictitious, arising out of the perception of significant political concerns. Yet unfortunately, but probably correctly, mainstream political philosophy is regarded as too narrow to afford them a place at the conceptual table.

The second reason relates to the deep interest in Western political philosophy in social contractarianism. This approach, based in the fiction of a social contract, which, if freely assented to, justifies a range of themes running from political formations, theories of justice and morality, is favored by some of the most important modern political thinkers, including Hobbes, Locke, Rousseau through Rawls, and more recently others such as Gauthier, Scanlon and Nussbaum. The approach to political philosophy through the device of a social contract is typically linked to the defense of property, a central theme in modern times. A long series of modern philosophers, from Hobbes and Locke through Hegel and Marx to Rawls and Nozick, construct political theories centering on property rights. I do not intend to suggest the formation of a state without property. Yet the theme of property must not usurp nor dominate the entire field of political philosophy to the exclusion of such other themes as happiness and freedom. Nor am I convinced that the fictional device of a social contract is now the most useful way to approach political philosophy. This concern is, for instance, hard to apply to the problem of a world in which the rising tide lifts all boats so to speak but the so-called bottom billion who live in the poorest countries of the world are continually sinking further and further in a terrible downward spiral.[9]

The third reason for reforming political philosophy at the present time derives from the formidable practical and conceptual challenges posed by 9/11. Socrates suggests that the unexamined life is not worth living. By 9/11 I will have in mind the events leading up to and leading away from that date. 9/11 is challenging on a number of different levels, of which I wish here to identify only two: an existential and a philosophical challenge. It is, to begin with, a tremendous difficulty for the US and its allies around the world, to which it presents an obvious danger, to what is often, but vaguely, characterized as "the democratic way of life." An obvious difficulty is the enormous bill still to be rendered, if Joseph Stiglitz and Laura Bilmes can

---

[9] See Paul Collier, *The Bottom Billion: Why the Poorest Countries Are Failing and What Can Be Done About It* (New York, NY: Oxford University Press, 2007).

be believed, as much as several trillion dollars merely for the still ongoing Iraqi War, the fiscal consequences of which for life in the United States is certainly significant.

To examine life means to take stock of where we are as the basis of raising questions about it. For the most part, we live at a time where at least in the West the constant element is steady, unremitting change, increasingly under the impulsion of capitalism that, since its emergence late in the eighteenth century, has increasingly tended to sweep away everything in its path. Though neither modern life nor politics can be reduced to economics, neither can they be conceptualized without it. Much of the twentieth century was taken up by a confrontation between two very different political systems, which, despite a series of major and minor crises, achieved a kind of perilous but fragile balance. This confrontation ended with the sudden, unforeseen, irremediable break-up of the Soviet Union and the end of the cold war. The emergence of a situation in which the entire world was dominated by a single superpower quickly led to new, often grave difficulties, as witness the often dramatic series of events loosely but universally known as 9/11.

9/11 presents an enormous conceptual challenge for a certain kind of political philosophy, which is, I believe, simply unable to grasp events such as 9/11, that is, events which arguably are among the most difficult and most important of the new century, perhaps, though it is still too early to say, among the most important of our time. An early hint of this predicament is the general silence about these events. According to Giovanna Borradori, these events issue a call to arms to philosophy, which has a unique role to play.[10] Yet it is unclear that philosophy, which has so far been distinguished by its deafening, nearly total silence about 9/11, is or is likely to play that self-assigned role.

9/11 concerns a series of events with a broadly political character. It is unclear that philosophy, or at least political philosophy as we now know it is well positioned to come to grips with a problem that runs against its grain so to speak. I will illustrate this in two ways. On the one hand, there are the rare comments of philosophers who have tried to say something intelligent about 9/11, including Habermas and Derrida, two of the best known thinkers of the last half of the twentieth century. According to the former, we are witnessing a conflict between Islam and the non-Islamic West, which represents an assault on the values of the Enlightenment by those who reject the Enlightenment commitment to reason. Habermas' premise is that Islamic terror is incompatible with the Enlightenment ideals incorporated in modernity. Yet the ideals of a life constructed on reason alone have notoriously lagged behind the claims made for them in countries that even now feature democracy, freedom or both as aims that can be brought about by through force from above, for instance in Iraq. One of the more disturbing consequences on 9/11 is that it has provoked a series of counter-measures that call into question the commitment to values so-called democratic countries claim to instantiate, including freedom of speech, due process, free elections decided by popular ballot, and so on. According to Derrida,

---

[10] See Giovanna Borradori, *Philosophy in a Time of Terror* (Chicago, IL: University of Chicago Press, 2003), p. xi. [Henceforth cited as *PTT*]

globalization is no more than a myth (*PTT* 121–124). Yet in branding as a myth the latest phase of capitalism, which is increasingly the main economic motor as well as the driving organizational force of the modern world, to which everything else is increasingly subordinated, Derrida unfortunately deflects attention away from a singularly important aspect of the current situation. In factoring out the economic component of the present situation as it were he makes it difficult to diagnose other than through such slogans as the axis of evil (George W. Bush); a difference in culture or civilization (Samuel Huntington); a failure to modernize leading to Muslim rage (Bernard Lewis), and so on.

I believe the inability to say more about the difficulties we are now facing derives from current political philosophy. Just as there is not philosophy, but philosophies, so there is not political philosophy but political philosophies. Yet just as the main thrust in philosophy, which, at least in the West, centers on a tradition created by and in reaction to Plato, so there is arguably a main thrust in Western political philosophy. Different kinds of political philosophy encompass a wide variety of different approaches. There is widespread agreement that the most important political philosopher of the last century is John Rawls.[11] Yet there seems no way to address the problems we are currently facing on the basis of Rawls' equality and difference principles,[12] his theory of justice as originally stated, or its later mutations.

Martha Nussbaum, who has written extensively on political philosophy, and who explicitly builds on Rawls, provides an interesting illustration of the relation of political philosophy to the surrounding world. In a very large book written well after 9/11 there is not a single word concerning these events. Nor is this a mere accident, an oversight as it were, but rather a result deriving from a well-known conception of political philosophy. It is then no accident that she begins a recent book, where she attempts to contribute to what she regards as three unsolved problems left by Rawls in further developing a variety of social contractarianism in saying that "Theories of social justice should be abstract."[13] Yet if political philosophy has nothing to say to us in this difficult time, then it seems difficult to avoid the inference that it is basically irrelevant to anyone other than philosophers.

On Recovering Philosophy After 9/11

I come now to my conclusion. The problems facing philosophy and especially political philosophy are not dissimilar but similar. The loss of relevance of a certain type of philosophy, whose model lies in the Platonic claims for absolute knowledge beyond any possibility of dialogue, is matched by the failure to be concerned

---

[11] See for example, Gerald Cohen, *Rescuing Justice and Equality* (Cambridge: Harvard University Press, 2009).

[12] See John Rawls, *A Theory of Justice* (Cambridge: Harvard University Press, 1971), p. 60.

[13] Martha C. Nussbaum, *Frontiers of Justice: Disability, Nationality, Species Membership* (Cambridge: Belknap Press, 2005), p. 1.

with the world in which we live. In turning away from problems, which arise in the daily round, political philosophy loses its social interest. If not the solution at least a first step for both philosophy in general and political philosophy in particular lies in returning from what Plato calls the world of reality to the world of appearance, in refusing monologue and in accepting dialogue, and in once again striving to come to grips with problems arising in appearance, the real problems of real human beings, that is human beings as they exist outside our philosophical theories, for example the problem of 9/11.

World Philosophy: On Philosophers Making Peace

Anton Hügli

Abstract Jaspers demands from philosophy to become world philosophy. The author follows the question, what is the difference between world philosophy and past forms of philosophizing, if it contains more than the not so new demand that future philosophy must care about world peace and unity of the world? The author comes to the conclusion that the Jaspersian project of world philosophy—to which Jaspers dedicated the last years of his life—can only be made understandable by taking into account the specific prerequisites of Jaspers' thinking. The crucial premise is that there cannot be world peace, unless it is preceded by making peace between the different philosophies and also between philosophy and religion—under the auspices of the truth, which connects all. This thought sheds a new light on the far reaching, partially gigantic projects and concepts of Jaspers philosophy: Periechontology, philosophical logic, the idea of a world history of philosophy, and foremost the concept of philosophical faith and the doctrine of ciphers.

The most insightful understanding of Karl Jaspers and a most comprehensive treatment of his project about a *World Philosophy* has already been accomplished by Hans Saner, particularly in his essay "Jaspers' Idee einer kommenden Weltphilosophie," published some 20 years ago.[1] Whoever wants to go beyond it must go to the literary archive in Marbach and intensively deal with the still unedited scripts stored there, such as Jaspers' gigantic and unfinished project of a world history of philosophy. My attempt here is more modest, as I explore to understand, from a contemporary point of view, how such world philosophy is at all possible.

---

[1] This essay and all quotations from German sources are translated by Mirko Wittwar with revisions by Helmut Wautischer. For Saner's essay see pp. 75–92 in Leonard Ehrlich and Richard Wisser, eds., *Karl Jaspers Today. Philosophy at the Threshold of the Future* (Lanham, MD: University Press of America, 1988). Probably the first explanation of Jaspers' project of a world philosophy is found in Hans Saner, *Karl Jaspers* (Rowohlt: Reinbek b. Hamburg, 1970), pp. 103–110.

A. Hügli (✉)
Basel University, Basel CH-4058, Switzerland
e-mail: anton.huegli@unibas.ch

H. Wautischer et al. (eds.), *Philosophical Faith and the Future of Humanity*,
DOI 10.1007/978-94-007-2223-1_27, © Springer Science+Business Media B.V. 2012

Historicity in Philosophy and the Prospect for a World Philosophy

Difficulties commence immediately with the term "world philosophy." After all, this philosophy is not termed world philosophy because it deals particularly with the topic of the world (and also not the traditional topics in philosophy, such as human nature, or God). Not by its subject but by its addressees is it defined as a world philosophy—it is meant to be a philosophy that includes and connects all humans, mankind as a whole. Thus it is not a philosophy *of* the world but a philosophy *for* the world. As it attempts to address everyone, world philosophy claims, by Jaspers' formulation, to be a communication in the name of truth that is meaningful to all humans, not just the intellectual elites. This claim also shows the way in which world philosophy as the future philosophy is different from prior philosophies. Explicitly no longer does it want to be a national philosophy or a European philosophy, for according to Jaspers, any national philosophy shows "some features of regional art (*Heimatkunst*)."[2]

The thesis expressed by the difference between a world philosophy, in contrast to a national philosophy or a European, occidental philosophy, is difficult to comprehend. For in what sense is philosophy supposed to have been national or, as we should rather say, local? This difference reminds us (by a reversed judgement) of some of the darkest chapters in more recent history of the sciences, for example German physics or Russian biology, and the exclusive use of scientific research to benefit one people only. Such judgment about earlier philosophies (and one may suppose that Jaspers' early philosophy is included as well), when seen from Jaspers' own vantage point, appears to be awkward in a double sense: already right from the beginning such a narrowing was far from Jaspers' thoughts, despite his declared appreciation of German culture and language; and secondly, he always understood his own philosophy to be a *philosophia perennis*, a philosophy aiming at the recurring existential problems of human beings throughout all times. But even if we do not use Jaspers as a benchmark, has there ever been a truly local philosophy? Also, the philosophers who were recognized to be national philosophers, when professing to belong to a certain state, a certain people, or a certain language, were usually not connected to a nationalist goal but instead to a world-missionary or universalist approach. For example, when Hegel has the world-spirit incarnated by Prussia, or Fichte envisions this rotten world to be cured by the German spirit, or ancient-minded philosophers like Heidegger support the thesis that after Greek language, only German could be the suitable language of philosophy.

From this a fundamental question can be posed: In what sense can we say that a philosophy is local, or respectively, since any locality is always also a spatial-chronological locality, in what sense is a philosophy historic? There are at least five answers.

---

[2] Unpublished works, quoted after Saner, ibid. p. 104.

First, philosophy itself is historic. It knows historic development in the sense that what was before determines that which is later, either to its advantage or disadvantage. Examples for such a way of understanding historicity are statements such as, "after Kant and Hegel it is impossible to philosophize in this way or that," or, that "with Plato's theory of ideas the forgetfulness of being commences." However, we may call philosophy historic also in a weaker sense, independent of all pondering about progress or decline. Philosophy is historic in itself also because every philosopher always takes up the ideas of other philosophers, engages with them for conversation, and such selection determines the shape of one's philosophy.

Second, philosophy is historic by intention. It is historically oriented, is "its own time expressed by thought," as Hegel said, and develops out of one's attempt to solve the social, cultural, and political problems of one's time.

Third, philosophy is contingently historic. Indeed, even if by its intention it is oriented towards the non-historical, such as the eternal fundamental questions of being, the way in which it asks questions and gives answers is determined, characterized, coloured by the respective age within which it finds itself. Time is always involved, and even though philosophy may be unaware of this, "philosophy is a child of its time."

Fourth, philosophy is historic by nature. It is always individual, it expresses the mind of a unique person, has a particular sound, and a particular voice. Fifth, philosophy is historic by its effects in as much as it identifies its time and works with it to bring forth change.

With all these different meanings of being historic one might ask: How can or should philosophy behave in view of the fact that, in this specific way, it is indeed historic? Should philosophy be interested at all in being anything other than historic?

As a minimal definition, we might agree that philosophy is an activity which is aware of itself. This means that one of philosophy's basic tasks is to become aware of its historicity. Such historic consciousness may then again influence philosophic activity, but it is far from being obvious that philosophy will ever be able to break out of its historicity or to change radically from what it is today. Let us briefly consider some of these variables.

That philosophy is historic in itself is a fact from which it will not escape. It will always be connected to a tradition, no matter how much it will open itself to other traditions. It will remain naturally historic, insofar as this is the case, even if it becomes aware of its historicity. Then, at best, and probably in vain, it may attempt to deny or dismiss some of its individual features.

Because of the fact that philosophy is contingently historic, a philosopher may behave in two ways by assuming the role of an observing third person, or taking the role of a first person. Acting from a third person perspective and taking a strictly scientific view, one may analyze individual philosophers in relation to others or being tied to their times. Here, one will treat philosophy as a cultural phenomenon, and define non-philosophical influences and effects that shape the thoughts of philosophers. Acting from a first person perspective, one will behave toward philosophy and other philosophers in a completely different way, indeed in an unhistoric way. Here, philosophic questions are pursued by consulting with other thinkers on themes considered to be helpful or to be touched by them, but neglecting them if their answers are not perceived to be helpful; in short, engaging in a monological conversation. In this case, the philosopher will not mind if an outsider, playing the role of third party, considers this conversation a cultural phenomenon of its time. He will only mind if there is the assumption that any of these influences of one's time might have had a disturbing influence on one's argumentation, and might have produced statements or decisions which cannot be justified. Thus, in a nutshell, being the third person, I speak *about* philosophers; being the first person, I talk *to* philosophers, I philosophize. When philosophizing, one can do nothing but ignore one's own historicity.

The situation is different with intentional historicity. In this instance, philosophy might actually be called on to care more about the world and the problems of its time. To some extent it is already doing so since, due to its immanent historicity, philosophy refers to its respective time, as was noticed already by Hegel in his famous dictum that philosophy is nothing else than its own age comprehended in thought. When philosophy is aware of its unavoidably intentional historicity, it will play the role of an interpreter of its time even more determinately. The situation is similar when philosophy directs its attention to the fact that it exerts influence on its times. Knowing this influence, it might also feel inclined to assume responsibility, for example, by actively engaging with public debate rather than to remain silent.

Recognizing these different types of historicity and possible dispositions toward historicity, where could there be a starting point located for a Jaspersian world philosophy with its rejection of local thinking? Such beginning is difficult to identify. Certainly, with respect to the contingently historic, Jaspers does include a demand to philosophize in the first person while talking to others, instead of considering philosophy as an established fact that one is to speak *about*.[3] But even in Jaspers, there is nothing specifically world-philosophical about such disposition. Rather, the first motivation in his philosophy is a philosophy of freedom, which first and foremost is due to caring about the well-being of the individual. For this he knows only one criterion of truth for philosophic thought, namely, that as an individual, I am ready to make my own life subject to these thoughts. Clearly world philosophical for Jaspers after World War II are the worries about saving the world, a world order, and world peace in the context of a fragile balance of terror which has come to the fore as mankind is threatened by the nuclear bomb. With his philosophy he feels called upon to become intentionally historic, endorsing the goal of a policy of world peace based on mutual understanding. Without referring to a God-given or allegedly historically immanent, necessary goal of history, this also means that Jaspers does not refer to an immanent historicity of philosophy.[4] Of course, the conclusion drawn from this direction of philosophy presupposes a clear awareness of the philosopher's

---

[3] Thus, according to Jaspers, a sufficient reason for "dealing significantly with the history of philosophy" can "only be philosophizing itself. This activity becomes meaningful when we face our own questions and answers in the course of history" (Hans Saner, ed., *Weltgeschichte der Philosophie. Einleitung* (München: Piper, 1982), p. 81).

[4] For example, Karl Jaspers, *Provokationen. Gespräche und Interviews*, ed. Hans Saner (München: Piper, 1969), p. 54.

particular responsibility with respect to working in the world as well as the appropriate will to have a voice in the public, as Jaspers repeatedly does in his political writings and with utmost determination.

The question remains, to what extent does Jaspers' approach introduce a new philosophy, albeit in dimly recognizable form, with a legitimate claim to be called world philosophy? Does this go beyond Kant's approach in his political writings, especially his writings on eternal peace? Is it not the case that Kants' project itself is already world philosophy in the best sense of the word? Identifying peace among nation states with trans-political peace among philosophers is a genuinely Kantian thought. Kant does not agree with Plato's claim (*Politics* 499) that constitutions will be imperfect until "philosophers become kings" or "kings become philosophers." Peace depends upon philosophy's abdication, so to speak, namely, by letting go of Plato's idea of the philosopher king.

Jaspers' Presuppositions for His Project of World Philosophy

If we take the idea of a world philosophy beyond the Kantian project, we need to address in more detail some premises of Jaspers' philosophizing. First of all, Jaspers understands philosophy as transcending thinking that goes beyond scientific reasoning. Science, he says, thinks strictly by categories of understanding (*Verstand*), is always oriented toward particular aspects within the world as it appears to us, and results in compelling knowledge from the process of consciousness. Philosophy, however, has to do with the faculty of reason (*Vernunft*) and asks about the origins of all being and about the all-encompassing One. It does not know any compelling knowledge but explores Being, illumination of existence, and world orientation. In sum, science has to do with immanence, and philosophy with transcendence. However, by asserting such competence, philosophy competes with the powers already occupying the field of transcendence, namely, religion in general, and particularly with theology, the science in charge of religion. But religion is a diverse power, divided into countless mutually exclusive groups, sects, churches, and other organizations with different ideas of gods and deities as well as different ways of life and life practices. There is a never-ending struggle and at times a state of war between religions. Such physical war might come to a standstill for reasons of survival, when different religious groups are forced to accept an external peace by the authority of a secular state (just as after the period of confessional wars in Europe), and where each group is ready to tolerate the existence of others as a necessary evil—in the sense of a so-called toleration. Nonetheless, the battle of faiths goes on, and its outcomes are anything but trivial—especially from Jaspers' perspective, who gives primary importance to such outcomes: It is the content and practice of beliefs that determines what kind of human one is, for one's own and others' benefit or disadvantage.[5]

---

[5] For example, Karl Jaspers, *Vom Ursprung und Ziel der Geschichte* (Zürich: Artemis, 1949), p. 273: "Nonetheless, it is the real . . . question of the future how and what man will believe."

Philosophy itself is just as torn and fragmented as religion with respect to its reception of the fundamental question about transcendence. In general, the following six positions can be identified.

First, the rejection of transcending thoughts, as it is generally practiced by positivists and naturalists. Here, a tree is a tree and the world as we recognize it is the world as such. One may call this the position of disbelief.

Second, transferring the distinction between immanence and transcendence to the former and perceiving as absolutely significant a certain set of facts about the world. This one may call the position of superstition, or as Jaspers calls it, "scientific superstition." Examples for such scientific superstition were beliefs in scientific methodologies that supposedly recognize a final meaning of history (as in Marxism and Leninism) or an absolute value of a race (as in Nazi biology).

Third, the belief in transcendence as a reality and one's ability to make well-founded, objective statements about such reality; for example in the form of rational proofs for the existence of God or theodicies. We may call this position that of rational metaphysics.

Fourth, the opposite position to the belief in transcendence, by making objective statements in denial of transcendence, namely, that there is no God and no reality which might be appropriate for a concept of transcendence. This is the position of atheists and nihilists.

Fifth, allowing for the possibility of transcendence but, in principle, rejecting the idea that convincing statements can be made on its reality. This is the position of sceptics and agnostics.

Sixth, and at the opposite end of all previously mentioned philosophical positions, there is the belief in revelation, in the possibility of making determinate statements on transcendence, due to a perceived fact that God reveals Himself to His chosen people, or that He came into this world as a human.

These positions are in a never-ending struggle with each other, a struggle that will continue even when religions have long made peace with one another. However, if peace in the world shall be lasting peace and not only a compromise of powers due to interest in survival (to my knowledge, this Jaspersian premise has never been explicitly expressed in this way), there must also be peace among religious and philosophical positions as well as religions and philosophies in general.[6] Such peace can be achieved only if the question of transcendence is not any longer the truth

---

[6] One support of my thesis is—apart from the significance Jaspers attributes to the so called transpolitical of today's world politics (see *Die Atombombe und die Zukunft des Menschen* (München: Piper, 1958), p. 309f)—for example, his programmatic sentence in the Preface to *Der philosophische Glaube angesichts der Offenbarung* (München: Piper, 1962), p. 7, [Henceforth cited as *PGO*]. "Today we seek that ground on which humans of all origins of belief might reasonably engage in communication across the world. . . ." As he explains further, it is about creating a necessary connecting environment of "communicability," in the form of his proposed "modern configuration" of philosophical "fundamental knowledge" as a "condition of mutual interaction with one another" (*PGO* 151), as "the bond of all encompassed modes of being, of reason" (*PGO* 127). Jaspers leaves no doubt that he is not interested in unanimity of beliefs: "The shared ground for diversity is in the clarity of thought, of truthfulness, and a shared fundamental knowledge"

that keeps us apart, but "the truth which binds us together." This is why Jaspers contradicts all these positions. What he offers instead is a position of philosophical faith.

Does this position open another front? For how is philosophical faith supposed to achieve the philosophical peace we seek? In Jaspers' answer I recognize the work of Jaspers, the Kantian. A short version of his answer, I think, is this: Each of the above listed positions shows one basic flaw in their own way, namely, the lack of serious engagement with Kant's critique of knowledge. All the positions lack insight in the boundary between that which can be justified and that which one cannot be justified but only believed. When Kant's methodological fundamental distinction, the distinction between the insight of understanding (*Verstand*) and the self-illumination of reason (*Vernunft*) is accepted, these positions cannot be sustained. This Kantian insight is the core of that what Jaspers calls "philosophical basic knowledge." It was only Kant, he says, "who achieved that liberation due to which we are able with any intellectual act to know what we are doing" (*PGO* 434). It makes the common space possible, where we may all meet in freedom, for

> only by clarifying the meaning of the validity of that what we say and hear we will be
> ... free of "fossilized assertions," of dictatorial claims for power, free of the constraint of
> logical forms whose preconditions we are not aware of. We will be liberated from all definite
> categories, from the restraints of language and one's own thoughts. We will not subject to
> any thought, except within its ever identifiable limits of meaning.[7]

Let me address this in terms of the above positions. Positivism and naturalism can proceed with their position because they reject a philosophically fundamental operation, namely, the insight of the subject-object split and the fundamental distinction between the world as it appears to us and the entirety of the world beyond the subject-object split. By denying transcendence, they also deny philosophy to function as the epitome of transcending-thinking and contribute to a loss of foundation for our existence. There is no peace among disbelief and philosophy, but only perpetual struggle.[8]

The situation is different for the various positions of belief referring positively or negatively to transcendence. Although philosophical faith contradicts also

---

[7] (*PGO* 7). At the level of content, i.e., in respect of that what is believed, there will be continuous struggle and unavoidable polemics. But no longer this will be a fight "for power, with one side being victorious, but for truth, where both sides come to realize themselves" (Karl Jaspers, *Weltgeschichte der Philosophie, Einleitung*, from his unpublished works, edited by Hans Saner (München: Piper, 1982), p. 74).

[7] (*PGO* 433). We owe this insight to Helmut Fahrenbach who pointed out this key role of philosophical basic knowledge in Jaspers' work. See Helmut Fahrenbach, "Das 'philosophische Grundwissen' kommunikativer Vernunft—Ein Beitrag zur gegenwärtigen Bedeutung der Philosophie von Karl Jaspers," in Karl Jaspers, *Philosoph, Arzt, politischer Denker* (München: Piper, 1986), pp. 232–280.

[8] This is the first struggle directed against both infidelity and revealed faith, the "struggle for the actuality and against any distortions and restrictions of transcendence" (*PGO* 196). This is the fight for the "purity of ciphers". The second struggle then is that of ciphers against each other (*PGO* 197ff).

these positions of belief, it may leave them their relative truth, however always under the condition that they are ready to accept the fundamental methodological insight in the irreconcilable difference between the insight of understanding and the thought of reason. The rational metaphysicians, just as the rational atheists and anti-metaphysicians, must go through the eye of the needle of skepticism in order to learn how to distinguish between the insight of understanding and the thought of reason, and to renounce the idea that there might be objective knowledge of transcendence that can be demonstrated to anyone. They are relatively justified in considering philosophy a rational activity which must follow a strict methodical discipline; their error is in equating this rational activity with that of conclusive scientific insight.

The so-called neutral common ground,[9] where all these positions meet and may start shared communication, is explored in three ways by Jaspers. One is his attempt, initiated by his *periechontology*, to produce a possible cartography of the infinite space of the imaginable, by way of distinguishing the different kinds of the encompassing. Another way is his gigantic project of a philosophical logic through which he wants to define the categories, concepts, procedures, and methods that make it possible to think about or recognise being within the different kinds of the encompassing.[10] This kind of logic was supposed to become the *organon* for reasoned thought as it self-reflectively illuminates itself. From the fundamental methodological insight of this logic results the third way that Jaspers presents as the all-connecting basis for communication, namely, his doctrine of ciphers. As shown by his philosophical logic, we do not have any language in which we can adequately speak about transcendence. If we try to do so with the help of concepts and categories of conventional logic, we end up in contradictions, circles, and tautologies.

At a first glance, Jaspers' position might appear to match what sceptics and agnostics say. Don't we have to give up on any way of speaking about transcendence and must simply be silent? Should we not agree with Jaspers' words, "Skepticism is an indispensable way of philosophizing. Thus, to a philosophical dogmatist real philosophy must appear as scepticism" (*PGO* 143)? Indeed, scepticism seems to be the philosophical attitude that alone does justice to the unachievable and distant

---

[9] Jaspers defends the idea of "philosophical foundational knowledge" against the objection that it is only one expression of belief among others by pointing out that only one belief is needed, the belief "in the possibility to understand each other without restrictions" (*PGO* 150). For all those sharing this belief it should basically be possible to achieve unanimity in respect of philosophical basic knowledge, for "if we move within this space, we seek to be able to operate by way of generally valid insights, and also we believe to be able to operate rationally and by way of ideas which are accessible for anybody" (Karl Jaspers/Rudolf Bultmann, *Die Frage der Entmythologisierung* (München: Piper, 1954), p. 109). This is "that field of philosophy where rational debating and agreement are perhaps possible, as opposed to the debate about faith" (ibid. p. 98).

[10] During his lifetime, only the first volume of this logic was published, the monumental work of more than one thousand pages (*Von der Wahrheit*) which was written during his forced retirement in the Nazi era. The dimensions Jaspers intended for this work become obvious in his "Nachlass zur philosophischen Logik" (*Unpublished Works on Philosophical Logic*), eds. Hans Saner und Marc Hänggi (München: Piper, 1991).

nature of transcendence. Jaspers draws a different conclusion from scepticism, one that matches the conclusion by so-called negative theology.[11] Precisely because any attempt of positively stating what transcendence is must be a failure, and in failing we become aware that transcendence is just the opposite of all we might imagine at all. For when imagining transcendence, we have the same experience as one who watches the sea, where the endlessly shifting horizon of the sea becomes the symbol for an infinite distance beyond all horizons.[12] Just like the experience of nature, also the failure of thought may become such a symbol, a cipher as Jaspers has it, which is permeable for something completely different, non-objectifiable and inexpressible, which makes us long for this distant *Other* that becomes present here and now precisely because I give in to this longing. That is why in the late period of his thought the ability to read ciphers and to read the traditional religious contents and ideas as ciphers becomes for Jaspers the main task of philosophy.[13]

Where Peace Is Possible and Where the Conflict Continues

Now, what has all this to do with world philosophy? I see the following context:

(1) *Philosophers themselves are making peace.* Periechontology and philosophical logic make possible the all-connecting communication within the medium of reason by confronting all participants with the *quaestio iuris*: How is it possible at all to gain a concept of transcendence and to speak about transcendence? Which methods of transcending thinking are available for us? So far this is still the Kantian approach. But now, moving to a meta-level, we add more detail. According to Jaspers' warning, we must be careful to avoid what Hegel tried to do, namely, to develop a closed system of all the allegedly imaginable and possible categories of being and thinking. We know that such a system is impossible. All we can do is to assume an eclectic way and collect and organize all materials that have been thought philosophically. The systems we sketch must be confronted with all categories that humans in different cultures have developed in the course of their respective histories. The approximation to truth of this system will be maintained only if we do not leave out any point of view, and if we try to philosophically appropriate everything that has been thought by all cultures at all times.[14] That is precisely why philosophy needs a world history of philosophy, and this is precisely why philosophy must

---

[11] See his appreciation of negative theology in *PGO* 388–390.

[12] The sea with its open horizons is one of the first experiences that, according to Jaspers' memories, for him became a cipher for freedom and transcendence (see *Schicksal und Wille. Autobiographische Schriften*, ed. Hans Saner (München: Piper, 1967), pp. 15f).

[13] For example, Karl Jaspers, *Kleine Schule des philosophischen Denkens* (München: Piper, 1965), p. 143f.

[14] See Jaspers in "The permanent search for a system of categories": "We are guided by pathos of never ending orientation in the service of existence which itself can only be illuminated, not objectively known. We seek the possibilities to read with open eyes the meaning of existing kinds

become world philosophy.[15] Only by visiting philosophy and all its phenomena will it be able to liberate itself from the bondage of its own historical contingency. However, this liberation is not accomplished by getting rid of everything historical, but rather by "newly appropriating, purifying, changing, and not giving up on one's own historical tradition" (*PGO* 7).

(2) *Peace among religion and philosophy and also among religions*. Philosophy's critical methodological consciousness, this has become obvious enough, is not by itself a way towards transcendence. It leaves us without images, without ideas, without any content and, so to speak, with empty hands. But as for us transcendence is only accessible by way of ciphers, we cannot live without these images and contents that provide evidence to the variety of ways in which transcendence has revealed itself to humans. If we try to philosophically read these traditional images and contents, they may become ciphers for us once again, referring to transcendence. And the more we face this variety of religious thought, the richer and more open we will be towards the way in which humans may be connected to transcendence. What makes a cipher may be most different for individual people, but the fact that their respective ciphers draw all of them towards transcendence is the truth that connects them all. When this happens, then even fundamental differences concerning what individuals believe may still be considered reasonable differences, differences within the range of transcendental reason. As always there are only ciphers for individual existence and not objective truths; no one will be able to claim privileged or preferential treatment or even sovereignty of interpretation on questions of transcendence: For all, transcendence is equally far away. When it comes to the nature and meaning of transcendence, there are no teachers, only students, and anyone may become a student. On the basis of this insight, peace among the religions is possible, and at the same time the conclusive reason is given to philosophically communicate with all religious positions, to understand their ways towards transcendence and appropriate or reject them for ourselves.

(3) *Positions without the possibility of peace*. There is only one great opponent of philosophical faith, the religions of revelation and the belief that transcendence is or has been alive in this world and that there exist individuals or institutions authorized immediately by God and having a monopoly of interpretation on the truth of transcendence. Those who claim that there is only one way and one truth and one life and that they alone know the way, do not need any communication with those believing in something else. Such individuals can do nothing but convert the Other

---

of knowledge and objects, without owning a comprehensive claim or even to envision such final ownership." (*Nachlass zur Philosophischen Logik*, ibid. p. 42)

[15] "The history of philosophy must be universal" because the "thinker" is necessarily interested "in everything which is essentially imagined on earth. . . . for him, all essential thinkers are helpers who find him even during the intellectual struggle, so that he may find himself. Really at home will be only he who has tried, extended and proven himself in all the world" (*Weltgeschichte der Philosophie*, ibid. p. 69).

and, if this is impossible, to merely tolerate their existence as one more obstacle in this world. In short, the truth of the religions of revelation is not of a connecting but of a separating kind of process. But it does not only separate us because it excludes the follower of a different faith. Moreover, it refers to a position which evades any philosophical approach, namely, that transcendence-itself is not only expressed as a cipher but, as in the incarnation, that God became man in Christianity, and that transcendence-itself has itself become a phenomenon of this world. Thus the religions of revelation (apart from the position of total disbelief) tend to be the great enemy of world philosophy. As long as faith in revelation is not transformed by philosophical faith, there will be no worldwide peace.

Thus, the circle is closed. The philosophy of Karl Jaspers, we have argued, is at first world philosophy in the intentional sense, insofar as it cares about the unity of humanity and worldwide peace. Based on the premise that there can be no peace without an all-connecting truth, and apart from caring about the world, there results the demand that any philosophy which might appear as a world philosophy, in the intentional sense, must be a philosophy of encompassing communication. Karl Jaspers dedicated his philosophical thought to this transformation of philosophy by developing periechontology, philosophical logic and the doctrine of ciphers.[16] By further developing Kant's approach and rejecting any final system, Jaspers was able to show why the transformation of philosophy might be successful only by way of a worldwide inclusion of all ways of thought. The unreachable enemies of this project remain, disbelievers who avow the philosophy of anti-philosophy, and the true believers with absolute faith in revelation. To philosophically engage these positions (and here we can only agree with Jaspers) remains the present and future task of philosophy.

---

[16] See Jaspers' self-evidence in the obituary he wrote himself: "All strength in these years he dedicated to carry on with his unfinishable philosophical work, by way of which he ... wanted to participate in the task of his age, to find the way from an ending European philosophy toward a coming world philosophy." (*Nekrolog, von Karl Jaspers selbst verfasst, in: Gedenkfeier für Karl Jaspers* (Basel: Basler Universitätsreden 60. Heft, 1969), p. 4)

Philosophical Faith as the Will to Communicate: Two Case Studies in Intercultural Understanding

Tomoko Iwasawa

Abstract This essay provides an analysis of historical examples that show how difficult it is to pursue Jaspersian "philosophical faith" in the real historic-political situation of intercultural understanding. The focus here will be the case of US-Japan communication both during and after World War II. After a brief identification of Jaspers' idea of boundless communication and its link to philosophical faith, the essay will comparatively analyze two studies of Japanese culture developed by American scholars in the 1940s, Ruth Benedict's *The Chrysanthemum and the Sword* and Helen Mears' *Mirror for Americans: Japan*, asking whether or not the realization of Jaspersian philosophical faith can be found in these two authors' use of reason.

Karl Jaspers' Concept of Philosophical Faith: Its Relevance for Contemporary Intercultural Dialogue

In *The Origin and Goal of History* (1949) Karl Jaspers pursues "the unity of history." His approach to this theme, however, is not like Hegel's who saw the culmination of history in the one exemplary form of civilization, i.e., the Christian civilization. Nor is it like Heidegger's who suggested an insurmountable gap between the Eastern and Western understanding of the world, and thus, the impossibility of finding the unity between them.[1] What, then, is unity and history for Jaspers?

---

[1] In his essay "A Dialogue on Language," Heidegger (represented by I = Inquirer) discusses this "insurmountable gap" with his Japanese interlocutor (represented by J = Japanese). I: "Sometime ago I called language, clumsily enough, the house of Being. If man by virtue of his language dwells within the claim and call for Being, then we Europeans presumably dwell in an entirely different house than Eastasian man." J: "Assuming that the language of the two are not merely different but are other in nature, and radically so." I: "And so, a dialogue from house to house remains nearly impossible." (p. 5) I: "The prospect of the thinking that labors to answer the nature of language is still veiled, in all its vastness. This is why I do not yet see what I am trying to think of as the nature of language is also adequate for the nature of Eastasian language." (p. 8) Quoted from *On the Way to Language* (New York, NY: Harper & Row Publishers, Inc., 1971).

T. Iwasawa (✉)
Reitaku University, Chiba, Japan
e-mail: iwasawa3@livedoor.com

H. Wautischer et al. (eds.), *Philosophical Faith and the Future of Humanity*, DOI 10.1007/978-94-007-2223-1_28, © Springer Science+Business Media B.V. 2012

In exploring the unity of history, Jaspers starts with the recognition that human historicity is essentially multiple:

> Man's historicity is, from the outset, multiple historicity.... Historical phenomena are immeasurably dispersed. There are many peoples, many cultures, and in each of these again an endless multiplicity of peculiar historical facts. Everywhere on the face of the earth where there was any possibility of gaining a livelihood, man has settled and brought himself to particular manifestation. There appears to be a multiplicity which develops and passes away concurrently and successively.[2]

Jaspers' thought does not stop with this *multiple historicity* of humans, but further seeks to discover their "enduring nature," which he ultimately grounds on the "demand for boundless communication" with others:

> The demand for boundless communication testifies to the solidarity of all men in potential understanding.... The ultimate question is then: Does the unity of mankind consist in unification on the basis of a common faith, in the objectivity of that which is thought and believed in common to be true, in an organization of the one eternal truth by an authority that spans the earth? Or is the only unity truly attainable to us humans unity through communication of the historically manifold origins, which are mutually concerned with one another, without becoming identical in the manifestation of idea and symbol—a unity which leaves the One concealed in manifoldness, the One that can remain true only in the will to boundless communication, as an endless task in the interminable testing of human possibilities? [*OGH* 263–264]

Needless to say, the unity for Jaspers means the latter. It is the unity that cannot be reduced either to "the one supreme faith" among various religious traditions, or to "the one eternal truth." Denying all these static notions, Jaspers' concept of unity claims to be evermore dynamic and dialogical. It is the unity attained "through communication of the historically manifold origins...without becoming identical in the manifestation of idea and symbol"—the unity "which leaves the One concealed in manifoldness, the One that can remain true only in the will to boundless communication."

This essay provides an analysis of historical examples that show how difficult it is to pursue Jaspersian "philosophical faith" in the real historic-political situation of intercultural understanding. The focus here will be the case of US-Japan communication both during and after WWII. After a brief identification of Jaspers' idea of boundless communication and its link to philosophical faith, I will comparatively analyze two studies of Japanese culture developed by American scholars in the 1940s, Ruth Benedict's *The Chrysanthemum and the Sword: Patterns of Japanese Culture* (1946) and Helen Mears' *Mirror for Americans: Japan* (1948).

Ruth Benedict (1887–1948), a well-known anthropologist and a leading figure in the study of Japanese culture, completed her influential book without ever visiting Japan or learning Japanese language in her life; she remained an outsider in interpreting her subject: Japan. As a result, *The Chrysanthemum and the Sword* consisted of nothing but emphasizing the foreignness and strangeness of Japanese culture for

---

[2] Karl Jaspers, *The Origin and Goal of History* (Westport, CT: Greenwood Press, 1976), p. 247. [Henceforth cited as *OGH*]

Americans. In contrast, Helen Mears (1898–1989), a member of the Labor Advisory Committee in Japan during the American occupation, had a unique experience of living among ordinary Japanese before WWII. From this experience, she analyzed Japanese culture, not as an outsider as in the case of Benedict, but as a participant observer (as defined by Clifford Geertz) who keeps in touch with the reality of people's concrete life, and thus, contemplates on the problem of how we can understand others even if at times they are considered to be an enemy.

After identifying the main thesis of Mears' argument in *Mirror for Americans* and analyzing how American and Japanese critics responded to her argument, I will then compare the work of Mears with that of Benedict—a contemporary of Mears who, as the writer of *The Chrysanthemum and the Sword*, was regarded as one of the leading figures on the study of Japanese culture. Interestingly, the comparison of these two works provides a contrastive model that shows two different attitudes of interpreting a foreign culture or civilization, which will further lead to asking whether or not the realization of Jaspersian philosophical faith can be found in these two authors' use of reason.

Communication and Philosophical Faith

The concept of "communication" becomes the primary category of Jaspers' philosophy, leading to his notion of philosophical faith. For Jaspers, philosophical faith means "the will to boundless communication"—"communication of the historically manifold origins" to understand one another. What supports and guides this faith is reason that engages in "an endless task in the interminable testing of human possibilities." Reason, for Jaspers, is a dynamic concept, which is more than the "abstract thinking of the mere intellect"[3]; it "absorbs the abstractions, transcends them, and returns with them to reality" (*AF* 210) as "a life-carrying basic mood." Jaspers defines reason as follows:

> Reason is more than the sum of acts of clear thinking. These acts, rather, spring from a life-carrying basic mood, and it is this mood we call reason. . . . Reason lies in the apperception of our environment, in constructive work, in earning for time and posterity, in peaceful competition, in the vision of beauty, in the contemplation of truth, in the fulfillment of one's destiny. Reason trusts in man and in his will to freedom, which receives intangible and incalculable aid from Transcendence. (*AF* 218)

Human beings as historic existence can live only in the world of *reality*, which can never claim to be eternal or universal. What can mediate this reality and the unfailing human desire for pursuing the unity in our historicity is reason, which remains universally "open and unbiased," but will always turn into "present historic existence." Jaspers asserts that this dynamic and dialogical movement of reason is essential to activating and developing our understanding of reality.

---

[3] Karl Jaspers, *The Atom Bomb and the Future of Man* (Chicago, IL: The University of Chicago Press, 1963), p. 210. [Henceforth cited as *AF*]

Reality lies in the movement of *reason*, which knowingly finds its way into every possibility, remains universally open and unbiased, but will always turn into present historic existence and thus is not universal. Our real existence is visible only in aspects of its historic appearance, and that only in retrospect. We cannot know it in its proper infinity and eternity. (*AF* 263)

Grounded on this concept of reality underlying human historicity, Jaspers' philosophical faith directed by reason is not abstract but concrete; it is not merely the philosophy of reason, but also the philosophy of action, and in this sense, political. The idea of reason as action is well articulated by Jaspers when he discusses the problem of ideology occurring in our historic-political understanding of the world. In the chapter, "Reason and Irrationality in Our Historic-Political Knowledge of the World" (*AF*), Jaspers calls our attention to the dilemma of never-ending ideological interpretations of reality:

The question always remains how ideologies are related to reality. Ideologies are products of thought; reality is the realm of action. Thinking itself is reality, though not unequivocally so; it detaches itself from reality, so as to produce two realities: the interpretation and that which is interpreted. In no case is an object of ideological interpretation identical with the reality occupied by its convinced protagonist.... The fact that we interpret reality and ourselves, and are human only by so doing, confronts us with an abysmal dilemma—for interpretation never comes to an end. (*AF* 275)

In turn, he emphasizes the importance of *critical rationality* that alone can save us from this dilemma:

As for theoretical insight, we can answer that the constructive analysis of ideologies in objectivized forms is neither deceptive nor ideologically distorted if we know what we are doing. We are putting up consistent constructions—ideal types—not in order to mistake them for realities, but to check the realities against them, to see where the realities fit them and where they do not. We are not seeing actual powers in these ideal types; we see them as tools for understanding. We must try them out, to see whether they will work. Ideologies cease being ideologies and become tools of understanding when reason takes hold and brings each one to the fore in its own special sense. (*AF* 276)

Jaspers knows the frailty of our thinking that easily creates ideologies excluding other views than our own. Facing such reality, Jaspers contends that philosophical faith alone yields clarity to "the perversions of reason," the lack of critical rationality or rationality perverted by emotions and propaganda. Thus, philosophical faith has to do with the hermeneutical rigorousness and sincerity that is required for anyone trying to engage in meaningful communication.

It is surprising to see what great importance Jaspers' philosophy acquires in the context of contemporary intercultural understandings. Let me introduce, for example, UNESCO's statement announced as the Final Communiqué at its international symposium held in Paris in 2005. The theme of this symposium is "Cultural Diversity and Transversal Values[4]: East-West Dialogue on Spiritual-Secular

---

[4] Michael Palencia-Roth, a speaker at this symposium, defines the term "transversal" as follows: "A transversal line is one that intersects a system of lines. The transversal is not altered by the lines it crosses. In axiological terms, transversal values are values that cross two or more cultures and

Dynamics." One will find how perfectly the philosophy of Jaspers resonates with this UNESCO statement, which emphasizes "unity in diversity"[5] in the contemporary intercultural understanding:

> *Cultural diversity* constitutes the raw material necessary for genuine dialogue. Without this fundamental prerequisite, so crucial to any exchange between peoples, cultures and civilizations, no attempt at international cooperation and mutual understanding is possible. In this context, encounters between civilizations occur through time and particularly long periods. Civilizations do not clash; instead it is the ignorance of civilizations that can lead to conflict...
>
> *Dialogue*, a means of verifying the validity of an idea shared by two or more people willing to confront their logical systems, is a difficult undertaking because the speaker runs the risk of witnessing his or her ideas transformed. Dialogue becomes an ever-evolving means of reviving the thought process, calling into question convictions and progressing from discovery to discovery....The emphasis should be placed on dialogue's remedial powers as a means of de-centering and stepping outside of one's cultural origins so as to plunge into a transversal dimension. In this way, we may go from a "dialogue of civilizations" to a "civilization of dialogue."[6]

The statement starts with recognizing that cultural diversity is the reality of our world. Then it goes on to say that the unity in this diversity is brought about by continuing dialogue between cultures—dialogue directed by the power of "reason" in the Jaspersian sense, which alone enables us to step outside of our cultural origins so as to plunge into the dimension of trans-cultural unity, i.e., the dimension underlying different cultures and civilizations as the common ground of humanity. As such, the unity is not a fact but a goal, which is pursued in the never-ending dialogical act of reason.

---

are common to them but they are not transformed into universal values. If a cultural transversal is to remain transversal, it must retain its specificity" (in *Cultural Diversity and Transversal Values: East-West Dialogue on Spiritual-Secular Dynamics* [UNESCO, 2006], p. 38). Here it should be noted that the concept of "transversal values" does not necessarily mean relativism. To the contrary, UNESCO's statement emphasizes on pursuing the unity, i.e., the common ground of humanity, among diverse cultures and civilizations in the world. Here the term transversal was chosen to avoid the connotation, historically embedded in the term universal, of unifying various values into the One, which has been supposed to mean the Christian value system (as discussed by Hegel). The philosophy of transversal values insists on finding the unity in diversity, but with an emphasis on "without negating the specific manifestation of each culture's way of being."

[5] This expression appears in UNESCO's statement in 1995, "Message from Tokyo—Science and Culture: A Common Path for the Future."

[6] Taken from the Final Communiqué at the UNESCO's international symposium on "Cultural Diversity and Transversal Values: East-West Dialogue on Spiritual-Secular Dynamics," held in Paris on November 7–9, 2005. The excerpt is from the book: *Cultural Diversity and Transversal Values: East-West Dialogue on Spiritual-Secular Dynamics* (UNESCO, 2006), pp. 206–207.

Helen Mears' Understanding of Japanese Culture in *Mirror for Americans: Japan*

Born in New York in 1898, Helen Mears studied at Goucher College in Baltimore, Maryland, hoping to become a journalist. Graduating from the college, she visited Beijing (China) with a friend, found a secretary job at a university, and stayed for a year. During this stay in China, she had a chance to travel to Japan for 10 days in 1925, which gave her an unforgettable memory of experiencing a culture totally different from her own, as well as from the Chinese. Upon her return to New York she worked for a publishing company, and again in 1935, she decided to visit Japan. At this time, she lived and worked among ordinary Japanese for eight months to observe concrete details of their everyday life. This record of her travel to Japan became her first book, *Year of the Wild Boar*, published by J.B. Lippincott Company in 1942. In this book, and in the manner of a cultural anthropologist, Mears explored, as objectively as possible, actual Japanese life that was so different from the then current image in the West of Japan as "a rapidly civilized, modern, aggressive nation." In the Foreword, she explains her intention of writing the book:

> One of the first questions asked by almost every Japanese I met who spoke English was, "What does America think of Japan?" If I had answered frankly I should have said that America was not thinking of Japan at all—was almost entirely unfamiliar with the facts of Japanese culture, institutions and history, and indifferent about them. This fundamental indifference lasted almost up to the moment of Pearl Harbor.... My intention was to set down as accurately as possible what I saw and heard while living in Japan, hoping to have a record of how the Japanese actually live their day-by-day round; since, however, there is almost nothing that the Japanese do today that does not have some political implication, a setting-down of their daily activities inevitably leads to politics and international relations.... This volume is a personal record, with the emphasis on how the Japanese behave in their daily affairs. It is also, I believe, a sensible explanation of why they behave that way.[7]

This introductory book on Japanese culture received a favorable review from American readers who looked for a clue to understand what they called "the sneak attacker" at Pearl Harbor in 1941.[8] Because of the success of this book, Mears thereafter became known as one of the specialists of Japanese studies. Her growing fame, after WWII, led to an appointment by the Supreme Commander of Allied Powers to serve as a member of the Labor Advisory Committee in Japan. This appointment

---

[7] Helen Mears, *Year of the Wild Boar* (Westport, CT: Greenwood Press, 1973), pp. 7–8.

[8] Here are several reviews on Mears' *Year of the Wild Boar*: "Ideas are our strongest weapons and our most deadly enemies". Hence the importance of this book, for unlike many authors who have rushed into print since Pear Harbor, Miss Mears knows that "It is not enough to hate aggressors; it is necessary also to understand them" (by M.S. Farley in *Far Eastern Survey*, Vol. 11, No. 21, 1942). Another book review says: "The book is not in the least journalistic or impressionistic. Rather is it searching and consciously analytic. Nor is it unsympathetic.... A fascinatingly live book by an author who employs extraordinary gift of observation of concrete detail significantly in a thoroughly honest endeavor to find more light in a great but murky national situation" (by A.L. Kroeber in *American Anthropologist*, New Series, Vol. 45, No. 2, 1943).

brought her to Japan for the third time in 1946, where again she experienced the conflict between the prevalent American image of the Japanese and what she observed as its reality. Her second book on the Japanese, *Mirror for Americans: Japan* (published in 1948), was created from the serious awareness as to how one might understand even "the enemy" rationally, without this image being perverted by emotions and by prejudice.

Mirror for Americans starts with the very controversial question: "What does Pearl Harbor mean for Americans?" Mears brings up this subject by saying: "Pearl Harbor was so much an unanswered question that, despite a half-dozen official investigation and reports,[9] with evidence and findings running into millions of words, the final answer was still as uncertain as ever."[10] Despite this uncertainty, what was certain was that this shocking affair became a satisfactory emotional release for Americans to wage a war against Japan:

> In the first emotion following the shock of the disaster, Americans were inclined to accept the attack as a bolt from the blue, almost as inevitable as an act of God with no conceivable rational explanation. The shock of the disaster had released such a burden of pent-up tension and emotion that all the issues and complexities of the period preceding it were canceled by an overwhelming outpouring of bitterness and hate. Pearl Harbor became the symbol of treachery, and the Japanese people became the focus for all our conflicting hates and fears, our insecurity and rage. A simple explanation for the disaster that relieved Americans of any responsibility whatsoever, and indicted a people, never popular, as the sole, deliberate, and unprovoked offender, was a satisfactory emotional release and a sure foundation for waging a war. (*MAJ* 13)

This emotional outburst was strong enough to paralyze people's critical mind to question any uncertainty hidden behind the Pearl Harbor event. Mears' sober eyes, without being distorted by emotion, try to elucidate this uncertainty by analyzing the US reports of the hearings before the Pearl Harbor investigation committees. Let me quote from her writing a rather long but important passage explaining the international power politics that had maneuvered around the time of Pearl Harbor:

> In general, these committees concerned themselves with a technical military problem. The question they tried to answer was, whose responsibility was it that an American military base had been caught by an attacking enemy with planes and ships assembled as though by deliberate design for target practice? Although their reports are far from simple reading, it was possible to discover that the Army and Navy, in excusing what looked like extreme negligence, insisted that a share of the responsibility must rest on the policy carried out by the State Department. In its official report, the Army claimed that our official policy toward Japan had been of a contradictory, dual nature which the Army report called a "Do, Don't" technique. This policy, the report said, was to make no open military moves against Japan, but to impose a series of progressively severe economic sanctions. By this policy, the report said, the Japanese were encouraged toward war and helped to arm themselves, while our own military preparation was still inadequate. Moreover, the report said, the seriousness of the disaster at Pearl Harbor was due in large degree to the fact that on November 26,

---

[9] Mears here refers to the Pearl Harbor Reports (including both Majority and Minority Reports) submitted by the Joint Investigation Committee of Both Houses in July, 1946.

[10] Helen Mears, *Mirror for Americans: Japan* (Boston, MA: Houghton Mifflin Company, 1948), p. 13. [Henceforth cited as *MAJ*]

Secretary Hull had presented Japan with an "ultimatum"—or what the Japanese thought was an ultimatum—without notifying the War Department. . . . The Army report, therefore, accepts the fact that an ultimatum was given and criticizes the Secretary for having delivered it before the date clearly stipulated to the President on November 28 by General Marshall and Admiral Stark. (*MAJ* 14)

From the analysis of these reports, Mears tries to show that Pearl Harbor was not "a bolt from the blue," but that the US military and civilian leaders had known that war with Japan was inevitable and coming up fast. By saying so, she is neither simply condemning the responsibility of the US leaders, nor defending the Japanese situation, but trying to keep her intellectual sincerity by not mythologizing Pearl Harbor. By mythologizing, I mean—following Jaspers—a situation of mentality that is clouded by irrational emotions so as to completely lose its critical rationality. When this happens one adheres to ideology as the unquestionable truth. Mears' attempt was to prevent such yielding to myth, which is another name for ideologically motivated propaganda:

In the light of our official statements, it seems obvious that "the sneak attack," the "Day of Infamy," must be reconsidered in somewhat new terms. There is considerable difference between an "unprovoked" treacherous attack by a savage people out to "conquer the world," and a counterattack against an economic blockade by a nation that believes it is involved in a complex game of power politics with an infinitely more powerful nation. It seems evident that Pearl Harbor was not the cause of our war with Japan, but only a move in a war America and Japan were already waging against each other. The question of "why did Japan attack us," therefore, must be supplemented by the question of "Why were we already waging war against Japan," if we want to solve the riddle of Pearl Harbor. (*MAJ* 16)

The myth of the Japanese thus incurred by Pearl Harbor proclaimed that the Japanese are "historically" and "traditionally aggressive," and therefore, "evil menace to the world." Mears tries to overturn this myth by objectively examining Japanese history. This essay does not intend to analyze Mears' entire discussion in detail, but an introduction of the following witty comment by Mears might help us perceive her rational advantage over the mythologizing mind:

During the war, our publicists, right down the line from our top policy-makers through every grade of popular press and publication, insisted that the Japanese had "historically" wanted "to conquer the world"; that they had "never been defeated," and that Pearl Harbor was therefore but an incident in a long continuous march toward world domination. . . . In normal times it would probably be obvious that such charges defeat their own claims, for how did it come about that the "world's most ruthless aggressors" had been trying "for twenty-six hundred years" to "conquer the world," "had never been defeated," and yet, as late as Pearl Harbor, had acquired an "Empire" made up only of their own small home islands, a handful of near-by, unimportant smaller islands and Korea. . . .[11] During Japan's pre-modern history, which covers a period around eighteen hundred years, the Japanese had acquired no territory outside their own home islands. (*MAJ* 122–123)

---

[11] It is in 1910 that Korea was annexed to Japan under the treaty made after the Russo-Japanese War.

According to Mears, contrary to "being *historically* aggressive," the Japanese continued to develop their civilization with long periods of internal peace and stability, and no foreign conquests for a historic period of at least eighteen centuries. Thus she strongly contends, "there is not a scrap of evidence to substantiate the charge that the Japanese people are inherently savage and fond of war, and that the history of their country and their traditional civilization are conclusive evidence against it" (*MAJ* 155). Be careful, however, in understanding that Mears' refutation is directed against the falsehood of interpreting the Japanese as being "inherently and historically" aggressive, and that she is not denying the fact that Japan's international behavior in the nineteenth and early twentieth centuries was unquestionably aggressive, and therefore, should be strongly criticized. Her question then becomes: What changed Japan to become so aggressive in the nineteenth and early twentieth centuries?[12]

After 200 years of isolation policy, Japan opened its door to the Western countries in 1854, when the American representative, Commodore Perry, succeeded in making a treaty, rather forcibly, which permitted Americans to trade at two Japanese ports. According to Mears, "this treaty marked the beginning of a new era for Japan" (*MAJ* 169). Mears describes the critical Japanese situation at that time:

> In October, 1854, the British secured a similar treaty; in February, 1855, the Russians secured one; and in November, 1855, the Dutch. In 1856, we (Americans) sent Townshend Harris as our first consul, and in 1857, he secured a new treaty which gave Americans the right to live and carry on trade at three ports; the next year he secured the first regular commercial treaty which opened five ports to Americans, where they could live under American law, not Japanese.... From this time on, till late in the 19th century, Japan had a semi-colonial status. (*MAJ* 169–170)
>
> The Japanese episodes represent their inability to resist encroachments of a group of foreign Powers acting in concert. The most energetic and independent Japanese realized that they had no chance of resisting Western demands. They reversed their policy and wholeheartedly submitted to Western "guidance." (*MAJ* 174)

Mears maintains that the Japanese aggressiveness as a modern nation was developed as they "worked conscientiously to learn what their Western teachers taught them" (*MAJ* 177), and that "the major objective for the Japanese in all this was their desire sufficiently to modernize themselves so that they could get free of the repressive and humiliating 'Unequal Treaties' and regain their sovereignty" (*MAJ* 177). She then argues:

> In condemning Japan today, we charge that they turned out badly on both the domestic and international fronts. We say that they became totalitarian at home and "violent and greedy" abroad. We explain this by saying that they are an inherently aggressive people and that their traditional civilization encouraged a "will to war." A study of the record suggests a very different answer. The modern Japanese developed a highly centralized regime because they were introduced into world society under conditions that made centralized control of both

---

[12] This essay does not have enough space or ability to analyze Mears' massive discussion on modern imperialism (i.e., the Spanish, Portuguese, British, Dutch, French, Russian, and even American expansion to the world) and the power politics of these nations to colonize the Asian countries. The main point of her argument, however, is very important.

government and economy essential to survival. They became "violent and greedy" because they were introduced into a world society in which violence and greed were standard and correct behavior; and they were taught the international techniques of organized violence and greed, literally, by experts. (*MAJ* 174–175)

Japan's real crime is not that she failed to profit by her first instruction in the ways of Western civilization, but that she made good. (*MAJ* 300)

Modern Japan holds up a mirror to Western civilization as it appears in its international relations in Asia. In indicting Japan's "inherent and traditional militarism," we have swung a boomerang. (*MAJ* 120)

As I have mentioned previously, Mears' intention is not to support or justify the Japanese expansionism and militarism. To the contrary, she is condemning Japan's crimes in the warfare as she criticizes any selfish and violent deeds in the war. And yet, she reproaches the simple attitude of victor nations to judge the defeated unilaterally as the most evil. For such one-sided judgment by the winner will hide the true problem that caused the disastrous warfare in the twentieth century—the problem of imperialism. Imperialism assumes the unequal relationship (i.e., the superior-inferior relationship) between a civilized and a so-called non-civilized country. Here, whether a nation is civilized or not is measured by the sole model of Western development. In this unequal relationship, the cultural identities of the colonized nations were marginalized, and their traditional values were subordinated to those of the colonialists. As Mears ironically describes the situation, Japan was a good student of the West, who learned this modern imperialism so quickly and skillfully. The condemnation of Japan by the West, however, is far from solving this fundamental problem of imperialism, which is based on the idea of discrimination between cultures, but blurring it. In the end, Mears argues:

A review of the crime and punishment of Japan proves that the principles of international law need sharper defining. In human terms the Japanese crime was that the nation put its assumed "national self-interest" ahead of the human rights of individual human beings, and sought to preserve its assumed "national vital interests" even to the extent of war. As long as this crime is accepted by all nations as a legal right, punishment of weaker nations by stronger ones will seem merely to represent a determination of the most powerful to preserve their own dominance. (*MAJ* 298–299)

The Reaction of American and Japanese Critics to Mears

It is interesting to see how American critics reacted to Mears' controversial work. *Mirror for Americans* was published in September 1948, two years after she returned from her duty in Japan as a member of the Labor Advisory Committee. Many reviews were written, both in newspapers and academic journals. Among the five reviews JSTOR retrieved, four reviews criticize Mears' work very negatively and harshly. For example, Earl Swisher at University of Colorado tries not to discuss Mears' historical analysis on the academic plane. He evades discussing how to interpret modern world history intellectually, but transforms the topic into how to solve the socio-political problems of post-war Japan practically:

Miss Mears introduces some very interesting and valuable materials, particularly the findings of the United States Strategic Bombing Survey, showing the large-scale destruction of Japanese industry as well as of Japanese cities, the paucity of Japanese naval and air strength, and the effectiveness of the Allied blockade, especially in preventing much-needed oil and gasoline from reaching Japan. She points out this exhaustion of Japan to prove that the use of atomic bomb was a tragic and barbarous blunder on the part of the United States. The facts are valuable and incontrovertible, but deductions are always dangerous. The atomic bomb question is sure to be perennial. It can be pointed out, however, that neither exhaustion nor peace feelers is conclusive "proof" that the war would have ended in terms acceptable by the Allies without either the atomic bomb or an invasion of the Japanese main islands... Of course, she urges that we "understand" the problem of Japan and Japan's attempts to solve them; but Americans would be more interested in the present dilemma of Japan than in a repetition of the arguments to justify the seizure of Manchuria, China, and the South Pacific in 1931 to 1941.[13]

John M. Maki at University of Washington opposes regarding Mears' massive analytic study as academically meaningful, and degrades it to "one woman's sentiments on the problems of international relations":

Her theme is that Japan has really not been responsible for what have been called her aggressive policies, but was forced by the West to become a practitioner of modern power politics and since her venture resulted so disastrously for her, the United States should profit from the Japanese example and refrain from the continued practice of power politics.... Miss Mears' book is a bold and sincere statement of one woman's sentiments on the problems of international relations in the modern world and of the occupation of Japan. To regard it as a serious analysis of those problems would be to place it in a category for which it was not intended and in which it would be exposed to damning criticism.[14]

John Morris in London does not seem to understand the intellectual complexity of Mears' argument, regarding it simply as an attack against the American and British policy during the war:

The greater part of [Mears'] book is devoted to attacking the United States and Britain, which, according to Miss Mears, were mostly responsible for Japan's decision to adopt a policy of aggression..... The fact is that Miss Mears has not the necessary knowledge (nor the properly-trained historian's lack of bias) to criticize the higher policy of the United States government, and her cynical and ill-informed attack upon the Department of State is not helpful in the settlement of world affairs.[15]

Richard W. Leopold at Northwestern University humiliates Mears' work as what "disgraces an undergraduate paper," which is never worthy of serious academic consideration:

She is convinced that not until we destroy our smug complacency, not until we free ourselves from wartime propaganda, not until we re-examine with humility our entire post-Perry performance can we hope to promote peace in the Far East or to convince

---

[13] Earl Swisher, "Book Review: *Mirror for Americans: Japan* by Helen Mears," *The Pacific Historical Review*, Vol. 18, No. 1, Rushing for Gold (February, 1949), pp. 148–150.

[14] John M. Maki, "Book Review: *Mirror for Americans: Japan* by Helen Mears," *Far Eastern Survey*, Vol. 18, No. 9 (May 4, 1949), p. 107.

[15] John Morris, "Book Review: *Mirror for Americans: Japan* by Helen Mears," *Pacific Affairs*, Vol. 22, No. 2 (June, 1949), pp. 200–201.

dependent peoples everywhere of the sincerity of our professed ideals.... The glaring
factual errors, gross oversimplification, and numerous non-sequiturs here noted would disgrace an undergraduate paper.... There is nothing here for the historian in his professional
capacity.[16]

A common element in the above four reviews is their *emotional* reaction against
Mears' thesis. As we have discussed, Mears' intention in *Mirror for Americans* was
not to defend Japanese expansionism and militarism during the war; rather, her purpose was to analyze modern world history as objectively as possible in the global
framework of imperialism, and not from an Anglo-American perspective. Contrary
to this intention, all the reviewers above criticize Mears for her discharging the
Japanese responsibility for the war and simply attacking the West—criticism derived
from an emotional distortion of Mears' thesis, and not upon objective analysis of her
thesis.

There was only one review that evaluated Mears' work positively. The reviewer
was John Fee Embree (1908–1950), the only American anthropologist who had
conducted fieldwork in Japan before the war. Visiting Japan in 1926, 1932, and
1935–1936, Embree's field research at a Japanese village culminated in the book
Suye Mura: A Japanese Village, and was published in 1939.[17] Richard H. Minear
(University of Massachusetts) evaluates *Sue Mura* as "a classic of descriptive
anthropology, warm and yet as objective as it is possible for anthropology to be."[18]
Here is Embree's review of *Mirror for Americans*:

While many of the data are old and familiar, her interpretation of these data are new enough
to have aroused most of the newspaper book reviewers to condemn *Mirror for Americans*
as dangerous thought.... A factor of real significance is that Japan, an Asiatic country,
was trying to behave as a political equal of a European nation. This fact, often overlooked,
probably accounts for a great deal of the conflict between Japan and the West and ultimately
may account for further trouble between other parts of Asia and the West. By the record, as
Miss Mears shows, Japan did nothing in the past century not done equally by Britain, France
and, by association, by the United States. But these were "white" nations. The problem of
race relations in international relations is a real one and Miss Mears' book is one of the first
to give it serious treatment. For the reason, *Mirror for Americans–Japan* is a contribution
to the sociology of nations.[19]

---

[16] Richard W. Leopold, "Book Review: *Mirror for Americans: Japan* by Helen Mears," *The
Mississippi Valley Historical Review*, Vol. 35, No. 4 (March, 1949), pp. 708–709.

[17] John F. Embree got his Ph.D. in anthropology from the University of Chicago in 1937. A junior
faculty member at the University of Toronto in 1941, he became a community analyst in 1942 for
the War Relocation Authority, the agency supervising the internment of the Japanese Americans;
later he taught in the Civil Affairs Training School set up by the Army to train future members
of the Occupation of Japan. He was Associate Professor of Sociology and Research Associate of
Anthropology at Yale from 1948 to 1950.

[18] Richard H. Minear, "Cross-Cultural Perception and World War II," *International Studies
Quarterly*, Vol. 24, No. 4 (December, 1980), p. 570.

[19] John F. Embree, "Book Review: *Mirror for Americans: Japan* by Helen Mears," *American
Sociological Review*, Vol. 14, No. 3 (June, 1949), pp. 439–440.

In discussing whether or not Mears distorts the historical facts as to why Japan went to war, it might be helpful to note the testimony of General Douglas MacArthur made after WWII (in 1951) at hearings before the Committee on Armed Services and the Committee on Foreign Relations, United States Senate. The hearings conducted an inquiry into the military situation in the Far East and the facts surrounding the removal of Douglas MacArthur from his assignments in that area. In this testimony, MacArthur admits that America's severe economic blockade encouraged the Japanese to arm themselves, and that Japan's purpose in going to war was largely for security reasons:

Strategy Against Japan in World War II
Senator Hickenlooper. Question No. 5: Isn't your proposal for sea and air blockade of Red China the same strategy by which Americans achieved victory over the Japanese in the Pacific?

General MacArthur: Yes, sir. In the Pacific we bypassed them. We closed in. You must understand that Japan had an enormous population of nearly 80 million people, crowded into 4 islands. About half was farm population. The other half was engaged in industry.

Potentially the labor pool in Japan, both in quantity and quality, is as good as anything that I have ever known. Some place down the line they discovered what you might call the dignity of labor that men are happier when they are working and constructing than when they are idling.

This enormous capacity for work meant that they had to have something to work on. They built factories, they had the labor, but they didn't have the basic materials.

There is practically nothing indigenous to Japan except the silkworm. They lack cotton, they lack wool, they lack petroleum products, they lack tin, they lack rubber, they lack a great many other things, all of which was in the Asiatic basin.

They feared that if those supplies were cut off, there would be 10 to 12 million people unoccupied in Japan. Their purpose, therefore, in going to war was largely dictated by security.[20]

In contrast, how did Japanese critics receive Mears' book? The book was actually banned from translation, publication, and distribution in Japan by General MacArthur himself during the American occupation. It was only in 1953, two years after the occupation ended, that the book's translation was first published in Japan.[21] Japanese readers at that time, however, showed little interest in this book, which had an indifferent market reception. In the 1950s, still devastated by the post-war situation, the Japanese mood was filled with strong aversion to all things military. Moreover, because of the hatred toward the totalitarian movement advanced by Imperial Japan prior to and during WWII, the Japanese public opinion began to attack and negate traditional Japanese values all together by maintaining that it

---

[20] *Hearings before the Committee on Armed Services and the Committee on Foreign Relations/* United States Senate / Eighty-second Congress First session to conduct an inquiry into the military situation in the Far East and the facts surrounding the relief of general of the Army Douglas MacArthur from his assignments in that area / Part I / May 3,4,5,7,8,9,10,11,12, and 14, 1951 / Printed for the use of the Committee on Armed Services and the Committee on Foreign Relations / United States Government Printing Office / Washington: 1951.

[21] The Japanese title of this book was *America no Hansei*, meaning "America's Self-Reflection." Translated by Momoyo Hara, it was published by Bungei-Shunju-Shinsha in 1953.

was those old values that had eventually created a hotbed of vicious totalitarianism. This anti-traditional tendency was strengthened by Japan's defeat in WWII and the forced democratization of Japanese society by the United States. The public sentiment, influenced by the so-called progressive intellectuals, showed strong aversion to discussing Imperial Japan's history in any other way than negatively. This emotional rejection of "the prewar Japan" was so powerful as to prevent the Japanese from reflecting their history objectively and constructively. In this postwar situation, it was impossible for Mears' book to get much attention and it soon passed into oblivion.

Indeed, it took almost 50 years for the Japanese to overcome their emotional block and begin to assess and evaluate Mears' work. In 1995, *Mirror for Americans* attracted a new publisher's attention, and was translated and distributed for the second time in Japan. This time, the book was widely welcomed by the Japanese and it received many positive reviews. The publication of the first book studying the life and works of Helen Mears in 1996 helped to enhance her public image.[22] Since then, *Mirror for Americans* has been widely circulated, with a paperback version published in 2005. More than 60 years after the war, the Japanese now encounter Mears' book objectively, regarding her as "the seeker of intellectual fairness by putting oneself in the perspective of *others*" (*WN* 184). In sum, when Mears poses the important question, how is it possible to acquire a strong rational mind that does not yield to the emotional perversion of reality, her book provides an eloquent answer.

Ruth Benedict's Interpretation of the Japanese

Two years before the publication of *Mirror for Americans*, Ruth Benedict published *The Chrysanthemum and the Sword*, arguably one of the most influential books on Japan by an American author. Benedict worked for the Office of War Information (OWI) between 1943 and 1945, and this book was one product of her work for the OWI. Contrary to the harsh criticism toward *Mirror for Americans*, Benedict's book enjoyed a warm reception by American readers. Many reviews praised the book glowingly, for example, by saying that *The Chrysanthemum and the Sword* is "a study of the utmost importance and a testimonial to the scholarship and literary skill of the author,"[23] that it is "a valuable book by virtue of its penetrating insight because it is a pioneer attempt to explore the basic patterns of a complex social world."[24]

---

[22] Takashi Mikuriya and Kazuto Oshio, *Wasurerareta Nichibei-Kankei: Helen Mears no Toi [A Forgotten Japan-US Relation: A Question of Helen Mears]* (Tokyo: Chikuma-Shobo, 1996). [Henceforth quoted as *WN*]

[23] Paul H. Clyde, *The American Political Science Review*, Vol. 4, No. 3 (June, 1947), p. 586.

[24] John Useem, *The Journal of American Folklore*, Vol. 62, No. 246 (October–December, 1949), p. 450.

In contrast to such a warm welcome in the US, Japanese scholars in the 1940s received Benedict's work rather negatively upon its translation and distribution in Japan in 1948.[25] The criticism of Japanese scholars was directed not only toward its methodology but also its content. Benedict's research materials were limited to works written in English (she could not read or speak Japanese), her informants were few and unrepresentative of the contemporary Japanese situation (she never visited Japan, and her informants were American Japanese detained in concentration camps), her discussion was prejudged (an "aggressiveness" of the Japanese was presupposed as she looked for reasons why it was nurtured), all of which oversimplified Japan's history and its cultural complexity.

Besides these criticisms, most interesting is the difference in attitudes of Benedict and Mears in their attempt to interpret a foreign culture. Part of the answer can be discerned in the opening remark of *The Chrysanthemum and the Sword* since it symbolizes Benedict's position. She begins her book by saying, "the Japanese were the most alien enemy the United States had ever fought in an all-out struggle. In no other war with a major foe had it been necessary to take into account such exceedingly different habits of acting and thinking.... We had to understand their behavior in order to cope with it."[26]

Benedict thus starts with the prejudgment that the Japanese are alien to the Americans, that they are too different in acting and thinking for Americans to understand them. So the purpose of her study is to show how one copes with such alien enemy. For this goal, she first addresses Japanese reliance on order and hierarchy, in contrast to American faith in freedom and equality. According to Benedict, even Pearl Harbor can be understood as the confrontation between the Americans' lofty pursuits of equality against a Japanese savage adherence to hierarchy. Here she explains Pearl Harbor, not in terms of politics and diplomacy, but in terms of the Japanese *pathological* character. When we compare this analysis of Benedict with that of Mears, their differences are clearly evident: Mears perceived Japan with sympathy, while Benedict confronted it with hostility. Such lack of tolerance for differences in cultural value, ethnicity, or religion brings not unity but despair in intercultural understanding. As Minear correctly comments on Benedict, "the element of pathology is strong in her work, and for her Pearl Harbor is a prime symptom of the Japanese disease."[27]

Another element of pathology that Benedict finds in Japanese culture is her assumption of some "traditional aggressiveness," which, she claims, was the cause of Japan's going to war. Most of *The Chrysanthemum and the Sword* is devoted to explaining how the Japanese have developed their aggressiveness. Benedict

---

[25] "Special Edition: On Ruth Benedict's *The Chrysanthemum and the Sword*," *Minzokugaku-Kenkyu* [Anthropological Studies], Vol. 12, No. 4 (May, 1949). A special edition with leading Japanese scholars of anthropology, such as Tetsuro Watsuji and Kunio Yanagita.

[26] Ruth Benedict, *The Chrysanthemum and the Sword: Patterns of Japanese Culture* (Boston, MA: Houghton Mifflin Company, 2005), p. 1. [Henceforth cited as *CS*]

[27] Richard H. Minear, "Cross-Cultural Perception and World War II," in *International Studies Quarterly*, Vol. 24, No. 4 (December, 1980), p. 564.

maintains that their peculiar culture made the Japanese warlike and aggressive as individuals and expansionist as a nation. From such standpoint, she justifies the American occupation of Japan as a necessary remedy for Japan's "dangerous disease":

> In the United States we have argued endlessly about hard and soft peace terms. The real issue is not between hard and soft. The problem is to use that amount of hardness, no more and no less, which will break up old and dangerous patterns of aggressiveness and set new goals. (*CS* 299–300)

Here let us recall that Mears' *Mirror for Americans* was an attempt to invalidate such myth, readily advertised by Benedict who proclaimed that the Japanese had been "traditionally and inherently aggressive." Indeed, this myth was so influential that even the Japanese (as earlier mentioned, the progressive intellectuals of the postwar period) gradually adhered to Benedict's theory as a good framework for self-understanding or, in other words, for denouncing such pathological traditional Japanese cultural patterns to become more democratized, i.e., Americanized. Accepting such myth also allowed the Japanese to avoid a reasoned self-assessment for almost 50 years, in the task of reflecting on their history objectively in a global framework.

Conclusion

What does the experience of these two American Japan scholars, Helen Mears and Ruth Benedict, suggest for us today? By interpreting Japanese culture, Mears maintained a position of critical rationality and objectivity without succumbing to the emotions and propaganda of her time. In contrast, Benedict embraced a mythologizing mind by losing objectivity and arriving at value judgments on the culture of an enemy nation. Mears set Japan into a global framework that transcended both Japan and America, while Benedict kept analyzing Japanese culture by reducing it to an American framework. As a result, Mears responded to Japan with sympathy, while Benedict confronted it with hostility.

What accounts for their difference? For one thing, the difference might come from how they committed themselves to the subject of their study. Mears lived and worked among ordinary Japanese for months to observe details of their everyday life, while Benedict never traveled to Japan. In other words, in interpreting the Japanese culture, Mears did not stay within abstract thinking of mere intellect, but contemplated by keeping in touch with the reality of people's actual life. Here we find the realization of what Jaspers called "the movement of reason" (*AF* 263). According to Jaspers, reason is more than the abstract thinking of the mere intellect. Reason absorbs the abstractions, transcends them, and returns with them to reality as a life-carrying basic mood. Here reality is where people's values exist—the values that have been developed and cultivated in each culture's long history. Reason that does not engage in a dialogical interaction with this reality, i.e., with values, is, therefore, powerless. Benedict's generalizations use abstract reasoning on the basis of normative assertions alone, without any foundation in reality (such as a knowledge of Japanese language and values), and thus, cannot generate a meaningful dialogue.

While abstract reason is value-free, as Max Weber said of science, philosophical reason will lose its humanity if it disregards communicating with values. Let us recall Jaspers' concept of philosophical faith again: what directs philosophical faith is reason that "remains universally open and unbiased, but will always turn into present historic existence" (*AF* 263). Here what Jaspers calls "present historic existence" consists of the wisdom of the past. As such, his emphasis is on that philosophy that does not engage in a dialogue with this wisdom of the past—i.e., the traditional values of various cultures and civilizations—would be totally irrelevant. It can be said that Mears has great respect for the values of other cultures and wants to understand them very much in the manner of Jaspers' concept of *Verstehen*. Indeed, what is required for contemporary intercultural understanding is such a concrete, all-around approach to the cultures of others as we have found in the attempt of Helen Mears.

The above quoted UNESCO statement correctly acknowledges that "civilizations do not clash; instead it is the ignorance of civilizations that can lead to conflict." To this Jaspers would reply that the way to overcome such ignorance consists in a never-ending dialogical act of reason, which alone enables boundless communication between different cultures and civilizations.

Faith as Humanity's Essential Communication Bridge

Hermann-Josef Seideneck

Abstract The existential experience of death as boundary situation makes it possible to ask the essential question about faith. Philosophical-theological considerations regarding the width and characteristic of faith are discussed in relation to Jaspers' concept "philosophical faith." In today's contrast between faith and knowledge an area of conflict opens up that brings significant relevance to pastoral efforts. At a deep level of deep faith that enables one to carry-on in difficult times, existential communication between humans of different cultures might develop.

Historical Orientation

When traveling the world, one can see many important old stone monuments: pyramids and temples in Egypt and Mesopotamia; temple-towers in India, Indochina, and Indonesia; grave-mounds in central Asia, China, and Korea; pyramids in Central America; and towering cathedrals in Europe. These visible signs of faith are all over the world and we struggle to understand their meaning. From time immemorial humans have included valuable objects into the tombs of their deceased. This makes it apparent that humans always had the awareness of living in the boundary situation between life and death, with death being the insurmountable limit situation, as Jaspers observed. Humans reflect on the finitude of existence again and again, man alone of all creatures ponders upon mortality. From this fact we conclude that man is *homo religiosus* and that the certitude of death is known to each of us.

The religious nature of humans is a significant part of the history of mankind and becomes especially significant with our view of death. A key phrase, which describes the old-Egyptian culture, reads: "You live, so that you die." On the west side of the Nile we see, as a sign of this attitude, the artifacts of death with innumerable monuments from simple graves to enormous tombs, throughout the Valley of the Kings with its pyramids and empty temples. The discovery of countless mummies continues to provide us with the message that humans believe in a life beyond death. Deep experience of the fact that humans have to die prepares our way to transcendence and opens a gate to faith.

H.-J. Seideneck (✉)
Ferna, Germany
e-mail: hermann-josef-seideneck@hotmail.de

H. Wautischer et al. (eds.), *Philosophical Faith and the Future of Humanity*,
DOI 10.1007/978-94-007-2223-1_29, © Springer Science+Business Media B.V. 2012

Also today, *nolens volens*, humans continue to live in the boundary situation of death. That we all have to die is indeed certain. Therefore we say, live each day in such way as if it would be your last. In the face of inevitable death, many are drawn nearer to God by religious faith. From its origin, the word *religio* means to absolutely entrust oneself to God in an unbreakable bond. We experience this insight in the fine arts, paintings, musical compositions, literature, sculptures, and so forth. A comprehensive view into the history of art points to an abundance of faith references worldwide. These paths of faith span from the myths of tribal peoples to world religions to new kinds of faith in modern times. Such fundamental faith disposition can lead to community bonding, so that faith becomes a key concept for mutual communication throughout time.

Karl Jaspers' notion of philosophical faith has its substantive roots in looking at the traces of faith in the intellectual traditions of mankind. Jaspers differentiates in principle between faith and knowledge: "Man, as a matter of principle, is more than he can know from himself"[1] and he also recognizes "man as a person with respect to God" (*EP* 63). Thus the experience of God and experience of freedom have proximity to each other. We understand our freedom as the gift of transcendence.

Jaspers finds the two fountains of freedom in the Occidental God and in historical thought, "the Bible and Greek Philosophy" (*EP* 38). Against this background the realm of the other-worldly and worldliness stand facing each other: "That God is, is enough" (*EP* 38). Here we note the idea of the *deus abconditus* formed by Nicolaus Cusanus. God is for us unattainably, incomprehensibly, invisibly, a perfectly mysterious God: "The believed God is the distant God, the hidden God, the unfathomable God" (*EP* 49). This God concept shows us the real nature of human freedom: "Freedom and God are inseparable" (*EP* 43). If we succeed in winning an intimate connection through faith in God, we achieve the highest experience of freedom.

Jaspers thinks from the historical beginnings of faith to a comprehensive faith in our time, which he calls philosophical faith. But what remains of this faith today? How do we describe the relationship between myth, religious faith, philosophical faith, and the other kinds of faith in our time?

Philosophical and Theological Aspects of Faith

There is a fundamental difference between knowledge and faith. What we know, we do not need to believe. Genuine faith is on a level different from knowledge. Jaspers emphasizes the fact that "faith demands *sacrificio dell intelletto*."[2] Both philosophy

---

[1] Karl Jaspers, *Einführung in die Philosophie* (Munich: R. Piper, 1953), p. 62. All translations by the author. [Henceforth cited as *EP*]

[2] Karll Jaspers, *Philosophie*, Volume 1 (Berlin: J. Springer, 1932), p. 304. [Henceforth cited as *P* with volume number.]

and religion have important mental aspects. Jaspers works out the differences in religion by focusing on prayer and cult, revelation, ecclesiastical community; while in philosophy he stresses the independence of existence and the way to transcendence. Their proximity, he notes, "recognizes the possibility of prayer" (*PI* 299), and he intensifies this thought when he observes, "praying has to do with possible reality, the lack of which we are painfully conscious of" (*PI* 311). Thus Jaspers recognizes the limits of philosophical thinking: "Philosophy cannot provide redemption, which happens in religious faith through overcoming tragedy."[3] Nonetheless, philosophy contains faith elements, and from this background Jaspers forms the basic terms of philosophical faith: "Philosophical faith, the faith of thinking humans, at all times has the feature that it is only possible together with knowledge."[4]

There are two aspects of faith that Leonard Ehrlich shares with Jaspers, viz., the contents of faith (*fides quae creditor*) and the existential experience of faith (*fides qua creditor*). This basic theological distinction originally is from Augustine[5] and it makes possible the further development of Augustine's terminology in dealing with the tension field between knowledge and faith, namely, *fides, credere* and *ratio, intelligere* as a basic rule with constant reference to the distinction between *pistis* and *gnosis* in Greek philosophy: "We know in order to believe; and believe in order to know (*Ergo intellige, ut credas, crede, ut intelligas*)."[6] Anselm of Canterbury develops the same formula in terms of faith-seeking understanding (*fides quaerens intellectum*). Thus we can differentiate between various possibilities for faith in God: as my reason for faith (*credere Deum*), from which I give testimony (*credere deo*), and as my faith intention (*credere in deum*). As Augustine states: "What therefore is belief in God? In faith go on loving, in faith go on esteeming, by faith go into God to become a part of his body."[7]

But Jaspers also reminds us: "Christian faith is but one faith, not the faith of all mankind."[8] By going beyond the Occidental horizon and considering the major religions worldwide, Jaspers locates the Axial Age (*Achsenzeit*) of religious consciousness several centuries before Christ: "The axle of world history seems approximately to lie...between 800 and 200 BC. There the deepest divide in history lies" (*UZG* 19). It is a time that includes the preaching of the Jewish prophets, pre-Socratic philosophy, the teachings of Zarathustra, Hinduism and Buddhism in India, and Confucius and Lao Tse in China. These signs of faith form the Axial Age for Jaspers. And into this theory he introduces the doctrine of the Encompassing in order to establish the ultimate horizon of thinking-faith. Only in the realm of

---

[3] Karl Jaspers, *Von der Wahrheit* (Munich: Piper, 1958), p. 965. [Henceforth cited as *W*]

[4] Karl Jaspers, *Der philosophische Glaube* (Munich: Piper, 1948), p. 13. [Henceforth cited as *PG*]

[5] Augustine, "De Trinitate 13,2," in Peter Eicher, *Neues Handbuch theologischer Grundbegriffe*, Volume 2 (Munich: Kösel, 1991), p. 238. [Henceforth cited as *NHG*]

[6] Augustine, Ep. 120 (*NHG* 238).

[7] *Quid est ergo credere in eum? Credendo amare, credendo diligere, credendo in eum ire, eius membris incoporari*, in Tract. Io. Ev. 29 (*NHG* 238).

[8] Karl Jaspers, *Vom Ursprung und Ziel der Geschichte* (Munich: R. Piper, 1949), p. 19. [Henceforth cited as *UZG*]

the Encompassing (*das Umgreifende*) can we attain philosophical faith, for the Encompassing has a double meaning: "The Being which encompasses us is the world as Transcendence; and the Being, which we are as life, consciousness and spirit, as Existenz" (*PG* 17). Within this field of tension—Transcendence and Existenz—philosophical faith can arise. "Faith has to do with living in view of the Encompassing, and possible Existenz is fulfillment by the Encompassing" (*PG* 20). The material contents of philosophical faith are the spiritual traditions of all humanity.

Jaspers describes the general characteristics of philosophical faith in terms of the following factors: (a) "the Transcendence beyond the world and before all worlds that is called God" (*PG* 29), (b) "the absolute demand that has its origin in me, bearing me along" (*PG* 31), and (c) "the reality of the world that is the vanishing of life between God and existence, the suspension of all recognized realities" (*PG* 32). Leonard Ehrlich describes two additional characteristics in Jaspers' *Introduction to Philosophy* and inserts them between (b) and (c), namely, that "humans are finite and unable to be perfect,"[9] and that "humans can live by the revelations of God" (*JÖG* 18). When considering of all these characteristics, Jaspers, like Cusanus, emphasizes that "we always remain in the suspense of unknowing" (*PG* 33).

Looking back favorably at the Biblical religions that have shaped occidental thinking, Jaspers notes, "the philosophical contents of Occidental philosophizing have their historical source not only in Greek, but also in Biblical thinking" (*PG* 34). He emphasizes the importance of one God, the transcendent creator God, the meeting of humans with this God, the commandments of God, the consciousness of historicity, suffering, and openness for paradox. Only thinking about this kind of God makes authentic human freedom possible: "The more humans are actually free, the more certainly of God. I am actually free and am certain that I am not free from myself, for God is for me the measure whereby I actually exist" (*EP* 63–64).

Jaspers also ponders the reality of a diminishing faith in our time and that "this loss of faith is a consequence of the Enlightenment" (*EP* 67). But he also differentiates thereby between true and false enlightenment. True enlightenment prepares a steady and appropriate place for faith. Here we feel the force of the injunction of Kant: "To limit knowledge in order to make room for faith."[10] For genuine faith is the indispensable basis for existential communication: "Only faith can understand belief" (*P2* 434). Even a conscious refusal of faith, the quest of absolutely atheistic thinking, saves an aspect of faith: "Nothing stands against God, which is not itself God; *Nemo contra deum nisi deus ipse*" (*P3* 73). Atheism therefore necessarily includes a content and attitude of mind oriented to the absent God.

It is important to consider the starting point of Jaspers. He develops the notion of philosophical faith for nearly 25 years prior to the end of World War II and the publication of *Der philosophische Glaube* (1948). During the subsequent 15 years

---

[9] Leonard Ehrlich, "Zu Jaspers' Idee eines Philosophischen Glaubens," *Jahrbuch der Östereichischen Karl Jaspers Gesellschaft*, eds. Elisabeth Salamun-Hybašek and Kurt Salamun, Volume 16 (Innsbruck: Studien Verlag, 2003), p. 17. [Henceforth cited as *JÖG*]

[10] Immanuel Kant, *Kritik der reinen Vernunft* (Leipzig: A. Kröner, 1925), p. 18.

we encounter the debate on demythologizing with Rudolf Bultmann and the publication of Jaspers' exhaustive work on *Philosophical Faith and Revelation* (1962) where he discusses the topic of faith in great detail.[11] In this work, Jaspers first asks whether it is possible to find faith in our time. The language of science can describe empirical facts clearly, but scientific exactitude cannot tell us what it means to be human and therefore remains existentially superficial. Only deep insight into vital truths can affect our subjectivity and make genuine communication possible.

Thus the question arises, how do philosophical and religious faith relate to each other, and is a fruitful meeting between them possible? Jaspers finds a progressive loss of faith in the world of modern humans as consequence of false enlightenment, but he also believes that it is possible for the two faiths to coalesce in the consciousness of many humans. He believes that revelatory faith can be thinking faith. Thinking faith unfolds in theology if it arises from historically determined revelation, while in philosophy, thinking faith arises from originary questions regarding the meaning of humanity. Philosophy can influence human orientation to revelation: "Philosophical faith has its own origin. But it permits revelation to be valid for other possibilities, even though philosophy cannot comprehend it" (*PGO* 38). On the other hand, revelation can become for philosophy a cipher that remains an unsolvable secret. In believing, one experiences a force from within that comes as a gift from elsewhere: "Faith is reason before all revelation. Its purpose is never to verify, but to recognize more luminously" (*PGO* 50).

Jaspers recognizes different approaches to theology and philosophy in the history of ideas. With reference to Bonaventure and Augustine he notes that theological thinking has its starting point from God; philosophy however leads to God. Theology therefore is the science of what is beyond reason, whereas philosophical thinking vis-à-vis theology is the science of human reason. Philosophy holds to fundamental knowledge which Jaspers, in his work, *Von der Wahrheit*, treats in detail: "Fundamental scientific knowledge, as to how we are in the world, tries to give us total knowledge which does not exist" (*PGO* 123). The tension between faith and knowledge thus informs Jaspers' thinking on ciphers—which, for our age, has special importance. Traces of Transcendence in ciphers are to be read ambiguously and never with total determinacy: "That which speaks in ciphers, and which desires sensuous material experience and proofs, cannot be understood; only the freedom of *Existenz* can hear the voice of Transcendence" (*PGO* 158).

Ciphers as the possible language of Transcendence, brings our thinking into a fruitful suspension and makes existential decisions possible. Thus important ciphers become, as mental realities, the foundation of human freedom. The strict constraints of ordered truths have to be waived so that genuine truthfulness can emerge. Thinking in ciphers can also prevent errors:

> The mischief of our time today has much to do with the diminishment of cipher language. The air that we breathe has become not only thin but also polluted by superstitious scientific

---

[11] Karl Jaspers, *Der philosophische Glaube angesichts der Offenbarung* (Munich: R. Piper, 1962). [Henceforth cited as *PGO*]

conceptions. Insight into the nature of the ciphers is a condition for the possibility that
ciphers can regain their existential force and the wealth of their language. (*PGO* 169)

Against this background Jaspers views positively those religious institutions in the
world that retain and transmit basic values. Concerning the Christian faith he says:

> The church still exists today. After the 18th century it seemed that the poetical and philo-
> sophical wealth of the Occident had been flushed away by the floods of the mentally superior
> world of freethinking and scientific positivism. But these floods have passed like a rock
> dipped into the spiritual-political waters of the church. (*PGO* 92)

Jaspers then draws a much larger circle than the one previously described by the
term "biblical religion." All "religions of the book" are taken into consideration by
way of philosophical faith. Here, the concept of God is of fundamental importance:
"The way of the person becoming human and the cipher of the personal God cor-
respond to each other" (*PGO* 221). Christian faith therefore is valid because "while
the nascent human God, Christ, is philosophically impossible, Jesus can speak to us
as a singular cipher" (*PGO* 225). Cipher thinking thus opens the area of freedom in
transcendence. It is here that the boundaries of any cipher language, originating in
an imperfect human nature, become clear:

> Only if a certain and real final conception becomes actual in the final representation of the
> cipher is there an awakening of Existenz. Then the final representation and internal reversal
> correspond. And in the reversal I am given to myself by another, as it were, in my freedom.
> (*PGO* 295)

In such a way humans remain in their everydayness; but if this mood breaks open in
the crisis times of life, transcendence can happen: "The stature of man lies in what he
becomes through the experience of boundary situations" (*PGO* 319). The insecurity
and transitory nature of human life is often displaced by the apparent successes
of science and technology which, erroneously accepted as final solutions, are the
product of scientific superstition. Cipher thinking saves us from the embarrassment
of scientific superstition and opens us to a further horizon: "Given to ourselves as
Existenz, the tradition of antiquity and the Bible have the power of fulfillment from
Transcendence" (*PGO* 421).

Thus the unfolding of cipher thinking points us to a boundary situation regarding
the meaning of Biblical statements where "the revealing reality does not speak more
than the possible cipher, since it is the experience of an uncanny boundary" (*PGO*
367). "The failure of each finite thought regarding the infinity of transcendence,
however, is also a way to become more clearly certain of its reality" (*PGO* 388).
Failure in this sense means shipwreck or foundering, grasping at the rubble and
remnants but with a positive view of what is happening throughout the experience.
For in failing or foundering, I obtain a positive orientation to my own life.

Beyond all ciphers understanding provides only what is not bound to words
but remains in silence: "In silence, nascent words lose their depth" (*PGO* 417).
This becomes clearly evident with participation in the spiritual exercises of Saint
Ignatius where, in the proximity of silence, the silence of the most internal God
opens itself. A quintessential point of Biblical faith directs our view to the freeing
of humans from their everyday activities: "The history of humans is the history of

freedom" (*PGO* 429). This freedom must be always achieved anew for otherwise the danger of an aversion to freedom arises that can be fatal for the world. The totalitarian dictatorships of the recent past indicate the future of humanity can be affected by "the most radical freedom that. . .can destroy the freedom of all humans" (*PGO* 462).

Thus in our technical age, internal freedom struggles to retain truth. This can only happen through communicative argumentation that has the character of a loving struggle: "Instead of having the benefit of an already completed truth, we humans stand for a struggle on the way to truth" (*PGO* 463). Here we meet the loving struggle of communication at the heart of the philosophy of Karl Jaspers. By this struggle humans have the possibility of an internal conversion "through overcoming the particulars standing in the way of communication and drawing nearer to philosophical thinking" (*PGO* 469). In the hope of meeting in positive communication, Jaspers bases his belief that "Faith in revelation and philosophical faith can become one" (*PGO* 479).

Jaspers esteems highly the values of Biblical tradition and demands their vital appropriation by humanity: "The bible has opened for us new depths into the reason of things" (*PGO* 496). He describes Christian communities as substantial components of human society and future tasks "that will perhaps determine the future fate of the Occident" (*PGO* 477). The pastoral activities of the clergy thereby are of paramount importance. The preaching of the Biblical tradition should not be neglected by secondary tasks that promote haste and discord: "The task of the priest is fulfilled in solitude. It is without noise. It lies where the origin the human existence is determined" (*PGO* 523) and "It is from these priests, and not the theologians, that the church develops" (*PGO* 524).

A significant discussion *Philosophical Faith and Revelation* took place in 1963 between the philosopher Karl Jaspers and the theologian Heinz Zahrnt. Their dialogue had to do with conditions for the promotion and encouragement of communication. The question as to the ultimate meaning of life, for Jaspers, is that "answers always remain in suspension."[12] The loving communicative struggle always hovers "around the cipher God" (*PK* 65). For humans this consciousness is crucial to the life "which always stands in the necessity of turning from the threat of loss from the outset" (*PK* 66).

"He who believes," Jaspers asserts, "believes by grace" (*PK* 68). In this manner, faith becomes the fundamental idea bringing human existence to the forefront: "Thus the contrast is not between faith and cognition, but the kind of faith which brings thinking itself to consciousness and this means a faith cognition neither philosophical nor theological" (*PK* 70). In scientific thinking, faith revolves around correctness; in philosophical thinking faith revolves around deep insight: "The truth character of faith and science are of an altogether different nature" (*PK* 72). By faith humans can experience fulfillment. No human can live his or her life from scientific

---

[12] Karl Jaspers, *Provokationen: Gespräche und Interviews* (Munich: Piper, 1969), p. 64. [Henceforth cited as *PK*]

results alone: "Every person needs a faith basis for everything that it is of major importance" (*PK* 72). Only faith opens the way to existential freedom, which we may accept as a gift from elsewhere. Like Kant, Jaspers believes "I cannot prove the reality of freedom" (*PK* 75). However freedom and faith point the way for action: "Faith proves itself in the actions of the humans who are doing it" (*PK* 76).

Zahrnt points to a particularly important aspect of Jaspers' thinking in this regard: "The hovering character of truth finds its expression in the language of the ciphers" (*PK* 76). This substantial understanding from theological side is most important because it is here that the possibilities of fruitful communication become manifest. As Jaspers puts it, "faith and truth can only become reality in communication" (*PK* 82), and further, "Truth is that which binds us together, and communication is the site of the truth" (*PK* 82). A vital faith therefore proves itself to be the basic foundation of the struggle for truth in community and the basis of the expectation that: "Philosophical faith and faith in revelation do not have to make humans enemies, but can provide a meeting ground" (*PK* 91).

The Starting Point and the Path of Practical Experiences

We have suggested that throughout human development religion is a fundamental feature of being human. The history of humanity demonstrates the indestructible traces of religious belief. Jaspers seizes upon this fact and places it into a universal framework by demonstrating the origin and development of philosophical faith. A critical feature of this faith is its readiness for comprehensive communication. Jaspers unfolds this path of thinking in a way that restores faith to philosophy. He commences on this path in his early works and completes it in the late works of the 1960s. Clearly, Jaspers succeeds in the task of integrating religious faith into philosophy in a comprehensive manner. Leonard Ehrlich is entirely true to Jaspers when he states: "Faith is a fundamental phenomenon of the historicity of human beings who, in the experience of freedom, founder on embracing transcendence. As a fundamental phenomenon faith appears long before the distinction between philosophy and religion" (*JÖG* 20). In this manner faith, as fundamental reason, proves to be something by which humans can inform themselves vitally, and it is faith that makes communication possible in the widest possible sense.

It is entirely valid to deepen the meaning of faith from the way it is understood in normal theological thinking. Ever since Tertullian this deepening has been associated with the saying, "I believe because it is absurd" (*Credo, quia absurdum*; *Gerade weil es Widersinn ist, glaube ich es*).[13] Here a radical contrast between faith and reason seems to obtain, but it also has to be understood in terms of Tertullian's struggle against docetic gnosticism.

---

[13] Two contributions by Gottlieb Söhngen in *Lexikon für Theologie und Kirche*, Volume 3, eds. Michael Buchberger, Josef Höfer, and Karl Rahner (Freiburg im Breisgau: Herder, 1986), p. 89. [Henceforth cited as *LTK*]

But there is also the position of Anselm of Canterbury, "I believe so that I can understand" (*Credo ut intelligam*; *Ich glaube, damit ich erkennen kann*) (*LTK* 89). It is the point already made by Augustine as the path of religious knowledge. Faith and understanding do not exclude but complement each other. In order to describe the special nature of both ways of mental experience, the following expression can be helpful: "I believe, because it concerns an eternal mystery" (*Credo, quia mysterium*; *Ich glaube, weil es ein bleibendes Geheimnis ist*) (*LTK* 90). The limitations of human understanding are recognized here and, at the same time, the unfathomable hidden nature of Transcendence is also recognized. In faith I can approach the Godhead, but I never am able to seize it. As a travel guide once expressed it on a visit to Delphi, "The man who wants to know like a god is a fool."

What are we to make of the status of faith in our world? In the West, a constant evaporation of faith is evident. Churches have lost their power and influence and the number of faithful members is reduced. The influence of science and technology and its rapid advance throughout the world makes faith appear to be superfluous and redundant. The spirit of the times does not lend itself to the asking of fundamental questions regarding Transcendence and Existenz, but seems concerned only with the interrupted pursuit of pleasure. Such developments lead the Western world to the edge of an abyss. Religious indifference aids and abets the dissolution of values and to relativism at all levels. Aggressive atheism has not proved to be the worst enemy, but rather a consumptive materialism that imbues all areas of life with superficiality. This has become evident, for example, in East Germany where 20 years of dictatorship were peacefully overcome only to be replaced by a new preoccupation with prosperity and material possessions.

In contrast we witness a radical religious awakening in the Islamic world of the 1980s. "He who denies the existence of God, in the Islamic view, is no longer human but degraded to the level of an animal."[14] Terrorist activities of some Islamic extremists have the unfortunate effect of covering up genuine faith concerns. As religious illiteracy spreads rapidly in Europe, the possibility of humans deepening their faith by understanding the faith of others is diminished. On a journey through Turkey, a native Muslim described the importance of faith to me in the following way: "Faith is like an organ of my body. If it does not work correctly, I become ill, and if it is taken from me, I must die."

These examples indicate that faith alone provides the possibility of genuine, loving, existential communication that always remains inaccessible to the strictly scientific horizon of understanding. Deep-seated communication and mutual understanding of human relationships, however, is imperative to find lasting solutions to the vital problems of today's world. It will only be through pastoral activity and providing a basic knowledge of the biblical message that the West will again understand the meaning of divine revelation. In the long run, this will be critical for the future

---

[14] Peter Scholl-Latour, *Allah ist mit den Standhaften* (Stuttgart: Deutsche Verlags-Anstalt, 1983), p. 699.

of Western civilization and for Jaspers' communicative reason. For only at the comprehensive level of faith is a depth of existential understanding attainable, achieved, so that the caller and the called can truly understand each other and not merely talk past each other. The lifelong struggle for such a ground of faith shows that spiritual greatness lies in man. Religious and philosophical faith can meet and then testify to a faith understood in an encompassing sense and that loving communication can bring the world's people of faith together.

Another personal experience can shed light on the importance of inter-faith dialogue. Travel bureaus in Ceylon provide tourists with the option of climbing to the top of Adam's Peak, the highest mountain in center of the island. Only a few travelers participate in this rigorous option, which includes traveling on primitive roads and, beginning at midnight, the difficult thirty-five hundred meter final climb to the summit. Both young and old were part of the pilgrim course in which I participated, and toward morning we reached the summit where a rock impression of a footprint is admired in different ways by the devoutly religious: by Jews, as the footprint of Adam, banished from Paradise; by Christians, as the footprint of the Apostle Thomas, in his mission to India; by Muslims, as the footprint of Mohammed, who taught from the Koran at this mountain; by Hindus, as the footprint of Shiva; and by Buddhists, as the footprint of Lord Buddha. Members of the great world religions participated in this pilgrimage, and on that bitterly cold morning we were united in a common faith.

Karl Jaspers and Leonard Ehrlich both recognize the abundant possibilities of meeting in the loving struggle for fruitful existential communication. Unfortunately communication in our time is all too often superficially misunderstood in terms of the ever more extensive technical capabilities. The tremendous advance in information technology is certainly helpful, but considered alone has nothing to do with improvements in communication, inter-human solidarity, understanding, and the continual struggle for a more deeply felt existential bond of humanity. The latter is possible only at the level of the faith, for faith is the foundation that opens up a future horizon for humanity. If philosophical faith, especially in the West, diminishes even more rapidly than is presently the case, then the deepest dangers develop for the future of humanity. Only faith can transform humanity from the inside and yield thereby improvements in existential communication. For this to happen, both religious faith and philosophical faith require mutual fertilization: philosophy needs fertilization by the word of revelation, and religion needs fertilization through the structures of critical thinking. Since only a thinking-faith can secure the future survival of humanity, I close this essay with famous words attributed to Andre Malraux—words entirely appropriate for understanding philosophical faith we find in Karl Jaspers and Leonard Ehrlich: "The 21st century will be religious or the 21st century will not exist; *Le XXIeme siècle sera religieux ou ne sera pas*; *Das 21. Jahrhundert wird religiös sein, oder es wird nicht sein.*"[15]

---

[15] Cited in Peter Scholl-Latour, *Kampf dem Terror—Kampf dem Islam?* (Berlin: Propyläen, 2002), p. 54.

Freedom in the Space of Nothingness

Malek K. Khazaee

Abstract This chapter contends that freedom can exist and thrive only in the space of nothingness. The latter is the antithesis of physical and metaphysical restraint in so far as freedom seems definable only as "the absence of restraint." The presence of this absence makes freedom what it is. While freedom is rooted in and desired by every sentient being, human and non-human, this chapter focuses only on the human side, the side that immediately involves personal as well as socio-political areas of life in the context of briefly discussing the national politics of a few States, with some consequential international issues.

Legend has it that when Nāsser-ed-Din Shah (reign 1848–1896) was advised to establish modern institutions of higher learning, he concluded sarcastically: "So, We shall spread consciousness and thereby occasion the downfall of Our own dynasty!"[1] A century and a half later, the protests of several million Iranians against the alleged widespread presidential electoral fraud were blamed by many officials on the Internet! The undercover and uniformed security forces have thus far raided, arrested and imprisoned several domestic protest sites and networkers, only to realize, each time, their inability to prevent the passing of the baton to the networking Diaspora and foreign service-providers—well beyond their reach. These electronic events have angered the government whose repeated attempts at interrupting socio-political networking have been frustrated by a geographically scattered but electronically connected group of savvy sympathizers providing service to and being fascinated to be a part of a historic protest movement as far away as thousands of kilometers.[2] Even on one occasion in the heat of the summer of 2009 the California-based Twitter delayed its scheduled maintenance for communication to flow uninterruptedly so that local protest organizers could continue circumventing the government's old-fashioned radio-television censorship by publishing online news, sending out messages to millions of desktops and laptops and cell phones in

---

[1] Paraphrased translation of one of his famous sayings.

[2] For example, Dina Bass and Pimm Fox of *Bloomberg News* refer to Jonathan Zittrain of Harvard Law School, and say that the "Iranians got around the clampdown by using servers outside the country to route Internet traffic around blocked Web sites." June 21, 2009.

M.K. Khazaee (✉)
California State University, Long Beach, CA, USA
e-mail: mkhazaee@csulb.edu

H. Wautischer et al. (eds.), *Philosophical Faith and the Future of Humanity*,
DOI 10.1007/978-94-007-2223-1_30, © Springer Science+Business Media B.V. 2012

homes and streets, thereby enabling more protest plans for gatherings in certain locations to follow. Meanwhile, the citizen-journalists have been filling in for the imprisoned national and expelled international journalists by transmitting their on-scene cellphone-camera recordings of the motorcycle police and plain-clothes Basij militiamen beating the protestors.

By repeatedly tearing down the government's firewalls, counter-measuring its crawling Internet slowdowns, breaking through its news blackouts, transmitting its violence, as well as twittering millions of tweets to wear the symbolic green, to write harmonious placards, and to mobilize massive demonstrations in certain streets, boulevards, public squares and parks, the Green Movement has been surprised at its own success. A proof of this is the cellphone videos sent out to YouTube and foreign TV stations, revealing the government's once invulnerable, consistent and iron-fisted stance now turned into a comical show of weariness and panic by its security forces, nervous reactions and contradictory statements by its public officials, finger-pointing and infighting in the Majles. This rapidly evolving struggle has led some of the movement's seasoned politicians to join in by text-messaging each other, twit on the election they believe stolen, and publically accuse the government of illegitimacy and national disgrace.[3] Amid the protests, it is no longer clear who the true leaders are: the same opposition politicians, or the newly social networking organizers? In the latest gatherings it has in fact been the politicians who have been joining the several hundred-thousand chanting crowds already in procession. In essence, it does not anymore matter who truly won the election. This sudden cyber-power shift has emboldened the youth with the self-awareness that their effective employment of computer technology is enabling them to bypass government censorship by doing and showing things to the world in ways hitherto unthinkable.[4] This phenomenon has in turn led the foreign newspaper reporters, TV anchors and commentators to herald the coming of a new age—that we are presently at the threshold of a true computer revolution, that virtual reality can now create actual reality, that we are finally witnessing the wedding of the PC with Grand Politics. The electronically powered peculiarity of this uprising is hailed particularly by the Western press as the opening of a political super-highway that eventually will wear-down and teardown oppressive regimes everywhere.

---

[3] With regard to the protestors' tenacity, *Washington Post* reporters Thomas Erdbrink and William Branigin write: "The government has struggled to quell protests for five months, deploying security forces on the streets of Tehran and officially banning opposition demonstrations. Yet, on Wednesday, anti-government demonstrators openly defied the ban, even as police fired tear gas and warning shots. In video clips captured by cellphone cameras, helmeted police officers could be seen beating protesters, including women, with batons." "In Iran, Rival Rallies Show Off Rift Endures: Clashes Erupt as Regime Marks 30th Anniversary of U.S. Embassy Siege," Thursday, November 5, 2009. About two months later, Diaa Haddid of Associated Press reports: "Iran's opposition has been heavily dependent on the Internet to organize protests and air the views of its leaders despite repeated attempts by authorities to block access to some sites." Sunday, January 10, 2010.

[4] This is a nation of approximately seventy-five million people, with an average age of thirty-three!

The upbeat tone of this prediction is not farfetched. The unprecedented nature of this ongoing phenomenon, which is bypassing the state-run media censorship and exposing the government's crackdowns in alleys and streets, must be a warning sign to all authoritarian rulers. The Chinese leaders, in particular, must be deeply worried about the inevitable fall of the political culture whose decades-old tendencies to secrecy, censorship, disinformation, tight grips on education and mind-control are now faced with Facebook, MySpace, Twitter, YouTube, etc.—the sort of things at first glance shallow and insignificant, but ultimately threatening to pull the rug from beneath the *ancient régime* altogether. China has always been authoritarian, xenophobic and obsessed with protecting its extensive borders, of which the Great Wall testifies. The question of its great firewalls, though, is now hanging in balance, as the tradition of controlling the physical borders and of state media are being bypassed via borderless and invisible waves received by and shown on millions of personal computers and cellphone screens on a wide variety of news and shows, like a parliamentary debate in Tokyo, a polling process in Warsaw, free-speech at the Hyde Park Corner, rioting in Lagos, elections in Seoul, the rugged life of Chechyan separatists, a rock concert in Johannesburg, terrorist bombings in Mumbai, spending sprees in Sao Paulo, Formula-1 racing in Dubai, fashion shows in Milan, or Monaco's leisurely lifestyles and casinos.[5] Among the many difficulties for the PRC Communist Party is how to deal with the rapidly growing Internet-savvy domestic bourgeoisie.

The leadership's strategy of liberalization has been nothing more than economic privatization. Because of its inflexibility in and inadaptability to the current political atmosphere, the government's initiating gradual and steady change toward a greater degree of freedom is unlikely. The Chinese leaders have apparently not learned Marx's lesson that a change in the economic infra-structure will inevitably lead to a change in the superstructure, including the class structure, social relations, and form of government—except that this time the direction is reversed, as the bourgeoisie is now a growing threat to the ruling Communist Party. Beijing is unwilling to politically adapt to its shifting infra-structure, since such adaptation would mean a resignation probably more destabilizing than the collapse of the Soviet experiment.[6] It is very ironic that the government, whose propaganda and agitations had

---

[5] Baidu, as China's state-run Internet search engine, is not a monopoly to control all the receiving information. Furthermore, the Chinese government's shared interest with the Iranian regime in controlling the country's Internet traffic has led to its publicly accusing the United State's government of cyber role in the Iranian upheaval—the same charge made by the Islamic Republic. For further details: "China Raises Stakes in Cyber War, Points to US Role in Iran," *The Economic Times*, January 26, 2010. Also, "China Paper Slams US for Cyber Role in Iran Unrest," *Strait Times*, January 24, 2010. On the Iranian charge, see: "Iran Accuses U.S. of creating 'Hacker Brigade,'" *PC Magazine*, January 25, 2010.

[6] In fact, from the Marxian perspective, the USSR and PRC had never been truly socialist. Russia and China, as agrarian/feudal states, had not gone through the capitalist mode of production to mature politically for the post-bourgeois, superstructural conditions of a true socialist society. So, as a phony socialist state, China, like Russia before her, will have to fail. Marx and Engels would have defended themselves by concluding that the return of Russia and China to capitalism is the

often been worded with excessive pride in being "Marxist," was in complete violation of Marx's materialist conception of history. Today, China is arguably the fastest
developing nation and greatest exporter on earth. The whopping computer sales in
this country of nearly one-and-a-half-billion people will inevitably lead to a nation-
wide liberal-democratic uprising that would miniaturize the June 4, 1989 Tiananmen
Square massacre. The more the political leadership stays rigid and unchanged, the
harder the impact of adjustment. Since the nation-state is still the sole powerhouse
of political and military forces, the PRC (or "People's Republic of Capitalism!")
could, if it so chose, shut down the Internet altogether—but at the cost of losing
much of its means of communication and the collapse of its financial institutions
and economy. Thanks to the inventions of electronics and fiber-optics, the world has
changed drastically since the reign of the Qing emperors—even beyond the wildest
imaginations of the nineteenth-century social and political European prophets.[7]

---

costly punishments for cheating on Mother History! This is true, in spite of the fact that on some
odd occasion Marx, who was disappointed and frustrated by his failed predictions of a socialist
revolution in the most industrially advanced Britain, and then the other Western nations, in the end
hoped for Russia to pioneer socialism.

[7] Obviously, the development and spread of cyber communication are not destabilizing or negative everywhere. For example, the connection of the cellphone to the Internet has been and will
continue to be a positive development for India. This most populous democracy is benefiting from
its colonial past by receiving numerous outsourced jobs, involving the latest instruments and gad-
gets whose primary language for communication is English. In fact, every walking and talking
Indian, in this nation of over a billion people, can carry fully customizable cellphones linked to
Facebook, MySpace, Twitter, text-messaging, emailing, every online newspaper, latest dictionaries
and encyclopedias—in a word, everything that is needed for information and communication—
stored in a tiny device held on the palm of a hand. All this, is at the disposal of numerous Indians
whose command of English is more methodical, and grammatically more accurate, than millions of
English speakers in the rest of the world. So, in contrast to the authoritarian regimes who perceive
the Internet as a serious challenge, the Indian government has no reason to fear but welcome it with
open arms. These tremendous opportunities, which have already led to a considerable economic
and financial success for this nation, will probably make it one of the world's two super-states.
Only China and India have the capacity of becoming "super-states"—the term whose application
requires a nation-state to be endowed with an exceptionally large population and a highly advanced
industrial output. Unlike the Western nations whose technological and social developments took
many decades of costly trial-and-error, these potential super-states, along with the smaller but
equally rapidly advancing East Asian and some Latin American nations are presently taking
shortcuts for development. For instance, instead of spending fortunes and decades for installing
numerous kilometers of telegraph cables or telephone-lines, they are using cellphones even in
remote villages; and instead of paying for mega-tons of paper and using costly, often inefficient
and time-consuming postal service, they are enjoying cost-free emailing with nearly the speed of
light. By benefitting from such innovations and shortcuts, some of these Third-World nations will
soon catch up and surpass a number of First-World countries. As time progresses, even newer, as
yet unknown techno-electronic horizons will be opening up for these developing nations, while
Europe's rusty industries and reverent old towns with narrow streets and alleys cannot simply be
bulldozed and leveled for post-industrial sites, or paved for wide and efficient traffic routes for
business and commercial transportation. The Third World does not have any aged industries to be
stuck with, or many structures blocking the way to development. Among the main reasons for the
astonishing postwar superiority of German and Japanese economies was their opportunity to build
anew on the ruins of World War II. It is widely believed that the rising China and India, which

Across this dynamic and complex landscape, there is one theme at play: freedom. It is rooted in and desired by every single being, human or non-human. Freedom, insofar as it is often defined by contrasting it with its antithesis as the "absence of restraint," depends on one entity who either enjoys the absence of restraint or suffers from its presence, and the other entity, the oppressor, who is either unwilling to or incapable of breaking that absence. Of course, an absence of this "absence" or the presence of restraint can occasion by a non-human animal, or even an insentient object. Hence, the two sides can be (1) both humans at each end, (2) a human and a non-human animal, (3) both sides non-human animals, (4) sentient and insentient, and (5) both insentient (e.g. the river held back by a mudslide, free air). In each case, though, only one side is in the position to restrain the other (although, in some sentient instances, both sides possess the ability to restrain, or avoid imposing restraint on the other party and bring peaceful coexistence or a balance of power).[8] As a deep seated proclivity, "freedom" has been regarded as a natural right and a precondition for the liberal-democracy. Now I am not particularly a diehard fan of democracy, having serious reservations about its odd economic partner, capitalism. Nonetheless, I would have to agree with Churchill, namely, that "Democracy is the worst form of government, except for all the others." Having just mentioned the necessity of "freedom" for every sentient being, I must add briefly that whenever as a child I had visited a zoo, I noticed that many birds were inexhaustibly running on their fragile feet from side to side in their cages. At the time appearing as a dumb show, it is still strong enough in its details to make me realize that the birds' desperate act must have been due to their hope of eventually running to a missing bar and flying away. Again as a child, whenever I walked toward our leashed golden-retriever, I witnessed his restless anticipation of getting unleashed and, when unleashed, he exploded, madly running around, ruining some shrubs and flowers while occasionally glancing at me gratefully with those naughty round eyes. Our daily experiences show that the human desire for freedom is shared with other animals, as the birds

---

make up 37% of the world population, will dominate the globe from the mid or late twentieth-first century onward. (Some of the information in this note on India and the other developing nations are my memories of watching Thomas L. Friedman's comments on the "Charlie Rose Show," Public Broadcasting Corporation, Thursday, March 26, 2009). Amid these global cyber movements and technical developments, the Online Jihadists have not been falling far behind. The "Twitter Terrorists" are filming explosive and bloody actions in Iraq and Afghanistan, and posting them on YouTube in order to expose the vulnerability of the Western forces. Through the website jihadica.com they are presently threatening to "invade Facebook" by their Wahabbi supporters and fanatics in the Middle East, North and Central Africa, South and East Asia, North and South America, and Western Europe. These are some unfortunate angry, intolerant, resentful, and dangerous inhabitants of the shrinking global village whose existence is becoming increasingly and equally intolerable to the rest of the world.

[8] In actual situations, the presence, absence, or degrees of restraint can change from time to time. For example, a lion, after having enough of a new kill, would normally impose no restraints on the nearby gazelles, and the gazelles are somehow aware of their freedom to continue playing around for a limited time. But when the time comes for the lion's next meal, the restraint fades away: then, the lion becomes the fearsome oppressor, and the gazelles, the terrified oppressed with no freedom of movement, except seeking shelter to hide or running away to safety.

of many feathers, mammals of many furs, and reptiles of many scales, either enjoy freedom in their natural habitats or strive to be free when in bondage.

In humans, this desire springs out as a faith in "freedom," especially under deprived conditions.[9] To believe otherwise is to deny the existence of this natural desire, and even the dignity of the individual. To view people as "herd-animals" (*Herdentiere*), as Nietzsche did, might be correct—but only to a certain extent. In so far as they are social animals, humans are herd-like; but as far as they individually display self-centeredness and value their personal privacy, they are solitary. The bloody uprisings give credence to these qualities, for what other reason do millions of revolutionaries risk their lives? Again, this is not to deny the need for a hierarchy in every society, since only an organized community can function practically for the benefit of all, including for those who love to lead. Yet even in the cruelest examples in the animal kingdom, in the wolf packs or among the wild dogs for example, the submissive inferiors always seem to try to challenge their superiors before they are beaten back—and this until the next opportune time to try again. Humans do not seem worse off than wolves and dogs. In the Judeo-Christian religion and in Kant there is the belief that no individual is to be underestimated and that the life of the single individual has infinite value. When life is secured in a civil society, freedom is taken to be next[10]; and when the need and hope in freedom remain unfulfilled, the faith in obtaining it usually becomes stronger and more resilient. Under the spell of oppression, the individual is impelled to seek remedies to overcome such consequent inner states as alienation, depression, feelings of worthlessness, emptiness and nothingness.

Among these states, emptiness and nothingness deserve immediate attention, especially in their non-psychological applications in relation to the psychological ones. In fact, the inner feeling of nothingness or emptiness tends to dissipate as external oppressive forces are reduced to zero. The inner zero of oppression is reached by the reduction and subsequent removal of the outer zero. In order to achieve this outer or external zero, which would dissipate the pressure from one's inner psyche, people, with an enlightened and effective leadership, can rise to eliminate an oppressive condition. Of particular interest here is freedom from that which is not, i.e. restraint. This negativity is a necessary condition for the general conception of freedom. In this sense, freedom can exist only when submerged in the state of nothingness or emptiness since this state is devoid of any restraint. To dispel restraint, willpower is needed to impose an antithetical pressure to tip the balance in favor of individual citizens. This antithetical force must void and null the core of the restraining, oppressive block, in order for freedom to be obtained. By weakening and eventually removing that which has been holding back and preventing the

---

[9] It is hard to know whether in that doghouse under those shading trees there was also a faith in freedom.

[10] After Life, Liberty is the most important element for all animals, including humans. The same order is to be found in John Locke, in the American Constitution, and in the Third Article of the Universal Declaration of Human Rights. The First Article starts by stating, "All human beings are born free and equal in dignity and rights...."

citizens from acting or doing what they wish, the antithetical force of liberation has the same negativity as that of freedom. In fact, this force must be identical with it, as a preliminary stage. Of course, no void, as no instance of nothingness, is, in and by itself, negative. Nothingness and void are like zero. But in order to dispel the restraining force of a tyranny, the void must be brought by an antithetical force to overthrow it. This antithesis would facilitate freedom, since freedom is meaningful only when it operates in a void—the void that is boundless, and its space akin to nothingness. As a result, the more personal empowerment there is by a greater degree of freedom, the weaker the restraint of the governing body. In a national or regional election-season, for example, the empty surrounding of freedom means that everyone, except the elector, must stay out of the electoral process so that the elector can exercise his or her right to vote without any restraining external pressure. Therefore, a running or retiring president (as the head of the republic) or prime minister (as head of the government of a constitutional monarchy), as well as any other official and officer, are obligated to avoid intervening during the electoral process and accept its results. The act of holding back, which in essence is to perform no act or avoidance from interfering or intervening in the election process, is the gap or emptiness at the issue here. If the notion of "holding back" is about the people in the sense that it is them who are being held back, then there is dictatorship or tyranny; but if it is the government that is being held back (by an uprising or by checks and balances), then freedom and democracy exist.

When we say the necessary condition for a free election is emptiness, we mean "emptiness of space" for the voter before and during the electoral process until the counting begins. Within this condition no governmental/non-governmental body is to fill the space between the voter and the vote, or between the ballots and the ballot-boxes. Here emptiness practically means that no external arms to get in the way, no hands be placing packs of readily filled-out votes in the ballot-boxes, no person throwing the ballots in the dumpsters, no uniformed and plain-clothed security force intimidating the voters, no misinformation about the polling locations, no polling station closes earlier than scheduled, and so on. This negativity is essential for a free polity to exist and function. It is essential to understand, however, that neither the desire per se, nor the emptiness into which the desire is imported, is freedom. Rather, freedom is the natural right of the citizen to exercise the act of voting through a non-restraining void. In non-election seasons the same emptiness, nothingness, void or gap between the government and the individual is necessary for his or her protection and privacy from the ruling authority, and for freedom to exist, to continue, and to thrive.

For example, one of the charges brought by the Green Movement in Iran is that a considerable number of sealed ballot-boxes across the country had been unusually heavy and became full too soon, indicating that they must have been stuffed before the election had begun. This grave charge, in addition to others, raises the suspicion that many agents of the sitting president and theocracy, namely the regional and local officials, as well as the Revolutionary Guard and their Basij militiamen across the country, must have been positioning themselves between the electorates and their votes, and between the casted votes and the ballot boxes by filling the

boxes with fraudulent ballots prior to the voting process, by replacing the legitimate ballot boxes with the phony ones, and so on. These allegations mean that those
who were given the responsibility of administering the election had been rigging
it! In a country like pre-revolutionary Egypt, on the other hand, the ballot boxes are
effectively meaningless, since the winner, who always happens to be the sitting president, or a handpicked candidate by the president, is announced by the state-owned
media as having received about 98–99% of the votes—a spectacular victory without anyone ever having witnessed the counting of the ballots! Similarly, the Green
Movement charges that, as shown on their country's state-controlled television and
also watched on the Internet and foreign media, there was no time between the start
of counting the approximately forty-five million votes and the announcement of
the winner by the government. In Afghanistan, Mexico, and many Latin American
states winning an election depends heavily on how much the running candidates
can afford and are willing to bribe the local constables and mayors to switch the
ballot boxes, or worse, how effectively they can intimidate these officials by threats
ranging from kidnapping their family members to murdering them. In Saudi Arabia,
China, and North Korea, things are more honest and straightforward: There are no
elections. The absence of freedom and democracy in all these nations are, again,
due to the existence of restraint (imposed by the local officials, military and security
apparatuses), by interference (in forms of widespread bribing, kidnapping, murdering), intervention of the external force (namely, the reigning authority pressuring
its weight), or simply the prevention (imposed by the central government) of any
election, of free speech, of open political discourse, and the like.

   The presence of emptiness or gap, as the necessary condition for freedom, would
obviously include things like nobody blocking an election process, no one disallow-
ing or censuring a political rally, nobody preventing a speech, or no one trespassing
through someone else's private property. In such cases, the conception of freedom
is akin to "ease or facility of movement" which, again, can occur in an empty space
or gap distancing the citizens' everyday activities from the heavy, intimidating (and
at times frightening) hand of the authority. In the restless Iran a considerable grass-
roots resistance against the restraining central power has generated from peaceful
street demonstrations.[11] In China the rapid rise in prosperity seems to be temporar-
ily distracting and delaying popular defiance against the single-party dictatorship,
while in Russia the majority appear apathetic toward the Kremlin's retrieving of earlier reforms for the sake of national security and control of the corrupt plutocrats.
Nonetheless, regardless of the differences between the internal political conditions
of these and other nations, no one is normally expected to desire bondage. In general, if the state's power becomes so overwhelming that even "an ease or facility of
movement" becomes a hurdle, the people would try to return the favor by making
it equally difficult for the government, especially in the tangible way of taking it

---

[11] This event is so fluid and contemporary that no book can be written on it for some time. Among
the newspaper reports, see "In Iran, Protests Gaining a Radical Tinge," *The New York Times*,
December 10, 2009.

to the street and public square, as currently in Iran, or like that single individual in the Tiananmen Square who blocked the military tank in that eternalized photograph. The man's act symbolizes one's physical restraining of an awesome military machine in a bitter exchange for the political restraining of him and his people by the power behind the tank.

Freedom is called "independence" for the nations, as "liberty" is meant for the individual. When colonized or under foreign occupation, a nation is restrained and unfree. How many wars of independence have we seen in late-modern history? The defeat of the Hungarian uprising in 1956 manifested itself in a bloody semi-final water polo match in the Melbourne Olympics of the same year, with the tearful Hungarian team smashing the Russians: 4-0. (The Hungarians went on to win the gold medal.[12]) What the people of Czechoslovakia were seeking in 1968 was to neutralize the restraining Soviet power so as to achieve "ease or facilitate movement" in their own country, without the eyeful KGB agents, and ending the humiliation of being a satellite-state. In essence, their aim was the same as the Yankees who were determined to expel the Redcoats, or the Parisian Partisans who tried to rush the German occupiers out of France. These are only a few examples that show the necessity of emptiness during the act of expelling the colonialists or foreign occupiers. Such examples are too many and historical details too much for the space of this paper. The point, however, should have been made so far that freedom—whether as liberty or as independence—is impossible without the space of nothingness. And to achieve freedom, the space of nothingness is to be brought by overpowering the restraining power, either by means of violence or by passive resistance. In America, for example, it was only after they expelled the British Army that the old "rebels" became known as "patriots" by attaining that which brought them ease and facility of movement, geographically and intellectually, and enabled them to expand and enjoy their territories through their independence and freedoms, while soon becoming the linguistic, cultural, political, and later the military allies of the former colonizer.[13]

Freedom is an urge from which one's will expresses itself by casting a vote in emptiness, to speak without fear, to live without persecution, to thrive through the void of non-intervention by the state, and to be independent from other states. Obviously freedom is not bound by the chain of causality. It operates in emptiness,

---

[12] For an historic report of this match: "Cold War Violence Erupts at Melbourne Olympics," *Sydney Morning Herald* (July 12, 1956). The fortieth anniversary of this most celebrated water polo event is remembered in "A Bloody War that Spilled into the Pool," by Ron Fimrite, *Sports Illustrated* (July 28, 1996). On the human "struggle for freedom," Jaspers says, "We have seen it in 1956, in Hungary. The agony of exploitation and economic distress, the accumulated despair of years, the unbearable loss of freedom, the enforced untruthfulness of life as a whole—all this brings matters to a point where a nation will dare all, will dare the impossible." *Die Atombombe und die Zukunft des Menschen*, translated by E.B. Ashton as *The Future of Mankind* (Chicago, IL: University of Chicago Press, 1961), p. 41.

[13] And, of course, the American Indians, African Americans, Mexicans, and later the Hispanic Americans, among others, including American women, had much to add concerning the restraints imposed on them.

but in practice it is not identical with it. Freedom is not independent from intentionality, and it is therefore subjective. In a free society one is able to transcend and thereby alter one's facticity through the non-restraining nothingness. Through one's intentional act of transgressing through the nothingness, the older facticity is altered and transformed into a new facticity. In this way, freedom is the ability to transcend from a particular facticity—through the nothingness or absence of an external interference/restraint—to a new facticity. The nothingness must either be already available for the subject or a people to exploit, or its space must be opened up forcefully by the personal and collective will, or both, i.e. a favorable condition like a restraining, old, exhausted and crumbling regime and one's determined will being supported in the company of likeminded allies. In international relations the same mechanisms exist for a rising power seeking self-transition, for it should create an open space of emptiness by repelling the straining force of an old, declining hegemonic nation, with a strong will and, preferably, with some help from allies for a more assuring and speedier success—at times, even if it takes to resort to war. World mastery certainly comes with more freedom in the community of nations, or a greater independence from international pressure, than nations who are weak and susceptible to be constrained and influenced by others.

"It is the emptiness that I create," says the street demonstrator, "by making the state and its security agents retreat." Her fellow demonstrator adds: "What I make is more than the physical representation—for what I intend is something other than this immediate act. I am seeking something more significant and abstract than the physical retreat of the enemy that I have forced out and expelled before my eyes, since my intent is to re-enforce the violated constitutional law, and if necessary, help to make a new set of laws at the end of the road." He, then, says: "The opening of this tangible, physical road, which is a mere street made of the asphalt and concrete structures, will end on the road ahead and beyond, where there is freedom." This is creative. Not just creating an event in the street, but ultimately making a change in the course of history. In this case freedom can also mean "immunity from the arbitrary exercise of power." If in the Chinese case this attempt was unsuccessful and got overpowered by the state, it is expected to come back and restart all over as long as the arbitrary exercise of power remains in place. In the Iranian system, where there are no bars, clubs, or other public places for recreation and entertainment—except the dark and morbid Shiite festivals mourning history's foreign, slain Imams—all that there is for the country's over third of the population under eighteen is playing with the computers, surfing the Net, and hoping for an opening space to make a fundamental change. Dictatorship has no place in modern history, especially in nations that have been seeking "freedom" since the nineteenth century. If the movement's leaders are nothing more than some intrigued observers, the social networking of a massive scale will continue to be mobilized and destabilize the country until new leaders will arrive to lead.

For all the Chinese citizens and all those young Iranian demonstrators born and raised in their respective totalitarian dictatorships, their feelings of alienation and anxiety show that no amount or kind of propaganda has succeeded in convincing them to be content with the political arrangements. They are estranged from that which is foreign to their very nature. They have the feelings of un-belonging to the government that has never been theirs. Their knowledge of the outside world, provided through the Internet, is a powerful source of making them feel deprived and humiliated before the world. Those several million fashion-conscious Iranian women under compulsory veils cannot take it anymore. So they rebel. China has come a long way since the Cultural Revolution. The many colors in the place of the Maoist gray uniforms are signs of not going back.

Now, the Western World, led by the United States, might try to agitate and rattle the potentially unstable nations by spreading the propaganda of freedom and help to overthrow their undemocratic governments, in hope of having them become either future politico-military allies, or politico-economic satellites, or a combination of the two in different proportions. (This third possibility in fact exists between the United States to its European partners, even though never publicly acknowledged.) As a natural and national tendency, there is nothing immoral about this tactic for a strategic advantage—granted that in international relations every nation-state is to seek maximum power. Here, the advent of computer technology is an incremental blessing for political destabilization and consequent economic and cultural penetration. While for China and India the foreign trade has been reversed to their advantage, in the political and cultural spheres the Chinese autocracy is, as suggested before, vulnerable. Vulnerable is, also, the Iranian theocratic-democracy, whose constitutional contradiction is currently playing out and being radicalized in streets and behind closed halls of power, with the theocratic part struggling to hold on to its slipping power and survive from its departing, grieved and furious democratic partner. While the West is the instigator, it can benefit immensely by having the seventy-five million, mostly educated, industrializing, geo-strategic nation to join its camp, amid the buffer, uncertain and unstable regions of Western/Southern/Central Asia and South-Eastern Europe. For the governments of China and Iran, the Internet is much more than an annoying instrument: It is a threatening reality, as unwelcome foreign highways going straight into people's homes.

Meanwhile, the military superpower Russia, which felt insecure in the early 1990s (following its loss of Soviet Socialist dominion in Eastern Europe and Central Asia), has defensively reversed most of its earlier democratic reforms. Of course, any democratic change in the Southern Caspian region could directly threaten the Russian heartland, a potential disaster being watched by the Kremlin. Meanwhile, Russia's former European satellites (including Ukraine and Georgia), which are struggling for establishing viable democratic institutions, have become junior and somewhat submissive partners of the West (especially in the region stretching from Poland to the Czech Republic). While these nations need to learn the essential civic values of individualism and tolerance on the path to democracy, their current Internet and Western dominated TV-watching youths are fascinated by blue jeans, hard-rock and Hollywood—the things that the French learned to despise decades ago. In Latin America, the nations that earlier in this century did practice some free elections have subsequently felt the danger of the return of imperialism, and therefore chose national freedom (independence) over individual freedom. This move typically has been either in variations of leftist popularism of anti-American charismatic leadership of Castro style (e.g. Venezuela and Bolivia), or in a slowly cautious and bumpy transitions to free elections (like the much larger South American nations of Brazil and Argentina). Lastly, there are those mostly impoverished nations for whom liberal-democracy is remote, and their dictatorial, corrupt and inefficient governments are completely dependent on Western support for survival. Located in parts of East and Southern Asia, most of the Middle East, some of Latin America, and nearly all of Africa—these states seem to be the last, if ever, to come to the idea and practice of liberal democracy. Nonetheless, the national aspiration for freedom in these countries and their individual citizen's faith in freedom might still be strong—remembering their struggles against European colonialism.

Meanwhile, the West's continuous economic decline and financial corruption will be coinciding with great opportunities in finding ideological allies in the ever-expanding democratic reforms in most of the world. Some indications are already present, although this does not necessarily mean that conflicts between democracies cannot happen. The ultimate challenge for the West is not to proactively try to convert the non-western nations to democracy, but rather how to appear non-interventional so as to prevent a backlash and a perception of pushing its own agenda. The opportunities seem infinite for the many nations of the world to take advantage of the emptiness and void in their own systems of government and transcend into the more representational and freer facticities.

Philosophical Faith: The Savior of Humanity

Indu Sarin

Abstract The chapter examines the challenges of the contemporary age on the future of humanity and shows the way of meeting them by taking Jaspers' rational holistic approach through philosophical faith. It explores the present shattering scenario in terms of the threat of the environment, unrestricted consumerism, religious violence information technology and unethical global flare-up with weapons of mass destruction, which are heading towards the end humanity. In this context questions arise such as, "How can there be harmonious interactions amongst man, nature, technology and culture?" Jaspers' concepts of philosophical faith and reason are compared with those of Paul Tillich, which become the fountainhead of freedom, creativity, and intrinsic values connecting man with other beings of the universe meaningfully.

This essay examines the challenges of the contemporary age on the future of humanity and shows the way of meeting these challenges by way of Jaspers' rational and holistic approach through philosophical faith. It reflects on the question: how can there be harmonious interactions amongst man, nature, technology and culture? Jaspers' concepts of philosophical faith and reason are compared with those of Paul Tillich, which become the fountainhead of freedom, creativity and intrinsic values connecting man with other beings of the universe meaningfully. Jaspers' holistic approach plays an important role in bringing peace and harmony in the universe that flowers open-mindedness and dignity of the individual as well as of mankind in general. The root of humanity extends beyond one's historically particular origin to the one origin that is common to all despite the manifoldness of historicity. This origin binds the people of all historical communities.

Philosophical faith is contrasted with fanatic religious faith that holds arrogance of one's own belief and uses force to rule humanity and gratify one's ego leading to the division of communities. It connects one with the other personally and makes present what is ordinarily not known. No doubt, commitment and devotion are common to both kinds of faith but the fanatic is close-minded, intolerant of other religions and becomes aggressive to the other ways of thinking. He is motivated by blind passion, partial and biased thinking whereas the philosophical faith is positive,

I. Sarin (✉)
Punjab University, Chandigarh, India
e-mail: indusarin@yahoo.com

H. Wautischer et al. (eds.), *Philosophical Faith and the Future of Humanity*,
DOI 10.1007/978-94-007-2223-1_31, © Springer Science+Business Media B.V. 2012

self-conscious, self-critical, open-minded, respects the other ways of thinking and is the synthesis of thought and feeling (deep passion).

The present situation is full of crises of various kinds. The threats of environment, unrestricted consumerism, religious violence, information technology and unethical global flare-up with weapons of mass destruction are heading towards the end of humanity. Weapons technology has injected fear of total destruction in the minds of people and also empowered the terrorists. The violence is increasing day by day. The threat is two-fold: first, a threat to the very survival of man and second, the threat to the value of being human, to freedom and dignity of the individual.

The term humanity can be interpreted in two senses: First, humanity is understood as the whole of mankind. In the present scenario, the very survival of man is in danger due to nuclear threat, horrors of terrorism, fanaticism and violence based on discrimination of race, class, gender and religion. Man is being killed brutally. Despite technological developments, the fear of losing life at any moment is haunting humankind. For Jaspers, "things are getting serious again—not only because of war, disease, and hunger, as in the past, but because of the real danger that mankind will perish."[1]

Second, the term humanity is also linked with the very notion of being human—characterization of man in terms of freedom and transcendence that lead to the realization of values and differentiate him from other beings in the world. Man has a responsibility towards himself in pursuing values and safeguarding freedom, dignity and the human rights of other human beings, as well as protecting other beings (animate and inanimate) of the world. Therein lay the humanity of man. To be human is to realize the value of being human and to transcend the narrow identities limited to race, class, gender, religion and nation. This would bring human integrity and shared humanity on a broader perspective based on justice, equality and fraternity—communication among all communities without producing mass-culture.

Humanity in both of the above senses is in danger. In fact, the first threat is due to the second. The threat to human life is due to a dissolution of human values. Thus the real cause of the present crisis is the loss of human values. According to Jaspers, all spheres of life are turning into "theaters of war." "In present world strategy we find not only a military theater, but economic, cultural, ideological, religious theaters of war" (*FM* 333). Jaspers' books *Man in the Modern Age*, *The Origin and Goal of History* and *The Future of Mankind* throw light on the contemporary crises. Jaspers analyses the cause of the crises in the following ways (*FM* 213–214): Psychological—"human ferocity, rapaciousness, love of adventure, the lust of feeling superior to life in flinging it away; and Economical"—"selfishness that lost its sense of values, subordinates everything to the great leveler, money, and alienates man from man himself. Technological"—"it may be the process of intelligent invention, which produces instruments of production and of destruction

---

[1] Karl Jaspers, *The Future of Mankind*, trans. E.B. Ashton (Chicago, IL: Chicago University Press, 1961), p. 203. [Henceforth cited as *FM*].

simultaneously, to the point where both unlimited production and total destruction are possible. Political"—"it may be a wrongly organized power practice, a way of government that induces the state to act ruinously even against the will of a vast majority of the people. Historical"—"ever recurring course of events in general terms and explanation within the historical process, what is new at a particular time."

The above spheres presuppose that things would happen according to cognoscible necessities, but they do not touch the reality as such or being as-such. Egoistical factors corrupt politics and mundane historical practices produce merely utilitarian relationships. Overly materialistic attitudes, dogmatic religions, and departmentalized thinking are also the enemies of man landing in various challenges:

(a) The challenge of demonic technologies in all walks of life: military crises and the prospect of nuclear war are hovering on the heads of man. Despite the technological progress in all walks of life, nobody is secure. "The atom bomb is today the greatest of all menaces to the future of mankind" (*FM* 4). One is in the world without knowing whence and wither. Technology produces mass-culture. Information-technology has revolutionized our whole way of thinking. Machines are replacing men. The individual is turned into an object among other objects.

(b) The challenge of marketing strategies. The individual is guided by publicity, propaganda and utilitarian considerations. Technology produces mass-culture governed by artificial modes. The focus is on the "show-off" activities. The individual wears different kinds of masks. Human ties are broken and no loyalty is left among people.

(c) The challenge to personal identity. The person wears so many masks and is not satisfied with his own self. He is too much bothered about his outward appearances and craves for more and more materialistic goods. Mechanization of man in the technological age and stereotyped mutual relationships produce the feeling of alienation. Human ties are broken.

(d) Conflicts among cultures: Discrimination amongst races, castes, classes and religions generates conflicts. The different cultures are at loggerheads with each other.

(e) Ecological crisis: It is produced by excessive exploitation of nature resulting in so many environmental problems. Consequently, the ecological balance is lost and man is not in harmony with nature. The desire to conquer nature has led to undesirable consequences. The imbalance in the planetary eco-system is produced. Nature is regarded as a resource to be used. Consequently, the physical reality of the objects and other forms of life are at the risk of destruction leading to environmental hazards. Nature is regarded as a resource to fulfill not only man's economic needs, but also his greed to have more and more goods.

(f) Dogmatic religion: Fanaticism leads to the horrors of terrorism and violence among communities.

(g) Departmentalized thinking: It produces a narrow horizon of cognition leading to disharmony amongst different spheres of life. Departmentalized thinking may claim mastery over a particular field of knowledge and handle specific skills. Though the present age can be called as the age of advancement of science and technology—attaining knowledge in different fields and mastery over skills, yet it is filled with many types of crises and fears. These are due to the crisis of values that cannot be overcome by any "task-force".

The function of value is to evaluate the decision regarding any knowledge or skill in terms of its intrinsic worth—is the pursuit of any knowledge or skill desirable for humanity as well as the environment around? It is not to undermine the importance of any knowledge or skill but rather to show that its evaluation is needed for its use in different realms of life. Life as a whole is to be respected.

The significant question is this: How ought we to use science and technology in desirable directions? Science and technology do not tackle this point—they "cannot show us the way out of doom" (*FM* 201). We need an axiology, which is the domain of intrinsic values. To save humanity from doom, Jaspers proposes a "new way of thinking" (*FM* 201) for the future of humanity. This new way of thinking is a step forward from intellectual thinking to encompassing rational thinking that "transforms man in his entirety" (*FM* 204). However, both are needed for the harmonious encounter of man with others. Reason presupposes intellect and the latter would remain empty without the former. Intellectual thinking, with "its research, its planning, and its technology" (*FM* 204), needs guidance. The knowledge of things and skills must invoke an "inner attitude of vision, of discrimination, and of judgment" (*FM* 204), which all belong to the realm of values that can transform humanity.

For Jaspers, "departmental thinking" grows like a "tumor in the living body" (*FM* 210), which is very harmful to the "spirit of the whole" (*FM* 210). Such thinking regards one standpoint to be the supreme and gets encaged in its mode. Consequently it ignores the other important aspects. Science and spirituality need to be integrated. The body-consciousness and mind-consciousness (intellect) are the necessary conditions of human life for the progress but man is not complete without soul-consciousness (depth of man's being above particular departments) that creates a unified and clear vision and brings harmony in both human and non-human relationships. This part of man, above merely departmental thinking, is the whole of man's being.

The whole being of man discriminates between right and wrong and critically reflects on one's doings and evaluates the worth of any pursuit. It rises above mere intellect to enter the realms of reason and philosophical faith. Reason discriminates between right and wrong. Faith adopts what is right and makes it the part of one's being. As Jaspers says, "the turning point—the transformation, or change, or jump—from outwardly productive to inwardly active thinking, from intellect to reason [is] the rational thought that opens all views and leads to creative decisions" (*FM* viii).

No doubt the specialized disciplines are needed to understand the nuance of each field. To have authority of expert knowledge and richness of different flavors, the divisions are made in sciences, arts, administrations, groups, communities and cultures. However, over-glorifying the divisions may lead to clashes and imbalanced growth, which may become harmful to both the human and non-human environment. The need of the hour is to awaken the being of man that understands the sense of man's existence (with the environment around) and to respect the dignity of each being. Jaspers makes a distinction between two ways of thinking:

> *Intellectual thought* is the inventor and maker. Its precepts can be carried out and can multiply the making by infinite repetition. The result is a world in which a few minds devise the mechanics, creating, as it were, a second world in which the masses then assume the operative function. *Rational thought*, on the other hand, does not provide for the carrying-out of mass directives but requires each individual to do his own thinking, original thinking. Here, truth is not found by a machine reproducible at will, but by decision, resolve, and action whose self-willed performance, by each on his own, is what creates a common spirit. (*FM* 7)

Intellect (discursive faculty) confines itself to "departmental thinking" and reason takes holistic approach. Science for Jaspers is "objectively compelling intellectual cognition; philosophy is rational self-enlightenment" (*FM* 9). Both are different, yet inseparable. The profound thought accompanied by faith leads to bright consciousness and vigorous creative actions.

The materialistic attitude is needed for the outer progress of both the individual and society. It is necessary because this approach is instrumental in producing things efficiently. However, in this process, it goes to the extent of treating others and even oneself as means to achieve the goals. The spiritualistic dimension is required for the inner development of man having an open perspective and taking into account all the dimensions of man. This approach regards oneself and also the other as an end-in-itself, making room for intrinsic values.

Jaspers distinguishes the above spiritual dimension from dogmatic religion where faith is communicated by the religions in a particular historic way. Jaspers is critical of dogmatic religion in general, and revealed theology in particular. He is critical of dogmatic and institutionalized religion because it is based on blind conformity to a set of beliefs and stifles freedom of the individual. It puts a barrier on healthy dialogical encounter among human communities and disvalues the real meaning of religion. The revealed theology makes the individual passive by coming between his personal and creative way of realizing God—a way from downward to upward. The meaning of Transcendence is not to be explained in terms of dogmatic and revealed theology. It is rather to be understood and experienced in terms of human freedom and faith: "common basis is an encompassing faith which nobody can call his own in definite form—faith in the road of truth on which all honest seekers for truth can meet."[2]

Jaspers' concept of philosophical faith is in contradistinction to both what is irrational (blind conformity) and purely intellectual, i.e., devoid of any feeling. Philosophical stands for rationality, faith stands for positive feeling and subjective certainty that strengthen the individual to overcome dogma, fear, and doubt. To have philosophical faith means to act vigorously with a positive, constructive

---

[2] Karl Jaspers, *Philosophy and the World*, trans. E.B. Ashton (Chicago, IL: Regnery, 1961), p. 294.

attitude and to show the path of transcendence. For Jaspers, faith needs philosophy and philosophy needs faith. Philosophy without faith is empty reflection and ends in skepticism without experiencing transcendence. Faith without philosophy may end in fanaticism and also lose the real meaning of transcendence.

The faith is called philosophical because it is grounded in reason, freedom and values. It is to be contrasted with a faith that is irrational, dogmatic and is motivated merely by group interests. The irrational faith turns values into disvalues and disvalues into values distorting the true meaning of religion. So many crimes are committed in the name of religion and theses acts are labeled as self-sacrifice, martyrdom, etc. It divides people on the basis of particular religions and injects hatred in different communities. It over-glorifies a particular religion or community and undermines the other, which can lead into a ghastly act of even taking the life of the other. Jaspers maintains, in the desire to gain worldly power, the religious institutions become inauthentic and corrupt. They become "dogmatic, doctrinaire, institutional modes of faith, secure in the sense of power they derive from membership of mighty organisms, that are effective in the world and at times omnipotent on a broad front."[3] Dogmatic faith is based on blind passion and produces massmen. Jaspers speaks of faith, which does not take the form of organized form in the religious institutions. Jaspers states:

> He who would like to live in the unclosed and unorganised and unorganisable community of authentic human beings–in what used to be called the invisible Church–does in fact live today as an individual in alliance with individuals scattered over the face of the earth, an alliance that survives every disaster, a dependability that is not fixed by any pact or any specific imperative. [...] It is as though everyone were charged by the Deity to work and live for boundless openness, authentic reason, truth and love and fidelity, without the recourse to force that is typical of the States and Churches in which we have to live and whose insufficiency we should like to oppose. (*GH* 228)

Philosophical faith is open to all communities and does not exclude one community from the other. It is linked with the concept of humanism, which emphasizes specificity, freedom and dignity of the individual in contrast to mass-culture and totalitarian inhumanity. It glorifies the intrinsic values that play a very significant role in meeting the challenges of the changing scenario. Since philosophical faith is not confined to a particular religion, it provides a platform where all religions can communicate to have healthy interactions and be in harmony with one another. It takes a move from the interior to the exterior, from the inner realm to the outer realm, from controlling the outer turmoil with the inner strength.

The starting-point is the individual. The inculcation of values is to be done by the each individual himself. No doubt that a change in the particular individual cannot change the world as a whole, but it certainly affects the people around. As Jaspers says, "It is true that the whole world will not change if I change. But the change in myself is the premise of the greater change . . . my general conduct in the community has political significance" (*FM* 325). The value-based humanism would move from

---

[3] Karl Jaspers, *The Origin and Goal of History*, trans. R. Manheim (London: Routledge and Kegan Paul, 1953), p. 225. [Henceforth cited as *GH*].

the private to the public realm turning into the politics of humanism that can put a check on the on-going atrocities. The external dangers to humanity can be regulated by practicing values, which demand internal realization and reach the depth of man's being—what is eternally present in man, Jaspers elaborates as follows:

> It is the clairvoyant love of humans sharing their destinies in rational union; it is the consciousness of doing right; it is the strength of advancing on the path of reason; it is the resistance that checks my self-will, my drifting, my untruthfulness, my anger, my arrogance, like the flaming sword of an angel parrying whatever would revolt in my existence; it is what happens in the deepest recesses of my being, by myself and not by myself alone; it is what guides my outward actions. (*FM* 341)

The problem of on-going atrocities cannot be overcome completely through stringent laws and political policies but through inner transformation of the individual. The former solution is temporary but the latter would be lasting. The "reliability of contracts and enforceable agreements" (*FM* 220) made by the political policies out of fear of war is only a transient solution. Jaspers maintains, "fear has become a political reality. We have peace today because of fear on both sides, due to the atomic balance of terror. But this in itself is not a peace to rely on" (*FM* 327).

Jaspers argues that fear may facilitate us to be aware of the dangers of humanity and to make the legal laws to secure the life of humanity. The real task is fulfilled by practicing human values and a "bright, transforming ethos" (*FM* 327). Such an ethos generates power within man in the face of Transcendence, which transforms him. There will be emergence of ethos, reason, self-sacrifice, faith and freedom within him. He should make values as indispensable part of his very being that ushers into a worthy life-style led by philosophical faith.

A lack of philosophical faith generates a nihilism that leads to dissolution of values and negativity "where faith is no longer the basis of the content of life, nothing is left but the vacuum of negation. When one is dissatisfied with oneself, the fault must be someone else's [. . .]. All the indissolubly intricate ramifications of causality or responsibility to which blame attaches are uncritically reduced to the blame of one single alien entity that is not oneself" (*GH* 134).

Thinking in terms of ideologies regarding one's standpoint to be the absolute leads to over-simplification and "the string by which one is guided like a puppet, incapable of development, empty and rigid [. . .] adheres to pseudo-scientific absolutes" (*GH* 134) and to mass-man. The individual degenerates into mass-man that leads to dissolution of his humanity. He does not have any hope within himself and looks at others for guidance. The anonymous mass regulates his behavior and guides him through propaganda and slogans. He becomes an exchangeable commodity and is thrown into "the current fashion, into the cinema, into the mere today [. . .] as mass I applaud the star on the conductor's dais [. . .] as mass I think in numbers, accumulate, level [. . .]. Human masses are easily able to lose the power of deliberation" (*GH* 129–130). Consequently, the individual succumbs to a blind faith.

Philosophical faith links man with the matrix of his being. Jaspers maintains, "Faith is the fulfilling and moving element in the depths of man, in which man is linked, above and beyond himself, with the origin of his being" (*GH* 215). Philosophical faith is "faith in God, faith in man (in one's own being and that of others), and faith in possibilities in the world" (*GH* 219). Faith in God gives peace of mind and security. Faith in one's own being is the assertion of one's own freedom. This freedom leads to authentic communication with others, which is more than mere contact, sympathy, interests and enjoyment. Jaspers says, "Without faith in God, faith in man degenerates into contempt for man, into loss of respect for man as man, with the final consequence that the alien human life is treated with indifference, as something to be used and destroyed" (*GH* 220).

Faith in "possibilities in the world" shows the significance of the world, which provides immense opportunities to man. No doubt faith implies transcendence but it is not renunciation of the present world—not concerned with the harsh realities of the present in the interests of an illusory future. For Jaspers, "without faith we are left with [...] mechanistic thinking, the irrational and ruin" (*GH* 220). Faith empowers man to face all odds. The empowerments of faith are strength in the face of ruin—faith is victorious over animal instincts, brutal force of the desire to dominate, delight in violence, cruelty, empty will to prestige, the desire for wealth and pleasure, the erotic instincts; tolerance and open-mindedness; and fulfillment as faith injects the feeling of fulfillment within man and connects him to the depth and origin of his being and to humanity at large.

Jaspers shares his views with Paul Tillich who also interprets the meaning of faith as the integration of all the dimensions of man. To have faith for Tillich also, is to take holistic view of life—a power that integrates all the dimensions of personality. Man is a unity of body, mind and spirit, which are within each other. Tillich holds, "Faith, therefore, is not a matter of the mind in isolation, or of the soul in contrast to mind and body, or of the body [...] but is the centered movement of the whole personality toward something of ultimate meaning and significance."[4] He continues, "Since faith is an act of the personality as a whole, it participates in the dynamics of personal life" (*DF* 4). For him, faith is the centered act of personality and state of being ultimately concerned, which is unconditional and accompanied by fulfillment. It touches the very being of the individual, which is not subject to any condition or limitation. It is the awareness of potential infinity.

Tillich distinguishes the ultimate concern from the preliminary concern that is conditioned. The ultimate concern "gives depth, direction and unity to all other concerns and, with them, to the whole personality" (*DF* 105), because it is center as well as the ground of all concerns. Tillich distinguishes faith as the ultimate concern from idolatrous faith. The latter has a preliminary concern and regards the preliminary concern to be the ultimate. It is not holistic—it is directed to something particular (limited element) and is extremely passionate to achieve that but without any integrating power. Consequently it breaks down sooner or later as it is attacked by some other particular element (limited). One preliminary concern stands against the other preliminary concern. The misguided idolatrous faith has dangerous consequences, which we are seeing in case of the religious fanatics. There is a conflict of one faith with the other and sometimes it takes the form of violence. The

---

[4] Paul Tillich, *Dynamics of Faith* (London: George Allen and Unwin Ltd., 1957), p. 106. [Henceforth cited as *DF*].

"fanatically defended doctrine" does not generate "acts of love." It excludes other contrasting claims and breeds hatred towards them.

Ultimate concern unites both the subjective (the act of faith) and the objective (toward which it is directed), therefore the polarity between subjective and objective breaks down. To have faith in something (objective) is to have faith in oneself (subjective). It is felt in the depth of man's soul. This depth is the point of contact "between the finite and the infinite," which makes the individual transcend all the divisions to have faith in humanity. The overcoming of cleavage between subjective and objective is the measure whether the concern is infinite, unconditional and ultimate. The cleavage between subjective and objective remains in case of finite, conditional and limited concern. In that case I look upon myself as a subject and the other as an external object to be used in any way I want. This is the ordinary way of looking at things. The idolatrous faith is not able to overcome the cleavage between subjective and objective. Even if there is too much identification in a particular case, that is only transient. It considers the finite concern as the ultimate and periphery as the center, which ends in "existential disappointment" (*DF* 12).

Faith as the ultimate concern is the awareness of the holy—awareness of the presence of the divine. Like Jaspers, Tillich is also critical of doctrinal formulations of faith manifested in religious institutions. Faith as the ultimate concern involves existential participation. In this sense it is closer to humanism. Since it is not limited to any religious doctrine and institution, it encompasses the humanity as such. Tillich says,

> Humanism is the attitude which makes man the measure of his own spiritual life, in art and philosophy, in science and politics, in social relations and personal ethics. For humanism the divine is manifest in the human; the ultimate concern of man is man. (*DF* 62–63)

Faith as the "state of being ultimately concerned" implies love and action. It is rather the ultimate power of the both. To have faith in something is that one has a desire to be united with it. This desire for the union is love—belongingness with the other. Love manifests in actions to actually fulfill love-relationship. The concern for the other leads to actions. Tillich further holds that humanism implies faith.

Tillich agrees with Jaspers that faith is not irrational. He holds that reason is the precondition of faith and the latter is fulfillment of reason (ontological). He distinguishes between technical and ontological reason. The technical reason is limited to instrumentality, explores the empirical realm and remains at the level of the preliminary concern. The ontological reason is ecstatic and comprehends the ultimate concern.

Like Jaspers, Tillich also holds that the nature of faith is dynamic because it involves the individual's participation. It realizes the ultimate concern though freedom, power and courage. It is the outcome of voluntary act of will and is not necessitated either by any internal psychic force or external agency. It comes from the inner power of one's being; the fulfillment is possible through courage. The fear generates negative energy that weakens the individual.

For Tillich, the dynamic power of faith is the foundation of true religion—it is the appearance of the unconditional in the conditional. It brings transformation within man that leads to the transformation of society—"man transforming in the face of the cosmos". Tillich holds that religion (understood in the above sense) should be the basis of any culture. He elaborates the meaning of religion as follows:

> Religion is the aspect of depth in the totality of the human spirit. What does the metaphor *depth* mean? It means that the religious aspect points to that which is ultimate, infinite, unconditional in man's spiritual life [. . .] ultimate concern is manifest in all creative functions of the human spirit. It is manifest in the moral sphere as the unconditional seriousness of the moral demand [. . .]. Ultimate concern is manifest in the realm of knowledge as the passionate longing for ultimate reality [. . .]. Ultimate concern is manifest in the aesthetic function of the human spirit as the infinite desire to express ultimate meaning.[5]

Religion for Tillich is the ground and depth of man's spiritual life that brings total transformation in the individual. The transformation of man is the dynamic process, fulfilled through love and faith that bind all the divisions and generate moral values in the present scenario of crises.

The crucial questions for the present generation are—how to create the better world while being in tune with technological developments and remain committed to intrinsic values? How to avoid the negative effects of technology—threatening disaster of the atom bomb? How to avoid violence? How to secure the future of humanity with peace and harmonious relationships with all kinds of beings in the world? This mission cannot be fulfilled either by science or dogmatic religion. The former is value-neutral and the latter because of its authority and orthodoxy ends in exclusivity.

The scientific attitude is dominated by uncontrolled power and lack of insensitivity towards others. As mentioned earlier, science tends to be governed by mechanization, atomization and piecemeal thinking. Scientific knowledge presupposes subject-object dichotomy, but their fusion is needed for the personal encounter. Scientific methodology is impersonal dominated by quantitative measurement and communicable in objective fixed manner ushering in generalization. Feelings hardly play any role in scientific understanding. Technological mode of producing attempts to control each and every phenomenon and makes it as a commercial object to gain more and more profit out of it. Man under the grip of marketing techniques reduces everything to mechanization and exploits all the resources for mass-consumption. Consequently there is no difference between machines and other living and non-living beings.

Can technology be counterbalanced by intrinsic rationality? Is it possible to realize Jaspers' vision of a new politics that rests on the principle of morality and brings "honest, rational communication and peace" (*FM* 333)? He pleads that politics be based on the suprapolitical—reason, morality and faith. It must feel responsible for human freedom and human rights. Reason takes holistic perspective and is grounded in freedom and faith. The community of rational persons should be the guiding force of politics. Jaspers suggests that reason should "prevail in all form of human order—in states, parties, churches, schools, unions, and bureaucracies" (*FM* 224).

---

[5] Paul Tillich, *Theology of Culture* (New York, NY: Oxford University Press, 1977), pp. 7–8.

> The political community of all can find the way of reason only where men who can trust each other in communication inspire trust in others. The germ of all public good, too, lies in the meeting of rational men [. . .]. The credibility of men begins in the narrowest circle of rational intimacy; it spreads in public, in conscious resistance to irrationality. (*FM* 225)

Jaspers advocates the "brotherhood of reasonable men," which is grounded in the depth of man's being and is the source of moral goodness that obliterates the distinction between the private and the public. This brotherhood is over and above material gains, and establishes a spiritual (deep) bond among human beings. Jaspers maintains that this is possible by faith in the "One of transcendence," which is the "origin and goal at one and the same time" (*GH* 264–265) of mankind and is not of the exclusive possession of a particular historical faith. He continues, "Thus this deepest unity is elevated to an invisible religion, to the realm of spirits, the secret realm of manifestation of Being in the concord of souls" (*GH* 265).

Man has a capacity for self-transformation to create a better future. Jaspers asserts that the contribution of each individual is very important for making a better future:

> [. . .] no law of nature and no law of history determine the course of events as a whole. The future depends on the responsible decisions and acts of men, and ultimately on each individual among the billions. Each individual counts. By his way of living, by his small daily actions and by his great decisions, he becomes his own witness to what might be. The present reality of his helps imperceptibly to shape the future. In this role he must feel no less important than in casting his ballot as one of an electorate of millions.[6]

Future disaster can be averted through each man's will power and integrity. Education can play an important role in bringing out the full potential of human beings at the grass root level. How to inculcate values in the young minds? Jaspers has also emphasized the significance of education. As he holds that the aim of education is not merely information transfer or learning technical skills but to develop the creative dimension of man (rising above dogmatism and developing critical ability) and awaken humanity within him. It should make the individual rise above narrow identities and embrace man as man and not his labels, respecting his freedom and dignity.

The education system today basically sharpens the intellect imparting information and teaching technical skills so that the students may become very good professionals. The good results are visible: some of them turn into highly creative intellectuals and economically also very sound. The question is—are they good human beings also? Unfortunately in the race of becoming good professionals, they have forgotten to be human in the true sense of the term. A new kind of capitalism is also developing, which is creating a gap between the rich and the poor. In addition, there is a great clash between different ideologies, civilizations and also with one's own civilization on petty interests and irrational grounds. The selfishness is increasing day by day. The exploitation of other human beings and even of nature and the

---

[6] *Philosophy and the World*, op. cit., pp. 277–278.

environment around has reached its climax. The materialistic attitude has overpowered human beings and turned this age to be the darkest. The religious fanaticism is one of acute problems. Jaspers pleads for the individual to wake up from dogmatic slumber and be rational.

The relationships in all spheres of life should be guided by reason and not by mere intellect or dogma. Jaspers argues that the intellect belongs to a specific field of comprehension whereas reason encompasses the whole being of man. The irrational, which is against both intellect and reason, lands into violent and irresponsible actions. The intellectual thinking is regarded as supreme because its opposite is regarded as irrational, which is to be condemned in all aspects. Dehumanization is inherent in the irrational, which though is not in the intellect yet the consequence of the latter may be inhuman because of its instrumental and compartmentalized approaches. Reason encompasses both history and transcendence enriching the world with discernible self-reflected norms that guide the individual's choices as well as bind him with the other beings.

What we need today is to take a step over and above intellectual thinking (without losing it) to what Jaspers calls rational thinking with philosophical faith that transforms man in his entirety. Scientific intellectual thinking follows the methodology of demonstration and proof of the external world and is concerned with outside visible achievements. This is not to undermine the importance of intellectual thinking but to show that it needs the guidance of "encompassing rational thinking," which is authentic and brings inner changes within man through faith. These changes become the eternal part of man's being which is not subservient to transient utilitarian considerations. It rises above the irrational or confused darkness, as well as above mere intellectual and technological labor of progress.

Man is born in a world, which is constituted by a network of relationships. All beings in the universe are variously interconnected and interdependent. The individual has lost harmonious relationships with others. The most dangerous thing is that man is not in harmony with his own self. The dissolution of values has generated the element of negativity within man leading to loss of faith. Jaspers' concept of philosophical faith awakens divinity within man inculcating intrinsic values. The axiological approach aspires for the outlook, which is eco-friendly, human-friendly and develops harmonious relationship with the world around—a healthy interaction amongst man, nature, technology and culture, which makes the individual dwell in the world by making fruitful contributions to enrich it.

The multilayered challenges can be met by developing the holistic approach that includes both the materialistic and spiritual dimensions of man. The individual is full of immense potentialities and cannot be reduced to merely an instance of any typical class, race, nation, gender or any such other category. Moreover, religious identity (living a particular religion) should not be socially recognized as the sole crucial identity of man. The inner transformation of the individual (through reason and the power of faith) opens the door for global communication. This would care for the values of being human to bring peace, harmony, and prosperity for the coming generations. Such positive and creative attitude brings hope for the future and inspires responsible action.

The Second Axial Age: Fulfilling the Human Destiny

Czesława Piecuch

Abstract The notion of Axial Age is the starting point for Jaspers' concept for a future world philosophy, and his vision of a united world based upon it. He argues that the first period (800–200 BC) referred to the common source of humankind, while the second one—marked with the development of modern technological civilisation—refers to the common goal, which is the union of the earth. The author poses the question, whether the future world philosophy is able to realize this great task, which manifested itself in the dawn of mankind: to bring about such union. Furthermore, which philosophical assumptions of this new thinking may help fulfill human destiny, and which render Jaspers' lofty project merely a beautiful utopia.

The great ancient civilizations of Greece, India, and China are a historical fact. They developed during the same period between the ninth and third centuries BCE, which Jaspers called the Axial Age. Jaspers believes that such synchronicity, coupled with the independence of these spiritual phenomena, is the primary argument for a common source of humanity. The true history of mankind takes its origin in this source, because it was during this period that the fundamental structures of human thought, the measure of the achievements for generations to follow, came into existence. Jaspers' concept of the Axial Age should not, however, be understood as analogous to the Nietzschean ideal of the Hellenist culture that was supposed to be an uppermost point of human development followed by the regressive history of the West. For Jaspers, the Axial Age is the opening phase in a long progression culminating in the second Axial Age, the latter marking the development of modern science and technological civilization. The second Axial Age is a new Promethean era, which is to transform history entirely so that it will gain a universal dimension. While the first Axial Age refers to the common source of humankind, the second one indicates a common goal, which is the union of the Earth. This aim requires a new way of thinking, brought by the future world philosophy, the outline of which Jaspers presents in his later writings.

This kind of thinking, democratic by assumption, includes the past and contemporary achievements of human thought, and it is to become the substructure for a universal world communication. Thus, the essential duty of world philosophy is

C. Piecuch (✉)
Pedagogical University of Krakow, Krakow, Poland
e-mail: cechnap@op.pl

H. Wautischer et al. (eds.), *Philosophical Faith and the Future of Humanity*,
DOI 10.1007/978-94-007-2223-1_32, © Springer Science+Business Media B.V. 2012

to lay the foundations for unity of the human community, which first manifested itself in the dawn of mankind. This key assertion should enable us overcome the Occidental claim of exclusivity, its tendency to separate cultures and nations, and its aspiration to dominate through claims of superiority and power.

In this essay I ask whether this lofty intention will prove to be nothing but utopian and, due to its monumentality, appear to us as yet another philosophical project never to be realized. Or, will it be the case that Jaspers' thinking can provide the way whereby a future spiritual union of Orient and Occident is possible and convincing?

The fundamental question is whether Jaspers' vision is more plausible than that of his modern predecessors. In the final passage of his *Obituary*, which Jaspers himself wrote some time before his death, he identifies the future of world philosophy as the last great philosophical issue to which he devoted himself.[1] In Jaspers' later works this theme figures prominently. And yet, since this future philosophy is to become a global philosophy, it is not yet present. Jaspers indicates a transitory period of the modern era, while for now, "we find ourselves on the road leading from the twilight of European philosophy through the darkness of the present age, to the dawn of World Philosophy."[2] Our age appears to him as still submerged in darkness, such as we do not even discern any light ahead of us, and proceed toward an unclear future.[3]

In Jaspers' thought, humanity is an ideal that continuously unfolds and is placed next to privileged, individual *Existenz*. It is the future of humankind that shall become the chief motif for Jaspers' philosophy of the world. Albeit new, we should stress that it is firmly rooted in history—both in the history of philosophy and in the history of humanity, both in the distant past and in the contemporary events that Jaspers personally witnessed. This is therefore an important turn in Jaspers' thinking, a turn toward social and political reality, which does not signify a departure from his fundamental philosophical beliefs, but rather constitutes a particular extension of these beliefs. We might attempt to transpose his term "philosophy of the world" into the expression "philosophy for the world," because a defined mission underlies this concept as expressed in Jaspers' work *The Origin and Goal of History* (1948). In time, as we shall see from the oeuvre he left behind, this mission will become monumental in character.

Jaspers' personal experience of World War II, as he writes in his *Philosophical Autobiography*, when the Americans saved him and his wife from dying at the hand of his compatriots, prompted him to look at historical events not from the perspective on an individual, or that of a single nation, but from the perspective of the world as a whole. Also, given the modern development of science and an unprecedented

---

[1] "Nekrolog, von Karl Jaspers selbst verfaßt," in *Gedenkfeier für Karl Jaspers* (Basel: Basler Universitätsreden, 60. Heft, 1969), p. 4.

[2] "Wir sind auf dem Wege vom Abendrot der europäischen Philosophie durch die Dämmerung unserer Zeit zur Morgenröte der Weltphilosophie" (all translations by the author). Karl Jaspers, *Rechenschaft und Ausblick* (München, 1958), p. 391.

[3] "Wir wandern in das Dunkel der Zukunft." Karl Jaspers, *Vom Ursprung und Ziel der Geschichte*, 8th ed. (München/Zürich, 1983), p. 284. [Henceforth cited as *UZG*]

rapid growth in technology, information technologies in particular, one becomes progressively more aware of the increasingly global character of history, and the increasing global relevance of events. In the contemporary era events cease to be local and instead form the history of the earth. While technology opens tremendous opportunities of growth for humanity, it also presents grave perils. In the presence of these contrary forces, it is philosophy that appears to Jaspers a cognitive foundation upon which humanity will build its future.

Jaspers perceives that the greatest of the perils faced by humanity is nuclear destruction leading to the annihilation of humankind. We should add that in spite of the time that has lapsed since Jaspers' diagnosis, his worries do not seem futile or exaggerated; on the contrary, they remain sensed and shared by most people. This is a good reason to take both his warning and his indications of possible solutions most seriously. Jaspers counterbalances the threat of disintegration with the perspective of unity. The possibility to come together appears realistic because, in Jaspers' own words, "the unity of the Earth is already a fact."[4] For the time being, it is only spatial and technological, while true unity is the question of the future. In fact, there is no guarantee that unification will come. Both options are open to mankind, either the disintegration of humanity, or its reconciliation. Because either one or the other is possible, Jaspers calls upon philosophy to develop the kind of thinking that may potentially save humankind. It becomes clear to Jaspers, though, that faced with a task so important, it can no longer be the thinking of only one tradition or pertaining to only one historical area; in other words, it cannot merely be Western philosophy that accomplishes this great task. Jaspers recognizes the limitations of Occidental thinking in the face of what the modern era demands, thus the source of his expression regarding the "twilight of European philosophy." This means that the kind of thinking capable of meeting this grand task must in itself cross the old limitations and traditions and become as broad and boundless as possible in order to encompass what has been thought before, and what is yet to be thought, from the perspective of the new task at hand.

At this point I would like to digress to indicate that this idea of Jaspers should not be construed as yet another attempt to plan the future, since any such planning or historical engineering, so to speak, disregards the limitations of human knowledge and human ability, and therefore must be doomed to failure by leading to the destruction of human freedom, creativity, and reason. We are reminded of a famous conviction formulated by Jaspers regarding the boundaries of human knowledge and of the possibilities to mould history based on that knowledge. He believes that it is impossible to set the goal of history and organize the world accordingly based on human understanding. Jaspers would say ultimately that both the origin and the goal of history remain unknown. At the same time, however, he confesses at the beginning of the aforementioned work, that while working on this concept he was guided by a doctrine of faith, that mankind has a common origin and goal.[5] This

---

[4] "Die Erdeinheit ist da" (*UZG* 163).

[5] "Bei meinem Entwurf bin ich getragen von der Glaubensthese, daß die Menschheit einen einzigen Ursprung und Ziel habe" (*UZG* 17).

is a declaration of faith, and it does not conflict with the other belief, of the two remaining unknown, because the fact that the origin and the goal remain unknown does not preclude the possibility to act. Philosophy is to play an important role, since through philosophical thinking we may approach it, and through philosophical discussion we are paving the path towards possible realization. Another reason why this quality of being unknown is not an obstacle, according to Jaspers' reasoning, is because what cannot be understood by ordinary knowing may be perceived and sensed through ambiguous ciphers and symbols.[6]

One may argue with Jaspers whether the entire great metaphysical and religious tradition of the West springs from one origin and one goal. Humanity has one source, and one objective, which is divinity. What is new in Jaspers' thought, however, is the belief that we can commune with the sacred or divinity through ciphers of transcendence, where they are heard, and through which we experience transcendence.[7] For Jaspers, therefore, faith is a necessary component in building the unity of the world. And yet by faith he understands not a belief based on dogmatic knowledge, but rather the faith through which man returns to his origin and by which he reconnects in the depth of his self with transcendence.

Seeing in contemporary circumstances the danger of the disintegration of all things resulting from raging nihilism, Jaspers turns to faith, because he believes that man cannot live apart from faith if he wants to preserve himself (*UZG* 209). It is worth noting that Jaspers rejects dogmatic faith mostly for the reason that it ceases to be convincing for modern man who is concerned above all with freedom, and freedom, it should be stressed, is the essential component of his vision of the future of humanity. He is more prone to refer to biblical faith than the dogmatic faith of the Church.[8] It is not that Jaspers is here repeating Kierkegaard's call for a return to early Christian practices, but rather a return to the foundation of the "great, simple truths" of the Bible, and to a new faith based upon but not identical with the primary religious tradition of the West. What shape this new faith should take, he does not want to determine in advance since he argues for manifold forms of faith, simultaneously coexisting and remaining in dialogue with one another. He will only insist that the new shape of faith needs to draw from the biblical tradition, because of its immense spiritual importance and influence, which must not be lost.

What then should this new faith be, and has Jaspers has left us any particular clues? Although Jaspers has not defined precisely what this new world philosophy, might be, he drafted a general plan.[9] What he shows in his work on the subject directs us initially to the distant historical past to what he himself terms the Axial

---

[6] "Die Welt ist Stätte von Aufgaben, ist selber aus der Transzendenz, in ihr begegnet die Sprache, auf die wir hören, wenn wir verstehen, was wir eigentlich wollen" (*UZG* 275).

[7] "Immer leben wir mit Symbolen. In ihnen erfahren wir und ergreifen die Transzendenz, die eigentliche Wirklichkeit" (*UZG* 274).

[8] "...im Bezug unseres Glaubens an die biblische Religion zuletzt die Entscheidung über die Zukunft unseres abendländischen Menschseins liegt, das ist gewiß" (*UZG* 281).

[9] Hans Saner writes about this in "Jaspers' Idee einer kommenden Weltphilosophie," *Philosophie der Freiheit*, ed. Rudolf Lengert (Oldenburg: H. Holzberg, 1983), p. 49. [Henceforth cited as *JIW*]

Age, a period which stretches between 800 and 200 BC. Let us note that in Jaspers' thinking, "Axial Age" has a double meaning. The first, basic meaning denotes the common origin of humanity. Therefore, it is not merely faith, but also an empirically verifiable event. In the axial time, parallel spiritual processes of unprecedented significance occurred, created by Socrates' predecessors in Greece, the prophets in Israel, the Buddha in India, and Confucius in China. These parallel events point to the beginning of humanity as such, as it was then that man acquired consciousness of one's own tragic self, when basic patterns and categories of culture and thinking took shape, the same patterns and categories we still use today. It is from that age that the history of human spirit derives, and when the notion of mankind was born. For Jaspers this is a particular proof of humankind's common origin, as the great creations of human spirit occurred simultaneously in parallel without influencing one another, as if they independently sprung from a primary source, which signifies that this real axial time would therefore be the embodiment of an ideal axis around which our human life circles in harmonious movement.[10] This coincidence cannot be explained in historical, immanent terms, because on that level it will always remain an enigma. We need to look for the answer outside history. Yet what is essential for Jaspers is that contemporary people will notice this common origin of humanity. Although this event has extraordinary significance, at the same time it is nothing exceptional.

Here we arrive at the second meaning of Jaspers' Axial Age, namely, its potential repeatability. As an ideal axis by definition, it would only require distinct real conditions to occur. By the same token, making people aware of this fact, of existence of their common source in the past, might help them to feel a reciprocal kinship and foster the sentiment of solidarity. Empirical observation of the present time indicates the actual scattering of individuals, cultures, nations, and religions. Yet in the face of this diaspora, the unity of the world becomes the goal of humankind. We should hasten to note that as a goal, this unity would not entail actual unification or uniformity which would always have to be forcibly imposed, especially if we consider the strong contemporary pull towards individuality, separation and freedom pertaining to individuals and nations alike. In the contemporary world, Jaspers notes the continuous struggle of contrary forces, yet unity may bring resolution either in the form of one global state, an empire created by force, or in the form of a global government of united states, giving up part of their particular independence for the benefit of a greater, pan-human independence, working the path towards the future of humanity based on consensus within the legal order. In the pulse of various—often contradictory—agendas, as well as religious, racial, or culturally motivated conflicts, we see the problem of unity intensifying. The problem of unity, therefore, may be solved either through violence, against which Jaspers warns us, or through the attainment of individual freedom, which he advocates. Jaspers, the philosopher of freedom, is a firm supporter of the latter solution, and he paints the picture of

---

[10] "Dann wäre diese reale Achsenzeit die Inkarnation einer idealen Achse, um die sich das Menschsein in seiner Bewegung zusammenfindet" (*UZG* 324).

an ideal world in which people meet for peaceful reasons, enter into agreement that decisions be made democratically and democratically transformed. Along with this utopian vision, we also find some particular, practical recommendations, namely, a world order in which states function independently while forming a federation based on natural law, which, according to Jaspers, reflects the universal bond connecting people, and providing foundations for human rights.

Such unity would not be achievable once and for all, but would have to be continually reestablished in a spirit of liberty and based on decisions made in the particular, ever changing social, economic, and cultural circumstances. It would be a neverending process, since ending it would be the end of history. In this process, the position of certain, definite knowledge, which is impossible to obtain, is now filled by the discussion of the new world order, carried within the framework of international communication and according to principles of democracy which guarantee the freedom of citizens and refer to the rule of law. For Jaspers, the Swiss federal state was the blueprint of such world unity. He was convinced that the model of such unity can be developed in technical, practical terms and, based on the achievements of civilization, could be implemented. But this is not sufficient. In order for basic values, such as human dignity, spiritual freedom, millennial traditions and national independence to be protected, the faith to evoke those values is absolutely essential. Because such a world order has never existed to date, Jaspers himself expresses some doubt whether it is possible to realize this. After all, it would require the political maturity of all states, and the general, popular awareness of liberty, for Jaspers, seems to be lacking in the Middle and Far East.[11] Jaspers sees obstacles on the road to such a system, but also is convinced, that there exists within people, so to say a priori, certain fundamental elements allowing them to overcome those obstacles. The first of these elements is the true desire of liberty, and the second is awareness that in spite of differences, the things we have in common are much more important and much more basic than what separates us. This awareness, which is now much more widespread thanks to the impact of mass media, counteracts the pull towards exclusivity, advantage, domination over others out of feelings of superiority and power. And while what is universal is also our origin, as he indicates through his notion of the Axial Age, that awareness helps the unification processes.

Here we return to the issue of philosophy's place in the future world order. According to Jaspers, philosophy should play a decisive role in this great endeavor. However, it must be a new kind of philosophy, focusing not only on an individual and his existential relation to transcendent Being, but also taking the responsibility for the world, and opening itself to humankind. Above all, it should clarify the awareness of historical breakthrough and the arrival of a new Promethean age, the second Axial Age, which has already been programmed or written into its very origin. While the first Axial Age manifested our common origin, the second will

---

[11] Jaspers is aware of dangers and difficulties mounting along this path, and always threatening to break it (*UZG* 199 ff). He is far from being naïve in his vision of the world. His intransigence in showing the misery of human life is best seen in this description of limit situations.

manifest our common goal. Although this may not be fully clear in the present, it challenges humanity as a task to be completed. We might say that the task, which Jaspers lays out for philosophy, appears in his thoughts almost as a fulfillment of destiny.

Is contemporary philosophy capable of this? In the notes he left behind as his testament, Jaspers drafts the outline of world philosophy. He is aware that his monumental project is not feasible, either as the achievement of a single individual, or is it possible as yet in the present time. On the other hand, he believes that although we are aware of the impossibility of the task at present, we contemporaries should at least initiate its realization (*JIW* 60). Jaspers himself takes first steps in that direction, and we can see how he is prompted alternately by a deep concern and by a greater dream. In order to perceive how great an undertaking this is, we reference the two most important tasks involved: first, world philosophy should turn to the past, and absorb everything which has been understood thus far; and second, philosophy should turn to the future and in order to discover new ways of thinking. This would entail the development of a world history of philosophy examining the significance of thinking, not just the thinking of philosophers, but of all creative people, in terms of how much it fosters trends launching communication processes, and to what extent it also interrupted those processes. We might dub it the history of thinking, pointing to the essential criteria already disclosed in the axial time. This would be the universal logic examining possibilities of thinking that would assist the proliferation of the idea of unity. Jaspers initiated, but only partly realized both these grand tasks—the fragments of which were published in his works *Vom Ursprung und Ziel der Geschichte, Die grossen Philosophen: Erster Band*, and *Von der Wahrheit*. These fragments are more than just seedlings and remain to be developed more clearly and completely (*JIW* 60).

Jaspers' idea of the future philosophy of the world is not only the philosophy of reason, showing the history of man's thought and its development perspectives; it is also the philosophy of action. In this respect, notions of communication and freedom, the primary categories of his philosophy, play an important role. In his work they were already featured prominently, but now, incorporated into the new project, they acquire additional meaning, as they are no longer linked solely to the notion of an individual *Existenz*, but to mankind as a whole. Therefore existential communication, described in the second volume of *Philosophie*, will become the new philosophy and universal communication of the world, and existential freedom will remain the core of the liberty for all people living in democratically governed states.

Theoretical philosophy is now fulfilled through the addition of practical philosophy. When we follow Jaspers' train of thought contained in his work on *The Origin and Goal of History*, we may conclude that this is not necessarily the result of one conditioning the other, of a theoretical plan preparing for a practical implementation. Considering the immensity of the theoretical task, we might rather say that the two should develop in parallel complementing one another; in other words, the increase of knowledge should gradually improve and deepen communication between people, fostering a freedom-based decision making process. This remains in harmony with the very principle of building unity according to Jaspers, as by definition it should be a living, ever-moving process, consisting of particular decisions people make here and now, while all the future options remain open.[12]

We now see that Jaspers finds the reasons for such a grand role of philosophy in constructing world unity within his own philosophy, because the latter brings arguments which render the decision making-process more profound. These are expressed by its categories, next to the aforementioned notions of reason, freedom, and communication, and also the notion of the One. The One manifests itself in its actuality during the Axial Age as the simultaneous occurrence of what people have in common, which gives rise to the belief in the original unity of humankind, anchored in a higher pre-source, which makes humanity the direct descendant of God.[13] Thus, for the person of faith, the Axial Age brings the testimony of the plan of divine Providence, while for the philosopher, Providence and its signs constitute symbols, which everyone may interpret freely in the desire to understand the truth, and present it for discussion with others. Therefore, although in terms of scientific knowledge neither the origin nor the goal of human history are empirically known, there are certain significant events occurring within this history, human achievements are accumulated, and become the shared inheritance of all mankind. Thanks to modern information technology, ever widening circles of people can partake in and draw from this wealth, and philosophy may clarify the meaning included therein, because philosophy possesses the tool of reason, and since its inception, communes with the mystery of transcendence. Thus a philosophical pursuit of the truth of transcendence, along the path of existential communication, is the pursuit, as Jaspers notes, "of the truth which we have in common." Hidden from objective knowledge, the meaning of the history of mankind calls for a limitless communication between people who can only discover it while engaging in what he called "the loving struggle."

As already mentioned, Jaspers' philosophy of the world appears to be the project of destiny. This destiny was already revealed in the first Axial Age, in a non-intentional manner, without people being aware of it; in the second Axial Age, philosophy should fulfill this destiny out of the awareness that it is a task of necessary for the world as a whole. In the first Axial Age, three independent roots of one human history manifested themselves, and thus the One was expressed in three different areas, in which a substantial metamorphosis of man was affected. Later, these paths began to diverge. In the second Axial Age, these diverging, different paths will lead to one goal, the One. According to Jaspers, being aware of this triple origin of the Axial Age gives rise to the need of boundless communication in which no one holds advantage over others, no one knows better than the others, even though Jaspers grants the lead in the path towards world unity to the Europeans, due

---

[12] "Die Tiefe des Jetzt wird offenbar nur ineins Vergangenheit und Zukunft, mit Erinnerung und mit der Idee, woraufhin ich lebe" (*UZG* 334).

[13] "Die Einheit also, auf die hin der Mensch lebt...kann nicht in einer Einheit biologischer Abstammung ihren Grund haben, sondern nur in dem höheren Ursprung, der den Menschen unmittelbar aus der Hand der Gottheit werden läßt" (*UZG* 309).

to their traditions of freedom and democracy, and the cultivation of personal love. However, what should be of paramount importance in this pursuit is the realization that all the great spiritual achievements of the Axial Age are essentially the same, and that in spite of the distance between them, they permeate one another (*UZG* 27). But the fact of similarity does not mean that history in these different areas would merely constitute a repetition. Jaspers believes that communication with other spiritual areas always enriches us, because it demonstrates human potential. What is therefore the meaning of "the same"? We may conclude that this is the very core of humanity, which manifests itself in different countries and eras in different ways. Here we encounter another interesting statement of Jaspers, namely, "that perhaps in every human being all the possibilities lie."[14] This would therefore mean that the way human potential develops depends on particular circumstances, on a particular time and place, this does not preclude the core of being one and the same, that is, our common humanity.

This leads us to the important conclusion that the cross-infusion of cultures, religions, and traditions, drawing from the past heritage of different nations, providing that it does not lead to uniformity, fosters the increase in the knowledge of what humans can become provided that conflicts, separatist tendencies, and wars do not bar the way to this goal. As we have seen, in Jaspers' concept of world philosophy, philosophical assumptions are interwoven with political beliefs, philosophical faith, and concern for the future of humankind. This monumental project raises doubts that do not only spring from the sheer magnitude of the task. Major doubt can be expressed in the question as to whether it is possible to reconcile his spirit of democracy and universal politics with philosophical elitism, in other words, whether it is possible to marry the global, democratic decision-making process and the postulate of universal communication with the wholly elitist concept of one, sole *Existenz* and irreplaceable existential experience of one's self in the face of transcendence and the unique reading of its ciphers? In sum, is it possible to reconcile Jaspers' idea of world philosophy with the fundamental concepts and beliefs of his philosophy of *Existenz*, which, after all, constitutes the core of the future world philosophy? We should note at this point that Jaspers himself is aware of the utopian character of his ideas, and yet he believes also that all the current obstacles on the way to unity, while seemingly dominant today, are merely a necessary intermediary stage. He always adds that while reason is the founding medium of philosophy, and that while communication is the way, they may prove to be insufficient. Therefore the ultimate factor is his faith in man, inseparable from his faith in transcendence, the Divine, which is "the origin and the goal" of all things. Thus faith is the guarantor of his belief in the world's future. He writes that what is important in building

---

[14] "Vielleicht sind in jedem Menschen alle Möglichkeiten, aber gewiß ist immer nur beschränkte Wirklichkeit" (*UZG* 276).

unity is the awareness of man who, in various historical periods, remains essentially the same, thanks to his faith, which connects him to Being itself.[15] From this belief in the common source, in the transcendental foundation of Being connecting all humankind, springs Jaspers' postulate to strive for the future of humanity with all people, without imposing one doctrine, one faith, or one religion as the basis of unity. He proposes to replace the rule of violence with the power of love, using reason. This stand permeates all his philosophizing. He promises it will guide us along the path, leading to the place where love gains its depth in true communication, and the truth which connects us will be revealed to those, as distant from one another as seems possible, as the basis of our common historical genesis.[16]

---

[15] "...[der Mensch,] der in mannighafen geschichtlichen Kleidern sich wesentlich gleich ist durch den Gehalt seines Glaubens, der ihn mit dem Grund des Seins verbindet" (*UZG* 272).

[16] "Und [Philosophieren] führt auf dem Weg dorthin, wo die Liebe ihre Tiefe gewinnt in wirklicher Kommunikation" (*UZG* 284).

Karl Jaspers' Philosophical Faith for the Global Age: The Idea of Civilizational Continuity

Joanne Miyang Cho

Abstract In the post-World War II era, Jaspers attempted to reformulate Western Christianity for an increasingly globalizing world. He was especially focused on overcoming its anti-Semitic legacy. His solution to it was the idea of civilizational continuity. Through it, he tried to reverse the directions of the German debate on civilization which had been dominated by Weimar historicists, especially Oswald Spengler and Ernst Troeltsch. While the latter emphasized the utter uniqueness of each civilization and thus denied any common elements between civilizations, Jaspers rejected their isolationist tendency by pointing to the historical reality of civilizational continuity. He found its best advocates in the Buddha.

Following World War II, Jaspers attempted to reformulate Christianity in the West in the context of Europe's recent past and present. How could it address its failures vis-à-vis the non-Christian world, the Holocaust, and colonialism? What kind of a new relationship can be established with the non-Christian world? Jaspers urgently explored these questions in many of his postwar writings. I will show how he addressed these issues effectively through the idea of civilizational continuity. Jaspers attempted to reverse the direction of German discourse on civilization which had been dominated by the Weimar historicists who emphasized the uniqueness of each civilization, denied a meaningful connection between civilizations, and proposed civilizational discontinuity. In contrast, Jaspers weakened their isolationist tendency by reformulating the idea of historicism. Historicism, he contended, should be connected to the idea of individuality and also to the idea of continuity.

In the following two parts, I discuss the meaning of civilizational continuity for Jaspers' notion of philosophical faith. In the first section to this chapter I situate Jaspers' idea of civilizational continuity in its historical context. Prior to Jaspers, the debate on civilization was dominated by two Weimar historicists, Oswald Spengler, author of the sensational work *The Decline of the West* (1919), and Ernst Troeltsch. Spengler viewed civilizations as entirely unique and isolated from each other. He recognized some cross-cultural adaptations, but dismissed them as superficial. Although Troeltsch represented Weimar liberals, in his critique of

J.M. Cho (✉)
William Paterson University, Wayne, NJ, USA
e-mail: choj@wpunj.edu

H. Wautischer et al. (eds.), *Philosophical Faith and the Future of Humanity*,
DOI 10.1007/978-94-007-2223-1_33, © Springer Science+Business Media B.V. 2012

Spengler's neo-conservative work, he did not entirely succeed in doing so,[1] for he shared with Spengler a rejection of civilizational continuity. In the second section I examine Jaspers' emphasis on civilizational continuity and his rejection of the Weimar historicists' isolationist tendencies. Unlike Spengler, he regarded cross-cultural adaptations as healthy. Unlike Troeltsch, he supported the cross-cultural adaptation from Westernized Christianity to Chinese Christianity. In this context I explore Jaspers' recommendation that the West learn Buddha's toleration of different perspectives and his avid practices of cross-cultural adaptation. These proposals place Jaspers among the strongest proponents of cosmopolitanism in post-World War II Germany.

The Weimar Historicists—The Idea of Civilizational Discontinuity

Several German historians and liberal theologians have become passionately interested in historicism since the 1880s.[2] Their emphasis on the individuality principle produced important works in history and theology. These historicists noted how the German tradition of individuality was different from, or even superior to, Western Europe's natural law tradition. Rejecting universal values and the idea of humankind, they held truths to be valid only within a given cultural context. Spengler and Troeltsch were at the forefront of this historicist movement. Despite Troeltsch's strong critique of Spengler's neo-conservative views, both shared a limited similarity in their rejection of cross-cultural adaptations; Spengler found them to be superficial and Troeltsch rejected them for his dislike of relativism.

Spengler's *Decline of the West* has often been regarded as a significant work in world history. This might appear ironical, since Spengler, in reality, rejected universal truths. He saw no common experiences across civilizations. Mankind, he argued, is "an empty word," having "no aim, no idea, no plan, any more than the family of butterflies and orchids."[3] Contrary to Hegel, he rejected "a linear graph" (*DW* 16) and meaning in history, for life experiences are "the expressions of its own and only its own time" (*DW* 31). Instead of a single truth applicable to all peoples, there are "the overwhelming multitude of the facts" and "the drama of *a number* of mighty cultures" (*DW* 17). Spengler found uniqueness to be present not only in artistic, but also scientific fields: "There is not one sculpture, one painting, one mathematics, one

---

[1] Ernst Troeltsch, book review of volumes I and II of Spengler's *Decline of the West*, in *Aufsätze zur Geistesgeschichte und Religionssoziologie. Gesammelte Schriften*, vol. IV, ed. Hans Baron (Tübingen: J.C.B. Mohr, 1925), pp. 677–684 and 685–691. [Henceforth cited as *AGR*]

[2] Michael Murrmann-Kahl, *Die entzauberte Heilsgeschichte. De Historismus erobert die Theologie 1880–1920* (Gütersloh: Gütersloher Verlagshaus Mohn, 1992).

[3] Oswald Spengler, *The Decline of the West*, an abridged edition, ed. Helmut Werner, trans. Charles Francis Atkinson (New York, NY & Oxford: Oxford University Press, 1991), p. 17. [Henceforth cited as *DW*]

physics, but many, each in its deepest essence different from the others, each limited in duration and self-contained" (*DW* 17). Each culture also makes "its own set of images of physical processes, which are true only for itself and only alive while it is itself alive" (*DW* 190). History possesses greater peculiarity than those "images of physical processes" (*DW* 78). Each culture has "its own conception of home and fatherland" (*DW* 174) as well as "its own systematic psychology just as it possesses its own style of knowledge of men and experience of life" (*DW* 160). After pointing out exhaustively the individuality principle everywhere, Spengler was justly proud of his historicist approach and called it "the Copernican discovery in the historical sphere" (*DW* 13–14).

Spengler does not totally deny cross-cultural adaptation, which he calls historical pseudomorphoses, but he finds it to be unimportant and accidental. Borrowing an analogy from mineralogy, he describes its formation: After a long period, crystals of a mineral embedded in a rock-stratum are gradually washed out. That hollowness is then filled up by molten masses during volcanic outbursts. But they are "not free to do so in their own special forms" due to pre-existing rock-stratum (*DW* 268). The result is a "distorted form" (*DW* 268). The same distorted process is happening to cultures as well:

> By the term "historical pseudomorphosis" I propose to designate those cases in which an older alien Culture lies too massively over the land so that a young Culture cannot get its breath and fails not only to achieve pure and specific expression-forms, but even to develop fully its own self-consciousness. (*DW* 268)

An example of historical pseudomorphosis is the Arabian Culture, which "lies entirely within the ambit of the ancient Babylonian Civilization" and thus it could not develop in a healthy way (*DW* 268). Despite his strong interests in several civilizations, Spengler was equally critical of civilizational grafting and sought to keep the purity of each cultural tradition.

Ernst Troeltsch published a book review of Spengler's *Decline of the West* in the leading historical journal of the time, *Historische Zeitschrift*. He was not a surprising choice as critic, since he, perhaps more than any other liberal theologians at that time, applied historical analysis to theology. He was regarded as the systematician of the History of Religions School (*religionsgeschictliche Schule*), which was formed by the young liberal theologians in the 1890s at the University of Göttingen. He was also considered as the leading philosopher of history in the early Weimar years. In the book review, Troeltsch clearly differentiated his liberal views from Spengler's neo-conservative ones. He connected himself to modernism, plurality, *Gesellschaft*, democracy, and scientific approach, while connecting Spengler to *Gemeinschaft*, "blood, romantic cynicism, amoral heroism" (*AGR* 691).

There was, however, an exception to this contrast, which Troeltsch failed to note. Like Spengler, Troeltsch applied the individuality principle to civilizations and noted that there is very little commonality between civilizations. Even science and logic are not universal, but culture specific:

> Indeed, even the validity of science and logic seemed to exhibit, under different skies and upon different soil, strong individual differences present even in their deepest and innermost

rudiments. What was really common to mankind [is found] to be at bottom exceedingly little, and to belong more to the province of material goods than to the ideal values of civilization.[4]

In a 1922 lecture, Troeltsch announced that due to the individuality principle, he could no longer claim even the relative superiority of Christianity over other world religions, as he had done in his 1902 *The Absoluteness of Christianity* (*CWR* 51). Now, he saw all world religions to be equally valid to their own believers. It would be wrong to apply Western categories to other cultures or religions. Westerners could find truths only within their Occidental cultures, whereas the non-Westerners could find theirs only within their non-Western cultures. Likewise, since Christianity was the dominant religion of Westerners for the last two millennia, Europeans, Troeltsch argued, could find salvation only through it (*CWR* 53). Yet Christianity is not valid for non-Westerners who could find salvation only through their non-Western religions.

In addition to differentiating Christianity from non-Western religions, Troeltsch even separated Europe's Westernized Christianity from various manifestations of Oriental Christianity: "The Christianity of the Oriental peoples—the Jacobites, Nestorians, Armenians, Abyssinians—is of quite a different type, indeed even that of the Russians is a world of its own" (*CWR* 52). The intention of his book, *The Social Teachings of Christian Churches* (1911), was to show Christianity in the West to be "thoroughly individual" (*CWR* 51). The West had developed its unique Christian social teachings while interacting with its unique socio-political and cultural developments during last 2,000 years. In this process, Troeltsch emphasizes, Christianity became "deorientalised," and from its origins as a "Jewish sect, Christianity has become the religion of all Europe. It stands or falls with European civilization; whilst, on its own part, it has entirely lost its Oriental character and has become Hellenized and westernized" (*CWR* 54). Consequently, Westerners, Troeltsch argued, could find salvation only through Westernized Christianity.

There is one notable inconsistency in Troeltsch's argument. Although in his early Weimar years he was opposed to the transfer of Westernized Christianity to the non-West, he had earlier accepted cross-cultural transfer in one instance; namely, Europe's borrowing of Semitic Christianity in the ancient world. Due to his growing objection to relativism, especially after World War I, he no longer supported cultural transfer. Instead, his idea of Europeanism linked Europeans to Christianity, as he feared that having non-Western religions as alternative religions would lead to relativism. Of course, one can see clearly that Troeltsch's isolationist position is counterfactual, since Westernized Christianity has spread to the non-West, as for example Chinese Christianity, Min Jung theology in South Korea, or Dalit theology in India. Thus, his assertion that Spengler's work belongs to literature, while his last major work, *Der Historismus und seine Probleme* (1922), was a work of science, may only be partially accepted.

---

[4] Ernst Troeltsch, "Christianity Among World Religions," in *Christian Thought. Its History and Application*, ed. Baron von Hügel (New York, NY: Meridian Books, 1957), p. 53. [Henceforth cited as *CWR*]

Along with Spengler, Troeltsch articulated the purest multiculturalist position in twentieth century Germany. The German historicist tradition enabled him to respect the uniqueness of other civilizations and to reject European imperialist politics and the Eurocentric Christian mission, and it also enabled him to deny any common understanding between civilizations. Troeltsch, supposedly a critic of Spengler, was actually similar to him. A number of historians have commented on that. Carlo Antoni harshly rejects Troeltsch's history of Europeanism as "only a revision of that chapter in *The Decline of the West* (*Untergang des Abendlandes*) which deals with our own civilization." In them, "the criteria and the methods" were the same.[5] Georg Iggers notes that neither Troeltsch nor Spengler accept "a single human history, but only the history of separate, closed cultures," thus contributing to the crisis of historicism.[6] Yet Troeltsch did so before Spengler.[7] Ernst Schulin, while chastising both for contributing to historical isolationism, criticized Troeltsch more because, due to his respected academic status at the University of Berlin, he had a greater influence on other academicians than did the private scholar, Oswald Spengler.[8]

Jaspers' Idea of Civilizational Continuity

After World War II, Jaspers, who had suffered during the Nazi period, along with his Jewish wife, became very critical of Christian anti-Semitism. Although German historicism was not responsible for this, he viewed its isolationist tendency as discouraging cultural integration between Christians and Jews in Germany and Europe. He thus tried to reformulate it so that it would be connected not only to the idea of individuality, but more importantly, to the idea of continuity. To strengthen the idea of continuity, Jaspers made two proposals that went against the isolationist position of the Weimar historicists. First, he partly criticized the historic in favor of the universal and emphasized the reality of human mobility. Unlike Troeltsch, he supported the transfer of Westernized Christianity to the non-West, as his example of Chinese Christianity shows. Secondly, Jaspers recommended that Christians in Europe learn from Buddha. Unlike Christians, Buddhists tolerated different views and actively practiced cross-cultural adaptations. Jaspers emphasized that Mahayana Buddhism, which actively adopted local cultures, was better than Hinayana Buddhism which

---

[5] Carlo Antoni, *From History to Sociology: The Transition in German Historical Thinking*, trans. Hayden V. White (Westport, CT: Greenwood Press, 1976), p. 83.

[6] Georg Iggers, *The German Conception of History: The National Tradition of Historical Thought from Herder to the Present*, rev. ed. (Middletown, CT: Wesleyan University Press, 1983), pp. 199, 240.

[7] Georg Iggers, *New Directions in European Historiography* (Middletown, CT: Wesleyan University Press, 1984), p. 30.

[8] Ernst Schulin, "Einleitung," in *Universalgeschichte*, ed. Ernst Schulin (Köln: Kiepenheuer & Witsch, 1974), p. 30. Ernst Schulin, *Traditionskritik und Rekonstrucktionsversuch. Studien zur Entwicklung von Geschichteswissenschaft und historischem Denken* (Göttingen: Vandenhoeck & Ruprecht, 1979), p. 183.

did not. Even so, Jaspers found different forms of Buddhism possessing a common spirit.

In his *Origin and Goal of History* (1949), Jaspers very sharply rejected the "absolute alienness" thesis which the Weimar historicists advocated:

> All assertions of absolute alienness, of the permanent impossibility of mutual understanding, remain the expression of resignation in lassitude, of failure before the most profound demand of humanity—the intensification of temporary impossibilities into absolute impossibilities, the extinction of inner readiness.[9]

Jaspers pilloried "Spengler's absolute separation of cultures standing side by side without relations" (*OGH* 277, Notes 3). Detecting the danger of civilizational isolationism, he was quite determined to fight against it. He was willing to perpetrate that violence against the historic in favor of the universal, the one historicity of being-human.[10] His presupposition was that "what is grasped and brought forth by the human race possesses a unity of meaning by virtue of the interrelatedness of everything" (*WHP* 19). Nonetheless, he was careful to point out his continuing commitment to history: "While we do not want to revert to history in the manner of historicism, or to substitute history of philosophy for philosophy, we also do not want to shut our eye to history."[11]

To demonstrate civilizational continuity, Jaspers pointed to the historical reality of human mobility. Humanity was "always mobile" and it "long ago has taken possession of the surface of the earth," except perhaps in Australia and America, but even the latter were "not absolutely isolated" and were still subject to "foreign influence" (*OGH* 254). He witnessed "the empirically demonstrable contacts, transferences, adaptations," such as "Buddhism in China, Christianity in the West" (*OGH* 277 Notes 3) and paid special attention to the transfer of Westernized Christianity onto Chinese Christianity crediting this to Matteo Ricci and other Jesuit missionaries in China during the sixteenth and seventeenth centuries. Their culturally sensitive mission succeeded at first, because they presented Christianity in terms of Confucian ideas and emphasized several similarities between Christian and Confucian ethics. Their mission succeeded in converting numbers of Chinese to Christianity, reaching about 200,000 at its height.[12] They also gained the support of Emperor Kangxi (1661–1722). The emperor allowed Christianity because of his enthusiasm for Western science and mathematics that the Jesuits brought with them. Jaspers clearly perceived mutual respect and learning between Jesuits and Chinese at this time.

---

[9] Karl Jaspers, *The Origin and Goal of History*, trans. Michael Bullock (New Haven, CT: Yale University Press, 1953), p. 264. [Henceforth cited as *OGH*]

[10] Karl Jaspers, "World History of Philosophy," in Karl Jaspers, *Philosopher Among Philosophers/ Philosoph unter Philosophen*, eds. Richard Wisser and Leonard H. Ehrlich (Würzburg: Königshausen & Neumann, 1993), p. 19. [Henceforth cited as *WHP*]

[11] Jaspers quoted in Leonard H. Ehrlich, "Philosophy and Its History. The Double Helix of Jaspers's Thought," in Karl Jaspers, *On Philosophy of History and History of Philosophy*, eds. Joseph W. Koterski, S.J. and Raymond J. Langley (Amherst, NY: Humanity Books, 2003), p. 21.

[12] Joanna Waley-Cohen, *The Sextants of Beijing* (New York, NY: W.W. Norton, 1999), p. 19.

However, Jaspers unhappily notes the end of "the creative Jesuit mission" due to the intolerance of the Vatican.[13] The Vatican objected to the Jesuits' tolerance of Chinese ancestor worship. Its legation, led by Carlo Tomasso Maillard de Tournor in 1705–1706, caused a "disastrous fallout" in Peking, as it insisted on the orthodox Catholic position on the Rites question. This alienated Emperor Kangxi.[14] When another Vatican legation arrived in the early 1720s, still insisting on the ortho- dox position, a new emperor, Yongzheng, lost his patience and issued Edicts in 1724 whereby all churches in the provinces were closed down and their resident Jesuits were expelled.[15] Jaspers pilloried the Vatican's intolerance of local culture for ending the Jesuit mission.

Another model for Jaspers' cosmopolitanism was the Buddha. Like the Jesuits who admired an Asian paradigmatic individual, Confucius, Jaspers found inspira- tion in another Asian paradigmatic individual, Buddha, whom he analyzed in *The Great Philosophers* (1957). He recommended that Western Christians and their leaders learn from Buddha. Jaspers' account of Buddha was unusual, in one regard, when compared to those of other scholars. For instance, Karen Armstrong was inspired by Jaspers' axial age for her book, *The Great Transformation*, and she, like Jaspers, focused on Buddha's compassion, enlightenment and the belief that there is no eternal self.[16] But she does not emphasize Buddha's cosmopolitanism, whereas it is the main focus of Jaspers. Buddha, Jaspers noted, addressed all men and "created for the first time in history the idea of humanity, of a religion for the whole world."[17] Buddha fought against anti-humanitarian traditions, such as "the caste system and the supreme power of the gods" (*SBC* 39).

Jaspers especially highlights Buddha's radical toleration of different perspec- tives. The best example is that Buddha did not conceive himself to be an exception, but only "a manifestation in a row of innumerable other Buddhas" (*PW* 143–145). Jaspers' emphasis on "innumerable other Buddhas" is clearly aimed at traditional Christology which believes in "the religion of Christ that sees God in Christ."[18] Buddha accepted that all human beings have "the prospect of becoming Budhisattas, or future Buddhas" (*SBC* 39). In this process, each person is helped by the grace of other human beings "who have already become Budhisattvas, to whom he prays" (*SBC* 39). Buddha's tolerance of different perspectives was made easier since

---

[13] Karl Jaspers, *Philosophy and the World. Selected Essays and Lectures*, trans. E.B. Ashton (Chicago, IL: Regnery, 1963), p. 143. [Henceforth cited as *PW*]

[14] Liam Matthew Brockey, *Journey to the East. The Jesuit Mission to China, 1579–1724* (Cambridge, MA: The Belknap Press of Harvard University Press, 2007), p. 165.

[15] Brockey, p. 165.

[16] Karen Armstrong, *The Great Transformation: The Beginning of Our Religious Traditions* (New York, NY: Alfred A. Knopf, 2006), pp. 274–288.

[17] Karl Jaspers, *Socrates, Buddha, Confucius, Jesus. The Paradigmatic individuals* [From *The Great Philosophers*, Volume I], ed. Hannah Arendt, trans. Ralph Manheim (San Diego, CA and New York, NY: A Harvest Books, 1962), pp. 34–35. [Henceforth cited as *SBC*]

[18] Jaspers, *The Perennial Scope of Philosophy*, trans. Ralph Manheim (Hamden, CT: Anchor Books, 1968), p. 105.

Buddha conceived the self to be transitory. The self is "made up of factors which form links in the chain of causality" and karma "in rebirth creates another transient combination" (*SBC* 30). There is "no permanence, nothing that remains identical" (*SBC* 30). For Jaspers, Buddha's sense of fluidity was important in preventing Buddhism from becoming dogmatic.

Jaspers also recommended that Christians in the West learn from Buddhism, which absorbed "alien elements" and tolerated "a great deal of diversity."[19] When it spread to different parts of Asia, Buddhism "assimilated ancient themes from the religious traditions of many peoples in all stages of cultural development" (*SBC* 38).

> His radical freedom from the world resulted in an equally radical tolerance toward the world....Thus Buddhism was able to assimilate all the religions philosophies, forms of life with which it came into contact. Every idea, every ethos, every faith, even those of the most primitive religions, was a possible preliminary stage, a jumping-off place, indispensable as such, but not a goal. (*SBC* 38)

As a result of active assimilation, Buddhism, Jaspers believed, possessed "a colorful medley of religious images" (*SBC* 38). Even "[F]oreign religious forms" which were supposed to be transcended became adopted by Buddhists. In Tibet, one can find "a striking example," for "even the old methods of magic became Buddhist methods, the monastic community became an organized church with secular rule" (*SBC* 38).

Jaspers was most different from the Weimar historicists when he argued that the active assimilation of local conditions created a better religious form than without it. For instance, Hinayana (Small Vehicle) or Theravada Buddhism, which can be found in Ceylon, Indochina, and Thailand, was "purer and closer to the forms of origins" than Mahayana Buddhism (the Great Vehicle) (*SBC* 36). Mahayana Buddhism, which was practiced in China, Korea, Vietnam, and Nepal, seems "like a fall into the mechanical forms of religion." Yet Hinayana Buddhism has contributed "nothing new" or at best had "a narrowing" effect, for it rigidly adhered to a once-acquired canon and emphasized the perfection of the individual (*SBC* 36). In contrast, Mahayana Buddhism has developed "certain of Buddha's ideas," "above all, his decision to bring salvation to all beings, god and men alike." Its "most important aspect" was the transformation of "Buddha's philosophy of salvation into a religion," thus "satisfying the religious needs of the masses" (*SBC* 36). In addition, Mahayana Buddhism "supplied the basis for a new flowering of sublimated speculative philosophy" (*SBC* 36).

Despite the varying merits of different types of Buddhism, Jaspers found a common spirit in them, just as he found a common spirit in different types of Christianity (*SBC* 39).

---

[19] *PW* 143–145. Like Jaspers, other Western observers were also impressed by the Buddhist's great toleration of other religions. For instance, Heinrich Dumoulin observed it in Japanese Buddhists: "The tolerance of Japanese Buddhists is indeed amazing. The warm hospitality which awaits the non-Buddhist, even the Christian priest or monk, in a Japanese Buddhist monastery, and the readiness for religious conversation are of immeasurable help in establishing contact." Heinrich Dumoulin, S.J., *Christianity Meets Buddhism*, trans. John C. Maraldo (La Salle, IL: Open Court, 1974), pp. 35–36.

The question arises: What has all this to do with Buddha? And we answer: In the world of the gods, the innumerable rites and cults, the institutions and sects, and the free monastic communities, a vestige of the philosophical origin remains discernible; something of the spiritual light first embodied in Buddha is reflected even in the most primitive figures of later Buddhism. (*SBC* 39)

What then, is, "the philosophical origin" which Jaspers saw in all types of Buddhism? In Buddhism, Jaspers detected "a trace of his wonderful self-abandonment, of the life that lets itself be wafted into eternity" and "the Buddhist love which partakes in the suffering and joy of all living beings" (*SBC* 39). Also there is Buddha's rejection of violence (*SBC* 39). Jaspers contrasted the lack of violence in Buddhism with several violent incidents in Christianity: It is "the one world religion that has known no violence, no persecution of heretics, no inquisitions, no witch trials, no crusades" (*SBC* 39).

Jaspers was not, however, without an awareness of difficulties which are connected to cross-cultural learning. He admitted that to participate in the essence of Buddha means "ceasing to be what we are," since Buddhism is "far removed from us." Jaspers saw no "quick, easy ways of coming closer to it." One should avoid "excessive haste and supposedly definitive interpretations" (*SBC* 40). In the end, Jaspers recommended learning from Buddha. He pointed out that "we are all men, all facing the same questions of human existence" (*SBC* 40). He added, "everything that is said in the Buddhist texts is addressed to a normal waking consciousness and must therefore be largely accessible to rational thought" (*SBC* 40). Emphasizing the open nature of human beings, he denied one objective essence for Western man. In the end, Jaspers perceived no fundamental hurdle in learning "a great solution" in Buddha and Buddhism, "Our task is to acquaint ourselves with it and as far as possible to understand it" (*SBC* 40). Just as Buddhism became "a reality in various parts of Asia down to our own day" (*SBC* 40). Buddhism, Jaspers suggested, could also become a reality in Europe.

Jaspers clearly preferred toleration over the purity of one's religion or culture. In contrast to Troeltsch, Jaspers urged Western Christians to go beyond the European framework by learning from Buddha's cosmopolitanism which avidly practiced cross-cultural adaptations. Comparing Troeltsch and Jaspers, Schulin rightly criticizes Troeltsch for narrowing universal history to the "universal history of Europe" but commends Jaspers' new impetus in German universal history.[20] Their different positions on civilizational relationship were also reflected in their different placements of Jews in European history. Although Troeltsch was not anti-Semitic and welcomed the improved situation of Weimar Jews, he excluded Judaism and Jews from the definition of Europeanism and regarded them as a cultural minority. In contrast, Jaspers pointed out an inseparable relationship between Jews and Christians;

---

[20] Schulin, *Traditionskritik und Rekonstrucktionsversuch*, p. 188.

"Jews are Westerners," and "Jesus was a Jew."[21] He believed that Jews and Judaism had positive influences throughout European history.

For Jaspers, toleration was a necessary condition for human co-existence at any time, but it became an urgent necessity in the historical context of the twentieth century. When Paul Ricoeur considered Jaspers to be a "Don Juan" for being too open-minded and thus lacking commitment,[22] Ricoeur set up a false opposition between toleration and relativism. Leonard Ehrlich is right in rejecting Ricoeur's framing Jaspers's philosophy in terms of "an alternative"—"either *this* faith based upon the highest authority of revelation, or many faiths; and if many faiths, then a Don Juanism of faith."[23] As Ehrlich notes, Ricoeur sought "one's certainties to the exclusion of others" and thus failed to presuppose "a diversity of faiths" and "a conception of freedom," which was the case with "the orthodox theologian" in general (*TP* 99). Instead, it is possible to commit to a particular tradition that best corresponds to our own historical and personal background, while still "leaving space for the other" (*TP* 99).

Jaspers' toleration cannot possibly be charged with relativism, it also cannot be compared to Don Juan's non-committed lifestyle. While Don Juan's life involved repeated conquests and abandonments without learning, in contrast Jaspers advocated tolerating different views and intensely committing oneself to cross-cultural grafting and learning. As Jaspers has exemplified in the cases of the Jesuits in China and Buddhism in Asia, the process of cross-cultural transfer requires intense involvement with local cultures. If cultural transfer is taken with a sensitive attitude, the philosophical core is maintained in different manifestations, which Jaspers detected in different types of Buddhism. While one's culture is important, Jaspers' cosmopolitanism provides room even for people who choose a religion outside of their historical and personal backgrounds. He believed that our common humanity is more fundamental than our civilizational identity. Consequently, Jaspers, after World War II, made a radical departure from the German historicist tradition that Spengler and Troeltsch represented after World War I, and provided an intellectual framework for global communication.

---

[21] Jaspers, "Die nichtchristlichen Religionen," in *Philosophie und Welt: Reden und Aufsätze* (München: R. Pier & Co. Verlag, 1958), p. 161.

[22] Paul Ricoeur, "The Relation of Jaspers' Philosophy to Religion," in *The Philosophy of Karl Jaspers*, ed. Paul Arthur Schilpp (La Salle, IL: Open Court, 1957), p. 611.

[23] Leonard H. Ehrlich, "Tolerance and the Prospect of a World Philosophy," in *Karl Jaspers Today. Philosophy at the Threshold of the Future*, eds. Leonard H. Ehrlich and Richard Wisser (Lanham, MD: University Press of America, 1988), p. 99. [Henceforth cited as *TP*]

The Factor of Listening in Karl Jaspers' Philosophy of Communication

Krystyna Górniak-Kocikowska

Abstract Jaspers' views on communication and his approach to the question of listening, both underwent an evolution in which World War II and the first years thereafter played a crucial role. In this process, Jaspers journeyed from listening to the great minds of the past, through an inward dialogue with them, to one-sided lecturing while his audience was engaged in a straight-line listening, to an intimate dialogue with those he considered like-minded, to a multi-faceted dialogue, and finally to listening to his contemporaries and learning how to practice transactional listening-in-conversation in the process of a multi-layered communication he called a loving struggle. This evolution, paralleled by the transition of Japers' philosophy from local-centered to world-centered makes his thinking attractive and useful today.

Dialogue, debate, and dispute—these are just a few forms of communication whose theoretical as well as practical sides were crucial in the development of philosophical tradition, especially the Western philosophical tradition. In one way or another, as theory or practice, communication is an indispensable part of philosophy. In short, it is the nervous system and blood of philosophy.

The subject of communication takes a prominent place in Karl Jaspers' philosophy as well; it is one of the factors (*the* factor, to some) that determine the identity of his philosophy. According to Jaspers' own testimony, communication played a very important role in his life from early on, at least since his school years during which he was "consumed by a longing for a communication which crosses over all misunderstanding, all merely transient, over every boundary of the all-too-obvious."[1] It also is one of the aspects of his philosophy that attracts growing attention from Jaspers scholars in recent years.

My focus in this essay is primarily on one form of communication; namely, on verbal communication, also called speech communication. I will ignore other

---

[1] Karl Jaspers, "Philosophische Autobiographie," in *Karl Jaspers: Werk und Wirkung*, ed. R. Klaus (Munich: R. Piper & Co., 1963), pp. 19–129 (p. 117). Unless otherwise noted, all translations in this essay are mine. [Henceforth cited as *PA*]

K. Górniak-Kocikowska (✉)
Southern Connecticut State University, New Haven, CT, USA
e-mail: gorniakk1@southernct.edu

H. Wautischer et al. (eds.), *Philosophical Faith and the Future of Humanity*,
DOI 10.1007/978-94-007-2223-1_34, © Springer Science+Business Media B.V. 2012

popular forms of communication such as, for instance, pictorial, bodily, senso-
rial, or telepathic, since verbal communication for Jaspers—like the majority of
philosophers—was of primary interest. Within the scope of communication, my
attention is devoted particularly to the problem of listening in the context of Jaspers'
views. I believe that the problem of listening as well as his awareness of this problem played an important if somewhat surprising role in the development of his
scholarship.

Listening and Philosophy

In every meaningful and purposeful form of communication there are two main
players, whether individual or collective: the communicator (sender) and the recipient (receiver).[2] Often, but not always, the participants switch roles in the process of
communication, from sender(s) to receiver(s) and vice versa. Usually, the speaker is
seen as an active participant in the communication process, while the listener is seen
as passive. Obviously, in terms of internal characteristics, esp. regarding thought
processes, a listener can be—and often is—as active as a speaker or perhaps even
more so. This, however, rarely has an impact on the process of communication at
the time when such process is taking place.

Professionally, Karl Jaspers was involved in the process of communication
mainly in two areas (in both almost exclusively in the role of sender/speaker): the
area of higher education and the area of public speaking. He developed a theory
of communication as part of his philosophy; it contained some views on listening,
but these played a rather marginal role in his theory. Within Jaspers' philosophy,
the problem of listening was not his primary focus. This subject was brought to
his attention later on—after World War II—when the issue of listening became an
obstacle in his own attempts at communication.

Despite the existence of two processes (speaking and listening) and two participants (speaker and listener) in the philosophical assessment of verbal communication there is an imbalance in the amount of attention devoted to each of these
processes, and this is also true for Jaspers' philosophy. The amount of attention
devoted to speaking by far exceeds the attention devoted to listening. Gemma
Corradi Fiumara, begins her book *The Other Side of Language: A Philosophy of
Listening* by presenting a view that this neglect of listening as a philosophical
problem is the result of the dominance of logos in the western philosophical tradition. "Among the widespread meanings of the Greek term *logos* there do not
appear to be recognizable references to the notion and capacity of listening; in
the tradition of Western thought we are thus faced with a system of knowledge

---

[2] See Krystyna Górniak-Kocikowska, "Problem z nazwaniem nowego globalnego spoleczenstwa,"
in *Osoba w Spoleczenstwie Informacyjnym*, ETHOS, Vol. 69–70 (Rome: John Paul II Institute
Catholic University of Lublin, John Paul II Foundation, 2005), pp. 77–99.

that tends to ignore listening processes."[3] She supports her statement by following Heidegger's views on logos and logic about their dominance in the Western philosophical tradition; and she concludes that logical thinking is "primary anchored to saying-without-listening" (*OSL* 3).

In accord with Corradi Fiumara's observations I contend that in the logos dominated (therefore mainly speaking-centered, not listening-centered) Western philosophical—or more adequately, intellectual—tradition, the primary purpose of communication is victory and domination rather than mutual understanding with existential insight. In a logos-centered paradigm, a speaker's objective is usually to prove, to convince, to make one understand, to make one follow the speaker's words or deeds. In contrast, a listener is supposed to pay attention (the compound "pay attention" is rarely an invitation to thinking things through, or to argue and debate an issue with the intention of influencing the speaker), to remember, to follow the speaker ("listen to me," not to mention the "I am telling you!" more often than not means "obey me"). Besides indicating the position of the listener as subordinate, these phrases indicate also that the role ascribed to the listener in the communication process is a passive one. In this context, Jaspers' insight nearly has a paradigm-shifting quality: "A violent struggle gets extinguished *in communication*. The result is a collective truth, *instead of a superiority in victory*."[4]

Corradi Fiumara published her book in 1990; one would like to assume that the situation has changed by today. There is a great amount of attention given to the issue of listening in various academic disciplines. Yet, even with the existence of professional organizations,[5] a multitude of publications, and specialized scholarly journals there is still little interest in the philosophical problem of listening. Corradi Fiumara's book stands out in this context; and it does not yet have much company from related philosophical works, even though she supports her views on language, listening, and communication by referring to philosophers like Jaspers—next to Gadamer, Heidegger, Kant, and Wittgenstein.

Several disciplines, especially psychology, education, medicine, and marketing, just to name a few, developed their own theories regarding the value of listening from within their own vantage point. Incidentally, Corradi Fiumara, besides being a philosopher, is also a psychoanalyst. Unfortunately, these theories are not very helpful for philosophy, since the concept of communication and consequently—to a large degree—the issue of listening are treated differently in these disciplines; and certainly not in the way Jaspers as thought of communication. For example, from a perspective of some of these disciplines, giving orders or providing information is seen as a correct form of communication. Similarly, fulfilling someone's orders swiftly and accurately, or taking into account facts one has been informed about is

---

[3] Gemma Corradi Fiumara, *The Other Side of Language: A Philosophy of Listening*, trans. Charles Lambert (London, New York: Routledge, 1990), p. 1. [Henceforth cited as *OSL*]

[4] Karl Jaspers, *Wahrheit, Freiheit und Friede* (Munich: R. Piper & Co. Verlag, 1958), p. 10 (my emphasis).

[5] For example The International Listening Association which "promotes the study, development, and teaching of listening and the practice of effective listening skills and techniques." (ILA website)

often seen as proof of effective listening. However, this is not the kind of communication or the kind of listening that Jaspers had in mind: "The threat to existential communication is not the reality of the dependencies but the temptation to find one's self-being fulfilled in the substance of unequal communication."[6]

Although humans are defined as a thinking species, thinking is in general a function of will—especially the existence-enlightening thinking that according to Jaspers leads to a path of existential truth. It rarely takes place unwanted, or unnoticed by the thinker, or on a whim. But this kind of willing thinking is a necessary condition for the type of communication Jaspers was most interested in. It is also a necessary condition for philosophy as Jaspers understood it. All other ways of thinking epitomize *Unphilosophie* "that doesn't want to know anything about truth."[7] In this sense, the will to listen (without which any meaningful communication is all but impossible) means also a will to think; not just a will to obey or to follow one's footsteps. The function of will for listening is very important indeed, especially in the context of Jaspers' philosophy of communication. Unfortunately, it cannot be explored in the scope of this essay.

Listening and Democracy

One of the philosophers interested in the problem of listening, albeit from a substantially different philosophical perspective than Jaspers, was John Dewey who developed significant contributions to the philosophical (and pedagogical) theory of listening. For example, he distinguished two main types of verbal communication based on the pattern and degree of active involvement by participants in the communication process. Henceforth, I will use some of Dewey's ideas and terminology.

At a presentation in 2009, Leonard J. Waks summarizes John Dewey's views on listening in the following way:

> Dewey's theory of listening rests on a distinction between *one-way* or *straight-line listening* and *transactional listening-in-conversation*. The former, he sees as the dominant feature of both traditional schools and undemocratic societies. Indeed, by fostering passivity, traditional schooling even in nominally democratic societies makes citizens vulnerable to undemocratic forces. Transactional listening, by contrast, lies at the heart of democracy.[8]

The fact that both Dewey and Jaspers explored the problem of communication within the context of democracy is, of course, of special value here.

---

[6] Karl Jaspers, *Philosophy*, trans. E.B. Ashton, Vol. 2 (Chicago, London: The University of Chicago Press, 1970), p. 83. [Henceforth cited as *P* with volume number]

[7] "...der nichts von Wahrheit weiß und wissen will." Karl Jaspers, *Vernunft und Widervernunft in Unserer Zeit: Drei Gastvorlesungen, gehalten auf Einladung des Asta an der Universität Heidelberg* (Munich: R. Piper & Co. Verlag, 1950), p. 55. [Henceforth cited as *VW*]

[8] Leonard J. Waks, (2009), *Hearing is a Participation: John Dewey on Listening, Friendship, and Participation in Democratic Society*, unpublished manuscript (my emphasis). I would like to express my sincere thanks to the author for allowing to quote from his work in progress.

John Dewey's views on listening, especially transactional listening, are part of the foundation of Jim Garrison's thoughts on the problem of listening in dialogues conducted under the conditions of democracy.[9] Like Waks, also Garrison refers to Dewey's philosophy in ways that are helpful in the examination of Jaspers' concepts of communication, dialogue, and listening. Garrison uses Dewey's distinction "between one-way or straight-line listening and transactional listening-in-conversation" to substantiate four basic claims about Jaspers: (1) Jaspers misjudged (underestimated) for many years the importance and power of transactional listening by focusing mainly on one-way listening. Dewey saw the straight-line listening as typical of and required by traditional education; this was one of his reasons for criticizing this type of education. In contrast, for many years Jaspers did not seem to see anything wrong with such method of teaching. It was the way he himself learned, and this was the way he taught for most of his life. (2) Such misjudgment was a significant factor in Jaspers' post WWII difficulties for addressing his targeted audience, especially in his radio speeches. (3) Jaspers devoted considerable effort during the last two decades of his life to revising his theory of communication. (4) This revision affected also his views on the university and the role of the philosopher in a future world society.

Jaspers' Concept of *Existential Communication*

Existence takes a central role in Jaspers' philosophy, just as existential communication (*existentielle Kommunikation*) is central to his understanding of human existence.[10] Jaspers established early on that human existence, as the true and authentic being-in-itself (*Selbstsein*), is only real and true in the process of communication with the *Selbstsein* of other human beings (*P2* 56–59). A human being cannot be truly herself in self-containment; this can only happen through relations with others. For Jaspers, the fullest, most fundamental, and most effective form of such a relation is existential communication. The superiority of existential communication over other forms of communication parallels Jaspers' hierarchy of types of truth and types of thinking, according to which existential truth and related to it reason (*Vernunft*) are supreme over other forms of truth and thinking.

For Jaspers, when existential communication takes place, it involves transactional listening, which is an active type of listening as the result of the listener's will to listen (as opposed to a situation when the listener is coaxed or forced into listening). Such existential communication is exceptional and takes place rarely, even for

---

[9] Jim Garrison, "A Deweyan Theory of Democratic Listening," *Educational Theory*, 1996, Vol. 46, No. 4, pp. 429–451.

[10] See Hasan Haluk Erdem, "Jaspers' Weltphilosophie und ihre Bedeutung für die universale Kommunikation," in *Karl Jaspers: Geschichtliche Wirklichkeit mit Blick auf die Grundfragen der Menschheit; Karl Jaspers: Historic Actuality in View of Fundamental Problems of Mankind*, eds. Andreas Cesana and Gregory J. Walters (Würzburg: Königshausen & Neumann, 2008), pp. 207–218 (here p. 213). [Henceforth cited as *WP*]

those who are capable and willing. The full extent of the importance of existential communication is apparent when one considers that

> properly speaking the existence as a being-in-itself of a human is real only in communication with the being-in-itself of other humans. The point of departure of Jaspers' philosophy is the conviction that a single human being cannot be who he/she really is for him(her)self alone, indeed he/she cannot be human. (*WP* 213)

This passage captures what Jaspers wrote about in many of his works, particularly in *Philosophy*, namely that

> Communication always takes place between two people who join but remain two, who come to each other out of solitude and yet know solitude only because they are communicating. I cannot come to myself without entering into Communication, and I cannot enter Communication without being lonely. (*P2* 56)

Jaspers addressed the problem of loneliness early in his career. In 1915–1916, at a time when he was still regarded as a psychologist rather than a philosopher, he presented a lecture *Individuum und Einsamkeit* which was first published posthumously in 1983 with the title *Einsamkeit*.[11] Gemma Corradi Fiumara takes the issue of the danger of self-absorbed solitude and the importance of transactional communication even further:

> The myth of Narcissus, who sees nothing but himself, might indicate the extreme opposite of an open dialogic field that unites the human race. . . . Narcissus perpetrates his own destruction (drowning) through the total absence of dialogue—the response of Echo being a fake; he aspires to isolated autarchy. (*OSL* 117)

One can find a similar thought in Jaspers:

> If I will not put up with my solitude, if I will not overcome it again and again, I choose either a chaotic ego dissolution or a fixation in forms and tracks without selfhood. If I will not risk abandoning myself, I perish as an empty, petrified I. (*P2* 57)

Yet, for Jaspers there exists still another dilemma with which he had to struggle for many years: "Either I keep risking loneliness over and over, to win my self-being in communication, or I have definitely voided my own self in another being" (*P2* 58). One needs to be aware that solitude and loneliness was not something Jaspers abhorred.

These remarks by Jaspers refer mainly to the metaphysical problem of communication, and the communication he had in mind was existential communication. There is a clear parallel between these thoughts and the way Jaspers approached the communication dilemma in his life. He was known to choose carefully with whom he would enter a real life communication (as opposed to a communication through books and other written texts) be it face-to-face, or in epistolary form. These individuals were the ones he would listen to, but they were also the ones who listened in a way Jaspers expected them to (otherwise, he would terminate the communication).

---

[11] Revue Internantional de Philosophie, 1983, Vol. 37, No. 147, pp. 390–409. Reprinted as Karl Jaspers, "Einsamkeit (Nachlassmanuskript)" in *Jahrbuch der Österreichischen Karl-Jaspers-Gesellschaft*, Jahrgang 1, eds. Elisabeth Hybašek and Kurt Salamun (VWGÖ: Innsbruck, 1988), pp. 20–31.

However, he was not used to, and did not explore a method of real life spontaneous communication with people who would try to engage in communication with him, but whom he did not know.

Practical Communication

The concept of existential communication belongs to Japers' metaphysics. There is, however, also an epistemological and—more importantly from the vantage point of this essay—a practical, utilitarian function of communication, of which Jaspers was well aware. Here, communication is primarily a tool and it is often the domain of (practical) intellect rather than (speculative) reason.

These two functions of communication, epistemological and practical (as opposite to existential communication) are also discussed in his works, although not as detailed as existential communication. Especially in his pre-World War II works, he treats the epistemological and practical function of communication somewhat marginally. I think there is a good reason for this; and it is found in Jaspers' own intellectual history.

From the perspective of communication as a tool, two issues are of special significance with respect to Jaspers' philosophy. One is the evolution, or rather—the expansion—of Jaspers' world and the way this process influenced his approach to communication. The other is the evolution of how Jaspers was both theorizing about communication as well as using it as a tool. I suggest there is a parallel between these two issues. Both of them illustrate the evolution of his approach to philosophy and to life, and they are intricately connected.

Jaspers' world (by which I mean less the world he felt at home, but rather the world he was concerned about) expanded from the internal world of thought through the familiar and exclusive world of Academia, to the world of his own nation, and finally the world of humankind. Throughout this process of expansion of a world with which Jaspers gradually identified himself, his thoughts also made a long journey. Starting inwardly with concerns about the individual human condition, and ending outwardly with concerns about the future of humankind. However, his concerns were of the same nature; they were primarily about the human condition, and about the deepest existential problems. Dealing with these concerns was, in Jaspers' view, a duty—in a Kantian sense—of any serious philosopher.

The above described process was paralleled by the evolution of Jaspers' views on the use of communication as a tool: From listening to the great minds of the past, through an inward dialogue with them, to a one-sided talking and lecturing (in the sense of dispensing knowledge while his audience was engaged in a straight-line listening); from an intimate dialogue with those he considered like-minded (e.g., Heidegger or Arendt) to a multi-faceted dialogue—with a hope, often futile, for an active reaction from his audience—and by listening to his contemporaries and learning how to practice transactional listening-in-conversation in the process of a multi-layered communication, which he called a loving struggle (*ein liebender Kampf*).

In this process, Jaspers did not abandon his concept of existential communication; rather, he enriched it. I contend that he did so mainly by expanding and enriching his concept of a human being. While in the earlier works his method could be seen as a form of existential reductionism, his later works indicated attempts at grasping the wholeness of a human existential phenomenon in its complexity, multifariousness, and dynamism. In this sense, his methodology shows—unsurprisingly—a close affinity with that of Max Weber and, reaching further back, with Hegel.

German Society—A Challenge to Jaspers' Concept of Communication

One could say that life forced the changes in Jaspers' idea of communication in a way unintended by the philosopher himself. It is always somewhat risky to play with these kinds of scenarios. I contend that there is enough evidence to support the claim that Jaspers would not have left speculative philosophy on his own initiative, solely as a result of a natural development of his philosophical agenda; and also that he would restrict his interest in the concept of communication exclusively to *existential communication*—if not for the direction taken by the Weimar Republic with all the ensuing events.

At the time of the Weimar Republic he still believed that public affairs and politics did not really belong to the domain of a true philosopher. So, he did not ask persistently enough, "Wohin treibt die Weimarer Republik?" He did not ask this of himself and not of his fellow citizens. It seems that he did not listen to the world carefully enough. He preoccupied himself, among other things, with promoting the idea of the university as foundation for a stable bourgeois State.[12] Consequently, he was not sufficiently prepared for the events that came when the Weimar Republic was replaced with a Nazi regime. After the war, after the years of semi-silence, when he finally could reenter the public discourse unhindered, it turned out that he was not prepared for it as well as he should have been, could have been, and desired to be. He was not ready for the type of communication he intended to have with his fellow Germans.[13]

Jaspers did not have a problem with listening, especially, when he was the one who listened to the great minds from the past. When it came to being heard, however, the story turned out to be quite different. Jaspers made this discovery at a time, when his need to be heard was most urgent, that is, after World War II.

---

[12] Karl Jaspers, *The Idea of the University*, trans. H.A.T. Reiche and H.F. Vanderschmidt (Boston, MA: Beacon Press, 1959).

[13] Krystyna Górniak-Kocikowska, "The Relevance of Jaspers' Idea of Communication in the Age of Global Society," in *Karl Jaspers' Philosophie: Gegenwärtigkeit und Zukunft; Karl Jaspers's Philosophy: Rooted in the Present, Paradigm for the Future*, eds. Richard Wisser and Leonard H. Ehrlich, co-eds. Andreas Cesana and Gregory Walters (Würzburg: Königshausen & Neumann, 2003), pp. 107–114.

He spent the years of the Nazi regime doing what he was doing earlier (minus teaching) namely, communicating with the great minds of the past. But this did not prepare him well enough for what he saw as his duty after the war: to define the concept of a future human society (and in particular the future German society). Yes, he listened to the world during the Nazi rule; he made moral choices and justified them; he thought-through the evils of its time and came up with a theory of how to root them out; he even thought of some practical ways to do so. However, he did not know how to involve people in this kind of communication he thought they ought to be engaged with. He did not learn what it takes to make people listen willingly and responsively; and he was still on very shaky ground when it came to transactional listening-in-conversation, not just with a selected few who were like-minded and like-educated and with whom he was comfortable, but with the reluctant, often unwilling, and sometimes contrary masses. In his words, "We are sorely deficient in talking with each other and listening to each other."[14] The fact that he used the word "we" rather than "you" or "they" reveals a profound change in Jaspers' perspective on his own position in the process of communication. Such a willingness to acknowledge one's own shortcomings and to learn from them also creates a new potential for communication. In the words of Leonard Ehrlich, "Man carries the task and the responsibility for the becoming of truth through the modes of Being which is man himself, which according to Jaspers is primarily that of communicative reason."[15] To my mind, by discussing a different problem in Jaspers' philosophy, Ehrlich captured the essence of Jaspers' post-World War II situation.

In his pre-WWII years as a university professor, Jaspers was used to speaking to and to speaking at; and he was used to being listened to in the one-way or straight line listening mode; he was not used to being spoken to or spoken at, even when the subject of his speaking was communication. Almost immediately after the war, he saw it as his task (not just his own, he actually saw it as a task, which "we professors" would have to fulfill) in changing "the very way of thinking" (*QG* 8) of the entire (German) population due to the new political situation. Jaspers was very careful and insistent (*QG* 8–17) in pointing out that although the situation in many aspects seemed to be as it used to be prior to 1933—when in fact it was not. Even if "we professors" were "free for truth" (*QG* 9) in this new situation, Jaspers did not think that it meant, "we are free to pass discretionary judgments" (*QG* 9). What he wanted to impress upon his colleagues was that "what we say ought to be unconditionally true" (*QG* 9).

On his part, he tried to learn the transactional listening-in-conversation for his own sake as well as for the sake of those whom he now perceived as his partners—actual or potential—in an honest and truthful dialogue on things that matter most to the future of Germany (West and East) and to the future of humanity.

---

[14] Karl Jaspers, *The Question of German Guilt*, trans. E.B. Ashton (New York, NY: The Dial Press, 1947), p. 122. [Henceforth cited as *QG*]

[15] Leonard H. Ehrlich, "Being and Truth: Heidegger vis-a-vis Jaspers," in *Philosopher among Philosophers; Philosoph unter Philosophen*, eds. Richard Wisser and Leonard H. Ehrlich (Würzburg: Königshausen & Neumann, 1993), pp. 121–138 (here p. 129).

Jaspers in the Post-WWII Period: The Problem of Listening

Jaspers was initially surprised and somewhat discouraged when he encountered indifference, even hostility towards his post-WW II speeches. When the Nazis had forbidden him to teach, they in a sense gave him a reason to believe that his university lectures could have propelled students, and also wider circles of German society, into action against the regime. If his lectures had no influence upon the students' minds there would be no need to remove him from the lectern—would there be now? Little wonder that such indifference and hostility, especially on account of *The Question of German Guilt*, caused Jaspers a disappointment. It turned out that he had to learn how to make people want to listen to him. He had to learn this because what he had to say was too urgent, too important for his time and also for the future of humankind to not let it be known. He saw it to be his moral duty as a philosopher and as a human being to warn people about the dangers he himself perceived. He had to find an effective way to do so, since talking to the elites was no longer sufficient in the epoch of the masses. So, he had to retool his language.

Partly, he learned from experience. During the war, he became an active listener—not merely a witness—to the events of the day. He continued this art of active listening after the war. However, unlike the period of his withdrawal from the public life enforced by the Nazis, he was now energetically trying to initiate a dialogue with his fellow citizens and beyond. He decided to become involved in a public debate and enter the political discourse.

Consequently, Jaspers' post-World War II works are the result, to a large extent, of the learning process he embarked on in order to amend these self-perceived failures. He did this mainly by focusing his attention on the question *Wohin treibt die Bundesrepublik?*, and published *The Future of Germany* where he tried to answer this question by focusing, among others, on issues like democracy and freedom, the army, forms of government, and education.[16] Understanding the role of the masses in this new post-WW II reality was of special interest and of special importance to him. It, too, required some significant changes in Jaspers himself, who was perceived by some as an elitist.[17] I do not mean to say that Jaspers became an aficionado of the masses, or that he now identified himself with the masses. Rather, he saw the masses as partner for his new approach to communication as transactional listening-in-conversation.

According to Paul Meyer-Gutzwiller—who worked for Radio Basel in a function of overseeing the Jaspers broadcasts at the time when Jaspers started this collaboration for his 1947 lectures on philosophical faith, followed by a series on philosophy and biblical religion, later on twelve lectures on philosophy (published in English

---

[16] Karl Jaspers, *The Future of Germany*, trans. and ed. E.B. Ashton (Chicago, London: The University of Chicago Press, 1967).

[17] See Jürgen Habermas, *Philosophisch-Politische Profile* (Frankfurt am Main: Suhrkamp Verlag, 1984) [Jürgen Habermas, ed. (1984), *Observation on 'The Spiritual Situation of the Age': Contemporary German Perspectives*, trans. Andrew Buchwalter (Cambridge, MA: The MIT Press).] and Golo Mann, *Erinnerungen und Gedanken* (Frankfurt am Main: Fischer Verlag, 1986).

as *Way To Wisdom*), and lectures on Schelling—Jaspers saw and appreciated "from the beginning" the importance "of these modern means of mass-communication,"[18] i.e., the press, radio, and television. In his short contribution to the book published in celebration of Jaspers' 80th Birthday, Meyer-Gutzwiller shares, among others, how he remembers a conversation with Jaspers after one of the recordings, where Jaspers "tried to formulate his thoughts in a way understandable to every listener, 'even to a chauffeur'" (*KJR* 170). This seems to be quite convincing proof to me that Jaspers was assuming, or at least hoping, that he would be listened to by a broad variety of people. Yet, philosophy seemed to have been always on his mind, it was part of his agenda. Meyer-Gutzwiller recalls what Jaspers had said about one of his popular lectures on Schelling in which "he placed the biographic information in the foreground 'but you would have noticed that I have smuggled a piece of philosophy into it'" (*KJR* 170).

And, as always, he remained steadfast in his fundamental metaphysical position; for instance, he did not change the view eloquently summarized by Ehrlich as follows: "One has to notice that Jaspers treats the true being's-thinking [*Seins-Denken*], which happens inescapably within the subject-object split, as a thinking-being [*Denkend-Sein*] whose truth requires proof of the thinking through the deed in communication with the other-being [*Anders-Seinden*]."[19] As mentioned earlier, this type of thinking is a necessary condition for the kind of communication Jaspers was most interested in, namely, existential communication. For Jaspers, this type of thinking is also a necessary condition for philosophy. All other ways of thinking epitomize *Unphilosophie* "that doesn't want to know anything about truth" (*VW* 55). Nonetheless, Jaspers observes that—from his point of view—when given a choice, the majority of people prefer such un-philosophy:

> What makes it worse is that so many people do not really want to think. They only want slogans and obedience. They ask no questions and they give no answers, except by repeating drilled-in phrases. They can only assert and obey, neither probe nor apprehend. Thus they cannot be convinced, either. How shall we talk with people who will not go where others probe and think, where men seek independence in insight and conviction? (*QG* 22–23)

People who "only want slogans and obedience" perhaps engage in such "listening to obey" that I had mentioned earlier, for lack of willingness or even capability for such listening that leads to true thinking and true communication, the kind of listening Jaspers needed and hoped for.

There is a dose of bitterness and disappointment in the passage quoted above, but it is by no means his excuse for giving up; more than anything, it is a reflection on his

---

[18] Paul Meyer-Gutzwiller, "Karl Jaspers und der Rundfunk," in *Karl Jaspers: Werk und Wirkung*, ed. Klaus Piper (Munich: R. Piper & Co., 1963), pp. 169–171 (here p. 169). [Henceforth cited as *KJR*]

[19] Leonard H. Ehrlich, "Heideggers Seinsdenken aus der Sicht von Arendt und Jaspers," in *Karl Jaspers' Philosophie: Gegenwärtigkeit und Zukunft; Karl Jaspers's Philosophy: Rooted in the Present, Paradigm for the Future*, eds. Richard Wisser and Leonard H. Ehrlich, co-eds. Andreas Cesana and Gregory Walters (Würzburg: Königshausen & Neumann, 2003), pp. 107–114 (here p. 113).

own shortcomings. It has become a challenge for Jaspers to find a way to "talk with people who will not go where others probe and think" (*QG* 23)—he accepted this challenge for his post-WWII years. Jaspers did not rest on his laurels as someone who had been right when so many others were wrong. A man, about whom Hannah Arendt once wrote that he was the only true student Kant had ever had, who saw it as his unconditional duty as a philosopher, a German, and a human being to roll up his sleeves and go to work on building the future for humankind. A man who could have claimed that he knew it all, accepted willingly that there are things he needed to learn (e.g., transactional listening-in-conversation), and he set up on a journey to learn them.

Jaspers' interest in the fate of humanity was demonstrated in his writings about international policy and relationships, and in his explorations of the threat posed to humankind from new weapons, specifically the atom bomb. Consistent with his practice, he did this by searching for answers in the thought of great philosophers of the past; but now he also added communication with his contemporaries. This was by no means an easy task as he was not immediately successful in finding ways of effective transactional communication.

Jaspers' Views on Education

Jaspers' idea of communication—and related to this essay, the problem of listening—along with the changes in his views are all closely linked with his under-standing of education in general, and higher education in particular. As several scholars noticed,[20] there was quite a remarkable change in Jaspers' pre-WWII and post-WWII views on the function of a university in society, from strict political neutrality to a limited political involvement. During the time of the greatest political involvement of university students after WWII, i.e., in the 1960s, Jaspers seemed to have found his solution to this problem. "With that the horizon delimited, within which Jaspers considered the political involvement of students to be legitimate. Their actions must stand *within the paradigm of communication and not of fight*" (*PB* 395, my emphasis). From my perspective, Jaspers' acceptance of a university as a place of discussion, of transactional listening-in-conversation, a place where stu-dents had the right to question professors and doubt their views, even to challenge them was short of being revolutionary.

The role of a teacher in Jaspers' ideal of education (and in accordance with his concept of communication), especially philosophical education that he considered to be the highest level of education, was not the one of a Socrates (albeit he was one of Jaspers' great role models), rather it was one of a wise teacher known, for instance,

---

[20] For example, Bernd Weidmann, "Karl Jaspers und die studentische Protestbewegung. Der Umschlag von Kommunikation in Kampf am Beispiel Rudi Dutschkes," in *Karl Jaspers: Geschichtliche Wirklichkeit mit Blick auf die Grundfragen der Menschheit; Karl Jaspers: Historic Actuality in View of Fundamental Problems of Mankind*, eds. Andreas Cesana and Gregory J. Walters (Würzburg: Königshausen & Neumann, 2008), pp. 385–405. [Henceforth cited as *PB*]

in Indian and Chinese philosophy. The difference is that Socrates actively, even aggressively, pursued his listeners and—through his maieutic method—engaged them in a form of transactional listening-in-conversation peculiar to him (the student was skillfully manipulated by Socrates into a particular way of thinking, the slave boy in *Meno* is but one instance of this procedure); whereas Dewey's concept of transactional listening-in-conversation, which is addressed in this essay, involves an act of will, even persistence and aggressiveness on the part of the listener as well as on the part of the speaker. This willing initiative of the student is also present in the Asian tradition. There, it is often the student (the listener) who initiates the communication.[21] As a university professor, Jaspers too, seems to have assumed that his students are willing and interested in listening to his lectures. He simply did not care for those who were not. Unlike Socrates, he did not attempt to spark their interest or thinking. Thinking is what students are supposed to do and then come prepared to listen to Jaspers—just like Svetaketu went to his teacher after studying for 12 years.

Actually, the position of a teacher-philosopher in Jaspers' view was not unlike that of a statesman (not merely a politician): "The statesman stands at the frontier of humanity, at the place where someone must stand so that all may live. The fate of all is determined by a few statesmen."[22] Like a statesman, a teacher-philosopher is beyond and above the ordinary, above the average. Like a statesman, a teacher-philosopher uses reason (*Vernunft*) and not merely intellect (*Verstand*), which is the tool of the ordinary. Like a statesman, a teacher-philosopher has an insight into subjects (current or future affairs of the world, or respectively of existence) that ordinary people cannot access without external guidance (of the statesman or teacher-philosopher). Like a true statesman (not a politician), a teacher-philosopher has the trust of listeners.

To Jaspers, the ideal teacher was definitely Max Weber.

> When Max Weber died in 1920, I felt as if the world has changed. The great man, who justified it and who made it soulful for my consciousness, was no more. . . . It was now, as if the instance vanished on which, in a reasonable discussion [*vernünftige Diskussion*], rested the absolutely trustworthy, not directly pronounced, leadership (*PA* 50–51).

After Weber's death Jaspers, like Svetaketu from the *Upanisad*, took it upon himself to find another teacher. To him, the choice was obvious; it had to be the man who was an authority to Max Weber, and he found this in Paul Rickert. The relationship did not work out—according to Jaspers (*PA* 51)—because of Rickert's unjust and incorrect opinion of Weber. Weber was for Jaspers still the measure of all things.

The teacher in Jaspers' view was not a sage, in the same sense in which Jaspers—according to William Kluback—thought of the Nazi-time Heidegger wanting to be a sage. Heidegger "retreated from dialogue to the silence of wisdom; he went from

---

[21] For example, Svetaketu, a character in the *Chandogya Upanisad*, Book Six, cited in John Koller and Patricia Koller, *A Sourcebook in Asian Philosophy* (New York, NY: Macmillan, 1991), pp. 25–30.

[22] Karl Jaspers, *The Atom Bomb and the Future of Man*, trans. E.B. Ashton (Chicago, IL: The University of Chicago Press, 1961), p. 237.

the thinker to the sage. The sage was beyond critical thinking; his pronouncement spoke from a mystical ground reached only by him and denied to others."[23] That kind of sage does not engage in communication, he does not listen, and he does not expect to be listened to—except for one student writes Kluback, which in Japsers' view of Heidegger is Hitler.

It seems that Jaspers himself was persuaded to give up the self-image of a sage (in the sense Kluback writes about), or a philosophical genius, relatively early in his life. He wrote in a letter to his wife on her 80th birthday: "As early as the first year of our marriage you said to me: A genius you are not."[24] He remembered her judgment after all these years; and he seemed to still be smarting from his wife's comment; could it be because this was what he was secretly dreaming or hoping for in his youth? But, no. Not for Jaspers the role of a genius or sage in the sense of someone who knows or possesses Truth and retreats "from dialogue to the silence of wisdom" (*PDV* 206). "Truth does not exist as merchandise ready-made for delivery" (*QG* 10), how could one possibly believe in possessing it?

For many years, Jaspers was hardly interested in going to the market place in search of a partner in dialogue, or a student, the way Socrates did. He prepared himself many years to be ready for students who would come to him in search of the wisdom he had acquired by listening to great philosophers of the past. As mentioned earlier, Jaspers' ideal student (listener) would be a person eager to listen and willing to change under the influence of teaching. Such a student would also be mature enough to form a dialogical partnership, a communication involving transactional listening-in-conversation. Heidegger and Arendt came closest to this model, and Jaspers himself was this kind of student-listener to Max Weber. All this changed after the war.

From *Existential Communication* to "Two-Way-Communication"

Following Bernd Weidmann's analysis of Jaspers' presence in the West German student press in the 1960s, especially during the period of student political protests, it seems to me that the philosopher succeeded in fulfilling the task of getting involved in a two-way-communication and in transactional listening to a commendable degree. Weidmann shows that, in his last years, Jaspers became one of the philosophers listened to by (West) German students, although he certainly did not

---

[23] William Kluback, "Philosophy's Discordant Voice. The Most Powerful Instrument of Perfidy: Language," in *Jahrbuch der Österreichischen Karl-Jaspers-Gesellschaft*, eds. Elisabeth Hybašek and Kurt Salamun, Jahrgang 3/4 (VWGÖ, 1990/1991), pp. 204–216 (here p. 206). [Henceforth cited as *PDV*]

[24] Karl Jaspers, "Letter to Gertrud Jaspers on Her Eightieth Birthday," trans. Edith Ehrlich in *Karl Jaspers' Philosophie: Gegenwärtigkeit und Zukunft; Karl Jaspers's Philosophy: Rooted in the Present, Paradigm for the Future*, eds. Richard Wisser and Leonard H. Ehrlich, co-eds. Andreas Cesana and Gregory Walters (Würzburg: Königshausen & Neumann, 2003), pp. 309–328 (here p. 316).

become one of the intellectual godfathers or gurus of the student movement. In Weidmann's estimation, the students saw Jaspers "in the best case" merely as a point of reference in matters of university politics, whereas they mostly ignored him in the socio-political context. (*PB* 389) It seems to me that this was the case, indeed. Nevertheless, this signals a major change in the place Jaspers occupied in the collective consciousness, especially of young people before and after World War II.

Before the war, Jaspers was perceived mostly as aloof and elitist; he was not known to relish in public dialogue; he was also a person who avoided, whenever possible, public gatherings (except for the lectures where he either would be the lecturer or a silent listener). He conducted a dialogue with some chosen individuals. He did so primarily in the form of letters. The most famous among them are the ones he exchanged over the years with Martin Heidegger and with Hannah Arendt.[25] After the war, his involvement and interest in the most burning issues concerning his nation and humankind in general, as well as his active efforts to reach out to those he wanted to communicate with brought him closer—although never close enough—to the young generation, especially university students, and to the masses. I tend to think that this happened not so much because the masses, his public, had changed but because Jaspers himself had changed.

He certainly made his mark on public discourse. In the early 1980s, several leading West German intellectuals published jointly a two-volume collection of essays, edited by Jürgen Habermas, *Stichworte zur 'Geistigen Situation der Zeit,'* which was a clear reference to Jaspers' 1931 book *Die geistige Situation der Zeit* (*Man in the Modern Age*). These essays were both a tribute to, and a wrestling with Jaspers' diagnosis of the ills of human existence in the modern age and a wrestling with his prescription for the cure of these ills, and with his thoughts concerning the future. For the authors, Jaspers' ideas were stimulating, important, relevant, and by no means outdated.

It seems to me that this acknowledgement of Jaspers' lasting relevance was a result of his changing position with regard to the relation between philosophy and politics as well as his changing views on the role of the university rather than any significant change in his concept of existential communication. If anything, I would venture a thesis that the bitter experiences with the unwilling, unresponsive listeners Jaspers had gone through after the end of World War II taught him about practical aspects of communication, about more effective ways of using communication as a tool in the process of exploring and spreading ideas vital for the existential self-consciousness of humankind in the second half of the twentieth century. It also certainly made him aware of the need for meaningful and effective multidimensional communication between large groups of people in the world who were already moving from a Euro-centric perspective toward a world-oriented one.

Jaspers seems to have been very well aware of the process of changes his thinking and his concept of communication went through. He also seems to have given it a

---

[25] Martin Heidegger/Karl Jaspers, *Briefwechsel 1920–1963*, eds. Walter Biemel and Hans Saner Hans (Frankfurt am Main: Vittorio Klosterman, 1990).

great deal of significance. In his eulogy, which he wrote on his own behalf and which was read at a 1969 memorial service held in his honor (*WP* 207), Jaspers wrote about himself during the years he lived in Basel:

> He gave all his strength of those years to the continuation of his unending philosophical work with which he wanted—more intuiting than already knowing, attempting, rather than holding—to participate in the task of the epoch, which was to find the way out of the end of the European philosophy into the approaching world philosophy. (*WP* 208)

It was to a very significant degree the journey Jaspers made through the various nuances of the philosophical idea and the practice of communication, whose immensity he recognized gradually over the decades that made him a visionary, a philosopher of the future, a world-philosopher (he belonged to one of the first ones who had abandoned Euro-centrism in favor of world-philosophy), and—let me add—a philosopher who could inspire those living in an era of information and communication technology. Indu Sarin summed it up in the following way: "He moves from the dreary dusk of European philosophy to the glowing dawn of a world-philosophy, from man to mankind, forming the framework of universal communication, which contributes significantly in bringing world peace."[26]

There is a growing interest in Jaspers as the world-philosopher. The creation of numerous Jaspers societies, the international Karl Jaspers conferences with publications resulting from them demonstrate a continuous interest. Also his idea of communication gains popularity, and it does so because it appeals to those interested in forming a world-philosophy through communication built upon transactional listening-in-conversation. That Jaspers himself made that journey from local-centered to world-centered philosophy, from communication built upon straight-line (one-way) listening to communication build upon transactional listening-in-conversation makes his philosophy especially attractive, promising, and useful.

---

[26] Indu Sarin, *The Global Vision: Karl Jaspers* (New York, NY: Peter Lang Publishers, 2009), p. 13.

Appendix

Photo 1 Gertrud Mayer and Karl Jaspers shortly after their marriage in 1910

Photo 2 Edith Schwarz and Leonard Ehrlich upon their engagement in Chicago, January 1944

H. Wautischer et al. (eds.), *Philosophical Faith and the Future of Humanity*,
DOI 10.1007/978-94-007-2223-1, © Springer Science+Business Media B.V. 2012

Photo 3 Leonard Ehrlich at the front in Germany in 1945 serving as a Medic for the US Army. Surprise visit by Marlene Dietrich, to boost the morale of the troops

Photo 4 Leonard Ehrlich and Richard Wisser in Worms, Germany, 2006

Photo 5 Leonard and Edith Ehrlich at the Nordsee (Neuharlingen near Oldenburg) in May 2008

Notes on Contributors

Andreas Cesana is Professor of Philosophy and Head of the *Studium generale* (Department for Interdisciplinary Studies) at the University of Mainz, having previously taught at the University of Basle. He is author of three books and over 90 papers in journals and collected works, many of which are studies on Karl Jaspers and Jacob Burckhardt; including *Johann Jakob Bachofens Geschichtsdeutung* (1983), *Geschichte als Entwicklung–Zur Kritik des geschichtsphilosophischen Entwicklungsdenkens* (1988), and *Neue Wege des Denkens* (2007, in Japanese). He is Chief Editor of *Jacob Burckhardt Werke: Kritische Gesamtausgabe*, (since 1988, 14 of projected 23 volumes completed), director of the International Association of Jaspers Studies, and the European International Delegate for the Fifth International Jaspers Conference, Istanbul, Turkey (2003).

Joanne M. Cho received her PhD from the University of Chicago. She is associate professor at William Paterson University of New Jersey, where she teaches modern German and European history. Her research focus is the debate on civilization in twentieth-century Germany. She is the recipient of several fellowships, including a Fulbright (Göttingen/Frankfurt-Oder), Max Planck Institut für Geschichte (Göttingen), Institut für Europäische Geschichte (Mainz), Deutscher Akademischer Austausch Dienst (Tübingen), and Karl Jaspers Center for Advanced Transcultural Studies (Heidelberg). She has published several articles on Karl Jaspers, Ernst Troeltsch, Oswald Spengler, and Albert Schweitzer. Her current research includes a monograph, *From German Guilt to World History in Karl Jaspers*.

Charles Courtney is Emeritus Professor of Philosophy at Drew University, New Jersey, where he taught from 1964 to 2004. His PhD is from Northwestern University where he first studied Jaspers with William Earle. A Fulbright Fellowship to Paris (1962–1964) allowed him to study phenomenology with Paul Ricoeur. He has served as President of the Karl Jaspers Society of North America. In addition to his 2003 World Congress paper on Jaspers and Ricoeur, his publications are in the areas of comparative philosophy of religion and human rights philosophy as it bears on the problem of poverty.

Leonard H. Ehrlich (1924–2011) was Professor of Philosophy and Judaic Studies, Emeritus, University of Massachusetts, Amherst. He is the author of *Karl Jaspers:*

Philosophy as Faith (1975), and numerous articles on Jaspers, fundamental philosophy, and the philosophy of Judaism. He was co-editor (with M. Ermarth) and co-translator (with E. Ehrlich) of Jaspers' *The Great Philosophers*, Vols. 3 and 4 (1993 and 1994); co-editor and co-translator, with E. Ehrlich and G. B. Pepper of *Karl Jaspers: Basic Philosophical Writings, Selections* (2nd edition, 1995). With R. Wisser, he has been chief co-organizer of the first five international Jaspers conferences (Montreal 1983, Brighton 1988, Moscow 1993, Boston 1998, Istanbul 2003) in connection with World Congresses of Philosophy, and co-editor of respective collections of conference papers. He was founder and co-director of the International Association of Jaspers Societies.

Stephen A. Erickson is Professor of Philosophy and the E. Wilson Lyon Professor of Humanities at Pomona College in Claremont, California. He received his PhD at Yale University (1964) and is author of *Language and Being* (Yale University Press), *Human Presence: At the Boundaries of Meaning* (Mercer University Press), and *The (Coming) Age of Thresholding* (Kluwer Academic Publishers), as well as numerous articles in journals such as *The Review of Metaphysics*, *Man and World*, *Philosophy Today*, *The Harvard Review of Philosophy*, the *International Philosophical Quarterly*, and *Existenz*. He served as Program Director of the Karl Jaspers Society of North America (1994–1996) as well as its President (1996–1998). In lectures throughout the United States, Europe, South America, and Asia, Erickson is reflecting on contemporary culture and its relation to spiritual life. His 24-lecture series "Philosophy as a Guide to Living" is available through *The Teaching Company*. He has been a guest-faculty member at several psychoanalytic institutes and is a member of the Editorial Advisory Board of *The Journal of Medicine and Philosophy*. He recently was an invited guest in Hong Kong and Xi'an, China to participate with other international and Chinese scholars in discussions concerning the Common Good and a Confucian approach to Chinese Family Health Care.

S. Nassir Ghaemi is Professor of Psychiatry at the Harvard Medical School and Cambridge Hospital, Cambridge, Massachusetts. In 1990 he received his MD from the Medical College of Virginia, completed an internal medicine internship at the Massachusetts General Hospital in Boston (MGH 1991), an adult psychiatry residency at Harvard-affiliated McLean Hospital in Belmont (1994), and a research fellowship in psychopharmacology at MGH (1995). He is a member of the Executive Council of the Association of Philosophy and Psychiatry (AAPP), co-founder of the Boston AAPP Chapter. He was co-recipient of the Karl Jaspers prize of the AAPP for his essay, "Mind/Brain Theories and Their Discontents," Integrative Psychiatry, 10 (1994): 52–57. His clinical work and research has focused on depression and manic-depressive illness, psychopharmacology, psychiatric phenomenology, and philosophical aspects of psychiatry. In this work, he has published over 100 scientific articles, over 30 scientific book chapters, and he has written or edited five books, including *The Concepts of Psychiatry: A Pluralistic Approach to the Mind and Mental Illness* (2003) and *The Rise and Fall of the Biopsychosocial Model: Reconciling Art and Science in Psychiatry* (2009). He serves on a number of editorial boards of psychiatric journals, is a Distinguished Fellow of the American Psychiatric Association, an elected officer of the International Society for Bipolar Disorders (ISBD), and chairman of the Diagnostic Guidelines Task Force of ISBD.

Andrew L. Gluck is an independent scholar who previously taught philosophy at Hofstra University and St. Johns University. He has Masters degrees in psychology, religion, and management and a doctorate in philosophy. He has published articles in medieval philosophy, philosophy of education, consciousness studies, philosophy of the social sciences and religion. He also does consulting work and has published numerous articles in the field of forensic vocational economics. Aside from journal articles, his works include: *The Kingly Crown, Damasio's Error* and *Religion, Fundamentalism and Violence: An Interdisciplinary Dialogue*. He is currently completing a book on Judah Abrabanel, a Renaissance philosopher. For many years he has been fascinated by the work of Karl Jaspers and addressed it in the contexts of the philosophy of the social sciences and consciousness studies.

Krystyna Górniak-Kocikowska is a Professor of Philosophy at Southern Connecticut State University, Director of the Religious Studies Program at the University, and Senior Research Associate in the Research Center on Computing & Society. Her degrees include an MA in German Philology and a PhD in Philosophy from the Adam Mickiewicz University in Poznan, Poland, and an MA Religious Studies from Temple University. Prior to her arrival in the United States, she was on the Faculty of the Philosophy Department at the Adam Mickiewicz University. She has received research grants from the Kosciuszko Foundation, the National Endowment for the Humanities, and the Metaphilosophy Foundation. She is actively involved in Computer (Information) Ethics research, and her main interest is on the impact of information technology on social justice issues related to globalization. She has co-edited and published (with Andrzej Kocikowski and Terrell Ward Bynum) a CD-ROM collection of "milestone" papers on Computer Ethics translated from English into Polish, and is on the Editorial Advisory Board of the *Journal of Information, Communication & Ethics in Society*.

Shinji Hayashida is Emeritus Professor at University of Electro-Communications, Tokyo Japan. He was the President of Jaspers Society of Japan 1995–2008, and participated with Leonard H. Ehrlich and Richard Wisser in the founding of the International Association of Jaspers Societies. He also served as President of the Japanese Society for Ethics, 1999–2003. He has published several works including *Karl Jaspers* (1968), *Jaspers no Jituzon-tetugaku (Jaspers' Existenz-philosophy)* (1971), and numerous articles on the philosophy of Karl Jaspers, existentialism, ethical problems, and also on the idea of existential ethics. He translated Jaspers' *Schicksal und Wille, Was ist Philosophie?* into Japanese, was also the co-translator of Jaspers' *Philosophie; Von der Wahrheit;* and *Der philosophische Glaube*.

W. Michael Hoffman is the founding Executive Director of the Center for Business Ethics at Bentley University in Waltham, Massachusetts. Since 1976, the Center has served as a research and consulting institute and an educational forum for the exchange of ideas and information in business ethics. He is the Hieken Professor of

Business and Professional Ethics at Bentley. He received his PhD in Philosophy at the University of Massachusetts/Amherst and has been a professor for 40 years in higher education. He has authored or edited 16 books, including *Business Ethics: Readings and Cases in Corporate Morality* (4th edition), *The Ethical Edge*, and *Ethics Matters: How to Implement Values-Driven Management*, and has published over 95 articles. He consults on business ethics for corporations and other organizations, and serves as an expert witness in litigation. Dr. Hoffman was co-founder and the first Executive Director of the Ethics & Compliance Officer Association and the Advisor to its board of directors for 10 years. He was co-founder and President of the Society for Business Ethics, served on the advisory board of the U.S. Sentencing Commission, and is frequently sought out globally for professional lectures and media interviews. Dr. Hoffman was named the 2007 Humanist of the Year by The Ethical Society of Boston, and received the 2009 Society for Corporate Compliance and Ethics Award for continuing contributions in the field of ethics and compliance.

Anton Hügli recently retired as Professor of Philosophy and Pedagogics at the University of Basle, having previously taught at the Universities of Münster and Bielefeld. He has published several studies on Karl Jaspers and, as the president of the *Karl-Jaspers-Stiftung Basel*, he is initially involved in the preparation of the commentary edition of the published and unpublished works and letters of Karl Jaspers. His books include: *Die Erkenntnis der Subjektivität und die Objektivität des Erkennens bei Søren Kierkegaard* and *Philosophie und Pädagogik*. He is Co-Editor of *Historisches Wörterbuch der Philosophie* and other lexical works, and also of *Studia philosophica*.

Tomoko Iwasawa is Associate Professor of Comparative Religions at Reitaku University, Japan. She received her MA and PhD in the Philosophy of Religion from Boston University. Her publications include Tama *in Japanese Myth: A Hermeneutical Study of Ancient Japanese Divinity* (2011) and "Jaspers' *Schuldfrage* and Hiroshima: Does the Concept of Guilt Exist for Japanese Religious Consciousness?" (2008). She is an executive board member of International Shinto Foundation.

Malek K. Khazaee earned his PhD from the Claremont Graduate University in 1988 and has been teaching philosophy in California State University at Long Beach since 1989. His publications are in Nineteenth Century German Philosophy, Contemporary Continental European Philosophy, Political Theory, and International Relations. His primary interests are in Nietzsche and Jaspers.

Suzanne Kirkbright graduated from the University of Surrey (Guildford), and completed her doctoral thesis on twentieth century German literature and philosophy in 1995 at Aston University, Birmingham. From 2000 to 2002, she worked at the University of Heidelberg as an *Alexander von Humboldt Research Fellow* and published the first English-speaking biography of *Karl Jaspers. A Biography: Navigations in Truth* (Yale 2004). In 2008, she was awarded the *Karl Jaspers Förderpreis* of the Universität Oldenburg. She has worked as a freelance author and translator since 2007 and is a Visiting Research Fellow at Queen Mary College, University of London.

Gerhard Knauss is Emeritus Professor of Philosophy at the University of Saarbrücken, Germany. He studied with Karl Jaspers in Heidelberg and Basel who was his dissertation advisor. He taught philosophy at Tohoku University in Sendai, Japan and at the University of Tokyo, Komaba. He is the author of *Gegenstand und Umgreifendes* (Basel 1954) as well as numerous articles on Jaspers' philosophy, including a chapter in Paul A. Schilpp's volume on *The Philosophy of Karl Jaspers* (La Salle 1981). During his time in Saabrücken he investigated analytically the Kantian problem of synthetic propositions a priori.

Raymond Langley is a Professor of Philosophy at Manhattanville College in Purchase, New York. He has published dozens of articles in encyclopedias, journals, and reviews. He has published or presented articles on Karl Jaspers on education and philosophy of history and philosophic faith, as well as comparative studies of Jaspers with Kant, Marx, Freud, William James, Sartre, and Foucault. Together with Joseph Koterski S.J. he is co-editor of *Karl Jaspers on Philosophy of History and History of Philosophy* (Humanity Books, 2003). He has served twice as President of the Karl Jaspers Society of North America.

Robert E. McNulty is the director of programs at the Center for Business Ethics (CBE), Bentley University. He joined CBE after many years in both business and academia. At CBE, he is responsible for managing many aspects of CBE's various programs and overseeing the Center's research activities. Some of his recent publications include "Business Ethics Perspectives on International Negotiations," "International Business, Human Rights and Moral Complicity: A Call for a Declaration on the Universal Rights and Duties of Business," and "A Business Ethics Theory of Whistleblowing: Responding to the $1 Trillion Question." all three co-authored with W. M. Hoffman. Besides teaching in Bentley's philosophy department, he has taught at Columbia University and at the State University of New York at New Paltz. Prior to entering academia he had a lengthy career in international business, specializing in the application of strategic communications to assist countries in their economic development efforts. He has also served as a consultant to many Fortune 500 and foreign-based firms. For the last decade and a half, the focus of his work has been ethics, both in its theoretical and applied forms. He founded and heads the non-profit organization Applied Ethics, Inc.

Alan M. Olson is a Professor of the Philosophy of Religion at Boston University. He was educated at Saint Olaf College, Luther Theological Seminary, Nashotah House, and Boston University where he received his PhD. At various times he has chaired the Departments of Religion and Philosophy at Boston University. He was Executive Director of the *20th World Congress of Philosophy* in Boston (1998), and is Director and Executive Editor of the *Paideia Project: Proceedings of the Twentieth World Congress of Philosophy* (12 vols, 2000). He served as Chair of the Committee on International Cooperation, American Philosophical Association (2002–2005) and served on the Board of Officers of the APA during the same period. He was the Benjamin Cardozo Lecturer, CCNY (1983); and the Karl Jaspers Lecturer at Oxford University (1989). He has twice been a Senior Fulbright Research Fellow, Tübingen

(1986), and Vienna, Austria (1995). He has authored and edited several books including: *Disguises of the Demonic* (1976); *Transcendence and Hermeneutics* (1979); *Myth, Symbol and Reality*, ed. (1980); *Transcendence and the Sacred* (1981); *The Seeing Eye: Essays in Hermeneutic Phenomenology* (1983); *Video Icons & Value*s (1990); *Hegel and the Spirit: Philosophy as Pneumatology* (1992); *Jaspers and Heidegger* (1994); *Educating for Democracy: Paideia in an Age of Uncertainty* (2004). He is past president of the *Karl Jaspers Society of North America* and co-editor, with Helmut Wautischer, of its on-line journal of philosophy, *Existenz*.

Filiz Peach completed her doctoral work on Karl Jaspers' existential philosophy at the City University in London UK, and now lectures in philosophy at the Mary Ward Centre and Kingston Adult Education both in London. She is the Vice President of *Philosophy for All*, an organization that provides a wide range of philosophical activities in London. She is also involved as an organizer for philosophical events in Kingston Philosophy Café. Her publications include *Existenz, Death and Deathlessness in Karl Jaspers' Philosophy* (Edinburgh University Press, 2008), a number of articles in *Jahrbuch der Österreichischen Karl Jaspers Gesellschaft, Analecta Husserliana, Philosophy Now,* and various other publications. She has presented papers on different aspects of philosophy at various seminars and conferences in Europe, Asia, and the United States.

George B. Pepper is Emeritus Professor at Iona College, New Rochelle, New York. He received his degree in philosophy from Fordham University and did postdoctoral study at Harvard and Columbia. He is a co-founder of the Karl Jaspers Society of North America, and co-editor with Edith and Leonard H. Ehrlich of Karl Jaspers: Basic Philosophical Writings (1994). Two additional papers on Jaspers have been published, and his work in the sociology of religion, "The Boston Heresy Case in view of the Secularization of Religion" was published in 1988.

Czesława Piecuch is Professor of Philosophy at the Pedagogical University, Kraków, and Head of Department of Contemporary Philosophy. She is founder and president of The Polish Karl Jaspers Society. She has published over 30 articles on the philosophy of Karl Jaspers, and translated into Polish the following books by Karl Jaspers: *Vernunft und Existenz* (1991), *Nietzsche und Christentum* (1991), *Chiffren der Transzendenz* (1999). She has published a book on the concept of man in the contemporary philosophy of existence entitled *Człowiek metafizyczny* (*The Metaphysical Man*) (2001), *Metafizyka egzystencjalna Karla Jaspersa* (Die existenzielle Metaphysik von Karl Jaspers) (2011), and *Karl Jaspers, Myślenie zaangażowane* (Karl Jaspers: engagiertes Denken) (2011).

Tom Rockmore is McAnulty College Distinguished Professor and Professor of Philosophy at Duquesne University and Distinguished Visiting Professor at the University of Peking. He is the recipient of numerous awards and fellowships including a Humboldt-Forschungsstipendium, Tübingen, 1981–1982, and Köln, 1996. His most recent books include: *Before and After 9/11: A Philosophical Analysis of Globalization* (2010), *Terror and History* (2009); *Kant* *and Phenomenology* (2008); *Kant and Idealism* (2007); *In Kant's Wake: Philosophy in the Twentieth Century* (1996); *On Constructivist Epistemology* (2005); *Hegel, Idealism, and Analytic Philosophy* (2005); *On Foundationalism: A Strategy for Metaphysical Realism* (2004); *Before and After Hegel: A Historical Introduction to Hegel's Thought* (2003); and *Marx After Marxism: An Introduction to the Philosophy of Karl Marx* (2002). Several of his books have been translated into Russian, Turkish, and Chinese.

Hans Saner studied philosophy, psychology, Germanic and Romance languages at the Universities of Lausanne and Basel. His doctoral dissertation was on the political philosophy of Kant, which appeared in English translation as *Kant's Political Thought: Its Origin and Development* (1973). During the period 1954–1959, he was an elementary school teacher near Interlaken; and in 1962–1969, he was the personal assistant to Karl Jaspers, whose literary estate he published in seven volumes on behalf of the Karl Jaspers Stiftung in Basel. From 1979 to 2008 he taught the philosophy of culture at the Basel Music Academy. He has published numerous books on history of philosophy, cultural criticism, and political and aesthetic philosophy, for which he has been awarded several prizes, including the Hermann-Hesse-Prize of the city of Karlsruhe; the Egner-Foundation-Prize, Zurich, and the *Grossen Kulturpreis* of the Canton of Solothurn, as well as an honorary Doctor of Political Science degree from the University of St. Gallen.

Indu Sarin is a retired Professor of Philosophy at Panjab University, Chandigarh, India. She chaired the Philosophy Department from 1991 to 1994. Her specializations include Existentialism, Philosophy of Religion, and Ethics. She has published two books: *Kierkegaard–A Turning Point,* and *The Global Vision–Karl Jaspers,* and also a paper on *Jaspers' Voice of Humanism in the Contemporary Crisis.* She has also published about 30 papers (including 9 papers on Jaspers' Philosophy) in Indian and International Journals and Volumes; and she has ninety-nine entries in *Dictionary of Philosophy.* She has participated in various national and international conferences and presented six papers at the International Jaspers Conferences held in Moscow, Graz, Boston, Istanbul, Oldenburg, and Seoul. At present, she is working on a book entitled, *Quest of Values in the Emerging Scenario.*

Wolfdietrich Schmied-Kowarzik is Professor of Philosophy at the University of Kassel and founder and first president of the *International Rosenzweig Society.* He has published several books on Schelling and Rosenzweig: *Sinn und Existenz in der Spätphilosophie Schellings* (1963); *Bruchstücke zur Dialektik der Philosophie* (1974); *Franz Rosenzweig: Existentielles Denken und gelebte Bewährung* (1991); *Von der wirklichen, von der seyenden Natur: Schellings Ringen um eine Naturphilosophie in Auseinandersetzung mit Kant, Fichte und Hegel (1996); Denken aus geschichtlicher Verantwortung: Wegbahnungen zur praktischen Philosophie* (1999); *Rosenzweig im Gespräch mit Ehrenberg, Cohen und Buber* (2006).

Reinhard Schulz teaches didactics in the Institute for Philosophy at the Carl von Ossietzky University Oldenburg. He has been Director of the "Karl Jaspers Lectures on Issues of the Times" since 1997. Following studies in biology, philosophy and sociology at Bielefeld University and the award of a doctorate in molecular biology at the University of Bremen (1984), he qualified as a grammar-school teacher. Prior to gaining his post-doctoral lecturer qualification in philosophy (2000) and his move to the Institute for Philosophy (2001), Schulz worked for the Student Advisory Office. He took up his professorship in 2006, and his primary research interests are natural philosophy, hermeneutics, anthropology, and research on Karl Jaspers.

Hermann-Josef Seideneck has been a Roman Catholic priest for over 20 years in several parishes and also as military and hospital chaplain. He completed a three-year basic study of the natural sciences in chemistry at Halle resulting in a 20-year academic relationship with Carl Friedrick von Weizsäcker in association with the Academy of Natural Scientists Leopoldina. He subsequently finished an eight-year study of philosophy and theology at Erfurt and Naumburg culminating in a thesis entitled: "A Venture of Suspense: The Concept of God in the Philosophical Work of Karl Jaspers," which was facilitated by way of a lengthy exchange of letters with Hans Saner in 1984. He has participated in all World Congresses of Philosophy (FISP) since 1988, and his essays have appeared in various anthologies including *Heidegger e la Theologia,* eds., Ott and Penzo (1995), *L'esprit d'aujourd'hui,* ed., Masubuchi (1995), and the *Yearbooks of the Austrian Karl Jaspers Society,* 3/4 and 7/8.

Chris Thornhill is Head of Politics and Professor of European Political Thought at the University of Glasgow, UK. He has previously held positions at the University of Sussex and King's College London. Recent and forthcoming publications are: (sole author) *Political Theory in Modern Germany* (1999); *Karl Jaspers: Politics and Metaphysics* (2002/2006); *German Political Philosophy: The Metaphysics of Law* (2007/2010); *A Sociology of Constitutions: Constitutions and State Legitimacy in historical-sociological Perspective* (2011); (co-author) *Niklas Luhmann's Theory of Politics and Law* (2003/2005); (co-editor) *Luhmann on Law and Politics: Critical Appraisals and Applications* (2006); *Legality and Legitimacy: Normative and Sociological Approaches* (2010). Articles on: constitutional history and theory; the history of fascism; historical sociology; European state building; legality and legitimacy; Niklas Luhmann; Carl Schmitt; Frankfurt School; Karl Jaspers; legal-political sociology in general.

Gregory J. Walters is Professor, Faculty of Philosophy, Saint Paul University/ Université Saint-Paul, Ottawa, Canada. He is the author of *Karl Jaspers and the Role of 'Conversion' in the Nuclear Age* (1987), *Equal Access: Safeguarding Disability Rights* (1992), *Human Rights in Theory and Practice* (1995), *Human Rights in an Information Age: A Philosophical Analysis* (2002). Editor and contributor to *The Tasks of Truth: Essays on Karl Jaspers's Idea of the University* (1996); Co-editor, with Carl Bankston et al., *Racial and Ethnic Relations in America* (2000), with Andreas Cesana, *Karl Jaspers: Geschichtliche Wirklichkeit mit Blick auf die Grundfragen der Menscheit / Karl Jaspers: Historic Actuality in View of Fundamental Problems of Mankind* (2008), and with Kurt Salamun, *Karl*

Jaspers's Philosophy: Expositions & Interpretations (2008). Recent publications are "Philosophy of Gene-Being: A Prolegomenon," in *Technology and the Changing Face of Humanity*, 2010, and "Police Brutality and Human Rights: A Dialogue," *Science et Esprit*, 2010. He held the Gordon F. Henderson Chair in Human Rights, University of Ottawa (1998), and was funded by the Canadian Foreign Affairs Department & Austrian-Canadian Studies Association (2006) for lectures at the Hörsaal des Instituts für Pathologie am LKH-Universitätsklinikum, the Institut für Philosophie at Karl-Franzens Universität Graz, and the Universities at Klagenfurt and Salzburg.

Helmut Wautischer is Senior Lecturer of Philosophy at California State University, Sonoma. In 1985, he received his PhD from the University of Graz, Austria, where he studied with Rudolf Haller and Ernst Topitsch. He is editor of *Tribal Epistemologies: Essays in the Philosophy of Anthropology* (Ashgate 1998), and *Ontology of Consciousness: Percipient Action* (MIT 2008), and has published essays in numerous venues, such as *Polylog*, *Prima Philosophia*, *Dialogue and Humanism*, *Anthropology of Consciousness*, *Shaman*, *Journal of Ritual Studies*, *Journal of Ethical Studies*. In 1996 and 1997 he was a guest lecturer at the University of Klagenfurt, Austria. He presented numerous papers at international conferences, such as the World Congresses of Philosophy (Moscow, Boston, Istanbul), Toward a Science of Consciousness (Tucson), American Philosophical Association, American Anthropological Association, Austrian Association for Philosophy, International Conference on the Study of Shamanism and Alternative Modes of Healing, and others. Currently he serves as president of the Karl Jaspers Society of North America, is co-Editor (with Alan M. Olson) of the online journal *Existenz*, and is Managing Editor of www.bu.edu/paideia.

Reiner Wiehl (1929–2010) studied philosophy, mathematics, and physics in Frankfurt am Main; Philosophy and Roman Languages in Pisa, 1949–1954. He received his Doctorate in Frankfurt, 1959, was Assistant Professor in the Department of Philosophy at the University of Heidelberg, 1961–1964, and completed his Habilitation in Heidelberg, 1966. He was Chair of the Department of Philosophy at the University of Hamburg in 1969, and Chair of the Department of Philosophy at the University of Heidelberg in 1976. His research interests include metaphysics and hermeneutics in modern philosophy (with special emphasis on aesthetics and ethics) and philosophical psychology. His publications include *Platos Sophistes*, Hamburg: Meiner, 1967; *Einleitung in die Philosophie A. N. Whiteheads*, Frankfurt: Suhrkamp 1971; *Die Vernunft in der menschlichen Unvernunft*, Göttingen: Vandenhoeck & Ruprecht 1982; *Metaphysik und Erfahrung*, Frankfurt: Suhrkamp 1996; *Zeitwelten. Philosophisches Denken an den Rändern von Natur und Geschichte*, Frankfurt: Suhrkamp 1998; *Subjektivität und System*, Frankfurt: Suhrkamp 2000. He has published numerous essays and articles on the philosophy of Hegel and the philosophy of the twentieth Century, especially the philosophy of Whitehead, Heidegger, Jaspers, and Rosenzweig. He was a member of the *Joachim Jungius Society of Sciences* in Hamburg, and the *Institut International de Philosophie*, Paris. He was President of the Karl Jaspers Foundation Basel; a

Researcher at Dr. Egner Foundation Zurich 1990; and a member of the European Academy of Arts and Sciences in Salzburg.

Armin Wildermuth is Emeritus Professor of Philosophy at the University of St. Gallen, Switzerland, where he lectured from 1973 to 1995. Earlier he was Assistant Professor of Philosophy at St. Johns University, New York (1967–1971) and at Central Michigan University, Mount Pleasant (1971–1973). He has published several books, including studies on Leibniz (*Wahrheit und Schöpfung*, 1960), Karl Marx (*Marx und die Verwirklichung der Philosophie*, 1970), contemporary art (*Vom Leib zum Bild: Maria Lassnings künstlerischer Erkenntnisprozess*, 1985), Karl Jaspers (*Karl Jaspers and the Concept of Philosophical Faith*, 2007), and on Jaspers' colleague at the University of Basel, Heinrich Barth (*Philosophie der Praktischen Vernunft*, 2009, originally published in 1927). His works are translated into several languages. He served as president of the Heinrich Barth Gesellschaft (1996–2008), is currently a Board member of Stiftung Lucerna in Switzerland, and since 2008 is president of Philosophische Gesellschaft Ostschweiz.

Richard Wisser is Professor of Philosophy at the University of Mainz, Germany. He has published over 100 papers on Karl Jaspers and, together with Leonard Ehrlich, was in charge of the First International Jaspers Conference which consequently met every five years. For the occasion of Jaspers' 100th Anniversary, he organized a 14-day symposium in Dubrovnik, Yugoslavia.

Michael Zank is Professor of Religion and Acting Director, The Elie Wiesel Center for Judaic Studies in the Department of Religion at Boston University. He received his PhD in Near Eastern and Judaic Studies at Brandeis University and holds a degree in Protestant Theology from the Evangelische Kirche der Pfalz in Speyer. He is the author of *The Idea of Atonement in the Philosophy of Hermann Cohen* (2000), the translator and editor of Leo Strauss's *The Early Writings (1921–1932)* (2002), and the editor of *New Perspectives on Martin Buber* (2006). He is a contributing editor of the *Journal for Jewish Thought and Philosophy*. Forthcoming work includes an anthology on *Jüdische Religionsphilosophie als Apologie des Mosaismus* (Siebeck Mohr) and a brief history of Jerusalem (Blackwell).

Name Index

NOTE: Locators from Appendix and Notes of Contributers are also added.

A

Albertus Magnus, 297
Apostle Peter, 117
Aquinas, Thomas, 96, 140, 218–219, 297, 300
Arendt, Hannah, 6, 45, 47–48, 204–205, 415, 429–430, 432–433
Aristotle, 46–47, 49, 91, 96, 139, 205, 209, 217–219, 242, 297, 325
Arnold, Matthew, 135
Augustine of Hippo, 116

B

Barth, Heinrich, 78, 161, 448
Barth, Karl, 40, 161
Benedict, Ruth, 348, 360–362
Berlin, Isaiah, 181
Böckenförde, Ernst-Wolfgang, 121
Boethius, 19, 49, 121
Bostrom, Nick, 273–274
Bruno, Giordano, 19, 37, 48–49, 112, 116–117, 276
Buddha, 97, 194, 205, 374, 403, 410, 413, 415–417
Buri, Fritz, 40, 86, 161, 184

C

Camus, Albert, 45, 73, 112
Cesana, Andreas, 87, 99–113, 121, 124, 227, 423, 426, 429–430, 432, 439, 447
Chan, Wing-Tsit, 206–207
Charlemagne, 116
Confucius, 97, 194, 203–209, 367, 403, 415
Constantine Copronymus, 116
Cusa, Nicholas, 38, 205

D

de l'Hopital, Michel, 121
della Mirandola, Pico, 23, 218
Descartes, René, 297–298

E

Ehrlich, Edith, 51, 53–54, 69, 71–72, 138, 179–180, 209, 211, 256, 277–278, 287, 432
Ehrlich, Leonard H., 35–44, 48, 51, 53, 66–67, 69, 79, 85, 99, 124, 138, 147, 156, 161, 175, 214, 239, 256, 277–279, 285, 414, 418, 426–427, 429, 432, 439

F

Feeney, Leonard Edward, 45, 50
Fichte, Johann Gottlieb, 82, 84, 103, 123, 185, 299–301, 336, 446
Freud, Sigmund, 285, 298

G

Gadamer, Hans-Georg, 68, 112–113
Galileo Galilei, 37, 45
Gehlen, Arnold, 313
Goethe, Johann Wolfgang von, 57, 186, 276, 291, 296

H

Hamlet, 14, 66, 71–72
Hegel, G.W.F., 125, 326
Heidegger, Martin, 45, 47, 80, 87–88, 126, 130–131, 303–304, 320, 433
Hitler, Adolf, 43, 51, 318, 432
Humboldt, Wilhelm v., 124, 323, 442, 445
Hus, Jan, 117

J

Jacobi, Carl Gustav Jacob, 83–84, 123
Jaspers, Karl, 4–7, 9, 11–74, 77–80, 83–97,
    99–121, 123–166, 168–169, 171–211,
    214–215, 217–218, 220–225, 227–234,
    236, 238–240, 251, 253–256, 259–266,
    269–272, 275–279, 281, 283–285,
    287–320, 335–336, 338–343, 345,
    347–351, 354, 362–363, 365–372, 374,
    383, 387–388, 390–435, 439–448
Jeremiah, 13–14
John Paul II, Pope, 49

K

Kant, Immanuel, 102, 136, 166, 177, 238, 288,
    291, 301, 305, 368
Kierkegaard, Søren, 152, 171, 230, 269,
    271, 442
Kretschmer, Ernst, 3

L

Leibniz, Gottfried W., 47, 92, 291, 300,
    323, 448
Luther, Martin, 61, 238, 292

M

Mayer, Gertrude, 36, 435
Mears, Helen, 348–349, 352–363
More, Sir Thomas, 18

N

Neville, Robert, 207
Nietzsche, Friedrich, 279, 285, 298

O

Olson, Alan M., 77–97, 124, 236, 256,
    443, 447

P

Parmenides, 15, 104, 148
Pascal, Blaise, 23, 119
Plato, 45–46, 97, 111, 127, 148, 204–205, 209,
    218–219, 276, 280, 294, 297, 321, 323,
    325, 327–329, 332
Pollock, Robert, 47
Pythagoras, 294

R

Ricoeur, Paul, 86, 89, 144, 265, 418, 439
Rosenzweig, Franz, 147–157, 193, 445–446,
    448
Rousseau, Jean-Jacques, 116
Ryan, Patrick J., 48

S

Saner, Hans, 9, 11, 99, 103, 106, 110–112,
    129–130, 295, 320, 335, 338, 341–343,
    402, 433, 445–446
Schelling, Friedrich Wilhelm Joseph von, 73,
    82–85, 92, 103, 123–124, 147–158, 299,
    301, 306, 429, 445
Schiller, Friedrich, 93, 215, 294
Schopenhauer, Arthur, 118–119, 186
Selten, Reinhart, 118
Shakespeare, William, 14, 71–73, 80
Simon, Herbert, 118
Socrates, 18, 26, 38, 45–46, 49, 52–53, 66,
    93–97, 111, 119, 121, 139, 205, 276, 285,
    321, 328–330, 403, 415, 430–432
Sommer, Johann, 291
Spengler, Oswald, 409–410, 413, 439
Spinoza, Baruch, 92, 116, 124, 205, 232,
    276, 325
Stevens, Wallace, 138

T

Thomas Aquinas, 96, 140, 297, 300
Tillich, Paul, 80, 85, 88, 93, 149, 238
Troeltsch, Ernst, 409–413, 417–418, 439

V

Valéry, Paul, 119
Vico, Giambattista, 297
Voltaire, 54
von Hildebrand, Dietrich, 47, 50
von Ranke, Leopold, 121

W

Wautischer, Helmut, 3–7, 11, 35, 45, 53, 115,
    123, 287, 299, 319, 335
Weber, Max, 94, 124, 173, 218, 222, 302–303,
    363, 426, 431–432
Wisser, Richard, 67–68, 79, 115, 287–298, 335,
    414, 418, 426–427, 429, 437, 440–441, 448
Wittgenstein, Ludwig, 105, 119, 421

Subject Index

NOTE: Locators from Appendix and Notes of Contributers are also added.

9/11, 86, 270, 319–333, 445

A

Absence, 26–27, 62, 120, 187, 257, 265, 288, 379, 382, 384, 424
Absolute consciousness, 37, 228, 271, 275, 277, 284
Active sufferance, 271, 282–284
Affirmation, 12, 16–17, 26, 28, 33, 106, 115–121, 143, 164, 276
Ambivalence, 166, 214
American Catholicism, 20
Animal rationale, 118
Apology, 26
Aufschwung, 15
Authority, 5–6, 13, 17, 26–27, 29, 39–40, 43–44, 49, 55, 81, 95–96, 99, 106, 110, 113, 120, 140, 143, 150, 189–190, 197, 199, 201, 204, 207, 216, 250, 255, 279, 299, 301, 312, 339, 348, 358, 381–382, 390, 396, 418, 431
Avowal, 115, 150
Axial age, 27, 184–185, 191–200, 203, 367, 399–408, 415
Axial age hypothesis, 191–192, 196–198
Axial mind, 198
Axial period, 204, 206
Axiom, 4, 15–16, 36–37, 250

B

Basel, 40, 55, 71, 78, 86, 160–161, 345, 400, 428, 434, 442–443, 445, 448
Bildung, 37, 93, 234, 294
Boundary situation, 19–20, 66, 71–72, 119, 125–126, 130–131, 133, 142–144, 255, 365–366, 370

Buddhism, 117, 237, 367, 413–414, 416–418
Business ethics, 235–252, 441–443

C

Cathar, 66, 72, 116
Certainty, 5, 15, 18, 21, 23, 25–27, 29–31, 57–58, 61, 66, 102, 104, 106–107, 109–111, 113, 123–135, 143, 145, 147, 152, 154, 156, 169, 172, 174, 181–182, 193, 214, 228, 255, 265, 271, 277, 283, 315, 353, 391, 444
Chaos, 6, 168, 182, 273
China, People's Republic of, 27, 30, 96–97, 183, 191, 194, 197–198, 201–202, 204–206, 276, 327, 352, 357, 359, 365, 367, 377–378, 382, 385, 399, 403, 414–416, 418, 440
The Chrysanthemum and the Sword, 348–349, 360–361
Ciphers, 33, 60, 85, 92, 97, 107, 110, 119, 125, 141, 144–145, 151–152, 155–156, 164, 232, 255–256, 259, 265, 277, 289, 307–308, 341–345, 369–370, 372, 402, 407
Common goal of humankind, 399, 405
Common source of humankind, 399, 403, 408
Communication
    existential, 5, 20, 24, 133, 255, 259, 262–264, 266, 309, 318, 368, 373–374, 405–406, 422–426, 429, 432–434
    philosophy of, 204, 419–434
    universal, 405, 407, 434
    US-Japan, 348

Community, 12, 19, 27–28, 36, 39–40, 42, 49,
    67, 97, 145, 151, 154–157, 207–208,
    252, 258–260, 262–263, 266, 309, 321,
    358, 366–367, 372, 380, 384, 392,
    396–397, 400, 416
Comprehensive ethics, 232–234
Confessio Augustana, 116
Confession, 12–13, 33, 38–39, 44, 49,
    115–117, 119–121, 140, 276,
    339
Corporate capitalism, 235–252
Corpus Christi, 26
Corruption, 50, 246, 386
Creed, 12, 90–91, 115–117, 119, 137, 140, 276
Criticism, 9, 39, 101, 161, 173, 206, 216, 219,
    357–358, 360–361, 445
Culture, 37, 90, 123, 125, 135, 139, 142,
    191–192, 198, 202, 225, 237–238,
    240–249, 257, 259–260, 262–263,
    299–318, 322–323, 332, 336, 348–349,
    351–352, 361–362, 365, 377, 387–389,
    392, 396, 398–399, 403, 411, 415,
    417–418, 440, 445

D

Daimon, 19, 26, 207
Death as a bounday situation, 365
De dignitate hominis, 118
Democracy, 5, 44, 170, 201, 261, 270, 279,
    302, 309–314, 316, 331, 378–379,
    381–382, 384–386, 404, 407, 411,
    422–423, 428, 444
Demonic technology, 389
Departmental thinking, 390–391
Depression, 246, 380, 440
Dialogue, 3, 6, 12, 32, 46, 66, 96, 107, 112,
    117, 126, 130, 154–155, 162, 166, 168,
    216–217, 222, 224–225, 262, 264, 287,
    289, 294, 319–333, 347–351, 363, 371,
    374, 402, 419, 423–425, 427–428,
    431–433, 441, 447
Die geistige Situation der Zeit (1931), 100,
    192, 308, 433
Dignity, 4–5, 40, 42, 58, 186, 191, 209, 236,
    242, 249–252, 359, 380, 387–388,
    391–392, 397, 404
Dogma, 4–5, 13, 28, 49–50, 78, 96, 107, 115,
    140, 255, 311, 391, 398
Domination, 42, 85, 282, 354, 404,
    421
Dover Beach, 138
Dutch rabbis, 116

E

Earnestness (*Ernst*), 128, 162–163
Ecological crisis, 389
Education, 6, 37, 135, 169, 175, 201, 209, 270,
    278, 288, 294, 298, 377, 397, 420–421,
    423, 428, 430–432, 441–444
Enactment, 148, 207, 214
Encompassing, 4–6, 18, 33, 39–40, 62, 67, 85,
    87, 92–93, 95, 97, 117–118, 126–128,
    139, 142–145, 148, 162–163, 208,
    227–228, 232–234, 255, 264, 276,
    278–280, 290, 318, 339, 342, 345,
    367–368, 374, 390–391
Encompassing, modes of encompassing,
    232–234
Enlightenment, 33, 57–58, 81, 84, 89, 96, 113,
    121, 178, 184–186, 200, 238, 302, 327,
    331, 368–369, 391, 415
Epistemology, 82, 93, 135, 217, 307
Ethics, 93, 139, 176, 216–217, 227–234,
    237–252, 313, 321, 395, 414
Ethos, 12, 40, 43, 56, 128, 164, 172, 198, 200,
    310, 393, 416, 420
Euphoria (deep passion), 388
Existential illumination, 152
Existentialism, 65–66, 69, 80, 125, 136, 142,
    165, 265, 290, 441
Existenz, 60, 65–67, 71–72, 86–88, 93, 95–96,
    103, 162, 187, 214, 227–228, 230, 233,
    283, 369, 400, 405, 407
Existenzerhellung, 100, 149, 152, 172

F

Faith
    in divine, 37, 40, 43, 89, 117, 140, 255,
        258, 373, 395, 406–407
    existential, 104, 109–110, 236–240
    reflected, 110–113
    religious, 4, 6, 13, 35–36, 39, 50, 84, 86,
        106–107, 112–113, 117, 121, 135, 138,
        141, 156, 219, 238, 251, 253–259,
        261–262, 264–266, 366–367, 369, 372,
        374, 387
Fanaticism, 20, 30, 388–389, 392, 398
Fear, 59, 143, 171–172, 174–175, 208, 215,
    258, 271, 273, 283, 378, 383, 388, 391,
    393, 395
Fides et ratio, 137
Fides qua creditur, 38, 277
Fides quae creditur, 38, 278
Finitude of man, 23–24
Foundering, 4, 7, 15, 67, 71–72, 85, 125, 134,
    142–145, 265, 269–286, 370

Four patterns of ethics, 233–234
Frankfurt School, 288
Freedom, 4–6, 14, 19–22, 24–26, 29–30, 37,
    40–44, 52, 66, 68, 70, 79, 95, 105,
    110–111, 121, 124, 128, 133, 137–138,
    141–142, 144–145, 149–151, 171–172,
    174, 176–177, 181–182, 195–196,
    198–202, 219, 224, 230, 255, 260, 265,
    270, 272, 278, 281–284, 301, 305–312,
    315–317, 330–331, 338, 341, 343, 349,
    361, 366, 368–372, 375–388, 391–397,
    401–407, 416, 418, 428
French Revolution, 181–182, 299, 305
Fulfillment of human destiny, 399–408

G
Game theory, 118
Germany, Federal Republic, 42
Geschichtlichkeit, 93, 99–100
Geschick, 185
Global catastrophic risks, 273–274, 284
Globalization, 42, 97, 113, 189, 194, 196,
    244–245, 328–332, 441
Glory, 23, 150
God, 9, 12–17, 21–23, 25–33, 40–42, 44, 48,
    51–52, 54–55, 62, 65, 72, 84, 86, 89,
    91–93, 95–97, 103, 107, 112, 117, 119,
    125–127, 135, 137–138, 140–141, 144,
    149–157, 162, 164, 174, 185–186, 191,
    201, 214–215, 219, 237, 241–242, 251,
    257–259, 264–265, 285, 302, 336, 338,
    340, 344–345, 353, 366–371, 373, 391,
    393–394, 406, 415, 446
Gott ist, 92
Grenzen, 66, 130

H
Historicity of philosophy, 338
Historiography, 190, 199, 201, 413
History
    of philosophy, 97, 101, 138–139, 203, 205,
        211–213, 216, 223–224, 287–298, 335,
        338, 343, 400, 405, 414, 443
    theory of, 192–198
Holy, 29, 32, 43, 85, 90–91, 166, 189–190,
    201, 395
Homo economicus, 118
Humanism, 96, 208, 299–308, 317–318,
    392–393, 395
Humanity, 5–6, 40–43, 45, 59, 71, 79–80,
    93, 96, 101–102, 104, 124, 136, 149,
    157, 160, 176, 178, 184, 193–201, 203,
    206–208, 225, 230, 235, 239, 242,

    251–252, 259, 262–263, 269–272, 275,
    284–285, 298, 301, 303, 307–308,
    312–313, 345, 351, 363, 368–369,
    371–372, 374, 387–388, 390, 393–397,
    399–403, 405, 406–408, 414–415, 418,
    427, 430–431
Humans are finite and unfinishable, 9, 22–25

I
Ideologies, 60, 128, 143, 350, 393, 397
Independence, 109, 150, 307, 367, 383–385,
    399, 403–404, 429
Inquisition, 37, 116–117, 120–121, 417
Integrity, 124, 209, 250, 388, 397
Intellect, 32, 63, 83, 85, 94, 109, 128, 219, 254,
    272, 276–277, 283, 297–298, 349, 362,
    390–391, 397–398, 425, 431
Intercultural understanding, 175, 347–363
International relations, 352, 356–358, 384–385,
    442
Internet advertisement and publicity, 269,
    280–282
Introduction to Metaphysics, 184
Iran, Islamic Republic of, 54, 59, 376–377,
    381–383, 385
Islam, 86, 88, 115, 154, 191–192, 200, 237,
    258, 331, 374

J
Jerusalem, 88, 96, 182, 186, 189–193,
    199–202, 284, 448
Jewish-Christian-Muslim relations, 45
Judaism, 15, 40, 86, 115, 155–156, 191–192,
    200, 213, 417–418, 440

K
Kin'en kyōkai kyōkai, 117
Know thyself, 46, 52
Kristallnacht, 43

L
Lebentragende Philosophie, 107
Liberty, 63, 181, 195, 201, 318, 380, 383,
    404–405
Limit situation, 72–73, 85, 143, 195, 198, 282,
    365, 404
Listening, 12, 29, 31, 94, 294, 419–434
Logos, 85, 153, 184–185, 420–421

M
Marketing strategies, 389
Mass-culture, 388–389, 392

Mass-man, 393
Materialistic, 389, 391, 398
Meaninglessness, 97, 118, 166, 208, 223,
    251, 382
Melancholy, 136
Meno, 140, 431
Metaphor, 65, 71, 83, 94, 143, 164, 247, 396
Methodology, 3, 129, 135, 212–214, 217, 220,
    230, 285, 361, 396, 398, 426
Mirror for Americans: Japan, 348, 352–353,
    357–358
Modernity, 50, 124, 179, 196, 236, 256–264,
    273, 331
Monotheism, 121, 189–190, 192, 195, 197

N

Nation-state, 378
Natura infinita, 116
Negativity, 380–381, 393, 398
New Promethean age, 404
New world order, 404
Nihilism, 17, 31, 43, 63, 141, 174, 239, 276,
    393, 402
Noble lie, 280
Nothingness, 15, 83, 124, 142, 163, 260, 271,
    285, 375–386

O

Obedience, 6, 17, 21, 28, 33, 110, 279, 429
Occident, 11, 14, 27, 30, 104, 116–117, 132,
    204, 289, 336, 366–368, 370–371,
    400–401, 412
The One, 17, 92, 164, 348, 351, 406
Open horizon, 67, 289, 343
Oppression, 48–49, 270, 380
Orient, 289, 400
Orientation, 72, 94, 100–101, 105, 107–109,
    112–113, 131, 133, 139, 142, 144,
    148–149, 152, 161–162, 166, 169–171,
    176–178, 194–195, 238, 251, 269, 276,
    279–280, 313, 339, 343, 365, 369–370
Origin, 12–15, 22, 27, 29, 32–34, 41, 45–46,
    78, 92, 109, 120, 129, 150, 160,
    162–164, 169, 186, 193–194, 198–199,
    201, 272, 275–277, 280, 288–289, 310,
    316, 366, 368–369, 371–372, 387,
    393–394, 397, 399, 401–407, 417
Otherness, 41, 54, 65, 73

P

Paradox, 91, 118, 139, 160, 165–166, 169, 174,
    260, 270, 278, 283, 317, 368

Periechontology, 127–128, 142–145, 227–234,
    276, 280–282, 335, 342–343, 345
Personal love, 407
Phaedo, 140
Phenomenology, 36, 39, 49–50, 79, 94, 132,
    136, 181–183, 235, 239–240, 252, 321,
    439–440, 444–445
Phenomenology of Spirit, 181, 183
Philosophia perennis, 87, 291, 336
Philosophical logic, 127, 342–343, 345
Philosophical thinking, 99, 101–102, 104, 107,
    153, 255, 261, 271, 367, 369, 371, 402
Philosophie der Offenbarung, 149, 151
Philosophischer Glaube, 80, 83
Philosophizing, 4, 7, 9, 11–34, 47, 57, 60–61,
    63–64, 94–95, 101, 104–107, 109–110,
    124, 128–129, 137, 139–145, 151–152,
    159–164, 174, 205, 229, 276, 287, 290,
    292, 295–297, 335, 338–339, 342,
    368, 408
Philosophy
    of communication, 204, 419–434
    future world philosophy, 399, 407
    life-sustaining philosophy, 107–108
Physis, 184–185
Political philosophy, 270, 289, 301, 308,
    319–334, 445–446
Politics, 35–36, 42, 44, 50, 59, 91, 94, 113,
    160, 162, 165, 174, 176, 191, 205, 258,
    260–261, 264, 270, 272–273, 279–280,
    283, 285, 299–318, 320, 331, 339–340,
    352–355, 357, 361, 375–376, 389, 393,
    395–396, 407, 413, 426, 433, 446
Practice, philosophizing as practice, 229
Predicament, 117, 331
Preliminary concern, 394–395
Prenzlau (Germany), 36
Presence, 15, 29–30, 33, 53, 95, 107, 126, 161,
    180, 239, 258, 261, 278, 375, 379, 382,
    395, 401, 432, 440
Pressure, 23, 79, 117, 131, 175, 216, 277,
    380–381, 384
Principles, 7, 9, 11–34, 39, 87, 95, 101, 105,
    108, 151, 162, 207, 237, 250–251, 264,
    279, 282, 300, 302–304, 307, 310, 313,
    316, 325, 332, 356, 404
Professio fidei Tridentina, 116
Profession, 57, 59, 117, 243
Protreptikos, 11
Provocation, 40, 66, 112, 155, 160, 167
Psychology, 19, 22, 108–109, 123, 125–126,
    128, 130–133, 160, 211, 214, 221–224,
    264, 285, 290, 411, 421, 441, 445, 447

Psychopathology, 3–4, 57, 90, 127–128, 133, 221
Public, 5–6, 12, 113, 121, 130, 135, 161, 165, 168–169, 173, 208–209, 213, 246, 250, 257, 259, 272, 281–282, 284, 300, 302, 311, 325, 338–339, 359–360, 376, 379, 383–384, 393, 397, 420, 426, 428, 433
Purpose, 5, 12–15, 17–19, 26, 32, 67, 127, 168–169, 176, 182, 185–186, 205, 225, 235–238, 240–244, 250, 280, 290, 294, 327, 358–359, 361, 369, 421

R

Reason, 4–5, 13, 15–16, 18, 27, 29, 33, 36, 39, 41, 47, 53, 57, 62–63, 78, 80, 82–86, 88–89, 91–96, 101–106, 110, 113, 119, 123–125, 127, 129–130, 133, 135–141, 143–145, 151–153, 160, 164, 172, 175–177, 184–186, 190, 196, 200, 206, 211–213, 218, 221, 224, 238, 254, 261, 265–266, 271–272, 274–276, 279–281, 283, 288, 290–291, 293–294, 296, 300–301, 303–312, 314, 316–318, 321, 325, 328, 330–331, 338–344, 349–351, 358, 362–363, 367, 369, 371–372, 374, 378, 380, 387, 390–393, 395–398, 401–402, 405–408, 423, 425, 427–428, 431
Rebellion, 269
Redemption, 27, 153–156, 164, 204, 206, 217, 251–252, 367
Release, 66, 272, 353
Religion, 7, 9, 12–13, 27, 35–36, 39, 43, 45, 50, 53–55, 57, 61–63, 77–79, 81, 83–84, 86, 89, 96–97, 100, 106–108, 110, 112–113, 121, 123–127, 129–130, 132, 142–144, 151–152, 156, 166–168, 185, 191–192, 197, 202, 212–213, 216–217, 219, 221, 224–225, 235–236, 238, 255–261, 265, 276–278, 284–285, 295, 314, 322, 339–340, 344, 361, 367, 370, 372, 374, 380, 388–389, 391–392, 395–398, 402, 408, 412, 415–418, 428, 439, 441–445, 448
Religious faith, 4, 6, 13, 35–36, 39, 84, 86, 106, 112–113, 117, 121, 135, 137–138, 141, 156, 219, 238, 251, 253–259, 261–262, 264–266, 366–367, 369, 372, 374, 387
Resistance, 19, 61, 70, 117, 139, 172–173, 382–383, 393, 397
Restraint, 379–382, 384

Revelation, 15, 26–29, 36–37, 39–40, 78, 85, 87–88, 95–97, 100–101, 103–107, 110, 120, 129, 137, 139–141, 143–144, 147–158, 162–163, 189–191, 228, 236, 255, 273, 276, 340, 344–345, 367, 369, 371–374, 418
Revocation, 17
Revolution, 59, 81, 93, 165–166, 181–182, 269–270, 273, 275, 277, 284, 299–300, 305, 326, 376, 378, 385
Risk, 28, 37, 43, 59, 63, 125, 138, 145, 147, 160, 206, 247–248, 274, 277, 351, 380, 389, 424

S

Science
    natural, 3, 37, 132, 167–168, 213–215, 225, 238, 322
    popular, 168
Scientific knowledge, 37, 56, 61, 101–102, 105, 108, 132–133, 165, 166, 168, 174, 177, 229, 312, 369, 396, 406
Second axial age, 399–408
Self-assertiveness, 29–30
Self-empowerment, 21–22, 28–29
Shipwreck, 65, 70–72, 142–143, 145, 284, 370
Silence, 14, 54, 72, 121, 183–184, 186, 193, 277, 281–282, 331, 370, 426, 431–432
Spiritual, 4, 35, 42–43, 53, 62, 70–71, 77, 82, 89, 132, 141, 143, 180, 185–186, 194, 201–202, 219, 221–222, 256–257, 275, 278, 350–351, 368, 370, 374, 391, 395–400, 402–404, 407, 417, 428, 440
Spiritual union of Orient and Occident, 400
Straight-line listening, 422–423, 425
Subject, ethical subject, 230–234
Subjective certainty, 111, 391
Summa Theologica, 140
Symbolum nicaenum, 116
Systems theory, 171–172

T

Technology, 82, 91, 142, 165–167, 170–173, 175, 177–178, 184, 193, 195, 227, 244, 246, 262–263, 273–275, 279, 312, 370, 373–374, 376, 385, 387–390, 396, 398, 401, 406, 434, 441, 447
Theology, 38, 40, 78, 85, 88–89, 93, 104, 123, 125, 135, 138, 140, 144, 156, 212, 228, 235, 239, 276, 291, 320, 322, 339, 343, 369, 391, 410–412, 446
Totalitarianism, 47, 279

Tradition, 13–14, 26–27, 33, 45, 48, 55, 57,
    61, 67, 74, 79, 81–83, 89–90, 92, 94,
    106–107, 127, 140–141, 147, 173, 190,
    196, 198–199, 203, 206–207, 217, 219,
    276, 278–279, 299, 304–305, 310, 314,
    320–321, 323–324, 327–328, 332, 337,
    344, 370–371, 377, 401–402, 410–411,
    413, 418–421, 431
Transactional listening-in-conversation, 419,
    422, 425, 427–428, 430–432, 434
Transcendence, 3–4, 21–22, 24, 62, 66–67,
    70, 86, 89, 92–93, 95, 97, 117, 120,
    137–138, 141–144, 187, 255–256,
    264–265, 283, 349, 368–370, 373, 391,
    393, 444
Transhumanism, 274–275, 284
Translation, 39, 67–73, 80, 89, 95, 147, 157,
    159, 165, 179–180, 191, 203, 206–207,
    211, 214, 256, 270, 277, 280, 285, 301,
    359, 361, 366, 375, 400, 419, 445
True language, 68, 70
Trust, 15, 42, 44, 80, 90, 123–134, 141,
    165–167, 169–172, 175, 177,
    397, 431
Truth, 5, 12–13, 40, 67–68, 80, 93–94,
    128–134, 141, 144, 155, 176, 269–286,
    372, 427, 432, 443, 447

U
Ultimate concern, 239–240, 245–246, 248,
    250, 394–396
Unconditional\unconditioned, 9, 13, 17–22,
    24–26, 28, 33, 40, 92, 94, 120–121,
    126, 129, 164, 174, 176–177, 208, 255,
    258, 278, 281, 284, 300, 317–318,
    394–395, 427, 430
Understanding, 224, 347–364
UNESCO, 201, 293, 350–351, 363
Unfinishable, 9, 22–25, 95, 345
United World, 402–403
University, 69, 77, 100, 160–161, 209,
    287–288, 290, 352, 356–358, 375, 411,
    413, 423, 426, 428, 430, 433
Unphilosophie (unphilosophy), 13, 78, 295,
    422, 429
Unselig, 120

Ursprung und Ziel der Geschichte (1949),
    191–192, 196, 199, 203, 339, 367,
    400, 405

V
Valuation, 211, 214–215, 217
Values, 5, 42–43, 61, 79–80, 82, 86, 92–97,
    107, 149, 170–171, 193, 196, 207, 217,
    220, 223–225, 250, 253, 258–263, 266,
    298, 303–305, 331, 350–351, 359–360,
    362–363, 370–371, 373, 387–388,
    390–393, 396–398, 404, 410, 412, 442,
    444–445
Vernunftglaube, 102
Verstehen, 82–83, 85, 211–226, 285, 363, 402
Virtue, 26, 32, 39, 93, 111, 129–131, 133, 139,
    170–171, 197, 244, 247, 250, 278, 281,
    294, 321, 347, 360, 414
Void, 16, 24, 39, 204, 206, 381, 383, 386

W
Weltphilosophie, 87, 95, 335, 400, 402, 423
Western thought, 99, 113, 420
Wissen, 37, 80–83, 113, 135, 301, 422
Wissenschaft, 37, 148, 166–168, 173
Work, 12, 36, 39, 41–43, 45–50, 53–54, 56,
    59–60, 62, 67–71, 82, 84, 86, 88, 90–91,
    100, 109, 124, 128, 130, 135, 143, 147,
    157, 160, 162, 165, 179–180, 192, 194,
    200, 203, 205, 211–212, 216–217, 219,
    221, 224, 228, 232, 235–252, 271–272,
    299, 304, 308–309, 311–312, 314–316,
    341–342, 345, 349–350, 356–361, 369,
    373, 392, 400–402, 405, 409–410, 412,
    422, 430–431, 434
World history, 154, 192, 195–196, 199, 258,
    264, 266, 356, 358, 367, 405, 410, 414,
    439
World history of philosophy, 139, 287–298,
    335, 343, 405, 414
Worldview, 90, 105, 108–109, 112, 116, 121,
    125–126, 128, 130, 132, 160, 191,
    220–223, 237, 253–254, 256, 259–264,
    266, 278, 295

Z
Zeitgeist (child of its time), 180, 182–183, 326,
    337